A COMMENTARY ON

ISAIAH

PETER A. STEVESON

BJU PRESS

GREENVILLE, SOUTH CAROLINA

Library of Congress Cataloging-in-Publication Data

Steveson, Peter A. (Peter Allan), 1934-
   Isaiah / Peter A. Steveson.
      p. cm.
   Includes bibliographical references (p.   ) and index.
   ISBN 1-57924-974-4
   1. Bible. O.T. Isaiah--Commentaries. I. Title.

   BS1515.53.S74 2003
   224'.107--dc21   2003012185

Isaiah
Peter A. Steveson, Ph.D.

*To Virginia Callahan,
my mother-in-law,
with deep appreciation
for her love, prayers,
and support over the years.*

TABLE OF CONTENTS

PREFACE

My study of the Book of Isaiah goes back well over thirty years, when I first taught the book to an adult Sunday school class. Since then I have taught large portions of the book for more than twenty years to students enrolled in my Major Prophets classes at Bob Jones University. The Book of Isaiah is never commonplace but always fresh and practical. The book demonstrates God's plan for His people in Old Testament times and in the kingdom age to come. Many basic New Testament truths have their roots in Isaiah. The book illustrates many principles for Christian living. Texts that cry out to be preached fill its pages. Believers today need to see the numerous messianic prophecies of the book.

There are many conservative commentaries on the book. At least in part for this reason, the question from many of my friends has been "Why Isaiah?" I have always pointed out that there needs to be a commentary that approaches Isaiah from a pre-Tribulation, premillennial viewpoint. Most of the existing books on Isaiah adopt an amillennial approach. In his excellent commentary on Isaiah, E. J. Young, for example, says that the millennial viewpoint "does violence of a serious kind to the general structure of Biblical eschatology."[1] Often, the kingdom passages in Isaiah become mere predictions of a return from the Babylonian captivity or a general statement of the eternal ages. It is rare to find any mention of the Tribulation period or the millennial reign of Jesus Christ over the earth. Where appropriate, I have tried to apply Isaiah's prophecies to these end-time events.

The Book of Isaiah is a treasure chest of prophecies relating to the atoning work of Christ. The Servant passages in chapters 42, 49, 50, and 52-53 set forth a clear teaching of the Lord's sacrifice for the sins of mankind. As with other passages in the Bible dealing with this, mere knowledge of the atonement is not enough. You must also accept Christ's sacrifice as the only means whereby God can forgive your sins. Having accepted the salvation made possible by Jesus Christ, you then receive the Holy Spirit to guide you in your study of God's Word. It is my prayer that the Spirit will use this book to help believers become spiritually stronger.

---

[1]Edward J. Young, *The Book of Isaiah*, I, 109.

As with any commentary, I owe a great debt to others who have helped in many ways. The library staffs at Bob Jones University and Furman University have given much assistance. In particular, Pat LeMaster of the Bob Jones University library staff has significantly helped me in gathering research materials. I have also drawn on the resources of numerous other college and university libraries. The editors at Bob Jones University Press, Suzette Jordan, Dr. Ron Tagliapietra and Marianne Appleman, have patiently corrected my grammar, spelling, and other human foibles. Others at the Press who have helped include Kelley Moore, Jennifer Hearing, and Jim Frasier in Composition, and Elizabeth Richardson in Ad + Design. My colleagues in the ministry—Mrs. Jackie Eaves, Edith Smith, Dr. Randy Jaeggli, and Dr. Robert Bell—have assisted my work. Finally, Bob Jones University has kindly given me a sabbatical leave to complete the book.

CHIEF ABBREVIATIONS

1QIsa^a	St. Marks Dead Sea Isaiah Scroll from Cave 1, Qumran
ANET	*Ancient Near Eastern Texts*
BASOR	*Bulletin of the American Schools of Oriental Research*
BDB	*A Hebrew and English Lexicon of the Old Testament*, ed. Brown, Driver, and Briggs
BZ	*Biblische Zeitschrift*
CBQ	*Catholic Biblical Quarterly*
G.K.	*Gesenius' Hebrew Grammar*, ed. E. Kautzsch and A. E. Cowley
HTR	*Harvard Theological Review*
HUCA	*Hebrew Union College Annual*
JAOS	*Journal of the American Oriental Society*
JBL	*Journal of Biblical Literature*
JBQ	*Jewish Bible Quarterly*
JETS	*Journal of the Evangelical Theological Society*
JNES	*Journal of Near Eastern Studies*
JNWSL	*Journal of Northwest Semitic Languages*
JQR	*Jewish Quarterly Review*
JSOT	*Journal for the Study of the Old Testament*
JSS	*Journal of Semitic Studies*
JTS	*Journal of Theological Studies*
KB	Koehler and Baumgartner
MT	Massoretic Text
NEB	New English Bible
NIV	New International Version
OTTP	*Old Testament Translation Problems*
REB	Revised English Bible
RSV	Revised Standard Version
SJOT	*Scottish Journal of Theology*
SVT	*Supplements to Vetus Testamentum*
Targum	*The Isaiah Targum*
TWOT	*Theological Wordbook of the Old Testament*
TZ	*Theologische Zeitschrift*
VT	*Vetus Testamentum*
WTJ	*Westminster Theological Journal*
ZAW	*Zeitschrift für die alttestamentliche Wissenschaft*

INTRODUCTION

The Book of Isaiah occupies the major position among the OT prophets.[1] Because of its heavy emphasis on the theme of salvation, especially concerning the coming Messiah, Isaiah has been called the "Evangelical Prophet."[2] His name "Isaiah" means "salvation of the Lord." The name is highly appropriate for one whose ministry would so heavily influence the declaration of salvation. The NT quotes or alludes to Isaiah at least fifty-eight times, more than any other OT book except the Psalms.[3]

We know little about the man himself. The opening verse tells us that he was the son of Amoz, 1:1. This man should not be confused with the prophet Amos. Jewish tradition says that Amoz was a brother of King Amaziah.[4] From the fact that Isaiah had access to the king, 7:3, this may well be the case. Isaiah held a high place in the court. He was a friend of the priest, 8:2. Hezekiah sent his officers to meet him, II Kings 19:2. Isaiah also kept the historical records of the court, II Chronicles 26:22; 32:32. Probably as part of his court responsibilities, he wrote biographies of Uzziah, II Chronicles 26:22, and Hezekiah, II Chronicles 32:32. Both of these have been lost.

Isaiah 6:1–8 indicates that he was called to prophesy in the last year of Uzziah's reign, ca. 740 B.C. He prophesied primarily to Judah. He mentions other nations as they relate to the plan of God for His people. He recorded the death of Sennacherib in 681 B.C., 37:38. Logically, if Isaiah's prophecies spanned the reigns of Jothan, sixteen years, Ahaz,

---

[1]Jesus, the son of Sirach, said that Isaiah was *hnbyʾ hgdwl*, "the great prophet," Ecclus. 48:22. Matthew Henry, *Commentary on the Whole Bible*, IV, 2, says that the book "is placed first, because it is the largest" of the prophetic books. While it does have more chapters than the other prophetic books, the Hebrew text is about 12 percent shorter than Jeremiah. Isaiah's prominence stems from its content and style more than its length.

[2]Jerome, *Against Rufinus* 2.32, says of Isaiah, "He was more of an evangelist than a prophet." Augustine, *City of God*, c. 29, wrote, "Some say he should be called an evangelist rather than a prophet." More recently, Albert Barnes, *Notes on the Old Testament: Isaiah,* I, 1950, 2, refers to Isaiah's "strongly evangelical character."

[3]James Flamming, "The New Testament Use of Isaiah," *Southwestern Journal of Theology* 11:89, states that "Isaiah is quoted more than twice as much as any other major prophet and more than all of the minor prophets combined." Later, p. 103, Flamming says that the NT quotes c. 1–39 148 times and c. 40–66 261 times. While Flamming includes some allusions as quotations, these figures show that the NT depended heavily on Isaiah. See also fn. 22.

[4]Babylonian Talmud, *Sota* 10b.

sixteen years, and Hezekiah, twenty-nine years, he could not have been an old man when he began to prophesy. If we assume he was about twenty years old when he first began, and if we accept the tradition that he was sawn in half with a wooden sword by Manasseh, cf. Hebrews 11:37, his life covered the years 760–680 B.C.[5] He would have been a contemporary of Micah and could possibly have known Hosea and Amos.

We know little of his wife. She is referred to only as "the prophetess," 8:3, probably because of her relationship to him. They had two sons, the names of whom were characteristic of Isaiah's message. The name of the older, Shear-jashub, "a remnant will return," shows the mercy of God toward His own, 7:3. The name of the younger, Maher-shalal-hash-baz, "swift the spoil, speedy the plunder," relates to God's judgment on His people, 8:3.

The prophecy of Isaiah is generally considered the greatest of the OT prophecies. Albert Barnes wrote, "In all ages Isaiah has been regarded as the most sublime of all writers. He is simple, bold, rapid, elevated; he abounds in metaphor and in rapid transitions; his writings are full of the sublimest figures of rhetoric, and the most beautiful ornaments of poetry."[6] William Kelly stated, "As Isaiah stands out from all the other prophets by the sublimity of his conception, the elevation of his sentiments, and the grandeur of his style, so is he by fulness and variety of subject matter. He was the suited vessel for the gift of inspiration which

---

[5]Justin Martyr, *Dialogue with Trypho* 120, in *Ante-Nicene Fathers*, I, 259, records the tradition: "whom [Isaiah] you sawed asunder with a wooden saw." He does not give any evidence for the statement. Origen, *Ante-Nicene Fathers*, IV, 388, refers to the "tradition . . . that Esaias the prophet was sawn asunder." The Talmud, *Yebamoth* 49b, records a fanciful account of Isaiah's death. Supposedly, Manasseh brought him to trial for contradicting Moses. Moses had taught that men could not see God and live, Exod. 33:20. Isaiah had claimed to have seen God, Isa. 6:1. Moses had taught that God was near Israel, Deut. 4:7. Isaiah said that God must be sought, Isa. 55:6. Moses taught that God would fulfill our days, not make additions, Exod. 23:26. Isaiah said that God would add fifteen years to Hezekiah, II Kings 20:6. Knowing that Manasseh would not accept anything he said, Isaiah "thereupon pronounced [the divine] Name and was swallowed up by a cedar. The cedar, however, was brought and sawn asunder. When the saw reached his mouth he died." In *Sanhedrin* 103b, another talmudic tradition says that the statement that Manasseh shed innocent blood every day, II Kings 21:16, was interpreted in Babylon to refer to killing Isaiah. Among others, Albert Barnes, I, 10; Page H. Kelley, *Isaiah*, in *The Broadman Bible Commentary*, V, 1971, 150; and George Rawlinson, *Isaiah*, in *The Pulpit Commentary*, I, iii, refer to the view that Heb. 11:37 refers to Isaiah's death.

[6]Barnes, I, 14.

set him in the front rank, but in the highest place of these eminent servants of God."[7] George Rawlinson commented, "It is generally allowed that Isaiah, as a writer, transcends all the other Hebrew prophets."[8]

Authorship

There is a vigorous debate as to the identity of Isaiah's author. Conservative authors hold to a single author, the biblical Isaiah. During the early part of the twentieth century, a critical view was widely popularized that there were two authors. First Isaiah wrote c. 1–39. He lived during the last half of the eighth century B.C. Second Isaiah wrote c. 40–66. He lived two centuries later, during the last part of the sixth century B.C.[9] In more recent years, critics have divided the authorship among three or more men.[10] This view holds that Isaiah, the son of Amoz, wrote c. 1–39. A second author, called Deutero-Isaiah, or Second Isaiah, wrote c. 40–55. The third author, Trito-Isaiah, or Third Isaiah, wrote c. 56–66.[11]

According to these views, the book was written over a period of more than two hundred years. First Isaiah wrote during the early reign of Manasseh, ca. 680 B.C. Second Isaiah wrote during the captivity, ca. 540 B.C. Third Isaiah followed over a period of time that concluded ca. 445 B.C.

Style and Language. Those who hold these views advance several arguments. One of the major arguments claims that there is a marked difference in the style and language between c. 1–39 and c. 40–66.[12] There

---

[7]William Kelly, *Exposition of the Book of Isaiah*, 1916, p. 70.

[8]Rawlinson, I, xii.

[9]Among others, the following hold variations of this view: G. Ernest Wright, *The Book of Isaiah*, in *The Layman's Bible Commentary*, 1982, pp. 7–8. Samuel R. Driver, *An Introduction to the Literature of the Old Testament*, 1913, pp. 236–46.

[10]This is the simplest suggestion. Many authors divide the book more extensively. Chapters 34 and 35 are often grouped with c. 40–55. The servant passages, 42:1–9; 49:1–13; 50:4–11; 52:13–53:12, are attributed to a different author. There is general but not unanimous agreement on the unity of c. 1–33, 36–39, and 40–55. Critics generally assign c. 56–66 to a group of authors.

[11]There are wide variations in the expression of this view. Some limit the second part to c. 40–48 and make c. 49–55 a third part. This makes c. 56–66 a fourth part. Some attribute the various parts to single authors; some make them collections of various prophetic oracles from different authors. Among those who suggest multiple authors for Isaiah are J. Skinner, *Isaiah XL–LXVI*, 1963, p. xxxi; John L. McKenzie, *Second Isaiah*, in *The Anchor Bible*, 1968, pp. xv–xxiii; and Emil G. Kraeling, *Commentary on the Prophets*, I, 1966, 33–37.

[12]Skinner, *Isaiah XL–LXVI*, p. xxii, says that Isaiah I "is distinguished by force and compression." Isaiah II, however, "is profuse and flowing, with a marked tendency to

are at least two answers to this claim. In the first place, there are numerous similarities in the style and language. For example, the phrase "Holy One of Israel," which occurs only four times in the rest of the OT, occurs twelve times in c. 1–39 and thirteen times in c. 40–66. Clear messianic prophecies occur in all sections, 7:14–16; 9:6–7; cf. 40:10; 52:13–53:12; 65:17–24. Word plays, e.g., 5:7, *mišpaṭ, mišpaḥ; ṣedaqâ, ṣeʿaqâ*; 49:10, *yenahªgem, yenahªlem*; 65:11–12, *menî, manîtî*; 66:1–2, *ʾê-zeh . . . ʾêzeh . . . ʾelˉzeh*, and repeated words and phrases, e.g., 27:5; 32:9–11; 40:1; 61:10 (*śôś ʾaśîś*), occur throughout the book.

Both parts of the book refer to creation, 29:16; 37:16; cf. 40:22; 45:12. Both refer to the "covenant," 24:5; 33:8; cf. 42:6; 61:8. Both refer to man's sin, 1:4; 30:9; cf. 43:24; 59:12; to the sovereignty of God, 14:27; 23:9; cf. 43:13; 46:11; and to the believing remnant, 1:26; 4:3; cf. 52:1; 60:21. Both sections deal with the themes of charity to the poor, 14:30; 25:4; cf. 41:17; 58:7. Both mention Babylon, 13:1; 29:9; cf. 43:14; 48:20; Egypt, 7:18; 19:12–25; cf. 45:14; 52:4; and Ethiopia, 18:1; 37:9; cf. 43:3; 45:14. The sections show no clear variation in the names of God. The name *yehwah* occurs in 203 verses in c. 1–39 and in 170 verses in c. 40–66. Variations of *ʾelohîm* refer to God 31 times in c. 1–39 and 51 times in c. 40–66. The name *ʾªdonay* occurs 34 times in c. 1–39 and 14 times in c. 40–66. These examples are only a small sample of the similarities between the two major parts of the book.

In the second place, there is a logical explanation for the differences in style and language that occur. Different themes require different styles and vocabulary.[13] There is no question but that c. 1–39 emphasize the history of the nation more than its future revealed through prophecy. At the same time, c. 40–66 stress messianic themes and Israel's future more than its historical past. We would not expect to find the same style or the same vocabulary.

---

amplification and repetition." Driver, p. 238, states that the dual authorship "is confirmed by the *literary style* of c. 40–66, which is very different from that of Isaiah." John Goldingay, *Isaiah*, in *New International Biblical Commentary*, 2001, p. 4, says that the writer of c. 40–55 "speaks more poetically or more lyrically than any of the other voices."

[13]Sir T. M. Knox, "The Computer and the New Testament," *Svensk Exegetisk Årsbok* 28–29:112, shows the fallacy of this approach in determining authorship. He refers to different studies of this kind. One proved that the *Iliad* and the *Odyssey* were by different authors. Another study showed that *Paradise Lost* and *Paradise Regained* could not have been written by the same author.

Could the same person write on different themes? Certainly! We have many examples of this elsewhere in the Bible. Moses authored five books. These books span the history of the world up to his time, at least two thousand years of history. Each of the books has a different emphasis. Solomon authored two psalms, most of Proverbs, Ecclesiastes, and the Song of Solomon. These have radical differences in style and vocabulary. Jeremiah wrote the Book of Jeremiah and also the Book of Lamentations. There are similar differences in the NT books.[14]

Historical Background. A second claim takes note of the apparent differences in historical background found in the major sections of Isaiah. Chapters 1–39 emphasize Israel's history during the reigns of Uzziah, Jotham, Ahaz, and Hezekiah. Chapters 40–55 draw upon the late exilic and early postexilic periods. A gap in time of about 150 years lies between c. 39 and c. 40. Chapters 1–39 address a people still living in Palestine. Chapters 40–55 supposedly address a people living in captivity in Babylon.[15] Chapters 56–66 address a returned people who worship in a rebuilt temple.

The differing historical emphases have led to a supposed law for prophecy. "A prophecy is earlier than what it predicts, but contemporary with, or later than, what it presupposes."[16] This looks good at first glance, but a little reflection shows the fatal error in the statement. Saying that a prophecy is "contemporary with, or later than, what it presupposes" limits the scope of prophecy. According to this rule, prophecy is limited to the next event, whatever that may be. No OT prophecy could foretell the Second Coming of Christ since that presupposes His first coming, an event that had not happened. In like manner, no prophecy

---

[14]To use a more modern example, the present author has written for national publications in the areas of the family, Bible exposition, mathematics, computer software, and astronomy. These books and articles display different styles and vocabulary, the differences coming naturally from the different themes. The differences in style and vocabulary do not prove that different men wrote the publications bearing my name.

[15]Portions of this section require the author to write from Palestine, e.g., 41:25; 46:11; 52:1, 2, 9; 54:3.

[16]So Wright, p. 8. Kelley, p. 160, also allude to this "law." Christopher R. North, *Isaiah 40–55,* in *Torch Bible Commentaries,* 1956, p. 15, comes close to this "law." He states, "The predictions of a prophet were always fairly closely related to the circumstances of his own time." After admitting that prophets sometimes predicted things that were centuries ahead of their own time, he explains this by saying they used "general or 'mythological' . . . terms."

could predict the return of Israel from Babylon since that presupposes the captivity.

There are examples elsewhere to show the fallacy of this "law." The Lord told Abram that his descendants would be in bondage in Egypt four hundred years and then would come out of their captivity, Genesis 15:13–16. The prediction that they would come out of captivity presupposes the Egyptian captivity. Acting on his belief of this promise, Joseph predicted that Jacob's descendants would return to the Promised Land, Genesis 50:24–26. This prediction was about three hundred years in advance of the Exodus and presupposes a lengthy stay in Egypt. Jeremiah predicted a seventy-year captivity followed by a return to Palestine, Jeremiah 29:10–14. The prediction of a return presupposes the captivity. Psalm 22 graphically describes the Crucifixion of Christ. This presupposes His birth and life. These few examples are enough to show that there is no law of prophecy that requires the prophet to live in the historical period presupposed by the prophecy.

The mention of Cyrus, 44:28; 45:1, opposes those who hold a liberal view of authorship. Liberal authors do not believe that Isaiah could refer by name to a man who lived more than a hundred years later.[17] This, however, ignores the examples given elsewhere in the Old Testament. Exodus 23:21 prophesies that the Lord would have the same name as Joshua.[18] First Kings 13:2 predicts the actions of Josiah, more than three hundred years later. The mere fact of prophesying a proper name gives no proof of different authorship.

In like manner, the fact that the major sections of Isaiah suggest different historical periods does not require different authors for each section. The guidance of the Holy Spirit allowed Isaiah to accurately predict the future. In some cases, the future was near, in some cases it lay more

---

[17]George W. Wade, *The Book of the Prophet Isaiah*, in *Westminster Commentaries*, 1911, p. xliv, refers to "Cyrus, the destined conqueror of Babylon, xliv. 28, xlv. 1–4, who is alluded to as though already known by reputation to the prophet's auditors or readers, and who is represented as already launched upon his successful career, xli. 2, 25, xlviii. 15." C. Von Orelli, *The Prophecies of Isaiah*, 1889, p. 255, comments: "This passage, where Cyrus is first named, does not give the impression of professing to mention miraculously the name of one yet utterly unknown to the world as that of a future deliverer of Judah, thus giving a miraculous proof of its own accuracy; but a well-known living prince seems meant. . . . Accordingly, Josephus, Ant. xi. 1, 2, is to be corrected."

[18]The proper name "Joshua," *yᵉhôšuaᶜ*, "Jehovah is salvation," means the same as "Jesus," Ἰησοῦς.

than two hundred years ahead, and in some cases it lay more than twenty-seven hundred years ahead.

The Lack of a Claim for Isaianic Authorship. Those who hold to multiple authors in the book note that Isaiah does not claim authorship of c. 40–66. While c. 1–39 mention Isaiah by name sixteen times, the final chapters do not mention him at all. This argument has a simple answer. Chapters 1–39 mention Isaiah since much of those chapters involve history in which he plays a part. He meets the king, 7:3. He acts out a prophetic sign, 20:2–3. He meets with the king's representatives, c. 37. In c. 40–66, the emphasis lies on future events in which he plays no part. There is no reason that he should mention his name. The NT, however, does mention his name several times when referring to c. 40–66.[19]

No part of the book places unusual emphasis on Isaiah. Chapters 1–36 mention him only six times. Large parts of this section, 7:4–12:6; 20:4–37:1, do not mention him at all. Only c. 37–39 stress the person of Isaiah. He is a major character there since the action described extensively involves the prophet.

The Unity of Isaiah. There are several positive arguments in favor of the unity of the book. In the first place all of the manuscript evidence supports the idea of a single author. There is no manuscript of any kind that suggests multiple authorship. The oldest Hebrew manuscript, the Isaiah Scroll found at Qumran, 1QIsa^a, begins c. 40 with a single line at the bottom of the page on which c. 39 ends. *Aleph*, *A* and *B*, the three oldest Greek manuscripts likewise support a single author for the book.

The book of II Chronicles accepts Isaiah's authorship. It is thought that Ezra wrote I and II Chronicles sometime in the first half of the fourth century B.C. Second Chronicles 26:22 and 32:32 mention the writings of "Isaiah the prophet."

In Ecclesiasticus 48:17–25, written ca. 180 B.C., the author not only refers to Isaiah by name but also speaks of his prophecies of comfort to the Jews. The statement reads,

17 Hezekiah fortified his city, bringing water within its walls; he drilled through the rock with tools of iron and made cisterns for the water.

18 In his reign Sennacherib invaded the country. He sent Rab-shakeh from Lachish, who made threats against Zion and grew arrogant in his boasting.

---

[19]See fn. 24 for the references.

19 Then they were unnerved in heart and hand; they suffered the anguish of a woman in labour.

20 So they called on the merciful Lord, spreading out their hands in supplication to him. The Holy One quickly answered their prayer from heaven by sending Isaiah to the rescue;

21 he struck down the Assyrian camp, and his angel wiped them out.

22 For Hezekiah did what was pleasing to the Lord, and kept firmly to the ways of his ancestor David, as he was instructed by Isaiah, the great prophet whose vision could be trusted.

23 In his time the sun went back, and he added many years to the king's life.

24 With inspired power he saw the future and comforted the mourners in Zion.

25 He revealed things to come before they happened, the secrets of the future to the end of time.[20]

The references to Hezekiah and the miracle of the sun's motion show clearly that his text of Isaiah included c. 36–39. Further, the statement in 24*b* that he "comforted the mourners in Zion" appears to allude to 40:1 or 61:2–3. The reference in v. 25 that "He revealed things to come before they happened, the secrets of the future to the end of time" alludes to prophecies of the future, e.g., 41:22–23; 42:9; 44:7; 45:21; or 46:10.

The first century A.D. Jewish historian Josephus also assigns the latter part of the book to Isaiah. In his *Antiquities of the Jews*, xi.1–2, he states that the Jews showed to Cyrus those writings of Isaiah that mention the king. This caused Cyrus to look with favor on returning the Jews to their homeland. This shows that Josephus considered Isaiah the author of the book.

The opening passage of c. 40 does not give an author or even an introduction to show that this is a new book. The opening passage of c. 56 is similar in form. If these portions of the book are by another author or authors, the omission of the author's name is unusual. The authors of the OT books of prophecy regularly introduce them by giving their name and something of their family background. This omission argues against new authorship.

Even those who hold to multiple authorship recognize that the evidence is against them. For this reason, some suggest that the book devel-

---

[20]The translation comes from John G. Snaith, *Ecclesiasticus*, in the *Cambridge Bible Commentary*, ed. P. R. Ackroyd, A. R. C. Leaney, and J. W. Packer (London: Syndics of the Cambridge University Press, 1974), pp. 242–43.

oped over a period of years.[21] A supposed school of Isaianic students added to the book until it assumed its present form. This approach, of course, assumes the conclusion and then argues its way to prove it.

A second positive argument comes from the New Testament's use of Isaiah. The Nestle-Aland New Testament has about six hundred quotations and allusions to all parts of the book.[22] Even granting that many of the allusions include coincidental groupings of words, it is clear that the NT authors considered the book important.[23] In nineteen references, the NT authors refer to Isaiah by name.[24] These references come from every major section of the book. Nine come from c. 1–39, eight from c. 40–55, and two from c. 56–66. This indicates the belief of the NT writers in a single author.

Included in these NT references are three quotations in which the Lord Himself referred to Isaiah, Matthew 13:14–15; 15:7–8; Mark 7:6–7. Some authors explain these away as the Lord accommodating

---

[21]For example, McKenzie, pp. xxi–xxii, concludes "that Second Isaiah not only knew the oracles of Isaiah of Jerusalem, but also that he thought of himself as the continuator of Isaiah . . . the authors and compilers of Third Isaiah thought of themselves as the custodians and the continuators of the Isaiah tradition, now expanded by the work of Second Isaiah." Kelley, p. 160, states, "The prevailing view at present is that chapters 56–66 should be dated in the early postexilic period—no earlier than 537 B.C. and no later than 445—and that they should be attributed to the disciples of Second Isaiah." Elmer A. Leslie, *Isaiah*, 1963, p. 205, says, "We cannot rightly refer to the writer of chs. 56–66, as it is practically certain that these chapters have more than one writer."

[22]Eberhard Nestle, Erwin Nestle, Kurt Aland, and Barbara Aland, *Novum Testamentum Graece*, 1979, pp. 758–62. Based on graduate work by Mark Kispert, James A. Sanders, "Isaiah in Luke," *Interpretation* 36:144, states that 590 references from Isaiah occur. These come "from sixty-three chapters of Isaiah . . . in twenty-three New Testament books, 239 from Isaiah 1–39; 240 from chaps 40–55; 111 from 56–66."

[23]Flamming, pp. 94, 97, credits the writers of the Gospels with quoting Isaiah "over one hundred times." He admits that "the exact number [depends] upon one's judgment of Isaiah as being the only source." He adds, "All four gospels use Isaiah. Matthew the most explicitly, and John the most implicitly . . . Matthew and Mark use Isaiah in a supportive way, that is to support the life, teachings, and work of Christ by prophetic referent. John and Luke, on the other hand, use Isaiah as a theological base, Luke to show the work of Christ, and John to show the person of Christ."

[24]Matt. 3:3; cf. Isa. 40:3; Matt. 4:14–16; cf. Isa. 9:1–2; Matt. 8:17; cf. Isa. 53:4; Matt. 12:17–21; cf. Isa. 42:1–3; Matt. 13:14–15; cf. Isa. 6:9–10; Matt. 15:7–9; cf. Isa. 29:13; Mark 7:6–7; cf. Isa. 29:13; Luke 3:4–6; cf. Isa. 40:3–5; Luke 4:17–19; cf. Isa. 61:1–2; John 1:23; cf. Isa. 40:3; John 12:38; cf. Isa. 53:1; John 12:39–41; cf. Isa. 6:10; Acts 8:28–33; cf. Isa. 53:7–8; Acts 28:25–27; cf. Isa. 6:9–10; Rom. 9:27–28; cf. Isa. 10:22–23; Rom. 9:29; cf. Isa. 1:9; Rom. 10:16; cf. Isa. 53:1; Rom. 10:20–21; cf. Isa. 65:1–2; Rom. 15:12; cf. Isa. 11:10.

Himself to the beliefs of the people.[25] This view, however, is unworthy of the Lord. He did not accommodate Himself to the prevailing belief about the Sabbath, Mark 2:23–28. He did not accommodate Himself to the pharisaical view toward eating with unwashed hands, Mark 7:1–8. He did not accommodate Himself to the current practice of selling things in the temple, John 2:13–17. Why would He have accommodated Himself to a mistaken view of Isaiah's authorship?

In addition, Matthew quotes Isaiah three times with the quotations coming from two major sections, 9:1–2 and 42:1–3; 53:4. The apostle John quotes from two major parts of the book, 6:10 and 53:1. Paul quotes Isaiah six times, drawing from all three sections, 1:9; 6:9–10; 10:22–23; 11:10; 53:1; 65:1–2.

The final argument for the unity of the book asks the question "What happened to Isaiah II and III?" How is it that the author, or authors, of such a great work as Isaiah 40–66 could have disappeared from Jewish history without a trace? The Jews have no tradition concerning Isaiah other than that a single Isaiah wrote the entire book. This is the inescapable conclusion.

Theology of Isaiah

As with most OT books, the theology of Isaiah is incomplete. The book builds on themes introduced in previous books. Some of these themes are basic—God, judgment of sin, and so forth. The eschatological emphasis of Isaiah, however, is unusual for a book this early in Israel's history. The later prophets develop this still more, but Isaiah has an unusually complete development for the OT. The following summary of Isaiah's theology sketches in the highlights. There are many areas that the reader may develop more fully for himself.

God

It is not surprising that Isaiah refers to God the Father. What is surprising, though, is the development that he gives to the Son of God and to the Holy Spirit. The prophet not only describes God in terms that refer to the Father, but He also gives details that can refer only to the Son or to the Spirit of God.

---

[25]For example, Kelley, p. 162, says, "Even if Jesus had believed in a 'Second Isaiah,' it is doubtful that he would have attempted to enlighten his disciples on this subject."

Names of God. Isaiah uses a wide variety of descriptive names for God. The dominant names, Yahweh, "Lord," and Elohim, "God," occur over four hundred times and almost one hundred times respectively. The name Adonai, "Lord," occurs thirty times. In addition, the names Yah, "LORD," 12:2; 26:4; 38:11 (two times), and Adon, "Lord," 1:24; 3:1; 10:16, 33; 51:22, also occur. Isaiah stresses the fundamental theme of God's holiness in connection with the names of God. He uses the name "Holy One" thirty times. Isaiah 57:15 mentions the "One . . . whose name is holy." Two other names describe God's position as head of the hosts of heaven and earth. The name "Lord of hosts" occurs fifty-three times, and the name "Lord God of hosts" occurs eight times.

Several names used by Isaiah point to the Lord Jesus Christ. The name "branch of the Lord" speaks of His divine origin in 4:2, while "branch" refers to His earthly heritage in 11:1. The well-known "Immanuel," "God with us," occurs in 7:14 and 8:8. In 11:10, He is the "root of Jesse," again suggesting His human origin. The richest name passage of the OT occurs in 9:6. The Lord there is the "Wonderful Counselor, the Mighty God, the Everlasting Father, the Prince of Peace." Four passages portray the Son of God as the "servant," 42:1–9; 49:1–13; 50:4–11; 52:13–53:12.[26]

Nature of God. Isaiah develops the nature of God in a reasonably full manner. He stresses the transcendental attributes over and over. We see the omnipotence of God in Creation, 40:26; 42:5. God is omniscient, 45:21; 46:9–10, and eternal, 43:10; 44:6. The prophet refers to the holiness of God extensively, e.g., 6:3; 57:15.

In His dealings with mankind, God acts sovereignly, 45:9, yet He allows man to exercise a free will, 6:8. He maintains control over individuals, 44:28: 45:1, and nations, 10:5–6; 13:17. Isaiah hints at God's revelation to him with the word "vision," 1:1; 21:2; 22:1, 5. He also records one clear vision in 6:1–13. Isaiah there sees the Lord in His

---

[26]There is wide disagreement over the Servant passages. Bernhard Duhm, *Das Buch Jesaja* (Göttinger: Vandenhoeck & Ruprecht, 1892), who originated the identification of the Servant passages, included 42:1–4; 49:1–6; 50:4–9; 52:13–53:12. Geoffrey W. Grogan, *Isaiah*, in *The Expositor's Bible Commentary*, ed. Frank E. Gaebelein, 1986, p. 18, includes 42:1–7; 49:1–9*a;* 50:1–11; and 52:13–53:12. F. Duane Lindsey, *The Servant Songs*, 1985, p. 60, includes 49:1–13 in the second song. Harry M. Orlinsky, *Studies on the Second Part of the Book of Isaiah*, in *Supplements to Vetus Testamentum*, Vol. XIV, Leiden: E. J. Brill, 1967, pp. 17–51, concludes that the final song includes only c. 53. Various authors also suggest other groupings of passages.

glory, seated upon His heavenly throne, with angelic attendants. The results of God's revelation to the prophet are inspired, 40:8.

Isaiah gives a limited development to the Trinity. The role of the Father naturally dominates the book. The prophet also mentions the earthly life and work of the Son and the work of the Holy Spirit. The Son will be born of "the virgin" (7:14; cf. Matt. 1:23). A forerunner will precede His ministry, 40:3–5; cf. Matt. 3:3. He will not be ostentatious, 42:1–4; cf. Matt. 12:18–21. He will depend upon the Lord, 50:7–9. He will heal many physically, 53:4; cf. Matt. 8:17.

The Spirit of the Lord commissions Him to preach and heal those who are spiritually bound by sin, 61:1–2; cf. Luke 4:17–19. He will preach in Zebulun and Naphtali, 9:2, and will use parables to illustrate His message, 6:9–10; cf. Matthew 13:13–15. His word will cut as a sword, 49:2. He will bring salvation to the earth, 49:6, 9–12; 53:10–11. He does this through suffering, 50:4–9; 52:13–53:12, vicariously for the sins of the people, 53:4–6. Isaiah vividly describes the Crucifixion of Christ, 50:6–9; 52:13–53:12. He includes such details as the spitting in His face, 50:6; cf. Matthew 26:67; the marring of His face, 52:14; cf. Matthew 26:67; 27:29–30; and the vicarious nature of His death on the cross, 53:4–6; cf. I Peter 2:24–25.

In general, His hearers will reject His preaching, 6:9, 10; 29:13; cf. John 12:40. He will thus be a stumbling block to the Jews, 8:14; cf. I Peter 2:8. Those who do believe on Him become His spiritual children, 8:18, cf. Hebrews 2:13, and He becomes the cornerstone of the church, 28:16; cf. I Peter 2:6. He is a covenant for the people, 49:8.

In view of the Holy Spirit's stated purpose to glorify Christ, John 16:14, it is not surprising that Isaiah does not stress the "Spirit of the Lord." Still, there are enough references to let us make some generalizations about His work. He is omniscient, 40:13–14. Not seeking His guidance leads to sin, 30:1. He is "vexed" by sin, 63:10. He sent the Messiah into the world, 48:16, and rested upon Him in His ministry, 11:2; 42:1; 61:1. During the kingdom, He will be poured out upon Israel, 32:15; 59:21.

The passage in 48:1–16 gives one of the clearest intimations of the Trinity in the OT. Beginning with v. 3, the first person singular pronoun occurs in a chain of statements that continues through the passage. This person is omniscient, 48:5–7, the judge of Israel, 48:10–11, eternal, 48:12, and the Creator, 48:13. Clearly, the statements refer to God. Yet, 48:16 says, "the Lord God, and his Spirit, hath sent me." We can give a clear explanation of the passage only by recognizing the Trinity. Other passages that mention the three members of the Godhead include 11:2; 42:1; 59:19–21; 61:1, and 63:7–14.

Judgment and Blessing

Despite His choice of Israel as His people, the Lord will not tolerate sin. For this reason, Isaiah predicts some of the judgments that God will pour out upon those who have turned from Him. He shows the judgment of God on sin in connection with three separate classes: individuals, foreign nations, and Israel and Judah. In addition, the prophet describes some of the blessings that God will give to those who are faithful to Him.

Upon Individuals. Two individuals make up the first group. Shebna, Israel's treasurer under King Hezekiah, is deposed from his position. This comes as judgment for his pride, 22:15–19. King Hezekiah, godly in much of his life, falls into the sin of pride while hosting messengers from Babylon. The Lord predicts that Babylon will bring judgment on the land, 39:1–8.

Upon Foreign Nations. The second group that faces judgment includes several foreign nations. These receive judgment because of their wicked actions toward Israel. Isaiah includes several nations: Assyria, 37:33–36; Moab, 15:1–16:14; Ethiopia, 20:2–6; Egypt, 19:1–17; Syria, represented by Damascus, 17:1–14; Edom, 34:5–17; Arabia, 21:13–17; Tyre, 23:1–14; and Babylon, 47:1–13. Although God sometimes used these nations to carry out His purpose of judging Israel for their sin, e.g., 10:5, they have not glorified Him, 10:13. This failure to see God's direction in their actions renders them liable to judgment.

Upon Israel and Judah. The nations of Israel and Judah make up the last class to receive judgment. Isaiah mentions Israel only briefly, 9:8–10:4. The judgment of Judah, however, is one of the major themes of the book. At least fifteen passages develop this topic, e.g., 3:1–9. In the course of the pronouncements of judgment, Isaiah records a catalog of sins. The people are guilty of murder, 1:15, 21; 59:7, and bribery, 1:23. They have oppressed the orphans, widows, and poor, 1:23; 10:2. They are greedy, 2:7, covetous, 5:8–10, and envious, 26:11. They have become proud, 9:9; 28:1, 3, and conceited, 5:21. The people have consulted familiar spirits and wizards, 8:19. They have practiced soothsaying, 2:6, and sorcery, 57:3. They are drunkards, 5:11–17; 28:7–8, and guilty of moral perversion, 5:20. They depend upon man, not God, 2:22.

Religiously, the people have forsaken the Lord, 1:2–5. They have failed to offer sacrifice, 43:23–24. What worship they offer is ritualistic,

29:13; 58:1–5. They worship idols, 2:8; 45:20; 57:5, and mock God, 5:18–19. Their leaders are guilty of making covenants with foreigners, 2:6; 31:1–3, even rejecting Jerusalem in favor of Syria, 8:6. They are unjust in their rule, 5:22–24. Because of these sins, the nation will reap what it has sown, 3:10–11.

Blessing of the Faithful. Despite the severity of the judgments, Isaiah holds out hope for Israel. God's purpose in the judgments is not national annihilation. He seeks rather to refine the people for Himself, 48:9–10. Repeatedly, Isaiah urges the people to repent, 1:16–20, and to forsake their sins, 55:6–7. He holds out the hope of mercy in the midst of judgment, 1:9. God will spare a remnant of His people, 10:20–23; 11:11–16.

Eschatology

While older books have introduced elements of eschatology, Isaiah is the first biblical author to develop it so completely. It is not possible to understand the book properly apart from this recognition. The Rapture of the church, the Tribulation era, the millennial kingdom, and the eternal ages are all present in varying degrees. The study of this topic is one of the most interesting approaches to the book.

The Return of the Lord. The prophet speaks of the Lord's return, 40:3, 9. He mentions that the saints will accompany Him at His return, 40:10. Over and over, it is assumed that the Lord returns and rules over mankind, e.g., 9:6; 33:22. Isaiah makes the soon return of the Lord motivation for right living, 56:1. The NT follows this same practice. The Lord may return at any time. In view of this, believers should live godly lives; cf. I John 2:28.

These passages do not all make a distinction between the return of the Lord for His saints and the return of the Lord with His saints. The fuller development of this doctrine comes from the NT teaching concerning the Lord's return.

The Rapture of Believers. Isaiah 26:19–21 gives a graphic picture of the pre-Tribulation rapture of believers. Verse 19 describes the resurrection of the "dead bodies," plural, not singular as in the AV. The Lord's invitation to His people is to "hide . . . until the indignation is past," v. 20. Verse 21 completes this brief thought by giving the reason for the Rapture. The Lord hides His people from His punishment of the wicked earth.

The Tribulation Era. Isaiah vividly describes the Tribulation. Several passages deal generally with the judgments that come upon the earth during this period. This period, called the "day of the Lord," 2:12; 13:6, 9, and the time of Israel's "travail," 66:7, will involve terrible devastation of the earth, 13:9, 11; 34:2–3, 8–10; 63:3, 6. The phrase "that day" also often refers to the Tribulation, e.g., 2:11, 17, 20; 3:18. A drought will come on the earth, 42:15. Heavenly disturbances, 13:10, 13; 51:6, and earthquakes, 13:13, will accompany the judgment.

Isaiah pays particular attention to the final days of this period. The nations of the earth gather themselves together from around the world to destroy the nation of Israel, 13:4–5. The Lord, however, exercises His judgment upon the nations, 24:1, 6; 24:17–20; 29:7–8. His judgment falls on both the spiritual realm, "the host of the high ones," the ungodly angels who have fought against the Lord, and the secular realm, "kings of the earth," those ruling over the world system at the time of the Lord's return, 24:21. The Battle of Armageddon climaxes the Lord's victory over His enemies, 30:25; 49:26. The Lord will return to destroy those who fight against Him, 66:15–16.

Millennial Kingdom. Isaiah devotes much of his eschatological emphasis to the kingdom age. The millennial reign of the Lord will follow the Tribulation, 61:2; 63:4. During the Tribulation, the Jewish nation will turn in repentance to the Lord, 30:19–22; 63:7–8; 66:8. He will preserve a remnant from the devastation, 27:2–5; 52:2. In the kingdom, he will "plant" them again in their land, 27:6; 60:21; 61:3–4. Jews from across the world will return to Palestine, 11:11–12; 51:11; 52:11–12. A road will join Egypt and Assyria to make travel easier for those who trust the Lord, 19:23; 35:8–9; 62:10. Gentile nations will help them return, 49:22–23; 60:10; 66:20. Israel will multiply in number, 9:3*a*; 49:18–21; 60:22. The borders of the land will be enlarged to hold the additional people, 33:17*b*; 54:2–3. There will be unity between Judah and Israel, 11:13.

Fire will cleanse the land from the effects of the Tribulation, 9:5. Physical changes will take place in the land, 43:19; 44:3; 52:9. Jerusalem will physically rise above the surrounding region, 2:2. The Lord will destroy the Gulf of Suez and break the Euphrates River into smaller streams, 11:15–16. The land will become more fruitful, 29:17; 35:1–2; 41:19; 55:12–13. The people will use valuable materials, 60:17*a*, to rebuild ruins in Palestine, 61:4.

The Lord will heal the physical infirmities of those who live in the land, 29:18, including the blind, deaf, lame, and dumb, 35:5–6. He will comfort His people, 57:18, and guide them in their decisions, 30:21.

There will be no more war or national punishment for sin, 40:1–2; 60:18. He will make provision for their needs, 4:6, including protecting them from their enemies, 33:21–22. He will bless them, 46:13; 49:13. The nation will be a blessing to the world, 19:24. The whole world will know that God has blessed them, 61:9; 62:2.

Those who live in the land will be godly, 57:13. Wicked men will no longer deceive others, 32:5–8. The nation will no longer worship idols, 2:18–21, but will worship the Lord, 12:1, 4–6. The spiritually lost will turn to the Lord, 42:16–17. Even Gentiles and eunuchs will worship the Lord, 56:3–7. The people will be righteous, 62:1, purified from past sins, 4:4. The godly will receive the Holy Spirit, 32:15, and have spiritual understanding, 29:22–24. They will see the Lord, 33:17a. The Lord will delight in them, 62:4, and they will praise Him, 42:10–12. The temple will be rebuilt, 60:13. The people will worship the Lord with their feasts, 33:20a. They will offer sacrifices, memorials of His sacrifice for their sins, 56:7; 60:7.

The King will rule in righteousness from His throne in Jerusalem, 2:2–4; 9:7; 16:5. Princes will rule under Him to dispense justice, 32:1. Righteousness will prevail, 11:4a; 51:5. Many Jews will return to live in Jerusalem, 30:19. The inhabitants of this city will be holy, 1:26; 4:3; 26:2, with no heathen being allowed to enter, 52:1. The redeemed from across the earth will come to Jerusalem, 35:10, and its gates will always be open to receive them, 60:11. This will be a time of peace for the world, 14:7; 54:10, 13–14. Even the animal kingdom will lose its natural animosity for mankind and for one another, 11:6–8; 65:25. The knowledge of the Lord will cover the whole earth, 11:9. He will be exalted, 12:4; 33:5, and the people will obey His Word, 2:3. God's people will no longer die or know sadness, 25:8; 35:10b; 65:20.

The Lord will include Gentile nations in the kingdom. The Egyptians will worship Him, 19:19–20, 22; 45:14. Ethiopia and the Sabeans, 45:14, will also be a part of Messiah's kingdom. There will be many Gentiles nations in the kingdom, 49:22–23; 56:3, 6–8; 60:6–9; 65:1. The Lord will send representatives throughout the earth to convert the nations following the establishment of some "sign," 66:19. Many will receive the Lord, 44:5; 60:3, and will worship Him, 11:10; 45:14. These nations will go to Jerusalem, 2:2, and will receive instruction from the Lord, 2:3. They will bring tribute to Israel, 60:5, 11, and render service to them, 61:5. The Lord will hold a feast to celebrate His union with the redeemed of all nations, 25:6. The New Jerusalem will be beautiful, 54:11–12.

Tragically, there will be those who will reject the rule of the Lord. At the end of the Millennium, these will gather together in rebellion against the Lord, 54:15. The Lord will defeat them. He will gather them together for the Great White Throne Judgment, 24:22; 66:18. Judgment will fall on Satan, 14:12–15.

Eternal Ages. Isaiah gives only limited space to eternity. Those who have rebelled against the Lord will suffer the eternal torments of the damned, 66:24. The Lord will create new heavens and a new earth for His people, 51:16; 65:17; 66:22. There will be no more sun or moon since the Lord Himself will give light to His people, 13:10; 24:23; 60:19–20. During this time all will worship the Lord, 66:23. The people of God will never again be cut off in judgment, 66:22. Those who enter into this new creation will no longer remember the cares and concerns of the former earth, 65:17.

Outline of Isaiah

The following outline gives a broad overview of the book. Additional details will be introduced in the discussions of the individual sections of the book.

I. Prophecies Concerning Judah and Jerusalem 1:1–12:6

    A. Judgment and Redemption 1:1–6:13

        1. Principles of Salvation 1:1–31

        2. Judgment and Glory 2:1–4:6

        3. Judgment of Israel 5:1–6:13

    B. Messiah's Coming and Kingdom 7:1–12:6

        1. Sign of the Virgin 7:1–25

        2. Comfort in the Darkness 8:1–9:7

        3. Judgment of the Wicked 9:8–10:4

        4. Judgment of Assyria 10:5–34

        5. Coming of the Messiah 11:1–16

        6. Chorus of Praise 12:1–6

ISAIAH 1

There is a logical development of the Book of Isaiah. Chapters 1–5 serve as an overview of Isaiah's ministry. This overview concludes in c. 6, where the prophet records his call into the prophetic ministry. This leads naturally into a series of messianic prophecies. Isaiah interweaves these with predictions of judgment, which will fall on the wicked both inside and outside the nation of Israel. Isaiah devotes c. 7–12 to the messianic hope and the judgment of evil men. Chapters 13–23 describe God's judgment of the nations. This serves to symbolize the eschatological judgments of c. 24. Isaiah follows this with the millennial kingdom and the final victory of the Lord over sinful man, c. 25–27. In c. 28–31, the prophet reemphasizes the fact of judgment for sin and then moves again to the hopeful future of the nation, c. 32–35.

Chapters 36–39 are a historical interlude. Isaiah concludes here his emphasis on Assyria and introduces Babylon. Beginning with c. 40, the book gives more stress to the comfort that God extends to His people. Chapter 41 introduces Cyrus, the king responsible for freeing Israel from their captivity. Chapter 42 introduces the Servant of the Lord, the Messiah, who brings ultimate comfort to God's people. The Lord will deliver His people from their enemies and bless them, c. 43–48. The Servant of the Lord will set up His kingdom and deliver Israel, c. 49–52*a;* He will redeem them, c. 52*b*–53; and He will bless redeemed mankind but judge the wicked, c. 54–57.

Isaiah rebukes the nation for its ritualistic worship, c. 58. If they will turn to the Lord, He will bless them with a blessing that extends into eternity, c. 59–60. There will be justice in the world, c. 61. Gentile nations will acknowledge the Lord, c. 62. He will judge the earth with the Tribulation judgments, c. 63. He will show mercy in preserving a remnant for Himself, c. 64–65. God's people will worship Him in the new creation, c. 66.

I. Prophecies Concerning Judah and Jerusalem 1:1–12:6
A. Judgment and Redemption 1:1–6:13

Isaiah begins his prophetic writing with the emphasis that has led to his reputation as "the evangelical prophet." After condemning the sin of the nation, vv. 1–15, he makes his first offer of forgiveness, vv. 16–19. Those who refuse this offer, v. 20, and continue in their sin will receive

*1 The vision of Isaiah the son of Amoz, which he saw concerning
Judah and Jerusalem in the days of Uzziah, Jotham, Ahaz, and
Hezekiah, kings of Judah.*

judgment, vv. 21–23. God's purpose is to cleanse the nation, vv. 24–26.
Those who respond to the Lord will experience His blessing, vv. 27–31.

1. Principles of Salvation 1:1–31[1]
a. Wickedness of the People 1:1–15

1 The opening chapter introduces the book by summarizing the sins
of Judah. Isaiah here condemns the ritualistic worship of the people. We
cannot be dogmatic as to the date. Verse 7 suggests that Isaiah may be
writing ca. 701 B.C., at the time of the Assyrian invasion of Judah. The
initial verse stands as a heading to the entire book.[2] This "vision of Isaiah" refers to events that occur throughout the reigns of Uzziah, Jotham,
Ahaz, and Hezekiah.[3] Isaiah elsewhere refers to visions, e.g., 21:2; 22:1.
That this revelation occurred in a "vision" suggests the inspiration of

---

[1]I have used a simplified transliteration system to indicate most of the Hebrew vowels.
The *a* indicates both the *qameṣ* and the *pataḥ*, the *e* indicates both the *segol* and the *ṣerê*,
the *o* indicates both the *ḥolem* and the *qameṣ ḥatup*, and the *u* indicates the *qibbuṣ*. The *ᵃ*,
ᵒ, or the *ᵉ* indicate the *šewa*. I have used *î* to represent the *ḥireq yod*, *ê* the *ṣerê yod*, and *â*
the *qameṣ hêʾ*. The *ô* indicates the *ḥolem waw* and the *û* the *šureq*.

[2]Among others, Kelley, p. 182; Skinner, *Isaiah I–XXXIX*, p. 1; and Owen C. Whitehouse, *Isaiah*, in *The Century Bible*, n.d., I, 1, suggest that the heading originally stood
before a shorter collection of oracles concerned with Judah and Jerusalem. This collection was combined with other collections and the heading became a heading for the entire book. Walter Brueggemann, *Isaiah 1–39* in *Westminster Bible Companion*, p. 12,
refers the heading to portions of c. 1–39. He attributes c. 40–66 to different authorship.
There is no evidence to support these views. Second Chron. 32:32 suggests that the title
was known by the late fifth century, the time for the writing of Chronicles.

[3]Otto Kaiser, *Isaiah 1–12*, 1972, p. 3, concludes that the statement reflects a later author since it mentions Jotham as a king. According to his chronology, Jotham served only
as regent under Uzziah and died before his father. There are two problems with the view.
In the first place, we cannot be certain of the chronology. Jotham may well have ruled in
his own right for a few years before his death. In the second place, even if Jotham was
the regent, his authority was that of a king. It would not be wrong to refer to him as king
since this was the position he occupied as regent. Brueggemann, *Isaiah 1–39*, pp. 11–12,
dismisses Jotham as "relatively unimportant and does not figure in the book of Isaiah."
He further dismisses the importance of Uzziah since Isaiah did not begin his ministry
until Uzziah's death. This leaves Ahaz, a weak king, and Hezekiah, a strong king. With
twisted logic, he concludes that Ahaz is a "metaphor for the refusal of Jerusalem to trust
Yahweh, whereby Israel comes to failure and exile." Hezekiah, however, is a "metaphor
for the trust that Israel may have in Yahweh, which makes possible an enduring commu-
nal existence into and beyond exile." We cannot take the approach seriously.

2 *Hear, O heavens, and give ear, O earth: for the Lord hath spoken, I have nourished and brought up children, and they have rebelled against me.*
3 *The ox knoweth his owner, and the ass his master's crib: but Israel doth not know, my people doth not consider.*
4 *Ah sinful nation, a people laden with iniquity, a seed of evildoers, children that are corrupters: they have forsaken the Lord, they have provoked the Holy One of Israel unto anger, they are gone away backward.*

Isaiah's message. God often used visions to give His revelation to the prophets; cf. Ezekiel 1:1; Daniel 2:19. Where there was no vision, the people lacked revelation from the Lord; cf. Proverbs 29:18. False prophets claimed to have visions in order to authenticate their prophecies, Jeremiah 14:14; 23:16.

The vision here concerns "Judah and Jerusalem," the primary subjects of God's revelation in the book. Later, Isaiah mentions other nations, e.g., Syria and Israel, 7:1; Assyria, 7:17; Babyon, 13:1. He includes these in his message because of their relationship to Judah. The nation chosen by God remains at the heart of Isaiah's writings.

As mentioned in the Introduction, Jewish tradition suggests that Amoz was the brother of King Amaziah. We have no evidence of this relationship. The fact, however, that Isaiah had access to the king and held a position at the court may support his relationship.[4] Whether it is so, it is clear that Isaiah was placed so that his prophecies touched the highest levels of Jewish society, v. 1.

2–4 The Lord calls on "the heavens" and "the earth," the whole of creation, to hear His indictment of the people; cf. Deuteronomy 32:1.[5] He has "nourished and brought up" His children.[6] Despite God's care,

---

[4]See the discussion on p. xi in the Introduction.

[5]Wright, p. 24, and T. R. Birks, *Commentary on the Book of Isaiah*, 1870, p. 19, refer the phrase to the angels in heaven and all the inhabitants of the earth. This is a possible view although I prefer to understand it as a poetical expression representing, by synecdoche, the whole of creation. Isaiah uses the expression this way in 13:13. See also 42:5. Judah Stampfer, "On Translating Biblical Poetry," *Judaism* 14:501, criticizes the translation "Give ear, O earth" as a "leisurely, detached gesture." I fail to see that his translation, "Attend me, O earth," gives any more vitality to the phrase. The AV accurately catches the sense of the denominative verb ʾazan, "to listen."

[6]Douglas R. Jones, "Exposition of Isaiah Chapter One Verses One to Nine," *SJOT* 17:469, translates the phrase "Sons I have made great and exalted." While this is technically correct, the context indicates that these are the words of a father to his children. The AV translation, "nourished and brought up," is more appropriate in this setting.

pictured as that of a father for his children, they had rebelled against Him, v. 2. The "ox" and the "ass" represent the dumb beasts of burden who are intelligent enough to know their owner and the source of their food. Israel, however, did not know as much as the animals. She did not "know" (*yada^c*) God nor did she consider her relationship to Him. The verb *yada^c* refers to an experiential knowledge. It is not that Israel did not know who God was. They knew quite well who He was. They did not, however, have an experiential knowledge of Him because they had rejected His Word and His prophets. As will become clear in vv. 11–15, Israel worshiped the Lord. But that was ritual worship and did not reflect a sincere heart worship of the Lord. Further, they did not "consider" (*bîn*), i.e., they did not understand the importance of their actions. The verb *bîn* refers to discerning the difference between opposites, often describing discernment between good and evil, v. 3.

Isaiah condemns the people with seven distinct phrases. The opening interjection "Ah" (*hôy*) normally expresses a lament or an announcement of trouble.[7] Here it refers to God's sorrow over His people's sin. The first four phrases describe the results of Judah's sin. (1) The "nation" (*gôy*)[8] has turned to sin and (2) has become loaded down with "iniquity" (*^cawon*). The term *^cawon* initially meant "to be bent, crooked"; cf. 21:3. This leads to the thought of "distortion"; cf. 19:14. In a moral sense, it refers to perverse behavior. It is often translated "iniquity." (3) They are "a seed of evildoers [*ra^ca^c*]." The word *ra^ca^c* in the *hip^cîl* refers to one that causes evil; thus these are offspring marked by wickedness.[9] (4) They are "children" (lit. "sons") who cause corruption.

The final phrases relate Judah's sin to its causes. (5) Judah has forsaken the Lord. (6) She has "provoked" (better, "despised") the Lord.[10]

---

[7]The word *hôy* occurs twenty-one times in Isaiah, more than in any other book. Only in 1:24; 18:1; and 55:1 is there a positive sense connected with it. Elsewhere, it is negative.

[8]Jones, p. 473, says that the use of "*gôi* suggests that those who should have been 'my people', *^cammi*, have become indistinguishable from the heathen nations." The problem with this view is that *gôy* refers to Israel elsewhere as well as to the Gentile nations, e.g., Exod. 19:6; Isa. 9:3; 26:2, 15. It is more likely used here in poetic variation with *^cam* and to achieve the assonance of *hôy gôy*.

[9]Barnes, I, 60, and Joseph A. Alexander, *Commentary on Isaiah*, 1867, I, 82, understand the genitive relationship to refer to source rather than species, i.e., the people had descended from evildoers. The parallelism with "sinful nation," "people laden with iniquity," and "children that are corrupters" argues that the genitive refers here to a people who are evil.

[10]The words "unto anger" are interpretive. Since the MT does not include the phrase, it is best left as above, "they have despised the Holy One of Israel."

5 *Why should ye be stricken any more? ye will revolt more and more: the whole head is sick, and the whole heart faint.*

6 *From the sole of the foot even unto the head there is no soundness in it; but wounds, and bruises, and putrifying sores: they have not been closed, neither bound up, neither mollified with ointment.*

7 *Your country is desolate, your cities are burned with fire: your land, strangers devour it in your presence, and it is desolate, as overthrown by strangers.*

8 *And the daughter of Zion is left as a cottage in a vineyard, as a lodge in a garden of cucumbers, as a besieged city.*

9 *Except the Lord of hosts had left unto us a very small remnant, we should have been as Sodom, and we should have been like unto Gomorrah.*

The phrase "Holy One of Israel" is one of Isaiah's favorite titles for God. He uses the phrase twenty-five times to describe God's nature as a holy God.[11] (7) "They are gone away backward," deserting God as they leave Him for other gods, v. 4.

5–9 Isaiah takes note of the judgment that has fallen upon Judah. He asks more literally, "why will ye be beaten any more [*meh . . . ʿôd*],[12] why will you continue with rebellion?" Both questions are rhetorical and assert that there is no good reason for Judah to continue their wayward way. The "head" and the "heart" (*leb*) both refer to Judah's emotions.[13]

---

[11]J. Alec Motyer, *The Prophecy of Isaiah*, 1993, p. 43, suggests that the title "*The Holy One of Israel* may well have been coined by Isaiah." While Isaiah uses the title more than all other OT authors combined, it does occur in Psalms, two of which are written by Asaph and Ethan more than two hundred years before Isaiah.

[12]Whitehouse, I, 90, translates the question "On what part (of the body) will ye be smitten yet?" The use of *meh* with ʿôd, however, regularly indicates time, "How long?" Cf. Bruce Waltke and M. O'Connor, *An Introduction to Biblical Hebrew Syntax*, 1990, p. 325.

[13]Edward J. Young, *The Book of Isaiah*, rpt. 1999, I, 50, understands the "head" and the "heart" to represent the outward and inward parts of the nation. W. E. Vine, *Isaiah: Prophecies, Promises, Warnings*, rpt. 1997, p. 6, compares the head to "the outward controlling power" and the heart to "the inward emotions." H. C. Leupold, *Exposition of Isaiah*, 1968, I, 58, refers the head to "those who are in positions of rule" and the heart "to courageous outlook, of which there is none left in the land." Franz Delitzsch, *Isaiah*, in *Commentary on the Old Testament*, trans. James Martin, rpt. 1978, I, 83, associated the head and the heart "as the noblest parts of the outer and inner man." Rawlinson, I, 3, relates the head and the heart to the "intellectual and moral natures." These are possible views. Elsewhere in the OT, however, the head primarily refers to an actual head, either the head of the human body or the leader of a group. When it has a figurative meaning, it generally refers to the emotions, e.g., Ps. 3:3; see also Isa. 58:5. The heart regularly refers to the emotions. For this reason, I prefer the above interpretation. I disagree with

The nation has rebelled against God and now is "sick" (*ḥºlî*) and "faint" from His judgment, v. 5. The people are filled with "wounds, and bruises [better 'welts,' raised by whips] and putrefying sores [better 'fresh wounds']." These have not been treated. They have not been "closed," or "pressed out," squeezing the pus from the sore. They have not been bandaged or covered with "ointment" ("oil"), used in biblical times as a medicine, cf. Luke 10:34; James 5:14, v. 6.

The land is desolate and the cities burned. The invading armies, "strangers," have devoured the crops. All is desolate, overthrown by the invaders. This likely refers to the Assyrian invasion described in II Kings 18:13–35, ca. 701 B.C., v. 7.[14] The "daughter of Zion," Jerusalem, has been left alone. The "cottage" and "lodge" were rude shelters placed in fields for watchmen who guarded the crops. Just as these were alone, surrounded by a large field, so Jerusalem is now alone, with no hope of help from other cities. She is "a besieged [*naṣar*] city." The participle form of *naṣar* refers to something that is watched. Here, it refers to a guarded city, v. 8. Excepting for the grace of "the Lord of hosts," who rules the hosts of heaven and earth,[15] in leaving a "very small remnant," the city would have become like Sodom and Gomorrah, gone from the face of the earth. Paul quotes the passage in Romans 9:29 as he magnifies the grace of God in leaving a remnant to Israel, v. 9.

G. R. Driver, "Isaiah I–XXXIX: Textual and Linguistic Problems," *JSS* 13:36, who relates *ḥºlî* to *heleʾ*, "sores," and *leb* to the Akkadian *libbu*, "intestines." He understands the phrase "sick head" as a head to be covered with "pustules" and the "sick heart" as a stomach disorder. Neither *ḥºlî* nor *leb* are rare and there is no reason to depart from their normal senses.

[14]The chronology of the individual chapters in Isaiah is difficult to establish. Edward J. Kissane, *The Book of Isaiah*, I, 9, suggests that this passage refers to the exile, not the invasion of 701 B.C. Robert Lowth, *Isaiah: A New Translation*, pp. 136–37, refers the passage to the end of Jotham's rule, when Israel and Syria invaded Judah. We simply do not have enough information to be certain.

[15]The OT calls the angels the "host of heaven," I Kings 22:19 (II Chron. 18:18); Neh. 9:6. Israel is called the "hosts of the Lord," Exod. 12:40–41. Whitehouse, I, 92, refers the word "hosts" to the stars "regarded as celestial spirits who fought under Yahweh's leadership." He cites Judg. 5:20 and Isa. 40:26 in support of his view. He fails to recognize the metaphorical use of "stars" in these passages.

10 *Hear the word of the Lord, ye rulers of Sodom; give ear unto the
     law of our God, ye people of Gomorrah.*
11 *To what purpose is the multitude of your sacrifices unto me? saith
     the Lord: I am full of the burnt offerings of rams, and the fat of fed
     beasts; and I delight not in the blood of bullocks, or of lambs, or of
     he goats.*
12 *When ye come to appear before me, who hath required this at your
     hand, to tread my courts?*
13 *Bring no more vain oblations; incense is an abomination unto me;
     the new moons and sabbaths, the calling of assemblies, I cannot
     away with; it is iniquity, even the solemn meeting.*
14 *Your new moons and your appointed feasts my soul hateth: they are
     a trouble unto me; I am weary to bear them.*
15 *And when ye spread forth your hands, I will hide mine eyes from
     you: yea, when ye make many prayers, I will not hear: your hands
     are full of blood.*

10–15 Isaiah calls upon the people to hear God's Word. He symbolically refers to Jerusalem as "Sodom . . . Gomorrah"; cf. Revelation 11:8.
This indicates the spiritual degeneracy of the city. The word "law" (*tôrâ*)
has "teaching" as a strong component of meaning. The purpose of God
here is to teach the people the error of their ways, v. 10.[16] Isaiah's question is rhetorical, meant to show the worthlessness of ritualistic "sacrifices" (*zebaḥ*);[17] cf. I Samuel 15:22–23; Psalm 51:16–17. Sacrifice has
value only when offered with a right attitude. This has always been a
principle in the worship of God; cf. Matthew 23:23; I Corinthians
11:28–30. To show that He rejects ritual worship, the Lord states His
displeasure with the sacrifices of the people. The term "fed beasts" (or
"fatlings, fat beasts," normally cattle) refers to animals that have been
separated from the flocks and fed only clean food in preparation for sacrifice, e.g., 11:6; Ezekiel 39:18; Amos 5:22. The Lord here rejects even
the choicest sacrifices, cf. Amos 5:22, v. 11.

The phrase "when ye come to appear [*ra²â*] before me"[18] refers to the
required attendance of Jewish men at the three major feasts. The men

---

[16]Grogan, p. 33, refers *tôrâ* to Mosaic Law. While this is possible, it seems rather to
refer to the whole teaching of God regarding worship. The people needed to learn that it
was the spirit of worship, not the letter of the law, that pleased God.

[17]The word *zebaḥ* regularly refers to the slaughter of animals for sacrifice. The word
came to refer generally to any of the bloody sacrifices.

[18]Whitehouse, I, 93; David Stacey, *Isaiah 1–39*, 1993, p. 7; and John D. W. Watts, *Isaiah 1–33*, 1987, p. 14, mention the possibility that the Massoretes pointed the verb *ra²â*

were to journey to the tabernacle (later, the temple) for the Feasts of Passover, Pentecost, and Tabernacles, Exodus 23:14–17; Deuteronomy 16:16. Here, however, the men come with a wrong attitude, and God considers their attendance no more than "tread[ing] [or trampling] my courts," v. 12. Their "oblations" were meal offerings, flour mixed with oil and frankincense.[19] God describes these as "vain" (*šaw˒*, or "lying"). The word *šaw˒* refers to something that has no value. While they appear to be sacrifices to God, they deceive their offerers. God considers the smoke of their incense (*q*e*toret*) "an abomination."[20] He rejects the worship services on the new moon (Num. 10:10; 28:11) and Sabbath days (Lev. 24:5–8; Num. 28:9) and "the calling of assemblies [*miqra˒*]."[21] The term *miqra˒* refers to various sacred convocations, including Sabbaths (Lev. 23:2–3), the first and seventh days of Passover (Lev. 23:6–8), the first and eighth day of Tabernacles (Lev. 23:34–36), and the seventh day of Pentecost (Lev. 23:21). A special convocation was called for the Feast of Trumpets (Lev. 23:24) and the Day of Atonement (Lev. 23:27). The Lord rejects all these. The phrase "I cannot away with; it is iniquity [*˒awen*], even the solemn meeting" is better "I cannot endure iniquity or the solemn meeting." The word *˒awen* occurs widely. It has a broad range of meanings connected with wickedness. It may have the sense of "deceit" and often refers to idolatry. The "solemn meeting" was also a special day of the great feasts. As such, it often refers to the *miqra˒*, e.g., the seventh day of Passover (Deut. 16:8) or the eighth day of Tabernacles (Num. 29:35). It could also include days of religious service proclaimed by civic leaders (II Chron. 7:9; Neh. 8:18). God rejects even the most special of days devoted to worship, v. 13. He rejects the worship at the

---

as a *nip˓al* to avoid a conflict with Exod. 33:20. With the passive *nip˓al*, the sense is appearing before God rather than looking upon God. The *nip˓al* of the verb refers to appearing before God in Exod. 23:15, 17; 34:20, 23, 24; Deut. 16:16; 31:11; I Sam. 1:22; and Ps. 42:2. There is no need to change it to the *qal* here.

[19]While the "oblation" (*minḥâ*) could include blood sacrifices, Gen. 4:4, it overwhelmingly refers elsewhere to grain offerings.

[20]A. S. Herbert, *Isaiah 1–39*, 1973, p. 29, comments on the NEB. Stacey, p. 8, comments on the Revised English Bible. Both translate the phrase "incense is an abomination to me" as "the reek of sacrifice is abhorrent to me." This takes *q*e*toret* as "reek of sacrifice," an interpretive sense not found elsewhere.

[21]The phrase "calling of assemblies" translates *q*e*ro˒ miqra˒*, both words from the same root. This repetition of roots characterizes Isaiah's style of writing. Repetition, word plays, and assonance occur in every major part of the book. This strongly argues for a single author.

16 Wash you, make you clean; put away the evil of your doings from before mine eyes; cease to do evil;
17 Learn to do well; seek judgment, relieve the oppressed, judge the fatherless, plead for the widow.

"new moons and the "appointed feasts." He hates the ritualistic worship of the people. It is "trouble" (or "a burden") to Him. He is weary with putting up with their sacrifices, v. 14. He will reject even the prayers of the people, a logical result of their sin; cf. Psalm 66:18. The very hands that they stretch out to God in prayer are "full of blood" (lit. "bloods"), an idiomatic reference to violent deeds that include even murder (cf. v. 21), v. 15.[22]

Note that Israel was a religious yet wicked people. The mere act of worship is meaningless without the right heart attitude. Israel went through the motions, doing all the right things but with a wrong spirit. For this reason, God rejected their attempts to worship Him. The principle is true today. God still hates ritualistic worship.

b. Invitation to the People 1:16–20

16–17 Washing often symbolizes purification, e.g., Exodus 19:14; 29:4. The people must put away their sin; cf. Romans 13:12–13. They should "cease to do evil [ra^ca^c, see v. 4]." This is the negative approach to cleansing, v. 16.[23] The people then must put on godly habits, a positive approach to godliness. Verse 17 lists five actions that the people must practice. These actions include (1) the practice of good works, (2) the pursuit of "judgment" (*mišpaṭ*, better "justice"),[24] (3) the relief of "the oppressed," i.e., the reproof of the ruthless,[25] (4) the defense of orphans,

---

[22]Kaiser, *Isaiah 1–12*, p. 16, understands the plural "bloods" to refer to the hypocritical sacrifices of the people. While the view is possible, most refer the passage to the murder of innocent victims.

[23]Kissane, I, 12, understands the passage from the Roman Catholic position that "the people must do penance for their sins." This reads the interpretation into a passage that says nothing about penance.

[24]The word *mišpaṭ* occurs more than four hundred times. It may be translated either "judgment" or "justice," depending on the context. The thought of "justice" is clear here and in most places that the word occurs in Isaiah.

[25]The phrase "relieve the oppressed" (*ʾašrû ḥamôṣ*) is better "reprove the ruthless." The phrase *ʾašrû ḥamôṣ* is lit. "set right the ruthless," i.e., correct them. The NIV translates "encourage the oppressed." This requires repointing *ḥamôṣ*, "ruthless," to *ḥamaṣ*, "oppressed." While the LXX supports this translation, it is not necessary to depart from the MT.

18 Come now, and let us reason together, saith the Lord: though your sins be as scarlet, they shall be as white as snow; though they be red like crimson, they shall be as wool.
19 If ye be willing and obedient, ye shall eat the good of the land:
20 But if ye refuse and rebel, ye shall be devoured with the sword: for the mouth of the Lord hath spoken it.

and (5) the "plead [ing]" (*rîb*)[26] on behalf of the widow. The list is representative, not exhaustive of God's requirements for His people, v. 17.

The Nature of Consecration

Separation from sin, v. 16

Separation to God, v. 17

18–20 The word "reason" (*niwwakḥâ*) is primarily a legal word.[27] The Lord does not invite the people to discuss their sins. He invites them rather to a trial in which He offers pardon to the guilty.[28] The contrast in colors brings out the stark contrast between sin and purity; cf. Psalm 51:7. The color "scarlet" comes from the kermes insect, *Coccus ilicis*. The insect lives on the kermes oak that grows in the Mediterranean region. The dried body and eggs of the female yield matter from which is made the dye used to color cloth. The color "crimson" comes from the same insect.[29] The phrases "white as snow" and "as wool" are both

---

[26]The word *rîb* often relates to a courtroom scene or controversy, e.g., Exod. 23:2, 6; Hos. 4:1. There is a legal sense connected with the pleading.

[27]George Buchanan Gray, *A Critical and Exegetical Commentary on the Book of Isaiah, vol. I,* in *The International Critical Commentary,* p. 27, argues that *yakaḥ* means "reproved" here. The word does have this meaning in the *hipᶜîl* as well as the sense "judge, decide, convince." The word, however, occurs in the *nipᶜal* here. The word *yakaḥ* occurs only twice elsewhere in the *nipᶜal*, Gen. 20:16 and Job 23:7. In neither case does the sense "reprove" occur. In Genesis, Sarah was "righted, cleared." It would also be possible to translate "reasoned with." Job wished to "reason" with God.

[28]Young, I, 76, and Leupold, I, 64, reject the idea of a trial. They understand the verse as an offer to Israel to make things right with God. The verb *yakaḥ*, however, has an overwhelming legal sense in the OT. In particular, Isaiah uses the word elsewhere in 2:4; 11:3, 4; 29:21; 37:4. In each case, there is a judicial sense connected with the word.

[29]Carl Wilhelm Eduard Näglesbach, *The Prophet Isaiah,* in *Commentary on the Holy Scriptures,* John Peter Lange, XI, 43, relates the red color to the bloodshed mentioned in

*21 How is the faithful city become an harlot! it was full of judgment;
    righteousness lodged in it; but now murderers.*
22 Thy silver is become dross, thy wine mixed with water:
*23 Thy princes are rebellious, and companions of thieves: every one
    loveth gifts, and followeth after rewards: they judge not the father-
    less, neither doth the cause of the widow come unto them.*

metaphors showing the purity of a heart when the Lord forgives sin, v. 18. The Lord offers cleansing.[30] If the people will be "willing and obedient," a mark of their repentance, God will bless them with an abundant harvest, v. 19.[31] If, however, they "refuse and rebel," He will devour them with the "sword," an emblem of judgment. The final phrase, "the mouth of the Lord hath spoken it," shows the certainty of this promise, v. 20.

c. Promise Concerning the People 1:21–31

21–23 Isaiah contrasts the glorious past of Jerusalem with her wicked present. She was once "faithful" to God but now is a "harlot"

---

v. 15. The sinner who is guilty of even such severe crimes is made pure when forgiven. While the view is possible, the connection to v. 15 is not clear.

[30]There are a variety of interpretations of the last part of the verse. (1) G. H. Box, *The Book of Isaiah*, p. 25, interprets the verse as a rhetorical question: "if your sins are as scarlet, shall they become white as snow? Be they red as crimson, shall they become as wool?" Wright, p. 25, and Leslie, p. 114, translate as a straight question: "Can they be white as snow . . . Shall they be like wool?" This makes Isaiah show the impossibility of cleansing sin by making ritual offerings. These views, however, face the problem that no interrogative particle signals a question. Further, the use of ʾim at the first to establish the condition suggests a following apodosis, not a question. (2) Watts, *Isaiah 1–33*, pp. 14–15, makes the verse conditional: "If your sins are like the scarlet . . . they may become white." (3) Whitehouse, I, 95, suggests treating the expression as "prophetic irony, though your sins be as scarlet, let them be white as snow." Nothing here, however, indicates either irony or a jussive sense. The use of the hipʿîl and the lack of any particle to signal potential argue against treating the verse this way. (4) R. B. Y. Scott, *The Book of Isaiah*, in *The Interpreter's Bible*, V, 174–75, sees the verse as the words of a judge scorning the hypocritical claim of the accused. The guilty claims that though he has sinned, he can still be forgiven. The judge replies: "Though your sins are like scarlet they shall be as white as snow[!] Though they are red like crimson they shall become like wool[!]." (5) Kissane, I, 13, makes the verse an exhortation, "If your sins are like scarlet, let them become white as snow. If they are as red as purple, let them become like wool." Again, the use of ʾim argues against taking the verbs in the following clauses as jussives. (6) Israel Wolf Slotki, *Isaiah*, 1983, p. 6, gives the rather curious view that there are two offers here. If you have sinned yourself and repent, your sins will be like snow. If you have caused others to sin, "your sins will not be forgiven completely, just as white wool is not pure white." The parallelism argues against this.

[31]Isaiah uses a play on words in vv. 19–20 that is characteristic of his style of writing. In v. 19, he states that obedience will let them "eat" (toʾkelû) the "good of the land." In

(*zonâ*).[32] The word *zonâ* occurs often to describe spiritual whoredom. Israel has left her first love and turned to other gods. She was once marked by "judgment" (*mišpaṭ*, better "justice," see v. 17). At one time the city was filled with "righteousness" (*ṣedeq*). The word *ṣedeq* describes conformity to an ethical or moral standard, especially the standard of God's Word. The city has gone away from this and now tolerates such sins as murder, v. 21.[33] Isaiah picturesquely continues this theme. Valuable silver now is worthless dross; tasty wine now is "mixed" (*mahûl*, or "weakened")[34] with water.[35] Both emblems represent the change from righteous to wicked leaders, v. 22.[36] Her "princes" (*śar*, or "rulers") now mingle with thieves. They love bribes and pursue the course that benefits them most; cf. Deuteronomy 10:17. They withhold justice from orphans and widows, v. 23.

---

v. 20, he warns that sin will cause them to "be devoured" (*teʾukkelû*). In both cases, he uses the root *ʾakal*. Robert B. Chisholm Jr., "Wordplay in the Eighth-Century Prophets," in *Vital Old Testament Issues*, ed. Roy B. Zuck, pp. 120–27, gives several similar examples of word play in Isaiah.

[32]Commentators suggest different times as the period of Jerusalem's faithfulness. Stacey, p. 11, thinks that Isaiah idealized the past. Kelley, p. 190, and many others suggest the rule of David. Näglesbach, p. 47, prefers the age of Melchisedec. Rawlinson, I, 7, refers to the times of Solomon and Jehoshaphat. I lean toward the time of David. The time, however, is not important. The point Isaiah makes is that Judah has departed from the faithfulness that identified them as the people of God.

[33]M. Friedländer, ed., *The Commentary of Ibn Ezra on Isaiah*, p. 11, understands the judges to be guilty of murder. They order the execution of innocent persons. While this is possible, there is no evidence in the text to support the view. It is just as likely that the murderers were simply wicked people living in the city.

[34]The word *mahûl* is a *hapax legomenon*. The Aramaic cognate *mehal* means "to circumcise." The thought of cutting, mutilating, leads to the idea of weakening, here by diluting with water.

[35]Mitchell Dahood, "'Weaker than Water': Comparative *beth* in Isaiah 1,22," *Biblica* 56:91–92, correctly argues that water mixed with wine is elsewhere seen as desirable, e.g., Prov. 23:31; II Macc. 15:39. For this reason, he understands the *be*-preposition before *mayim* as a comparative, "your choice wine is weaker than water." Neither Ronald J. Williams, *Hebrew Syntax: An Outline*; E. Kautzsch, *Gesenius' Hebrew Grammar*; or Waltke and O'Connor give a comparative use for the *be*-preposition. The solution probably lies in the use of *sobeʾ* rather than *yayin* for "wine." The OT associates *sobeʾ* with drunkenness, Deut. 21:20; Prov. 23:20, 21; Nah. 1:10. Cutting the *sobeʾ* with water would weaken its strength and make drunkenness unlikely.

[36]Among others, Delitzsch, I, 102, and Näglesbach, p. 47, relate the silver and the wine to the noble men who led the nation. Derek Kidner, *Isaiah*, in *The New Bible*, ed. D. A. Carson, 1994, p. 635, and Stacey, p. 11, refer them to justice and righteousness. Either view is possible. It is a question of whether the symbols illustrate v. 21 or introduce v. 23. The use of metals later, in v. 25, supports the view that leaders are in the Lord's mind.

24 *Therefore saith the Lord, the Lord of hosts, the mighty One of Israel,*
  Ah, I will ease me of mine adversaries, and avenge me of mine
  enemies:
25 *And I will turn my hand upon thee, and purely purge away thy dross,*
  and take away all thy tin:
26 *And I will restore thy judges as at the first, and thy counsellors as at*
  the beginning: afterward thou shalt be called, The city of righteous-
  ness, the faithful city.

24–26 The Lord promises judgment upon the wicked. The repetition
of the divine name three times emphasizes that God is speaking. This is
"the Lord," the master of Israel who has the right to command them. He
is "the Lord of hosts," ruler of the hosts of heaven and earth. He is "the
mighty One of Israel," the one who has strength to supply to His people.
The judgment is therefore sure. He will "ease" (*naham*)[37] Himself, bring
rest to His feelings, by judging His enemies, v. 24. He will "turn [His]
hand" upon the people. The idiom signals a change in His relationship to
them. He will now judge those who have led the nation into sin. The
Lord's "hand" often represents His power; cf. 8:11; 45:12. This will
cleanse Israel from its "dross" and "tin." The second phrase is better "I
will refine your dross as with lye [*bor*]." The word *bor* occurs only here
and Job 9:30. The feminine form occurs at Jeremiah 2:22 and Malachi
3:2. In every case, the word has the sense of a cleansing agent. He will
also take away their "tin" (*bedîlayik*, or "alloy," an impurity that robs a
precious metal of its value). The "dross" and "alloy" represent the leaders of the nation, v. 25. The Lord will take away these wicked leaders
and will replace them with godly men such as the nation had at its beginning. While partial fulfillments have come with such leaders as
Zerubbabel and Ezra, the complete fulfillment is yet future, in the Millennium. It is at that time that Jerusalem will be called "the city of righteousness [*sedeq*, see v. 21], the faithful city," v. 26.[38]

---

[37]Where the word *naham* refers to comfort, it signals the emotional support and encouragement given to the recipient. The one responsible for giving the comfort supplies
the help and guidance needed to gain this change of emotions. The Lord Himself both
supplies and receives comfort here from His actions in judgment.

[38]Rawlinson, I, 8, refers the passage to the heavenly Jerusalem, which he interprets as
the church. Young, I, 87–88, argues against a millennial position saying that this would
have given no comfort to sinful Judah. Much of prophecy, however, was not meant for
the OT community. Most commentators simply avoid the eschatological teaching at this
point. This ignores the fact that no OT setting suits naming Jerusalem as "the city of
righteousness. . . ."

*27 Zion shall be redeemed with judgment, and her converts with right-
    eousness.*
*28 And the destruction of the transgressors and of the sinners shall be
    together, and they that forsake the Lord shall be consumed.*
*29 For they shall be ashamed of the oaks which ye have desired, and ye
    shall be confounded for the gardens that ye have chosen.*
*30 For ye shall be as an oak whose leaf fadeth, and as a garden that
    hath no water.*
*31 And the strong shall be as tow, and the maker of it as a spark, and
    they shall both burn together, and none shall quench them.*

27–31 This passage gives the final promise, that of national redemption. The word "redeemed" (*tippadeh*)[39] expresses the concept of trans-
ferring ownership by the payment of a price. The word often has the
sense of "ransom." The Lord will redeem her with "judgment" (*mišpaṭ*,
better "justice," see v. 17). The "converts" (*šûb*) are those who have returned to the land from other nations. The word *šûb* refers to those who
"turn" from their sin. The word occurs often of turning from sin and
turning to God, e.g., 6:10; 19:22. These will come in "righteousness,"
v. 27. In contrast, those who forsake the Lord will receive judgment.[40]
The "destruction" (or "crushing") of the wicked will take place. The
"transgressors," those who have rebelled against God, and "sinners,"
those who have fallen short of God's standards, will fall "together."[41]
Those who forsake the Lord will "be consumed" (or "come to an end"),
v. 28. At that time, the people will be "ashamed" (*bôš*) of the sins that

---

[39]The word *padâ* is one of the great theological words of the OT. It describes the trans-
fer of ownership upon the payment of a price. The firstborn child belonged to God but
could be redeemed by paying a price, Exod. 13:13. A firstborn clean animal could not be
redeemed but was sacrificed to God, Num. 18:17. The Lord redeemed Israel from their
bondage in Egypt, Deut. 15:15. The Lord redeemed David out of difficulty, II Sam. 4:9.
The psalmist looked forward to the time when God would redeem him from death,
49:15. The Lord rebuked Israel for failing to walk in fellowship with Him when He had
redeemed them from their bondage, Hos. 7:13. The verse here looks forward to the redemption of the people from their sin. The sacrificial death of Christ is the great price
paid for our redemption.

[40]Vine, p. 9, applies the verse to those who follow Antichrist. While the context supports the view, the verse does not actually mention Antichrist. It is as possible that the
wicked simply follow their own sinful will.

[41]Henry Cowles, *Isaiah*, 1869, p. 11, does not see the destruction of transgressors together with sinners. He understands the word "together" to join the destruction of v. 28
with the redemption of v. 27. While this is possible, the Massoretic accents do not support the view.

14

have led them away from the Lord. The word *bôš* refers to the public shame that comes from some failure, either one's own failure or the failure of something in which trust was placed. The "oaks" and "gardens" refer to the groves where the people had worshiped idols; cf. Jeremiah 2:20; 3:6.[42] These represent many other temptations that could have been mentioned, v. 29. The ungodly will be as the "oak" (better "terebinth"; cf. 6:13; 61:3) or "garden" that lacks water; contra. Psalm 1:3; Isaiah 58:11. The terebinth tree grows up to forty feet high, has dark green foliage, and bears red berries. It is sometimes called the turpentine tree from the fact that turpentine may be obtained from it, v. 30. The self-sufficient man, "strong" (*ḥason*) in his own strength, will be as "tow," short or broken strands from flax.[43] Tow is highly combustible. The "maker of it" (*poʿalô*, better "his work") will be as a spark. Both the mighty man and his work will quickly burn.[44] No one will stop this judgment, v. 31.

---

[42]Kidner, p. 635, understands the "oaks" and the "groves" on the basis of v. 31 to represent "human strength and organization." Kraeling, p. 48, suggests that the verse alludes to "the rich and their country estates." Vine, p. 9, makes the "oaks" represent the "Man of Sin and the leaders under him." The "gardens" symbolize "the pleasures and glories of the world." John Mauchline, *Isaiah 1–39*, 1962, p. 58, sees the oaks and gardens as "an allusion to illicit fertility cults practised under every green tree." While these views are possible, the above view agrees more with references to trees and gardens elsewhere; cf. 57:5; 65:3; 66:17.

[43]Näglesbach, p. 49, makes the "strong" an idolater who is ruined by his idol worship. Delitzsch, I, 109, understands him as a "prosperous idolater" who can afford gold and silver idols. Leupold, I, 71, views him as the ruler who introduces idolatry into the land. Barnes, I, 80, broadens this to include "rulers, princes, and the commanders of their armies." The people rely on these for protection. Mauchline, p. 58, states that in the passage, the "strong" can refer only to the "oak" of v. 30. Ibn Ezra, p. 13, refers to the idols "which are made strong." Vine, p. 10, ignores the lack of a context and identifies the "strong" as the two great "beasts" of Rev. 13. Homer Hailey, *A Commentary on Isaiah*, 1992, p. 44, and Von Orelli, p. 23, understand the "work" as the idols that the man has made. Gray, I, 39, sees it as "preparations for war, alliances, and so forth." Clearly, it is hazardous to be dogmatic. Without being specific, I have referred the "strong" to self-sufficient men and the "work" to their evil works.

[44]M. Tsevat, "Isaiah I 31," *VT* 19:261–62, understands *poʿel* as God. He equates *ḥason* with *ḥwsn*, "flax," a word that appears in rabbinical Hebrew but not in the OT. The flax and the tow are metaphors for the high and low classes of people. God "sparks" these so that they burn together. His position is weak in that he relies on a nonbiblical word for support. The word *ḥason* and related words occur several times in the OT, and there are Aramaic and Arabic cognates with the same meaning. Further, Tsevat mistakes the burning of a spark as a momentary thing, which is not satisfactory as a punishment. In fact, it starts a conflagration that represents the punishment. Samuel E. Loewenstamm, "Isaiah I 31," *VT* 22:247, gives several other weaknesses in Tsevat's argument.

Practical Applications from Chapter 1

1. Turning Away from the Lord (1:4). This action leads only in one direction—downward to sin, iniquity, evil, and corruption. This is the fruit that grows in the life of those who turn from God.
2. The Grace of God (1:9). God's chastisement often has the purpose of turning man back to Him. The withholding of complete judgment is an act of grace that gives time for men to come back to God.
3. Ritual Worship (1:10–15). Those who merely go through the motions of worship do not please God. He wants our love, our obedience, and our sincere desire to honor Him. Our worship pleases the Lord only when we worship Him with the right attitude.
4. Repentance and Renewal (1:16–20). The Lord invites sinners to turn to Him. When we repent of our sins and show our sincerity by a renewed manner of life, He gives us His blessing. When we refuse to repent and continue to practice ungodly habits, He gives us His judgment.
5. The Messianic Hope (1:25–27). The "glorious appearing of the great God and our Saviour Jesus Christ" will initiate His one-thousand-year rule over the earth. He will rule from Jerusalem, at that time called "the city of righteousness, the faithful city." Righteousness will mark the land.
6. The Weakness of Idolatry (1:28–31). When the Lord is exalted, He will reveal the weakness of false gods. Men who have followed idols will be ashamed of their choices in that day, but it will be too late to avoid judgment.

1 The word that Isaiah the son of Amoz saw concerning Judah and Jerusalem.

2 And it shall come to pass in the last days, that the mountain of the Lord's house shall be established in the top of the mountains, and shall be exalted above the hills; and all nations shall flow unto it.

ISAIAH 2

As is so often true in the prophets, Isaiah now turns from the sin of the nation to its future glory. This change in emphasis carries a clear message with it. Although the Lord will judge His people when they sin, He will not cast them off forever. His plan for them involves their future blessing. Isaiah emphasizes this messianic element here for the first of many times in the book.

2. Judgment and Glory 2:1–4:6
a. Messianic Age 2:1–5

1–2 Isaiah sees "the word," apparently referring to a vision from God.[1] The heading is similar to that in 1:1. The heading there stands at the beginning of the book. The heading here is a subtitle that introduces the next major section of the book.[2] In 1:1, Isaiah sees a "vision." Here, he sees a "word." This is undoubtedly idiomatic. Words are verbal symbols of mental images. Isaiah saw the word in that he understood its meaning.[3]

The subject of the word concerns "Judah and Jerusalem," v. 1.[4] The rest of the section, vv. 2–4, occurs with several differences in Micah 4:1–3.[5] In all likelihood, both Isaiah and Micah draw on an earlier writing

---

[1]Wade, p. 14, says that "the term *word* is equivalent to *revelation* . . . the verb *saw*, used in connection with it, merely visualizes the prophet's intuitions." This view ignores the inspiration of the Holy Spirit and makes the book merely a human production.

[2]Among others, Herbert, *Isaiah 1–39*, p. 34; Gray, p. 40; and Kaiser, *Isaiah 1-12*, p. 23, see the heading as evidence that the book is not a unity but a collection of sermons of Isaiah. While the view is possible, it ignores the fact that subtitles and section headings are common in literature.

[3]Isa. 13:1 and Hab. 1:1 refer to seeing a "burden." Jer. 2:31; Amos 1:1; and Mic. 1:1 refer to seeing words. Num. 24:4, 16 refer to hearing words while seeing a vision.

[4]Young, I, 95, states that the prophecy "is a confirmation of the doctrine of the church." His view is the standard position held in covenant theology. It reads the interpretation into the text. So far as the wording of the book is concerned, Isaiah's prophecy relates primarily to Judah and Jerusalem and, where the content suggests, to eschatological events. We should not place the church in matters spoken to Israel.

[5]Commentators divide over the source for the passage. Grogan, p. 34, mentions the possibility that both men received "independent revelation in the inspiration." Näglesbach,

3 And many people shall go and say, Come ye, and let us go up to the mountain of the Lord, to the house of the God of Jacob; and he will teach us of his ways, and we will walk in his paths: for out of Zion shall go forth the law, and the word of the Lord from Jerusalem.
4 And he shall judge among the nations, and shall rebuke many people: and they shall beat their swords into plowshares, and their spears into pruninghooks: nation shall not lift up sword against nation, neither shall they learn war any more.
5 O house of Jacob, come ye, and let us walk in the light of the Lord.

by an unknown prophet. The phrase "in the last days," together with the content of the paragraph, sets the fulfillment in the millennial kingdom, when Christ rules the world. At that time, the Lord's house will "be established" on the peak of Mt. Zion; cf. Joel 3:16–17; Zechariah 8:3.[6] This is an "exalted" position. It is physically exalted above the surrounding mountains and spiritually exalted because of the Lord's presence and the worship offered Him there. The nations of the world will "flow" (or "stream") to Him either in worship or to receive guidance, v. 2.

The "mountain" from which the Lord rules towers over other mountains at that time; cf. Zechariah 14:10. Isaiah 40:4 indicates that the terrain of the earth during the Millennium will be like that of the original creation. At that time, the earth seems to have had gentle rolling hills and a semitropical climate, v. 2.[7]

3–5 The nations will go to Jerusalem, to the mountain on which He has located His "house." This is the millennial temple, where He receives

---

p. 54; Delitzsch, I, 204; and Young, I, 112, accept Micah as the original author. Kelley, p. 193; Lowth, p. 149; and Kissane, I, 22, assign it to Isaiah. Leupold, I, 75; Kaiser, *Isaiah 1–12*, p. 25; Kraeling, p. 49; and Wade, p. 14, assign the passage to a third party. While the two passages are similar, they are not identical. This supports the idea that both Micah and Isaiah called to mind a well-known prophecy that both had heard. They paraphrased rather than slavishly reproducing the original. Also, the fact that Joel 3:10, a ninth-century B.C. prophecy written a century before Isaiah, is similar to v. 4 suggests that Joel likewise quotes from this earlier source.

[6]Young, I, 100, argues that the verb "established" (*nakôn*) does not refer to a future passive but to a condition that already exists when this age ends. The use of *hayâ* with the verb indicates an existing condition rather than something yet future. The problem he faces is that it is the imperfect form of *hayâ* that occurs here. When the imperfect *yihyeh* occurs with the verb, it indicates a future action. Cf. G.K. 116 r. In addition, the *nip‘al* participle *nakôn* suggests a passive sense, "be established."

[7]Rawlinson, I, 31, spiritualizes the passage. He makes "the mountain of the Lord's house" represent the church while the other mountains "are the kingdoms, or perhaps the

worship and also the location of the throne from which He governs, v. 2.[8]
There the nations will learn about God and His Word. The word "law"
(*tôrâ*; cf. 1:10) is better "instruction." The nations will come to
Jerusalem to learn the principles by which the Lord wishes them to govern. The desire of the nations to do the will of God sets this in the millennial kingdom of Christ, v. 3. The Lord will judge national disputes
and will "rebuke" (*yakaḥ*, or "decide between," see 1:18) the people. As
a result, there will be no need for war. Weapons will be turned into
peaceful tools: the nations will turn their swords into "plowshares"
(*ʾittîm*, or "mattocks")[9] and their spears into "pruninghooks" (or "pruning knives"). The Prince of Peace will do away with the need for
weapons, v. 4.[10] Isaiah exhorts the "house of Jacob," Judah, to follow the
example of the Gentiles and walk "in the light of the Lord," the revealed
Word of God, v. 5.

---

religions, of the earth." Kelley, p. 194, also spiritualizes the passage. He sees the exaltation as "poetic hyperbole" simply meaning that the glory of the Lord will be revealed to
mankind everywhere. Nothing in the passage points to a poetical interpretation. Scripture
elsewhere suggests the literal exaltation of the physical mountain, e.g., 27:13; Zech.
14:9–10; Rev. 21:10–27.

[8]Motyer, *The Prophecy of Isaiah*, p. 51, makes the "house" the dwelling of God and
the temple a separate place of worship. Since "mythologically, mountains were the
homes of the gods . . . the supreme exaltation of his mountain home expresses the Lord's
triumph over all the so-called gods on their mountains." The view is another spiritualiza-
tion of the passage. In addition, it makes an unnecessary distinction between "house"
and "temple." Ezek. 43:7–12 speaks of the Lord's "house" on a mountain where He
dwells with His people. The passage immediately goes on to describe the altar and sacrifices that people offer there.

[9]We do not know the exact sense of *ʾittîm*. From I Sam. 13:20–21, it must be some sort
of farm instrument different from a "[plow]share." "Mattock" is as good a guess as any.

[10]Delitzsch, p. 116, advocates a millennial view in which "the true humanity which sin
has choked up will gain the mastery, and the world's history will keep Sabbath." Young,
I, 102, draws a distinction between the Millennium and the "Messianic age." Barnes, I,
87, writing in a different generation, argues that "the tendency of things now is towards
peace" and "wars are far less barbarous now than they were formerly." While the Bible
mentions the Millennium only in Rev. 20:1–7, there is no warrant for spiritualizing it
away. Numerous passages throughout Isaiah are satisfactorily explained only with the
thousand-year kingdom rule of Christ.

6 Therefore thou hast forsaken thy people the house of Jacob, because
   they be replenished from the east, and are soothsayers like the
   Philistines, and they please themselves in the children of strangers.
7 Their land also is full of silver and gold, neither is there any end of
   their treasures; their land is also full of horses, neither is there any
   end of their chariots:
8 Their land also is full of idols; they worship the work of their own
   hands, that which their own fingers have made:
9 And the mean man boweth down, and the great man humbleth himself: therefore forgive them not.

b. Day of the Lord Judgments 2:6–4:1
(1) Judgment of Idols 2:6–21

6–9 Isaiah now justifies his exhortation to Judah.[11] They should walk
in the light of God's Word because He has "forsaken" His people.[12] The
idea is not that He has totally abandoned them. Rather, He has let them
go their own way to supply their own needs. Isaiah gives three reasons
for the statement. In the first place, Israel has been "replenished [lit.
'filled'] from the east [qedem],"[13] i.e., influenced by heathen customs.

---

[11]R. Davidson, "The Interpretation of Isaiah II 6ff," *VT* 16:1–7, argues that the phrase
"house of Jacob" refers to the Northern Kingdom of Israel. He builds on a review by
Henri Cazelles of W. Eichrodt, *Der Heilige im Israel, Jesaja 1–12, VT* 12:350, who
refers to "la maison de Jacob" as "l'ensemble d'Israel." Davidson draws heavily on the
use of the phrase in Amos and portions of Micah that he dates prior to 721 B.C. (when Israel ceased to be a nation). It is not surprising that the phrase "house of Jacob" refers
elsewhere to Israel. Originally, the phrase identified the family and descendants of Jacob,
Gen. 46:27; Exod. 19:3; Ps. 114:1. After the division of the nation into Judah and Israel,
the phrase identified the descendants of Jacob in both kingdoms. The key is not how
Amos and Micah use the phrase but how Isaiah uses it. Davidson dismisses v. 5 as "an
editorial link" joining 2:2–4 to vv. 6ff. There is, however, no textual evidence for this. In
addition, Isaiah (who uses the phrase more than any other OT author) refers it to Judah
(8:17; 10:20; 46:3; 48:1; 58:1) or to the restored nation in the millennial kingdom (14:1;
29:22).

[12]Isaiah begins his statement with *kî*, "therefore" (better "because" or "for"). Leupold,
I, 79, makes the phrase apply to Israel—they have abandoned their own people. The
closest antecedent, however, is "the Lord." Further, the reasons for the abandonment—
being influenced from the east, practicing divination, and agreements with the heathen—
are spiritual reasons that would cause the Lord to pass judgment.

[13]In a widely adopted change, the RSV assumes that *qesem*, "diviners," has dropped out
because of its similarity to *qedem*, "east." They insert *miqsam* before *miqqedem* and translate, "full of diviners from the east." The emendation does not have significant textual
support. Barnes, I, 87, translates *qedem* with the alternate meaning "old," a possible
translation. The mention of "Philistines" and "children of strangers" later argues for location rather than time. In a unique interpretation, Henry, p. 15, understands "filled" as

Such countries as Arabia, with its nomadic tribes, Assyria, Babylon, and Persia all lay to the east of Palestine. As Judah interacted with these nations, they adopted many of their customs. Next, they had become "soothsayers" (*ʿonᵉnîm*),[14] i.e., diviners, like the Philistines; cf. I Samuel 6:2; II Kings 1:2. Finally, they "please themselves" (*yaśpîqû*, or "strike hands"),[15] i.e., enter into agreements with foreigners, v. 6. Through their commercial activities, they have become wealthy. The land is filled with silver, gold, treasures of various kinds, horses, and chariots, v. 7. While not wrong in itself, this wealth was wrong since it had turned them from the Lord. They now worship idols (*ʾᵉlîlîm*). The word *ʾᵉlîlîm* refers to something worthless, weak, or feeble, then by extension, an idol. This is seen in that the people of Judah have made their own idols, v. 8.[16] The "mean man" (*ʾadam*) humbles himself. The word *ʾadam* is the most often used word for "man." It may refer to "mankind" in general, to man as created in the image of God, or to other nuances relating to man. The sense of mankind contrasts nicely here with the following *ʾîš*. The "great man" (*ʾîš*, or "man" as an individual) abases himself as he bows before the idols.[17] The final phrase, "therefore forgive them not" is jussive. This

---

replenishing. Israel encourages foreigners to live among them. While this is true, the idea of filling here refers to foreign influence, not the relocation of foreigners into the country.

[14]The meaning of the participle *ʿonᵉnîm* is uncertain. This leads to various translations: "observers of times" (Deut. 18:14); Meonenim (Judg. 9:37); "enchanters" (Jer. 27:9); "divination" (NIV); "barbarians" (NEB); "telling fortunes" (Watts). Isa. 57:3 translates the feminine participle "sorceress." Whatever the correct translation, Lev. 19:26 and Deut. 18:10–14 forbid the practice. The various contexts are consistent in indicating some form of heathen magical practice.

[15]Rawlinson, I, 32, thinks the striking of hands refers only to a show of familiarity. The word *śapaq* does not have this sense anywhere else. Jeffrey S. Rogers, "An Allusion to Coronation in Isaiah 2:6," *CBQ* 51:232–36, argues from synonyms that *śapaq* refers to "the clapping of hands associated with coronation." He refers the passage to the coronation of Pekah in Israel. His argument suffers in that it rests on the use of synonyms rather than *śapaq*. It further requires that the passage refer to the Northern Kingdom rather than Judah. As shown in note 11, this is a weak position.

[16]The suffixes in vv. 7–8 are generally singular: "his land . . . his treasures . . . his land . . . his chariots . . . his land . . . his hands . . . his fingers." The suffixes have a distributive force that refers to the class of idolaters. The plural verbs in v. 8 clearly influence the translation. See G.K. 145 *m*.

[17]The word *ʾadam* lays the emphasis on man's humble beginning, Gen. 2:7. The word *ʾîš*, however, stresses man's greatness, e.g., Ps. 49:2 (where "low and high" are lit. "sons of *ʾadam* and sons of *ʾîš*"); 62:9 (where "men of low degree" are "sons of *ʾadam*" and "men of high degree" are "sons of *ʾîš*"). Isaiah uses the two words in contrast here and in 5:15; 31:8; and 44:13.

*10 Enter into the rock, and hide thee in the dust, for fear of the Lord,
and for the glory of his majesty.*

*11 The lofty looks of man shall be humbled, and the haughtiness of
men shall be bowed down, and the Lord alone shall be exalted in
that day.*

conveys a mild imperative sense, "and do not forgive them," v. 9.[18] With
the statement, Isaiah recognizes that the holiness of God precludes offering forgiveness to those who delight in sin.

Sources of Sin

The verb *male²*, "fill," occurs four times in the passage.

1. Full of heathen influence, "filled from the east," v. 6
2. Full of greed, "full of silver and gold," v. 7*a*
3. Full of materialism, "full of horses . . . chariots," v. 7*b*
4. Full of idolatry, "full of idols," v. 8

Such wickedness brings the judgment of God, "thou wilt
not forgive them," v. 9*b*.

10–11 In biblical times, people sometimes hid in caves to escape
danger; cf. Judges 6:2; I Samuel 13:6; 22:1. Caves suitable for this occur
in the mountainous region west of the Dead Sea. In addition, burying
one's face in the sand was the way to preserve life during a sandstorm.
Isaiah draws on these figures as he urges the people to hide from God's
wrath. The "fear [*pahad*][19] of the Lord" here is literal dread or terror, not
the reverence that is so often meant by the phrase. The "glory of his
majesty" refers to God's glory as He sends judgment. Verses 19*b* and

---

[18]The meaning of "forgive," *tiśśa²*, comes from a root meaning "to lift, raise." The NEB
translates, "how can they raise themselves?" referring to their humbled position. Gray, I,
18, mentions favorably the suggestion that there is no "uplifting" for these who have
been humbled. Driver, *JSS* 13:37, likewise understands this as a question, "'How can
there be lifting up for them?', i.e. 'how can they ever be raised from the mean estate to
which they have been reduced?'" He understands *²al* as an interrogative, a use not sup-
ported by G.K., Williams, or Waltke and O'Connor. There is no *h^e*-interrogative in the
verse to suggest a question. Further, the use of *²al* with the jussive normally expresses a
negative.

[19]The word *pahad* includes a strong emotional component of terror. It is more than a
mere intellectual knowledge of some danger.

12 For the day of the Lord of hosts shall be upon every one that is
   proud and lofty, and upon every one that is lifted up; and he shall be
   brought low:
13 And upon all the cedars of Lebanon, that are high and lifted up, and
   upon all the oaks of Bashan,
14 And upon all the high mountains, and upon all the hills that are
   lifted up,
15 And upon every high tower, and upon every fenced wall,
16 And upon all the ships of Tarshish, and upon all pleasant pictures.
17 And the loftiness of man shall be bowed down, and the haughtiness
   of men shall be made low: and the Lord alone shall be exalted in
   that day.

21b virtually repeat v. 10b. The Lord will judge the proud of the land.
He will bring low the "lofty looks of man [ʾadam, see v. 9]" and the
"haughtiness of men [ᵃnašîm]." The word ᵃnašîm often lays stress on
man's frailty or mortality. These who have been proud in themselves will
bow before the Lord in that day, cf. Philippians 2:10–11, v. 11.

   12–17 The theme of judgment continues. For the first time in the
book, the "day of the Lord" comes into view.[20] The phrase is often eschatological. It refers to the Tribulation judgments (Jer. 46:10; Joel 2:31;
II Pet. 3:10) and to the millennial reign of Christ (Joel 3:14–17; Zeph.
3:8–13; Hag. 2:6–7). The focus here is on the judgments that fall upon
the land and its people. This will be a time of judgment upon those who
are proud, v. 12. Nature is bound together with man. When one suffers,
so does the other; when one receives glory, so does the other. Here, the
works of nature suffer from the day of the Lord judgments. The "cedars
of Lebanon" were abundant in biblical times; cf. Judges 9:15; Psalm
29:5; 104:16; Isaiah 14:8. Likewise, the "oaks of Bashan" were plentiful
in that period; cf. Ezekiel 27:6; Zechariah 11:2. The mountains as well
suffer judgment, vv. 13–14. The works of man also receive judgment.
The "high tower" and "fenced [better 'fortified'] wall" were built to defend cities. These will suffer judgment, v. 15. Moreover, the Lord will
judge the "ships of Tarshish [taršîš]." The word taršîš undoubtedly indicates a place, e.g., 23:6; 66:19.[21] The phrase "ships of Tarshish," however, refers to the purpose of ships. These were built to carry ore to
Israel, where it was smelted. These were large ships, yet they suffer

---

[20]The phrase occurs here and at 13:6, 9; and 34:8.

[21]Young, I, 128, locates Tarshish in northern Africa near modern-day Tunis. Josephus,
Antiquities 9.9, identifies it as Tarsus in Cilicia, probably from the similarity of sound.

18 *And the idols he shall utterly abolish.*

19 *And they shall go into the holes of the rocks, and into the caves of the earth, for fear of the Lord, and for the glory of his majesty, when he ariseth to shake terribly the earth.*

20 *In that day a man shall cast his idols of silver, and his idols of gold, which they made each one for himself to worship, to the moles and to the bats;*

21 *To go into the clefts of the rocks, and into the tops of the ragged rocks, for fear of the Lord, and for the glory of his majesty, when he ariseth to shake terribly the earth.*

judgment. From the parallelism with "ships of Tarshish," the phrase "pleasant pictures" (*śᵉkîyot haḥemdâ*) refers to ships used for pleasure.[22] These as well come into judgment, v. 16. Isaiah repeats the refrain of v. 11 in almost identical words. Sinful "man" (*ᵃnašîm*, see v. 11) will be humbled while the Lord will be exalted, v. 17.

18–21 Isaiah ends this section by predicting a time when the Lord will completely do away with "idols" (*ᵉlîlîm*, see v. 8). From the con-

---

Ross E. Price, *Isaiah*, in *Beacon Bible Commentary*, ed. A. F. Harper and W. T. Purkiser, 1966, p. 39, locates it as Tartessus in Spain. Without being specific, Ibn Ezra, p. 278, locates it "near Palestine." Yohanan Aharoni and Michael Avi-Yonah, *The Macmillan Bible Atlas*, ed. Anson F. Rainey and Ze'ev Safrai, pp. 88–89, locate it as the town of Tharros on the island of Sardinia. William F. Albright, "New Light on the Early History of Phoenician Colonization," *BASOR* 83:21, identifies Tarshish as the town of Nora in Sardinia. He explains Tarshish as a loan word from Akkadian, meaning "smelting plant, refinery." The word occurs often in the OT in connection with a "navy," e.g., here and I Kings 10:22; 22:48; Psalm 48:7. The use of the phrase elsewhere argues that Tarshish is not a destination but rather a type of ship. First Kings 22:48 (II Chron. 20:36) says the ships were built at Ezion-geber, on the Gulf of Aqaba. It would be well nigh impossible for ships built there to sail to Spain or Cilicia. On the other hand, ships of Tarshish dock at Tyre after sailing on the Mediterranean and therefore grieve at its judgment, Isa. 23:1, 14. The existence of these ships in two separate bodies of water argues that the phrase "ships of Tarshish" does not refer to a location. Phoenician inscriptions refer to boats carrying ores smelted in Spain and Cilicia. The "ships of Tarshish" may have been named for their journeys to and from this location. Later, however, the term became generic, referring to the purpose of the ships in carrying ore. Elsewhere, e.g., 66:19, Tarshish refers to a destination, no doubt the place from which the ships acquired their name.

[22]The word *śᵉkîyot* occurs only here. Thomas O. Lambdin, "Egyptian Loan Words in the Old Testament," *JAOS* 73:154–55, understands it as an Egyptian loan word meaning "ships." Karl Budde, "Zu Jesaja 1–5," *ZAW* 49:198, quotes J. Begrich, stating that *śᵉkîyot* is "ein ägyptisches Lehnwort." God will destroy not only commercial ships but also ships used for pleasure. Slotki, p. 14, relates it to *śakâ*, "to see," thus images attractive to the eye. Motyer, *The Prophecy of Isaiah*, p. 58, opts for "desirable human artistic achievements." Herbert, *Isaiah 1–39*, p. 39, speculates that the phrase means "dhows [sailing vessels] of Arabia." The word is difficult but the parallelism supports the view given

22 Cease ye from man, whose breath is in his nostrils: for wherein is he to be accounted of?

text, this refers to the Tribulation and millennial kingdom although Israel has not generally worshiped idols since the Babylonian captivity, v. 18. Their "fear [*paḥad*, see v. 10] of the Lord" will cause men to try to hide from God as He shakes the earth with judgment. The word "caves" (*meḥillâ*) occurs only here with this sense. The difference between "holes" (*mecarôt*) and "caves" (*meḥillôt*) is not clear. Perhaps *meḥillôt* refers to something pierced into the earth by man, an excavation. God's ability to shake the earth reveals His power, v. 19. Realizing now the worthlessness of "idols" (*elîlîm*, see v. 8), men cast them "to the moles [*laḥpor perôt*][23] and to the bats," i.e., into the holes and caves of these animals, v. 20. Men will go into hiding places because they "fear" (*paḥad*, see v. 10) the Lord. Once more, He will show His power by shaking the earth, v. 21.

(2) Judgment of Evil Leaders 2:22–3:15

22 The verse introduces the next section, continued in c. 3. Isaiah appeals to the people, "Cease ye from man [*adam*, see v. 9]," i.e., stop depending on man. The phrase "whose breath is in his nostrils" emphasizes man's frailty and indicates that man lives only as long as he has breath, cf. Psalm 104:29, v. 22.

---

above. In vv. 12–15 there are ten objects of judgment. These form five groups of two each: the proud, v. 12; the mighty trees, v. 13; the mountains, v. 14; buildings, v. 15; and ships, v. 16. If *sekîyot* does not refer to a ship in some way, it breaks the parallelism.

[23]The Hebrew *laḥpor perôt* should be read as *laḥaparparot*. The word refers to a digging animal of some kind. Herbert, *Isaiah 1–39*, p. 40, commenting on the NEB, accepts "dung beetle." Motyer, *The Prophecy of Isaiah*, p. 58, suggests either "rodents" or "some burrowing insect." Young, I, 131, tentatively suggests "shrewmouse." The translation "moles" is untenable. Since no variety of moles live in Palestine, the text must have some other animal in view. The point lies not with the name of the animal but with the fact that it is a digging animal. Men will hide their idols in the holes dug by this animal.

Practical Applications from Chapter 2

1. The Nature of the Millennium, vv. 2–5. Physical changes will occur, v. 2. The nations will accept the Lord's rule. They will go to Him to receive guidance. His Word will be the ultimate authority, v. 3. He will solve the conflicts of nations, and peace will exist over all the earth, v. 4. In view of this, should we not follow the Lord now, v. 5?

2. The Judgment of God, vv. 10–17, 21. People will no longer be self-sufficient. They will fear the wrath of God and will exalt Him in the Day of Judgment, vv. 10–11, 17. Nature will suffer in the judgment, vv. 13–14. The works of mankind will suffer as well from God's judgment, vv. 15–16. Man will try to escape, v. 21*a*. God will show His power as He shakes the whole earth, v. 21*b*.

1 For, behold, the Lord, the Lord of hosts, doth take away from
   Jerusalem and from Judah the stay and the staff, the whole stay of
   bread, and the whole stay of water,
2 The mighty man, and the man of war, the judge, and the prophet,
   and the prudent, and the ancient,
3 The captain of fifty, and the honourable man, and the counsellor,
   and the cunning artificer, and the eloquent orator.
4 And I will give children to be their princes, and babes shall rule
   over them.

ISAIAH 3

The prophet continues the theme begun at v. 22 in the last chapter.
Isaiah describes here several groups of people who will come under the
judgment of God. He focuses his words on the nation of Judah. The
people are wicked and are therefore deserving of punishment. Isaiah
summarizes this judgment in the chapter.

1–4 The introductory "for" indicates that the passage continues 2:22.
Isaiah cautions there against depending on frail man. He now completes
the thought. Weak man is about to receive God's judgment. "The Lord
[ʾadôn], the Lord of hosts [yᵉhwah ṣᵉbaʾôt]" combines two names of
God, Adonai and Jehovah of Hosts. This particular combination occurs
five times in Isaiah, here and at 1:24; 10:16, 33; and 19:4. It does not
occur elsewhere in the OT. Adonai lays stress on God's position as the
Master, the owner of mankind. Jehovah reveals God's nature as a redemptive God. The name occurs in conjunction with the sacrifices and
as God interacts with His people. The combination of the two names establishes God's right to punish Judah. He has redeemed them and is their
Master. They have a double responsibility to obey Him.

The Lord will bring judgment upon the land. He will take from Judah
even the bare necessities for life, bread and water. The words "stay" and
"staff" are the masculine and feminine forms of the same word, both indicating "supply." The use of both genders with the same root indicates
totality, here all kinds of support for life.[1] The occurrence of the phrase
"staff of bread" elsewhere (Ps. 105:16; Ezek. 4:16; 5:16) suggests that it
was proverbial in Judah. Isaiah uses it here in the normal way and adds

---

[1] Isaiah uses the masculine and feminine gender of the same word root in the combination "sons . . . daughters," 43:6; 49:22; 56:5; 60:4. In each case, the idea of totality is apparent. He coordinates the masculine ʾomen with the feminine ʾemûnâ at 25:1. Cf. G.K.
122 v; Waltke and O'Connor 6.4.3.

the thought of water to intensify the judgment. Isaiah mentions "bread" and "water" specifically. These are the minimum support for life, v. 1.

Isaiah lists the leaders of the people who will fall in the judgment. The "mighty man" (*gibbôr*, often a warrior or valiant person) and the "man of war" are proven warriors.[2] The "judge" and the "prophet" are the judicial and religious leaders of the people. The "prudent" is better a "diviner," a heathen means of discerning the future. The "ancient" is better "elder," broadly used of various leaders. The "captain of fifty" is a leader of fifty soldiers; cf. II Kings 1:9–13. The "honourable man" (or "recognized man," lit. "leader of faces") is a civic leader. The "counsellor" is an advisor to the king or other eminent person. The "cunning artificer" is a skilled craftsman. The "eloquent orator" (*nᵉbôn laḥaš*) is better a "clever enchanter."[3] The enchanter used magical incantations to call the spirits to obey him. The law forbad the practice, Deuteronomy 18:10. The existence of diviners and enchanters in Jewish society showed the spiritual decay of the people. There is no special order to the list of leaders, vv. 2–3.

As an additional aspect of the judgment, the Lord will give "children . . . and babes [*taᶜᵃlûlîm*],"[4] immature leaders, as "princes" (*śar*, or "rulers") to the nation. After Hezekiah, the oldest king was only twenty-five years old at the time of his inauguration as ruler.

---

[2]Wade, p. 21, understands the "mighty man" as representing the "royal bodyguard" and the "man of war" as representing the "national militia." While this is possible, there is nothing in the text that requires this symbolism.

[3]The word "orator"(*laḥaš*) can mean "whisper" or "charm." It refers to one who tries to cast a spell by whispering, an enchanter; cf. Ps. 58:4–5; Eccles. 10:11; Jer. 8:17. He is "eloquent" (*nᵉbôn*) in that he has understanding of the practice.

[4]The word "babes" (*taᶜᵃlûlîm*) is from the unused root ᶜalal, "to act childishly." Skinner, *Isaiah I–XXXIX*, p. 23, relates it to ᶜalal, "to glean." He translates, "outrage." Whitehouse, I, 105, and Leupold, I, 90, suggest "willfulness." The root also occurs in contexts that suggest something to do with children, 3:12; 66:4. Kaiser, *Isaiah 1–12*, p. 39, suggests "capricious persons." Leslie, p. 37, and Stacey, p. 23, suggest "caprice." Alexander, I, 11, suggests "childishness." Birks, p. 31, gives "follies" or "childishness," contemptuous for "frivolous childish persons." The parallelism with "children" clearly indicates the idea of a person rather than a trait. I would translate "youngsters" while understanding that this poetically interprets the word.

5 *And the people shall be oppressed, every one by another, and every one by his neighbour: the child shall behave himself proudly against the ancient, and the base against the honourable.*

6 *When a man shall take hold of his brother of the house of his father, saying, Thou hast clothing, be thou our ruler, and let this ruin be under thy hand:*

7 *In that day shall he swear, saying, I will not be an healer; for in my house is neither bread nor clothing: make me not a ruler of the people.*

Name	Age	Reference
Manasseh	12	II Kings 21:1; II Chronicles 33:1
Amon	22	II Kings 21:19; II Chronicles 33:21
Josiah	8	II Kings 22:1; II Chronicles 34:1
Jehoahaz	23	II Kings 23:31; II Chronicles 36:2
Jehoiakim	25	II Kings 23:36; II Chronicles 36:5
Jehoiachin	18	II Kings 24:8; II Chronicles 36:9[5]
Zedekiah	21	II Kings 24:18; II Chronicles 36:11

This succession of immature leaders continues God's judgment on the nation. With the exception of Josiah and the partial exception of Manasseh, who repented after his captivity, these leaders were uniformly wicked, v. 4.[6]

5–7 Not only do the leaders suffer judgment, the people also are "oppressed" (*nagaś*)[7] for their sins. Neighbors oppress neighbors, children rise up against the "ancient" (*zaqen*, better "elders," see v. 2), and the

---

[5]Second Chron. 36:9 gives the age of Jehoiachin as "eight years old." This copyist error for "eighteen" has crept into the text. Ezek. 19:5–9 portrays him as a "lion" that catches the "prey" and "devoured men." This suggests an older person. In addition, archeology has uncovered tablets listing sons of Jehoiachin, some of which were born before 592 B.C., when he would have been about twenty-three years old. With the younger age, this would have been impossible. See "Jehoiachin," in *Unger's Bible Dictionary*, ed. Merrill F. Unger, 1957.

[6]While only two in this list would normally be thought of as children, all were young to become kings. Alexander, I, 111, appropriately comments: "The most probable opinion is that the incompetent rulers are called boys or children not in respect to age but character."

[7]The word *nagaś* means "to exert pressure, exact." It occurs in Exod. 3:7 of Israel's oppression as the Egyptian overseers demanded the same number of bricks without straw being supplied.

8 *For Jerusalem is ruined, and Judah is fallen: because their tongue and their doings are against the Lord, to provoke the eyes of his glory.*
9 *The shew of their countenance doth witness against them; and they declare their sin as Sodom, they hide it not. Woe unto their soul! for they have rewarded evil unto themselves.*

"base" (or "lightly esteemed") rise against the "honourable" (*kabed*),[8] the more noble, v. 5. The oppression is so great that one who has "clothing" is thought to be more able than others in his family. His brother will urge him to lead the family, saying, "Let this ruin be under thy hand." The word "ruin" embraces all of the problems facing the family—legal, financial, physical, moral, and so forth, v. 6. He, however, will refuse to become the "healer" (lit. "binder up"), used poetically of a leader who heals the ills of society. He will "swear" (lit. "lift up"), raising his voice in protest.[9] He points out that he has no food or "clothing" in his house. Since v. 6 has just stated that he had "clothing," the thought here is of extra clothing that could be shared with others, v. 7.

8–9 Once more, Isaiah announces the judgment of the nation. The cause is "their tongue and their doings. . . ." The phrase relates to Israel's idolatry, which resulted in their words and their works opposing God. These have provoked "the eyes of his glory," the glorious eyes of the Lord that see all that man does, v. 8. The sin of the people is evident on their faces. Even worse, they "declare their sin [*ḥaṭṭaʾt*] as Sodom," boldly stating their sinful desires; cf. Genesis 19:5. The word *ḥaṭṭaʾt* is the most common word for "sin." The word originally meant "to miss the mark"; cf. Judges 20:16. From this, it came to describe a falling short of the righteous standards set by God for His people. Isaiah announces "woe" (*ʾôy*) upon them. When used with the second or third person pro-

---

[8]The word *kabed* means "heavy." The word occurs widely with various senses. It may refer, as here, to having "weight" as a person, being honorable, or God, having glory. It may refer to "heavy," i.e., severe, behavior. It may refer to literal weight, heaviness. It may refer to parts of the body that are slow or dull. It may refer to size, i.e., someone "heavy of sin." It may refer to "heaviness of splendor," i.e., beauty. In each case, the context indicates its sense.

[9]The object "voice" is supplied. John Gill, *An Exposition of the Books of the Prophets*, rpt. 1979, I, 18, suggests that "the hand" is the object. Lifting the hand was connected with taking an oath. Here, the man takes an oath that he cannot meet the needs of his family. While the lifting of the hand indicates an oath in the OT, Isaiah never refers to lifting the hand. Elsewhere, the phrase refers to lifting the voice, e.g., 10:30; 24:14; 42:2, 11.

10 Say ye to the righteous, that it shall be well with him: for they shall eat the fruit of their doings.
11 Woe unto the wicked! it shall be ill with him: for the reward of his hands shall be given him.
12 As for my people, children are their oppressors, and women rule over them. O my people, they which lead thee cause thee to err, and destroy the way of thy paths.

noun, the word *ʾôy* always indicates a warning of judgment or an accusation. Thus, they have brought "evil" (*raʿ*) upon themselves. The word *raʿ* has a broad range of meanings, including physical, emotional, or spiritual evil. In the context here, it indicates a form of judgment, v. 9.

10–12 In light of the judgment that he has just announced, it is appropriate that Isaiah state the general law of sowing and reaping. The righteous will enjoy the fruit of their labors, v. 10.[10] The phrase "woe [*ʾôy*, see v. 9] unto the wicked [*lᵉrašaʿ*]"[11] anticipates the punishment of God. It will be "ill" (*raʿ*, see v. 9) with the wicked. He will receive the "reward" of his labors. Clearly, this is not a desirable reward. This principle of sowing and reaping occurs widely throughout the Bible, e.g., Job 4:8; Proverbs 22:8; Hosea 8:7; 10:12–13; Galatians 6:7–8. It appropriately states the judgment of the wicked and holds out hope for the righteous, v. 11.

Isaiah returns to the thought of v. 4. The "children" (*mᵉʿôlel*) and "women" (*našîm*) are not fitted to lead.[12] In addition to the children listed

---

[10]W. L. Holladay, "Isa. III 10–11: An Archaic Wisdom Passage," in *VT* 18:481–87, argues that "say," *ʾimrû*, has an archaic sense here, "see." He translates, "See the righteous man, that he is good." He understands Isaiah as quoting an ancient proverb. His view, however, ignores the obvious parallelism with v. 11. The Hebrew phrasing is irregular but the meaning is clear.

[11]Ibn Ezra, p. 21, prefers to translate *ʾôy lᵉrašaʿ raʿ* "woe to the hardened sinner." Taking the verse by itself, the translation is possible. The parallelism with v. 10, however, supports the supply of the verb and prepositional phrase as in the AV.

[12]Kaiser, *Isaiah 1–12*, p. 43, understands "children" (*mᵉʿôlel*) as "to maltreat someone." He interprets "oppressors" (*nagaś*) as "governors" and translates, "everyone of their governors is a tormentor." While the interpretation is technically correct, it discards the more common meaning of *nagaś*, "to exact, oppress." The word occurs at 3:5; 9:4; 14:2, 4; 53:7; 58:3; 60:17 with this sense. It never refers to "governors" elsewhere. Wade, p. 23, calls the plural participle *nogeś* a "plural of dignity." He translates, "their oppressor plays the child." Again, the explanation is technically correct but unlikely. It is easier to make the singular *mᵉʿôlel* a collective than to understand the plural participle *nogśayw* as a singular. The word "women" (*našîm*) is debated. Among others, Stacy, p. 25, and Kelley, p. 199, repoint the word to *nošîm* and translate, "usurers." This has the support of the LXX

13 *The Lord standeth up to plead, and standeth to judge the people.*
14 *The Lord will enter into judgment with the ancients of his people,
and the princes thereof: for ye have eaten up the vineyard; the spoil
of the poor is in your houses.*
15 *What mean ye that ye beat my people to pieces, and grind the faces
of the poor? saith the Lord God of hosts.*

above at v. 4, Jezebel (I Kings 18:4; 21:25) influenced her husband and
the nation, and Athaliah (II Kings 11:1; II Chron. 22:10, 12) ruled over
the nation. These wicked leaders are "oppressors" (*nagaś*, see v. 5) and
"destroy" (*billeʿû*, or "swallow up") the people. They "destroy" (*billeʿû*)
their paths. The root *balaʿ* normally means "to swallow up." Here it
metaphorically refers to swallowing up the paths of righteousness,
engulfing them so that the people no longer know how to live, v. 12.

13–15 The Lord stands up to "plead" (*rîb*, see 1:17) His case against
the "people" (*ʿammîm*, lit. "peoples").[13] While the judgment includes all
nations, the focus here is on Israel. He accuses them, and then pronounces judgment on them, v. 13. He pronounces "judgment" (*mišpaṭ*,
see 1:17) on the "ancient," the elders (*zaqen*; cf. v. 2) of the people, and
the "princes" (*śar*, or "rulers"). They have "eaten up" (*biʿartem*) the
"vineyard," a common symbol of Israel; cf. 5:1–7; 27:2–3; Psalm 80:8;
Jeremiah 2:21. Instead of cultivating and bringing forth fruit from the
nation, they have used it for their own good. They have taken advantage
of the "poor" (*ʿanî*). The *ʿanî* is someone under physical or material distress, v. 14. They "beat" (*tedakkeʾû*, better "crush") the people. The verb
dakaʾ often has a metaphorical sense. It may refer to emotional suffering; cf. 53:10; Psalm 143:3; oppression, Psalm 89:10; Proverbs 22:22; or
even destruction, Job 6:9. They "grind" (*tiṭḥanû*, the process by which
something is reduced to powder by rubbing it between harder objects,
e.g., Exod. 32:20; Num. 11:8) the "poor" (*ʿanî*). Both *tedakkeʾû* and
tiṭḥanû refer to extreme oppression of the poor and defenseless, v. 15.[14]

(πρακτορε) and some Hebrew texts. The Vulgate, however, gives *mulieres*, "women."
The history of the nation gives evidence for retaining the MT. The thought of children
and women ruling the people accurately sums up the later history of Judah.

[13]There is widespread agreement that the singular *ʿam* should stand here instead of the
plural *ʿammîm*, e.g., NASB, NIV. The NEB follows the LXX in translating *ʿammô*, "his
people." There is no compelling reason to leave the MT. The Lord announces here a uni-
versal judgment, then lays the stress on Israel in the following verses.

[14]Alexander Scheiber, "Zwei Bemerkungen zu Jesaja," *VT* 11:455, argues that the verb
ṭaḥan hints at making an exception for the poor. His reasoning, however, rests on a grammatical construction not found here.

16 Moreover the Lord saith, Because the daughters of Zion are haughty, and walk with stretched forth necks and wanton eyes, walking and mincing as they go, and making a tinkling with their feet:
17 Therefore the Lord will smite with a scab the crown of the head of the daughters of Zion, and the Lord will discover their secret parts.

(3) Judgment of Proud Women 3:16–4:1

16–17 The Lord singles out proud women for judgment. They walk in a way to draw attention to themselves. The "stretched forth necks" refers to their holding high their heads, not wrong in itself but wrong if done with a proud motive. The phrase "wanton [$m^e\acute{s}aqq^er\hat{o}t$] eyes" occurs only here. On the basis of an Aramaic cognate, the root *śaqar* has the sense of "looking about," perhaps seeing whether others notice them. They walk with "mincing" steps, an affected, delicate stride designed to draw attention. They make a "tinkling [^cakas] with their feet," shaking the bangles worn on their feet. The word ^cakas refers to chains or rings worn about the ankles, possibly with bells or something else that would create a noise with each step, v. 16.[15] With poetic judgment, the Lord will openly humiliate them. He will strike them with a scalp disease to destroy the beauty of their hair. In addition, He will "discover their secret parts" (*pot*). This word occurs elsewhere only at I Kings 7:50, where it refers to "sockets" or "hinges." Apparently, the idea here is that the joints of the legs will be uncovered, i.e., exposing the private parts, openly shaming the people, v. 17.[16]

---

[15]Kissane, I, 45, suggests the translation "fetter their feet." Chaining the feet together would lead to the short, mincing steps of the previous phrase. We do not know enough to be dogmatic as to the meaning of ^cakas. The root occurs only at 3:16, 18 and Prov. 7:22, where it does refer to "fetters." The noun in 3:18 supports the sense of "anklets" or "tinkling ornaments" although Kissane prefers "step-chain" there. Since v. 20 uses another word ($\d{s}a^cad$) for step-chain, it is unlikely to find that meaning here.

[16]On the basis of an Akkadian cognate, *putu*, "face, front, edge," some, e.g., NASB, NEB, NIV, relate *pothen* to the forehead and translate something like "make bare their foreheads." This has the advantage of paralleling v. 17*a*. The word does not occur enough to be dogmatic as to its meaning. Understanding the word to refer to the forehead, however, robs the verse of its force. It is not as dramatic as the threat to expose the nakedness of the women. The AV is defensible.

18 *In that day the Lord will take away the bravery of their tinkling ornaments about their feet, and their cauls, and their round tires like the moon,*
19 *The chains, and the bracelets, and the mufflers,*
20 *The bonnets, and the ornaments of the legs, and the headbands, and the tablets, and the earrings,*
21 *The rings, and nose jewels,*
22 *The changeable suits of apparel, and the mantles, and the wimples, and the crisping pins,*
23 *The glasses, and the fine linen, and the hoods, and the vails.*

18–23 In the day when He brings judgment, the Lord will judge the women by removing their jewelry.[17] He will take away the "bravery" (lit. "beauty, glory") of their jewelry. Isaiah lists twenty-one items used by the women in their dress. The items are listed randomly. The "tinkling ornaments about their feet" refer to bangles, worn as anklets. The Hebrew term (ʿakas) is from the same root used in v. 16. The "caul" (šabîs) seems to be related to šabaṣ, "to weave." This would indicate a woven band of silver or gold, a headband, worn by women.[18] The "round tires like the moon" were crescent-shaped ornaments, v. 18. The "chains" (neṭîpâ) were pendant earrings. The word neṭîpâ is from naṭap, "to drop," and thus a pendant or drop-shaped earring. The "bracelets" (šêrôt)[19] were similar to those worn by women today. The "mufflers" (harʿalôt) were costly veils, v. 19.[20] "Bonnets" (peʾer) were linen headdresses, probably

---

[17]Elizabeth Ellen Platt, "Jewelry of Bible Times and the Catalog of Isa. 3:18–23," part I, *Andrews University Seminary Studies* 17:82–83, understands the collection of jewelry and clothing as associated with those who hold positions of leadership in Jerusalem. She views the passage as "the denunciation of those who hold aristocratic office in the royal city of Jerusalem and the disruption of societal roles." With this in mind, she applies the passage to both men and women. To reach this conclusion, she divorces the passage from its context ("daughters of Zion," vv. 16–17). She admits that several of the items mentioned belonged to women only but still applies the passage to both men and women.

[18]The word occurs only here and is therefore obscure. Others make šabîs a diminutive of šemeš, "sun," and understand it as sunlike ornaments. So NEB, Näglesbach, p. 74; and Von Orelli, p. 30. Platt, part II, *Andrews University Seminary Studies*, 17:194–98, has an extended discussion of sunlike pendants found in the ancient world.

[19]BDB, *A Hebrew and English Lexicon of the Old Testament*, rpt. 1974, p. 1057, relates šêrôt to šor, "navel-string," i.e., umbilical cord; šerâ, "bracelet"; and šarîr, "sinew, muscle." It translates šêrôt as "bracelet." Platt, part I, 74, understands it as "necklace cords." The Akkadian šeršerratu supports the meaning of "chains."

[20]The word harʿalôt is a *hapax legomenon*. The related verb raʿal, "to shake, tremble," occurs only once, Nah. 2:4. Other related words also occur but all with the sense of "reeling." The meaning of "veil" here comes from the motion of the veil as a person

turbans.[21] The "ornaments of the legs" (*ṣaʿad*) were ankle chains.[22] The "headbands" were sashes, bound about the body in some way. The "tablets" (*batê hannepeš*, lit. "the houses of breath," i.e., an aroma) were perfume boxes.[23] The "earrings" were charms of some kind, probably worn as ornaments rather than as protection against some disease or enemy, v. 20.

The "rings" were similar to those worn today on the fingers. The "nose jewels" were rings worn as ornaments on the nose, cf. Genesis 24:47; Ezekiel 16:12, v. 21. The "changeable suits of apparel" (or "stately robes") were festive robes; cf. Zechariah 3:4 ("change of raiment"). The "mantles" (*maʿⁿṭapôt*) were tunics, worn outside the normal robes.[24] The "wimples" were cloaks; cf. Ruth 3:15 ("vail"). The "crisping pins" (*ḥᵃrîṭîm*) were bags, possibly decorated to enhance their appearance, v. 22.[25] The "glasses" (*gillayôn*) were highly polished mirrors made from bronze.[26] The "fine linen" was a linen wrap; cf. Judges 14:12, 13.

---

moves. Barnes, Ibn Ezra, and Kissane relate the word to some kind of ornament. Platt, part II, 198, relates *harᶜalôt* to hanging beads, a possible view.

[21]Näglesbach, p. 74, calls the *pᵉʾer* a diadem or tiara, worn as part of the headdress. Exod. 39:28 and Ezek. 44:18 state that they were made from linen and thus were not items of jewelry. Men could also wear them, 61:10; Ezek. 44:18. This leads to the thought that these were turbans, wound about the head as an item of beauty.

[22]The root *ṣaʿad* refers to stepping or marching. From this, it is thought that these chains were meant to shorten the step. This encouraged the mincing step that was thought attractive. Platt, part I, 76, follows the RSV in translating "armlets." She relates the word to *ʾeṣʿadâ* in Num. 31:50 and II Sam. 1:10 although she admits that there is no prosthetic *aleph* there.

[23]Israel Eitan, "A Contribution to Isaiah Exegesis," in *HUCA* XII–XIII, p. 57, and Motyer, *The Prophecy of Isaiah*, p. 64, understand *nepeš* as "throat." The word "houses" then becomes the housing (or holder) of the throat. From this, the phrase *batê hannepeš* is a "collar" or "high collar. The view is unlikely. The word *nepeš* is well established as "breath, soul, person, emotion, etc." Platt, part II, 195, 198–99, cites examples from archaeology of small amulets that held charms written on small papyri. She would understand *batê hannepeš* as "'soul' cases." Her view is possible.

[24]Platt, part II, 200, relates *maʿⁿṭapôt* to *ᶜaṭap*, "to envelop," and understands a cape. This is also an outer garment.

[25]G. R. Driver, p. 37, understands *ḥᵃrîṭîm* as "flounced skirt" on the basis of a cognate *harâṭatu*. He feels that a "bag, purse" is "out of place between various articles of clothing." The word occurs again only in II Kings 5:23, where it clearly refers to a bag. It is not uncommon for women to take great care about choosing a purse as an accessory to their clothing.

[26]On the basis of an Arabic cognate, Kissane, I, 46, understands *gillayôn* as "a fine garment." The LXX supports this sense. On the basis of 8:1, where the word occurs again ("roll"), it is better to retain the traditional sense of "mirror."

24 *And it shall come to pass, that instead of sweet smell there shall be*
   stink; and instead of a girdle a rent; and instead of well set hair
   baldness; and instead of a stomacher a girding of sackcloth; and
   burning instead of beauty.
25 *Thy men shall fall by the sword, and thy mighty in the war.*
26 *And her gates shall lament and mourn; and she being desolate shall*
   sit upon the ground.

The Talmud describes this as the summer dress of a person. The "hoods"
were headdresses of some kind, possibly turbans. The "vails" were light
shawls, v. 23.

24–26 The Lord announces poetic justice. Instead of the elements of
dress that reflect joy and a self-satisfied attitude, the people will know
these matters that come with judgment. Rather than the sweet smell of
perfume, there will be "a stink" (lit. "decay, rottenness"), leading to the
smell of putrefaction. Instead of a "girdle," a belt to hold in their robes,
will be a "rent" (better a "rope") wrapped around them. Instead of "well
set hair" will be "baldness," a direct blow at the element of beauty in
which most women glory. Instead of "a stomacher," an expensive robe,
will be "a girding of sackcloth," coarse, dark cloth made from goat's hair
and normally worn as a sign of sorrow; cf. I Kings 20:31–32. Instead of
"beauty" will be "burning," a brand, the mark of a slave, v. 24.[27] In addition, the men of the land will fall by the sword. Even their "mighty"
(*gᵉbûrâ*, see v. 2), strong and successful warriors, will likewise fall in battle, v. 25. The "gates" of Jerusalem were the place for transacting public
affairs. They thus were a place of conversation between people. These
will mourn in sorrow over the judgment that has fallen upon the land.
"She," Zion, sits "desolate" from the loss of her men in battle, v. 26.

The passage closes with 4:1. For the sake of organization, the next
chapter discusses this verse.

---

[27]Watts, *Isaiah 1–33*, p. 44, and Kelley, p. 201, follow 1QIsaᵃ by taking "burning" (*kî*)
as a conjunction and adding *bošet*, "shame." The form of *kî*, however, follows the form of
other doubly weak *lamed-hê* hollow verbs. The *hê* ending assimilates to form the *ḥireq*
yod. See *ʾawâ* and *ʾî*, *rawâ* and *rî*, *ʿawâ* and *ʿî*. With no other textual support, it seems
likely that the Qumran scribe misunderstood the *kî* and added the *bošet* to clarify the
passage.

Practical Applications from Chapter 3

1. The Judgment of Sin, 3:1–9, 12–15. The judgment will be devastating, v. 1. God will include all classes of wicked leaders, vv. 2–3, and replace them with less qualified leaders, v. 4. This causes unprecedented oppression, vv. 5–8. People openly declare their wickedness, v. 9. Evil leaders cause the people to sin, v. 12. The Lord pronounces judgment of the leaders for their sin, vv. 13–15.

2. The Law of Sowing and Reaping, vv. 10–11. See footnote 8.

3. Misplaced Emphasis on Dress, vv. 16–26. The proud women have emphasized their outward appearance, v. 16; therefore, the Lord will judge their outward appearance, vv. 17, 24. He will take away the jewelry and clothing in which they delighted, vv. 18–23. The men they had tried to impress will fall in battle, v. 25, and the city will be desolate, v. 26.

1 *And in that day seven women shall take hold of one man, saying, We will eat our own bread, and wear our own apparel: only let us be called by thy name, to take away our reproach.*

2 *In that day shall the branch of the Lord be beautiful and glorious, and the fruit of the earth shall be excellent and comely for them that are escaped of Israel.*

3 *And it shall come to pass, that he that is left in Zion, and he that remaineth in Jerusalem, shall be called holy, even every one that is written among the living in Jerusalem:*

4 *When the Lord shall have washed away the filth of the daughters of Zion, and shall have purged the blood of Jerusalem from the midst thereof by the spirit of judgment, and by the spirit of burning.*

ISAIAH 4

1 Verse 1 properly closes the section dealing with the judgment of proud women. The phrase "seven women" figuratively refers to a group of women. Following the judgment and the captivity, the land lacks men. These women beg the man who does remain to take them as wives. They will furnish their own food and clothing if he will become their husband. By this means they hope to bear children and to lose the "reproach" of childlessness; cf. Genesis 16:4; 30:1, 23. The scene shows the tragic conditions remaining after God's judgment has fallen on Judah, v. 1.

c. Kingdom Vision 4:2–6

The final paragraph in this second major section of the book logically follows the previous material. After condemning the ritualistic worship of the people, 1:1–15, Isaiah offers cleansing, 1:16–20, and restoration, 1:21–31. He then introduces the final end of restoration, the millennial kingdom, 2:1–5. As a warning, Isaiah turns to the heavenly judgments. God will judge the wicked and their idols, 2:6–21; the wicked leaders of the land, 2:22–3:15; and the proud women, 3:15–4:1. Isaiah now returns to the kingdom with which he began in c. 2.

2–4 In contrast to the judgment that falls upon the wicked nation, the Lord will establish His kingdom for those who trust Him. The phrase "in that day" occurs widely in Isaiah. In the previous six times it occurs (2:11, 17, 20; 3:7, 18; 4:1), it refers to the Day of Judgment. For the first time, the phrase now refers to the kingdom era. At that time, the "branch of the Lord" and the "fruit of the earth" will be "beautiful and glorious." The "branch" elsewhere occurs as a messianic title; cf. Jeremiah 23:5; 33:15; Zechariah 3:8; 6:12. By parallelism, the "fruit of the earth" is also a messianic title.[1] The first phrase stresses Christ's relation to the Father, the second His relation to the earth. It is reasonable to understand "branch of the Lord" as referring to the deity of the Lord. The "fruit of the earth" refers to the humanity of Christ.[2]

"Them that are escaped of Israel" are those who have survived the Tribulation judgments. To these, the Lord is "beautiful and glorious" and "excellent and comely," v. 2. Those that are left in the land are "holy." They have accepted Jesus Christ as their Savior and therefore have their sins cleansed. They are "written among the living" (better "all who are written for life"). This refers to the Book of Life, which contains the names of all the godly. This would include the Old Testament saints as well as those who have received Jesus Christ as their Savior, v. 3.[3]

The judgments of the Tribulation period have purged the wicked from the land. The phrase "daughters of Zion" refers to the people who live in the land. The Lord has "washed" (raḥaṣ)[4] their "filth," their

---

[1]J. J. M. Roberts, "The Meaning of 'צמח ה' in Isaiah 4:2," *JBQ* 28:20–27, points out that parallelism may relate identical terms, as in A = B, or present complementary terms, as in A + B. He sees the "fruit of the earth" as the growth of the human population of the land. The "branch [or 'shoot'] of the Lord" is messianic. Leupold, I, 102–3, follows this position. While the view is possible, I have chosen here to make both phrases name the Lord. The word "fruit" refers to the Lord in Ps. 132:11. In addition, the phrases "them that are escaped," "he that is left," and "he that remaineth" in vv. 2–3 stress the few that are in the land, not the many.

[2]Many commentators take the phrase "the branch of the Lord" parallel to "the fruit of the earth." Both refer to the abundant produce brought forth by the land during the kingdom. Among others, Arthur E. Cundall, *Proverbs—Isaiah 39*, in *Bible Study Books*, p. 62; Kaiser, *Isaiah 1–12*, pp. 54–55; and Kissane, I, 48, adopt this position. Mauchline, p. 76, makes the "branch of the Lord" the righteous remnant of Israel. The "fruit of the earth" is the renewed fruitfulness of the land. Näglesbach, p. 80, spiritualizes the "branch of the Lord" and refers it to the sphere of conscious life. He refers the "fruit of the earth" to the sphere of unconscious life. Gray, I, 78, rejects a messianic application. He makes both phrases refer to the promise of fruitfulness in the land if Israel walks with the Lord. In the light of the kingdom emphasis in vv. 3–6, I prefer to parallel both phrases and refer them to Christ. Many conservative commentators likewise take this approach, e.g., Vine, p. 15; Delitzsch, pp. 151–53; Motyer, *The Prophecy of Isaiah*, p. 65.

[3]There are numerous references to the "book of life" in the Bible, e.g., Exod. 32:32–33; Ps. 69:28; Dan. 12:1; Mal. 3:16; Luke 10:20; Phil. 4:3; Rev. 3:5; 13:8; 17:8; 20:12, 15; 21:27. Gray, I, 79, after referring to the many references mentioning the Book of Life, specifically applies the passage here to "life on earth as a member of the holy Jewish community." In view of the fuller development elsewhere, the view is too restricted.

[4]Joyce G. Baldwin, "ṣemaḥ as a Technical Term in the Prophets," *VT* 14:97–99, argues that raḥaṣ refers to "sacrificial washing, which would enable the remnant to be called holy." The problem with this view is that raḥaṣ occurs widely in various contexts to refer

5 And the Lord will create upon every dwelling place of mount Zion, and upon her assemblies, a cloud and smoke by day, and the shining of a flaming fire by night: for upon all the glory shall be a defence.
6 And there shall be a tabernacle for a shadow in the daytime from the heat, and for a place of refuge, and for a covert from storm and from rain.

moral depravity.[5] In addition, He cleanses the "blood [lit. 'bloods'] of Jerusalem." The plural of blood most often indicates blood shed by violent means. Here, it refers to murderous activities in the city. These now have been purified by the work of the Holy Spirit. Isaiah names Him "the spirit [rûaḥ] of judgment [mišpaṭ, see 1:17] . . . the spirit [rûaḥ] of burning" because of His work in cleansing the people from their sin, v. 4.[6]

5–6 The Lord will create upon "every dwelling place" (lit. "the whole area") in Jerusalem and upon the "assemblies" (miqraʾ, see 1:13), the gatherings of the people for worship, His glory cloud. In the wilderness wanderings, the cloud showed God's presence with Israel, Exodus 13:21. Once more, the cloud will show His presence among His people. The glory will shine through the cloud by day and by night. "Upon all the

---

to both sacrificial washing and washing in general. Cf. Gen. 18:4; 19:2; Judg. 19:21; Ruth 3:3; Ezek. 16:4, 9; 23:40. She parallels it with dûaḥ, "purged," which refers elsewhere only to "priestly washing." The word duah, however, occurs only three other times, II Chron. 4:6; Jer. 51:34; and Ezek. 40:38. In one of these, Jer. 51:34, it refers to the Jews being "cast out," i.e., purged, rather than priestly washing. The sample is too small to prove her argument.

[5]Hailey, p. 61, limits the "filth" to the list given in 3:16–23. This is too restrictive. Stacey, p. 30, refers Israel's "filth" to their "ritual impurity" and "blood" to "bloodstains," a violation of the rituals for handling blood. While his view is included within the more general view expressed above, it is too specific to limit the interpretation to violations of the ritual. Brueggemann, Isaiah 1–39, p. 43, refers "filth" to the menstrual emissions of women. The word never has this meaning elsewhere. Brueggemann takes the phrase "daughters of Zion" too literally. It normally refers to inhabitants, not simply women.

[6]Vine, p. 16, relates the "spirit of burning" to the baptism of fire, foretold by John the Baptist, Matt. 3:11. While it is true that fire elsewhere refers to purification, e.g., 10:16–17; Deut. 32:22, it also represents other things as well. Among these are God's holiness, Exod. 3:2–5; God's glory, Exod. 24:17; angels, Ps. 104:4; judgment, Isa. 33:12, 14; and God's Word, Jer. 23:29. In view of this, it is likely that the NT reference is coincidental, not specially drawn from the Isaiah passage. Näglesbach, p. 77, and Delitzsch, I, 155, translate "fire" (baʿer) as "sifting." The infinitive baʿer, however, regularly refers to "burning." Kissane, I, 49, translates rûaḥ inconsistently, "spirit of judgment . . . wind of burning." While rûaḥ may mean either "wind" or "spirit," the parallelism argues against giving it both senses here. Grogan, p. 46, understands it as "a blast of judgment and a blast of fire" rather than a reference to the Holy Spirit. This is possible. In view of the similar use in 42:1, I prefer to make rûaḥ refer to the Holy Spirit.

glory" (ʿal⁻kol⁻kabôd, better "over all the glory") will be a "defence" (huppâ, lit. "canopy"), a protective covering to shield the people; cf. Zechariah 2:5. This undoubtedly is the Lord Himself as He furnishes protection and guidance to His people, v. 5.

A "tabernacle" (or "booth") will provide shade and refuge for the people. It will give them protection from the elements. The idea is that the Lord anticipates all the needs of the people—He cares for His own. The passage looks forward to the Millennium. During the kingdom, the Lord provides the needs of His people, v. 6.

Practical Applications from Chapter 4

1. The Nature of Jesus Christ. He is "the branch of the God" and the "fruit of the earth," the God-man, appropriately described as "beautiful and glorious . . . excellent and comely," v. 2.

2. Characteristics of the Millennium. The people who live then are "holy," with their names written in the Book of Life, v. 3. Their sins have been cleansed by the work of the Holy Spirit, v. 4. The Lord is present in glory to guide His people, v. 5. He provides protection for them, v. 6.

1 Now will I sing to my wellbeloved a song of my beloved touching his vineyard. My wellbeloved hath a vineyard in a very fruitful hill:
2 And he fenced it, and gathered out the stones thereof, and planted it with the choicest vine, and built a tower in the midst of it, and also made a winepress therein: and he looked that it should bring forth grapes, and it brought forth wild grapes.

ISAIAH 5

Isaiah turns back to the sins of the nation. In 2:1–5 and 4:2–6, he has looked at the future blessing of the nation. To keep the people from focusing exclusively on their privilege as a nation belonging to the Lord, the prophet now reminds them of their moral failures. He begins with a poetical picture of their sin (vv. 1–7), moves to a sequence of woes on various groups within the nation (vv. 8–24), and concludes with a statement of judgment (vv. 25–30).

3. Judgment of Israel 5:1–6:13
a. Poetical Statement of Wrath 5:1–24
(1) Parable of the Vineyard 5:1–7

1–2 The parable occurs elsewhere in the OT as a poetical form, e.g., Judges 9:7–15. Ezekiel 17:1–10 also relates a parable that uses the vine to represent Israel. Isaiah here sings to his "wellbeloved" (*dôdî*), the Lord.[1] The song concerns the vineyard of His beloved. The vine elsewhere occurs as a symbol of Israel, Psalm 80:8–16; Jeremiah 2:21; 12:10–11; Hosea 10:1.[2] The vineyard stands on "a very fruitful hill." The phrase is literally "on a horn of a sun of oil," i.e., the brow of a fertile region on a hill. The "horn" is a projection, a peak jutting out where it receives the sun. This is a likely place on which to plant a vineyard, v. 1.

Isaiah describes the care given the vineyard by the Lord. He had "fenced" (*ʿazaq*) it. The word *ʿazaq* occurs only here. From an Arabic cognate, it seems to mean "digged." The Lord had digged the soil, preparing it to receive the plants. He had gathered out the stones, necessary because of the rocky soil in Palestine; cf. II Kings 3:19, 25. He planted it with the very best slips of vine (*śoreq*). The word *śoreq* occurs

---

[1]The threefold repetition of "beloved" is characteristic of Isaiah's style of writing, e.g., 6:2 ("twain"); 8:9 ("broken in pieces"); 51:9 ("awake"); 63:7 ("Lord").

[2]Skinner, *Isaiah I–XXXIX*, p. 32, suggests that the idea of Israel as the Lord's vineyard originated with Isaiah. Chronologically, however, Psalm 80:8–16 is earlier. Asaph lived in the time of David, about two hundred years earlier.

3 *And now, O inhabitants of Jerusalem, and men of Judah, judge, I*
pray you, betwixt me and my vineyard.
4 *What could have been done more to my vineyard, that I have not*
done in it? wherefore, when I looked that it should bring forth
grapes, brought it forth wild grapes?
5 *And now go to; I will tell you what I will do to my vineyard: I will*
take away the hedge thereof, and it shall be eaten up; and break
down the wall thereof, and it shall be trodden down:
6 *And I will lay it waste: it shall not be pruned, nor digged; but there*
shall come up briers and thorns: I will also command the clouds
that they rain no rain upon it.
7 *For the vineyard of the Lord of hosts is the house of Israel, and the*
men of Judah his pleasant plant: and he looked for judgment, but
behold oppression; for righteousness, but behold a cry.

only here and at Jeremiah 2:21 with related words at 16:8; Genesis
49:11. Judges 16:4 refers to the "Valley of Sorek," a place of vineyards.
The Sorek River runs through this valley, which begins about ten miles
west of Jerusalem and extends in a west-northwest direction to the
Mediterranean. The word *śoreq* refers to a small reddish blue grape of
fine quality. Quite possibly using the stones He has gathered from the
vineyard, the Lord has built a tower for the watchman to stand in during
the harvest. He had "made a winepress" (*yeqeb ḥaṣeb*, lit. "hewn out a
wine vat"), a place for collecting the juice of the grapes. The *yeqeb* was a
hollowed-out place in the rocks. The workers placed the grapes in an
upper hollow; cf. Joel 3:13. They then crushed them by walking over
them. As the juice drained, it was caught in the *yeqeb*, the lower recep-
tacle. From here, containers were filled with the juice.

Despite the Lord's care for the vineyard, it had failed in its purpose.
When He "looked" (*qawâ*) for the grapes, He found "wild grapes"
(*beʾušîm*, lit. "stinking things"),[3] a vivid picture of Israel's sin. The verb
"look" (*qawâ*) has the sense of eagerly looking or hoping with an attitude
of expectancy. Note that the Lord did not plant the vine for its beauty. He
did not plant it to create shade or to provide protection from wild animals. His purpose in planting the vine was to bring forth fruit. So it is
with God's children today. His purpose is still to produce fruit, v. 2.

3–7 The Lord now begins to speak. He laments over Judah. He invites
the people to "judge" between Him and His vineyard, still a symbol of
the nation, v. 3. Rhetorically, He asks if more could have been done for

---

[3]While *beʾušîm* occurs only in vv. 2, 4, related words occur elsewhere, e.g., Exod. 7:18,
21; 16:20, 24; Eccles. 10:1. It refers to something loathsome or with a foul odor.

8 Woe unto them that join house to house, that lay field to field, till there be no place, that they may be placed alone in the midst of the earth!

them. The expected answer is no! He has "looked" (*qawâ*) for fruit but they have produced only *beʾušîm*, "stinking things." Despite this hope of the Lord, the nation had failed Him, v. 4. For this reason, He plans to take "away the hedge," a planting of prickly growth designed to keep wild animals from the vines, and to "break down the wall," a defense against intruders. It will then become a place to be trodden down, trampled by animals or men who wish to come in, v. 5. He will devastate the vineyard. He will not prune the vines or dig about them to keep the weeds down but will let the "briers and thorns" grow and keep the "clouds" (*ʿab*) from raining on them. This last statement shows the control of God over the judgment. When *ʿab* refers to clouds, it is normally rain clouds, e.g., Judges 5:4; I Kings 18:45. God, however, turns the clouds away from their normal purpose, v. 6.

Verse 7 applies the passage. The "vineyard" is Israel. The "men of Judah" have been "his pleasant plant" (better "a planting of his delight"), the planting from which He had long anticipated delight. The second half of v. 7 involves a play on words. "He looked [*qawâ*, see v. 2] for judgment [*mišpaṭ*, better 'justice,' see 1:17] and, behold, oppression [*mišpaḥ*, better 'bloodshed'];[4] for righteousness [*ṣedaqâ*] and, behold, a cry [*ṣeʿaqâ*, better 'a cry of distress']." It is as though the Lord looked for justice and found injustice, for righteous speech and found complaining words, v. 7.

(2) Proclamation of Woes 5:8–24[5]
(a) Against the Covetous 5:8–10

8–10 The series of six "woes" in this section follow naturally the statement of Israel's sin in vv. 1–4 and the promise of judgment in

---

[4]The word *mišpaḥ* occurs only here in the OT. It apparently comes from the unused root *šapaḥ*, "to pour out," seen in the substantive *sapîaḥ*, Job 14:19, "outpourings." The sense of "bloodshed" is appropriate. KB, II, 641, suggests "legal infringement," a contrast with "justice." The LXX translates ἀνομίαν an obvious contrast with "justice." Delitzsch, I, 166, relates it to *sapaḥ,* which he understands as "sweep away." He interprets this as sweeping away another man's property, thus "grasping." While it is not possible to be certain, I feel that the evidence supports "bloodshed," the pouring out of blood.

[5]Robert B. Chisholm Jr., "Structure, Style, and the Prophetic Message: An Analysis of Isaiah 5:8–30," in *Vital Old Testament Issues*, pp. 131–35, divides vv. 8–30 into three

9 *In mine ears said the Lord of hosts, Of a truth many houses shall be
desolate, even great and fair, without inhabitant.*
10 *Yea, ten acres of vineyard shall yield one bath, and the seed of an
homer shall yield an ephah.*
11 *Woe unto them that rise up early in the morning, that they may follow strong drink; that continue until night, till wine inflame them!*
12 *And the harp, and the viol, the tabret, and pipe, and wine, are in
their feasts: but they regard not the work of the Lord, neither consider the operation of his hands.*

vv. 5–7.[6] The section lists several representative sins and announces
judgment on each. The first "woe" condemns the covetousness of the
people. They sought to acquire additional property until "there be no
place," i.e., no place for others. They wished to be "placed alone" with
no one owning property near them, v. 8. The Lord speaks "in mine ears"
so that Isaiah may hear. The supplied verb "said" is obvious; cf. 22:14.
God's judgment will leave many houses "desolate" (*šammâ*). The word
šammâ refers to devastation or desolation that comes as the result of
judgment, normally divine judgment. This will include even the homes
of the wealthy and influential, v. 9. To show the extent of His judgment,
the Lord describes a lean harvest. The word "acres" (*ṣemed*) literally
means "yoke." It refers to the amount of land a yoke of oxen could plow
in a day; cf. I Samuel 14:14. A vineyard occupying ten *ṣemed* of ground,
five-to-ten acres, will yield only "one bath," a little more than eight gal-
lons of wine. A "homer," ten ephahs (Ezek. 45:11) of seed, about eight
bushels, will yield only one-tenth as much, v. 10.

(b) Against the Drunkards 5:11–17

11–12 The Lord condemns those who spend day and night in drinking alcoholic beverages. The phrase "strong drink" (*šekar*) refers to wine
made from fermented grains or fruits, not to the stronger forms of alcohol so often consumed today. Distilled alcohol, as we know it today, was

---

parts, vv. 8–10, 11–17, 18–30. He uses "rhetorical criticism" to isolate three "judgment
speech[es]." Each involves "an accusation and an announcement of judgment." The division, however, is arbitrary. It imposes an unnatural structure on the passage in order to
couple an announcement of judgment with each accusation. Isaiah's repetitive use of *hôy*
seems more naturally to support the six paragraphs given in the discussion.

[6]Wright, p. 32, understands the "woe" (*hôy*) of the chapter (5:8, 11, 18, 20, 21, 22) as
an exclamation, "alas," rather than an imprecation, "woe." The context has to determine
the sense of *hôy*. In my view, the promises of judgment that occur through the rest of the
chapter, e.g., vv. 9–10, 13–17, make this an imprecation.

13 *Therefore my people are gone into captivity, because they have no knowledge: and their honourable men are famished, and their multitude dried up with thirst.*

14 *Therefore hell hath enlarged herself, and opened her mouth without measure: and their glory, and their multitude, and their pomp, and he that rejoiceth, shall descend into it.*

15 *And the mean man shall be brought down, and the mighty man shall be humbled, and the eyes of the lofty shall be humbled:*

16 *But the Lord of hosts shall be exalted in judgment, and God that is holy shall be sanctified in righteousness.*

17 *Then shall the lambs feed after their manner, and the waste places of the fat ones shall strangers eat.*

invented in the Arabian world in the Middle Ages. The "wine" (*yayin*) is the more common wine normally developed from fermented grapes, v. 11. Music with various instruments accompanies the revelry, all taking place without concern for the Lord. The "harp" is a lyre with ten strings made from the small intestine of a sheep.[7] These were stretched over a sounding board and plucked either with a plectrum or the fingers. The "viol" was probably a twelve-stringed harp with a rounded shape. The "tabret" was a small drum that was struck with the hand. The "pipe" was similar to a flute. Music accompanied the "wine" (*yayin*) drinking. In all of this rejoicing, the people failed to see the work of God in their nation, v. 12.

13–17 The Lord will send the people into captivity. The verbs in the passage are prophetic perfects. They show a future condition as though it has already happened. The people "[go] into captivity" (*galâ*)[8] because "they have no knowledge" of spiritual truth; cf. Hosea 4:1, 6. The judgment will include both honorable men and the masses. The picture of men being "famished" and "dried up with thirst" briefly sums up the hardships of captivity, v. 13. Isaiah pictures "hell" (*šᵉʾôl*), literally "sheol," here referring to the grave, as a ravenous beast.[9] She "enlarges

---

[7]Josephus, *Antiquities* vii.12.3, gives a brief description of the lyre and harp.

[8]Driver, *JSS* 13:38, interprets *galâ* as sweeping the people "away in death." He argues that the warning of a captivity that would "not happen for over a century will not have been an effective deterrent to the prophet's hearers." Many prophecies of judgment, however, relate to the long-range future of Judah. In addition, the verb *galâ* regularly refers to going into exile, e.g., Judg. 18:30; II Kings 15:29; 16:9; Jer. 1:3; 13:19. The participle form of *galâ* also refers to an exile, II Sam. 15:19; II Kings 24:14; Isa. 49:21; Amos 6:7.

[9]Whitehouse, p. 116, wrongly describes the Jewish view of sheol as "the mysterious dark abode of the dead beneath the earth, where they led an obscure, joyless existence.

18 *Woe unto them that draw iniquity with cords of vanity, and sin as it*
   were with a cart rope:
19 *That say, Let him make speed, and hasten his work, that we may see*
   it: and let the counsel of the Holy One of Israel draw nigh and come,
   that we may know it!

herself"[10] and opens her mouth to swallow the wicked; cf. Proverbs
1:12; 27:20. The pronouns are singular, not plural, and refer to the glory,
the number, and the "pomp" (or "noise") of Jerusalem. All who now rejoice will go into "it," the grave, v. 14. All classes of society, low and
high, will be humbled; cf. 2:11, 17. The judgment includes the "mean
man" (*ʾadam*, see 2:9) and the "mighty man" (*ʾîš*, see 2:9). These two
words rightly draw a contrast between the common man and the more
successful man. All who lift themselves up in pride will be humbled,
v. 15. The "Lord of hosts," the ruler of the heavenly and earthly hosts,
alone will be exalted as the "judgment" (*mišpat*, see 1:17) of those who
have opposed Him. The "God that is holy" (or "the Holy God") will be
"sanctified," set apart in that day, by His righteousness, v. 16. The desolate land will become a pasture for sheep. The "fat ones," the wealthy
who have gone into judgment, leave their harvest for the "strangers,"
wanderers in the land, to eat, v. 17.[11]

(c) Against Those Who Defy God 5:18–19

18–19 The Lord pronounces "woe" on those who draw "iniquity"
(*ʿawon*, see 1:4) and "sin" (*hattaʾâ*, see 3:9) after themselves. The terms

---

From this dark region it was supposed that spirits might be summoned back to the earth
by the arts of the necromancer (I Sam. xxviii)." The OT makes sheol the abode of both
the righteous (Ps. 16:10; 30:3) and the wicked (Num. 16:33; Ps. 9:17). There was a difference in the condition of the righteous and the wicked in sheol (Ps. 28:1, 3–5). The
Lord will take the righteous out of sheol (Ps. 49:15; 86:13; Prov. 15:24; Hos 13:14). The
difficulty in understanding sheol lies partly with the fact that it sometimes refers to the
grave (e.g., 28:15, 18), which receives the dead without measure (5:14). At other times, it
refers to the eternal abode. It is the home of the debased (57:9). There is a conscious existence of the dead and a personal identity (14:9, 15).

[10]Based on the Akkadian *napištu*, Eitan, p. 57, understands "herself" (*nepeš*) as
"throat." He translates, "Sheol hath enlarged her throat and opened her mouth without
measure." While this brings the two phrases into parallel thought, it requires us to neglect the traditional meaning of "soul," and thus translate "self" for *nepeš*. The Akkadian
napištu means "soul" far more often than "throat." The Hebrew *nepeš* does not refer to
the "throat" at all.

[11]This is not a description of blessing as though the righteous will enjoy the fullness of
the land after the judgment of the wicked. Henry, p. 34, and A. R. Fausset, *Isaiah*, in

20 *Woe unto them that call evil good, and good evil; that put darkness for light, and light for darkness; that put bitter for sweet, and sweet for bitter!*
21 *Woe unto them that are wise in their own eyes, and prudent in their own sight!*

"cords of vanity [*šawʾ*, see 1:13]" (or "cords of falsehood") and "cart rope" suggest the strength found in sinful habits. As was said by the educator Horace Mann, "Habit is a cable. We weave a thread of it each day until at last it binds us." While the "cords of falsehood" and "cart rope" may be metaphorical here, these ropes are just as strong as the ropes that would be used to lead animals, v. 18. These wicked ones challenge God to speed His work and to show them His counsel (cf. II Pet. 3:3–4). Clearly, they do not believe that God will judge them for their actions, v. 19.

(d) Against Moral Perversion 5:20

20 The ungodly pervert good and evil. The words "light" and "sweet" symbolize good (cf. Ps. 112:4). The words "darkness" and "bitter" symbolize evil (cf. Prov. 2:13; Jer. 2:19). These wicked individuals ignore common standards of behavior. They substitute good for evil and evil for good. God pronounces "woe" on them, v. 20.

(e) Against the Self-Sufficient 5:21

21 God now condemns those who trust themselves completely. They consider themselves "wise" and "prudent" (*bîn*, see 1:3, discerning, intelligent, understanding). This implies that they feel no need to rely upon the Lord for guidance. The theme occurs often elsewhere in both the OT and NT, e.g., Proverbs 1:7; 3:7; 26:12, 16; Jeremiah 9:23–24; Romans 1:22; 12:16; I Corinthians 3:18–20, v. 21.

(f) Against Unjust Rulers 5:22–24

22–24 Judah's leaders are drunken degenerates. They are "mighty" in drinking wine and "men of strength" in mixing strong drink. As before, v. 11, the "wine" refers to fermented grape juice, and "strong drink" refers to the fermented juices of grains or fruits. The rulers "mingle" their wine, mixing in spices to flavor it, e.g. Psalm 75:8; Proverbs 9:2, 5;

A Critical and Experimental Commentary on the Old and New Testaments, 1967, p. 579, so understand the verse. It is rather a picture of the land after the judgment of God leaves it without inhabitants.

22 *Woe unto them that are mighty to drink wine, and men of strength to*
mingle strong drink:
23 *Which justify the wicked for reward, and take away the righteous-*
ness of the righteous from him!
24 *Therefore as the fire devoureth the stubble, and the flame consumeth*
the chaff, so their root shall be as rottenness, and their blossom shall
go up as dust: because they have cast away the law of the Lord of
hosts, and despised the word of the Holy One of Israel.
25 *Therefore is the anger of the Lord kindled against his people, and he*
hath stretched forth his hand against them, and hath smitten them:
and the hills did tremble, and their carcases were torn in the midst
of the streets. For all this his anger is not turned away, but his hand
is stretched out still.

Song of Solomon 8:2, v. 22.[12] This reliance on alcohol leads the nation's
leaders to accept bribes and to render unrighteous judgments (cf. Prov.
31:4–5), v. 23. The Lord compares their judgment to the burning of stubble or chaff and to the rotting of a plant. The rotting of the roots of the
plant and the drying up and decaying of the flower back into the dust
suggest the completeness of the judgment (cf. Mal. 4:1). This judgment
comes because the people have rejected God's "law" (*tôrâ*, see 1:10).
The parallelism with "word of the Holy One" suggests that this is more
than the Mosaic Law. It is the general teaching of God by which He reveals Himself and His will, v. 24.

b. Pronouncement of Wrath 5:25–30

25 Isaiah closes his message by proclaiming judgment upon wicked
Judah. He describes the judgment in terms of an earthquake shaking the
land. The earthquake is a means of judgment elsewhere; cf. Numbers
16:32; Joel 3:16.[13] The carcases of the dead are "torn" (*kassûḥâ*, better

---

[12]Only a limited number of references mention the mixing of wine. Isa. 1:22 and Ps.
102:9 connect the mixing of wine with water as an indication of judgment. Neither of
these verses, however, uses *yayin* to refer to "wine." Also using a different word, Prov.
23:30 mentions the woe of those who drink "mixed wine" excessively. Song of Sol. 8:2
refers to spiced wine at a time of rejoicing. The context here relates more to a social occasion at which spiced wine would be desirable.

[13]Motyer, *The Prophecy of Isaiah*, p. 73, and Fausset, p. 580, suggest this might be the
same earthquake mentioned in Amos 1:1; Zech. 14:5. Cowles, p. 37, does not mention
the earthquake of Amos but he sets the events of the verse in the past. The passage here
is a prophetic perfect. It looks to the future even though it states the earthquake as an accomplished fact. Cowles understands the trembling of the hills to indicate "the appalling
majesty of these inflictions of divine judgment," as though the hills respond in awe to the

26 *And he will lift up an ensign to the nations from far, and will hiss*
unto them from the end of the earth: and, behold, they shall come
with speed swiftly:
27 *None shall be weary nor stumble among them; none shall slumber*
nor sleep; neither shall the girdle of their loins be loosed, nor the
latchet of their shoes be broken:
28 *Whose arrows are sharp, and all their bows bent, their horses' hoofs*
shall be counted like flint, and their wheels like a whirlwind:
29 *Their roaring shall be like a lion, they shall roar like young lions:*
yea, they shall roar, and lay hold of the prey, and shall carry it away
safe, and none shall deliver it.

"as refuse")[14] in the streets. Yet the Lord does not end His wrath at this point. He is still angry at the sin of the nation, v. 25.[15]

26–29 For the first time, Isaiah describes the judgment as an invasion of nations. He lifts "an ensign," a banner, to show the nations where they should go. He signals them "from far," hissing to them as a signal. Although Egypt and Rome later conquered Palestine, the thought here is most likely of the Assyrian and Babylonian nations. Both of them invaded Palestine in the OT and brought significant judgment upon Judah. They will "come with speed swiftly," an indication that the judgment will fall soon, v. 26.

The nations are ready for the battle. They are rested so that they do not need delay, "slumber nor sleep." They have fastened the "girdle of their loins," the leather belt that kept the flowing robe from impeding the soldier. The cords that bind their shoes are unbroken, preventing any hindrance to their work of judgment, v. 27. Their arrows are sharp and their bows "bent" (*darak*).[16] The hoofs of their horses are like flint, trampling the people. Their chariots sweep across the land like an unstoppable whirlwind, v. 28. The phrase "their roaring" is better "its roaring," referring to the noise as it comes into the nation. Like a lioness, it approaches

---

Lord's work. This view is unlikely. The passage describes actual events rather than giving metaphorical pictures.

[14]The AV translates *kassûhâ*, "to cut off, cut away, cut down" as "torn." The initial *k*, however, is the preposition "as." The word *suhâ* occurs again only at Ps. 80:16. In form, it is from the unused root *suah*, probably related to *sahâ*, "to sweep."

[15]Isaiah uses the phrase "his hand is stretched out still" here and at 9:12, 17, 21; and 10:4. See also 14:21.

[16]The use of *darak* here is interesting. The root means "to tread." Here, it refers to stepping on the lower end of the bow while pulling the upper end to bend it so that it may be strung.

*30 And in that day they shall roar against them like the roaring of the
sea: and if one look unto the land, behold darkness and sorrow, and
the light is darkened in the heavens thereof.*

the land. The "roar" (or "growl") is like that of "young lions." It will
"carry it away safe" (or "carry it off"). No one will deliver Judah, v. 29.

30 The phrase "they shall roar" is better "it shall growl." This again
refers to the noise of the army as it approaches.[17] The noise is like the
roaring of the ocean waters as they beat against the shore. The judgment
leaves the land in "darkness and sorrow [or 'darkness of distress']." This
metaphorically pictures emotional gloom that spreads across the land.
Even the light becomes dark "in the heavens thereof" (*ʿarîp*, better "by
its clouds"),[18] again poetically stating the gloom of the nation, v. 30.

Practical Applications from Chapter 5

1. The vineyard, a picture of Israel and an illustration of people today,
   v. 7a. God plants it, v. 1, and cares for it, vv. 2a, 3–4a, yet it brings
   forth stinking fruit, vv. 2b, 4b; cf. v. 7b. God will judge it, vv. 5–6.

2. The "Woes" of Judgment, vv. 8–30

   a. Upon the covetous, vv. 8–10

   b. Upon the drunkards, vv. 11–17

   c. Upon those who defy God, vv. 18–19

   d. Upon moral perversion, v. 20

   e. Upon the self-sufficient, v. 21

   f. Upon unjust rulers, vv. 22–24

   Those who live in sin will receive judgment, vv. 25–30.

3. Even those who belong to God will receive judgment for their sin.
   The chapter speaks of "his vineyard," v. 1; "my vineyard," vv. 3, 4, 5;
   "his pleasant plants," v. 7; "my people," v. 13; and "his people,"
   v. 25. Judgment still comes on those who sin.

---

[17]Wade, p. 37, makes the Lord the subject of the verb. While this is possible, the context favors relating the noise to the approach of the enemy troops.

[18]Whitehouse, p. 120, and Kissane, I, 66, translate *ʿarîp* as "gloom." Slotki, p. 28,
translates as "skies." Watts, *Isaiah 1–33*, p. 64, gives "spray," a word that does not fit
with "light." While the word *ʿarîp* occurs only here, there are related words that also
occur in the OT. The root *ʿarap* is "to drip, drop." This supports the translation of
"clouds," the heavenly storehouse of drops of water.

1 In the year that king Uzziah died I saw also the Lord sitting upon a throne, high and lifted up, and his train filled the temple.

2 Above it stood the seraphims: each one had six wings; with twain he covered his face, and with twain he covered his feet, and with twain he did fly.

3 And one cried unto another, and said, Holy, holy, holy, is the Lord of hosts: the whole earth is full of his glory.

4 And the posts of the door moved at the voice of him that cried, and the house was filled with smoke.

ISAIAH 6

It may seem strange that Isaiah's call to the prophetic ministry should occur here and not at the beginning of the book.[1] The reason rests with the literary structure followed by Isaiah. He begins with an overview of his ministry. In c. 1–5, he has introduced both current and future themes. He has rebuked the people for their sin and warned them of coming judgment. He has prophesied the captivity and the return to Palestine. He has introduced the Millennium. Now he cycles back to begin more detailed looks at each of these themes.

c. Prophetic Vision of Wrath 6:1–7

1–4 King Uzziah died ca. 742 B.C.[2] The Lord often uses trial to prepare hearts for rich spiritual experiences. Here, Isaiah sees a vision of the Lord in the heavenly "temple" (*hêkal*).[3] The heavenly temple is the original of which the earthly tabernacle was a partial copy, Psalm 11:4; cf. Exodus 25:9, 40.[4] Isaiah sees the Lord seated upon His throne. This must be a vision of Jesus Christ, the second person of the Trinity. Isaiah

---

[1] Amos 7:14–15 also records the call of the prophet significantly after beginning his writings.

[2] There is disagreement regarding the date of Uzziah's death. Wright, p. 34, sets it at 734 B.C. Goldingay, p. 58, places the death between 742 and 735 B.C. Slotki, p. 28, fixes the date at 739 B.C. Grogan, p. 5, gives 740 B.C. Mauchline, p. 89, and Herbert, *Isaiah 1–39*, p. 58, date it at 742 B.C. Ivan Engnell, *The Call of Isaiah*, 1949, p. 25, makes it 748 B.C. Fortunately, the exact dating of the chapter does not affect its message.

[3] Rawlinson, I, 106, understands the Lord as being in His heavenly palace since He sits upon His "throne." The word *hêkal* may mean either "palace" or "temple." The presence of the "altar," v. 6, and the emphasis on cleanliness from sin suggest that this is the temple. It would not be out of place for the Lord to sit on a throne in the heavenly temple while He receives worship.

[4] Among others, Engnell, p. 28; Price, p. 49; and Kaiser, *Isaiah 1–12*, p. 74, make this the earthly temple. Rolf Knierim, "The Vocation of Isaiah," *VT* 18:51, states that "door"

sees Him, yet elsewhere the Bible says that no man has seen God; cf. Exodus 33:20; John 1:18; 6:46; I Timothy 6:16; I John 4:12. The Being here speaks and has a body wearing a robe. Elsewhere God the Father is a spirit, John 4:24; I Timothy 1:17; 6:15–16. John 12:40 settles the identity. After referring to this passage, John says that Isaiah saw the glory of the Son of God, John 12:41.

The Lord is "high and lifted up," exalted in His glory.[5] His "train," the trailing part of His regal vestments, fills the temple, v. 1. Taking the pronoun "it" (*lô*) as "Him" rather than the throne, the "seraphims" (better "seraphs") fly about the Lord.[6] There is no indication of the total number of seraphs. Since this is a glorious scene, it is reasonable that there are many of them.[7] This is the only mention of seraphs in the Bible although the creatures in Revelation 4:6–8 are similar in their ministry. The root *śerāpîm* means "burning ones," indicating their color. The noun occurs several times referring to snakes, Numbers 21:6, 8; Deuteronomy 8:15;

(*sap*), in v. 4, occurs elsewhere referring only to the earthly temple. The word, however, occurs in Ezek. 40:6, 7; 41:16; and 43:8, where the millennial temple is in view. The presence of a throne upon which the Lord sits and the continuing worship of the seraphim (not cherubs as in the earthly temple, e.g., Exod. 25:18–22) make the heavenly temple more likely. With no justification, Henry, p. 38, makes the temple represent the church on earth. This spiritualizes the text.

[5]Skinner, *Isaiah I–XXXIX*, p. 44; Herbert, *Isaiah 1–39*, p. 58; and Barnes, I, 138, make the phrase "high and lifted up" modify the throne rather than the Lord. Delitzsch, I, 190, makes the "high and exalted throne" the "heavenly antitype of the earthly throne which was formed by the ark of the covenant." From the Hebrew, it is possible that the phrase modifies the throne. However, the same phrase refers to the Lord in 57:15 and a similar phrase to Him in 52:13. Since Isaiah's primary focus is on the Lord, I prefer to make the phrase relate to Him.

[6]The *îm* ending on *śerap* makes the Hebrew word plural. Adding an "s" to seraphim is unnecessary. These are seraphs, not seraphims.

[7]Engnell, pp. 34–35, argues that there were but two seraphs. He bases the view on the phrase "one called to another," on archaeological discoveries relating angelic creatures to heathen kings, to a variety of biblical references including Luke 24:4 (John 20:12) and the two witnesses of Rev. 11, and on the two cherubs in the holy of holies. Karen Randolph Joines, "Winged Serpents in Isaiah's Inaugural Vision," *JBL* 86:410, also concludes that there were two. She mentions only the phrase "one called to another" in support. This phrase, however, may also be general, describing two groups singing to one another. Other appearances of angels often include many of them, Gen. 28:12; 32:1–2; I Kings 22:19; II Kings 6:16–17; Rev. 5:11. It is reasonable to understand it so here. E. Lacheman, "The Seraphim of Isaiah 6," *JQR* 59:71–72, also argues for two seraphs. He understands them as the two golden cherubs in the holy of holies mounted above the ark of the covenant. Isaiah poetically describes them as flying about the Lord. This does not explain the cry of the seraphs, "Holy, holy, holy" or the cleansing of the prophet by the seraph.

Isaiah 14:29; 30:6. Once again, the word refers to the color of the serpents.[8] Some think that these are cherubim, described from their appearance rather than their work.[9] They cover their feet, as if to hide that which was soiled from daily service.[10] They cover their faces, shielding themselves from the divine glory. With their remaining wings, they fly, keeping themselves in readiness to serve the Lord, v. 2.[11]

The seraphs sing of the holiness of God. Their color of fire is appropriate in view of the association of fire with the holiness of God, Exodus 3:2–5; 19:18; Deuteronomy 32:22; Isaiah 10:16–17. Possibly, the singing "one to another" indicates that the seraphs were on either side of the throne. The singing may have been antiphonal, alternating between the groups. While not a clear doctrinal statement, the phrase "holy, holy, holy" hints at the Trinity.[12] The thrice-repeated "holy" conveys an unusual emphasis. Normally, a single repetition in Hebrew is emphatic. The double repetition is rare.[13] The scene must have impressed Isaiah. He refers to God over and over as "the holy One of Israel," more than

---

[8]Among others, Joines, p. 411; Kelley, p. 209; Gray, I, 105; and Kraeling, p. 62, visualize the seraphs as winged serpents with feet and faces. This gives too much emphasis to the root elsewhere referring to serpents and not enough to its indication of color. Joines, pp. 411–14, summarizes archaeological evidence from Egypt showing the association of the uraeus with the pharaohs. She concludes that the winged serpents here are "royal symbolism," the Lord. The evidence, however, is from Egypt, not from Judah. In addition to the difficulty in identifying seraphs as serpents, no evidence identifies them as symbols of the Lord.

[9]*TWOT*, II, 884.

[10]Kelley, p. 210; Kraeling, p. 62; and Engnell, p. 16, understand the feet as a euphemism for the genitalia. The seraphs cover themselves to maintain their modesty. There is nothing in the context here, however, to suggest a metaphorical use. It is not likely that the feet stand for anything more than feet.

[11]Jerome held a curious view of the event. He applied the pronoun "his" to God. The seraphim cover God's face and His feet with their wings. In some unexplained way, covering God's face kept them from knowing "His beginning." Covering His feet kept them from knowing "His bounds," the work of God throughout eternity *(The Letters of St. Jerome*, trans. Charles Christopher Mierow, in *Ancient Christian Writers: The Works of the Fathers in Translation*, ed. Johannes Quasten and Walter J. Burghardt [Westminster, Md.: The Newman Press, 1963], p. 86). The view suffers in that it requires God to have a body. Jerome refers to God here as though he thinks of God the Father rather than God the Son.

[12]*The Isaiah Targum*, trans. Bruce D. Chilton, in *The Aramaic Bible*, Vol. 11, ed. Kevin Cathcart, Michael Maher, and Martin McNamara, p. 15, relates the thrice repeated holy to God's holiness in the heavens, in the earth, and in eternity.

[13]The similar pattern occurs in Jer. 7:4; 22:29; Ezek. 21:27. Close parallels occur in II Sam. 18:33 and Ps. 113:1. There is a NT parallel in Rev. 4:8.

5 Then said I, Woe is me! for I am undone; because I am a man of unclean lips, and I dwell in the midst of a people of unclean lips: for
mine eyes have seen the King, the Lord of hosts.
6 Then flew one of the seraphims unto me, having a live coal in his
hand, which he had taken with the tongs from off the altar:
7 And he laid it upon my mouth, and said, Lo, this hath touched thy
lips; and thine iniquity is taken away, and thy sin purged.

any other title used by him of God. The seraphs as well sing of God's
glory filling the earth, v. 3.

The "posts [*ammôt*] of the door [*sippîm*]" shake at the pronouncements of the Lord. The word *ammôt* is from *aman*, "to confirm, support." By extension, it refers to the "foundation" of the building and not
merely the upright parts of the door. In this context, *sippîm* is better
"thresholds," a meaning it often takes elsewhere, e.g., Judges 19:27;
Ezekiel 40:6–7. The idea is that the very foundations of the building
shake. The building fills with smoke, a sign of God's presence (cf. Gen.
15:17; I Kings 8:10–11). A similar scene occurs in Revelation 15:8, v. 4.

5–7 In God's presence, Isaiah senses his own sin. He is "undone"
(*nidmêtî*, or "cut off").[14] The root *damâ* II has the basic sense "to cut
off " and always occurs in a context of judgment. Isaiah senses that he
faces judgment for his sinfulness. In contrast with the seraphs, whose
lips sing the praise of God, Isaiah's own lips and the lips of his people
are "unclean" (*tame*). The word *tame* may refer to someone who is ritually impure or to wicked individuals. In the presence of the seraphim
who praise God with their lips, Isaiah is conscious of his failure and the
failure of the nation toward God. He has seen the King, the Ruler of the
hosts of heaven and earth, and is conscious of his own sinfulness. It is
worth noting that Isaiah here uses the titles of "King" and "Lord of
hosts" for Jesus Christ. The Son is the visible member of the Godhead,
the one Isaiah sees sitting upon His throne in heaven; cf. v. 1.

Isaiah has confessed his sin, v. 5. The sacrifice of confession always
pleases God (cf. Lev. 26:40–42; Ps. 51:3–5; Prov. 28:13). A seraph now
takes a "coal" from the heavenly altar of incense and "laid" (better

---

[14]Watts, *Isaiah 1–33*, p. 75, translates *nidmêtî* as "I am silent." He states that Isaiah
wanted to praise the Lord but dared not do so because of his sinfulness. The root *damâ*
occurs seventeen times in the OT with the basic sense of "to cut off." Often it is translated "to be silent" because a body of people no longer exist. In particular, the root occurs in the *nipʿal* ten times, as here, eight of them outside of Isaiah. In every case, the
sense "cut off " is appropriate.

8 Also I heard the voice of the Lord, saying, Whom shall I send, and
   who will go for us? Then said I, Here am I; send me.
9 And he said, Go, and tell this people, Hear ye indeed, but understand not; and see ye indeed, but perceive not.
10 Make the heart of this people fat, and make their ears heavy, and
   shut their eyes; lest they see with their eyes, and hear with their
   ears, and understand with their heart, and convert, and be healed.

"touched") it to Isaiah's mouth. Symbolically, this shows Isaiah's cleansing; cf. 4:4; Malachi 3:2. His "iniquity" (ᶜawon, see 1:4) is "taken away"
in the sense that God has forgiven it. The sin no longer is a barrier to
Isaiah's service. His "sin" (ḥaṭṭaʾt, see 3:9) is "purged" (kapar, or
"atoned for"). The word kapar is one of the great theological words of
the OT. It means "to make an atonement, reconciliation." The word most
often occurs in connection with sacrifice. It also occurs generally referring to atonement. Here, Isaiah's confession shows his acceptance of
God's holiness and his consciousness of sin. God accepts this as the
basis for his atonement. The seraph announces this to Isaiah, vv. 6–7.

d. Personal Record of Isaiah 6:8–13

8 The Lord calls for a volunteer to deliver His message to the people.
The phrase "who will go for us?" suggests the triune God.[15] Isaiah readily
responds: "Here am I; send me." The order of this incident is significant.
First, Isaiah confesses his sin (v. 5). The Lord responds by cleansing him
from sin (vv. 6–7). Isaiah then responds to the call for service (v. 8). The
passage shows the influence of sin, keeping God's children from doing
His will.

9–10 The Lord sends Isaiah to deliver a message to the people. They
will hear (šimᶜû šamôaᶜ) the message but not "understand" (bîn, see 1:3)
it. They will look (rᵉʾû raʾô) for something to help them but not "perceive" (yadaᶜ, see 1:3) anything in what they see. The grammatical construction in both cases, the imperative followed by the infinitive absolute

---

[15]Delitzsch I, 198, relates the plural pronoun to God and the seraphs "who formed, together with the Lord, one deliberative council." Näglesbach, p. 108; Hailey, p. 77; and
Leupold, I, 136, take similar positions. Kraeling, p. 63, and Engnell, p. 41, include Isaiah
in the divine council. Nowhere in the OT, however, does God confer with heavenly beings or prophets in order to determine His will. The NT recognizes the members of the
Godhead here. John 12:41 refers to the failure to see "his [Christ's] glory." Acts 28:25
refers to the Holy Spirit speaking the passage through Isaiah.

11 Then said I, Lord, how long? And he answered, Until the cities be wasted without inhabitant, and the houses without man, and the land be utterly desolate,
12 And the Lord have removed men far away, and there be a great forsaking in the midst of the land.
13 But yet in it shall be a tenth, and it shall return, and shall be eaten: as a teil tree, and as an oak, whose substance is in them, when they cast their leaves: so the holy seed shall be the substance thereof.

of the same root, intensifies the thought. They "hear indeed." They "see indeed."[16] In neither case do they comprehend.[17]

The NT quotes the passage five times. In Matthew 13:14–15; Mark 4:11–12; and Luke 8:10, the Lord explains His use of parables. This form of teaching hides divine truth from those who lack spiritual sensitivity. In John 12:39–40, the passage shows why the Jews could not believe in Christ as the Son of God. In Acts 28:25–28, Paul quotes the passage to show why the Jews reject his preaching of the gospel. Because of this, the gospel now goes to the Gentiles who will receive it, v. 9.

As Isaiah delivers God's Word to the people, he becomes the means whereby their hearts are hardened. Their rejection of God's message makes them less able to receive truth. Their hearts become "fat," insensitive to divine communication; cf. Deuteronomy 32:15; Jeremiah 5:28. Their ears are "heavy" (*kabed*, see 3:5), dull, unresponsive to the Lord's directions; cf. Exodus 7:14; 9:34 (both "hardened"). The eyes are "shut," smeared with paste and thus blinded to spiritual truth; cf. 29:10. They lose their spiritual sight, their spiritual hearing, and their spiritual understanding. The result of this is their inability to "convert" (*šûb*, or "to turn," see 1:27), v. 10.

11–13 Sensing the seriousness of this judgment, Isaiah asks, "How long?" The question relates to the length of the judgment. The Lord

---

[16]G.K.113 *r* recognizes the possibility of this construction intensifying the verb elsewhere. Here, however, he takes the construction as expressing "the long continuance of an action." The NASB follows this, translating, "Keep on listening . . . keep on looking. . . ." Waltke and O'Connor, pp. 584–86, understand the construction as intensifying the verbal idea. I have followed this view as being more in keeping with the repetition of roots elsewhere. Herbert, *Isaiah 1–39*, p. 57, suggests a question in the translation, "but how will you understand . . . but how will you know?" The repetition of the verbs, the omission of the interrogative particle, and the NT use all argue against this.

[17]Andrew F. Key, "The Magical Background of Isaiah 6 9–13," *JBL* 86:198–204, rather astoundingly considers Isaiah's words as having magical power. He speaks in order to

answers that there will be national disaster. Cities will be wasted, houses emptied, and the land left desolate, v. 11. The people will be taken "far away," fulfilled in the Babylonian captivity. There will be a "great forsaking" (or "many forsaken places") in the land, v. 12. Only "a tenth," a small remnant, will be left in the land. Even this remnant will suffer further judgment. It will "return, and shall be eaten" (baᶜar, or "again be for burning"), a statement of future suffering.[18] It will be as "a teil tree" (or "terebinth"; cf. the description at 1:30) or "as an oak." There are several varieties of oak growing in Palestine. There is no way to know whether Isaiah had a specific variety in mind. Both of these trees have their "substance" (better "stump") when "they cast their leaves" (better "it is felled"). The idea is that the stumps left when the trees are cut down become the source of new growth. In like manner, Israel ("the holy seed") is the "substance" (better "stump"). God will resettle the land from this "stump," the remnant left after the judgment, v. 13.[19]

---

bring the judgment to pass. Isaiah, as with all the prophets, served as representative of the Lord. Their words were those given by God. There is authority in the words but no magical power.

[18]The verb baᶜar, "to burn, consume," often has a figurative sense. Isaiah frequently uses it with the sense "consume," e.g., 9:18; 34:9; 42:25; 62:1. G. W. Ahlström, "Isaiah VI. 13," JSS 19:170, understands the burning as an agricultural practice, burning a field in order to gain a better yield in the future. While this is a valid agricultural practice, it is difficult to see anything other than judgment here. The captivity of v. 12 does not increase the population later. Further, there is no other place in the OT that refers to burning a field in order to improve its yield.

[19]Herbert, Isaiah 1–39, pp. 57, 60, commenting on the NEB, calls the final phrase "obscure." It is obscure in the NEB: "a sacred pole thrown out from its place in a hillshrine." This translation rests on 1QIsaᵃ, which is interpretive, developing the oak and the terebinth as though they were idols. Barnes, I, 145, understands the remnant as a group of people returning from Egypt; cf. II Kings 25:26. He assumes Jer. 40:11–12 includes this group in the return to Palestine. They return only to be destroyed. From the few that are left, the nation rises again.

Practical Application from Chapter 6

The Call into the Ministry. While there will always be unique features of God's call to a person, there are also features that are common to every call.

1. Isaiah received a vision of the glorious Lord, vv. 1, 3*b*.

2. He understood the holiness of God, vv. 2–3*a*.

3. He confessed his sin and unworthiness, v. 5.

4. The Lord cleansed him from his sin, vv. 6–7.

5. He experienced a definite call, v. 8*a*.

6. He responded to the call, v. 8*b*.

7. He had God's message to declare, v. 9*a*.

8. Some would not respond, vv. 9*b*–10 (although some will respond, Isaiah focuses on the lack of response).

9. There will be a final judgment, vv. 11–13.

1 And it came to pass in the days of Ahaz the son of Jotham, the son of Uzziah, king of Judah, that Rezin the king of Syria, and Pekah the son of Remaliah, king of Israel, went up toward Jerusalem to war against it, but could not prevail against it.
2 And it was told the house of David, saying, Syria is confederate with Ephraim. And his heart was moved, and the heart of his people, as the trees of the wood are moved with the wind.

ISAIAH 7

The next group of chapters (7–12) relates to events happening during the reign of Ahaz. This twelfth king of Judah came to the throne in perilous times. In the nation's recent history, both Syria and Israel had won victories over Judah. In one battle, 120,000 men of Judah had died, II Chronicles 28:5–6. These nations have now joined forces to meet the threat from Assyria. To gain strength, Syria and Israel try to force Judah to join them. When Ahaz refuses, they threaten him with military action. In the midst of these events, the mysterious Immanuel appears. Isaiah introduces Him in c. 7, mentions Him briefly in c. 8 (vv. 8, 10), and develops Him further in 9:6–7. Chapter 10 describes the Assyrian threat while c. 11–12 focus on the future work of Immanuel.

B. Messiah's Coming and Kingdom 7:1–12:6
1. Sign of the Virgin 7:1–25
a. Promise of Safety 7:1–9

1–2 Verse 1 introduces the passage. Rezin was the last king of Syria. During his rule, under the leadership of Tiglath-pileser III, Assyria attacked Syria. Rezin was defeated and slain, II Kings 16:9. Pekah had usurped the throne of Israel from Pekahiah, II Kings 15:23–25. Second Chronicles 28:5 indicates that both Pekah and Rezin had defeated Ahaz separately in earlier battles. Now the two join forces. They seek to make Judah help them against Assyria.

Despite the power held by the two nations, they cannot conquer Judah. This reflects the outcome after Ahaz appeals to Tiglath-pileser, II Kings 16:7. Assyria then attacked Damascus, II Kings 16:9. This forced the coalition to turn back from their invasion of Judah, v. 1. Ahaz receives the news that "Syria is confederate with Ephraim." The word "confederate" is lit. "rests upon." This most likely indicates that the Syrian soldiers

3 Then said the Lord unto Isaiah, Go forth now to meet Ahaz, thou, and Shear-jashub thy son, at the end of the conduit of the upper pool in the highway of the fuller's field; .

were camping in Israel, just a few days away. At the news of the Syro-Israelite invasion, Ahaz is "moved" (better "shaken"), fearing the threat. The people likewise are "moved," pictured by the motion of trees swaying in the wind. So the people shake in fear of the invaders, v. 2.

3 The Lord leads Isaiah to give an object lesson to Ahaz.[1] He takes his son Shear-jashub with him. They meet king Ahaz by the "end of the conduit of the upper pool." Tradition places this pool outside the Jaffa Gate in the west wall of the city.[2] The "fuller's field" was an open area where vats were set up for washing and bleaching clothes. It is mentioned again in 36:2; II Kings 18:17. Ahaz may have been inspecting the city in preparation for the coming attack. The prophet's message to the king is one of encouragement. It stands to reason that the presence of his son was meant to reinforce this idea. The name "Shear-jashub" means "a remnant will return."[3] The presence of Isaiah's son visually conveys to Ahaz that Judah will not be overcome. Although they may face a threat from Assyria, God will preserve a remnant for Himself, v. 3.[4]

---

[1]Kaiser, *Isaiah 1–12*, p. 89, and Kissane, I, 80, suggest that referring to Isaiah in the third person reflects the work of an editor. It is just as likely that Isaiah, looking back in time, tells the story as a historian, as in 20:2–3; 38:4. In this role, he would naturally refer to himself in the third person. Isaiah never says, "The Lord said to me."

[2]Watts, *Isaiah 1–33*, p. 91, locates the pool to the northeast of Jerusalem. Skinner, *Isaiah I–XXXIX*, p. 52, mentions the possibility that it was to the south of the city. Because we lack clear knowledge of the city at that time, we are not certain of the location.

[3]The names of children often have meaning in the OT. Cf. Isaac, "he laughs," Gen. 17:19; the sons of Jacob, Gen. 30; Immanuel, Isa. 7:14. In addition, the children of Hosea have prophetic significance, Hos. 1:4, 6, 9.

[4]Generally speaking, the interpretations of the name Shear-jashub make it either a promise or a warning. They differ, however, in the nature of the promise or warning. In the first group, Stuart A. Irvine, "Isaiah's She'ar-Yashub and the Davidic House," *BZ* ns 37:87, considers the name "a hopeful message, announcing the sure survival of a remnant," likely "the Davidic house." Ahaz faces opposition from his own people; cf. 8:6. Isaiah's son is a sign of victory if he does not give in to the pressures to join the alliance. Fausset, p. 584, views it as a promise that the nation will not be completely destroyed. Ibn Ezra, p. 42, accounts the name as a promise that some will repent. In the second group, Herbert, p. 62, thinks the name is "a warning of the consequences of the royal policy" of relying on Assyria, II Kings 16:7–8. Brueggemann, *Isaiah 1–39*, p. 65, understands the name to convey the thought that "*the exile is certain*, and from exile *only a small portion will survive* as identifiable Jews." Kelley, p. 213, sees the name as a warning that only a remnant will

*4 And say unto him, Take heed, and be quiet; fear not, neither be faint-
hearted for the two tails of these smoking firebrands, for the fierce
anger of Rezin with Syria, and of the son of Remaliah.*
*5 Because Syria, Ephraim, and the son of Remaliah, have taken evil
counsel against thee, saying,*
*6 Let us go up against Judah, and vex it, and let us make a breach
therein for us, and set a king in the midst of it, even the son of
Tabeal:*
*7 Thus saith the Lord God, It shall not stand, neither shall it come to
pass.*
*8 For the head of Syria is Damascus, and the head of Damascus is
Rezin; and within threescore and five years shall Ephraim be broken, that it be not a people.*
*9 And the head of Ephraim is Samaria, and the head of Samaria is Re-
maliah's son. If ye will not believe, surely ye shall not be established.*

4–9 Isaiah urges the king not to show fear. Ahaz should "take heed"
(or "keep yourself"). The phrase "be quiet" (*šaqaṭ*) has the sense of
being calm or at peace. The word *šaqaṭ* suggests the absence of conflict,
either the conflict of war or the conflict of worry. Ahaz should not be
faint of heart, concerned over the threat of invasion from Rezin and
Pekah.[5] His enemies are "two tails [or 'stumps'] of . . . smoking firebrands." The thought is that these firebrands have burned down to their
ends and have no great capacity to harm, v. 4. They have planned to
march against Judah to "vex it" (or "cause loathing"). They will "make a
breach" in it, to cleave the nation apart. They plan to set up "the son of
Tabeal," an unknown person, as king, vv. 5–6.[6] Because of this evil plan,
the Lord promises to deliver Judah, v. 7.

---

escape if Ahaz fails to trust the Lord. Goldingay, p. 64, gives an ambiguous message to
the name. "Only a remnant of the Assyrians will return to their land if Ahaz trusts in
Yahweh; only a remnant of Judah will survive if he does not." Others, including
Delitzsch, I, 209, combine both promise and warning. This makes the name an attempt
"to drive the king to Jehovah by force, through the threatening aspect it presented," while
Isaiah's "name pointed to salvation, [and] was to allure him to Jehovah with its promising
tone." I understand the name as a promise as discussed above.

[5]Kaiser, *Isaiah 1–12*, p. 92, understands that at the coronation of the king, he was proclaimed the "adopted son of God;" cf. Ps. 2:7 ff. He now urges him to live as though this
was a fact. He refers to II Kings 16:7, in which Ahaz identifies himself as the "son" of
Tiglath-pileser as he seeks the help of Assyria. Isaiah warns Ahaz against this breach of
loyalty to God. This is an extreme interpretation of Ps. 2, a messianic psalm that applies
to Christ, not to Ahaz.

[6]The spelling "Tabeal" in the AV reflects the pausal position at the end of the verse.
The original spelling, "*ṭabʾel*," means "God is good." The meaning of "Tabeal" is

The phrase "the head of Syria is Damascus" has the sense that Damascus is head *only* over Syria. The phrase "the head of Damascus is Rezin" shows that Rezin is head *only* over Damascus. Within sixty-five years, Israel will be "broken" (*ḥatat*),[7] completely destroyed.[8] The fulfillment of this promise took place in stages. Initially, the Assyrians defeated Syria, ca. 732 B.C., II Kings 15:29; 16:9.[9] Sometime after this, the Assyrian army under Sargon II defeated Israel, 722 B.C., II Kings 17:4–6.[10] Following this, colonists from other lands repopulated the region. This was done under Sargon II, II Kings 17:24; under Esarhaddon,

---

"not good" or "nothing is good" or, with a slight stretch, "good for nothing." Brevard S. Childs, *Isaiah*, 2001, p. 64, adopts this sense. This is an unlikely name for a child. Herbert, *Isaiah 1–39*, p. 62, and Gray, I, 120, reject the influence of the pause and suggest instead that the spelling was deliberate to create the meaning "No-good." While a clever thought, there is no reason to reject the pausal influence. In spite of the meaning "God is good," Price, *Isaiah,* p. 62, and Gray, I, 118, consider the phrase "son of Tabeal" a contemptuous way of referring to the man. This is a weak idea. If it were true, we would have to say that "son of David," "son of man," and even "Son of God" were contemptuous. It is more likely that the phrase simply identifies the man whose father Ṭabʾel was well known. W. F. Albright, "The Son of Tabeel (Isaiah 7:6)," *BASOR* 140:34–35, makes Ṭabʾel a "location north of Ammon and Gilead." He identifies the "son of Ṭabʾel" as "a prince of Judah whose maternal home was in the land of Ṭabʾel." He suggests that he was a son of Uzziah or Jotham by a princess of Ṭabʾel. Herbert, p. 62, makes him "a son of Uzziah by a Syrian princess." Robert I. Vasholz, "Isaiah and Ahaz: A Brief History of Crisis in Isaiah 7 and 8," *Presbyterion* 13:80, suggests that "he was another of the king's sons by a foreign wife." He would thus have a claim to the throne after removing Ahaz. Irvine, p. 82, suggests that "he may have been a member of the house of Tubail, the Phoenician royalty in Tyre and staunch allies of Syria during the 730s." We cannot be certain of any identification.

[7]The verb *ḥatat* means "to break, shatter." The word may refer to the shattering of nations or to people broken in spirit, i.e., dismayed. In each case, the context determines the nature of the "breaking."

[8]Robert Althann, "*Yôm,* 'Time' and Some Texts in Isaiah," *JNWSL* 11:6, divides *šiššîm,* "threescore," into *šeš* and *yôm.* He translates "six cycles, even five years." Aside from the fact that no mss evidence supports him, he views *yôm* as a collective singular, accepts it as defectively written, and interprets "times" as "cycles." The view is forced in order to make the statement "fit the historical facts, as we know them." It is, however, not necessary since the sixty-five-year period already agrees with the historical fall of Israel.

[9]The records of Tiglath-pileser III state, "I laid siege to and conquered the town of Hadara, the inherited property of Rezon of Damascus. . . . I brought away as prisoners 800 (of its) inhabitants with their possessions . . . their large (and) small cattle, 750 prisoners from Kurussa (. . . prisoners) from Irma, 550 prisoners from Metuna I brought (also) away. . . . 592 towns . . . of the 166 districts of the country of Damascus . . . I destroyed," *ANET*, p. 283.

[10]Sargon's records claim that he carried away 27,290 inhabitants of Israel along with great amounts of spoil. He placed the region under an Assyrian governor.

10 Moreover the Lord spake again unto Ahaz, saying,
11 Ask thee a sign of the Lord thy God; ask it either in the depth, or in
the height above.
12 But Ahaz said, I will not ask, neither will I tempt the Lord.

Ezra 4:2; and Ashurbanipal ("Asnapper"), Ezra 4:10. All of this was effectively completed within the sixty-five years of the prophecy, v. 8.

Continuing the thought, Samaria is the head *only* over Ephraim, used representatively of the nation of Israel. Pekah, "Remaliah's son," is the head *only* over Samaria. The implied thought is that Judah does not need to fear. In fact, if the nation does not "believe" (*hipᶜil* of *ʾaman*) this promise, it will not "be established [*nipᶜal* of *ʾaman*]." The verb *ʾaman* in the *hipᶜil* has the sense "to believe, to be certain." This faith is necessary; otherwise, the kingdom will not continue.[11] It is worth noting that God sent Judah into captivity only after they abandoned their faith in God, v. 9.

b. Pronouncement of the Sign 7:10–16

10–12 Verse 9 asks Ahaz to believe. Knowing the weakness of his faith, the Lord now asks him to set his own "sign" (*ʾôt*) as an encouragement to him. The word *ʾôt* occurs seventy-nine times in the OT. Overwhelmingly, it refers to a religious sign of some sort. Ahaz may ask for a sign "in the depth" (*haᶜmeq šᵉʾalâ*). The phrase *haᶜmeq šᵉʾalâ* is better "make it deep in sheol." He may ask for a sign "in the height above," in the heavens, vv. 10–11. Ahaz piously refuses, saying that he will not

---

[11]Both "believe" and "established" translate the verb *ʾaman*. The first is the *hipᶜil taʾᵃmînû* and the second *nipᶜal teʾamenû*. There is an obvious play on words to tempt the translator. Leslie, p. 49, suggests, "If you will not have faith, Surely you shall not have staith [a northern England word for steadiness]." Price, p. 56, paraphrases, "If [Ahaz] will not *affirm* his faith in the true God, his kingdom will not be *confirmed*." The NEB offers, "have firm faith, or you will not stand firm." The NIV gives, "If you do not stand by faith, indeed you will not stand at all." Vine, p. 25, translates, "If ye are not firm in faith, ye shall not be made firm in fact." On a more serious note, Young, I, 277, relates the statement to predestination: "If he does not believe, it is because he is not in a condition of firmness, in which alone he is able to believe. . . . Only established men, those who have been brought into a believing condition, are able to believe." It is highly unlikely that the passage relates to the doctrine of predestination. Isaiah here warns the nation simply that unbelief will lead to their downfall.

13 And he said, Hear ye now, O house of David; Is it a small thing for you to weary men, but will ye weary my God also?
14 Therefore the Lord himself shall give you a sign; Behold, a virgin shall conceive, and bear a son, and shall call his name Immanuel.

"tempt the Lord." His refusal is unbelief since the Lord Himself has invited him to ask for the sign, v. 12.[12]

13–14 Isaiah rebukes the king, the representative of the "house of David." The pronouns "ye" and "you" are plural. They embrace all of the wicked kings of the nation. Ahaz is only the latest representative of this group. The rhetorical question, "Is it a small thing for you to weary [*la'â*] men [*'enošîm*, see 2:11]," requires a negative answer. The verb *la'â* may refer either to physical tiredness or to mental wearying. The latter idea is in view here. The kings have imposed a burden on the people through their failure to give spiritual leadership. Not only this, they have burdened God by their refusal to accept His Word, v. 13. Isaiah declares that the Lord will give a "sign" (*'ôt*, see v. 11) anyway. The plural word "you" has as its antecedent the "house of Israel." The sign of the "virgin" (*'almâ*) birth therefore prophesies to "you," the nation. The fulfillment is to the nation, not the individual king. The word *'almâ* always indicates a virgin in the OT.[13] No other Hebrew word adequately

---

[12]Richard Niessen, "The Virginity of the עַלְמָה in Isaiah 7:14," *BibSac* 137:142, suggests that Ahaz refused a sign since this would have shown his trust in Yahweh. This would have kept him "from calling in the Assyrians which he was determined to do anyway." Charles P. Price, "Immanuel: God with Us," *Christianity and Crisis* 23:222, concludes, "Ahaz meant that he did not believe the Lord could or would deliver him." While these views are speculative, either explains the action of the king.

[13]The word *'almâ* occurs nine times in the OT: here and Gen. 24:43; Exod. 2:8; I Chron. 15:20; Ps. 46:1 (title); 68:25; Prov. 30:19; Song of Sol. 1:3; 6:8. In I Chron. 15:20 and Ps. 46:1, the word is transliterated, "Alamoth," an unknown musical term. It may refer to the key in which the song was to be sung. So Niessen, p. 136. Gen. 24:43 refers to Rebekah, the virgin selected as a bride for Isaac. Verse 16 tells us "neither had any man known her." Miriam, Exod. 2:8, is certainly a virgin, unmarried and living with her parents. Ps. 68:25 refers to "damsels" involved in the worship of God. It would not be appropriate for impure women to participate in this. In Prov. 30:19, Agur admits that he does not understand the development of love between a man and a maid. Again, this is a chaste and pure woman. In Song of Sol. 1:3, the unmarried women exclaim in delight at the possibility that they might come into a union with Solomon. In 6:8, Solomon contrasts the *'almâ* with his wives and concubines. His "dove" (v. 9) excels all these in beauty. Summing this up, there is no reference in which the translation "virgin" is not appropriate. The NT makes this more certain by using παρθένος. This word occurs thirteen times in the NT, always meaning "virgin." Among others, Stacey, p. 55, and Kelley, p. 215, explain Matt. 1:23 as quoting the LXX. They insist that *'almâ* means "young

describes this woman. Any attempt to apply it to Ahaz or to the time of his reign meets difficulties.[14]

To further indicate the nature of the child, His mother will call Him "Immanuel." The name means "God is with us."[15] The *ʾel* ending of *ʿimmanû ʾel* normally indicates deity in Isaiah, e.g., 5:16; 9:6; 46:9. Names in the OT have theological significance. This name agrees with numerous prophecies that refer to God's presence with His people, e.g., 8:8, 10 (a translation of *ʿimmanû ʾel*); Leviticus 26:12; Psalm 46:5. The name is therefore an indication of the child's deity. Isaiah develops this aspect further in c. 9 and c. 11, v. 14.

---

woman" rather than "virgin." This, however, ignores the fact that the LXX translation παρθένος clearly understood *ʿalmâ* as "virgin." Kaiser, *Isaiah 1–12*, pp. 102–3, adopts a "collective interpretation." He understands *ʿalmâ* to refer to all of the women in Judah who now are with child. The danger to the nation will disappear so rapidly that they will name their sons "Immanuel." This expresses their gratitude for God being with the nation. Among others, Von Orelli, p. 53; Kissane, I, 89; and A. R. Hulst, *OTTP*, p. 139, make *bᵉtulâ* the word to express "virgin" while *ʿalmâ* represents merely the "young woman." The word *bᵉtulâ*, however, is not limited to pure women. Esther 2:17 ("virgins") refers to those who had been with the king. Joel 1:8 speaks of the "virgin" whose husband has died. Ezek. 23:3, 8 give a parable that refers to women who commit "whoredoms," whose "teats of their virginity" have been caressed. Clearly, *bᵉtulâ* is not limited to a "virgin."

[14]There are numerous attempts to understand *ʿalmâ*. Several authors relate it to a virgin either in the court or known to the king. (1) Leslie, p. 49, relates the prophecy to a new wife of Ahaz. (2) Fausset, p. 586, refers it to a virgin about to become Isaiah's "second wife." (3) Delitzsch, I, 219, refers this to some maiden in the house of David with Ahaz fathering the child. (4) Barnes, I, 157, thinks it is some woman, then a virgin, who will conceive and bring forth a child. There are also a variety of other views. (5) Watts, *Isaiah 1–33*, p. 101, thinks that the queen will give birth to a son. (6) Gray, I, 125, mentions the possibility of some pregnant women standing near while Isaiah and Ahaz talked. The prophet predicts that she will have a son. (7) Whitehouse, p. 134, holds the view that the "virgin" refers to "the Jewish community in Jerusalem, out of which the ideal ruler with the name Immanuel was to be born." (8) Kraeling, p. 63, suggests the passage is "a legendary offshoot of the incident of 8:1–4," the birth of Isaiah's child. (9) Ibn Ezra, p. 41, makes the child a third son of Isaiah. (10) Goldingay, p. 64, generalizes the prophecy to include any woman who will soon marry, conceive, and bear a son. Other views as well have been expressed. Robert L. Reymond, "Who Is the עלמה of Isaiah 7:14?" *Presbyterion* 15:10, points out that v. 14 indicates that "the עלמה was to be a virgin not only at the time of her marriage but also *at the time of her conception and her delivery*." The subject עלמה governs both verbs, i.e., the virgin conceives and the virgin bears a son. This eliminates any attempt to find the fulfillment in a natural birth.

[15]Frank Zimmerman, "The Immanuel Prophecy," *JQR* 52:156–58, argues that *ʿimmanû ʾel* should be divided as *ʿam nôal*, "foolish nation." Since the *nipʿal* participle of *yaʾal* does not occur in the OT, there is no textual evidence to support his suggestion.

15 *Butter and honey shall he eat, that he may know to refuse the evil, and choose the good.*
16 *For before the child shall know to refuse the evil, and choose the good, the land that thou abhorrest shall be forsaken of both her kings.*

15–16 The phrase "butter [or 'curds,' thickened milk] and honey" refers to natural food, eaten by all in the land; cf. v. 22. The word "that" is better "when." When the child matures enough to know to choose good and reject evil, He will live on a simple diet. This hints at His birth into a poor family, v. 15.[16] Before He grows to the time that He can refuse evil and choose good, the land will lose her kings, both Rezin and Pekah.[17] The period between birth and the development of moral consciousness is only a few years.[18] While Ahaz would not have grasped the messianic nature of the prophecy, he would have understood the time involved in maturing morally. The time suggested by the prophecy allowed for both the fall of Syria in 732 B.C. and the fall of Israel in 722 B.C., v. 16.

---

[16]Young, I, 291–92, suggests that a diet of curds and honey was symbolic of a royal diet. The diet, then, brought out the "regal character of the Messiah." Mauchline, p. 99, suggests this is the "food of Paradise." Brueggemann, *Isaiah 1–39*, p. 71, likewise considers "curds and honey" as indicating "a time of abundance, prosperity, and well-being." I feel that v. 22 argues more for poverty than for plenty. In any case, the point of the prophecy is that the child will know good from evil when he is old enough to eat curds and honey.

[17]Vasholz, pp. 82–83, makes the passage two prophecies, a long-range one in vv. 14–15 and a short-range one in v. 16. He argues that "the child" in v. 16 should be translated as an indefinite, "a boy." See G.K. 126 *p-r* in support. This is the sign for Ahaz. In just a few years, the Syro-Israelite coalition will end. While Vasholz's argument is grammatically correct, there is no signal in the text to indicate that the child in v. 16 differs from the child in vv. 14–15.

[18]Gene Rice, "The Interpretation of Isaiah 7:15–17," *JBL* 96:363–69, understands that knowing the difference between good and evil is the same as being able to distinguish between "the pleasant and the painful." He makes this "a period of approximately a year, the time required by an infant to distinguish between the pleasant and the painful." This period of time is too short! The time required to rid the land "of both of her kings" must embrace both 732 B.C., when Syria fell, and 722 B.C., when Israel fell. Joseph Jensen, "The Age of Immanuel," *CBQ* 41:224–25, suggests a better view. He argues from the use of the phrase elsewhere, e.g., Num. 14:31; Deut. 1:39, that it refers to the age of adulthood.

17 The Lord shall bring upon thee, and upon thy people, and upon thy father's house, days that have not come from the day that Ephraim departed from Judah; even the king of Assyria.

18 And it shall come to pass in that day, that the Lord shall hiss for the fly that is in the uttermost part of the rivers of Egypt, and for the bee that is in the land of Assyria.

19 And they shall come, and shall rest all of them in the desolate valleys, and in the holes of the rocks, and upon all thorns, and upon all bushes.

c. Prediction of Destruction 7:17–25

17–19 Judah will not escape God's punishment of their sin. The people will go into captivity. This will be a time such as has not been seen since Israel ("Ephraim") went into captivity. The Lord will bring the "king of Assyria" upon them. Nebuchadnezzar, the king of Babylon, is in view. He was the "king of Assyria" in that Assyria was the parent of Babylon. Babylon was the successor to the Assyrian scourge, v. 17. In that day of judgment, the Lord will "hiss" (*šaraq*) for the "fly" from Egypt and the "bee" from Assyria.[19] These insects are abundantly present in these countries. The "fly" is a pest in the "uttermost part of the rivers of Egypt," the delta. The "bee" swarms throughout Mesopotamia. These insects here represent the military might of the nations, v. 18. Their armies swarm over the land in conquest. They rest in "desolate valleys" (*naḥᵃlê habbattôt*, better "steep ravines"),[20] in the "holes [or 'clefts'] of the rocks," on the "thorns" (*naᶜᵃṣûṣîm*, or "thorny bushes"), and on the "bushes" (*naḥᵃlolîm*, or "watering-places").[21] Even in unlikely places, the enemy may be found. Israel's position between Egypt and Mesopotamia has made it a natural target. Armies from the two regions

---

[19]Many authors and versions translate *šaraq* "whistle," e.g., Young, Kaiser, NASB, NIV. While this is possible, I feel that "hiss" better captures the thought of signaling the nations. There is no place in the OT that requires "whistle" rather than "hiss."

[20]The word *naḥal* refers to a wadi that is dry much of the year but which may become filled with a torrent of water after a rain. While the translation "wadi" is more precise, modern translations use "ravine" more often because of its familiarity. The descriptive word *battâ* occurs only here. There is an Arabic root cognate to *batat,* which means "to cut off." This leads to the idea of a valley whose sides have been cut off, a precipitous drop. Here it refers to the abrupt drop-off of the wadi, i.e., its steepness.

[21]The word *naᶜᵃṣûṣ* occurs only here and at 55:13. The context there indicates an undesirable plant of some kind. "Thorny bushes" is an appropriate gloss. The word *naḥᵃlol* comes from the root *nahal,* "to lead to a watering-place." The point of the verse is that the enemy armies camp throughout the land.

20 *In the same day shall the Lord shave with a razor that is hired,*
namely, by them beyond the river, by the king of Assyria, the head,
and the hair of the feet: and it shall also consume the beard.
21 *And it shall come to pass in that day, that a man shall nourish a*
young cow, and two sheep;
22 *And it shall come to pass, for the abundance of milk that they shall*
give he shall eat butter: for butter and honey shall every one eat that
is left in the land.
23 *And it shall come to pass in that day, that every place shall be,*
where there were a thousand vines at a thousand silverlings, it shall
even be for briers and thorns.
24 *With arrows and with bows shall men come thither; because all the*
land shall become briers and thorns.
25 *And on all hills that shall be digged with the mattock, there shall not*
come thither the fear of briers and thorns: but it shall be for the
sending forth of oxen, and for the treading of lesser cattle.

have conquered Palestine and taken spoil several dozen times in history, both in the OT and in the intertestamental period, v. 19.

20–22 The Lord will shave the nations with "a razor that is hired," here referring to "the king of Assyria," Tiglath-pileser. Ahaz hired Tiglath-pileser to deliver him from the joint invasion of Syria and Israel; cf. II Kings 16:7–8. Assyria's king, however, will not stop with Syria and Israel. He will "shave" Judah's head, his beard, and "the hair of the feet." This last is a euphemism for the pubic hair. The shaving pictures the open humiliation of the nation, v. 20. As a result, the land will be impoverished. A young man will own only a few animals, v. 21. These, however, will be enough to provide the food that he needs for life. He will make butter from the milk of the cow and will eat the "butter," again, "curds" (see v. 15). Those who are left in the land will eat curds and honey, food readily available to them, v. 22.

23–25 The land will become overgrown. A "silverling" (*kesep*) was a piece of silver of an unknown weight. In Song of Solomon 8:11, the annual rent of the king's vineyard was a thousand pieces of silver. Here, only a thousand vines have this value. This valuable vineyard will be overtaken with "briers and thorns," v. 23. Men will hunt in the land since it has returned to its wild state, v. 24. The final verse should read something like this: "And all the hills that were digged with the mattock, you will not go there for the fear of briars and thorns; but they will be for the pasturing of oxen and the trampling underfoot of sheep." The idea is that the hills that formerly were "digged with the mattock," cultivated for the crops, are now deserted. The animals roam amid the thorns that have grown up, v. 25.

Practical Applications from Chapter 7

1. God's Care of His People (illustrated by His care for Judah), vv. 1–9. God's people often fear when facing trials, v. 2. God, however, does not want us to fear, v. 4. Although enemies may come against us, they will fail, v. 7. Only by believing God's promises will we have the confidence that will make us secure, v. 9.

2. God's Word Is Trustworthy, vv. 10–16. The test of prophecy is whether it agrees with other Scripture; cf. Deuteronomy 13:1–3; and whether it comes to pass; cf. Deuteronomy 18:22. The prophecies of Christ, though remarkably detailed, agree with other Scripture and have come true: the Virgin Birth, v. 14; cf. Matthew 1:22–23; His name Immanuel, v. 14; cf. Matthew 1:23; John 1:14; I Timothy 3:16; born into a poor family, v. 15; suggested by His birth in a manger, Luke 2:7, 16; the deliverance and preservation of the nation, v. 16; cf. 8:4.

3. God's Judgment of Sin (illustrated by Judah's captivity), vv. 17–25. Once more, God's Word of judgment is accurate. Judah's judgment will be like Israel's judgment, v. 17. God controls the affairs of nations so that they accomplish His will. Here, He brings nations several hundred miles to bring judgment on Judah, vv. 18–19. The judgment humiliates His disobedient people, v. 20, and is severe, vv. 21–25.

1 Moreover the Lord said unto me, Take thee a great roll, and write in it with a man's pen concerning Maher-shalal-hash-baz.
2 And I took unto me faithful witnesses to record, Uriah the priest, and Zechariah the son of Jeberechiah.

ISAIAH 8

The chapter continues to treat the Syro-Israelite alliance introduced in c. 7. The people of Judah should not fear this alliance. The Lord will judge those who support the confederation of Israel and Syria. He will also bring to nothing their plan to conquer Judah. Isaiah will not follow the people; he purposes to place his faith in the Lord. He and his sons will act as signs to the people. Those who reject God's Word will receive judgment. There will be no deliverance.

2. Comfort in the Darkness 8:1–9:7
a. Proclamation of the Destruction 8:1–8

1–2 The Lord commands Isaiah to write on "a great roll" (*gillayôn*), probably to be hung by the gates of the city for all to see. The *gillayôn* is a "tablet" here likely made of wood. He is to write "with a man's pen [*ḥereṭ*]." The *ḥereṭ* is a metal stylus or engraving tool. Isaiah apparently cuts the letters into a wooden surface. The phrase "man's pen" (*ḥereṭ ᵓenôš*) is an idiom referring to "ordinary writing," easily understood by the readers.[1] He is to write "Maher-shalal-hash-baz," here better translated according to its meaning, "swift is the spoil, speedy is the prey."[2] This is an obscure prediction that Assyria soon would overcome Judah's enemies, Syria and Israel. At that time, the Assyrians will gather booty from both nations, v. 1.[3]

---

[1]Frank Talmage, "חרט אנוש in Isaiah 8:1," *HTR* 60:467, revocalizes *ᵓenôš* as "*ānūš*" and relates it to cognates with the meaning "to be weak." From this, he draws the meaning "blunt," as with a weak, i.e., blunt sword. He suggests that *ḥereṭ ᵓenôš* is a "broad nibbed, flexible pen capable of making the bold stroke expected in the context." It is difficult to see how a "weak" pen can make a "bold stroke." Since the word "*ānūš*" does not occur elsewhere, we should not find it here.

[2]Kraeling, p. 69, understands the name as two phrases "because it was to apply to two kingdoms, the one to be totally destroyed, the other damaged." It is common, though, in Hebrew to emphasize something by doubling the text. In this case, both phrases apply to both kingdoms, Syria and Israel, the nations threatening Judah.

[3]Brueggemann, *Isaiah 1–39*, p. 76, makes "spoil" refer to wealth gathered from the capital of Syria and "prey" to booty from the capital of Israel. The passage, however, does not make these terms specific. We could just as well reverse the terms from

3 And I went unto the prophetess; and she conceived, and bare a son. Then said the Lord to me, Call his name Maher-shalal-hash-baz.
4 For before the child shall have knowledge to cry, My father, and my mother, the riches of Damascus and the spoil of Samaria shall be taken away before the king of Assyria.

The phrase "I took unto me" is better "I will take to Myself." The Lord speaks here, indicating that He will call witnesses to Isaiah's writing. Uriah, the high priest, later cooperated with Ahaz in making a heathen altar for the temple (II Kings 16:10–16). Zechariah was apparently the father-in-law of King Ahaz (II Kings 18:2). These are "faithful witnesses," men not particularly friendly to Isaiah and thus not open to a charge of favoring the prophet, v. 2.

3–4 Isaiah and his wife, called "the prophetess," conceive a child. The title "prophetess" is appropriate because of the part she plays. She gives birth to a son whose name points to Judah's deliverance.[4] The Lord directs Isaiah to name him Maher-shalal-hash-baz. The name reemphasizes Isaiah's earlier writing: "swift is the spoil, speedy is the prey," v. 3.[5] Before the son is old enough to call to his parents, the "king of Assyria" will spoil Syria and Israel. The "king of Assyria" here refers to Tiglath-pileser III. He led Assyria to victory over Syria and parts of Israel in 732 B.C. (cf. II Kings 16:9), v. 4.[6]

Brueggemann's application. The words "spoil" and "prey" should be understood generally, referring to plunder from both Syria and Israel.

[4]Among others, Kaiser, *Isaiah 1–12*, p. 111; Watts, *Isaiah 1–33*, p. 113; and Von Orelli, p. 60, understand "prophetess" to indicate that Isaiah's wife also prophesied from time to time. A. Jepson, "Die Nebiah in Jes 8 3," *ZAW* 72:268, suggests "sollte Jesaja eben eine solche nebiah geheiratet haben," that Isaiah may have married a prophetess. The word, however, has a broad span of meanings in the OT. The title applies to Miriam, Moses's sister, Exod. 15:20–21, although she simply leads the women of Israel in a chorus praising God. Deborah is a "prophetess," Judg. 4:4, although she judges the nation rather than foretelling the future. Huldah is a "prophetess," II Kings 22:14, with a single prophecy recorded. Isaiah's wife has the title because of her role in bearing the child whose name is prophetic.

[5]Herbert M. Wolf, "A Solution to the Immanuel Prophecy in Isaiah 7:14–8:22," *JBL* 91:454–55, concludes that Maher-shalal-hash-baz is another name for Immanuel, both referring to Isaiah's son by "the prophetess." The name Immanuel, given by the mother, expresses the promise aspect of the sign, while Maher-shalal-hash-baz, given by Isaiah, relates to its judgmental side.

[6]Stacey, pp. 62–63, states that an editor has compressed history here since Tiglath-pileser III defeated Syria ca. 733 B.C. but did not defeat Israel until eleven years later. The Assyrian records, however, mention the conquest of Naphtali along with the defeat

5 *The Lord spake also unto me again, saying,*
6 *Forasmuch as this people refuseth the waters of Shiloah that go softly, and rejoice in Rezin and Remaliah's son;*
7 *Now therefore, behold, the Lord bringeth up upon them the waters of the river, strong and many, even the king of Assyria, and all his glory: and he shall come up over all his channels, and go over all his banks:*
8 *And he shall pass through Judah; he shall overflow and go over, he shall reach even to the neck; and the stretching out of his wings shall fill the breadth of thy land, O Immanuel.*

5–8 The Lord continues to speak to Isaiah, v. 5. Likely fearing the threat, some of the people have cast their lot with Rezin and Pekah, "Remaliah's son." They have rejected the "waters of Shiloah [*šiloah*]."[7] The name "Shiloah" does not occur again. It probably refers to the pool of Siloam, a source of water inside the walls of Jerusalem. The name *šiloah* comes from *šalah*, "to send." The name indicates the waters sent through the tunnel under the walls into the city. The phrase "waters of Shiloah" symbolizes the Davidic leadership of Judah. The people had rejected this in favor of the Syro-Israelite leadership.

The water came from an underground tunnel that led to Gihon, a spring in the Kidron Valley. The tunnel was the "gutter," II Samuel 5:8, through which David's men entered in their capture of Jerusalem. Water from Siloam was carried to the temple during the Feast of Tabernacles. The Lord drew on this during the Feast of Tabernacles when He stood in the temple and cried, "If any man thirst, let him come unto me, and drink" (John 7:37).[8]

---

of Syria. From the geography of the area, it is reasonable that Assyria would also have taken spoil from the tribes east of the Jordan River.

[7]Irvine, p. 86, suggests that the waters of Shiloah came from the Gihon spring, where Davidic kings were ritually anointed, I Kings 1:33–40. The statement is then symbolic for rejecting the Davidic monarchy. In view of the contrast with the "waters of the river," v. 7, Irvine's suggestion is likely.

[8]Young, I, 305, and Gray, pp. 145–46, identify the "waters of Shiloah" with a spring that flows from a cave east of Jerusalem about 350 yards south of the temple area. Kaiser, *Isaiah 1–12*, p. 113, rejects an identification with Hezekiah's tunnel. He refers the term to the waters coming from Gihon by the side of the eastern hill of Jerusalem. These views are possible. I identify it with the waters flowing through Hezekiah's tunnel because of the name "Shiloah."

At the same time, the people "rejoice in Rezin and Remaliah's son,"
Pekah; cf. 7:1.[9] There is apparently a party in Judah that wants to join
Israel in aligning themselves with Syria. Isaiah warns them of the judg-
ment that will fall on them for their unfaithfulness in failing to trust the
Lord, v. 6.

Water often represents nations; cf. 17:12–13; 59:19; Jeremiah 46:7–8;
Amos 8:8; 9:5. The Lord will judge the nation. The "waters of the river"
are the waters of the Euphrates River. These are "strong and many [or
'abundant']." The symbolism becomes clear with the explanatory phrase
"even the king of Assyria, and all his glory." The contrast is stark. The
people of Judah must choose the gently flowing waters of Siloam or face
the deluge of the Euphrates as it sweeps over the land, v. 7.[10] The judgment will pass to the "neck" of Judah, inflicting serious harm on the nation. The picture is of the Assyrian armies conquering almost the whole
land. Only Jerusalem remains. The Lord adds a second symbol to the
picture of judgment. A bird with stretched out wings will fill the land.
This represents the Assyrian army as it flies across the land.[11] Isaiah addresses the statement of judgment to "Immanuel," showing by this that
the mysterious figure of 7:14 is Lord of the land, v. 8.[12]

---

[9]Von Orelli, p. 61, and Motyer, *The Prophecy of Isaiah,* p. 91, refer "this people" to
Israel, the Northern Kingdom. While this is possible, it is just as likely that Isaiah refers
to a party in Judah who have followed Israel's example. The context does not identify the
group clearly.

[10]Barnes, I, 175; Motyer, *The Prophecy of Isaiah,* p. 91; and Fausset, p. 589, refer the
prophecy to the whole nation of Israel, not merely Judah. Verse 8, however, focuses on
Judah rather than Israel. Isaiah thus warns his nation against following the example of
the Northern Kingdom.

[11]Zöckler, *The Prophet Isaiah,* p. 132; Von Orelli, p. 61; and Delitzsch, I, 234, consider
the "wings" as the sides of the Assyrian army. These spread out from the main body like
the two wings of a bird. The view is possible although it may read too much into the
image. Isaiah uses the figure of a bird attacking its prey as a threat elsewhere, 46:11.

[12]Gray, I, 149, rejects a messianic idea here: "To base a far-reaching construction of
messianic belief on so ambiguous a passage is a mistake." His view is wrong. It stems
from the idea that prophecy did not reach far into the future. The MT is accurate in addressing the prophecy to the one to whom the land belongs. G. C. I. Wong, "Is 'God with
Us' in Isaiah VIII 8?" *VT* 49:430, considers "Immanuel" as "an exclamation of grief and
a cry for mercy . . . May God be with us!" His view faces the problem that the early versions, e.g., Vulgate, translated ʿimmanû ʾel as a vocative. The Targum translated "O Israel"
and the LXX "O God with us." These are interpretive but still evidence of the vocative.

9 *Associate yourselves, O ye people, and ye shall be broken in pieces;*
and give ear, all ye of far countries: gird yourselves, and ye shall be
broken in pieces; gird yourselves, and ye shall be broken in pieces.
10 *Take counsel together, and it shall come to nought; speak the word,*
and it shall not stand: for God is with us.

b. Denunciation of the Confederacy 8:9–15

9–10 Isaiah challenges the nations by means of several imperatives.
The initial phrase depends on the derivation of the imperative "associate" (*roʿû*.)[13] The verb is from *raʿaʿ* II, lit. "break," apparently referring
to Judah as the object of the threat. In turn, they will "be broken (*ḥatat*,
better 'be shattered,' see 7:8) in pieces." The nation who would break
others will themselves be broken. The double imperative used here indicates a certain consequence. Judgment upon God's enemies is sure.[14]

Distant countries should "give ear," listen to the announcement of
judgment imposed on the nation that turned from God. They may "gird
themselves," yet they will be "broken in pieces" (again "be shattered").
The repetition of the phrase "gird yourselves, and ye shall be broken in
pieces [again, 'be shattered']" gives emphasis to the warning. No matter
what the nations may do, girding themselves for war, v. 9, taking counsel
together as they make their plans, or speaking threatening words, all will
fail. The last phrase, "God is with us," is a play on words that draws on
the literal meaning of "Immanuel," v. 10.

---

[13]Driver, p. 40; Gray, I, 149; and Kaiser, *Isaiah 1–12*, p. 115, follow the LXX in reading *deʿû*, "know," for *roʿû*, "break." While this does not change the meaning, the LXX
alone is not strong evidence for leaving the MT. The translators likely misread *dalet* for
rêš. Barnes, I, 178, and George Adam Smith, *The Book of Isaiah*, I, 1896, 124, follow the
AV in deriving the verb from *raʿaʿ* II, "to associate." The verb, however, is not pointed as
a reflexive conjugation. Motyer, p. 94, and Watts, *Isaiah 1–33*, p. 116, translate as from
the verb *rûaʿ*, "to make an uproar." This verb, however, always occurs in the *hipʿîl*, not
the *qal* as here. Alexander, I, 188–89, and Young, I, 307, derive the word from *raʿaʿ* I,
"to be evil." This leads to something like "be wicked" or, paraphrasing, "do harm," a
possible view. Delitzsch, I, 234, and Skinner, *Isaiah I–XXXIX*, p. 68, also locate the verb
from *raʿaʿ* I but translate it too freely, "Be exasperated." The translation of the RSV and
NASB, "be broken," parallels the last part of the stich, "and be shattered." We should
not, however, translate the imperative here as a passive.

[14]Vine, p. 29, goes too far in applying the passage to Armageddon. The context applies
the passage to the Syro-Israelite confederation.

11 For the Lord spake thus to me with a strong hand, and instructed me
    that I should not walk in the way of this people, saying,
12 Say ye not, A confederacy, to all them to whom this people shall say,
    A confederacy; neither fear ye their fear, nor be afraid.
13 Sanctify the Lord of hosts himself; and let him be your fear, and let
    him be your dread.
14 And he shall be for a sanctuary; but for a stone of stumbling and for
    a rock of offence to both the houses of Israel, for a gin and for a
    snare to the inhabitants of Jerusalem.
15 And many among them shall stumble, and fall, and be broken, and
    be snared, and be taken.

11–15 Isaiah emphasizes the divine authority behind his words. The
Lord has spoken to him "with a strong hand," i.e., with mighty power.
Isaiah should not follow the way of the people, v. 11. Specifically, he
should not admit to a "confederacy" (*qešer*, better "conspiracy") when
the people accuse him of conspiring.[15] Isaiah's warning against the plans
of allying with Syria and Israel might well have been considered treason
by some. He should not "be afraid" (*ʿaraṣ*) of them. The verb *ʿaraṣ* in the
hipʿîl means "regard with awe." There is no reason for holding the people
in awe, v. 12. Rather than fearing what the people fear, he should "sanctify" the Lord, setting Him apart as holy. He should hold Him in awe, cf.
Proverbs 29:25, v. 13. He is a "sanctuary" for those who follow Him, but
for those who do not fear Him, He is "a stone of stumbling and a rock of
offense." He is "a gin" (better "trap") and a "snare," i.e., one who brings
judgment. Romans 9:33 and I Peter 2:7–8 make the passage messianic.
Jesus Christ is the "stone" over which men stumble on their way to judgment. He is a "snare," a trap to those who refuse Him, v. 14. Failing to
accept God's Words, they will stumble into punishment. The repetition,
"fall . . . be broken . . . be snared . . . be taken," emphasizes the certainty
and the strength of the judgment, v. 15.

---

[15]G. R. Driver, "Two Misunderstood Passages of the Old Testament," *JTS* 6:82–83,
fails to see a relationship between v. 12 and vv. 13–14. He understands *qešer* as "difficulty" on the basis of the LXX, which translated as σκληρόν, "hard, difficult." This requires him to read *qdš* in vv. 13–14 as *qšr*. This is an unnecessary correction to the MT.
Craig A. Evans, "An Interpretation of Isa 8, 11–15 Unemended," *ZAW* 97:112–13, correctly answers Driver. Isaiah urges his followers not to call his policy of separation from
Syria and Israel "treason." They should not fear what the leaders of the nation fear. They
should rather fear the Lord and they should regard the Lord as holy and as a sanctuary
for His people.

16 Bind up the testimony, seal the law among my disciples.
17 And I will wait upon the Lord, that hideth his face from the house
of Jacob, and I will look for him.
18 Behold, I and the children whom the Lord hath given me are for
signs and for wonders in Israel from the Lord of hosts, which
dwelleth in mount Zion.

c. Declaration of the Guidance 8:16–22

16–18 The Lord commands Isaiah to "bind up the testimony."[16] He
should "seal the law [*tôrâ*, see 1:10]."[17] Both phrases refer to stopping
his public preaching. Instead, he should concentrate on the disciples,
v. 16. Isaiah determines that he will wait for further revelation from
God. The verb "will look" (*qawâ*, see 5:2) conveys Isaiah's sense of expectancy, v. 17. At the same time, he and his sons will bear the character
of "signs [*ʾôt*, see 7:11] and wonders" to Judah. The one son, Shear-
jashub ("a remnant will return"), reminds of the Lord's grace in keeping
the nation in existence. The other son, Maher-shalal-hash-baz ("swift is
the spoil, speedy is the prey"), reminds of the judgment that will come.
Isaiah's own name, meaning "salvation," suggests the forgiving nature of
the Lord.

Hebrews 2:13 gives the verse a messianic emphasis. The passage there
describes the church as the children given to Christ. Just as Isaiah and his
children bore a continuing witness to Israel, so the Lord and His church
are a continuing testimony of God's gracious work in this world, v. 18.[18]

---

[16]Delitzsch, I, 237, and Whitehouse, I, 144, see Isaiah as speaking to his disciples.
While this is possible, the phrase "my disciples" more readily refers to the Lord's disciples. There is no indication that Isaiah encouraged others to follow him.

[17]C. F. Whitley, "The Language and Exegesis of Isaiah 8 16–23," *ZAW* 90:29, understands the binding as "the 'tying' and 'sealing' of the book or scroll in which they were
written." Kaiser, *Isaiah 1–12*, p. 120, varies this slightly. He also makes the "binding" a
physical act. Isaiah should take his written-out prophecies, wrap them in linen, place
them in a pot, and close it with a clay seal. Kraeling, p. 72, suggests that Isaiah should
tie up the scroll containing his prophecies and seal it with a clay seal. While these views
are possible, Isaiah's response in v. 17 suggests the approach discussed above. God has
commanded him to stop his public ministry. He obeys with the intention of listening for
God's voice. The presence of Isaiah and his family bears a continuing reminder to the
nation of the words from the Lord that he has told them.

[18]Since Heb. 2:13 quotes the passage as the words of Messiah, Alexander, I, 192, understands the speaker in vv. 17–18 to be Messiah. Nothing in the context here suggests
Messiah. The passage states clearly that Isaiah and his sons are "for signs and wonders
in Israel." While it is appropriate to see the family as a picture pointing to Christ, it is
not appropriate to replace the picture with the application.

19 And when they shall say unto you, Seek unto them that have familiar spirits, and unto wizards that peep, and that mutter: should not a people seek unto their God? for the living to the dead?
20 To the law and to the testimony: if they speak not according to this word, it is because there is no light in them.
21 And they shall pass through it, hardly bestead and hungry: and it shall come to pass, that when they shall be hungry, they shall fret themselves, and curse their king and their God, and look upward.
22 And they shall look unto the earth; and behold trouble and darkness, dimness of anguish; and they shall be driven to darkness.

19–22 Although Isaiah ceases his public ministry, this does not give the people license to consult the spirit world for guidance. The words "familiar spirits" apply to witchcraft or necromancy, consulting the dead. The "wizards" attempted to predict the future. These "peep" (better "chirp" or "whisper") and "mutter" as they carry out their incantations and rituals. Isaiah answers them with two rhetorical questions. "Should not a people seek unto their God?" Yes, they should! "[Should they seek] for [i.e., on behalf of] the living to the dead"?[19] The answer is clearly no! Isaiah 2:6; 19:3; and 29:4 also speak critically of spiritism, v. 19.

Instead of demonic rituals, Isaiah holds up the "law" (tôrâ, cf. 1:10), God's instructions, and the "testimony," here a synonym of "law," as the right standard. Those who differ from this have "no light [šaḥar] in them." The verb šaḥar has the regular meaning "to seek early." The noun "dawn" comes from this root. This leads to the translation "[these] do not have the dawn in them."[20] Not having revelation from the Lord, they walk in darkness, v. 20. They will walk through "it," the land, in great distress. They will be "hardly bestead," hard-pressed, and "hungry." They will "fret" (qaṣap). The idea of "fretting" is too gentle. The verb qaṣap refers to a burning anger, rage. This will lead them to curse their king and God because they have failed to ease their hunger. Isaiah refers to the condition of the people in the midst of the Assyrian invasion of 701 B.C. The people look up to the heavens, v. 21, and they look about them in vain for deliverance, but they find only the continuing darkness of judgment, v. 22.

---

[19]Childs, p. 70, translates ʾelohîm as "gods," referring to the heathen deities rather than as a plural of majesty, "God," referring to the true God. Grammatically, either view can be true. The question is whether this phrase continues the reply of the people or gives the answer of Isaiah. The contrast with the final question argues that this is Isaiah's answer.
[20]Kissane, I, 109, translates šaḥar as "witchcraft." He bases the view on an Arabic cognate. The word šaḥar, however, occurs widely in all parts of the OT with the sense of "dawn." There is no reason to emend the word linguistically here.

Practical Applications from Chapter 8

1. God Will Protect His People. Both the name of Isaiah's son Maher-shalal-hash-baz and the direct statements of vv. 4, 9–10, point to the destruction of the confederacy between Israel and Syria. While the Lord may let His own go through trials as He punishes their sin, e.g., vv. 6–8, He will not let the enemy gain a permanent victory.

2. God's People Should Obey the Lord and His Word. Rather than fearing man, v. 12, we should fear the Lord, v. 13. He is our "sanctuary," v. 14a. Those who do not fear Him will come into judgment, vv. 14b–15. Because we belong to Him, we should establish His Word as the standard by which we judge all things. Those who go contrary to His Word are in darkness, v. 20, and will come into judgment, vv. 21–22.

1 Nevertheless the dimness shall not be such as was in her vexation, when at the first he lightly afflicted the land of Zebulun and the land of Naphtali, and afterward did more grievously afflict her by the way of the sea, beyond Jordan, in Galilee of the nations.
2 The people that walked in darkness have seen a great light: they that dwell in the land of the shadow of death, upon them hath the light shined.
3 Thou hast multiplied the nation, and not increased the joy: they joy before thee according to the joy in harvest, and as men rejoice when they divide the spoil.

ISAIAH 9

Verse 1 is a summary statement. In the Hebrew, it is v. 23, closing chapter 8.[1] Verses 2–7 (vv. 1–6 in Hebrew) expand the summary, giving details of the blessing that will come to Palestine. The passage reaches its climax in vv. 6–7, a marvelous messianic prophecy of the reign of Christ. This will be a righteous rule over the earth, a time when sin will no longer run rampant. To illustrate this, Isaiah describes several classes of sinners that will receive judgment: the proud, vv. 8–12; wicked leaders, vv. 13–17; wicked people, vv. 18–21; and continuing in c. 10, unjust judges, 10:1–4.

d. Annunciation of the Child 9:1–7

1–3 Chapter 8 ended by describing God's judgment on the people. The opening phrase of c. 9 is a promise: "There will be no gloom to her who was in distress." The judgment will not continue forever. Although the Lord had "lightly afflicted" (better "treated with contempt") the regions of Zebulon and Naphtali, to the west and north of Galilee, he later will bring blessing. He will "more grievously afflict" (better "make glorious") the "way of the sea."[2] This is the road leading north along the western side of Galilee.[3] Since directions in the Bible are oriented to-

---

[1]Following the Jewish division of the verses, Price, p. 61, makes v. 1 close the preceding passage. The division of the English version makes v. 1 an introduction to the messianic message of vv. 2–7. The NT usage of 9:1–2 in Matt. 4:15–16 makes the connection clear. This division is more logical. Otherwise, the transition is too abrupt.

[2]Wade, p. 63, makes the glory "the restoration of the northern tribes and their re-union with Judah in the messianic age." The NT use of the passage, however, in Matt. 4:15–16, applies it to the ministry of Christ.

[3]Commenting on the NEB, Herbert, *Isaiah 1–39*, pp. 72–73, describes "two stages in Tiglath-pileser's invasion," the first lighter and the second heavier. It is possible to trans-

ward the east, the phrase "beyond Jordan" indicates the eastern shore of the Sea of Galilee. Thus, the area occupied by the half tribe of Manasseh will benefit from this blessing.[4] Finally, "Galilee of the nations," the northern portion of the land bordered by heathen nations, will also be blessed, v. 1.[5]

The people who once "walked in darkness" will see "a great light." There is both an OT and a NT fulfillment of this. Assyria had swept across the land in judgment. A "great light," however, of blessing will come when the Lord releases His people from their captivity. In addition, Matthew 4:15–16 makes the passage messianic.[6] This is a prophecy of Christ, who grew up in Nazareth, a city in Zebulon, darkened because of its lack of spiritual light. The people there live in the land of the "shadow of death [*salmawet*][7]." The "light" of the Lord shines upon them. From Nazareth, the Lord enters into His public ministry (Luke

---

late *kabed* with the NEB as "dealt heavily." This requires historical pronouncements that we have no evidence for. Translating *kabed* as "bring to glory" smoothly introduces v. 2, where there is no question of the messianic application.

[4]Barnes, I, 187, rejects the thought that "beyond Jordan" refers to land east of the Jordan. He refers it simply to the upper part of the country. The phrase, however, occurs several times in the OT to indicate land east of the Jordan River, e.g., Deut. 3:20, 25; Josh. 9:10; 13:8; 18:7.

[5]The word "Galilee" is from *galîl,* which can mean "circle." Delitzsch, I, 244, thinks of it as that portion of Palestine circled by Gentile nations. Mauchline, p. 110, suggests it is "the circle of nations (Moab, Ammon, Edom, Philistia, etc.), against which Amos, for instance, delivered words of judgment." Kraeling, p. 73, refers to a "district encircled by cities with diverse political affiliation." Fausset, p. 593, speaks of the region inhabited by both Jews and Gentiles circling the northern part of Palestine. This is the only time the phrase occurs. There is not enough information to choose between these suggestions. I accept the view expressed by Delitzsch.

[6]Stacey, pp. 69–70, redefines messianic as "an OT conception." He refers it to the accession of kings, not to prophecies of Christ. "Long-term forecasts of an individual in the distant future, and, even more, precise forecasts of Jesus himself are not to be found there." He argues that the NT writers read prophecies of Christ into the OT. The statement, of course, reflects his theological view. A conservative view would see the NT writers as recognizing the prophecies of the OT. Jewish teachers had not understood them because they lacked knowledge of spiritual truth. Their rejection of Christ made it impossible to understand spiritual matters.

[7]The word *salmawet* is a compound of *sal,* "shadow," and *mawet,* "death." Despite the fact that *salmôt* does not occur elsewhere, Watts, *Isaiah 1–33,* p. 131, revocalizes the word and translates "[land of] shadow." Mauchline, p. 111, and Kaiser, *Isaiah 1–12,* p. 124, translate similarly. Matthew 4:16, however, translates the phrase as σκιᾷ θανάτου. This leaves no doubt that "shadow of death" is correct.

> 4 For thou hast broken the yoke of his burden, and the staff of his shoulder, the rod of his oppressor, as in the day of Midian.
> 5 For every battle of the warrior is with confused noise, and garments rolled in blood; but this shall be with burning and fuel of fire.
> 6 For unto us a child is born, unto us a son is given: and the government shall be upon his shoulder: and his name shall be called Wonderful, Counsellor, The mighty God, The everlasting Father, The Prince of Peace.

4:16), v. 2.[8] Under His leadership, the nation multiplies, a kingdom prophecy.[9] At that time, there will be general rejoicing in the land. The phrase "not increased the joy" (lo' higdalta haśśimḥâ) is better read with the q^{e}rê, lô higdalta haśśimḥâ, "to it, You have increased the joy."[10] Isaiah illustrates the joy. He compares it to the joy of an abundant harvest or the joy that comes from dividing the spoil of a conquest, v. 3.

4–5 To illustrate how the "oppressor" (nagaś, see 3:5) will be broken, Isaiah makes a comparison. The "yoke . . . staff . . . rod" will be overthrown "as in the day of Midian." This refers to the time when Gideon delivered Ephraim from the Midianite invasion (Judg. 6:1–8:21), v. 4. Verse 5 is better translated "For every boot [s^e'ôn][11] of the tramping one [i.e., the soldier] in the confusion [of battle] and the cloak rolled in blood shall be for burning, fuel for the fire." This describes the cleansing of the land with fire after the great battle that closes the Tribulation (Rev. 19:11–21). The Lord will overcome opposition as He prepares to rule the earth, v. 5.

6–7 The source of this deliverance now appears. The child of 7:14 will Himself carry the "government" (miśrâ); cf. 22:22.[12] The word miśrâ

---

[8]Kelley, p. 223, makes the passage refer to a king contemporary with Isaiah "rather than to an ideal king of the future." He bases this conclusion on the use of perfect tense verbs in the passage. It is, however, common to express future thoughts with the perfect tense in prophecy. These are matters so certain in the mind of God that they can be spoken of as having taken place.

[9]Leslie, p. 61, applies the passage to the accession of Hezekiah. The NT application, however, makes the passage messianic.

[10]While there are some who accept the k^{e}tîb, e.g., Fausset, p. 593, and Henry, p. 58, the overwhelming majority of authors and translations read the verse with the q^{e}rê.

[11]Fausset, p. 594, translates s^e'ôn as "greave" rather than "boot." The word occurs only here (twice). There is, however, an Akkadian cognate, śênu, "shoe, sandal," which points to "boot." The context requires military equipment of some kind that will burn.

[12]Understandably, the Jewish commentators Slotki, p. 44, and Ibn Ezra, pp. 51–52, reject the idea that the verse refers to Christ. They see Hezekiah as the logical fulfillment

*7 Of the increase of his government and peace there shall be no end,
upon the throne of David, and upon his kingdom, to order it, and to
establish it with judgment and with justice from henceforth even for
ever. The zeal of the Lord of hosts will perform this.*

occurs only here and in v. 7. It may, however, be related to the assumed
root *śarar*, from which *śar*, "chief, ruler," comes. The Akkadian *šarru*,
"king," further supports the idea of ruling. This will occur during the
kingdom. A fourfold description shows His qualifications.[13] He is "Wonderful, Counsellor" (better, "a wonderful Counselor), with wisdom to
govern; cf. 28:29.[14] He is the "mighty God," with power to carry out His
will. He is the "everlasting Father." The phrase refers not only to His
care for His children, the members of the church, but also to His role as
the second Adam, the Father of the redeemed; cf. I Corinthians 15:45.

---

of the prophecy. Skinner, *Isaiah I–XXXIX*, p. 76, likewise denies that the person here
prophesied is God. He sees only that "the divine energy works through him and is displayed in his rule." Kaiser, *Isaiah 1–12*, p. 128, views the passage as describing "the
adoption of the [earthly] king by God in the moment in which he ascends the throne."
The titles "set out the programme for his reign and promise him good fortune." On the
basis of the "fivefold Egyptian throne name," Kaiser, p. 129, suggests that a fifth name
has fallen out of the text. These views require that we explain away the names pointing
to Deity.

[13]John Goldingay, "The Compound Name in Isaiah 9:5(6)," *CBQ* 61:240–43, understands the names to refer to God, not the child. They declare "what God will be for the
child." He further considers the names as two noun clauses rather than four phrases. He
translates, "One who plans a wonder is the warrior God; the father for ever is a commander who brings peace." Taking the names as two noun clauses does not give a logical
translation. Why should one who plans a wonder be a warrior God? Why should the
everlasting Father be a commander who brings peace? There is no connection between
the subject and the predicate. Retaining the asyndetic nature gives us four parallel names
describing the child from different aspects. As for naming the Father rather than the Son,
the natural antecedent to the phrase "his name" is the child spoken of earlier in the verse.

[14]Among others, Cowles, p. 72; Rawlinson, I, 166; and Hailey, p. 102, retain the separation between "Wonderful" and "Counsellor." The parallelism in the verse, however,
supports the idea that there are four names, rather than five. In addition, the accents support four names. Slotki, p. 44, takes a different approach. He translates, "Wonderful in
counsel is God the Mighty, the Everlasting Father, the Ruler of Peace." The translation,
however, ignores the opening part of the verse, "And his name shall be called." We cannot take the names as an independent sentence. The Talmud, *Sanhedrin* 94a, takes still
another approach, understanding eight names. The presence of "God" and "Father"
argues against this. It is not necessary to say that Messiah is God and the Father. The
Vulgate translated as six names: *Admirabilis, Consilarius, Deus, Fortis, Pater futuri
sæculi, Princeps pacis* (Wonderful, Counselor, God, Mighty, Everlasting Father, Prince
of Peace). This ignores the parallelism.

He is the "Prince of Peace [*šalôm*]," governing the world to secure world peace; cf. 2:4. The idea of *šalôm* includes not only the absence of war and violence but also the thought of fulfillment, satisfaction, and wholesome relationships with others. It expresses a blessing that has its source in a right relationship with God. All of these descriptive phrases in the name find their fulfillment in Christ.[15]

Verse 6 actually has two prophecies. The first speaks of the birth of Christ. This is followed by a gap in time before the prophecy of Christ as King over the earth. The church age falls between the words "given" and "and." The two prophecies embrace the first coming of Christ and His Second Coming in glory, v. 6.

His rule will be everlasting, marked by "peace" (*šalôm*).[16] This rule fulfills the Davidic covenant; cf. II Samuel 7:12–16. He will establish His government with "judgment" (*mišpat*, better "justice," see 1:17) and "justice" (*ṣedaqâ*, or "righteousness," see 1:21) forever. This points to the kingdom, when Messiah rules with justice and righteousness. The Lord will bring this to pass by His "zeal" (*qinʾâ*), a strong emotion of burning desire, v. 7.

3. Judgment of the Wicked 9:8–10:4

Righteousness requires the punishment of sin. Isaiah now gives several representative judgments to show the Lord's desire that sin be put away. The judgment includes both Israel (vv. 8, 9) and Judah (vv. 8, 21). The re-

---

[15]Smith, I, 136, rejects the names as prophecies of Christ's deity. He argues that each of the names can be applied to man. In particular, he points out that the words translated "mighty God" here in Ezek. 32:21 refer to a man. It is also true, however, that these same words refer to God in Isa. 10:21 and Jer. 32:18. While it is true that the individual names could refer to a man, the heaping of name after name conveys the idea that this is more than a man. Smith, I, 140, also argues that Isaiah was the prophet of God's unity. "It is inconceivable that if Isaiah, the prophet of the unity of God, had at any time a second Divine person in his hope, he should have afterwards remained so silent about Him." Smith overlooks the servant passages in the last half of the book and the several clear presentations of the Trinity. See 11:2, note 4.

[16]The *mêm* in *lᵉmarbeh* ("increase") is written as an unusual final *mêm*, which has led to a variety of treatments. The LXX deleted the first two consonants as a dittography, translating μεγάλη ἡ ἀρχὴ αὐτοῦ, "great is His rule." Wade, p. 66; Gray, I, 176; and Whitehouse, I, 151, follow this translation. Von Orelli, p. 65, states that the *mêm* rises from an ancient reading *lam rabbâ* or *rabbeh* with *lam* = *lahem*. This follows an older rabbinical explanation. The simplest approach follows the *qᵉrê*, writing the final *mêm* as a normal *mêm*. The form in the MT may well show the influence of the final *mêm* in the previous verse. The verse repeats the *lamed* preposition in the next clause, *lᵉšalôm*, supporting the form of *lᵉmarbeh*.

8 The Lord sent a word into Jacob, and it hath lighted upon Israel.
9 And all the people shall know, even Ephraim and the inhabitant of Samaria, that say in the pride and stoutness of heart,
10 The bricks are fallen down, but we will build with hewn stones: the sycomores are cut down, but we will change them into cedars.
11 Therefore the Lord shall set up the adversaries of Rezin against him, and join his enemies together;
12 The Syrians before, and the Philistines behind; and they shall devour Israel with open mouth. For all this his anger is not turned away, but his hand is stretched out still.

curring phrase "For all this his anger is not turned away, but his hand is stretched out still" (vv. 12, 17, 21, 10:4) marks each of the sections.

a. Upon Pride 9:8–12

8–10 The Lord directs His message to both Judah and Israel, although the further development of the paragraph focuses on Israel, v. 8.[17] This gives the people the knowledge of God's standards. They are, therefore, without excuse, v. 9a. The specific object of His wrath is the pride of the nation, v. 9b. Tiglath-pileser III brought the Assyrian army into the land, ca. 732 B.C. Massive destruction occurred at that time, although Menahem purchased Israel's safety by paying Assyria a thousand talents of silver, II Kings 15:19. The people now arrogantly propose to build better in place of that which has been destroyed. Instead of "bricks" and "sycomores," common building materials, they will use "hewn stones" and "cedar," more expensive materials. They do not see the hand of God's judgment in the destruction, v. 10.

11–12 To rebuke this attitude, the Lord promises judgment by the "adversaries of Rezin," i.e., Assyria. Rezin, of course, is the king

---

[17]The following four paragraphs each end with the refrain "For all this his anger is not turned away, but his hand is stretched out still" (vv. 12, 17, 21; 10:4). This same refrain occurs in 5:25. For this reason, many commentators feel that 9:18–10:4 should be moved to c. 5. Smith, I, 48, moves 9:18–10:4 to follow 5:25 so that 5:26–30 concludes the whole passage. Motyer, *The Prophecy of Isaiah*, p. 112, suggests that 5:25–30 once followed 10:4. This lets 5:26–30 conclude the passage that now ends with a condemnation of the judiciary. Gray, I, 95, 96, 179–80, omits vv. 25a–c, 30 as editorial additions and moves 5:25d–29 to follow 10:4. He understands 5:25d as the conclusion to a lost strophe or the last strophe of 10:4. Kraeling, pp. 60, 76–77, moves 5:25–29 to follow 9:8–21. He thinks the refrain in 10:4 "was falsely recopied from 9:21b when 10:1ff was injected." Other suggestions to join these two sections have been made as well. All of these rest on the repetition of the phrase "For all this. . . ." This denies Isaiah the right to repeat himself. In addition, the passage in c. 5 deals with Judah (5:7) while the four paragraphs here focus on Israel (9:12, 14, 21). There is no textual support for joining the passages in any way.

13 For the people turneth not unto him that smiteth them, neither do they seek the Lord of hosts.
14 Therefore the Lord will cut off from Israel head and tail, branch and rush, in one day.
15 The ancient and honourable, he is the head; and the prophet that teacheth lies, he is the tail.

formerly joined with Israel against Judah; cf. 7:1. The same enemies that judged Syria will now come "against him," against Israel. The Lord will bring their enemies together, v. 11. He mentions Syria and Philistia, representative nations, located "before," on the east, and "behind," on the west of Israel. They devour Israel with "open mouth," a picture of their ravenous appetite for their enemy. It is possible that the word "Israel" here represents the whole of Israel and Judah since there is no recorded attack of Philistia against Israel.[18] It is equally possible, however, that we do not have enough information about the relationship between Philistia and Israel. Amos 1:6 may hint at an invasion of Israel although the passage is not clear. This judgment, however, does not satisfy God's anger toward Israel's sin, v. 12.

b. Upon Leaders 9:13–17

13–15 The people do not turn to the God who has punished them nor do they seek the Lord of the hosts of heaven and earth, v. 13. For this reason, judgment will come. The Lord will cut off "head and tail, branch and rush," cf. 19:15, v. 14. These terms represent differing groups of leaders in Israel. The "head" is the honorable leader; the "tail" is the false prophet who speaks "lies" (*šeqer*).[19] The noun *šeqer* refers to untruthfulness, speech that has no basis in fact. Drawing on the parallelism, the "branch" (better "palm branch"), growing high in the tree, also represents the upper class, the leaders in society. The "rush" (better

---

[18]Delitzsch, I, 258, suggests this view. Young, I, 350, also adopts this suggestion. Näglesbach, p. 146, disagrees with the position.

[19]Hailey, p. 107, understands the "head and tail" as representing the animal realm while the "branch and rush" represent the vegetable world. Motyer, *The Prophecy of Isaiah*, p. 108, explains both figures as representing totality. The "head and tail signify from one end to the other while branch and reed . . . signify from the eminent to the lowly." While these views are possible, the symbolism is not clear. It is just as valid to understand the symbols as standing for high and low groups within the nation.

16 For the leaders of this people cause them to err; and they that are led of them are destroyed.
17 Therefore the Lord shall have no joy in their young men, neither shall have mercy on their fatherless and widows: for every one is an hypocrite and an evildoer, and every mouth speaketh folly. For all this his anger is not turned away, but his hand is stretched out still.
18 For wickedness burneth as the fire: it shall devour the briers and thorns, and shall kindle in the thickets of the forest, and they shall mount up like the lifting up of smoke.
19 Through the wrath of the Lord of hosts is the land darkened, and the people shall be as the fuel of the fire: no man shall spare his brother.
20 And he shall snatch on the right hand, and be hungry; and he shall eat on the left hand, and they shall not be satisfied: they shall eat every man the flesh of his own arm:
21 Manasseh, Ephraim; and Ephraim, Manasseh: and they together shall be against Judah. For all this his anger is not turned away, but his hand is stretched out still.

"bulrush"), growing in the marsh, stands for the baser elements of leadership; those who falsely claim to represent God, v. 15.[20]

16–17 Those who lead the people astray, and those who have followed these leaders, will be destroyed (*bala͛*), v. 16. The nature of their sin is such that God will turn even from His normal mercy toward the helpless. Everyone is a "hypocrite" (*ḥanep*). The word *ḥanep* refers to godless or profane individuals. All are "evil doers" (*ra͛a͛*, see 1:4). All have spoken foolishly. They deserve punishment. Yet, even this will not satisfy God's anger toward sin, v. 17.

c. Upon the People 9:18–21

18–21 The fire of wickedness rages throughout the land. It consumes all in its path, including the "briers and thorns," the common people; cf. 27:4; Ezekiel 2:6; and the "thickets of the forest," the leaders; cf. 10:34. The judgments "mount up" (*yit͗ab͗ekû*) like a cloud of smoke, v. 18.[21]

---

[20]Delitzsch, I, 259, and Näglesbach, p. 147, understand the "rush" to represent the lower classes of people. While the view is possible, it requires different symbolism for the parallel phrases in v. 14. Isaiah explains the symbolism of the first two pictures. After that, there is no need to explain the symbolism of the second two expressions.

[21]The verb *͗abak* occurs only here. There is, however, an Akkadian cognate, *abaku*, "to bring along, drive away." The passive sense of the *hitpa͛el* verb supports the idea that these caught in the judgment "are driven away" like a cloud of smoke.

The Lord sends His own fire of judgment, causing the land to be "darkened" (ʿatam).[22] The context suggests a meaning of "burned, scorched." The word "darkened" of the AV reflects the idea of blackening the land through burning.

The people are fuel for the fires of judgment. They turn on one another: "no man shall spare his brother," v. 19. The people "snatch" (better "cut off") on the right without satisfying their hunger. They eat on the left with no resulting satisfaction. Each one eats "the flesh of his own arm," picturesquely describing their willingness to turn against their own family, v. 20. Manasseh and Ephraim, despite their common heritage, turn on one another. Together, they turn against Judah. Even this desperation of the people does not satisfy the Lord's anger toward the sin of His people, v. 21.

Practical Applications from Chapter 9

1. God's Plan for This World. He will bless the nations, v. 1, by sending His Son into the world, v. 2. This will bring joy to His people, v. 3. He will overcome the opposition of Antichrist to His work, vv. 4–5. His Son will then govern the world. The wise, mighty, eternal Son will bring unending peace to this world, vv. 6–7.

2. God Will Judge the Wicked, 9:8–10:4.

   a. Proud individuals, vv. 8–12

   b. Evil leaders, vv. 13–17

   c. Wicked people, vv. 18–21

   d. Unjust judges, 10:1–4

---

[22]The word ʿatam is also a *hapax legomenon*. The LXX translated συγκέκαυται, "burnt." Kaiser, *Isaiah 1–12*, p. 132, follows William L. Moran, "The Putative Root ʿtm in Is. 9:18," *CBQ* 12:153–54, in locating the word as the 3fs of nuaʿ, "to reel," with an enclitic *mêm*. Moran translates, "the earth reeled." Kaiser freely translates, "bent down." The context supports better the idea of burning.

*1 Woe unto them that decree unrighteous decrees, and that write
 grievousness which they have prescribed.*
*2 To turn aside the needy from judgment, and to take away the right
 from the poor of my people, that widows may be their prey, and that
 they may rob the fatherless!*
*3 And what will ye do in the day of visitation, and in the desolation
 which shall come from far? to whom will ye flee for help? and where
 will ye leave your glory?*
*4 Without me they shall bow down under the prisoners, and they shall
 fall under the slain. For all this his anger is not turned away, but his
 hand is stretched out still.*

ISAIAH 10

The first paragraph in the chapter concludes the final thought of c. 9,
the judgment of various wicked groups of people. Verses 5–34 develop a
single idea, the judgment of the Assyrians. Rather than glorifying God
for His goodness to them, they had arrogantly concluded that they were
the cause of their success. In the midst of their planned conquest of
Judah, God intervenes to show His power over the heathen. The chapter
develops the arrogance of Assyria, their approach to Judah, and the following destruction of the Assyrian army.

d. Upon Injustice 10:1–4

1–4 This final paragraph in the pronouncements of judgment on Israel focuses on those who have perverted judgment and oppressed the
helpless.[1] From the context of v. 2, the "unrighteous decrees" refer to
court decisions. The last half of v. 1 reads something like "the writers
who write mischief," i.e., creating problems for others by their unjust decisions, v. 1. Isaiah expands on the nature of their injustice. They take
"right" (*mišpaṭ*, or "justice," see 1:17) from the "needy" (*dal*) and rob the
"poor" (*ʿanî*, see 3:14) of their rights. The *dal* is someone without material possessions or social influence. The wicked use legal means to oppress the widows and orphans, v. 2.

---

[1]Leupold, I, 197, makes this final section directed against Judah rather than Israel.
Nothing in the text, however, supports his view. The context of the prior three judgments
(9:8–12, 13–17, 18–22) argues that this fourth statement also has Israel in view.

5 O Assyrian, the rod of mine anger, and the staff in their hand is mine indignation.
6 I will send him against an hypocritical nation, and against the people of my wrath will I give him a charge, to take the spoil, and to take the prey, and to tread them down like the mire of the streets.

Isaiah asks, "What will ye do . . . ?" This rhetorical question shows that there will be no safety for the oppressors when God sends judgment. The "day of visitation" is that day when God visits the land with judgment. The "desolation" (or "devastation") will come "from far," a hint that Assyria is in view. The questions that follow parallel the opening question. There will be no escape from the judgment. The words "your glory" refer to Israel's wealth. The enemy will seize this, v. 3. Israel will go into captivity. They will "bow down" among other prisoners or fall among the slain.[2] What a change! At one time, they arrogantly oppressed those without power to resist them. Now they themselves have no power against Assyria. They hide among the prisoners and dead in an attempt to escape. As in the first three statements of judgment in c. 9, the punishment does not satisfy God's anger against sin, v. 4.

4. Judgment of Assyria 10:5–34
a. Arrogance of Assyria 10:5–11

5–6 The phrase "O Assyrian" is lit. "Woe to Assyria." With this, the Lord introduces a proclamation of judgment. Assyria has been God's "rod" and "staff" to chasten Israel, v. 5. God will send them against His people, a "hypocritical" (or "godless," ḥanep, see 9:17) nation, people who were the object of God's wrath. They are to plunder the nation and to trample the people underfoot, v. 6.

---

[2]Leslie, p. 36, accepts the suggested emendation in BH. He translates "Beltis is crouching, Osiris is shattered" for the first part of the verse. Not only is there no textual support for this but there is no indication in the OT that Israel worshiped either of these gods. The problem in this verse stems from the use of biltî, "without me," and the change from singular to plural in the verbs. The particle biltî clarifies the rhetorical questions of v. 3: "where will you flee . . . where will you leave your glory, unless he bows down beneath the prisoners and they lie under the slain?"

7 *Howbeit he meaneth not so, neither doth his heart think so; but it is in his heart to destroy and cut off nations not a few.*
8 *For he saith, Are not my princes altogether kings?*
9 *Is not Calno as Carchemish? is not Hamath as Arpad? is not Samaria as Damascus?*
10 *As my hand hath found the kingdoms of the idols, and whose graven images did excel them of Jerusalem and of Samaria;*
11 *Shall I not, as I have done unto Samaria and her idols, so do to Jerusalem and her idols?*

7–11 Assyria does not recognize this sacred trust.[3] She looks on the conquest of Israel as only one more step in a grand plan of conquest in which she overcomes "not a few" nations, v. 7. She exalts her leaders. She makes her "princes" (or "captains"), not necessarily members of the royal family, rule as kings over the conquered nations, v. 8. She dwells on the power that has brought her past conquests. The six cities named all fell to Assyria. "Calno," identified with "Calneh," was located fifty miles southwest of Carchemish in upper Mesopotamia. It was one of the cities of Nimrod, Genesis 10:10. If Calno is the Kullani mentioned in Assyrian texts, Tiglath-pileser III conquered it, ca. 738 B.C. Carchemish stood on the banks of the upper Euphrates River. It had been a chief city of the Hittites. Sargon conquered it, ca. 717 B.C. Hamath was a Syrian city, located on the Orontes River in northern Syria. It also had been a Hittite city. Sargon conquered it, ca. 720 B.C., beheading its king and reducing it to ruins. Arpad was one of the northernmost cities of Syria. It fell to Tiglath-pileser III, ca. 740 B.C., and again to Sargon, ca. 720 B.C. Samaria, the capital of Israel, fell to Shalmaneser in 722 B.C.; cf. II Kings 17:5–6. Damascus, one of the major Syrian cities, was conquered by Tiglath-pileser III, ca. 732 B.C., cf. II Kings 16:9, v. 9. The Assyrians think of these past conquests as defeating "the kingdoms of the idols [*ᵊlîlîm*, see 2:8]." The phrase reflects the thinking that each nation had its own gods. The Assyrians considered the gods of these nations superior to those in Palestine, v. 10. For this reason, they are confident that they will conquer Judah. Just as they had conquered Samaria with her "idols" (*ᵊlîlîm*, see 2:8), they will now conquer Jerusalem, v. 11.

---

[3]J. Dwight Pentecost, *Things to Come: A Study in Biblical Eschatology*, 1958, p. 334, goes too far in making "Assyrian" in 10:5–12 a name for the man of sin. The context supports the idea given above, the condemnation of Assyria for her pride.

12 *Wherefore it shall come to pass, that when the Lord hath performed his whole work upon mount Zion and on Jerusalem, I will punish the fruit of the stout heart of the king of Assyria, and the glory of his high looks.*

13 *For he saith, By the strength of my hand I have done it, and by my wisdom; for I am prudent: and I have removed the bounds of the people, and have robbed their treasures, and I have put down the inhabitants like a valiant man:*

14 *And my hand hath found as a nest the riches of the people: and as one gathereth eggs that are left, have I gathered all the earth; and there was none that moved the wing, or opened the mouth, or peeped.*

b. Judgment Against Assyria 10:12–19

12–14 The Lord will let Assyria perform His "whole work" of judgment on Judah. After that, however, He will "punish" (*paqad*)[4] the "stout heart" (lit. "great heart"), i.e., the arrogant attitude, of Assyria's king.[5] The parallel phrase "glory of his high looks" again brings out the pride of the king, v. 12.[6] To emphasize Assyria's haughtiness, Isaiah uses nine personal pronouns to refer to the nation. The repetition of "my" and "I" in vv. 13–14 shows their arrogance. The Assyrian king, and through him the nation, will claim credit for the conquest of Israel. They will not think of themselves as only instruments of God.[7] The word "valiant" (*'abbîr*) is lit. "bull" or "stallion." It often refers poetically to "strength" or "might," e.g., Job 24:22; 34:20; Jeremiah 46:15. Here, the Assyrians apply it to themselves, v. 13. They will boast of their might in plundering the wealth of the nation. No one has withstood Assyria, v. 14.

---

[4]The word *paqad* is translated by such words as "number," "want," "punish," "visit," etc. The basic sense of the word seems to be an inspection of something with a view toward making some decision. Sometimes the decision is simply numbering, sometimes a judgment, sometimes to exercising care. The broad semantic range of the word leads to uncertainty in many passages. Here, the idea is that of punishment.

[5]The shift between speaking of the Lord in the third person, then in the first person, is not significant. Isaiah first reports the word of the Lord to him. He then completely identifies himself with the Lord and speaks in the first person.

[6]Once again, Pentecost, pp. 326, 355, is extreme when he identifies Assyria here with the northern confederacy of nations in the end times. The context does not support more than the fall of Assyria in OT times.

[7]There is a sharp contrast between the heathen king and the divine King of kings. The heathen king claims credit for himself. The King of kings recognizes the work of God's Spirit through Him, 4:4; 11:2; 48:16; 61:1.

15 *Shall the axe boast itself against him that heweth therewith? or shall the saw magnify itself against him that shaketh it? as if the rod should shake itself against them that lift it up, or as if the staff should lift up itself, as if it were no wood.*
16 *Therefore shall the Lord, the Lord of hosts, send among his fat ones leanness; and under his glory he shall kindle a burning like the burning of a fire.*
17 *And the light of Israel shall be for a fire, and his Holy One for a flame: and it shall burn and devour his thorns and his briers in one day;*
18 *And shall consume the glory of his forest, and of his fruitful field, both soul and body: and they shall be as when a standardbearer fainteth.*
19 *And the rest of the trees of his forest shall be few, that a child may write them.*

15–19 The Lord asks rhetorically if the weapon is greater than the one wielding it. Is the axe greater than the hewer? The saw greater than the one who "shaketh it," drawing it back and forth? The next two clauses more literally read, "Like the rod brandishing the one who lifts it? Like the staff lifting him who is not wood." This would be like the "rod," referring to a club, waving back and forth the one who holds it. It would be like the "staff," or rod, lifting the one who is "not wood," i.e., the human wielder of the rod, v. 15.[8] Assyria has failed to recognize that God is the power behind her. For this reason, He will judge her. He will send "leanness," a wasting away from disease. This will strike his "fat ones," the well-fed leaders of the nation.[9] "Under his glory" (*taḥat kᵉbodô*),[10] the wealth of the nation, the Lord will set a fire of judgment, v. 16.[11] The "Lord," the one to whom Judah belongs, and "the Lord of

---

[8]Delitzsch, I, 270; Leupold, I, 205; and Young, I, 365, are extreme when they relate the phrase "no wood" to God, as if the Assyrians think that they control God. The phrase "him who is not wood" parallels the one who "shaketh" the saw. Both phrases refer to the human who normally wields the club or the rod.

[9]In general, authors hold one of three views regarding the "fat ones." Some apply the phrase to the Assyrian leaders, e.g., Cowles, p. 82; Delitzsch, I, 270; and Ibn Ezra, p. 56. Some relate the phrase to the Assyrian army, e.g., Von Orelli, p. 76; Skinner, *Isaiah I–XXXIX*, p. 88; and Leupold, I, 205. Some apply it to the Assyrian nation as a whole, e.g., Näglesbach, 155; Price, p. 67; and Slotki, p. 52. While any of these views explains the passage, the context of v. 18 better supports the first view.

[10]The Talmud, *Shabbath* 113*b*, sets forth a peculiar view. This understands the preposition *taḥat* as "beneath" and *kᵉbodô* as "clothes." "Beneath the clothes" are the bodies that will be burned in judgment.

[11]The fire is a symbol of the judgment. The phrasing of this is typically Isaianic: *yeqad yᵉqod kîqôd*. The triple use of *yaqad* emphasizes the severity of the judgment.

20 And it shall come to pass in that day, that the remnant of Israel, and such as are escaped of the house of Jacob, shall no more again stay upon him that smote them; but shall stay upon the Lord, the Holy One of Israel, in truth.
21 The remnant shall return, even the remnant of Jacob, unto the mighty God.
22 For though thy people Israel be as the sand of the sea, yet a remnant of them shall return: the consumption decreed shall overflow with righteousness.
23 For the Lord God of hosts shall make a consumption, even determined, in the midst of all the land.

hosts," the ruler of the heavenly and earthly hosts, will be the fire that burns the common people ("his thorns and his briers"; cf. 9:18). He therefore has the right and the power to discipline the nation. The phrase "in one day" tells us that the judgment is quick. This may suggest the loss of 185,000 soldiers at Jerusalem, v. 17. In addition, the Lord will consume the leaders, the "glory of his forest, and of his fruitful field [or 'garden']." It will be as when the "standardbearer fainteth" (better "when a sick man wastes away"), v. 18. The destruction will be so complete that "a child may write them." The remaining number of leaders, "the trees of his forest," will be so small that even a child will be able to list the remnant. Assyria's fall at her invasion of Judah fulfills this promise, v. 19.

c. Deliverance of the Remnant 10:20–27

20–23 In that "day," the day of Assyria's judgment, the remnants of Israel and Judah will no longer trust in Assyria; contra. II Kings 16:7–9.[12] They will rather trust the Lord "in truth," with a sincere heart, v. 20. The remnant of Judah will return to the Lord, v. 21. Although there are a large number of Israelites, only the remnant will return. A "consumption" (better "destruction") has been decreed for them. The Lord will bring the exact measure of satisfaction on the nation that is necessary to vindicate God's righteousness. In Romans 9:27–28, Paul applies vv. 22–23 to the believing remnant. He argues there that God's

---

[12]The Scofield Reference Bible, ed. C. I. Scofield (New York: Oxford University Press, 1945), pp. 722–23, assigns vv. 20–34 to the Tribulation. The cities mentioned in vv. 28–32 do not fit into an approach to Megiddo, where the final battle will be centered. For this reason, it is better to relate the passage to the miraculous victory of God over the Assyrians at the time of Hezekiah.

24 *Therefore thus saith the Lord God of hosts, O my people that dwellest in Zion, be not afraid of the Assyrian: he shall smite thee with a rod, and shall lift up his staff against thee, after the manner of Egypt.*
25 *For yet a very little while, and the indignation shall cease, and mine anger in their destruction.*
26 *And the Lord of hosts shall stir up a scourge for him according to the slaughter of Midian at the rock of Oreb: and as his rod was upon the sea, so shall he lift it up after the manner of Egypt.*
27 *And it shall come to pass in that day, that his burden shall be taken away from off thy shoulder, and his yoke from off thy neck; and the yoke shall be destroyed because of the anointing.*

plan has always been to save a remnant of the nation, v. 22.[13] God will bring a "consumption," again "destruction," on the land, v. 23.

24–27 The people need not fear the Assyrians. He will punish them "after the manner of Egypt," in the same cruel manner as in the Egyptian bondage, v. 24. After a short time, however, the "indignation," the punishment of Judah, will stop. God will then direct His "anger" toward Assyria's destruction, v. 25. The Lord will punish Assyria in the same way that He slaughtered Midian at "the rock of Oreb," where a Midianite prince was slain; cf. Judges 7:25. Just as He rolled back the waters of the Red Sea, cf. Exodus 14:21–22, so He will roll back the waters of oppression that have threatened to engulf them, v. 26. In that day, He will take Israel's "burden" from them. He illustrates this deliverance as the removal of the yoke from the shoulders and neck of the ox. This will occur "because of the anointing" (*šemen*). The word *šemen* occurs elsewhere in Isaiah with a sense of fatness, 5:1; 25:6; 28:1, 4. The phrase then is "because of the fatness." The fatness of the neck implies strength sufficient to break the yoke placed upon it.[14] Verse 27c parallels 27a and b as it describes the lifting of the Assyrian yoke of bondage, v. 27.

---

[13]It is not right, as Pentecost, p. 476, to find the fulfillment of vv. 21–22 in the Millennium. While it is true that the Jews will worship God during the kingdom, the nation will be converted during the Tribulation, Zech. 12:10; 13:1.

[14]Rawlinson, I, 189, understands "the anointing" as symbolic of Hezekiah "but with a future reference to the Messiah." Nothing in the context suggests that the verse is messianic. Henry, 71, refers the "anointing" to both Hezekiah and David, probably a symbolism that is too general. While the view of Rawlinson is possible, I prefer a more literal understanding of the phrase.

28 He is come to Aiath, he is passed to Migron; at Michmash he hath
laid up his carriages:
29 They are gone over the passage: they have taken up their lodging at
Geba; Ramah is afraid; Gibeah of Saul is fled.
30 Lift up thy voice, O daughter of Gallim: cause it to be heard unto
Laish, O poor Anathoth.
31 Madmenah is removed; the inhabitants of Gebim gather themselves
to flee.
32 As yet shall he remain at Nob that day: he shall shake his hand
against the mount of the daughter of Zion, the hill of Jerusalem.

d. Description of the Judgment 10:28–34

28–32 Isaiah describes the latter part of Assyria's approach to
Judah.[15] All of the towns mentioned are close to Jerusalem. Aiath is Ai,
about ten miles north of Jerusalem near Bethel. Migron is an unknown
city, located in Benjamin from the context. Michmash was seven miles
north of Jerusalem. The enemy lays up "his carriages" ($k^e l\hat{i}$)[16] there, i.e.,
stores his baggage, v. 28. The "passage" was the pass through the moun-

---

[15]According to 36:2 (II Kings 18:17), the Assyrian army came from the southwest
rather than from the north as they traveled from Lachish to Jerusalem. Leupold, I, 211,
explains the difference by making this passage "a poetic phantasy." Goldingay, p. 82,
calls it "an imaginary picture of the Assyrians' closer advance." Young, I, 374, calls this
"an ideal picture . . . designed by the prophet to express the thought that the enemy when
he comes will take over the whole land." Smith, I, 170, says, "This is not actual fact; but
it is vision of what may take place to-day or to-morrow." He understands this as showing
the uselessness of Judah's treaty with Assyria, II Kings 16:7–8. Hailey, p. 118, concludes
that Isaiah "is not describing the actual coming but an approach that would strike terror
in the hearts of the towns that he mentions." These views are hard to accept. Nothing in
the passage hints at a poetic or imaginary description. Wright, p. 49, and Herbert, *Isaiah*
1–39, p. 88, make the approach that of Pekah and Rezin in the days of Ahaz; cf. 7:1. The
context of vv. 5, 12, 24, however, places Assyria in view. D. L. Christensen, "The March
of Conquest in Isaiah X 27c–34," *VT* 26:389–90, 398, thinks that the passage describes
"the Divine Warrior" in a march against His people. Again, the context suggests Assyria
as the enemy, not the Lord. Kelley, p. 230, defends the account. He proposes "a two-
pronged attack upon Jerusalem, sending one force down the central mountain range that
ran from Samaria to Jerusalem" and "another force against the city from the southwest."
Kaiser, *Isaiah 1–12*, p. 151, suggests that the Assyrians deviated from the shorter path in
order to punish "the border towns of the northern kingdom." It is equally possible that a
part of the Assyrian army traveled from the north to prevent the people of Judah from
fleeing. While we do not know the details, we may accept the description here with
confidence.

[16]The word $k^e l\hat{i}$ has a broad meaning in the OT. Elsewhere it refers to jewels (Gen.
24:53), household items (Gen. 31:37), tabernacle vessels (Exod. 27:3), furniture (Exod.
31:8), drinking vessels (Ruth 2:9), armor (I Sam. 14:6), a bag (I Sam. 17:40), musical instruments (I Chron. 15:16), etc. For this reason, we cannot be certain as to what it refers

33 Behold, the Lord, the Lord of hosts, shall lop the bough with terror:
and the high ones of stature shall be hewn down, and the haughty
shall be humbled.
34 And he shall cut down the thickets of the forest with iron, and
Lebanon shall fall by a mighty one.

tainous area near Michmash.[17] Geba, Ramah, and Gibeah were all north
of Jerusalem, six, five, and four miles respectively. The people of
Ramah fear the approach of the enemy. The people of Gibeah flee, v. 29.
Other small towns along the way weep at the prospect of facing the Assyrians. Gallim is an unknown city that must have been near Jerusalem.
Anathoth was two and a half miles northeast of Jerusalem. Laish,
thought to have been a small town about one and a half miles northeast
of Jerusalem, hears their weeping. It is likely that the people of Anathoth
come through there on their way to safety in Jerusalem, v. 30. The location of Madmenah is not certain other than that it must have been north
of Jerusalem. Those who live there flee from the enemy. The people of
Gebim, six miles north of Jerusalem, likewise flee, v. 31. The Assyrians
reach Nob, a priestly city (I Sam. 22:19) whose location has been lost.
They "remain at Nob that day" apparently resting before the final thrust
at Jerusalem.[18] They "shake their hand," a threatening gesture, against
"the mount [*har*] of the daughter [*bayit*] of Zion, the hill of Jerusalem,"
v. 32.[19]

33–34 "The Lord, the Lord of hosts," now steps in; cf. v. 16. He
strikes down the Assyrians, humbling them for their arrogance. Isaiah
uses the figure of a woodsman cutting down trees to describe the

---

to here. In general, *kᵉlî* refers to equipment, tools, or vessels. Grogan, p. 86, argues for
the translation "he examines his weapons." Although an unusual sense of *kᵉlî*, the view is
possible.

[17] The NEB transliterates *maᶜbarâ*, "passage," as "Maabarah." We know of no town by
this name. The word is not rare. It regularly refers to a "ford" or "pass" in the historical
and prophetic sections of the OT, Gen. 32:22; Josh. 2:7; Isa. 16:2; Jer. 51:32.

[18] The Talmud, in *Megillah* 31a, has an interesting interpretation of "that day." It makes
the fall of Sennacherib, prophesied here, occur on the day of Passover. While this may be
true—we have no way of knowing—it is unlikely that "day" here refers to anything more
than the arrival of the Assyrian forces at Nob.

[19] The AV along with virtually everyone else reads the *qᵉrê, bat*, "daughter," rather than
the *kᵉtîb, bayit*, "house." Watts, *Isaiah 1–33*, pp. 160, 164, combines *har* and *bayit* and
reads either *hirbît* or *harbôt*. He translates "to make Zion large." He understands this as
the Lord's signal that Zion should grow in anticipation of the predicted fruitfulness of
11:1. There is no textual support for this reading.

destruction of the Assyrians. The Lord will "lop the bough [*pu²râ*][20] with terror." The trimming here is done with "terror" (better "a terrible crash"), hinting at the great fall of these mighty ones, v. 33. The "thickets of the forest," cf. v. 19, again referring to the Assyrian leaders, are cut down as with an iron axe. The (implied) forests of Lebanon likewise fall. Second Kings 19:35–36 describes the fulfillment of this promise. The "mighty one" who accomplishes this is God, v. 34.

Practical Applications from Chapter 10

1. Verses 1–4 (included with c. 9)
2. The Destruction of Self-exaltation. The Assyrians gave credit to themselves for their success. God was going to send them against Judah to judge the nation for its sin, v. 6. They, however, did not recognize God's commission. They considered this only one more victory in a long record of conquest, vv. 7–10. They considered Israel's gods to be weaker than the gods of other conquered nations, v. 10. They would do to the Jews as they had done to other countries, v. 11. God will use them to judge His people, v. 12. They, however, will give Him no credit, vv. 13–14. God will therefore judge them, vv. 15–19. Those in Judah who escape the judgment will turn back to God, vv. 20–23. The Assyrians will fall, vv. 24–27. God will give them partial victory. He will let them approach Jerusalem, vv. 28–32. He will then strike them and they will fall in judgment, vv. 33–34.

---

[20]The noun *pu²râ,* "boughs," occurs only here. Related nouns, however, occur elsewhere, Ezek. 17:6; 31:5. The context of Deut. 24:20 shows that the verb *pa²ar,* from which *pu²râ* comes, can mean "glean."

1 And there shall come forth a rod out of the stem of Jesse, and a
Branch shall grow out of his roots:
2 And the spirit of the Lord shall rest upon him, the spirit of wisdom
and understanding, the spirit of counsel and might, the spirit of
knowledge and of the fear of the Lord;

ISAIAH 11

Isaiah now returns to the work of the Messiah. He has introduced
Him in c. 7 and developed His work briefly in 8:8, 10; 9:6–7. Chapter 10
has dealt extensively with the Assyrian threat to Judah. The victory of
the Lord over His enemies leads naturally into His future reign over the
whole earth. Chapter 11 focuses on this theme and prepares for the note
of praise to God sounded in c. 12.

5. Coming of the Messiah 11:1–16
a. Character of His Reign 11:1–9

1–2 A "rod," the trunk of a tree, comes from the "stem [better
'stump'] of Jesse."[1] This pictures the growth of a tree from the stump of
a tree that has been cut down. In a sense, the tree of Jesse was cut down
when the monarchy was overcome. The new tree is the restored monarchy under Christ. This comes from the "stump of Jesse" in that the Lord
descended from Jesse. In synonymous parallelism with the first clause, a
"Branch" (*neṣer*, a fresh sprout), grows from the "roots" (*šoreš*, see
53:2).[2] The word *neṣer* is the basis for the statement that Jesus would be
called a "Nazarene," Matthew 2:23. The prophecy here is therefore messianic, fulfilled in Christ, v. 1.[3]

---

[1]Hailey, p. 120, thinks that the "house of David will fall into such a state of dishonor
. . . that the prophet here does not refer to it by its proper name, but by the name of
David's father." This presupposes that Jesse's house was not one of honor, a view not
taught in the OT. The phrase "stock of Jesse" allows the introduction of the "rod" and the
parallel title of "Branch," a messianic name.

[2]Gray, pp. 214–15, states that the mention of a branch coming from the stump means
that a descendant of David is not reigning. He therefore dates the prophecy after Judah's
fall in 586 B.C. Herbert, *Isaiah 1–39*, p. 91, thinks that this view goes too far. He simply
makes the branch a symbol of Hezekiah. These views fail to understand the symbolism
of the passage. The Jewish commentator Slotki, p. 56, does better by recognizing the
passage as a prophecy of Messiah. He does not, however, recognize Christ as the fulfillment of the prophecy.

[3]Leslie, pp. 62–63, redefines the idea of a messianic hope: "We are not to think here of
a messianic age remote in the future." Rather, he considers this a description of the king

The Holy Spirit will "rest upon him," anointing Him for His earthly ministry. The seven names given to the Spirit correspond to the seven-fold reference to the Holy Spirit given in Revelation 1:4; 3:1; 4:5; 5:6. The initial name, "Spirit of the Lord," notes the nature of the Spirit as the indwelling presence of God in the Son.[4] Isaiah arranges the final six names in three groups of two names each. In each case, the first characteristic is the source from which the second characteristic flows.

The first group, "the spirit of wisdom and understanding," relates to the intellect of the Holy Spirit. He has "wisdom," the practical ability to apply knowledge. This gives Him "understanding," the ability to discern the differences, particularly the rightness or wrongness, in various situations and matters. As a consequence of this, the Holy Spirit is omniscient. The second group relates to the practice of the Holy Spirit. He has "counsel," the ability to form right conclusions. This gives Him "might," the ability to carry out His plans since He bases them on right plans. As a consequence of this, the Holy Spirit is omnipotent. The final group relates to the deity of the Holy Spirit. He has "knowledge" (*da^{c}at*, from *yada^c*, see 1:3). By virtue of the grammatical construction, this is the "knowledge of the Lord." We may say that the Spirit possesses the full knowledge of God. This leads to the conclusion that the Spirit is God; cf. I Corinthians 2:11. He has the "fear of the Lord," a reverence for the things that concern God. His knowledge of God and His reverence for God reflect His own deity. He is separate from God yet has the nature of God, v. 2.

The Character of Messiah 11:2

Omniscience: "The Spirit of wisdom and understanding"

Omnipotence: "The Spirit of counsel and might"

Deity: "The Spirit of knowledge and of the fear of the Lord"

---

who was adopted by the Lord on his accession to Israel's throne. This, of course, denies the reality of messianic prophecy.

[4]Note that the verse mentions all three members of the Godhead: "Spirit," "Lord," and "Him [Messiah, the Son]." This is the first mention of the Trinity in Isaiah. See also 42:1; 48:16; 59:19–21; 61:1; 63:7–14.

3 *And shall make him of quick understanding in the fear of the Lord: and he shall not judge after the sight of his eyes, neither reprove after the hearing of his ears:*
4 *But with righteousness shall he judge the poor, and reprove with equity for the meek of the earth: and he shall smite the earth with the rod of his mouth, and with the breath of his lips shall he slay the wicked.*
5 *And righteousness shall be the girdle of his loins, and faithfulness the girdle of his reins.*

3–5 The Holy Spirit will "make Him of quick understanding" (*rîaḥ*, lit. "cause Him to smell"). The word *rîaḥ* occurs elsewhere with a metaphoric sense of "delighting," Amos 5:21. With this sense, the Son here delights in the "fear of the Lord." He has a reverence for God and for the things of God. This leads Him to avoid judging according to the outward appearance of matters.[5] Likewise, He will not "reprove" (*yakaḥ*, or "decide," see 1:18) on the basis of what He hears, v. 3. He rather judges the "poor" (*dal*, see 10:2) according to "righteousness" (*ṣedeq*, see 1:21). He will "reprove [*yakaḥ*] with equity" (better "decide with uprightness") on behalf of the "meek" (*ʿanaw*, see 3:14). He strikes the "earth" in judgment "with the rod of His mouth," an expression that refers to His speech; cf. Proverbs 14:3. Revelation 19:15 alludes to this verse with its statement that the Lord strikes the nations with the "sharp sword" of His mouth. From the parallelism with "wicked," the "earth" (*ʾereṣ*) represents the world system that opposes God. This is a meaning *ʾereṣ* has elsewhere, e.g., Genesis 9:17; Isaiah 45:22, v. 4.[6]

Righteousness and faithfulness characterize Messiah's rule. The "girdle" (or "belt") was a leather band that gathered in the robes to keep them from hindering a man's actions. Here, "righteousness" (*ṣedeq*, see 1:21) serves as the belt about the "loins" (or "waist") so that He may act without hindrance. In like manner, "faithfulness" (*ʾemûnâ*) is a belt

---

[5]David Noel Freedman, "Is Justice Blind? (Is 11,3 f.)," *Biblica* 52:536, comments, "In the Bible, justice while impartial is not blind." For this reason, he understands *lôʾ* in both phrases as an asseverative particle. He translates, "And strictly in accordance with what his eyes see shall he judge, and strictly in accordance with what his ears hear shall he decide." This assigns an unusual use to the common negative particle *lôʾ*.

[6]Vine, p. 39, and Delitzsch, I, 284, understand the "wicked" as Antichrist. While the view is possible, the parallelism here argues against anything more than judgment of the wicked on the earth. The millennial kingdom will be an era of enforced righteousness. While men will continue to sin, they will not sin with impunity. The Lord will see that overall righteousness governs the actions of mankind.

6 *The wolf also shall dwell with the lamb, and the leopard shall lie down with the kid; and the calf and the young lion and the fatling together; and a little child shall lead them.*
7 *And the cow and the bear shall feed; their young ones shall lie down together: and the lion shall eat straw like the ox.*
8 *And the sucking child shall play on the hole of the asp, and the weaned child shall put his hand on the cockatrice' den.*
9 *They shall not hurt nor destroy in all my holy mountain: for the earth shall be full of the knowledge of the Lord, as the waters cover the sea.*

about his "reins" (or "loins"). The word *ᵉmûnâ* comes from the verb *ᵓaman*, "to confirm, support" and, in the *nipᶜal*, "to be faithful." As such, it represents His desire to do the Father's will. So Messiah's "righteousness" and "faithfulness" keep Him from turning aside from the will of God, cf. Revelation 19:11, v. 5.

6–9 These verses describe the peaceful nature of Messiah's kingdom.[7] Animals that now are natural enemies will live in peace with one another.[8] The wolf no longer preys on the lamb; the leopard and young male goat will sleep together. The young lion will be between a calf and a "fatling" (*mᵉrîᵓ*, see 1:11), a cow that has been fattened in its stall.[9] A "little child" (*naᶜar qaton*) will lead these animals. The diminutive *qaton* may refer to age and *naᶜar* relates to children of all ages, including young men. The phrase describes youths that care for the flocks, v. 6. The cow and bear will graze together and their young will sleep together. The lion will change his diet, eating the same fodder as the ox, v. 7. The nursing child plays by the hole of the "asp," an unknown poisonous

---

[7]Young, 1, 391, argues that the passage cannot apply to the millennial kingdom. He believes that the passage describes a day "in which there is no sin." This, however, misunderstands vv. 5, 9. The fact that "the earth shall be full of the knowledge of the Lord" does not mean that there will be no sin. Rev. 20:7–9 reveals the true nature of man at the close of the Millennium. These who do not know the Lord as their Savior will follow Satan rather than God.

[8]Hailey, p. 123, rejects a literal interpretation, then expresses the view that the passage refers to the peace of the Lord's kingdom. While he winds up at the right place, he takes a wrong turn getting there. The kingdom will involve peace among the animals, 65:25, and the absence of war among the nations, 2:4.

[9]Henry, p. 74, spiritualizes the passage. He makes the wolf and lamb represent violent men and gentle men. The peace between the animals pictures the peace that will one day exist between the Jews and Gentiles. There is no need to abandon the literal application of the passage.

10 *And in that day there shall be a root of Jesse, which shall stand for an ensign of the people; to it shall the Gentiles seek: and his rest shall be glorious.*

11 *And it shall come to pass in that day, that the Lord shall set his hand again the second time to recover the remnant of his people, which shall be left, from Assyria, and from Egypt, and from Pathros, and from Cush, and from Elam, and from Shinar, and from Hamath, and from the islands of the sea.*

12 *And he shall set up an ensign for the nations, and shall assemble the outcasts of Israel, and gather together the dispersed of Judah from the four corners of the earth.*

snake, perhaps an adder or a viper. The weaned child will "put" (*hadâ*)[10] his hand into the "den" (*me'ûrâ*) of the "cockatrice," again an unknown poisonous snake, also possibly an adder or a viper. The *me'ûrâ* is lit. "light-hole," i.e., a hole through which, looking upward, light is visible. It refers to the underground lair of a serpent, v. 8. The animals will not cause "hurt" (*ra'a'* I, see 1:4) in the kingdom. The verb *ra'a'* simply refers to harm of some kind. Even the animals will sense the Lord's presence in that time, v. 9.[11]

b. Coming of His People 11:10–16

10–12 The phrase "in that day" here points to an eschatological fulfillment. The "root of Jesse," Messiah, referring to His earthly heritage cf. v. 1, will be an "ensign," a rallying point for the people in the millennial kingdom.[12] The Gentiles will come "to it," better "to Him." The

---

[10]The word *hadâ* is a *hapax legomenon*. On the basis of Arabic and Aramaic parallels, BDB, p. 213, gives the meaning "stretch out." From the context, it is clear that the child is playing in some way near the viper's lair.

[11]The question here is whether we should limit the verse to animals or to man as the subject. Either view gives a correct thought. Leupold, I, 220, refers the verse to man on the basis that Hab. 2:14 makes this application. In the only other similar passage in Isaiah, 65:25, the thought is of animals. It is therefore more consistent to make that same application here.

[12]With doubtful logic, Brueggemann, *Isaiah 1–39*, p. 104, states that "the poem is not a prediction of Jesus, nor even an anticipation of one so remote." Then he notes that the church has seen Jesus in the text and comments: "Such a rereading of the text is legitimate and proper, for these great texts evoke and permit many rereadings. That is not the same, however, as treating it as a 'prediction,' but it is a responsible way of interpretation that establishes linkage between Jewish expectation and the powerful, compelling reality of Jesus." Let me simply say that Brueggemann's comments are not "a responsible way of interpretation."

"rest" that He gives in that day will be "glorious."[13] When we consider that it will be a time of worldwide peace, 2:4, a time when man himself will be free from the physical infirmities of sin, 32:3–4; 35:5–6, and a time when the earth is free from the curse of sin, 55:12–13, the word "glorious" is appropriate. Paul in Romans 15:12 makes the passage an explicit prophecy of the reign of Christ, v. 10.

At that time, "in that day," the Lord gathers His people, believing Israel, from across the world. The locations given here are a representative, not an exhaustive, list. Assyria and Egypt (*miṣrayim*) were the two great world powers at the time Isaiah writes. Pathros was the ancient name for Upper Egypt, the land south of the delta. In view of this, the name *miṣrayim* likely refers to Lower Egypt, the delta region. Cush is modern Ethiopia, the land south of Egypt. Elam was a dominant world power in the third millennium B.C. It lay to the east of Babylon, beyond the Tigris River. In Isaiah's day, it was bounded on the north by Media and Assyria, on the south by the Persian Gulf, and on the east by Persia. Shinar was the ancient name for the area later occupied by Babylon in the southern part of the Tigris-Euphrates Valley. Hamath was the northernmost city-state of Syria. The "islands [ʾî]"[14] of the sea" include the occupied islands and coastal areas of the Mediterranean Sea, v. 11.

The Lord gathers in Israel those of the nation who have been dispersed throughout the world. He Himself is the "ensign," a rallying point for the people.[15] To "it," again, better "to Him," cf. v. 10, the nations will come; cf. 60:3, 5. They bring to Judah the "outcasts," those who have been banished from Palestine. They assist those who have been "dispersed" in prior times. These come from the "four corners" (*kanap*) of the earth. The

---

[13]Henry, p. 76, gives the passage a double fulfillment, first with Hezekiah, then with Messiah. The journey of the Babylonian representatives to Hezekiah, II Kings 20:12–13, does not even come close to fulfilling the scope of the passage. Rawlinson, I, 204, finds the fulfillment in the development of the church as Gentiles accepted Christ. Alexander, I, 256, makes the "ensign" the preaching of the gospel. The church then becomes glorious as Gentiles become believers. These views overlook the fact that there has not been the worldwide return of Jews to Palestine as prophesied in v. 11. It is best to make the eschatological application alone without finding an earlier fulfillment.

[14]The word ʾî refers to the shores of the Mediterranean and then, by synecdoche, to the whole of the area bounding the Mediterranean Sea.

[15]Leupold, I, 223, makes this a signal of some kind set on an elevated point. Not only would this be impossible to see from distant nations but also the nearness to v. 10 makes it unlikely that this signal would differ from the signal there.

13 The envy also of Ephraim shall depart, and the adversaries of Judah shall be cut off: Ephraim shall not envy Judah, and Judah shall not vex Ephraim.

14 But they shall fly upon the shoulders of the Philistines toward the west; they shall spoil them of the east together: they shall lay their hand upon Edom and Moab; and the children of Ammon shall obey them.

15 And the Lord shall utterly destroy the tongue of the Egyptian sea; and with his mighty wind shall he shake his hand over the river, and shall smite it in the seven streams, and make men go over dryshod.

16 And there shall be an highway for the remnant of his people, which shall be left, from Assyria; like as it was to Israel in the day that he came up out of the land of Egypt.

word *kanap* means "wings." It occurs here in a metaphoric sense, representing the north, east, south, and west, i.e., from all over, v. 12.

13–16 The ancient enmity between "Ephraim," the Northern Kingdom of Israel, and "Judah," the Southern Kingdom, will vanish, v. 13.[16] Now united under Messiah's leadership, they will dominate the other nations of the world. Once again, the nations listed are representative, not exhaustive. The "shoulders [*katep*, singular, thus 'shoulder'] of the Philistines" describes the low ridge that leads from Judah to the coastal plain occupied by Philistia toward the "west" (better "sea"). Israel will control this area and will also gain wealth from the "east" (lit. "sons of the east"). The people in the regions of Edom, Moab, and Ammon will submit to her authority. Verses 13–14 summarize the conditions in Palestine during the kingdom. Israel will be unified and will dominate the surrounding people, v. 14.

At that time, the Lord will destroy (*heḥᵉrîm*) "the tongue of the Egyptian Sea." This poetic statement refers to the Gulf of Suez, a hindrance to travel north to Palestine. The *hipᶜîl* verb *heḥᵉrîm* normally means "to place something under a ban." It refers to something wholly devoted to God, either for His service, e.g., Leviticus 27:28, or for total destruction, e.g., Numbers 21:2–3. Here, the waters interfere with the return of the Jews to Israel and must be destroyed. In addition, the "mighty [*ᶜᵃyam*, or

---

[16]Fausset, p. 604, understands "the adversaries of Judah" as "the adversaries from Judah," those of Judah who are hostile toward Ephraim. The grammatical construction, however, of the phrases "envy of Ephraim" and "adversaries of Judah" is identical. In both cases, there is a construct relationship. This suggests that we should interpret both in the same way. Ephraim will no longer envy Judah, and Judah will no longer be an adversary of Ephraim.

'scorching']¹⁷ wind" of the Lord will break up "the river," the Euphrates River, into "seven streams [*nahal* see 7:19]." The number "seven" here is symbolic for completeness. The river is turned into a number of small streams flowing in shallow ravines that let men cross without removing their sandals, v. 15. These actions allow unhindered travel between Egypt and Assyria through Israel, cf. 19:23; 35:8–10, v. 16.

Practical Applications from Chapter 11

1. The Character and Work of Christ

   a. Descended from David, v. 1*a*

   b. Restoration of the monarchy, v. 1*b*

   c. Prophecy of the Nazarene, Matthew 2:23, v. 1*b*

   d. Filled with the Spirit (omniscient, omnipotent, Deity), v. 2

   e. Mention of the Trinity, v. 2

   f. Reverent toward God, v. 3

   g. Righteous, vv. 4*a*, 5*a*

   h. Judge of the wicked, v. 4*b*

   i. Faithful, v. 5*b*

2. Nature of the Kingdom

   a. Peacefulness of the kingdom, vv. 6–9

   b. Worship of the Gentiles, v. 10

   c. Return of the Jews to Palestine, vv. 11–12

   d. Peace in the land, v. 13

   e. Dominance of nearby nations, v. 14

   f. Unity with Egypt and Assyria, vv. 15–16

---

¹⁷The word *ᶜayam* is a *hapax legomenon*. Possible Arabic cognates relating to "heat" or "thirst" suggest the meaning of "scorching." The LXX translated πνεύματι βιαίω, "violent wind." The Vulgate gives *in fortitudine spiritus sui,* "in the might of his wind." Along with the AV, these apparently emend *ᶜayam* to *ᶜoṣem,* "mighty." A "scorching wind," however, amply satisfies the action of breaking up the river.

1 *And in that day thou shalt say, O Lord, I will praise thee: though*
thou wast angry with me, thine anger is turned away, and thou com-
fortedst me.
2 *Behold, God is my salvation; I will trust, and not be afraid: for the*
Lord Jehovah is my strength and my song; he also is become my
salvation.
3 *Therefore with joy shall ye draw water out of the wells of salvation.*

ISAIAH 12

Isaiah concludes the first section of the book with a song of praise.
Having focused on the person and work of Christ in c. 11, it is appropriate to close the thought with this note of praise. Isaiah stresses the salvation that the Lord has provided to His people. In view of what He has
done, He is "great" and therefore worthy to receive praise.

6. Chorus of His Praise 12:1–6

1–3 The Jews ("thou") will praise the Lord in "that day," the kingdom
age described in c. 11 and in the numerous individual prophecies in
c. 1–10.[1] The people ask the Lord to turn away His anger from them.[2]
This indicates that they see their need to turn from their sinful worship
to worship the Lord alone. Instead of judgment, the Lord now "comfort-
edst" (*naham* see 1:24) the people. Because of His comfort, they fear the
judgment of God no longer, v. 1.

God is the "salvation" of the people. He has delivered them from their
enemies and redeemed them from their sins. This gives them confidence.
They trust Him and are not "afraid" (*pahad*, see 2:10). The name "Lord
Jehovah" (*yah y^ehwah*) is a doubled name, lit. "the Lord, the Lord."[3] The

---

[1]Rawlinson, I, 218, makes the passage apply directly to the church. While it is true that
the church will praise God in the kingdom, this is no reason to make c. 12 directly refer
to the church. The development of the church is a NT teaching.

[2]Isaiah uses the jussive form of the verb "turned away" (*yašob*) where we would expect
an ordinary imperfect verb. This may simply be poetic (so Delitzsch, I, 292). G.K. 109 *k*
explains this on "rhythmical grounds." Waltke and O'Connor, 34.2.1.c, suggest that it
may "represent vestiges of an earlier verbal system." Young, I, 402, understands it as introducing an apodosis. He translates, "Thou wast angry, let thine anger return (i.e., thine
anger must return), and do thou show comfort to me." If we understand the earlier *kî* as
introducing a conditional rather than a concessive clause, the jussive may be retained
naturally: "if you are angry with me, let your anger turn away, and you will comfort me."

[3]Skinner, *Isaiah I–XXXIX*, p. 103, suggests that someone added the name *y^ehwah* as an
explanation of *yah*. Wade, p. 90, concludes that one of the names should be omitted. They

4 *And in that day shall ye say, Praise the Lord, call upon his name, declare his doings among the people, make mention that his name is exalted.*

5 *Sing unto the Lord; for he hath done excellent things: this is known in all the earth.*

6 *Cry out and shout, thou inhabitant of Zion: for great is the Holy One of Israel in the midst of thee.*

combination of divine names occurs only here and in 26:4. This doubling stresses the source of Israel's blessing. It is the Lord Himself who is Israel's strength, their source of joy, and their Savior.[4] The last half of the verse comes from the Song of Moses, Exodus 15:2, cf. also Psalm 118:14, v. 2.

Verses 1–2 have used singular verbs as Isaiah speaks to each individual Israelite. Beginning with v. 3, he uses plural verbs. He now addresses his comments to the nation as a whole. The nation will draw joyously on this inexhaustible supply of salvation; cf. John 4:13–14.[5] The "well" (*ma⁽yan,* better "springs") provides fresh-flowing supplies of water rather than a reservoir of water. The ongoing flow of "water" from the "springs" poetically portrays the unending supply of salvation, v. 3.[6]

4–6 In "that day," again the kingdom, cf. v. 1, the people will "praise" (*hip⁽îl* of *yadâ*) the Lord. The verb *yadâ* can mean either "praise" or "give thanks." Here, with the *l⁽*-preposition, the thought of thanking the

---

cite the LXX and other versions that give only one divine name here. The evidence from Hebrew supports the MT. It is likely that the LXX and other versions simply interpreted the double name rather than giving an exact translation.

[4]Grogan, p. 93, limits the thought of salvation to "the deliverance of the people from all their enemies." There is no reason, however, to place this restriction on the verse. This is a kingdom note of praise. The people then will know full well the extent of God's deliverance, both from their enemies and from their sins.

[5]The Talmud, *Sukkah* 48*b,* records a curious interpretation of the verse. The argument rests on the use of the *b⁽*-preposition with "joy." The conclusion is that wineskins will be made from the skins of apostates, i.e., Jews who have converted to Christianity. The Jews will draw water with them.

[6]Herbert, *Isaiah 1–39,* pp. 93–94, thinks that vv. 3–6 refer to "some ritual act performed at the New Year Festival at the Gihon spring." Through this "acted symbol Israel expressed its confidence in the coming of the rain upon which all life depends." It is true that at the Feast of Tabernacles, the Jews drew water from the Pool of Siloam. This was carried in a golden pitcher to the temple. The Feast of Tabernacles, however, was not the New Year feast. At no other time was water drawn for a ritual use. Moreover, there is no hint that this song is anything other than a song of praise to a gracious God, who has saved His people from their sin.

Lord is the better choice.[7] They "give thanks to the Lord" as they recognize all He has done for them. The people will call upon Him in prayer.[8] They will openly proclaim His works among the peoples of the earth. They will "make mention" (or "remember") that His name is exalted, v. 4. They will sing His praises for the excellent works He has done.[9] The last phrase, "this is known," is better "let this be known [$m^e yuda^c at$] in all the earth," v. 5.[10] In view of this future note of praise to the Lord, Isaiah commands the people of his day to give a "shout" of rejoicing.[11] The "Holy One of Israel," who dwells among them, is great. The implied thought is that He is deserving of praise, v. 6.

---

[7]In 29 references, when the l^e-preposition follows *yadâ* in the *hip^cîl*, the AV translates "give thanks to." There are only a few cases, in most of which the translation "give thanks to" would be suitable, that the AV translates "praise."

[8]Leupold, I, 232; Cowles, p. 102; and Delitzsch, I, 293, understand "call" (*qir^'û*) as "proclaim." The phrase refers to proclaiming the Lord's name throughout the earth, a thought that the rest of the verse develops. This is a possible view. In my judgment, however, the following b^e-preposition makes it more likely that prayer is in view here. This construction occurs elsewhere only in I Kings 18:25; I Chron. 16:8; and Ps. 105:1, all of which refer to prayer.

[9]Delitzsch, I, 293, translates *zamm^erû* as "harp," an instrumental act of praise to the Lord. The verb *zamar*, however, often represents simple praise without any limitation to an instrument, e.g., Ps. 101:1; 104:33; 146:2. There is no reason to restrict *zamar*. The broad application of praise from all people is appropriate.

[10]The $k^e tîb$, $m^e yuda^c at$, the *pu^cal* participle, elsewhere refers to an acquaintance or kinsman, a less intimate relationship. The $q^e rê$ *muda^c at*, a *hop^cal* participle, brings out the intimacy of the relationship with the Lord. This idea is appropriate here.

[11]J. Alec Motyer, *Isaiah: An Introduction and Commentary*, 1999, p. 110, notes that the word "inhabitant" is feminine. He concludes that Isaiah draws his thought from Miriam's song, Exod. 15:20–21. This is a trivial point upon which to base the connection. Because of the feminine noun, Wade, p. 90, translates, "inhabitress of Zion." It is more probable that the noun refers collectively to Israel, the "inhabitant" of Zion. The OT often uses the feminine participle, as here, to express a collective sense; cf. G.K. 122 s, Waltke and O'Connor 6.4.2c.

Practical Application from Chapter 12

It is right to praise the Lord! In the kingdom age ("in that day"), when the people receive His salvation, they will ask Him to turn His anger away from them, v. 1. God is their Deliverer, both from their enemies and from sin. He Himself is the source of their strength, their joy, and their salvation, v. 2. With joy, they draw on His unending salvation, v. 3. In the kingdom age ("in that day"), the people will give thanks to Him. They will pray. They will tell others of His works and exalt His name, v. 4. They will sing praises to Him for His works, and tell this throughout the earth, v. 5. In view of this future note of praise, Isaiah commands the people of his own day to praise the Lord, who is great and therefore worthy of praise, v. 6. Should we not praise the Lord now?

1 *The burden of Babylon, which Isaiah the son of Amoz did see.*
2 *Lift ye up a banner upon the high mountain, exalt the voice unto them, shake the hand, that they may go into the gates of the nobles.*
3 *I have commanded my sanctified ones, I have also called my mighty ones for mine anger, even them that rejoice in my highness.*
4 *The noise of a multitude in the mountains, like as of a great people; a tumultuous noise of the kingdoms of nations gathered together: the Lord of hosts mustereth the host of the battle.*
5 *They come from a far country, from the end of heaven, even the Lord, and the weapons of his indignation, to destroy the whole land.*
6 *Howl ye; for the day of the Lord is at hand; it shall come as a destruction from the Almighty.*
7 *Therefore shall all hands be faint, and every man's heart shall melt:*
8 *And they shall be afraid: pangs and sorrows shall take hold of them; they shall be in pain as a woman that travaileth: they shall be amazed one at another; their faces shall be as flames.*

ISAIAH 13

Chapter 13 begins a series of oracles against the nations. These include Babylon and Assyria (13:1–14:27); Philistia (14:28–32); Moab (15:1–16:14); Syria, represented by Damascus, and Israel (17:1–11); a second oracle against Assyria (17:12–18:7); Egypt (19:1–25); Egypt and Ethiopia (20:1–6); a second condemnation of Babylon (21:1–10); Edom (21:11–12); Arabia (21:13–17); Jerusalem (22:1–25); and Phoenicia, represented by Tyre (23:1–18). This leads naturally into the third major section of the book, 24:1–27:13, in which Isaiah moves to eschatological events. The judgments of the OT serve as symbols for the greater judgment that lies in the future.

II. Prophecies Against the Nations 13:1–23:18
A. Against Babylon and Assyria 13:1–14:27
1. Desolation of Babylon 13:1–22
a. Day of the Lord 13:1–13

1–8 Isaiah mentions Babylon here, then does not mention it again until v. 19. The section introduces the "day of the Lord" judgments; cf. v. 6.[1] Babylon's fall foreshadows this time of tribulation on the earth. Isaiah describes this as a "burden" (*maśśa᾽*, or "oracle") that concerns

---

[1]See the summary of the Day of the Lord at 2:12.

Babylon, v. 1.[2] The verse does not identify the speaker but it is undoubtedly the Lord. Only He has the power to command the nations. He calls the nations to raise a "banner" (or "standard"), a signal to direct the troops to their destination. They raise the standard on a "high mountain" (better "wind-swept mountain"). They raise their voice to urge the soldiers on. They "shake the hand," cf. 10:32, motioning to their troops to enter "the gates of the nobles," the main gates of the city, v. 2.[3] The Lord has called the Median and Persian soldiers, His "sanctified ones," so named because they are set apart for His work. He has called His "mighty ones" (*gibbôr*, see 3:2) and "them that rejoice in my highness" (better "my proudly rejoicing ones") because of His anger toward Babylon, v. 3.

The armies noisily gather together "in the mountains." These mountains are likely the Zagros Mountains, south of the Caspian Sea on the border between Media and Assyria. The noise is like that of a great crowd. The various national groups ("the kingdoms of nations") in the Median army come together as the "Lord of hosts" prepares for the battle, v. 4. The soldiers come from far-off lands, poetically described as from "the end of heaven." They represent the Lord. They are the "weapons of his indignation," brought together to destroy the land of Babylon, v. 5.

The people wail as they face the judgment. This is the "day of the Lord," the time when He destroys His enemies. In keeping with the general theme of the passage, the destruction here represents the destruction that one day will engulf the earth during the Tribulation. The name "Almighty" (*šadday*) occurs appropriately here.[4] The LXX translates it as

---

[2]The word *maśśaʾ* occurs widely in all parts of the OT. It may signal a "burden," a metaphorical emblem of judgment, or an "oracle," a divine message that generally deals with judgment. In Isaiah, it best represents an "oracle" except where the context supports the meaning of "burden," 22:25; 46:1, 2. Isaiah 30:27 is a special case (see notes). Wright, p. 53, dismisses the meaning "oracle" as used only in the later prophets. Actually, the word has this sense in Nahum (ca. 625 B.C.) and Habakkuk (ca. 625 B.C.), both within a century of Isaiah.

[3]Watts, *Isaiah 1–33*, p. 196, makes the "gates" the entrances to the camp of the soldiers, also a possible view. I prefer to understand the *waw* as a simple *waw*-consecutive, "and go into the gates of the nobles." In either case, the shaking of the hands gives directions to the group.

[4]Whitehouse, I, 186, suggests that *šadday* was the name by which Israel worshiped God before they came under the influence of the Kenites; cf. Judg. 1:16; 4:11, 17. His suggestion fails to account for Exod. 6:3, in which the Lord states that Israel is about to

9 *Behold, the day of the Lord cometh, cruel both with wrath and fierce anger, to lay the land desolate: and he shall destroy the sinners thereof out of it.*

10 *For the stars of heaven and the constellations thereof shall not give their light: the sun shall be darkened in his going forth, and the moon shall not cause her light to shine.*

11 *And I will punish the world for their evil, and the wicked for their iniquity; and I will cause the arrogancy of the proud to cease, and will lay low the haughtiness of the terrible.*

12 *I will make a man more precious than fine gold; even a man than the golden wedge of Ophir.*

13 *Therefore I will shake the heavens, and the earth shall remove out of her place, in the wrath of the Lord of hosts, and in the day of his fierce anger.*

παντοκράτωρ, "all powerful," v. 6. All will fear the judgment. Isaiah describes this with the phrases "all hands be faint" and "every man's [ʾᵉnôš, see 2:11] heart shall melt," cf. Ezekiel 21:7, v. 7. Pain, like the anguish of a woman giving birth, will accompany the fear.[5] The people will be "amazed" (or "astonished") at one another. Their faces will be "as flames," flushed with their terror, v. 8.

9–13 The thought now moves beyond the destruction of Babylon to the eschatological judgment of sinners in the Tribulation. The "day of the Lord" is a cruel time that leaves the land "desolate" (šammâ, see 5:9) and destroys the sinners in it, v. 9. The sun, moon, and stars cease to give their light; cf. Joel 2:31; 3:15; Matthew 24:29 (Mark 13:24; Luke 21:25); Acts 2:20; Revelation 6:12.[6] The term "constellations" (kᵉsîl) occurs elsewhere three times. In each case, it refers to the single constellation Orion. Here, then, the plural word refers to the Orion-like groupings of stars, the constellations, v. 10.

---

know Him as Jehovah, the name associated with God's grace and with His interaction with mankind. The Lord appears as Jehovah on numerous occasions to the patriarchs, Abraham, Isaac, and Jacob, then to the nation from its beginning.

[5]Driver, *JSS* 13:43, interprets "pangs" (ṣîrîm) on the basis of an Arabic cognate, maṣârru, as "intestines." He translates, "entrails are disturbed and pangs seize them." The word ṣîr, however, occurs four times elsewhere, including two times in Isa. 21:3, in which the meaning "pangs" cannot be disputed. There is no reason to abandon the plain meaning here for one that occurs nowhere else in the OT.

[6]Barnes, I, 252, denies that the verse is literal. He asserts that it "is a metaphorical representation of the calamities that were coming upon Babylon." This view fails to see the eschatological application of the passage. The references given above make it clear that there will be cataclysmic changes in the heavens during the Tribulation that will cause men to fear.

14 And it shall be as the chased roe, and as a sheep that no man taketh up: they shall every man turn to his own people, and flee every one into his own land.

15 Every one that is found shall be thrust through; and every one that is joined unto them shall fall by the sword.

16 Their children also shall be dashed to pieces before their eyes; their houses shall be spoiled, and their wives ravished.

The Lord speaks directly, warning that He will "punish" (*paqad*, see 10:12) the world for its "evil" (*ra*, see 3:9). He will judge the wicked for their "iniquity" (*awon*, see 1:4). He places special emphasis on the sin of pride. He will bring down the "terrible" (or "mighty") person, v. 11. The population will become so small that a "man" (*enôš*, see 2:11) will be more "precious" (*yaqer*)[7] than gold. We do not know for certain the location of "Ophir." It is thought to have been in southwest Arabia on the coast by the Red Sea, modern Yemen.[8] It was noted for its gold, e.g., Job 22:24; Psalm 45:9, v. 12. The Lord will shake the heavens and the earth in His wrath; cf. Joel 3:16; Haggai 2:6, 21. The phrase "the earth shall remove out of her place" looks forward to an earthquake; cf. 24:20. These things will take place in the "day of his fierce anger," the Day of the Lord, introduced earlier (v. 9), v. 13.

b. Destiny of Babylon 13:14–22

14–16 From the context, vv. 17, 19, the thought of the passage returns to Babylon. The city, "it," will flee like the "chased roe" (or "frightened gazelle") or as untended sheep. Men will return to their own homelands, v. 14. Those who are captured, however, will be killed, v. 15, even children. The houses will be plundered and the women ravished (*tiššagalnâ*), v. 16.[9]

---

[7]The root *yaqar* is similar to *kabed*. It can mean "heavy" and, by extension, "honor, precious, valuable." In each case, the context determines the sense.

[8]Others locate it in either Africa or India. We do not have enough information to be certain.

[9]Von Orelli, p. 91, accepts the *qerê*, *tiššakabnâ*, lit. "be lain with" but euphemistically "dishonoured." The *ketîb tiššagalnâ*, "raped," accurately expresses the actions of the soldiers toward the conquered women.

17 *Behold, I will stir up the Medes against them, which shall not regard silver; and as for gold, they shall not delight in it.*

18 *Their bows also shall dash the young men to pieces; and they shall have no pity on the fruit of the womb; their eye shall not spare children.*

19 *And Babylon, the glory of kingdoms, the beauty of the Chaldees' excellency, shall be as when God overthrew Sodom and Gomorrah.*

20 *It shall never be inhabited, neither shall it be dwelt in from generation to generation: neither shall the Arabian pitch tent there; neither shall the shepherds make their fold there.*

21 *But wild beasts of the desert shall lie there; and their houses shall be full of doleful creatures; and owls shall dwell there, and satyrs shall dance there.*

22 *And the wild beasts of the islands shall cry in their desolate houses, and dragons in their pleasant palaces: and her time is near to come, and her days shall not be prolonged.*

17–18 For the first time, Isaiah identifies the Medes as the conquerors of Babylon.[10] They do "not regard silver" or "delight" in gold. Their primary goal is revenge rather than spoil, v. 17. The bow was the chief weapon of the Medes. They use this effectively, the arrows tearing flesh from the young men in Babylon's army.[11] They kill pregnant women as well. They will not spare children, v. 18.

19–22 Complete destruction will come on glorious Babylon. To vividly portray this, the Lord compares it to Sodom and Gomorrah. The Lord destroyed those cities, Genesis 19:24–25. No trace of them remains today, v. 19. In like manner, people will not live in Babylon. Even nomads and shepherds will not use it as a camp. After the conquest by Cyrus, 539 B.C., Babylon was conquered a second time by Darius Hystaspes, 518 B.C. At this time, the walls were mostly torn down. In 482 B.C., Xerxes plundered the city, taking a large gold statue weighing almost 1800 pounds from the temple of Bel. In 312 B.C., Seleucus I

---

[10]Kelley, p. 237, and Stacey, p. 102, state that Cyrus the Persian took Babylon, thus the record here is not accurate. Cyrus, however, forged a coalition between the Medes and the Persians. The Medes were therefore involved in the conquest of Babylon. In addition, Darius the Mede became the king of Babylon, ruling under Cyrus, Dan. 5:31. The MT is accurate.

[11]The MT reads *ûqšatôt n^e^{c}arîm t^{e}raṭṭašnâ*, "the bows the young men they tear in pieces." The easiest way to treat *na^{c}ar* is as the direct object of *raṭaš*. While perhaps it is not as precise as we would like, the passage must be translated something like "The bows dash in pieces the young men." The implied thought is that they dash the enemy in pieces, ripping flesh from him as the arrows pass through him.

conquered Babylon for the final time. He made Antioch his capital, causing Babylon's influence to wane. By the time of the Greek geographer Strabo, ca. 63 B.C.–A.D 24., Babylon was a complete ruin. It will never be inhabited, v. 20. The "wild beasts of the desert" (ṣîyîm) will live in its ruins. The ṣîyîm cannot be identified with any specific creature. Here and in its other occurrences (Ps. 72:9; Isa. 23:13; 34:14; Jer. 50:39) ṣîyîm simply indicates "desert creatures." The "doleful [ʾoḥîm, 'howling']¹² creatures," possibly hyenas, will live there. The "owls" (bᵉnôt yaᶜᵃnâ, lit. "daughters of the owls," an unclean bird, Lev. 11:16; Deut. 14:15, but not clearly identified) will dwell there. The "satyrs" (śaᶜîr, "goats") will skip about the ruins, v. 21.¹³ The "wild beasts" (or "jackals" or "wolves") will howl "in their desolate houses." Other beasts, including "dragons" (tannîm, most likely "serpents" although many translate "jackals") will also live there. The time of Babylon's judgment is "near" from God's perspective. He will not let its days "be prolonged," v. 22.

---

¹²The meaning of ʾoḥîm is doubtful since the word occurs only here. Delitzsch, I, 305, suggests "horned owls." Leupold, I, 249, adopts "howling creatures." Grogan, p. 107, suggests a connection with the onomatopoeic ʾaḥ, "ah!" He refers it to "a howling or screeching creature." Based on a rare Akkadian cognate, BDB, p. 28, suggests "jackal." The context requires some wild animal or bird. We cannot be dogmatic beyond that.

¹³Stacey, p. 103, concludes that the satyr was "a mythical deity with both human and animal features." Gray, I, 244, thinks of "demonic animals, howling after the wont of demons and jinn in unfrequented places, of a hairy nature and perhaps goat-like in form." Wade, p. 97, suggests demons "in the shape of he-goats." He also mentions the possibility that the demons have "human shapes, with the horns and tail and feet of goats." There is nothing in the text, however, to indicate that śaᶜîr refers to anything other than goats. The surrounding context focuses on various animals. The "dance" of the goats is simply the graceful movement of these animals as they pass through the ruins of the city.

Practical Applications from Chapter 13

1. The Final Judgment of the Nations, vv. 1–13. The battle against Babylon serves to illustrate the "day of the Lord," v. 6. The Lord calls the nations to raise a signal to their troops. They should urge on their troops in the battle, v. 2. The Lord has called those set apart for the battle. These warriors reflect God's anger toward His enemies, v. 3. The armies gather together, v. 4, to destroy the land, v. 5, in this "day of the Lord" judgment, v. 6. The people fear the judgment, v. 7, and experience pain. They are astonished and flushed with terror, v. 8. The "day of the Lord" is a cruel time. The land will be desolate. Sinners will be destroyed, v. 9. There will be signs in the heavens, v. 10. The Lord will judge the wicked for their "iniquity" (ᶜawon, see 1:4), v. 11. Men will be so scarce in number that a single man will be more precious than gold, v. 12. The Lord will shake the heavens and the earth as He executes His wrath upon sin, v. 13.

2. The Illustration of Judgment, vv. 14–22.

   a. God's judgment is thorough, vv. 14–22a. Babylon will flee as a frightened gazelle or stray as sheep with no shepherd. Men will return to their homelands, v. 14. Those who are captured will be killed, v. 15. Children will die, houses plundered, and women ravished, v. 16. God will raise the Medes against Babylon. Their motive will be revenge rather than gold, v. 17. Using their bows, they will rip the flesh from the Babylonian soldiers. They will kill pregnant women and not spare the children, v. 18. Babylon will be as Sodom and Gomorrah, destroyed and no more inhabited, v. 19. No one will live there. Not even nomads or shepherds will camp there, v. 20. Wild beasts will live amid the ruins. Howling creatures, birds, goats, and snakes will dwell there, vv. 21–22a.

   b. God sets the time of judgment, v. 22b. The judgment is near. Babylon will not prolong her days past the time set by God for judgment, v. 22b.

1 *For the Lord will have mercy on Jacob, and will yet choose Israel,*
and set them in their own land: and the strangers shall be joined
with them, and they shall cleave to the house of Jacob.
2 *And the people shall take them, and bring them to their place: and*
the house of Israel shall possess them in the land of the Lord for ser-
vants and handmaids: and they shall take them captives, whose cap-
tives they were; and they shall rule over their oppressors.

ISAIAH 14

The opening of c. 14 naturally follows c. 13. After Israel's major enemies fall, God will raise up the nation again. This took place historically
when Cyrus the Great gave permission to the Jews to return to Palestine,
vv. 1–2. Isaiah then summarizes the fall of Babylon, vv. 3–11. In his
doing this, the thought passes from the king of Babylon to the destruction of Satan. The one who had thought to supplant God is himself cast
into hell, vv. 12–15. Returning to Babylon, Isaiah describes the humiliation of Babylon's king, vv. 16–21. Babylon will become a place of desolation, vv. 22–23. Assyria, vv. 24–27, and Philistia, vv. 28–32, will also
fall in judgment. The fall of the nations that have opposed God's people
should serve as an encouragement. God has not left His people alone.
While He punishes them for their sins, He will complete His plan
through them.

2. Restoration of Israel 14:1–23
a. Israel's Exaltation 14:1–2

1–2 When the Jews return to their homeland, "strangers" (*ger*) will
become Jews so as to enjoy their blessings. The word *ger* refers to one
outside the normal class, here those not Israelites by birth, v. 1. The
"people," heathen nations, will help Israel return to their "place," Palestine. The heathen in the land of Palestine will serve the Israelites. This
reverses the former situation. Israel now has dominion over those who
once were their "oppressors" (*nagaś*, see 3:5). The ultimate fulfillment of
this lies in the millennial kingdom. At that time, Israel will be the dominant nation in the world, v. 2.

3 *And it shall come to pass in the day that the Lord shall give thee rest*
   from thy sorrow, and from thy fear, and from the hard bondage
   wherein thou wast made to serve,
4 *That thou shalt take up this proverb against the king of Babylon, and*
   say, How hath the oppressor ceased! the golden city ceased!
5 *The Lord hath broken the staff of the wicked, and the sceptre of the*
   rulers.
6 *He who smote the people in wrath with a continual stroke, he that*
   ruled the nations in anger, is persecuted, and none hindereth.

b. Babylon's Degradation 14:3–23

3–6 In the time that Israel receives deliverance from her bondage, she
will enjoy rest from the burdens she has borne in judgment. Whereas
this life has brought Jews "sorrow . . . fear . . . hard bondage," the kingdom will bring them "rest," v. 3. Israel will speak a "proverb" (*mašal*)
against the "king of Babylon."[1] The word *mašal* refers normally to a
short, pithy saying that briefly gives some lesson drawn from life. It is
meant to instruct—to give an object lesson, a parable, a poem, an extended teaching, and so forth. Occasionally, as here, the word has the
sense of a "taunt," e.g., Job 17:6; Psalm 44:14. Israel will note that
Babylon is no longer their "oppressor" (*nagaś*, see 3:5). The phrase
"golden city" (*madhebâ*) is better "raging."[2] This also has stopped, v. 4.
The Lord has "broken" (*šabar*) Babylon's "staff" and "sceptre," the symbols of her power. The word *šabar* is strong, often indicating complete
destruction of idols or kingdoms, v. 5. Babylon formerly struck the nations "with a continual stroke," an unceasing persecution. She formerly
ruled the nations with anger. The phrase "is persecuted, and none

---

[1]It is extreme to understand the "king of Babylon" at this point as a reference to Antichrist. So Pentecost, p. 334 ("14:2," *sic*). The passage later applies to Satan. Here, however, the emphasis is on an OT type of Satan, the Babylonian king.

[2]The word *madhebâ* occurs only here. There is no root *dhb*. The AV apparently conjec-
tured *dahab* = *zahab* and read the form as a participle, the "place of Gold," i.e., the
"golden city." Delitzsch, I, 308, suggests that the root *dahab* = *daʾab*, "to pine away." The
participle is the place of pining away, i.e., "the place of torture," a rather free translation.
Seth Erlandsson, *The Burden of Babylon: A Study of Isaiah 13:2–14:23*, 1970, pp. 29–31,
has an extended discussion in which he concludes that the meaning is "gold tribute." The
Vulgate translates the word as *tributum*, "tribute," possibly understanding *middâ*. The Isaiah Scroll as well as the LXX support reading the form as *marhebâ*, raging or boisterous
behavior. Harry M. Orlinsky, "*MADHEBAH* in Isaiah XIV 4," *VT* 7:202–3, suggests that
the early versions interpreted *madhebâ* with "oppressor," *nagaś*, rather than understanding
marhebâ. He conjectures that *madhebâ* is from the root *dbʾ*, "to be strong, mighty."

7 *The whole earth is at rest, and is quiet: they break forth into singing.*
8 *Yea, the fir trees rejoice at thee, and the cedars of Lebanon, saying,*
  Since thou art laid down, no feller is come up against us.
9 *Hell from beneath is moved for thee to meet thee at thy coming: it*
  stirreth up the dead for thee, even all the chief ones of the earth; it
  hath raised up from their thrones all the kings of the nations.
10 *All they shall speak and say unto thee, Art thou also become weak as*
  we? art thou become like unto us?
11 *Thy pomp is brought down to the grave, and the noise of thy viols:*
  the worm is spread under thee, and the worms cover thee.

hindereth" is better "with unrestrained persecution." It also describes Babylon's treatment of the nations. The unstated thought is that this powerful nation will be brought low, v. 6.

7–8 The passage now takes on an eschatological sense. The entire earth is at rest and "quiet" (*šaqaṭ*, see 7:4). "They," all the members of the earth, rejoice at the peace that it enjoys, v. 7. The "fir trees" (*bᵉrôšîm*, better "cypress trees") and the "cedars of Lebanon" represent the trees throughout the land. These rejoice at Babylon's fall. Since Babylon has been laid low, "no feller," no cutter of trees, comes to chop down the wood for use by the army, v. 8.[3]

9–11 The word "hell" (*šᵉʾôl*, see 5:14) here refers to the region of the dead.[4] The members of sheol meet the dead Babylonian king at his arrival.[5] The "chief ones," formerly leaders of the earth, and the now dead "kings of the nations" in *šᵉʾôl* rise in anticipation of the judgment of

---

[3]Grogan, p. 105, and Kraeling, pp. 86–87, understand the trees as symbols of the Babylonian kings. This leads naturally into v. 9, in which kings are clearly in view. On the other hand, taking v. 8 literally completes the thought of v. 7, in which nature rejoices. Since the Babylonian kings cut down the trees of Palestine for their own use, the view expressed above is preferable.

[4]Rawlinson, I, 244, locates sheol in the center of the earth. While it is not possible to refute this location, since no one has been to the center of the earth, it is unlikely that *šᵉʾôl* has a physical location. The fact that it houses the soul, the immaterial part of the body, together with the fact that the fires of judgment do not burn up the body, makes it likely that *šᵉʾôl* refers to a place totally outside man's experience. It is a real place of real punishment. The nature and location, however, must remain a mystery for now.

[5]Stacey, p. 105, describes sheol as a place "of such low quality that it can hardly be called survival." It is "a place where there was no joy, no memory, where one is not remembered by God, nor able to worship him." Kelley, p. 238, describes sheol similarly: "The scene shifts to Sheol, the eternal abode of the ghostly dead . . . [this] reflects the early Hebrew concept of the afterlife, a concept that was simple but depressing." In most places that *šᵉʾôl* occurs, it refers to the grave. Views such as those of Stacey and Kelley confuse these references with the place of life after death. See 5:14, note 6.

12 How art thou fallen from heaven, O Lucifer, son of the morning! how art thou cut down to the ground, which didst weaken the nations!

13 For thou hast said in thine heart, I will ascend into heaven, I will exalt my throne above the stars of God: I will sit also upon the mount of the congregation, in the sides of the north:

14 I will ascend above the heights of the clouds; I will be like the most High.

Babylon's king, v. 9. They taunt him with the fact that he has joined them in death. Despite his position of power in life, he has become "weak" (*ḥalâ*) like them, v. 10.[6] The glory that he once knew is now gone, "brought down to the grave" (*šeʾôl*). The music of his court, the "viols" (better "harps" or "lutes") has now ceased. The "worm" (or "maggots") and the "worms" now feast upon his corpse, v. 11.

12–14 While vv. 12–14 could represent the continued speech of the fallen kings, it is more logical to make it a prophecy of judgment. The emphasis here passes to Satan, here called "Lucifer" (*hêlel*, lit. "shining one").[7] He is the "son of the morning [*šahar*, 'dawn', see 8:20]," the brightly shining planet Venus.[8] The name is appropriate since Satan attempts to take the place of that one who is the true "morning star," Revelation 22:16. He who has brought weakness to the nations himself is now cut down, v. 12.

---

[6]Eitan, p. 62, understands *ḥalâ* as "to be left alone." He argues from an Arabic cognate. The meaning "to be sick," thus "weak," is well established in Hebrew. There is no need to change the sense based on a relatively rare cognate word.

[7]Hailey, pp. 139–40, and *TWOT*, I, 217, refer the passage to a Babylonian king. Young, I, 441, denies that the passage refers to Satan. He feels the passage describes simply the downfall and removal of an earthly king. Among others, Smith, p. 411; Cowles, p. 118; and Barnes, pp. 271–72, also refer the passage to an earthly king. The arrogant claims of vv. 13–14, however, go beyond the ordinary claims to deity of heathen kings. The historical view, since the time of the church fathers, applies the passage to Satan.

[8]Kelley, p. 239, suggests that Isaiah uses a "mythological story from Canaanite religion to illustrate the fall of the king of Babylon." A minor Canaanite god named *Helal ben Shahar* tried to make himself like "the chief god in the Canaanite pantheon." His proud attempt was overcome and he was cast into sheol. John Gray, *Near Eastern Mythology* (New York: The Hamlyn Publishing Group, Ltd., 1973), p. 128, likewise relates the account to a Babylonian myth. Marvin E. Tate, "Satan in the Old Testament," *Review and Expositor* 89:467–69, refers to several myths involving a god who usurped power. He concludes that 14:12–17 makes use of "widely known traditional elements." These views, however, overlook the possibility that these myths may well have developed from the rebellion of Satan, which the Bible records. This is similar to the mythological accounts of Creation and of the worldwide Flood. In both cases, the myths pervert the true account given in Scripture. Isaiah's account here of Satan's fall is the accurate statement.

15 Yet thou shalt be brought down to hell, to the sides of the pit.

16 They that see thee shall narrowly look upon thee, and consider thee, saying, Is this the man that made the earth to tremble, that did shake kingdoms;

17 That made the world as a wilderness, and destroyed the cities thereof; that opened not the house of his prisoners?

With a series of five "I will" statements, Isaiah shows Satan's attempt at self-deification. Satan ascends into the highest heaven, from which God will one day cast him out, Luke 10:18. He exalts his rule above the "stars of God," the angelic hosts, Job 38:7. He purposes to sit on "the mount of the congregation," the seat of supreme judgment, Psalm 82:1. This is located in the "sides [*yarkâ*, or 'extremities']⁹ of the north," poetically considered the home of God, v. 13.¹⁰ He plans to dwell above the "heights of the clouds," in the heavens. He thinks he is equal to "the most High," to God Himself, thus deserving of man's worship, v. 14.¹¹

15–17 Despite Satan's pride, he will fail. The Lord will cast him into "hell" (*šeʾol,* see 5:14). He will be sent to "the sides [*yarkâ*, or 'extremities,' see v. 13] of the pit [*bôr*]." The word *bôr* normally refers to a cistern or well, but it also indicates a dungeon or place of captivity, e.g., Psalm 7:15; Lamentations 3:53, 55. As such, it may refer to the place of the dead, Psalm 88:4, 6; Proverbs 1:12. In that Satan is sent to the extremities of the pit, he receives the greater punishment of *šeʾôl*, cf. Luke 12:47–48, v. 15.¹²

---

⁹The word *yarkâ* occurs in Isaiah only in vv. 13, 15, and 37:24. The word *yarkâ* refers generally to the part of something that is farthest away, e.g., distant parts of the earth, Jer. 6:22; rear of the tabernacle, Exod. 26:22; the farthest border of Zebulon, Gen. 49:13. Here, the extremity of the north represents the highest part of heaven.

¹⁰Pentecost, p. 431, calls this "the seat of divine government in the earth." The context, however, locates this in the heavens: "into heaven . . . above the stars of God . . . above the heights of the clouds . . . like the most High."

¹¹Stacey, pp. 106–7, misses the point when he makes the title "most High" refer to "the highest deity in the pantheon." He considers the title "of Canaanite origin." The title, however, occurs more than forty times in every section of the OT, e.g., Num. 24:16; Ps. 9:2; Lam. 3:35, 38; Dan. 4:24–25; Hos. 7:16. There is nothing to indicate that Isaiah adopts a heathen title here.

¹²In keeping with his view that the passage refers to a heathen king, Barnes, I, 274, understands the phrase "sides [*yarkâ*] of the pit" to refer to tombs dug around the sides of a cavern. Kings, however, were not buried in common tombs in mass burial areas. More elaborate sepulchres were built for the bodies of royalty. Here, *yarkâ* refers to the extremities of sheol, the place of greatest punishment.

18 All the kings of the nations, even all of them, lie in glory, every one in his own house.

19 But thou art cast out of thy grave like an abominable branch, and as the raiment of those that are slain, thrust through with a sword, that go down to the stones of the pit; as a carcase trodden under feet.

20 Thou shalt not be joined with them in burial, because thou hast destroyed thy land, and slain thy people: the seed of evildoers shall never be renowned.

21 Prepare slaughter for his children for the iniquity of their fathers; that they do not rise, nor possess the land, nor fill the face of the world with cities.

The scene now shifts back to the fall of Babylon's king. Others look in amazement on his unburied corpse and recall his conquests. They remember the fear that he aroused in others, v. 16. They bring to mind the destruction caused by his conquests. They think of the multitudes of prisoners that he kept from returning to their homelands, cf. II Kings 25:27–30, v. 17.

18–21 Other kings who have died lie buried in glorious tombs, in their "own house," i.e., their own grave, v.18. In contrast, the king of Babylon has no tomb. He is like "an abominable branch," one growing in the wrong place on a tree and therefore cut off and thrown away. He is a "branch" from the royal tree but not deserving of honor. He is like "the raiment of those that are slain," i.e., his corpse lies with the bodies of those who have died from wounds caused by a sword. These bodies form the "raiment" of others who have died. Those carcasses are buried with the "stones of the pit [bôr, see v. 15]," i.e., moved into a depression and covered with stones thrown over them; cf. Joshua 7:26; 8:29; II Samuel 18:17; Jeremiah 41:7, 9; Ezekiel 32:23.[13] The body of Babylon's king, however, lies unburied, trodden underfoot by others, v. 19. His actions in life deserve special condemnation. Because he has brought destruction to his land and people, he will not gain honor in his death. His corpse will not be joined with others in burial. As additional disgrace, the "seed of evildoers [ra‘a‘, see 1:4]," his descendants, will not "be renowned" (better "be mentioned"). The thought is that his descendants will not

---

[13]Motyer, *The Prophecy of Isaiah*, p. 145, understands "stones of the pit" as the "rock bottom of the pit of Sheol." While this is possible, the OT nowhere represents sheol as a literal pit with a rocky bottom. The numerous mentions elsewhere of covering a body with stones argue for that meaning here. Erlandsson, p. 38, understands the phrase as "a stone-lined grave." Since the passage describes a dishonorable death, the phrase does not refer to an honorable tomb.

22 *For I will rise up against them, saith the Lord of hosts, and cut off*
from Babylon the name, and remnant, and son, and nephew, saith
the Lord.

23 *I will also make it a possession for the bittern, and pools of water:*
and I will sweep it with the besom of destruction, saith the Lord of
hosts.

follow him as rulers of the land, v. 20. They will be cut off "for the
iniquity [*ʿawon*, see 1:4] of their fathers." The implied thought is that
they have adopted the wicked beliefs and practices of their ancestors and
are therefore judged. They will not rule the land or build great cities
throughout the world, v. 21.

22–23 The "Lord of hosts," the ruler of heaven and earth, will rise
up against his family. The "name" of the ruling family will be cut off.
The surviving remnant, the "son," an offspring who remains, and the
"nephew" (better "posterity"), will fall in the judgment, v. 22. The city
of Babylon itself will become the home of animals. The "bittern"
(*qippod*),[14] an unknown bird, will dwell there. It will be a place of "pools
of water," swampy from standing water. The Lord will sweep it with the
"besom [better 'broom'] of destruction," a poetic description of judgment, v. 23.[15]

---

[14]The identity of the *qippod* is not clear. The LXX translates *qippod* with ἐχίνους,
"hedgehog." So NASB, NRSV. Some translate *qippod* as "owls." So NIV. 1QIsaᵃ has
qippoz, "arrow snake," probably a misreading of the MT. The root *qpd* refers to gathering
together, perhaps rolling something up. This has led to the suggestion of the porcupine or
hedgehog. The passage here associates the *qippod* with water. Zeph. 2:14 refers to
dwelling in a high place. The grouping together with the other birds in 34:11 suggests
that this also is a bird.

[15]The Talmud has an interesting note: "The Rabbis did not know what was meant by
we-teṭethia bemaṭaṭe *of destruction* till one day they heard the handmaid of the household of Rabbi say to her companion, Take the *ṭaṭitha* [broom] and *ṭaṭi* [sweep] the
house," *Rosh Hashana* 26b. Hollis R. Johnson and Svend Holm-Nielsen, "Comments on
Two Possible References to Comets in the Old Testament," *Scandinavian Journal of the
Old Testament* 7:103, suggest that Isaiah may have seen "a comet, with its broom-shaped
tail and terrifying appearance." While the suggestion is possible, we do not have evidence that would allow us to make a firm conclusion.

24 *The Lord of hosts hath sworn, saying, Surely as I have thought, so shall it come to pass; and as I have purposed, so shall it stand:*

25 *That I will break the Assyrian in my land, and upon my mountains tread him under foot: then shall his yoke depart from off them, and his burden depart from off their shoulders.*

26 *This is the purpose that is purposed upon the whole earth: and this is the hand that is stretched out upon all the nations.*

27 *For the Lord of hosts hath purposed, and who shall disannul it? and his hand is stretched out, and who shall turn it back?*

28 *In the year that king Ahaz died was this burden.*

29 *Rejoice not thou, whole Palestina, because the rod of him that smote thee is broken: for out of the serpent's root shall come forth a cockatrice, and his fruit shall be a fiery flying serpent.*

30 *And the firstborn of the poor shall feed, and the needy shall lie down in safety: and I will kill thy root with famine, and he shall slay thy remnant.*

3. Proclamation Against Assyria 14:24–27

24–27 Isaiah now takes up Judah's most immediate threat, the Assyrian nation. To show the certainty of the promise, the Lord has taken a solemn oath; cf. 45:23; 54:9; 62:8. What He plans will come to pass, v. 24. He will "break" (*šabar*, see v. 5) the Assyrian army and will do this "in my land" and in "my mountains." This breaking undoubtedly refers to the events described in II Kings 19:35 and releases Judah from the Assyrian "yoke," the "burden" placed upon them, v. 25.

Since Assyria will be the dominant power in the Mediterranean world at that time, their fall will result in worldwide changes in the relationships between the nations. God has purposed this. This judgment of Assyria is the "hand" that will be stretched out upon the nations. The symbolism of the Lord's "hand" moving in judgment occurs frequently in Isaiah, e.g., 5:5; 9:12, 17, 20, 21; 10:4; 51:17, 22, v. 26. To give emphasis to this certain promise, Isaiah repeats the promise that the Lord has determined to accomplish the judgment. The rhetorical question, "Who shall turn it back," must be answered, "No one," v. 27.

B. Against Philistia 14:28–32

28–30 Ahaz, the twelfth king of Judah, died ca. 725 B.C. From the phrase "messengers of the nation" in v. 32, we surmise that the Philistines had sent a delegation to mourn the king's death. The Lord chooses this time to declare this "burden" (*maśśaʾ*, cf. 13:1). The word *maśśaʾ* has the sense here of an oracle, a message of reproof for the Philistines, v. 28.

Isaiah warns all of the Philistines ("whole Palestina") not to rejoice over the death of Tiglath-pileser III, the "rod" that had smitten them.[16] From the "serpent's root" will come another poisonous snake. The "cockatrice," possibly an adder, cannot be identified with certainty. Likewise, the "fiery flying serpent" (lit. "a fiery flying one") pictures an aroused viper. The word "fiery" refers to the burning of the poisonous bite.[17] The easiest way of understanding the succession of serpents takes them as poetic references to a series of Assyrian kings. The sequence—the general serpent, the poisonous adder, the aroused and striking viper—suggests an intensification of the danger posed by the kings. After Tiglath-pileser III, a later Assyrian king, Sargon, conquered Philistia and carried away many of its leaders to Assyria. Sargon's son, Sennacherib, also conquered Philistia, v. 29.[18]

The "firstborn of the poor [dal, see 10:2]" will feed in that time. The child of the poor has no prospect of wealth, yet he will feed. The expression "firstborn of the poor" idiomatically represents the poorest of the poor. The "needy" (ʾebyôn) will have "safety" (beṭaḥ). The ʾebyôn is someone who is poor, in need of protection or material help. The word beṭaḥ refers to confidence, a sense of security that comes from trust in a person or thing. Both of these descriptive terms refer to Israel, a people harassed by Philistia during the reign of Ahaz, II Chronicles 28:18–19. In sharp contrast, the Lord will bring famine upon the Philistines, causing many to die. Their "root" and their "remnant," their children, will die of starvation, v. 30.

---

[16]Motyer, *The Prophecy of Isaiah,* p. 148; Barnes, I, 281; and Mauchline, p. 144, refer the broken rod to the death of Ahaz. The mention in v. 31 of the invasion coming from the north argues against this view. It is more consistent to apply the rod to one of the Assyrian kings.

[17]Stacey, p. 109, views the third serpent as "a mythical monster." Kaiser, *Isaiah 13–39,* p. 54, considers it a "fabulous winged, fiery serpent, the dragon,." Kraeling, p. 90, calls it "a product of mythical fancy." These views are extreme. The NIV translates "darting, venomous serpent," apparently referring to the swift strike of the serpent. This is a possible interpretation.

[18]Delitzsch, I, 318, and Näglesbach, pp. 318–19, refer the final two serpents to Hezekiah and Messiah. They make the first serpent represent the house of David. This is a general reference with no specific connection to Philistia. Watts, *Isaiah 1–33,* p. 219, understands the serpent as Shalmaneser. He makes both the cockatrice and the flying serpent refer to Sargon. While possible, the sequence rather suggests three Assyrian kings. Hailey, pp. 139–40, refers the rod to Assyria, the adder to Babylon, and the final serpent to an unspecified power that completes the destruction. Failing to identify the third serpent is unsatisfactory.

31 Howl, O gate; cry, O city; thou, whole Palestina, art dissolved: for there shall come from the north a smoke, and none shall be alone in his appointed times.

32 What shall one then answer the messengers of the nation? That the Lord hath founded Zion, and the poor of his people shall trust in it.

31–32 The Lord urges the Philistine cities to lament because they will be "dissolved" (*mûg*, or "melt away"). The verb *mûg* expresses the fact that God will "cause their melting," i.e., their weakening, as He judges them. A "smoke," the Assyrian army, will come from the north. The final phrase of the verse, "none shall be alone in his appointed times," is better "none shall be alone in his appointed place," i.e., his "ranks." The idea is that there will be no stragglers in the Assyrian army, v. 31. The "messengers of the nation" apparently refers to a delegation sent from Philistia to Judah seeking help against the Assyrian army. While we do not have a biblical record of this, it may well have happened.[19] The answer to them is that the Lord has founded Zion, Jerusalem, and the "poor [*'anî*, see 3:14] of His people" will trust in "it" (better "Him"), v. 32.[20]

Practical Applications from Chapter 14

1. God's Millennial Plan for His People. After the enemies of Israel fall in judgment, the Lord will extend mercy to His people. He will restore them to the land of Palestine. Some of the Gentiles will become Jews, v. 1. Others will become servants to Israel. Those who at one time ruled the Jews are now themselves ruled by the Jews, v. 2.

2. The Judgment of Satan.

   a. The overthrow of the king. In the time that Israel enjoys rest from her trials, v. 3, she will taunt the king of Babylon. He no longer rages against her or oppresses her, v. 4. The Lord has broken his power, v. 5. He had formerly persecuted the nations. Now he himself is persecuted, v. 6.

   b. The rejoicing of the earth. The earth itself rejoices over Babylon's fall, vv. 7–8.

---

[19]Leupold, I, 271, mentions the possibility that the delegation may have come after the destruction of the Assyrian army. The passage speaks of God's protection of Jerusalem, not of what may have happened after Assyria's destruction.

[20]Numerous commentators and translations refer the pronoun to Zion. It is, however, God who protects. It is more logical to refer the pronoun to Him.

    c. The taunt by the dead. The members of sheol meet the Babylon-ian king at his arrival into "hell." Those who formerly ruled nations of the earth, v. 9, now taunt Babylon's king. Despite his former power, he has become weak like them, v. 10. His earthly glory and the music of his court are gone, v. 11.

    d. The fall of Satan. He who had brought weakness to the nations himself is humbled, v. 12. He had attempted to usurp the place of God (note the five "I will" statements), vv. 13–14. He now goes to the extremities of sheol, v. 15.

3. Judgment of the Wicked

    a. The fall of Babylon. Men look in amazement on the unburied corpse of Babylon's king. They recall his conquests and the fear that he stirred in others, v. 16. They recall his destruction of cities and the prisoners that he took captive, v. 17. Other kings who die lie buried in glorious tombs or graves, v. 18. The king of Babylon, however, lies in dishonor on the open ground. He lies surrounded with the bodies of others who have died. They are covered with stones thrown over them, v. 19. He has brought destruction to his land and people. His body will not be joined with others in its burial. Further, his children will also not receive honor, v. 20. They will die in judgment, v. 21. The Lord of hosts will rise up against Babylon, v. 22. The city will become a place for birds to dwell. It will become swampy from standing water. The Lord will sweep it with a broom of destruction, v. 23.

    b. The fall of Assyria. The Lord has sworn a solemn oath, v. 24. He will break the Assyrians "in my land"; cf. 37:36. This will release His people from the yoke placed upon them by the Assyrians, v. 25. This judgment will affect the whole earth, v. 26. The Lord of heavenly and earthly hosts has purposed this judgment. No one can keep it from happening, v. 27.

    c. The fall of Philistia. Isaiah reproves the Philistines, v. 28. They should not rejoice over the death of the Assyrian king because additional kings will arise to strike them, v. 29. Israel will have food and safety but the Philistines will know famine and danger, v. 30. The Assyrian army will cover the land, v. 31. The Philistines will plead with Judah to help them. The Jews, however, will trust in the Lord, not in an alliance with a heathen nation, v. 32.

1 *The burden of Moab. Because in the night Ar of Moab is laid waste,*
and brought to silence; because in the night Kir of Moab is laid
waste, and brought to silence;
2 *He is gone up to Bajith, and to Dibon, the high places, to weep:*
Moab shall howl over Nebo, and over Medeba: on all their heads
shall be baldness, and every beard cut off.

ISAIAH 15

Isaiah now prophesies judgment on Moab. From its sordid beginning, Genesis 19:31–37, Moab opposed Israel throughout its history. During the reigns of Omri and Ahab, Israel oppressed the Moabites. An archaeological find, the *Mesha^c* inscription, line 5, states that "Chemosh was angry with his land for many days."[1] Mesha^c, king of Moab, rebelled against Israel, taking territory back from the Jews, II Kings 1:1; 3:5. This led to an invasion by Israel and Judah, placing the Moabites in subjection again, II Kings 3:6–25. Later, Babylon defeated Moab.[2] Many of the Moabites fled to Egypt at this time, and Moab declined as a nation. Archaeological evidence shows that they were virtually gone by the early sixth century B.C.

Not only was Moab an enemy of Israel but they also worshiped a heathen god. The religion of Moab centered on the god Chemosh. The *Mesha^c* inscription mentions him twelve times. Mesha^c portrays him as his sovereign: "Chemosh lived in it [Medeba, an old Moabite town] in my days" (lines 8–9). "Chemosh said to me, Go, seize Nebo against Israel" (line 14). "Chemosh drove him out before me" (line 19). "Chemosh said to me, Go, fight in Haronen" (line 32). This wickedness lies behind Isaiah's oracle of judgment.

C. Against Moab 15:1–16:14
1. Cry of Distress 15:1–9

1–4 Isaiah proclaims a "burden" (*maśśaʾ*, see 13:1) to Moab. The city of Ar has not been positively identified but is thought to have been located about twelve miles south of the Arnon River. Kir may have been the capital of Moab, Kir-Haraseth, II Kings 3:25 (or Kir-Heres,

---

[1] The Moabite stone has a record of Mesha^c, the king of Moab, in the late ninth century B.C. The stone was discovered in 1868 by F. A. Klein, a German missionary at Diban, north of the Arnon River about thirteen miles east of the Dead Sea.

[2] Josephus, *Antiquities* 10.9.7.

3 *In their streets they shall gird themselves with sackcloth: on the tops of their houses, and in their streets, every one shall howl, weeping abundantly.*
4 *And Heshbon shall cry, and Elealeh: their voice shall be heard even unto Jahaz: therefore the armed soldiers of Moab shall cry out; his life shall be grievous unto him.*

Jer. 48:31, 36). It lay about eighteen miles south of the Arnon River. Both of these cities will be destroyed and "brought to silence" (lit. "cut off"), v. 1. The Moabites will go to "Bajith," lit. "the house," referring to a temple, probably of Chemosh, their chief god. They also go to Dibon, apparently the location of the "high places," places of heathen worship.[3] Dibon lay about three miles north of the Arnon River. The people weep over the loss of Nebo and Medeba. We do not know the location of Nebo. Logically, it must have been near Mt. Nebo, about fifteen miles due west of the northern tip of the Dead Sea. Medeba was three miles southeast of Mt. Nebo. The Moabites cut their hair and shave their beards, marks of their sorrow, cf. Ezra 9:3; Jeremiah 16:6; 47:5; 48:37; Amos 8:10, v. 2. They put on "sackcloth," a dark garment made from coarsely woven goat's hair. It was worn as a sign of mourning; cf. Genesis 37:34; I Kings 21:27. The people weep throughout the cities, on their housetops and in the "streets" (*reḥôb*). The word *reḥôb* refers to an open place in the city. This likely refers to the area inside the city gate that often served as a market, a meeting place, and the seat of government, v. 3. Heshbon, three miles northeast of Mt. Nebo, and Elealeh, a mile north of Heshbon, join in the weeping. The people of Jahaz hear of their grief as fugitives from the other towns pass through it. Jahaz lay about eleven miles south of Heshbon. Even the Moabite soldiers cry out in sorrow. The phrase "his life [better 'soul']" refers to Moab as a nation. They grieve over the national threat, v. 4.

---

[3]The grammar is difficult. The phrase *ʿalâ habbayit weḏîbon* is lit. "the house [or temple] goes up and Dibon." Leupold, I, 276, translates, "She went up to the sanctuary and Dibon [went up] to the high places to weep." This reads the 3ms verb as a 3fs and assumes the omission of a preposition and a verb in the second clause. Delitzsch, I, 324, translates, "They go up to the temple-house and Dibon. . . ." This either reads the 3ms verb as a 3mp or, more probably, understands it as a collective. Herbert, *Isaiah 1–39*, p. 107, follows the NEB, "The people of Dibon go up to the hill-shrines to weep." This omits the *waw*-consecutive and paraphrases the rest. Other authors adopt additional approaches. The AV follows the MT. This assumes that *habbayit* is the proper name Bajith, which is possible although we do not know of such a place. Since we do not have much archaeological or textual evidence from Moab, this is possible. With Delitzsch, I translate *habbayit* as "the house" and refer it to a heathen temple.

5 *My heart shall cry out for Moab; his fugitives shall flee unto Zoar,*
an heifer of three years old: for by the mounting up of Luhith with
weeping shall they go it up; for in the way of Horonaim they shall
raise up a cry of destruction.
6 *For the waters of Nimrim shall be desolate: for the hay is withered*
away, the grass faileth, there is no green thing.
7 *Therefore the abundance they have gotten, and that which they have*
laid up, shall they carry away to the brook of the willows.
8 *For the cry is gone round about the borders of Moab; the howling*
thereof unto Eglaim, and the howling thereof unto Beerelim.
9 *For the waters of Dimon shall be full of blood: for I will bring more*
upon Dimon, lions upon him that escapeth of Moab, and upon the
remnant of the land.

5–9 The first-person pronoun indicates that Isaiah sympathizes with
Moab in her trial.[4] Her people flee to Zoar, a small city located south of
the Dead Sea in biblical times; cf. Genesis 19:22–23. The phrase "an
heifer of three years old" should be transliterated from *ʿeglat šelišîyâ*,
"Eglath-Shelishiyah."[5] This town apparently lay south of the Dead Sea.
The people flee here as well. They weep as they go to Luhith, an unknown location at the top of some ascent ("mounting up"). They go to
Horonaim, probably near Luhith. As they go, they "raise" (*yeʿoʿerû*) a
"cry of destruction," i.e., a cry caused by the destruction that has come
on them, v. 5.[6] In addition, a drought causes the "waters of Nimrim," a
fertile area thought to lie southeast of the Dead Sea, to dry up; cf. Jeremiah 48:34. The vegetation withers, v. 6. The Moabites carry their

---

[4]Motyer, p. 150, and Goldingay, p. 108, understand the Lord as the one expressing His
grief. The statement here, however, is similar to that of 16:9, 11. It is best to attribute
both passages to Isaiah.

[5]Whitehouse, I, 208; Grogan, pp. 115–16; and Skinner, *Isaiah I–XXXIX*, p. 126, translate *ʿeglat šelišîyâ* something like "the third Eglath," an unknown location. It is hard to defend the view when we do not know of two other Eglaths. Barnes, I, 291; Rawlinson, I,
269; and Fausset, p. 614, understand the fugitives as raising their voices like a three-
year-old heifer. The suggestion requires that we read too much into the verse. Vine,
p. 47, understands the "heifer [or ox] of three years old," an ox in the fullness of its
strength, as a description of Zoar. The view is doubtful. The phrase occurs again in Jer.
48:34, where it clearly does not refer to Zoar.

[6]The verb *yeʿoʿerû* is unique. BDB, p. 735, locates it as a *pilpel* from *ʿûr*, "raise." KB,
II, 802–3, locates it similarly but proposes "to keep busy." The form is apparently con-
tracted from *yeʿarʿerû*. The form is exceptional, occurring only here.

"abundance" (*yitrâ*), their food, with them as they flee.[7] They go to the "brook [*naḥal*, see 7:19] of the willows [*ᶜᵃrabîm*]," an unknown location, trying to escape the threat to Moab. We do not know the exact nature of *ᶜᵃrabîm*. The root *ᶜarab* is "to be dark." Apparently, it refers to trees with dark wood, perhaps poplar, v. 7.[8] Their sorrow goes throughout the land of Moab. It reaches Eglaim, an uncertain location. The cries likewise reach Beer-elim, "well of trees." Once more, we do not know the location. From the context, both of these places are thought to lie south of the Dead Sea, v. 8. The "waters of Dimon," a stream east of the Dead Sea, run red with blood.[9] The Lord now speaks directly. He promises to bring "more" (lit. "additions"), added trials, to Dimon. He will bring "lions" (*ᵓaryeh*, better "a lion") upon those who flee. The use of a singular word here suggests that the "lion" should be understood poetically. It likely refers to an additional invasion of Moab by an Assyrian or Babylonian king. We cannot, however, identify the king with certainty, v. 9.[10]

---

[7]The form *yitrâ* occurs only here. The root *yatar* means "to be left over," leading to the idea of abundance. Näglesbach, p. 201, understands the "abundance" as the valuables of the people. This is a possible view.

[8]Fausset, p. 614, and Barnes, I, 292, transliterate *ᶜᵃrabîm* as Arabians. Mauchline, p. 147, and Whitehouse, I, 209, refer it to the Arabah, the depression south of the Dead Sea extending to the Gulf of Aqaba. Kaiser, *Isaiah 13–39*, p. 69, and Grogan, p. 117, identify this as the Wadi el Ḥesa on the southern border where Moab joins Edom. Delitzsch, I, 328, and Hailey, p. 147, view the wood as willow. Price, p. 79, suggests oleanders. We cannot be dogmatic.

[9]Rawlinson, I, 269, and Delitzsch, I, 329, among others, understand Dimon as Dibon and identify the waters with the nearby Arnon River. Näglesbach, p. 201, identifies the waters as tributaries of the Arnon since blood shed in Dibon would not reach the Arnon. It is tempting to identify Dimon with Dibon. Unfortunately, we do not know enough of the geography of Moab in biblical times to be sure.

[10]Henry, p. 93, and Barnes, I, 293, misunderstand the singular form of *ᵓaryeh* and so relate it to wild beasts. Rawlinson, I, 269, suggests either Nebuchadnezzar or Ashur-banipal. Whitehouse, I, 209, thinks it is Tiglath-pileser III. Delitzsch, I, 329, relates the lion to the nation of Judah. There is clearly no way of identifying the king represented by the lion.

Practical Application from Chapter 15

Once more, the Lord encourages His people with the knowledge that He will protect them from their enemies. He will destroy the major cities of Moab, v. 1. The Moabites will call to no avail on their false gods for help. They will weep over the fall of their cities. They will openly show the signs of their grief, v. 2. They put on sackcloth to show their sorrow. The people weep on the tops of their houses and in the streets. They are overcome with grief, v. 3. The people of their cities will cry out in sorrow. Their soldiers will grieve, v. 4. Isaiah sympathizes with the Moabites because of their trials. The Moabites flee to other cities, lifting their voices as they lament the destruction that has come on them, v. 5. To add to their affliction, the Lord allows a drought to come on them, v. 6. The Moabites carry their food with them as they flee, v. 7. The grieving of Moab reaches new cities, v. 8. The blood of the slain colors the waters, yet the Lord promises to bring additional destruction on Moab, v. 9.

a. Note the grief caused by the punishment. Moab had lived with no thought of God. Now they grieve as He sends punishment to them.

b. Note the rightness of God's punishment. Moab had begun with the knowledge of the true God. Later, they turned their back on Him and worshiped false gods. Now the true God pours out His wrath on them for their sin.

c. Note the completeness of God's punishment. He will not allow sin to go unpunished.

1 *Send ye the lamb to the ruler of the land from Sela to the wilderness,*
  unto the mount of the daughter of Zion.
2 *For it shall be, that, as a wandering bird cast out of the nest, so the*
  daughters of Moab shall be at the fords of Arnon.

ISAIAH 16

Chapter 16 continues the thought introduced in c. 15, God's judgment on Moab. Isaiah advises the Moabites what to do to gain the favor of God. If they will come to Judah for help, if they will forsake their sins and begin to worship the true God, they can find deliverance. If not, the judgment from God will soon fall upon them.

2. Conditions for Deliverance 16:1–5

1–2 Chapter 15 had made it clear that Moab faces the prospect of national judgment. There is only one hope. Isaiah advises the Moabites to send tribute lambs (*kar*) to the king of Judah.[1] The word *kar*, "the lamb," is a collective singular referring to many tribute lambs.[2] The Moabites should send them from "Sela," the Hebrew name for Petra and the capital of Edom.[3] The Moabites apparently have hidden themselves in Edom. From there, the lambs will be driven north through the wilderness and then to the city of Zion, Jerusalem, v. 1. The Moabites face danger from the invading Assyrians. As a "wandering bird" (*ʿôp̄ nôḏēḏ*) that has been "cast out of the nest" (*qēn mᵉšullāḥ*, or "scattered nestlings"), so the Moabites will come to the fords of the Arnon River as they flee.[4] The

---

[1]Young, I, 461; Alexander, I, 321; and Brueggemann, *Isaiah 1–39*, p. 141, understand the passage as the words of the Moabite leaders advising the nation to accept the rule of Judah. Their tribute would acknowledge this. The view is possible although elsewhere Moab seeks freedom from Judah's control, II Kings 3:5; 13:20; 24:2.

[2]The noun *kar* is masculine singular. The OT often uses the ms noun as a collective while the fs denotes an individual member of the class. Cf. Williams, *Hebrew Syntax: An Outline,* II.2 (b), 27; Waltke and O'Connor 6.3.2c; 7.2.1c; and G.K. 122 *t*.

[3]Rawlinson, I, 276, understands *selaᶜ* as a collective singular indicating the "rocks" of Moab. While this is possible, it then becomes difficult to locate the "wilderness" since the natural route from Moab would go toward the ford of the Jordan River north of the Dead Sea. Slotki, p. 77, mentions that older Jewish commentators understood *selaᶜ midbarâ* as a proper noun, Sela-Midbarah. It is better to understand the *hê* at the end of *midbarâ* as expressing direction toward the *midbar*, the "wilderness" between Edom and Jerusalem. See G.K. 26 *h*, 90 *c*.

[4]Both *ʿôp̄* and *qēn* should be understood as collectives. The phrase reads "as wandering birds, as scattered nestlings."

3 *Take counsel, execute judgment; make thy shadow as the night in the midst of the noonday; hide the outcasts; bewray not him that wandereth.*
4 *Let mine outcasts dwell with thee, Moab; be thou a covert to them from the face of the spoiler: for the extortioner is at an end, the spoiler ceaseth, the oppressors are consumed out of the land.*
5 *And in mercy shall the throne be established: and he shall sit upon it in truth in the tabernacle of David, judging, and seeking judgment, and hasting righteousness.*

Arnon River was the northern border of Moab. Apparently, the "daughters of Moab," the Moabite women, take the shortest route to Judah to find safety, v. 2.[5]

3–5 The Moabites appeal to the Israelites to "take [*habî'û*, 'cause to bring,' i.e., 'give'] counsel," advising them on their efforts to escape. Israel should "execute judgment" (*ᶜaśû pᵉlîlâ*, better "make a decision"), again guiding the Moabites to safety.[6] They plead with Israel to become a shade to them, protecting them from the sun of Assyria's heat. They seek to hide themselves in Judah and ask that the Jews not betray them, v. 3.

Verse 4 continues Moab's plea. The first part, "Let mine outcasts [*niddaḥay*] dwell with thee, Moab" is better "Let my outcasts, the ones of Moab, dwell with you."[7] Isaiah asks that Moab's "outcasts," driven

---

[5]Among others, Fausset, p. 615, and Rawlinson, I, 276, refer the phrase "daughters of Moab" to the general population of Moab. While the singular "daughter" may refer to people, the plural "daughters" normally refers to women, e.g., 3:16–17; 4:4.

[6]The verb in the first phrase is an mp imperative with the *qᵉrê* an fs imperative. Since the sense of the first two phrases is parallel, I would read the first verb with the *kᵉtîb*, *habî'û*, and apply the thought of the passage to the Moabites. Näglesbach, p. 203, applies the passage to Isaiah as he urges the Moabites to place themselves in subjection to Judah. The third and fourth verbs are fs imperatives: "hide . . . bewray. . . ." Moab here appeals to the nation of Israel considered as a unit rather than to individual members of the nation.

[7]In form, *niddaḥay* has the personal pronoun modifying the participle, "my banished ones." If we understand Moab as a vocative, the verse is the Lord's speech to Moab that they should shelter those who flee from Judah. This does not fit the context. We may also understand Moab in apposition to *niddaḥay*, explaining who the outcasts are: "my outcasts, i.e., Moab." Fausset, p. 615, understands the *ay* as an old construct ending, "the outcasts of Moab." In either of these last views, we arrive at the position expressed above. Another approach repoints *niddaḥay* to make it construct, *niddaḥê*, and lets v. 4*a* continue the plea begun in v. 3. Mauchline, p. 147, and Rawlinson, I, 277, adopt this change. The LXX supports this but it may be interpretive. At the same time, the MT makes sense if we understand "Moab" in apposition to "outcasts."

away from their homes by the enemy, might stay in Judah.[8] Let Judah be a "covert" to them, a shelter from the "spoiler" (or "destroyer"). The "extortioner" (*hammeṣ*), the Assyrian oppressor, will soon come to an end, no more spoiling others.[9] The "oppressors" (*romes*) themselves will be consumed. The word *romes* refers to those who trample on others. They will be taken away where they can trample others no more, v. 4.

The thought of deliverance from Assyria causes Isaiah to look into the future. He sees the time when the Lord will establish His throne in "mercy" (*ḥesed*). The word *ḥesed* occurs widely to refer to lovingkindness, mercy, or goodness. There is a strong component of loyalty in the word. Often, it may be translated "loyalty." The king will rule from the "tabernacle [better 'tent'] of David," i.e., continue the Davidic line of rule; cf. II Samuel 7:16. He will sit upon the throne to bring "judgment" (*mišpaṭ*, better "justice," see 1:17) and "righteousness" (*ṣedeq*, see 1:21) to the people. From the description—a loyal Ruler, ruling from the "tabernacle of David," justice and righteousness—it is clear that Isaiah describes the millennial reign of Christ. He will be swift to execute righteousness. The implied thought of this is that Moab should enter into the worship of Israel's God, v. 5.[10]

---

[8]Vine, p. 48, gives v. 4 an eschatological meaning. The Lord asks Moab to shelter His people during the persecution of Antichrist. Pentecost, p. 334, refers the name "spoiler" to Antichrist. It is, however, arbitrary to pick one name from the verse as naming Antichrist. While v. 4 leads into a messianic thought, the context thus far is specific to Moab.

[9]The word *hammeṣ* is a *hapax legomenon*. It apparently is a *qal* participle from the root *mîṣ*, "to press, squeeze," which occurs only in Prov. 30:33. The root meaning of "press, squeeze," together with the parallel terms "spoiler" and "oppressors" lead to the meaning "extortioner." Leupold, I, 284; Watts, *Isaiah 1–33*, p. 224; and Barnes, I, 300, suggest "oppressor," also a possible translation.

[10]Alexander, I, 324, understands the verse as a promise to the Jews. If they will shelter the fugitives of Moab, their own government will grow stronger. One from the house of David will appear to rule the land. Young, I, 463, adopts much the same position. Watts, *Isaiah 1–33*, p. 232, simply states that "aggression will cease when the Davidic dynasty holds sway over the territory again." Mauchline, p. 148, suggests that this is a "compliment to Judah to the effect that such a deliverance for Moab with their aid would be to the glory of the house of David and to its establishment in justice and righteousness on the throne of Judah." Kaiser, *Isaiah 13–39*, p. 73, states that the "hope is really of comfort only to the Jews. They can look beyond the distress which is coming upon them . . . to the age of salvation. It is of no benefit to the Moabites who beg for protection in their need." Since the verse does not mention Moab, it is not possible to be dogmatic. Since, however, the context deals with Moab, it is reasonable to assume that they will in some way be involved with Messiah's kingdom. This is possible only if they worship the God of Israel.

6 *We have heard of the pride of Moab; he is very proud: even of his*
haughtiness, and his pride, and his wrath: but his lies shall not be so.
7 *Therefore shall Moab howl for Moab, every one shall howl: for the*
foundations of Kir-hareseth shall ye mourn; surely they are stricken.
8 *For the fields of Heshbon languish, and the vine of Sibmah: the*
lords of the heathen have broken down the principal plants thereof,
they are come even unto Jazer, they wandered through the wilder-
ness: her branches are stretched out, they are gone over the sea.

3. Cause of Disaster 16:6–12

6–8 Isaiah returns to the thought of c. 15, giving the cause of Moab's
judgment as their pride ($g^{e\jmath}\hat{o}n$). By repeating variants of $g^{e\jmath}\hat{o}n$, Isaiah
emphasizes Moab's arrogance: $g^{e\jmath}\hat{o}n$ ("pride") . . . $ge^{\jmath}$ ("proud")[11] . . .
$ga^{\jmath a}wat\hat{o}$ ("haughtiness") . . . $g^{e\jmath}\hat{o}n\hat{o}$ ("pride"). Despite their boasts, "his
lies shall not be so," i.e., his empty words will not come to pass, v. 6.
The judgment that comes on Moab will cause them to howl with grief.
They will "mourn" (or "groan") for the "foundations" ($^{\jmath a}\check{s}\hat{i}\check{s}$, better
"raisin cakes"). Raisin cakes are delicacies made from grapes from the
vineyards of Kir-hareseth, v. 7. The fields of Heshbon, cf. 15:4, and the
vines of "Sibmah," an unknown location but probably near Heshbon,
will suffer destruction.[12] The "lords of the heathen," commanders of the
various groups in the Assyrian army, will break down (*halam*, "to hammer," thus "trample down") the "principal plants" (*śaroq*, lit. "vines").[13]
These had reached to Jazer, a city north of Moab, in the region occupied
by Gad. On the east, they grew as far as the "wilderness" between Palestine and Babylon. On the west, the vines grew on the other side of the
Dead Sea, v. 8.[14]

---

[11]The word *ge$^{\jmath}$* occurs only here. It is widely assumed to be a misspelling of *ge$^{\jmath}$â*.
Jer. 48:29, which repeats much of the verse, reads *ge$^{\jmath}$â*. 1QIsa^a and some Hebrew
manuscripts also include *ge$^{\jmath}$â*. No matter what the reading, the thought of pride does
not change.

[12]Stacey, p. 113, and Kaiser, *Isaiah 13–39*, p. 73, suggest that the vineyards represent
the land and the vines the people. The context, however, of vv. 6–10 gives too many details relating to the vines to let us take vines and vineyards symbolically.

[13]Among others, Mauchline, p. 149; Skinner, *Isaiah I–XXXIX*, p. 130; and Brueggemann, *Isaiah 1–39*, p. 144, understand "lords of the heathen [or 'nations']" as the object
rather than the subject. They think that Isaiah speaks of the influence that the wine has
on the heathen leaders. Verses 9–10, however, refer to the grief that comes over the destruction of the vines. Why would the heathen destroy that which brought them pleasure?

[14]Delitzsch, I, 334, and Whitehouse, I, 213, understand the phrase "gone over the sea"
as hyperbole. The vines grow close to the sea, not on the other side. Delitzsch further
cites Jer. 48:32, which refers to the "Sea of Jazer." The "sea" here is thus not the Dead

9 *Therefore I will bewail with the weeping of Jazer the vine of Sibmah:
I will water thee with my tears, O Heshbon, and Elealeh: for the
shouting for thy summer fruits and for thy harvest is fallen.*

10 *And gladness is taken away, and joy out of the plentiful field; and in
the vineyards there shall be no singing, neither shall there be shouting: the treaders shall tread out no wine in their presses; I have
made their vintage shouting to cease.*

11 *Wherefore my bowels shall sound like an harp for Moab, and mine
inward parts for Kirharesh.*

12 *And it shall come to pass, when it is seen that Moab is weary on the
high place, that he shall come to his sanctuary to pray; but he shall
not prevail.*

9–12 The prophet grieves with the Moabites.[15] Although the wickedness of Moab has forced such judgment, Isaiah still expresses his sorrow
at what they must go through. He will grieve with the Moabites in Jazer
over the loss of their vines. He will weep with those in Heshbon and
Elealeh; cf. 15:4. There is no longer "shouting" (*hêdad*) over the summer
crops (*qêṣek*) and the harvest (*qᵉṣîrek*).[16] The wordplay with *qêṣek* and
qᵉṣîrek is typical of Isaiah's style of writing, v. 9. There is no longer joy
in the fields and in the vineyards. Those who tread the juice from the
grapes no longer tread the presses (*yᵉqabîm*, see 5:2). There would normally be rejoicing at this time. Now, the Lord has made their joyful
"shouting" to cease, v. 10. The prophet continues to grieve for Moab.
His "bowels" (*meᶜeh*, metaphoric for emotions) vibrate like the strings of
a "harp"; cf. 5:12. His "inward parts," again representing his emotions,
are stirred, v. 11. Moab will continue to rely on her gods. He will weary
himself with prayer in the "high place," the heathen place of worship.
The principle Moabite god was Chemosh, Numbers 21:29. Among other
forms of worship, Chemosh required the sacrifice of children, II Kings

---

Sea but some unknown body of water near Jazer. Barnes, I, 302, argues similarly. Jeremiah, however, distinguishes the Sea of Jazer from the phrase "over the sea." There is no
reason to identify the Sea of Jazer as the "sea" mentioned here.

[15]As in 15:5, Motyer, *The Prophecy of Isaiah,* p. 154, makes this refer to the Lord as
He grieves over Moab. Ibn Ezra, p. 80, makes the verse refer to the Moabites, "whom the
prophet represents as speaking." It is more likely that Isaiah speaks here, expressing his
grief over the fate of the Moabites.

[16]Delitzsch, I, 335, makes *hêdad* the subject and treats it as the shout of the enemy
falling upon the vineyards of Moab as he takes them for himself. Kelley, p. 244, and
Kraeling, p. 93, treat the verse similarly. The word *hêdad* regularly refers to the shout of
the workers as they harvest the vines. It is also unlikely that Isaiah would give a different
sense here from what he gives the same word in v. 10.

13 This is the word that the Lord hath spoken concerning Moab since that time.

14 But now the Lord hath spoken, saying, Within three years, as the years of an hireling, and the glory of Moab shall be contemned, with all that great multitude; and the remnant shall be very small and feeble.

3:27. Moab will not, however, prevail over his enemy by relying on Chemosh, v. 12.

4. Coming of Destruction 16:13–14

13–14 The previous verses in c. 15–16 have been general as to the time of Moab's judgment. The Lord now gives Isaiah a new prophecy to make the prediction definite, v. 13.[17] Within three years, the judgment will come upon Moab. The three years are as "the years of an hireling." Just as a hireling serves for a definite number of years, so the judgment will come in a definite number of years. At that time, the "glory of Moab" will "be contemned" (better "be dishonored"). The phrase "great multitude" likely explains the "glory of Moab." The "great multitude" of inhabitants in Moab will be reduced to a "very small and feeble" remnant. Her nobles, her soldiers, her leaders, all will suffer in the judgment.

The problem introduced by the definite time is that Moab's judgment did not take place until the twenty-third year of Nebuchadnezzar, ca. 582 B.C.[18] Jeremiah, writing ca. 600 B.C., repeats much of Isaiah's prophecy concerning Moab (Jer. 48:1–46). How, then, do we explain the reference to "three years"? The easiest way is to relate it to an interim judgment, the details of which we do not know. This judgment will take place three years from Isaiah's prophecy. Because of continuing sin, Jeremiah was later called to prophesy an additional judgment, v. 14.[19]

---

[17]Cundall, *Proverbs–Isaiah 39*, p. 74, makes the startling claim that Isaiah admits here "that his prophecy concerning Moab including probably **15**.1–**16**.12, was not original." Rather than an admission that he has copied someone else's prophecy, it is more likely that Isaiah himself added vv. 13–14 to his own words. This would as well account for the change in form from poetry to prose.

[18]So Josephus, *Antiquities* 10.9.7.

[19]Näglesbach, p. 207, finds the fulfillment in some "fact which bore with it in principle the fall of Moab." We do not know of such a fact. Barnes, I, 305, quotes Jerome

Practical Applications from Chapter 16

1. The Hope of the Wicked. If we let Moab represent the wicked, the chapter gives guidance on avoiding the judgment of God. While the principles given in the chapter are specific to Moab, they stand for steps that will always bring God's favor to the wicked.

   a. Place yourself in submission to the people of God. Isaiah advised the Moabites to send tribute lambs to the king of Judah, v. 1. They should accept guidance from Israel and place themselves under Israel's protection, v. 3. They ask the Jews to take them into their country until the oppressor himself is overcome, v. 4.

   b. Begin to worship the true God. Moab worshiped false gods. We know of their chief god, Chemosh, mentioned in the Moabite stone and in the OT, e.g., Numbers 21:29; Jeremiah 48:7, 13, 46. There may well have been other gods. Isaiah tells them of Messiah's kingdom. He will establish His rule in loyalty. He will continue the line of David. He will judge in truth and righteousness. Moab should worship this true God.

2. The Judgment of the Wicked. Chapter 16 continues the thought of judgment seen throughout c.13–23. While this application is much the same from chapter to chapter, it is always appropriate to remind the wicked of their future.

   a. The cause of the judgment. Isaiah denounces the pride of Moab. The repeated words for "pride" give emphasis to the thought, v. 6.

   b. The result of the judgment. The Moabites come to the fords of the Arnon River, the northern border of the land, as they flee, v. 2. They howl with grief over the destruction of their fields and crops, vv. 7–8. The Moabites will no longer rejoice in their vineyards since the Lord has taken fruit from them, v. 10. The Moabites will call to their gods but to no avail, v. 12. The Lord has set the time of judgment. The great multitude will become a small remnant, v. 14.

---

to say that the judgment took place during the reign of Hezekiah under Sennacherib. Fausset, p. 616, views this as an example. Just as a hireling has a fixed term of employment, so the Lord has fixed the time for Moab's fall. Leupold, I, 289, understands the reference to "hireling" as indicating three toilsome years. After three hard years, Moab will fall. The time is not made clear as to when this takes place.

c. The compassion of the prophet. Isaiah weeps over the sin that requires Moab's punishment. He grieves with them over the loss of their vines and harvest. He weeps with the people in their cities, v. 9. The Lord has taken their harvest away, v. 10. Isaiah laments with them over the judgment, v. 11. It is their sin that causes His sorrow. If they will repent, there will be no need for judgment.

1 The burden of Damascus. Behold, Damascus is taken away from being a city, and it shall be a ruinous heap.
2 The cities of Aroer are forsaken: they shall be for flocks, which shall lie down, and none shall make them afraid.
3 The fortress also shall cease from Ephraim, and the kingdom from Damascus, and the remnant of Syria: they shall be as the glory of the children of Israel, saith the Lord of hosts.

ISAIAH 17

Isaiah denounces Damascus, one of the chief cities of Syria. The city lay east of the anti-Lebanon mountains, on the Abana River. The trade route passed through her. The city was about forty miles east-northeast of Dan, the northernmost city in Israel. This made Damascus the closest major city of Syria to Israel. It stands here as the representative of the whole nation. In Isaiah's day, Rezin ruled the city-state from Damascus. He and Israel had formed an alliance against Judah, 7:1–9. The first three verses focus on Syria. The remainder of the chapter takes up God's plan to judge Israel.

D. Against Syria and Israel 17:1–11
1. Ruin Predicted 17:1–3

1–3 Isaiah proclaims a "burden" (*maśśaʾ*, see 13:1) for Damascus. She will be "taken away" (*mûsar*).[1] She will become a "ruinous heap [*meʿî*]."[2] The conquest of Tiglath-pileser III fulfiled this prophecy in 732 B.C. One Assyrian inscription describes this: "I laid siege to and conquered the town Hadara, the inherited property of Rezon of Damascus, [the place where] he was born. I brought away as prisoners 800 (of its) inhabitants with their possessions, . . . their large (and) small cattle. 750 prisoners from Kurussa [. . . prisoners] from Irma, 550 prisoners

---

[1]Watts, *Isaiah 1–33*, p. 236, notes that the masculine form of *mûsar* is a problem since *dammeśeq*, Damascus, is a feminine noun. There are numerous examples, however, of gender disagreement in the OT for a variety of reasons. Isaiah may have used the masculine in direct contrast with the future weakness of the city, a condition normally expressed in the feminine.

[2]The form *meʿî* is a *hapax legomenon*. The noun is from *ʿawâ*, "to bend, twist," a doubly weak verb that often gives rise to unusual forms. There are related forms translated "heap" or "heaps." It is entirely possible that Isaiah chose the word because of its assonance with *meʿîr*, "city." Watts, *Isaiah 1–33*, p. 236, derives it from *maʿâ*, a root that does not occur in the OT but underlies nouns that refer to the inward organs. He translates, "twisted," an adjective modifying *mappalâ*, "ruin."

from Metuna I brought (also) away. 592 towns . . . of the 16 districts of the country of Damascus I destroyed (making them look) like hills of (ruined cities over which) the flood (had swept)," v. 1.[3]

There are at least three "cities of Aroer" in the OT. There was an Aroer on the north bank of the Arnon River, which belonged to the area occupied by Reuben (Deut. 2:36; 3:12; 4:48; Josh. 13:15–16). A second Aroer, modern Ararah, lay twelve miles southeast of Beer-sheba, I Samuel 30:28; I Chronicles 11:44. There was also an Aroer in the area occupied by Gad (Num. 32:34; Josh. 13:25; II Sam. 24:5). We do not know the location of this today. It is likely that Isaiah thought of the northernmost Aroer in Gad since the Assyrians would come to it first.[4]

The "cities of Aroer" include the smaller cities in that region.[5] No matter which Aroer is in view, the point is that it will become desolate, a place in which flocks will graze in peace, v. 2.[6] Isaiah introduces Ephraim here since she allied herself with Syria; cf. 7:1–2, 5–6. Ephraim, representing the whole nation of Israel, will lose her "fortress" (*mibṣar*), probably referring to her capital, Samaria. We do not know of any one "fortress" that distinguished Israel. The word *mibṣar* indicates a "fortified city," II Kings 17:9; Jeremiah 5:17, a defense in which Israel might well trust.[7] The Lord will remove this. He will also take away the self-rule of Damascus. The city's "remnant" will go into captivity. The

---

[3]Adapted from *Ancient Near Eastern Texts*, ed. James B. Pritchard, p. 283.

[4]Rawlinson, I, 289, identifies Aroer as Gargar, a town mentioned in the annals of Sargon as allied with Damascus and Samaria. While this is possible, we do not have enough information to make the identification certain.

[5]Näglesbach, p. 210; Delitzsch, I, 341; and Von Orelli, p. 108, suppose that the "cities of Aroer" include both of the northern Aroers. The phrase "cities of . . ." occurs over one hundred times in the OT. It commonly refers to cities belonging to something or someone else. This includes belonging to another city, II Sam. 2:3; cf. Num. 21:25; Josh. 13:17; 15:44; to a region, Josh. 15:9; 17:9; to a king, Josh. 13:10, 31; II Sam. 8:8; to a nation, I Sam. 6:18; 30:29; and to a purpose, Num. 35:11; I Kings 9:19. It is reasonable to so understand the phrase here with the "cities of Aroer" being the cities belonging to Aroer.

[6]The opening part of the verb illustrates Isaiah's use of assonance. The phrase "the cities of Aroer are forsaken" reads *ᶜᵃzubôt ᶜarê ᶜᵃroᶜer*. This is typical of Isaiah's writing style.

[7]Among others, Leupold, I, 293–94; Leslie, p. 45; and Wade, p. 116, understand the "fortress" as Damascus itself, a buffer that stood between Assyria and Israel. Näglesbach, p. 211, interprets *mibṣar* as a collective, "all defense." These are also possible views of the "fortress."

4 *And in that day it shall come to pass, that the glory of Jacob shall be made thin, and the fatness of his flesh shall wax lean.*

5 *And it shall be as when the harvestman gathereth the corn, and reapeth the ears with his arm; and it shall be as he that gathereth ears in the valley of Rephaim.*

6 *Yet gleaning grapes shall be left in it, as the shaking of an olive tree, two or three berries in the top of the uppermost bough, four or five in the outmost fruitful branches thereof, saith the Lord God of Israel.*

Syrians will become "as the glory of the children of Israel," something that was no longer significant, v. 3.

2. Reaping Accomplished 17:4–11

4–6 The next section focuses on Israel, allied with Syria to their own hurt. The phrase "in that day" naturally sets off the paragraphs, vv. 4, 7, 9. In the first paragraph, Isaiah pictures the distress of the nation in three ways: (1) some sickness causing the leanness of a fat man; (2) the reaping of a harvest; and (3) the gleaning of olives from the tree. The Lord will include "the glory of Jacob," Israel, in the judgment.[8] The judgment will reduce his "glory." It will be "made thin" (*dalal* or "brought low"). The root *dalal* often refers to material loss, e.g., Judges 6:6; Proverbs 14:31, v. 4. Just as the farmer harvests his grain in the "valley of Rephaim," so the enemy will harvest the spoil from Israel.[9] The name Rephaim ("giants") came from the giants who lived in Palestine. The "valley of Rephaim" was about three miles long. It ran southwest from Jerusalem toward Bethlehem, v. 5. Isaiah next compares the land to a tree from which olives are gleaned. The workers are "shaking" (better "striking") the tree, beating off the olives, so that only a few remain on the branches. In the same way, only a few people will be left to live in the land, v. 6.

---

[8]While the term "Jacob" normally refers to Judah, the context here makes it clear that Isaiah speaks of Israel. Leupold, I, 294, and Näglesbach, p. 212, consider the phrase "glory of Jacob" rhetorical variation referring to Israel. Young, I, 470, relates the phrase to Israel as descended from Jacob. Brueggemann, *Isaiah 1–39*, p. 147, relates the passage to both Judah and Israel.

[9]The AV along with most other translations reads the MT *qaṣîr*, "harvest," as *qoṣer*, "reaper." The 3ms pronoun later in the verse supports this change in the vowel pointing.

7 *At that day shall a man look to his Maker, and his eyes shall have respect to the Holy One of Israel.*

8 *And he shall not look to the altars, the work of his hands, neither shall respect that which his fingers have made, either the groves, or the images.*

9 *In that day shall his strong cities be as a forsaken bough, and an uppermost branch, which they left because of the children of Israel: and there shall be desolation.*

10 *Because thou hast forgotten the God of thy salvation, and hast not been mindful of the rock of thy strength, therefore shalt thou plant pleasant plants, and shalt set it with strange slips:*

11 *In the day shalt thou make thy plant to grow, and in the morning shalt thou make thy seed to flourish: but the harvest shall be a heap in the day of grief and of desperate sorrow.*

7–8 At that "day" of judgment, the "man" who has escaped the enemy will glory in his Creator God, v. 7. He will no longer trust in the "altars" that he himself has made; cf. II Kings 16:10–16. He will not "respect," look with favor on the idols made with his hands. The "groves" (*ᵓašerîm*, better transliterated Asherim) were wooden poles erected to represent the goddess Asherah, who was both a fertility and war goddess. The OT also refers to her as Ashtoreth and Astarte. The "images" (*ḥammanîm*) are thought to be incense altars, v. 8.[10]

9–11 In the time that God judges the land, the cities will become as "a forsaken bough [better 'wood']," no longer used by people. They will become as "an uppermost branch" (better "summit," the barren crest of a mountain). Isaiah relates these abandoned places to the wooded areas and mountaintops left by the Canaanites when they fled before Israel.[11]

---

[10]The word *ḥammanîm* is also thought to refer to sun idols. The root *ḥamam* means "to be hot." We may easily relate it either to the sun or to the burning of incense. The OT is not clear. Older commentators, e.g., Von Orelli, Whitehouse, tend to translate as sun idols. More recent authors, e.g., Mauchline, Watts, tend to interpret it as incense altars.

[11]Kelley, p. 245; Watts, *Isaiah 1–33*, p. 240; and Childs, p. 135, follow the LXX and emend *kaᶜᵃzûbat ḥaḥoreš weḥaᵓamîr*, "strong cities be as a forsaken bough, and an uppermost branch," to *kᵃᶜazabot haḥiwwî wᵉhaᵓemôrî*, "like the deserted cities of the Hivites and the Amorites." The NEB translates similarly. The emendation has the support of the LXX but not the Isaiah Scroll. We may explain the confusion of the LXX translators because of the rare word *ᵓamîr*, which occurs only in vv. 6, 9. The context in v. 6 forces a meaning something like "uppermost branches." It is unlikely that Isaiah would adopt a meaning totally different in v. 9. Since the combination of "Amorite" and "Hivite" occurs in that order fifteen of the sixteen times it appears in the OT, the LXX translators reversed the order of the words here, translating Αμορραῖοι καὶ οἱ Ευαῖοι. The change is not necessary.

As the land was before, so it will become again, v. 9. This judgment comes because the people have forgotten the God who has delivered them in the past. They have not remembered the "Rock" of their strength, a certain place of safety.[12] The parallelism between "God of thy salvation [*yašaᶜ*]"[13] and "Rock of thy strength" suggests that the "Rock" is a name for God. Forgetting Him, they had turned to heathen forms of worship. They had planted "pleasant plants" (*niṭᶜê naᶜᵃmanîm*) in their gardens, places of heathen worship; cf. 1:29; 65:3; 66:17.[14] They had set out "strange slips [*zᵉmôrâ*, or 'branches'],"[15] from the parallelism again referring to heathen worship, v. 10. They will devote themselves to the growth of their plants. The phrase "to grow" is better "you made a fence." They cared for the seed so that it would "flourish" (or "blossom"). Despite their care, the Lord will judge their work. Their harvest will be a "heap," plants uprooted and piled up. This will be a "day of grief [or 'sickliness'] and of desperate sorrow [or 'incurable pain']," v. 11.

---

[12]Isaiah also refers to God as the Rock in 8:14; 26:4 ("strength"); 30:29 ("mighty One"); and 44:8 ("God"). A summary occurs at 30:29.

[13]The word *yašaᶜ* occurs widely to refer to deliverance or salvation. The context tells whether physical deliverance or spiritual deliverance is in view. The one who brings deliverance is a "Savior." The word occurs several times in this sense to refer to the Messiah, e.g., 60:16; 63:8.

[14]Watts, *Isaiah 1–33*, p. 240, interprets *naᶜᵃmanîm* as "Beloved," the name of a fertility goddess. Among others, Herbert, *Isaiah 1–39*, p. 114; Stacey, p. 117; and Kraeling, p. 95, refer *niṭᶜê naᶜᵃmanîm*, "pleasant plants," to Adonis, the Greek name of the god Tammuz, Ezek. 8:14. Kaiser, *Isaiah 13–39*, p. 80, translates *naᶜᵃmanîm* as "anemones," a meaning it has nowhere in the OT. He then relates this to the worship of Adonis. While it is possible that the Jews worshiped Adonis, we cannot be dogmatic. Birks, p. 98, spiritualizes the passage. The "pleasant plants" and "strange slips" are those "worldly alliances and expedients, whereby they hoped to regain their lost honour and greatness." The word *naᶜᵃmanîm* is plural and should not be translated as the singular Adonis. In addition, the noun and adjectival forms of *naᶜem* occur widely as "pleasant, delightful." There is no reason to abandon the ordinary meaning for an unusual meaning here. From the context of the verse, it is clear that "pleasant plants" refers to heathen worship of some kind. We cannot be specific as to the nature of the worship.

[15]Delitzsch, I, 343–44, translates *zᵉmorâ* as "strange vines" and suggests that these were "sensual accompaniments" to heathen worship. Näglesbach, p. 214, considers these foreign grapevines "connected with heathen life to whose culture Israel devoted itself." Leupold, I, 297, translates, "slips for an alien god" and relates the phrase to heathen worship. The NASB combines these thoughts with its translation "vine slips of a strange god." The idea is of branches or shoots cut for planting in preparation for heathen worship.

12 *Woe to the multitude of many people, which make a noise like the noise of the seas; and to the rushing of nations, that make a rushing like the rushing of mighty waters!*

13 *The nations shall rush like the rushing of many waters: but God shall rebuke them, and they shall flee far off, and shall be chased as the chaff of the mountains before the wind, and like a rolling thing before the whirlwind.*

14 *And behold at eveningtide trouble; and before the morning he is not. This is the portion of them that spoil us, and the lot of them that rob us.*

E. Against Assyria 17:12–18:7
1. Rebuke of the Nation 17:12–14[16]

12–14 Isaiah extends the judgment of Syria and Israel naturally to Assyria, the nation who themselves judged other peoples. He pronounces "woe" on the "multitude" (lit. "tumult") of "many people." The Assyrian army included soldiers from the many nations they had conquered. As the army moved, tumult was natural. The use of waters to represent people occurs elsewhere in the book; cf. 8:7; 48:1; 59:19. The army moves with the force of mighty waters tumbling along the riverbanks, v. 12. The nations involved in the army move like many waters joining together to form one great river. Despite their might, the Lord's rebuke causes them to flee. Isaiah pictures their flight as "chaff" blown by the wind and "a rolling thing," whirling dust or a tumbling weed, before the storm, v. 13. Trouble comes upon them in the evening. In the morning, the army is "not," devastated. This is the future of those who set themselves against the people of God. This last verse virtually requires us to relate the passage to the deliverance described in II Kings 19:35–36, v. 14.

---

[16]There is widespread dispute about the purpose of vv. 12–14. Barnes, I, 312, thinks that they are unconnected with what goes before. He sees the passage as describing Sennacherib's invasion of Judah and the overthrow of his army. Skinner, *Isaiah I–XXXIX*, p. 137, sees no connection either with vv. 1–11 or with c. 18. Alexander, I, 339, thinks that c. 17 and 18 form a single prophecy. Kaiser, *Isaiah 13–39*, p. 85, and Whitehouse, I, 221, make vv. 12–14 introduce 18:1–6. Fausset, p. 618, and Cundall, *Proverbs—Isaiah 39*, p. 75, treat vv. 12–14 as the conclusion to vv. 1–11 although they understand it differently. Fausett makes it a promise that Judah will not be "utterly destroyed." Cundall sees the passage as the Assyrian army sweeping away the apostate people of Judah. I understand the paragraph as the introduction to c. 18.

Practical Applications from Chapter 17

1. The heathen are destroyed. The wicked may triumph for a while. God, however, will bring judgment upon them. Verses 5–6 aptly compare this to a harvest. The farmer reaps his corn and gathers his grapes and olives. He leaves only a few berries. In the same way, God will reap His harvest of judgment upon the heathen.

2. The purpose of judgment is to punish wickedness and to purify the people. When God punishes the people, those who are left will recognize Him as the Creator God and the "Holy One of Israel," v. 7. Men will leave their idols and heathen places of worship as they turn to the Lord in worship, v. 8.

3. Men must have a god, either the true God of Creation or a false god created by man. When men forget the God who has delivered them in the past, the God who is a "Rock of strength," they will turn to a god of their own making. They will build their heathen centers for worshiping this god, v. 10. They will devote great care to these places. The end, however, will be ruin and great tragedy, v. 11.

1 *Woe to the land shadowing with wings, which is beyond the rivers of Ethiopia:*

2 *That sendeth ambassadors by the sea, even in vessels of bulrushes upon the waters, saying, Go, ye swift messengers, to a nation scattered and peeled, to a people terrible from their beginning hitherto; a nation meted out and trodden down, whose land the rivers have spoiled!*

ISAIAH 18

Isaiah now turns to the nation of Ethiopia. His remarks here, however, do not pronounce judgment. That will come in c. 20. Isaiah encourages the nation. At this time, Ethiopia was an independent nation that was powerful enough to control Egypt. The warlike tendencies of Assyria must have brought concern to them. Isaiah now writes to assure the people that Assyria will not trouble them. The Lord will judge the Assyrians. This will free Ethiopia from any possible immediate threat.

2. Confidence of the Lord 18:1–7

1–2 The initial particle "woe" (*hôy*, see 1:4) should be translated "Ho," as in 55:1.[1] Isaiah encourages "the land shadowing with wings" (better "the land of whirring [*ṣilṣal*] wings").[2] The phrase refers to Ethiopia, a land characterized by insects; cf. 7:18. Ethiopia lay south of

---

[1]Watts, *Isaiah 1–33*, p. 245, translates *hôy* as "Woe" but does not consider it as pronouncing a curse on Ethiopia. Rather, he sees it as a "cry of dismay" by the Jews at the news that a delegation approaches from Ethiopia. They fear the prospect of military operations. The natural connection, however, is with Ethiopia: "Ho, O land of whirring wings!" Delitzsch, I, 348, translates "woe" but considers it "an expression of compassion . . . rather than of anger" since Ethiopia is oppressed by Assyria. At the time of Isaiah, though, Ethiopia was not under Assyrian control.

[2]Henry, p. 102, makes the phrase apply to Assyria as God pronounces a "woe" on it. It is, however, difficult to see how Assyria lay "beyond the rivers of Ethiopia." Possible interpretations tend to fall into three groups. (1) G. R. Driver, *JSS* 13:45, translates *ṣilṣal* "a land of sailing boats." KB, III, 1031, derives the word from a different root than in Deut. 28:42. They acknowledge the disputed meaning but support "whirring boats," i.e., light boats. The LXX translates πλοίων πτέρυγες, "winged [or 'sailing'] ships." Price, p. 83, gives "land of many sails," an interpretation rather than a translation. (2) Rawlinson, I, 304, translates "the land of the noise of wings." This derives *ṣilṣal* from *ṣalal*, "to quiver," and understands it as the clashing sound of the cymbals, a use seen elsewhere, e.g., II Sam. 6:5.; Ps. 150:5. Rawlinson sees this as representing the warriors of Ethiopia. Motyer, *The Prophecy of Isaiah*, p. 161, translates, "whirring wings" and sees these as symbolic of the "busy, restless world." Young, I, 474, translates "whirring wings" and views these as representing the "swarming hordes" of Ethiopia, its armies that can go

the first cataract of the Nile River, the site of the modern Aswan dam. Its major rivers, the White Nile, Blue Nile, Sobat, and Atbara, all flow into the Nile River. Isaiah introduces Ethiopia here in preparation for continuing his message of judgment on Assyria.[3]

The people of Ethiopia came from Noah's son Ham through his son Cush, Genesis 10:6. The Cushites migrated south into Arabia. From there, some crossed to the area presently known as Ethiopia and mingled with the people already living there. The nation was subject to the Egyptian rulers during its early history. About 1000 B.C. Ethiopia gained its independence. Around 750 B.C., under King Kashta, Ethiopia conquered Upper Egypt, south of the delta. His son Piankhi followed him ca. 745 B.C. He gained control of much of Lower Egypt. His successor Shabako is the biblical So, II Kings 17:4. He gained control of all Egypt by defeating Bochoris ca. 708 B.C. Isaiah's prophecies come about the time of Piankhi, v. 1.

The Ethiopians had sent ambassadors "by the sea," the Nile River; cf. 19:5; Nahum 3:8.[4] These had traveled along the Nile River in "vessels of bulrushes [better 'papyrus']," boats made by tying reeds together and caulking them. Apparently, these messengers have come to Judah. From vv. 3–7, we see that the great concern was Assyria. Quite possibly, these Ethiopians have come to persuade Judah to join them in opposing Assyria.

We may omit the supplied word "saying." Isaiah speaks to the ambassadors, the "swift [qallîm] messengers."[5] They should "go," return home to "a nation scattered [muššak] and peeled [môraṭ]" (better "a tall and

---

forth to pillage other nations. Meir Lubetski, "Beatlemania of Bygone Times," *JSOT* 91:3–26, understands the word to refer to the beetle. He makes this a symbol of the Egyptian sun god, appropriate in view of Ethiopia's connection with Upper Egypt. (3) Fausset, p. 619, defends the translation "shadowing with wings." He derives ṣilṣal from another meaning of ṣalal, "to be dark." The shadowing of the land with "wings," a dual word, is the protecting of the land with its armies and its ships. Ibn Ezra, p. 85, understands ṣilṣal as reduplicating ṣel, "shadow." He interprets the "shady land" as "a wide land."

[3]Stacey, p. 118, identifies the country as the Sudan, a land "beyond the rivers" in the south. The Sudan, however, was not a mighty nation. It does not figure into the biblical narrative elsewhere; cf. v. 2.

[4]Watts, *Isaiah 1–33*, p. 244, thinks that the "sea" refers to the Mediterranean coastal area. Barnes, I, 316, mentions the possibility that it means the Red Sea. These are possible although the Ethiopian envoys would surely have traveled the Nile River first.

[5]Barnes, I, 319, understands Isaiah to direct his speech to the "light messengers," the light boats made from papyrus. The word qallîm, from qal, "to be slight, swift," normally refers to speed rather than weight.

smooth nation").[6] The phrase describes the physical stature and looks of the Ethiopian people. They are tall and with smooth skin, not disfigured with excessive hair, perhaps even with oil applied to produce a shining appearance. Herodotus described them as "the tallest and most attractive people in the world."[7] This is "a people terrible," noted for their fierceness. They are feared "from their beginning hitherto" (*min⁻hû' wahal'â*), better "from here and abroad" or, idiomatically, "widely (feared)."[8] It is "a nation meted out [*qaw⁻qaw*] and trodden down" (or "a mighty and destructive nation").[9] It is a land "spoiled" (*baz'û*, better "divided") by its rivers, v. 2.[10]

---

[6]Henry, p. 102, applies the phrase to Judah. They are "trampled on as a nation scattered and peeled." Vine, p. 49, follows this view. Motyer, *The Prophecy of Isaiah*, p. 161, argues that *muššak* never means "tall" elsewhere. He opts for "drawn out," i.e., a nation with a long-standing history. The *pu'al muššak* occurs only once (Prov. 13:12) outside vv. 2, 7. The argument is therefore weak. In addition, Ethiopia was not notably ancient in its history. Motyer also argues that *môraṭ* refers to a sharpened sword, here indicating a nation prepared for battle, "stripped down for action." While *môraṭ* refers to a polished sword elsewhere, that sense occurs only in Ezekiel, where another word is translated "sword." The sense of "bare, polished, bald" is more normal, I Kings 7:45; Ezek. 21:10, 11.

[7]Herodotus, *The Histories* iii.20.

[8]The idiom *min⁻hû wahal'â* is variously taken as spatial, "near and far," or temporal, "then and now." The interpretation rests on *hal'â*, a word that elsewhere indicates space or time. Without exception (Lev. 22:27; Num. 15:23; I Sam. 18:9; Ezek. 39:22; 43:27), however, when time is in view, the word "day" is in the context to point to time. Elsewhere (18:7; Gen. 19:9; 35:21; Num. 16:37; 32:19; I Sam. 10:3; 20:22; Jer. 22:19; Amos 5:27), where space is in view, the context lacks this clue.

[9]The word *qaw⁻qaw* occurs only here and in v. 7. It is a reduplicated form, apparently related to an Arabic root meaning "strength." The repetition of the entire stem intensifies the meaning, thus "mighty." Alexander, I, 344, also refers it to the Arabic root but understands the reduplication as "double strength." Delitzsch, I, 351, derives it from *qaw*, "line." He understands the line to give direction, thus "command." The duplication gives it the sense of "a commanding nation." The nation here is one that commands and treads down, "a ruling and conquering nation." Näglesbach, p. 217, compares it to 28:10, 13, where the construction is *qaw laqaw*, "line upon line." He understands it here as "line, line," thus a normative measure, again a commanding nation. Watts, *Isaiah 1–33*, p. 245, thinks that 28:10, 13 are only a "meaningless sound." He follows BDB and the Arabic cognate, understanding it as "strong." Barnes, I, 320–21, understands *qaw⁻qaw* as "line, line," measuring others for destruction. Herbert Donner, *Israel unter den Völkern*, in *SVT* (Leiden: E. J. Brill, 1964), XI, 122, calls it likely an onomatopoetic form indicating an unidentified language. While the derivation of *qaw⁻qaw* is vague, the sense of the word is clear. From the context, it refers to a powerful nation.

[10]Rawlinson, I, 305; Hailey, p. 158; and Näglesbach, p. 218, understand *baz'û* as "erode" or "spoil," washing the soil of Ethiopia into Egypt. This passage, however, praises Ethiopia rather than dwelling on her negative points. The rate of erosion is, as

3 All ye inhabitants of the world, and dwellers on the earth, see ye,
when he lifteth up an ensign on the mountains; and when he bloweth
a trumpet, hear ye.
4 For so the Lord said unto me, I will take my rest, and I will consider
in my dwelling place like a clear heat upon herbs, and like a cloud
of dew in the heat of harvest.
5 For afore the harvest, when the bud is perfect, and the sour grape is
ripening in the flower, he shall both cut off the sprigs with pruning
hooks, and take away and cut down the branches.
6 They shall be left together unto the fowls of the mountains, and to
the beasts of the earth: and the fowls shall summer upon them, and
all the beasts of the earth shall winter upon them.

3–6 In vv. 3–7, Isaiah reveals why there is no need for an alliance between Ethiopia and Judah.[11] Isaiah calls upon the nations of the world to
hear the Lord's message. Ethiopia is no doubt included among these although Isaiah does not single out the nation. Poetically, "he," the Lord,
will raise a signal on the mountains of Judah. He will blow a trumpet
(šôpar) to announce the message. The šôpar was made from the curved
horn of the ram. Its sound called the people together, e.g., Judges 3:27;
6:34. It gave signals in war, e.g., II Samuel 18:16; 20:22. It announced
certain festivals, e.g., Leviticus 25:9; Psalm 81:3. It called the attention
of the Lord to His people, e.g. Joshua 6:5; Judges 7:18. It warned of
danger, e.g., Ezekiel 33:3–6; Joel 2:1. The Lord here calls the nations of
the world to listen, v. 3. The Lord has no concern over the Assyrian
threat to Judah. He will take His "rest" (šaqat, see 7:4), letting the danger posed by Assyria develop fully. He "will consider" (or "regard") the
actions of Assyria. He compares His delay to the "clear [sah, or 'daz-
zling'][12] heat" of the sun "upon herbs" (better "upon light"), i.e., the heat

---

well, debatable. The major river, the White Nile, rises in Africa and likely carries as
much sediment in as it carries out.

[11]Watts, *Isaiah 1–33*, p. 246, thinks that the messengers come to Judah to make an alliance against Egypt. Judah sends them on to Assyria, the nation that controlled them at
this time, and therefore the only nation that could make an agreement with Ethiopia. The
view is unhistorical. Ethiopia, under Piankhi, ruled most of Egypt. There was no need for
an alliance against Egypt.

[12]Kaiser, *Isaiah 13–39*, pp. 90, 95, transliterates sah, "like the heat of Zach above the
light." He understands Zach as the Akkadian name of a summer month. It is highly unlikely that Isaiah would use an Akkadian name here, especially when the Hebrew meaning makes sense.

> 7 In that time shall the present be brought unto the Lord of hosts of a people scattered and peeled, and from a people terrible from their beginning hitherto; a nation meted out and trodden under foot, whose land the rivers have spoiled, to the place of the name of the Lord of hosts, the mount Zion.

that slowly warms the day. His delay is like the dew that nourishes plants in the warmth of the harvest time, v. 4.

At the proper time, before the Assyrians "harvest" the spoil of Judah, the Lord will act. Isaiah describes His work poetically. The bud develops; the grape ripens. The Lord will then prune the Assyrian army and cut off its branches, v. 5.[13] The bodies of the Assyrians will serve as feed for the birds and "beasts" (*b^ehemâ*) of the field. The word *b^ehemâ* may refer to either wild or domesticated animals. Here, wild animals are in view. The passage is a clear prophecy of the events summarized in II Kings 19:35. With 185,000 Assyrian soldiers dying suddenly, the corpses will serve to feed the animals in both the summer and winter, v. 6.

7 Verse 7 identically repeats the description of the Ethiopians given in v. 2.[14] There, the messengers returned to Ethiopia. Here, Ethiopia brings a "present" to the Lord and carries it to the place that bears His name, the temple. We have no record of such a gift being brought at the time of Judah's deliverance unless II Chronicles 32:23 includes it. It is likely that the Ethiopians would have rejoiced in the defeat of Assyria. Other OT passages suggest that this is eschatological, a gift brought to the Lord in the kingdom; cf. 45:14; Psalm 68:31; Zephaniah 3:10. The gift in this case reflects an act of worship as the Ethiopians recognize the position of the Lord as King of kings in the earth.

---

[13]Stacey, p. 119, makes the branches stand for "meddlesome allies who try to accelerate God's purposes." He gives no details other than specifically rejecting Assyria. Among others, Kraeling, p. 97; Leslie, p. 66; and Brueggemann, *Isaiah 1–39*, p.154, refer this to the destruction of Ethiopia. Herbert, *Isaiah 1–39*, p. 119, allows for either Assyria or Egypt. The description of the defeat in v. 6 indicates Assyria.

[14]In keeping with his view of v. 2, Watts, *Isaiah 1–33*, p. 247, identifies those bringing gifts as Assyrians. Fausset, p. 621, makes the gift the restoration of Jewish outcasts who had escaped from the Assyrian army to Ethiopia. There is, of course, no evidence either for or against these views.

Practical Application from Chapter 18

The Lord controls human history! While Assyria was a mighty war-like nation, the prophet confidently proclaims their coming defeat.

1. The Lord's Control of Immediate History. Isaiah speaks to Ethiopia, v. 1. Ambassadors from Ethiopia had traveled to Palestine, v. 2. Isaiah now speaks to the nations of the world. Ethiopia is logically among these. The Lord will announce His message, v. 3. He has no concern over the Assyrian threat. He in fact will take His rest while the Assyrians develop their threat, v. 4. Before the Assyrians take a harvest of spoil from Judah, He will act. He will prune their army, v. 5. The dead bodies of the Assyrians will serve to feed the birds and beasts of the field, v. 6.

2. The Lord's Control of Future History. Isaiah's thought now leaps into the future. He sees the Ethiopian ambassadors returning to Palestine. This time is in the millennial kingdom. The ambassadors will bring a gift to the Lord as they acknowledge His position as King of kings, v. 7.

1 *The burden of Egypt. Behold, the Lord rideth upon a swift cloud, and shall come into Egypt: and the idols of Egypt shall be moved at his presence, and the heart of Egypt shall melt in the midst of it.*

2 *And I will set the Egyptians against the Egyptians: and they shall fight every one against his brother, and every one against his neighbour; city against city, and kingdom against kingdom.*

3 *And the spirit of Egypt shall fail in the midst thereof; and I will destroy the counsel thereof: and they shall seek to the idols, and to the charmers, and to them that have familiar spirits, and to the wizards.*

4 *And the Egyptians will I give over into the hand of a cruel lord; and a fierce king shall rule over them, saith the Lord, the Lord of hosts.*

ISAIAH 19

The Lord now turns to the land of Egypt. The initial part of the chapter, vv. 1–15, poetically describes the judgment that will come upon the nation for its sin. By civil war, the rule of a tyrant, natural calamities, and a lack of leadership, the Lord will punish the Egyptians. The people and their leaders will have no solutions to help them. The Lord, however, intends to restore Egypt to Himself, vv. 16–25. He describes the change that will come upon them in the end times. They will turn to Him and gain His favor.

F. Against Egypt 19:1–25
1. Promise of Judgment 19:1–15

1–4 Isaiah proclaims a "burden" (*maśśaʾ*, see 13:1) on Egypt. The Lord will come swiftly into Egypt to overthrow her false gods. As is often the case, e.g., 17:10–11; 40:6–8, Isaiah uses a picture drawn from nature. The Lord rides into Egypt upon a "swift cloud," a cloud that moves briskly across the sky. The "idols" (*ʾĕlîl*, see 2:8) of Egypt "shall be moved" (better "tremble") at His arrival. The Egyptians themselves "melt," showing their fear at the Lord's presence, v. 1. The Lord causes civil war to break out. The levels of this civil war increase in their scope. It begins in the family, moves to include neighbors, broadens to take in cities, and finally pits "kingdom against kingdom." While we cannot be certain, it is likely that this refers to the nomes or provinces that divided Egypt.[1] The biblical Shishak, II Chronicles 12:2–9, unified Egypt after

---

[1] Motyer, *The Prophecy of Isaiah,* p. 164; Hailey, p. 161; and Fausset, p. 622, understand this as a conflict between Upper and Lower Egypt. Since Ethiopia ruled Upper Egypt at this time and partially controlled Lower Egypt, the view is entirely possible.

years of weak pharaohs. His successors in the twenty-second dynasty maintained this unity. The rulers of the twenty-third dynasty lost this control. Rival pharaohs set up their kingdoms. Tefnakht ruled from Sais, in the western part of the delta. In Lower Egypt, Piankhi, the Ethiopian king, gained wide control. The nomes under the control of nobles gained in strength. Bochoris was the only king of the twenty-fourth dynasty. He ruled six years, 713–708 B.C., before being defeated and put to death by the Ethiopian king Shabako, first king of the twenty-fifth dynasty.

The Assyrians under Ashur-banipal invaded Egypt ca. 663 B.C. He conquered south to Thebes, the biblical No-Amon, Nahum 3:8. He appointed the Egyptian Psammeticus I as king. With the decline of the Assyrian presence, Psammeticus I (663–610 B.C.) unified the nation under his rule and brought the nomes back under his control, v. 2.

The spirit of the Egyptians will "fail," lack confidence. The Lord will "destroy" (*bala^c*, better "swallow up," see 3:12) their counsel, making it of no effect. The Egyptians will turn to their false gods in the hope of gaining deliverance from the invading army. They consult "idols" (*^elîlîm*, see 2:8) and "charmers" (*^ittîm*).[2] They turn to "familiar spirits," who consult the dead, and "wizards," possibly male witches, v. 3.[3] The Lord, however, will bring these resources to naught. He will give the Egyptians to a "cruel [*qašeh*] lord [*^adonîm*]." The plural *^adonîm* is a plural of majesty. The singular adjective *qašeh* joined to the plural of majesty is normal. The parallel "fierce king" shows that only one king is in view.[4] This king is likely Psammeticus I, who ruled the nation after the Assyrians. He is known to have executed the kings who opposed

---

[2] The word *^ittîm* occurs only here. It comes from a root meaning "to be gentle, soft." It is thought to refer to the low muttering of various ritual incantations.

[3] The precise distinction between these wicked practices is obscure. While we can make educated guesses at the exact nature of these evil works, we cannot be certain.

[4] Hailey, p. 162, understands the singular "king" as a collective referring to several Assyrian kings who conquered and ruled Egypt. While the view is possible, the parallelism with "cruel lord" supports rather a single king. Näglesbach, pp. 221, 224, notes that "lord" is plural. He understands this in an abstract sense, "dominion," and refers it to Psammeticus I and his descendants who also ruled. Rawlinson, I, 313, and Grogan, p. 126, think it was Esarhaddon who conquered Egypt. Young, II, 19, makes this refer to the four great world powers; cf. Dan. 2:38–40. In keeping with his idea of a late date for the passage, Kraeling, p. 98, suggests Cambyses or Artaxerxes III, Persian kings. Leslie, p. 67, thinks it is one of the Ethiopian kings, Piankhi or Shabako. Whitehouse, I, 230, suggests either Cambyses or Xerxes. Brueggemann, *Isaiah 1–39*, p. 157, identifies the king as "any from

5 *And the waters shall fail from the sea, and the river shall be wasted*
and dried up.

6 *And they shall turn the rivers far away; and the brooks of defence*
shall be emptied and dried up: the reeds and flags shall wither.

7 *The paper reeds by the brooks, by the mouth of the brooks, and*
every thing sown by the brooks, shall wither, be driven away, and be
no more.

8 *The fishers also shall mourn, and all they that cast angle into the*
brooks shall lament, and they that spread nets upon the waters shall
languish.

9 *Moreover they that work in fine flax, and they that weave networks,*
shall be confounded.

10 *And they shall be broken in the purposes thereof, all that make*
sluices and ponds for fish.

him.[5] Notice that it is "the Lord," the Master of Israel, and "the Lord of hosts," the Ruler of the heavenly and earthly hosts, who plans this judgment on Egypt. He therefore has the right to defend His people and the power with which to do it, v. 4.

5–10 The Lord sends drought to "the sea," the Nile River; cf. 18:2. Normally, the Nile rises over several months, June through October, from the melting snows on the mountains of Ethiopia and Africa. This water gave Egypt the name "gift of the Nile," v. 5. The drought brings serious problems. The "far away" rivers, probably the irrigation canals, will "turn" (*heʾeznîḥû*, better "stink"), stagnating and becoming foul from the rotting vegetation left as the waters recede.[6] The "brooks of defense," better "rivers of Egypt [*maṣôr*],"[7] the arms of the Nile in the delta, cf. 7:18, are "emptied" (*dalal*, see 17:4), i.e., dry up. This causes

---

Tiglath-pileser III to Ashurbanipal." Price, p. 248, gives either Piankhi or Esarhaddon. Other kings as well have been suggested. We cannot be sure since most foreign rulers of that time could have been described as "cruel."

[5]*Diodorus of Sicily*, trans. C. H. Oldfather (Cambridge, Mass.: Harvard University Press, 1968), I, 231.

[6]The form of *heʾeznîḥû* is unusual, occurring only here. G.K. 19 *m* and 53 *g* explain the form as including a prosthetic aleph. Waltke and O'Connor, p. 445, suggest that it reflects either Arabic or Aramaic influence. The meaning follows an Arabic equivalent, "to become rancid."

[7]The name "Egypt" normally occurs in a dual form, *miṣrayim*, thought to include both Upper and Lower Egypt. Here, however, the singular form *maṣôr* occurs. It is possible that Isaiah uses this deliberately to refer to Lower Egypt, the delta.

the "reeds and flags" by the river to "wither" (*qamal*),[8] v. 6. The "brooks" (*ye'ôr*, lit. "river," each time referring to the Nile) will dry up.[9] This causes the "paper reeds" (*'arôt*, lit. "bare places"),[10] places with grassy vegetation only, or the growth at the "mouth" (or "edge") of the Nile, and all sorts of plants along the Nile to shrivel up and die, v. 7.

Industries that depend on the Nile will die. Fishermen will suffer, and those who use the "angle" (or "fishhook") in the "brooks" (again *ye'ôr*, "river") will lament. Likewise, those who use nets to catch the fish will grieve, v. 8. Those who use "fine [*še'rîqôt*, better 'combed']"[11] flax" to weave linen garments, cf. I Kings 10:28; Proverbs 7:16; Ezekiel 27:7, and those who weave "networks" (lit. "white cloth"), cotton fabric, will be "confounded" (*bôš*, or "dismayed," see 1:29). The plants that produce this have died, v. 9. Verse 10 reads, "And they shall be broken in the purposes thereof, all that make sluices and ponds for fish." This is better translated, "And the foundations [*šatoteyha*] of it [i.e., Egypt] shall be shattered, all that make wages will be grieved in soul [*nepeš*]." The "foundations" (*šatoteyha*)[12] are the leaders of society, the employers and the wealthy. The wage earners represent a lower class of society, those who work for others. All suffer the effects of the drought, v. 10.

---

[8]The root *qamal* occurs only here and in 33:9. BDB, p. 888, relies on a Syriac cognate for the meaning "decay." KB, III, 1109, translates "wilt" or "blacken." The parallelism suggests something like "wither."

[9]Barnes, I, 331, refers to *ye'orê*, a plural form meaning "rivers." He then refers these to the irrigation canals along the Nile. The word, however, is singular, not plural. In addition, it is common for *ye'ôr* to refer to the Nile River, e.g., 23:3; Ezek. 29:9.

[10]This is the only place that *'arôt* occurs. The NIV renders it as "plants," and the NASB as "bulrushes." KB II, 882, gives "reed." The root *'arâ*, however, means "to empty out, lay bare." Related words occur widely to indicate nakedness, e.g., 20:4; 47:3. The meaning "bare places," indicating places without heavy vegetation, is appropriate here.

[11]The adjective *še'rîqôt* is a *hapax legomenon*. Based on an Arabic cognate, BDB, p. 977, suggests "carded, combed." This fits well with the manufacturing process in which flax was prepared for spinning by separating its fibers. Egypt perfected the art of preparing fine linen for clothing used for the living and also for mummies.

[12]Barnes, I, 334, derives *šatoteyha* from *šatat*, "to place, lay." He refers the word to "the banks or dykes that were made to retain the waters in the canals." These will "be trodden down." Watts, *Isaiah 1–33*, p. 251, follows the LXX and emends to *še'tîteyha*, "her weavers." The NIV is similar, "the workers in cloth." Hailey, p. 162, and Mauchline, p. 157, derive the word from *šatâ* but parallel the meaning with "all that make wages" so that both terms refer to the same group. Ibn Ezra, p 89, understands the word to refer to "the buildings which they erect to take the fish in." More probably, the source of *šatoteyha* is *šît*, "to put, set" and thus something placed, a foundation.

*11 Surely the princes of Zoan are fools, the counsel of the wise counsel-
lors of Pharaoh is become brutish: how say ye unto Pharaoh, I am
the son of the wise, the son of ancient kings?*
*12 Where are they? where are thy wise men? and let them tell thee now,
and let them know what the Lord of hosts hath purposed upon Egypt.*
*13 The princes of Zoan are become fools, the princes of Noph are de-
ceived; they have also seduced Egypt, even they that are the stay of
the tribes thereof.*
*14 The Lord hath mingled a perverse spirit in the midst thereof: and
they have caused Egypt to err in every work thereof, as a drunken
man staggereth in his vomit.*
*15 Neither shall there be any work for Egypt, which the head or tail,
branch or rush, may do.*

11–15 The nation's leaders have no solution. Zoan also has the biblical
name of Rameses and the nonbiblical names of Tanis and Avaris. The city
lay in the eastern part of the delta. It was one of the pharaohs' treasure
cities. Its leaders are "fools" (*ᵉwilîm*), morally corrupt persons with no
fear of God. Other counselors to Pharaoh are "brutish," careless individuals of low moral condition; cf. Proverbs 12:1. Isaiah asks rhetorically how
these men can boast of their descent from wise men and royalty. In
essence, they boast of themselves in an effort to impress Pharaoh, v. 11.[13]
Isaiah speaks to Pharaoh, again rhetorically. Where are Pharaoh's wise
men? Let them tell Pharaoh what the Lord has planned for the nation,
v. 12. Repeating the thought of v. 11*a,* Isaiah calls the leaders of Zoan
"fools." The leaders of "Noph," also called Memphis, located on the western bank of the Nile River just south of the delta, have been deceived. For
this reason, these who are the "stay" (better "cornerstone") of the nation
have "seduced Egypt," led her astray, v. 13. The Lord has allowed a "perverse spirit" (*ᶜiwᶜîm,* or "twisted spirit, distorted spirit") to influence these
leaders. The plural *ᶜiwᶜîm* intensifies the nature of the wicked spirit. This
has caused Egypt to go astray, making faulty judgments. They stagger as a
drunk in his own vomit, v. 14. The people can do nothing to correct their
problems. The expression "head or tail, branch or rush" is identical to the
same phrase in 9:14. As there, the idea here is that the upper class and the
false prophets can offer no help, v. 15.

---

[13]Barnes, I, 335, makes the courtiers remind Pharaoh that he is descended from wise
men. This is an attempt to flatter him. This overlooks the presence of *ᵓanî,* "I." The
speech is in the first person as these courtiers try to influence Pharaoh.

16 In that day shall Egypt be like unto women: and it shall be afraid and fear because of the shaking of the hand of the Lord of hosts, which he shaketh over it.

17 And the land of Judah shall be a terror unto Egypt, every one that maketh mention thereof shall be afraid in himself, because of the counsel of the Lord of hosts, which he hath determined against it.

2. Prophecy of Restoration 19:16–25

16–17 The first part of the chapter has been poetic in form. Isaiah now shifts to prose. The phrase "in that day" occurs again in vv. 18, 19, 21, 23, and 24. In each case, this looks forward to the Day of the Lord in the end times. Taken as a whole, the section spans the range from the judgment of Egypt to its restoration and full blessing from the Lord.

> **The Nature of Consecration**
>
> Conviction of Sin, vv. 16–17
>
> Conversion of the Lost, vv. 18–19
>
> Consecration of the Saints, vv. 20–22
>
> Unity of Believers, v. 23
>
> Blessing of the Kingdom, vv. 24–25

This will be a time that brings great "fear" (*pahad*, see 2:10) to Egypt. They tremble as God shakes His hand over them. The shaking of God's hand idiomatically portrays His judgments of their sin; cf. 10:32; 11:15. It is the "Lord of hosts" who does this, the powerful Ruler of heaven and earth, v. 16. God's blessings on Judah bring "terror" (*hagga*)[14] to Egypt. She becomes fearful that God will bring judgment upon her. The mere

---

[14]The word *hagga* occurs only here. The word is from *hagag*. BDB, p. 290, gives "make a pilgrimage, keep a pilgrimage-feast" but also "reel." KB, I, 290, suggests "shame, confusion." G. R. Driver, *JSS* 13:46, compares the word to an Arabic cognate. He gives "shock." Ps. 107:27 shows that this root may mean something like "reeling" as from the drunkenness that would be associated with feasting. The Egyptians here "reel" in fear.

18 In that day shall five cities in the land of Egypt speak the language of Canaan, and swear to the Lord of hosts; one shall be called, The city of destruction.

mention of Judah causes Egypt to "be afraid" (*paḥad*, see 2:10) that the "Lord of hosts" has determined punishment for their land, v. 17.[15]

18 In that day, "five cities" in Egypt "speak the language of Canaan." The five cities represent the beginning of Egypt's conversion.[16] The parallel phrase "swear to the Lord of hosts" shows that their willingness to speak Canaan's language is equivalent to worshiping the Lord.[17] One city will be called "the city of destruction" (*ʿîr haheres*).[18] This is a play on words that involves the city of Heliopolis, the city of the sun god (*ʿîr haheres*). This city was destroyed during the Persian invasion and occupation of Egypt. Now, however, this destroyed city will be restored to the worship of the Lord, v. 18.[19]

---

[15]Henry, p. 107, relates this to Sennacherib's invasion of Judah. Egypt fears that they will be next. I feel, however, that the context makes the passage eschatological. It looks to the distant future.

[16]Rawlinson, I, 315 makes "five" a round number, the first few cities to turn to the Lord. He also finds the fulfillment in the number of Egyptian cities that were settled by Jews, e.g., Alexandria and smaller cities near the Jewish temple built by Onias during the rule of Ptolemy VI (Philometer). There is not enough historical information about the Jews in Egypt to be certain of this. The view, however, goes against the context that supports an eschatological understanding of the passage.

[17]Hailey, pp. 165–66, argues that "the language of Canaan" never refers to the language of Israel. He argues that it was the trade language. Since the merchants did not generally worship the Lord, he concludes that this is "a mongrel speech, the expression of a mixed or impure religion." If we accept a messianic application of the passage, there is no difficulty in letting the "language of Canaan" be the speech of Israel.

[18]Price, p. 88, and Kaiser, *Isaiah 13–39*, pp. 104, 107, read *ʿîr haṣṣedeq* with the LXX and translate, "the city of Righteousness." The LXX, however, is likely interpretive. Because of the difficulty in understanding the phrase "city of destruction," Delitzsch, I, 363, and Skinner, *Isaiah I–XXXIX*, p. 150, emend to *ʿîr haheres* and refer it directly to Heliopolis, "the city of the sun." Vine, p. 50, thinks that the phrase relates to the destruction of idols. This is possible if we neglect the eschatological application.

[19]Henry, p. 108, and Alexander, I, 359, suggest that for every five cities in Egypt that accept the Lord, one will reject Him. Those cities will be called cities of destruction because they have refused the salvation offered by the Lord. The view reads the interpretation into the text.

19 *In that day shall there be an altar to the Lord in the midst of the land of Egypt, and a pillar at the border thereof to the Lord.*
20 *And it shall be for a sign and for a witness unto the Lord of hosts in the land of Egypt: for they shall cry unto the Lord because of the oppressors, and he shall send them a saviour, and a great one, and he shall deliver them.*
21 *And the Lord shall be known to Egypt, and the Egyptians shall know the Lord in that day, and shall do sacrifice and oblation; yea, they shall vow a vow unto the Lord, and perform it.*
22 *And the Lord shall smite Egypt: he shall smite and heal it: and they shall return even to the Lord, and he shall be intreated of them, and shall heal them.*

19–22 An altar will be built in the land and a pillar erected at the border. On the basis of this passage, Onias IV, the Jewish high priest, appealed to Pharaoh Philometer for permission to build a temple to the Lord in Egypt. The temple was built near Heliopolis.[20] The true fulfillment of the passage, however, is yet future. In the kingdom there will be places of worship to the Lord erected in Egypt. The pillar at the border marks the land as devoted to the Lord, v. 19.[21]

The presence of these religious elements witnesses to Egypt's faith in the Lord. As visitors come to the land, they see the "sign" (*ʾôt*, see 7:11) of Egypt's devotion to God.[22] When Egypt turns to the Lord for deliverance from their "oppressors," He will send them a "saviour" (*yašaʿ*, see 17:10).[23] Daniel 11:42–43 shows that Antichrist will oppress Egypt during

---

[20]Josephus, *Wars of the Jews* VII.x.2–3.

[21]Gray, I, 337, refers the verse to Jewish worship in the land. He rejects the idea that Egyptians will worship the Lord. On the other hand, Barnes, I, 340, and Fausset, p. 625, make the altar a memorial only since the Jews were to worship only at the altar in Jerusalem; cf. Deut. 12:13–14; 16:22 ("image," same word translated "pillar" here). When we project the passage into the kingdom, worship by the Egyptians is appropriate.

[22]Delitzsch, I, 365, understands the altar as the sign and the pillar as the witness. Näglesbach, p. 229, thinks the pillar is the sign and the altar the witness. Motyer, *The Prophecy of Isaiah*, p. 169, considers the altar alone to be both sign and witness. The difficulty in identifying the subject is at least partially related to the gender of the words involved. The altar is a masculine noun, the pillar is a feminine noun, and the verb is masculine. The sign is a feminine noun and the witness is a masculine noun. Trying to match these leads to the different approaches. The easiest approach simply takes "it" as referring to the presence of the altar and the pillar in Egypt. This is both sign and witness of Egypt's acceptance of the Lord.

[23]Kraeling, p. 100, ignores the prophetic nature of the passage by making the "saviour" an Egyptian pharaoh, possibly Philadelphus. Barnes, I, 341, and Fausset, p. 625, suggest

23 *In that day shall there be a highway out of Egypt to Assyria, and the Assyrian shall come into Egypt, and the Egyptian into Assyria, and the Egyptians shall serve with the Assyrians.*
24 *In that day shall Israel be the third with Egypt and with Assyria, even a blessing in the midst of the land:*
25 *Whom the Lord of hosts shall bless, saying, Blessed be Egypt my people, and Assyria the work of my hands, and Israel mine inheritance.*

the Tribulation. The passage here looks forward to Egypt's deliverance from Antichrist. At that time, the Lord Himself, "the great one," will be their "saviour," v. 20. The Lord will then "be known" (*nôda*ᶜ) to the Egyptians. The *nip*ᶜ*al* verb from *yada*ᶜ suggests that the Lord makes Himself known to the Egyptians. They, in turn, come to "know" (*yada*ᶜ) Him. In both cases, the verb *yada*ᶜ indicates an experiential rather than theoretical knowledge; cf. 1:3. Egypt then will worship the Lord. They will offer "sacrifice" (*zebah*, see 1:11) in remembrance of His atoning death. They will make "oblation," grain offerings, as they worship the Lord[24] and will make vows of dedication to Him, v. 21. The Lord's judgment of Egypt is likely that carried out through Antichrist. This will bring spiritual healing to Egypt. The people will "return" (*šûb*, see 1:27) to the Lord; cf. Hebrews 12:11; Revelation 3:19. They will plead with Him in prayer for deliverance, a prayer that He will answer, v. 22.

23–25 In the kingdom, a highway will join Egypt, Palestine, and Assyria; cf. 11:16; 35:8–10.[25] Both Egypt and Assyria will serve (ᶜ*abad*) the Lord, v. 23.[26] Israel will rise to the same level as Egypt and Assyria,

---

Alexander the Great as the "saviour." Alexander, I, 361, makes the word "generic." He applies it to all that have delivered Egypt down through the years. Young, II, 40, applies the term to Christ as the only one who can provide salvation to the heathen. There are too many details of the passage that were not fulfilled during OT times. Zech. 10:10–11 makes it clear that the Lord will deliver Egypt from Antichrist during the Tribulation.

[24]Young, II, 41, understands the language here as metaphoric rather than literal. Although Isaiah describes Egypt's worship by using OT terms, this does not mean that they "offer literal sacrifices upon actual altars." The OT elsewhere teaches, however, that God's people will offer literal sacrifices during the kingdom, e.g., 56:6–7; Jer. 33:17–18; Ezek. 43:18. There is no need to understand the passage here as metaphoric.

[25]Stacey, p. 125, considers the highway "more metaphorical than real." He views it as implying an economic and religious bond between Egypt and Assyria. Young, II, 43, understands the road as a symbol of "friendly and brotherly intercourse."

[26]Watts, *Isaiah 1–33*, p. 257, feels that "the context calls for a cultic meaning" of worship rather than service. The word ᶜ*abad* occurs widely, however, with a meaning of service. Rev. 22:3 speaks of eternal service to the Lord. While God's children will undoubtedly worship Him, they will also serve Him in unspecified ways.

large and influential lands. They will no longer be a dependent nation that lies between hostile powers. They will now be a blessing to all nations "in the midst of the land" (better "earth"), v. 24. These nations occupy an exalted position because the Lord "shall bless" (lit. "has blessed") them. Egypt is "my people," a nation belonging to the Lord. Assyria is "the work of my hands" as He has turned them from their pagan heritage to Himself. Israel is "mine inheritance," given to Him by the Father, cf. Deuteronomy 4:20; 9:29; 32:9; I Kings 8:51, v. 25.

Practical Applications from Chapter 19

1. The Scope of Judgment. The opening part of the chapter develops the judgment of Egypt more fully than most pronouncements of judgment. The variety developed here shows the broad range of options available to God as He punishes those who refuse Him.

    a. Civil war. The Lord overthrows the false gods of Egypt, v. 1. He brings internal strife into the land. This begins small, involving only family members and rapidly spreads to neighbors, cities, and even kingdoms, v. 2.

    b. Rule by a tyrant. Even though the Egyptians consult their false gods and those who have false spiritual power, all will be vain, v 3. A cruel ruler will rise to direct the nation, v. 4.

    c. Calamity in nature. The Lord will send a drought to the Nile River, v. 5. The irrigation canals will stink from the rotting vegetation. The arms of the Nile in the delta will dry up, v. 6. Vegetation along the Nile will wither and die, v. 7. Those who rely on fish from the river will suffer, v. 8. Those who depend on flax for weaving will be dismayed since none is available, v. 9. Both the upper and lower classes of society will suffer, v. 10.

    d. Lack of leadership. The leaders of the land have low morals, yet they boast of their wisdom and heritage, v. 11. Isaiah challenges Pharaoh to have his wise men tell what God has planned for Egypt, v. 12. They are fools and have been deceived. They therefore have led Egypt astray, v. 13. A wicked spirit has led them. This has caused Egypt to make wrong decisions and has led to erratic behavior, v. 14. No one can help them, v. 15. The wicked often look at themselves with satisfaction. The job is secure; the income is good; the future looks rosy. But God does not set limits upon His judgment. What we see with Egypt can be multiplied many times. God can bring judgment in many ways as He judges the wicked.

2. God's Work in the End Times. We often think that the end-time events involve only Israel and Christians. God's plan, however, involves the conversion of many people that today are steeped in heathen practices. Egypt is such a nation. God will work with them in such a way as to bring them to Himself. The outline given at the discussion of v. 16 develops this plan.

1 In the year that Tartan came unto Ashdod, (when Sargon the king of Assyria sent him,) and fought against Ashdod, and took it;

ISAIAH 20

The historical reference in v. 1 lets us date this chapter with some certainty. The "Tartan" was a title given to the commander of the Assyrian troops; cf. II Kings 18:17. He served under the emperor but often had complete authority over an army. The Philistine city of Ashdod had rebelled against Assyria in 714 B.C. by refusing to pay tribute. They had sought instead the aid of Egypt. At this time, Egypt and Ethiopia were unified. Ethiopia lay to the south of Egypt, which had ruled it for several hundred years. About 725 B.C., however, the Ethiopian king Piankhi gained control over most of Egypt. His successor, Shabako, defeated the Egyptian king Bochoris, ca. 708 B.C., and united the country. Confident of their strength, Egypt led a rebellion against Assyria. Ashdod, in Philistia, was part of this rebellion.

G. Against Egypt and Ethiopia 20:1–6

1 Sargon II (722–705 B.C.) gained the throne of Assyria after the death of Shalmaneser V.[1] While not a son of Shalmaneser, his position as leader of the army gave him a basis upon which to claim the rule of the nation. He sent the "Tartan," the commander of the army under Sargon, against Ashdod, then ruled by Azuri. After conquering the city, Sargon replaced Azuri with his brother Achimiti. Shortly afterwards, the people of Ashdod rebelled against Achimiti and replaced him with Iamani. Sargon then moved against the rebels and severely punished them. Isaiah's message here refers to this later campaign in 711 B.C.

The Annals of Sargon record these events:

> Azuri, king of Ashdod, had schemed not to deliver tribute (any more) and sent messages (full) of hostilities against Assyria to the kings (living) in his neighborhood. On account of the misdeed which he (thus) committed, I abolished his rule over the inhabitants of his country and made Ahimiti, his younger brother, king over them. But the(se) Hittites, (always) planning treachery, hated his reign and elevated to rule over them a Greek who, without claim to the throne, knew, just as they (themselves), no respect for

---

[1]Barnes, I, 344, an older commentator, misidentifies Sargon as Sennacherib. Historical information now available makes Sargon II the successor to Shalmaneser V. Sennacherib followed Sargon II as the ruler of Assyria.

2 *At the same time spake the Lord by Isaiah the son of Amoz, saying,*
  Go and loose the sackcloth from off thy loins, and put off thy shoe
  from thy foot. And he did so, walking naked and barefoot.
3 *And the Lord said, Like as my servant Isaiah hath walked naked and*
  barefoot three years for a sign and wonder upon Egypt and upon
  Ethiopia;
4 *So shall the king of Assyria lead away the Egyptians prisoners, and*
  the Ethiopians captives, young and old, naked and barefoot, even
  with their buttocks uncovered, to the shame of Egypt.
5 *And they shall be afraid and ashamed of Ethiopia their expectation,*
  and of Egypt their glory.
6 *And the inhabitant of this isle shall say in that day, Behold, such is*
  our expectation, whither we flee for help to be delivered from the
  king of Assyria: and how shall we escape?

authority. [In a sudden rage] I marched quickly—(even) in my state-chariot and (only) with my cavalry which never, even in friendly territory, leaves my side—against Ashdod, his royal residence, and I besieged and conquered the cities Ashdod, Gath (and) Asdudimmu. I declared the gods residing therein, himself, as well as the inhabitants of his country, the gold, silver (and) his personal possessions as booty. I reorganized (the administration of) these cities and placed an officer of mine as governor over them and declared them Assyrian citizens and they bore (as such) my yoke.[2]

By his message here, the Lord keeps Judah from joining in the rebellion against Assyria, v. 1.

2–6 The Lord commands Isaiah to act out a prophecy to Judah. Other examples in the OT show that this was a common way of prophesying. Both true prophets (cf. Jer. 13:2–11; 32:7–15; Ezek. 4:1–17; 5:1–4) and false prophets (cf. I Kings 22:11–12; Jer. 28:10–11) used the technique of acted-out prophecies.

Isaiah here is to remove his "sackcloth," cf. 3:24; 15:3, and "shoe" (or "sandals"). Prophets often wore sackcloth, apparently to show their grief over Israel's sin, Daniel 9:3; Zechariah 13:4. Isaiah is to walk about partially naked and barefoot, v. 2.[3] He is to do this for three years, probably

---

[2] Adapted from Pritchard, *ANET*, p. 286.
[3] Stacey, p. 126, argues that Isaiah was "ready to behave immodestly, if he was so instructed." God, however, will never instruct His servants to act contrary to His Word. While ᶜarum may indicate full nakedness, e.g., Gen. 2:25; Job 1:21; Eccles. 5:15, it also refers to partial nakedness, e.g., Exod. 28:42; I Sam. 19:24; Job 22:6; 24:7, 10; Isa. 58:7; Mic. 1:8. Isaiah would have considered total nakedness a shameful thing; cf. 20:4; Gen. 3:7, 10–11; 9:22.

from 713–711 B.C. until Ashdod rebelled again against Assyria, v. 3*a*.[4] Isaiah's actions are a "sign" (*'ôt*, see 7:11) to Judah "upon" (*'al*, better "against") Egypt and Ethiopia. His prophecy shows the people what will happen to the people of Egypt and Ethiopia, v. 3*b*. The Assyrian king will take away prisoners from Egypt and Ethiopia. They will go into captivity barefoot and naked, some even baring their " buttocks," a shameful condition for the people, cf. II Samuel 10:4, v. 4. Those in Israel who trusted in Egypt and Ethiopia will "be afraid" (*ḥatat*, or "be dismayed," see 7:8). They will be "ashamed" (*bôš*, see 1:29) that they have trusted in such a weak defense, v. 5. The "inhabitants of this isle" (*'î*, better "coastland," see 11:11), the Philistines who lived in the coastal region, will wonder why they trusted Egypt and Ethiopia. Seeing the weakness of these nations, they ask, "how shall we escape," v. 6.

Practical Application from Chapter 20

The Foolishness of Relying on Human Resources. The Egyptians were unified under the control of the Ethiopians. Thinking this strength enough, the Philistines join them in rebellion against Assyria. This is all to no avail. The Assyrians send their army under its leader to Ashdod and defeat the town. They set up their own ruler over the Philistines, v. 1. The Lord leads Isaiah to act out a prophecy against the Philistines and Egyptians. He removes part of his clothing and walks about partially naked and barefoot, v. 2. He does this for three years, v. 3*a,* to show what will happen to Egypt and Ethiopia, v. 3*b*. The Assyrians will take prisoners from Egypt and Ethiopia. They will go into captivity naked and barefoot, v. 4. Those who trusted Egypt and Ethiopia will be ashamed, v. 5. The people of the coastlands will wonder that they had placed their confidence in Egypt and Ethiopia. They will ask, "How shall we escape?"

The chapter illustrates the weakness of human resources. While the Lord can use weak humans for His glory, we should be sure that He is leading us to rely upon human resources. Human wisdom will fail us. We need to rely on the Lord.

---

[4]Alexander, I, 368, and Cowles, p. 152, think that Isaiah partially exposed himself once. This continued to be a sign to the people for three years. This is unlikely. People tend to have short memories. It is doubtful that Judah would have kept Isaiah's actions in mind for three years.

1 The burden of the desert of the sea. As whirlwinds in the south pass through; so it cometh from the desert, from a terrible land.

ISAIAH 21

The chapter includes three oracles against heathen nations. The major oracle is against Babylon, vv. 1–10. Warnings of judgment against Edom, vv. 11–12, and Arabia, vv. 13–17, also occur. Babylon was not the enemy of Judah during Isaiah's lifetime. They gained control over Assyria about the time of Isaiah's death. The Lord, however, leads the prophet to look at the future enmity that would take place between the nations. As a result, the Lord would send the judgment prophesied here. In general, both Edom and Arabia were enemies of the Jews in the OT. The Lord elsewhere accuses Edom of "perpetual hatred" (Ezek. 35:5) toward His people. The Arabians often fought against Judah, II Chronicles 21:16; 26:7, although they were also tributaries at times, II Chronicles 9:14; 17:11. The Lord now announces judgment on both of these regions.

H. Against Babylon 21:1–10

1 Isaiah declares a "burden" (*maśśaᵓ*, or "oracle," see 13:1) concerning "the desert of the sea," Babylon. The city stood on land reclaimed from water by the building of dams and irrigation canals. Some Assyrian monuments call it a "sea" or "sea-country"; cf. Jeremiah 51:13. Isaiah calls it "the desert [or 'wilderness'] of the sea." The title looks forward to the time Babylon will become a wilderness. To distinguish it from other barren places, he calls it the "wilderness" built upon the "sea."[1] The "south" (*negeb*) here points to the Arabian desert, located south of Babylon. Like a storm blowing from the south, an invading army will

---

[1]Näglesbach, p. 238, suggests that John understood the passage differently. In Rev. 17:1, 3, Babylon, the symbol of religious evil, sits on many waters, interpreted in 17:15 as people. At the same time, she is in the "wilderness." While the symbolism is appropriate, there is nothing in Rev. 17 to suggest that John drew from Isaiah. Similarly, there is nothing in Isaiah to suggest that the waters should be taken any way but literally. Ibn Ezra, p. 93, suggests that *yam* has an alternate meaning of "west." This leads to the "desert of the west." He refers this to Babylon that lies to the west of Persia and Media. In his note, Friedländer suggests that Isaiah considered the Euphrates River a "sea" because of its width. While Ibn Ezra's suggestion correctly refers the phrase to Babylon, the details are unlikely. Isaiah uses the word *yam* twenty-nine times to refer to a "sea." Only at 11:14 and 49:12 is the translation "west." In both places, "sea" is a better translation. Friedländer's view requires an unnecessary poetic view of *yam*.

169

2 *A grievous vision is declared unto me; the treacherous dealer dealeth treacherously, and the spoiler spoileth. Go up, O Elam: besiege, O Media; all the sighing thereof have I made to cease.*

3 *Therefore are my loins filled with pain: pangs have taken hold upon me, as the pangs of a woman that travaileth: I was bowed down at the hearing of it; I was dismayed at the seeing of it.*

4 *My heart panted, fearfulness affrighted me: the night of my pleasure hath he turned into fear unto me.*

come upon Babylon.[2] To make clear what he says, Isaiah identifies this storm as coming from a "terrible land." Verse 2 identifies this as the land of the Elamites and Medes. While Cyrus, king of Persia, led the conquest, he allied himself with Elam and Media. The army naturally moved through those lands as it approached Babylon, v. 1.

2–4 Isaiah sees the invasion in a "grievous vision," one that is hard to bear because of its content.[3] He shows the cause of Babylon's fall by repeating the descriptive terms: "the treacherous dealer dealeth treacherously, and the spoiler spoileth" (*habbôged bôged weḥaššôded šôded*). The repetition here is a mark of Isaiah's style. Babylon has been greatly unfaithful. She has greatly plundered other nations.[4] The Lord therefore calls on Elam and Media to rise against her. Elam lay to the east of Babylon between the Persian Gulf and the Zagros Mountains. The Medes came from the region northeast of Babylon, north of the Zagros Mountains below the Caspian Sea. The conquest of Babylon by this coalition causes the "sighing" (*ʾanaḥâ*)[5] of Babylon's victims to cease, v. 2.

---

[2]Näglesbach, p. 238, refers the *negeb* to Arabia Petræa, the region south of Judah. He then makes Isaiah say that as the storms in Judah come from the south, so a storm will come to Babylon from a terrible land. The mention of Arabia is not necessary. Isaiah refers to the Median army as they approach Babylon from the south (or southeast).

[3]Watts, *Isaiah 1–33*, p. 272, identifies the first-person speakers in c. 21–22 as Shebna, mentioned in 22:15. It is unlikely, however, that a new speaker would be introduced anonymously.

[4]It is grammatically possible to apply the words to the Elamites and Medians as they attack Babylon, so Delitzsch, I, 379; Cowles, p. 153. The words are more natural, however, when applied to Babylon's unfaithfulness to God in failing to see themselves as an instrument in His hands and to the unrestrained plundering in their conquests.

[5]Driver, *JSS* 13:47, understands *ʾanaḥâ* as "weariness" on the basis of an Akkadian cognate. He considers this "a summons to the Elamites and the Medes." The verbal root in Hebrew, however, occurs twelve times, all with the sense of "sign, groan." In addition, there is also an Akkadian cognate with the same meaning. The noun occurs in the book here and at 35:10 and 51:11. In all three cases, the sense of "sighing, mourning" is appropriate.

5 *Prepare the table, watch in the watchtower, eat, drink: arise, ye princes, and anoint the shield.*

Isaiah responds emotionally to what he has seen. The loins elsewhere are the place of pain or fear, e.g., Psalm 38:7; 66:11; Jeremiah 30:6. Sackcloth was frequently worn upon the loins, e.g., Genesis 37:34; Isaiah 32:11; Amos 8:10. Isaiah is filled with "pain" (*halhalâ*). The word *halhalâ* is strong. It suggests anguish that affects the body, a writhing in pain. He compares this to the pain of a woman in childbirth. Isaiah is "bowed down," emotionally devastated by what he hears. He is "dismayed" at what he sees, v. 3. His "heart panteth" (or "mind staggers"). He is consumed with horror. The restful night that he looked forward to has become a fearful thing, v. 4.

5 Isaiah briefly summarizes the activities of Babylon. They set their table with food, preparing a banquet at which they will enjoy themselves. They "watch in the watchtower" (*sapoh hassapît*), better "spread the carpet," preparing for the feast.[6] Their thought is of eating and drinking. Isaiah commands the princes to leave their tables. They should "anoint the shield," rubbing oil into their leather shields to keep them from becoming brittle; cf. II Samuel 1:21.[7] This action should be carried out well ahead of battle. Isaiah seeks to awaken them to the coming attack, v. 5.[8]

---

[6]The noun *sapoh* occurs only here although the root *sapâ* II occurs often with the sense "to lay out, overlay." This leads to the meaning of something laid out, i.e., "carpet." The AV translates *sapâ* I, "to watch." This leads to the conjecture of "watchtower" for *sapoh*. The idea of stretching out a carpet to lie on suits the context of eating and drinking better.

[7]Von Orelli, p. 124, and Slotki, p. 96, think that the oiling of the shields prepared the soldiers for close conflict. The shields were then smooth enough to make the enemy darts slide off. I cannot see that oiling a leather shield would cause arrows to slide off. Kraeling, p. 102, suggests that the oiling sanctified the shields in preparation for battle. Wade, p. 138, calls this "a religious rite." There is no indication elsewhere that this is a holy war.

[8]Motyer, *The Prophecy of Isaiah,* p. 175, makes the passage symbolic of the church fighting its battles with carnal weapons. When there is an obvious literal meaning, we should not turn to symbolism.

6 *For thus hath the Lord said unto me, Go, set a watchman, let him declare what he seeth.*

7 *And he saw a chariot with a couple of horsemen, a chariot of asses, and a chariot of camels; and he hearkened diligently with much heed:*

8 *And he cried, A lion: My lord, I stand continually upon the watchtower in the daytime, and I am set in my ward whole nights:*

9 *And, behold, here cometh a chariot of men, with a couple of horsemen. And he answered and said, Babylon is fallen, is fallen; and all the graven images of her gods he hath broken unto the ground.*

6–9 The Lord commands Isaiah to set someone to watch for the coming army, v. 6. He will see a "chariot" (*rekeb*, better "riders," likely a procession of riders on various animals), "a couple of horsemen" (or "pairs of horsemen"), with others riding asses or camels.[9] The verb is a prophetic perfect, something so sure that Isaiah describes it as though it has already happened. The watchman "hearkened diligently," listening intently to the vision as it unfolds, v. 7. He cries "a lion [*ʾaryeh*, or, 'as a lion']," with a lionlike voice.[10] He is impatient, having watched several days and nights, v. 8.[11] Now, however, the watchman announces the arrival of the Babylonian scouts.[12] Isaiah responds to this, saying that "Babylon is fallen."[13] The repetition "is fallen, is fallen," intensifies the thought. Complete destruction awaits Babylon and her idols. Revelation

---

[9]Vine, p. 52, and Henry, p. 113, translate *rekeb* as "chariot." The word, however, may denote "riders" as well. With asses and camels being involved, it is likely that Isaiah sees riders of various animals. The word *rekeb* occurs as a collective singular here. See the discussion of the grammar of a collective in c. 16, note 2.

[10]Motyer, *The Prophecy of Isaiah,* p. 175, understands *ʾaryeh* as the subject and translates "the lion shouted." He takes *ʾaryeh* as describing the watchman as a lionlike person, one of great strength. Taking *ʾaryeh* as the subject, however, creates an awkward symbolism. It is grammatically correct to supply the comparative "as."

[11]Stacey, p. 129, mistakenly identifies the watchman in v. 8 as Isaiah. This leads him to conclude that vv. 6, 8 contradict one another. In both cases, however, the third person indicates that the watchman is someone other than Isaiah.

[12]Kaiser, *Isaiah 13–39*, p. 127, understands the "chariot of men," *rekeb ʾîš*, as chariots drawn by men. While the phrasing is not identically the same in v. 7, it is close enough that we should interpret it in the same way.

[13]Young, II, 72, and Näglesbach, p. 241, make the watchman the one who speaks. Delitzsch, I, 382, makes the speakers the advancing part of Babylon's army. Kraeling, pp. 102–3, makes Isaiah the watchman who reports what he sees to the Lord. The Lord then proclaims the fall of Babylon. Kelley, p. 253, makes Isaiah the watchman who announces Babylon's fall. Grammatically, it is not clear who announces Babylon's fall. The point is not who announces the fall but that Babylon falls.

10 O my threshing, and the corn of my floor: that which I have heard of the Lord of hosts, the God of Israel, have I declared unto you.
11 The burden of Dumah. He calleth to me out of Seir, Watchman, what of the night? Watchman, what of the night?
12 The watchman said, The morning cometh, and also the night: if ye will enquire, enquire ye: return, come.

14:8 and 18:2 quote the phrase. This makes Babylon's fall and the destruction of her gods in the OT a picture of the end-time destruction of Rome, spiritual Babylon, v. 9.

10 Isaiah speaks to "my threshing, and the corn [lit. 'son'] of my floor." The idiom "son of . . ." in the OT refers to a thing that comes from something else.[14] Here, the "corn" comes from the threshing floor. The words of the prophet are God's message to His people. Judah had been threshed by their captivity in Babylon. They were the children who had experienced the threshing floor of Babylon. Isaiah has delivered the Lord's message to them, a message of hope that tells them of Babylon's destruction, v. 10.

I. Against Edom 21:11–12[15]

11–12 Isaiah declares the "burden [*maśśaʾ*, again 'oracle,' see v. 1] of Dumah." The word "Dumah" (*dûmâ*) means "silence."[16] It occurs again at Psalm 94:17; 115:17, both times referring to the silence of death. The seriousness of the oracle suggests that *dûmâ* has this sense here, the silence of death. The mention of Seir shows that this refers to Edom. Seir, also known as Edom, was the mountainous region south of the Dead Sea. Isaiah's use of *dûmâ* may well be a play on the name *ʾedom*. The oracle predicts the coming judgment of the land.

---

[14]E.g., the "sparks," Job 5:7, are lit. "sons of the burning coal." The "arrow," Job 41:28, is lit. a "son of the bow."

[15]Because of their brevity, Alexander, pp. 375–76, takes vv. 11–12 as a continuation of vv. 1–10. Nowhere else in Isaiah, however, does the word *maśśaʾ* occur without beginning a new topic.

[16]Whitehouse, I, 246, suggests that *dûmâ* is a corruption of *ʾedôm*, "Edom." The LXX supports this with its translation Ἰδουμαίας. The LXX, however, is likely interpretive, based on the mention of Seir in v. 11. Goldingay, pp. 125–26, gives *dûmâ* a double meaning. He refers it to an oasis near Babylon and also to the silence of death. Fausset, p. 629, refers *dûmâ* to "a tribe and region of Ishmael in Arabia." There is evidence of Dumah as a place name. The oasis Dumat al-Jauf is in Arabia, east of Edom. The name occurs as one of Ishmael's son, Gen. 25:14; I Chron. 1:30. The place name likely derives from this. There was also a Dumah located in Judah, Josh. 15:52. If Isaiah refers to a place name, the name is only a symbol of Edom. The mention of Seir virtually demands this.

13 The burden upon Arabia. In the forest in Arabia shall ye lodge, O ye
travelling companies of Dedanim.
14 The inhabitants of the land of Tema brought water to him that was
thirsty, they prevented with their bread him that fled.
15 For they fled from the swords, from the drawn sword, and from the
bent bow, and from the grievousness of war.

Isaiah, the "watchman" who sees into the future, hears a call from
Edom. "What of the night . . . what of the night?" Edom's repeated question emphasizes the somber nature of the matter. The "night" of judgment has come upon them, and they want to know how long it will last.
While we cannot be specific, it is likely that some Assyrian conquest is
in view. Assyria was the dominant power in the biblical world at this
time. We know of campaigns in Edom by Sargon, 715 B.C., and Sennacherib, 701 B.C., v. 11.

Isaiah, still the "watchman," responds to Edom's question. A "morning" comes, relief from the trials of Assyria. Another "night," however,
will follow the morning.[17] Again, we may not be specific. The second
"night" may refer to conquests by Babylon, Persia, Greece, Judah, or
Rome, all of which oppressed Edom. Isaiah has nothing further to tell
them. If they wish to inquire, they may. They may "return, come," asking
additional questions.[18] Isaiah, however, holds out no hope for the
Edomites, v. 12.

J. Against Arabia 21:13–17[19]

13–15 Isaiah announces another "burden" (*maśśaʾ*, see v. 1), this time
concerning the people of Arabia (*ᶜarab*).[20] The OT region of Arabia

---

[17]Scheiber, *VT* 11:456, understands the *gam* in *gam⁻layᵉlâ*, "also the night," as the *qal*
perfect from the unused verb *gamam*, "to become much, abundant." He then translates,
"Es kam der Morgen und vollendet is die Nacht," "the morning has come and the night
is over." This avoids the symbolism of the second "night." It is doubtful that the well-
known *gam* should be related to a verb not found elsewhere in the OT.

[18]Young, II, 78, spiritualizes the "morning" to mean the light of salvation. He makes
Isaiah say "Return" (or "turn") to the Lord, "come" to Him in repentance. Delitzsch, II,
385–86, agrees with this last part although he makes the "morning" refer to relief from
their enemies. I cannot see any call to salvation in the verse, especially in view of other
OT passages that refer to Edom's desolation, e.g., Ezek. 35.

[19]Kaiser, *Isaiah 13–39*, p. 133, translates *ᶜarab* as "desert," an unusual meaning. Although BDB, p. 787, suggests this meaning here, the masculine form of *ᶜarab* refers elsewhere to desert dwellers, the Arabian peoples. It is the feminine form *ᶜarabâ* that refers
to the desert.

[20]The grammar is unique here among the oracles pronounced by Isaiah. Only here is
the subject of the oracle introduced by the *bᵉ*-preposition. Delitzsch, I, 386, thinks that

*16 For thus hath the Lord said unto me, Within a year, according to the
years of an hireling, and all the glory of Kedar shall fail:*

*17 And the residue of the number of archers, the mighty men of the chil-
dren of Kedar, shall be diminished: for the Lord God of Israel hath
spoken it.*

refers primarily to Arabia Petræa, the rocky portion of the Arabian
Peninsula adjacent to Judah. This area embraced several tribal groups of
people. The first group mentioned is Dedan. The Dedanites were merchants; cf. Ezekiel 27:15, 20; 38:13. The "forests of Arabia" refers to the
thickets of shrubs and scrub trees found in that area. Actual forests are
rare in that wilderness. Isaiah's mention of "travelling companies" refers
to the trading caravans as they journeyed to other regions. To escape
their enemies, they will "lodge" (*lîn*, better "spend the night") in the
brush, away from the normal road they would travel, v. 13. As they continue to the south, hoping to escape their enemies, the people of Tema
bring them bread and water. Tema was a town about three hundred miles
southeast of Jerusalem. They "prevented" (better "met") the Dedanites
with provisions, v. 14. The Dedanites have fled from the weapons of the
invaders and the warfare that would beset them, v. 15.

16–17 Isaiah predicts the fall of Kedar, a people of the wilderness.
They are thought to have lived in the northwest part of the Arabian Peninsula although we have no archaeological evidence of them. They lived in
villages, 42:11, but also dwelled in tents, Psalm 120:5. They grazed animals, 60:7; Jeremiah 49:29, which they traded with other nations, Ezekiel
27:21. Although Kedar was a specific tribe, they here represent the Arabs
in general. According to the oracle, the tribes will evade their enemies for
a time. Within a year, however, "according to the years of an hireling," a
definite time, cf. 16:14, the region will fall, v. 16. At that time, their
"mighty men" (*gibbôr*, see 3:2, warriors) will be reduced in number. The
destruction is certain since the Lord God has decreed it, v. 17.

---

this is for the purpose of making it symbolic. Herbert, *Isaiah 1–39*, p. 132, makes the
first mention of the Arabs a prepositional phrase that completes the second mention: "In
the scrub with the Arabs you will camp." This ignores the ʾathnaḥ as well as departs
from the form used by Isaiah to introduce the other oracles. It may well be that the *bᵉ*
limits the oracle to Arabia Petræa, the northwest portion of Arabia. The southern part is
Arabia Felix and the northeastern part Arabia Deserta.

Practical Application from Chapter 21

Judgment of the Wicked

1. Judgment of Babylon. Isaiah announces judgment on the nation that will become a wilderness, v. 1. He will bring the armies of Cyrus against it, v. 2. Isaiah experiences pain and terror at what he sees in the vision, vv. 3–4. He urges the Babylonians to prepare for the attack, v. 5. The Lord has told the prophet to set a watch for the coming army, v. 6. He sees riders on animals, v. 7. He cries out with impatience, v. 8. The announcement comes that Babylon has fallen, v. 9. This message of judgment should encourage the nation, v. 10. The practical lesson here is that God will right the wrongs of this life.

2. Judgment of Edom. The Edomites seek to know how long the judgment will last, v. 11. Isaiah responds that additional judgment will follow the reprieve from Assyrian judgment, v. 12. The practical lesson here is that God's judgment is complete.

3. Judgment on Arabia. The people of Arabia will flee, hiding in the thickets to escape their enemy, v. 13. The Edomites will help them, v. 14, as they flee from their enemies, v. 15. The nation will fall soon to their enemies, v. 16. Their warriors will be diminished. God Himself has decreed the judgment, v. 17. The practical lesson here is that God's judgment is certain.

1 *The burden of the valley of vision. What aileth thee now, that thou*
   art wholly gone up to the housetops?
2 *Thou that art full of stirs, a tumultuous city, a joyous city: thy slain*
   men are not slain with the sword, nor dead in battle.
3 *All thy rulers are fled together, they are bound by the archers: all*
   that are found in thee are bound together, which have fled from far.
4 *Therefore said I, Look away from me; I will weep bitterly, labour not*
   to comfort me, because of the spoiling of the daughter of my people.

ISAIAH 22

Isaiah directs the final messages of judgment in this part of the book against two of the evil cities in Palestine, Jerusalem and Tyre. Chapter 22 focuses on Jerusalem and c. 23 on Tyre. The message of vv. 1–14 relates to the invasion of the Assyrian army under Sennacherib, ca. 701 B.C. Instead of recognizing the sin that had brought judgment upon the land, the Jews concerned themselves only with the threat to their freedom. When the threat was gone, they gave no further thought to the judgment. God gives Isaiah a message of further judgment. Judah must know that God will judge their sin.

The second half of the chapter, vv. 15–25, focuses on two individuals, Shebna and Eliakim. The judgment that will fall on Shebna illustrates the judgment that will fall upon the nation. The promotion that comes to Eliakim illustrates the reward that God bestows upon the faithful. Sin in every form will receive punishment and faithfulness in every area will receive reward.

K. Against Jerusalem 22:1–25
1. Fall of the City 22:1–14

1–4 Isaiah begins by declaring a "burden" (*maśśaʾ*, or "oracle," see 13:1) for the "valley of vision," another name for Jerusalem. It is the place at which God gives Isaiah this vision of judgment to come.[1] It is a

---

[1]Leslie, p. 69, states that this refers to an altar in the Valley of Hinnom where divination took place. It is unthinkable that Isaiah would locate his oracle by a heathen altar. Herbert, *Isaiah 1–39*, p. 135, suggests that "vision" (*ḥizzayôn*) is a "deliberate distortion of *ḥinnom*, a place where human sacrifice was offered to a pagan deity." Since Isaiah repeats the phrase in v. 5, we may reject this. The prophet surely would not repeat such a distortion. Grogan, p. 140, broadens the thought of "vision" to include all visions received at Jerusalem—"both Isaiah's and other prophets." The view is possible. Based on the LXX, Whitehouse, I, 250, makes *ḥizzayôn* a corruption for *ṣîyôn*. The LXX, however, probably interprets the phrase "valley of vision." It is unlikely that such a corruption

"valley" in that Jerusalem both lies about the Tyropœon Valley and is surrounded by valleys. From vv. 9–10, we see that the city is Jerusalem. Isaiah rebukes the people for going to the housetops to view the enemy camp. This places the time after the flight of the Assyrian army, II Kings 19:35–36. The people have no concern over the experience they have endured. They think now only of the joy of deliverance, v. 1.[2]

While Isaiah begins with the joy of the people at the lifting of the Assyrian siege, he rapidly moves to a future judgment.[3] A likely possibility for this future judgment is the Babylonian siege of Jerusalem at the time of Zedekiah. This siege effectively ended with Zedekiah's attempt to escape, II Kings 25:4–5. If this is the case, Isaiah uses the prophetic perfect to describe the scene. The certainty of the future allows him to portray the scene as past.

Isaiah rebukes the people for rejoicing. The city is filled with "stirs." They are "tumultuous." From the mention of joy, it seems that the city exults over their escape from the Assyrian siege. Isaiah, however, speaks of the coming judgment. Their "slain men" will not die in battle but in a siege. They will not die honorably in war; rather, they will waste away from the lack of food or from pestilence, v. 2.

Their chief men will try to flee. Instead of gaining safety, they will be "bound by the archers" (lit. "they have been taken prisoner [ʾussarû] without the bow"). Although they try to flee far away, they will be taken prisoner (ʾussarû) together, v. 3.[4] Judah's plight affects Isaiah emotion-

---

would occur in both v. 1 and v. 5. Motyer, *The Prophecy of Isaiah,* p. 182, rejects the thought that the valley is the place where Israel received the vision. He sees it as metaphorical, representing "life's darker experiences." While this is possible, nothing forces us to abandon a literal view here.

[2]There are a variety of other interpretations to the passage. Birks, p. 115, makes the "valley of vision" the "valley of Samaria at the close of its three years' siege by the Assyrians." Kelley, p. 255, and Leupold, I, 346, relate it to the withdrawal of the Assyrian troops after paying them tribute, II Kings 18:14–16. Delitzsch, I, 391, makes this the approach of the Assyrian troops. The people rejoice at their safety, having no idea of the deprivations that await them. This is a possible view, but it is unlikely that the people would rejoice at the sight of an enemy. Kraeling, p. 104, assumes a temporary withdrawal of Assyria due to the reported arrival of Egypt. There is no evidence of this. Cundall, *Proverbs—Isaiah 39,* p. 78, considers this the actions of people who feast with no concern for the consequences. This is unlikely.

[3]Clues in the passage set the fulfillment in the future. The walls of Jerusalem will be broken down, v. 5. The Elamites and men of Kir will be the enemy, v. 6. The nearby valleys will fill with enemy chariots, v. 7. This all foretells the invasion of Babylon into Judah.

[4]Driver, *JSS* 13:47, interprets the puᶜal ʾussarû on the basis of a cognate as "huddled together." Although the puᶜal of ʾasar occurs only here, the verb itself occurs over sixty

5 *For it is a day of trouble, and of treading down, and of perplexity by the Lord God of hosts in the valley of vision, breaking down the walls, and of crying to the mountains.*
6 *And Elam bare the quiver with chariots of men and horsemen, and Kir uncovered the shield.*
7 *And it shall come to pass, that thy choicest valleys shall be full of chariots, and the horsemen shall set themselves in array at the gate.*

ally; cf. 21:3–4. He seeks privacy so that he may "weep bitterly." He rejects any "comfort" (*naḥam*, see 1:24) that others might give him. The "spoiling" (better "destruction") of Judah is reason enough for him to grieve. The designation of Jerusalem as a "daughter" is common, cf. 1:8; 10:30, 32, v. 4.

5–7 This future judgment is a "day of trouble" (*meḥûmâ*, or "turmoil"), a time of great disturbance leading to a general uproar among the people.[5] It is a time of "treading down" (*mebûsâ*, or "subjugation"), when the enemy will trample down the people. It is a period of "perplexity" (*mebûkâ*, or "confusion"), when the people do not know what to do.[6] The Lord has allowed this to come upon Judah in the "valley of vision," Jerusalem; cf. v. 1. The enemy is "breaking down the walls" (*meqarqar qir*)[7] either by siege machines that cast boulders at them or by digging under the walls to destroy their foundations. The people of the city cry

---

times. Consistently, it has the sense of "binding," a sense that is suitable here. There is no need to assume a meaning that does not clearly appear elsewhere.

[5]The Hebrew of 5a reads *meḥûmâ ûmebûsâ ûmebûkâ*. The NIV captures the assonance by translating "tumult and trampling and terror." The NEB translates "tumult . . . trampling . . . turmoil." Kaiser, *Isaiah 13–39*, p. 137, offers "tumult and trampling and turbulence." Motyer, *The Prophecy of Isaiah*, p. 183, gives "trampling . . . treading under foot . . . terror." While these alliterative efforts capture the poetry of the phrase, they do not accurately convey the sense of the text.

[6]Henry, p. 117, thinks that the enemy causes "trouble" and "treading down." He distinguishes the "perplexity" as that of Israel's friends who do not know how to relieve their burdens. The parallelism suggests rather that all of these problems belong to Israel.

[7]Both the verb *meqarqar* and the noun *qir* occur only here. Kaiser, *Isaiah 13–39*, p. 137, and Childs, p. 156, rely on an Arabic word *qarqara*, referring to noises, and Ugaritic *qr*, noise, sound. Kaiser understands both *meqarqar* and *qir* to refer to noise and so translates, "an outcry rings out." Watts, *Isaiah 1–33*, p. 279, finds the source of *meqarqar* in *qur*, "to dig." He makes *qir* a shortened form of *maqôr*, "spring, fountain," and translates, "digging a ditch." Von Orelli, p. 128, derives *meqarqar* similarly but understands *qir* as a defective form of *qîr*, "wall." He translates, "undermining the main walls." This is a possible interpretation. The phrase is difficult since neither word occurs again. The similar form *qarqar* in Num. 24:17 argues that *meqarqar* is a pilpel participle from *qarar*, "to tear down." The object *qir* could well be a variant spelling of *qîr*, "wall."

179

8 *And he discovered the covering of Judah, and thou didst look in that day to the armour of the house of the forest.*

9 *Ye have seen also the breaches of the city of David, that they are many: and ye gathered together the waters of the lower pool.*

10 *And ye have numbered the houses of Jerusalem, and the houses have ye broken down to fortify the wall.*

11 *Ye made also a ditch between the two walls for the water of the old pool: but ye have not looked unto the maker thereof, neither had respect unto him that fashioned it long ago.*

"to the mountains" (*har*). The word *har* is singular, "the mountain." The people direct their "crying" (*šôaᶜ*) for help to the mountain on which the temple stands, and thus to the Lord of the temple. The noun *šôaᶜ* occurs only here. Related verbal forms, however, occur regularly when people cry for help. This need for help suggests that it is the people of the city that cry out, v. 5.[8]

Representing the armies of the enemy, Isaiah names "Elam," cf. 11:11, and "Kir," likely an Assyrian province near Media; cf. II Kings 16:9; Amos 1:5; 9:7. While the enemy is Babylon, the armies used people from many nations. They "bare" (i.e., "bear, take up") their quivers. They bring their "chariots of men and horsemen" (or "chariots, men [i.e., soldiers], and horsemen"). They prepare themselves for battle by removing the covering that protects their shields, v. 6. The "choicest valleys," fertile valleys convenient to the city, fill with enemy "chariots." The horsemen take up positions outside the gates of Jerusalem, v. 7.

8–11 The Lord "discovered" (or "removes") the "covering" (*masak*) of Judah.[9] The word *masak* here has a metaphoric sense, apparently rep-

---

[8]Leupold, I, 347, thinks the calls come from the enemy during siege operations as they mutually encourage one another with cries that echo from the surrounding hills. Stacey, p. 133, makes the cries those of the victims of Assyria *before* the armies reach Jerusalem. Herbert, *Isaiah 1–39*, p. 136, views the calls as coming from fugitives in the hill country. Motyer, *The Prophecy of Isaiah*, p. 183, considers the cries as "screams for help resounding to the encircling *mountains* from the sack of the city." Alexander, I, 381, specifically rejects the notion that the mountain is Mt. Zion. He makes the cries echo from the surrounding mountains. These views all require us to understand *har* as a collective, a possible but unlikely view since the plural *harîm* occurs widely. Smith, I, 315, sees the cries as "an appeal to the hills to fall and cover us," an improbable view.

[9]Leslie, p. 70, understands *masak* as a covering of "terror." He translates, "thy terror, O Judah, was revealed." The translation, however, ignores the ᵓet, the sign of the direct object, and the active verb tense. It is improbable that *masak* is the subject. Gray, p. 370, and Price, p. 96, along with the NEB and NIV take this same approach. Kelley, p. 255, refers "he" to the enemy, a possible view although v. 7 speaks of him only in the plural.

resenting the defense of the people that they were relying on for safety.[10] Realizing now their plight, the people put their hope in the weapons stored in the "house of the forest." The "house of the forest" was Solomon's armory and treasury, I Kings 7:2–5; 10:17, 21; II Chronicles 9:16, 20. From its size, 50 × 100 cubits and 30 cubits high, it may well have had other uses also. It was built from cedars from Lebanon. The upright cedars with their appearance of trees side by side gave it the name, v. 8.

The people see the breaches in the defenses of the city. They gather "the waters of the lower pool," the pool of Siloam, storing them in preparation for a siege, v. 9.[11] The people count the houses in the city. They tear down extra houses and use the building materials to strengthen the city's defenses, v. 10.[12] They make a "ditch," a reservoir, "between the two walls" to store water. We cannot identify this place; the "two walls" may refer to a corner where two walls intersect or to a double wall.[13]

With all of the emphasis on preparing to meet the enemy, the people will forget their primary defense. They will fail to seek the Lord's protection and guidance; cf. Psalm 127:1. He is the one who long before has arranged these events, v. 11.

---

[10]It is equally possible that *masak* refers to the covering of Judah's ignorance. Removing this lets the people see their weaknesses. Older commentators, e.g., Näglesbach, p. 250; Leupold, I, 349; and Delitzsch, I, 394, take the verse in this sense. Newer commentators, e.g., Motyer, *The Prophecy of Isaiah,* I, 184; Young, II, 98; and Kelley, p. 255, follow the view expressed above.

[11]Among others, Rawlinson, I, 353; Herbert, *Isaiah 1–39,* p. 136; and Fausset, p. 631, relate the gathering of the waters to Hezekiah's day. This is possible only if the paragraph is considered historical and not prophetic. The references to Elam and Kir in the previous verse support the idea that this is prophetic.

[12]Childs, p. 156, understands the houses as those built outside the city but near the wall "at its base." Removing them makes the wall more difficult to reach. The view is possible although nothing in the text tells us which houses the Jews remove.

[13]Delitzsch, I, 395, and Näglesbach, p. 250, identify the reservoir with a pool outside the Joppa gate in the upper part of Jerusalem. Alexander, I, 384, thinks it is a wall built out from the city around a reservoir and returning to the city. He explains the lack of such a wall by making it a temporary defense. We have, however, no archaeological or biblical information on such a wall. Wright, p. 63, identifies it with the pool of Siloam. Stacey, p. 134, refers this to flooding the space between the double wall of Jerusalem. There is not enough information to let us be certain of the location.

12 *And in that day did the Lord God of hosts call to weeping, and to mourning, and to baldness, and to girding with sackcloth:*

13 *And behold joy and gladness, slaying oxen, and killing sheep, eating flesh, and drinking wine: let us eat and drink; for to morrow we shall die.*

14 *And it was revealed in mine ears by the Lord of hosts, Surely this iniquity shall not be purged from you till ye die, saith the Lord God of hosts.*

15 *Thus saith the Lord God of hosts, Go, get thee unto this treasurer, even unto Shebna, which is over the house, and say,*

16 *What hast thou here? and whom hast thou here, that thou hast hewed thee out a sepulchre here, as he that heweth him out a sepulchre on high, and that graveth an habitation for himself in a rock?*

17 *Behold, the Lord will carry thee away with a mighty captivity, and will surely cover thee.*

18 *He will surely violently turn and toss thee like a ball into a large country: there shalt thou die, and there the chariots of thy glory shall be the shame of thy lord's house.*

19 *And I will drive thee from thy station, and from thy state shall he pull thee down.*

12–14 The Lord's purpose is to call the people to repentance. He wants them to grieve over their sins. They should cut their hair, a mark of grief, cf. 15:2, and put on sackcloth, also an outward sign of inward grief, cf. 15:3, v. 12. Instead, they enjoy themselves. The mention of "oxen" and "sheep," "flesh" and "wine" (*yayin*, see 5:11) suggests banqueting, more than normal meals. They eat and drink with no concern that the next day might bring their death. Paul quotes the second half of the verse, I Corinthians 15:32. Here, men have rejected the spiritual in favor of the fleshly. There, Paul makes the point that man might as well abandon himself to enjoyable pursuits if there is no resurrection, v. 13. The Lord promises judgment upon the people. Their "iniquity" (*ʿawon*, see 1:4) will not be forgiven. The phrase "till ye die" does not suggest that the sin would be forgiven after the death of the people. The phrase states rather the impossibility of forgiveness. Judah's refusal to repent made their condition hopeless, v. 14.

2. Fall of Shebna 22:15–25

15–19 Isaiah gives a specific example of Israel's sin. The Lord sends him to rebuke Shebna.[14] The name "Shebna" is Aramaic, but there is no

---

[14]See also the notes on 36:3 in which Isaiah mentions Shebna again.

mention of his father's name or his background. This leads to the thought that he was a foreigner who had risen to a position of authority. He was the king's "treasurer" (*soken*). The word *soken* comes from the verb *sakan*, meaning "to be of use, serve" in the *qal*. It means something like "steward" here, v. 15. Isaiah meets Shebna. The repeated word "here" indicates that the meeting takes place by a tomb Shebna is preparing for himself. Isaiah rebukes Shebna for his pride.[15] The evidence of this comes from the preparation of the tomb "on high," apparently in an area used by royalty, cf. II Chronicles 32:33 ("chiefest" = "highest"), v. 16. The Lord will punish him. The choice of grammar creates a picturesque image. The Lord "will carry thee away with a mighty captivity [*meṭalṭelka ṭalṭelâ geber*]." The phrase involves the repeated verb *ṭal*, "to cast, throw, hurl." The verb occurs only here in the *pilpel* but the meaning is clear. The doubling of *ṭal* indicates that the Lord will "vigorously hurl" Shebna like a ball. The word *geber* is a vocative, "O mighty man!"[16] Afterward, the Lord will "surely cover thee" (*ᶜoṭᵉkâ ᶜaṭoh*). The repetition of the verb *ᶜaṭâ* gives emphasis. Shebna will be covered, buried in obscurity, v. 17.[17] The Lord will "violently turn and toss" (*ṣanôp yiṣnopka ṣᵉnepâ*) Shebna into a "large country." The threefold use of the root *ṣanap* also gives emphasis. He apparently refers to sending Shebna to Assyria.[18] There, in captivity, he will die. The chariots

---

[15]Skinner, *Isaiah I–XXXIX*, p. 168, assumes that Shebna advocates an alliance with Egypt while Eliakim supports the view held by Isaiah. Replacing Shebna with Eliakim is therefore a major change in Hezekiah's policy. While this may have been true, Isaiah does not give us any information about it. The only reason given here is the arrogance of Shebna.

[16]Young, II, 109, understands *geber* as an adverbial accusative, "as a man." The view is possible although it does not seem right to use *geber* to express the idea "as a mere man" since *geber* normally refers to a "mighty man."

[17]Young, II, 110, and Leupold, I, 353, understand *ᶜaṭâ*, "to grasp," as though the Lord tightly grasps Shebna in preparation to hurl him. The verb follows the act of hurling away, the opposite of grasping firmly. This would also give the verb a sense it does not clearly have elsewhere. In addition, the parallelism of v. 18 suggests Shebna's humiliation. I take *ᶜaṭâ* in its more normal sense "to wrap, cover." Kaiser, *Isaiah 13–39*, p. 148, translates *ᶜoṭᵉkâ ᶜaṭoh* "and rids oneself vigorously of lice." While the image picturesquely illustrates 17*a*, it is extreme to so translate the phrase.

[18]Slotki, p. 103, identifies the "large country" as "Casiphia, a Babylonian city," where many Jews later settled; cf. Ezra 8:17. The text literally says "to a land wide on two sides," i.e., a broad land, not a city. Leupold, I, 353, identifies it as Babylon, the threat earlier in the chapter. The date of Babylon's invasion is more than a hundred years later, too late to make this the place of Shebna's captivity.

20 And it shall come to pass in that day, that I will call my servant Eliakim the son of Hilkiah:
21 And I will clothe him with thy robe, and strengthen him with thy girdle, and I will commit thy government into his hand: and he shall be a father to the inhabitants of Jerusalem, and to the house of Judah.
22 And the key of the house of David will I lay upon his shoulder; so he shall open, and none shall shut; and he shall shut, and none shall open.
23 And I will fasten him as a nail in a sure place; and he shall be for a glorious throne to his father's house.
24 And they shall hang upon him all the glory of his father's house, the offspring and the issue, all vessels of small quantity, from the vessels of cups, even to all the vessels of flagons.

in which he had gloried will go as spoil to the Assyrians. They will stand there as memorials testifying to the shame Shebna had brought upon Hezekiah's house, v. 18. In the first half of v. 19 and in vv. 21–23, Isaiah completely identifies himself with the Lord. "I," the Lord Himself, will bring these things to pass. He reverts to the third person in 19*b:* "He" will bring Shebna down, v. 19.[19]

20–24 The Lord will replace Shebna with the godly Eliakim. The phrase "my servant" marks him as a faithful man; cf. 20:3; 49:6; 52:13. He is the son of Hilkiah, an unknown Israelite, not the father of Jeremiah, who lived about a century later, v. 20. The Lord will give him the "robe" and "girdle" of Shebna to mark him as the officeholder. The "government" of Judah will be in his hand as he leads the nation. He will be a "father" to the people, protecting and guiding them, v. 21.

The Lord will give Eliakim "the key of the house of David." Because the key controls the access to the treasures of a city, it is an apt symbol of power and authority; cf. Matthew 16:19. He bears the key on his "shoulder." The thought suggests the weight of the power that he bears. He opens and shuts with no one to undo his actions.[20] Eliakim here be-

---

[19]The change of person is not unusual in poetic or prophetic literature, cf. G.K. 144 *p.*

[20]Grogan, p. 143, understands the picture literally. The steward carries the "large master key of the palace fastened to the shoulder of his tunic." Only in Rev. 3:7 does this become symbolic. There is, however, no reason that the steward would need to carry the key with him throughout the day. While the key was undoubtedly given to him upon his investiture into office, it is unlikely that he would carry it on his shoulder. The "key" is elsewhere symbolic, Matt. 16:19. It stands here to show Eliakim's power in his governmental role to open or shut. It is appropriate to understand it as a symbol of power and authority.

*25 In that day, saith the Lord of hosts, shall the nail that is fastened in
the sure place be removed, and be cut down, and fall; and the burden that was upon it shall be cut off: for the Lord hath spoken it.*

comes a picture of the Lord, the one who holds the power over death and
hell, cf. Revelation 1:18; 3:7, v. 22. Eliakim will be a "nail in a sure
place," a peg driven into a wall and firmly fixed in its position. As well,
he will be a "glorious throne," a source of honor, to his family. He therefore is one that the nation can depend upon, v. 23.

Isaiah now warns Eliakim. Verse 24 should be understood in a conditional sense. The "glory of his father's house," Eliakim's relatives, will
rely upon him. The following word pictures clarify "the offspring
[*se^{ʾe}ṣaʾîm*] and the issue [*ṣ^epiʿôt*]."[21] Isaiah compares them to "vessels of
small quantity" (or "small containers"), to "vessels of cups" (or "bowls"),
and to "vessels of flagons" (or "jars, pitchers"). The collection of undis-
tinguished containers suggests that Eliakim's family had no notable
achievements, v. 24.

25 Isaiah now gives the inevitable result of nepotism. If Eliakim lets
his relatives take advantage of his position, judgment will result. "In that
day" when he allows his relatives to use his position of influence, this
"nail" will be cut off. The family "burden" (*maśśaʾ*, see 13:1) that rested
upon it will fall, v. 25.[22]

---

[21]Herbert, *Isaiah 1–39*, p. 137, is extreme when he translates *haṣṣe^{ʾe}ṣaʾîm w^ehaṣṣ^epiʿot*
as "dung and excrement." He understands this to refer to "the lowest dregs" of the fam-
ily. The word *ṣe^{ʾe}ṣaʾ* occurs elsewhere in Isaiah, e.g., 44:3; 48:19, and in Job to indicate
"offspring." The parallel "issue" (*ṣapîaʿôt*) can mean "excrement," but the context here
argues for "issue," that which comes forth. The following reference to various containers
establishes the lack of accomplishments in the family apart from Eliakim.

[22]Rawlinson, I, 355, makes the "day" the day of Christ's crucifixion in which He was
"cut off" for the sins of mankind. The lack of a context to distinguish v. 25 from v. 24
makes this view unlikely. Among others, Vine, p. 53; Alexander, I, 391; and Slotki, p.
105, apply v. 25 to Shebna, a view that ignores the context. Pentecost, p. 334, includes
the name in a list given by Arthur Pink of names for Antichrist. Again, the context does
not support this.

Practical Applications from Chapter 22

1. God Judges a Variety of Things. The people, vv. 1–8*a;* the plans, vv. 8*b*–11; the pleasure, vv. 12–14; the pride, vv. 15–19; the position, vv. 20–25. God will judge sin in all its forms.

2. The Brevity of Life. "Let us eat and drink; for to morrow we shall die," v. 13. In view of this, why should we focus on the pleasures that are available to mankind? Why should we not focus instead on eternal matters?

3. Eliakim

   a. A godly character: "the son of Hilkiah." The name Hilkiah means "my portion is the Lord." This may suggests a godly background for Eliakim. The name Eliakim means "God raises up." In addition, God calls him "my servant," v. 20.

   b. A faithful service: not only the overseer of Hezekiah but also one of three representatives to the Assyrians, 36:3, 22; 37:2.

   c. A sobering warning, vv. 24–25.

1   *The burden of Tyre. Howl, ye ships of Tarshish; for it is laid waste,*
    so that there is no house, no entering in: from the land of Chittim it
    is revealed to them.
2   *Be still, ye inhabitants of the isle; thou whom the merchants of*
    Zidon, that pass over the sea, have replenished.
3   *And by great waters the seed of Sihor, the harvest of the river, is her*
    revenue; and she is a mart of nations.

ISAIAH 23

Isaiah directs his final "burden" (or "oracle") against Tyre.[1] Of all the
nations that c. 13–23 mention, the situation of Tyre is perhaps the sad-
dest. Despite their knowledge of the Lord, they had chosen to worship
false gods. Tyre had been closely involved with the Jews. In early days,
David had friendly relations with Tyre, II Samuel 5:11. Solomon allied
himself with Tyre, I Kings 5:12. Despite these relationships, the Phoenicians had not come to worship Israel's God. The marriage between Ahab
and Jezebel likely encouraged the worship of Baal and Asherah in Israel;
cf. I Kings 18:19. The Phoenicians later succumbed to greed and traf-
ficked in Hebrew slaves, Joel 3:4–6; Amos 1:9–10. For these reasons,
the Lord now denounces Tyre, one of two major Phoenician cities and
representative of the nation.

L. Against Tyre 23:1–18
1. Fall of Tyre 23:1–14

1–3 Isaiah announces a "burden" (*massaʾ*, or "oracle," see 13:1) concerning Tyre. He poetically pictures the "ships of Tarshish," cf. 2:16,
wailing over the destruction of their home port. As the ships sail home,
they hear that the houses in Tyre have been "laid waste," devastated, and
the port obstructed and there is "no entering in."[2] The news of Tyre's fall
has come to the sailors in the "land of Chittim," the island of Cyprus,

---

[1]Various attempts to date the prophecy relate it to the fall of Tyre. Rawlinson, I, 371,
dates it ca. 710 B.C., at the invasion of Sargon. Kelley, p. 257, puts it at 701 B.C., after
the approach of Sennacherib. Watts, *Isaiah 1–33*, p. 306, dates it ca. 677 B.C., after the
attack by Assyria under Esarhaddon. Leslie, p. 257, places it after 332 B.C., when Tyre
fell to Alexander. The chapter, however, is not history but prophecy. There is no compelling reason to relate the text to an invasion by some specific nation.

[2]Young, II, 123, makes the phrase "no entering in" dependent on the phrase "no
house," i.e., there is no entrance into the houses of Tyre. While the view is possible, the
repetition of the *min* preposition suggests parallelism rather than dependence. The ships
grieve because of the loss of the houses and the loss of the port.

4 *Be thou ashamed, O Zidon: for the sea hath spoken, even the strength of the sea, saying, I travail not, nor bring forth children, neither do I nourish up young men, nor bring up virgins.*
5 *As at the report concerning Egypt, so shall they be sorely pained at the report of Tyre.*
6 *Pass ye over to Tarshish; howl, ye inhabitants of the isle.*

about 120 miles west of Tyre in the Mediterranean. This was the natural last trading stop before completing the voyage home, v. 1. The prophet orders the people of the "isle" (אִי, occurs regularly in Isaiah to refer to the coastal regions of the Mediterranean, see 11:11)[3] to be "silent" (*dommû*).[4] These who have been supplied by the merchant trade from "Zidon," i.e., the Phoenicians, now should remain quiet as they consider the fate of Tyre, v. 2.[5] The mention of the Phoenician merchant trade causes Isaiah to describe further their commercial activity. Her trade reached the "great waters" of Egypt, the Nile River. The word "Sihor" (*šihor*, lit. Shihor) means "black." It refers to the black dirt carried by the Nile and, by extension, to the river itself. Joshua 13:3 suggests that Sihor was on the eastern side of the delta ("before Egypt").[6] If this is so, we could possibly identify Sihor with the Pelusiac arm of the Nile in the eastern delta. The harvest from around the river was a valuable trade item. This let her become a "mart of the nations," a source for the trade carried on by the Phoenicians, v. 3.

4–6 The Phoenicians should be "ashamed" (*bôš*, see 1:29) at Tyre's fall. Poetically, the "strength [or 'stronghold'] of the sea" laments the loss of her "children," her "young men," and her "virgins," the inhabitants of Tyre. The fact that the sea does not "travail," "bring forth," "nourish," or

---

[3]Grogan, p. 148, identifies the "isle" as the offshore island on which New Tyre was built. The word אִי, however, normally refers to the coastal areas rather than an actual island.

[4]Mitchell Dahood, "Textual Problems in Isaia," *CBQ* 22:400–4, understands *dommû* on the basis of Akkadian and Ugaritic cognates to mean "weep." He considers it "passing strange" that Isaiah begins in v. 1 with "Howl, ye ships . . . ," then urges the coastal areas to be "silent." It is not, however, strange that two groups will react differently to the same event. Here, one group bewails their loss while the other is struck dumb. The *qal* imperative of *damam* occurs seven more times in the OT. In every case, the meaning "silence, rest, wait" is appropriate.

[5]Zidon was the mother city of Phoenicia. According to Herodotus, the founding of Zidon took place ca. 2750 B.C. The term "Sidonian" often stands for the Phoenicians in general; cf. I Kings 5:6; 16:31. Isaiah mentions them here in this sense.

[6]Vine, p. 54, does not take this into account. He makes Sihor the Hebrew name for Siris, the Egyptian name for the Upper Nile River.

7 *Is this your joyous city, whose antiquity is of ancient days? her own feet shall carry her afar off to sojourn.*

8 *Who hath taken this counsel against Tyre, the crowning city, whose merchants are princes, whose traffickers are the honourable of the earth?*

9 *The Lord of hosts hath purposed it, to stain the pride of all glory, and to bring into contempt all the honourable of the earth.*

10 *Pass through thy land as a river, O daughter of Tarshish: there is no more strength.*

11 *He stretched out his hand over the sea, he shook the kingdoms: the Lord hath given a commandment against the merchant city, to destroy the strong holds thereof.*

12 *And he said, Thou shalt no more rejoice, O thou oppressed virgin, daughter of Zidon: arise, pass over to Chittim; there also shalt thou have no rest.*

13 *Behold the land of the Chaldeans; this people was not, till the Assyrian founded it for them that dwell in the wilderness: they set up the towers thereof, they raised up the palaces thereof; and he brought it to ruin.*

14 *Howl, ye ships of Tarshish: for your strength is laid waste.*

"bring up" relates to the lack of people in Tyre. It is as though the sea never has had the Phoenicians as children to sail her waters, v. 4. The phrase "As at the report concerning Egypt" is better "When the report is to Egypt," i.e., reaches Egypt. Hearing of Tyre's fall, they will grieve at the report. No doubt because of the loss of trade, Egypt mourns over the fate of Tyre, v. 5. The Phoenician survivors of Tyre's destruction should find refuge in Tarshish. The people who live in the "isle" (ʾî, the coastal area, see 11:11) will weep over the city's fall, v. 6.

7–14 Isaiah contrasts the fallen Tyre with its former greatness as an ancient city. Its "antiquity [*qadmatah*][7] is of ancient days." The city was more than two thousand years old in Isaiah's time. The verb "shall carry" is better "carried." In those older times, she had colonized far-off places, v. 7. Isaiah asks who has planned the overthrow of Tyre. This is a great city, one that has bestowed crowns, i.e., kingships, on her colonies, giving them independent government. Her "merchants are princes," not actual rulers but ruling over the commerce of the Mediterranean. They

---

[7]Wilfred G. E. Watson, "Tribute to Tyre (Is. XXIII 7)," *VT* 26:372–74, understands *qadmatah* as "presentation" and thus "tribute." He argues that the verb *yabal* requires an object. Since he makes "her" a dative, he understands "tribute" as the object. The verb, however, has the object "her" with the traditional understanding. In addition, Aramaic and Arabic cognates support the meaning "antiquity" for *qadam*.

are "traffickers," the "honourable" (*kabed*, see 3:5) who received honor for their trading pursuits, v. 8. Such a great city could only be destroyed by a great power. Isaiah identifies this power as that of the "Lord of hosts," the ruler of heavenly and earthly powers. He will humble Tyre's pride. He will "stain" [*halal*] the pride of all glory." The word *halal* refers to uncleanness or to something common in contrast with something holy. Here, the Lord considers Tyre's pride unclean. The parallelism with the phrase "all the honourable [*kabed*] of the earth" makes Tyre's "glory" (*ṣᵉbî*)[8] the merchant princes who had exalted themselves. The Lord will bring them low, v. 9.

The colony of Tarshish is now free to move like (lit.) "the river," i.e., the Nile River, which overflows its banks each year. Tyre no longer has "strength" (*mezaḥ*)[9] to restrain her in any way, v. 10. The Lord has reached from Tarshish "over the sea," across the Mediterranean, the primary area of Tyre's influence, to shake the kingdoms. There is no doubt but that Tyre's fall brought economic harm to the lands that depended upon her for trade. The Lord, however, has purposed to destroy "the merchant city" (*kᵉnaᶜan*, lit. "Canaan," the region in which Tyre was located). He here focuses primarily on Tyre, one of the major cities in the area, v. 11.

Tyre is the "oppressed virgin," the "daughter of Zidon." The word "oppressed" has the sense here of "crushed." Until this time, Tyre has been as a "virgin," not overcome by anyone.[10] Now, she has been "crushed." The phrase "daughter of Zidon" refers to Tyre's mother city. Zidon lay about twenty miles north of Tyre on the coast. Zidon, apparently the one for whom the city was named, was the firstborn son of Canaan, Genesis 49:13. The city early became a "great" city; cf. Joshua 11:8; 19:28. Tyre was a colony of Zidon, thus its "daughter." To this time of prophesied judgment, she has overcome all attempts to defeat her. Now, however,

---

[8]Driver, *JSS* 13:49, unnecessarily makes *ṣᵉbî* refer to the "gazelle." In turn, he understands this as a symbol for the nobles of the land. While the AV sometimes translates *ṣᵉbî* as "roe" or "roebuck," better "gazelle," e.g., 13:14; Prov. 6:5; Song of Sol. 2:7, the word often indicates "glory," e.g., 13:19; 24:16; 28:1, 4, 5. The parallelism here gives us the symbolism. There is no need to understand "gazelle."

[9]The root of *mezaḥ* occurs elsewhere as a "girdle," Ps. 109:19. This leads to a metaphoric picture of a restraining influence, a bond no longer possessed by Tyre. The NEB follows the LXX in reading *maḥoz*, "market." The NIV emends similarly but understands it as "harbor." There is, however, no compelling reason to abandon the MT. The defeat of Tyre means there is no longer a restraint to keep the Tarshians at home.

[10]The idea of a "virgin city" is unusual but see 37:22.

15 *And it shall come to pass in that day, that Tyre shall be forgotten seventy years, according to the days of one king: after the end of seventy years shall Tyre sing as an harlot.*

16 *Take an harp, go about the city, thou harlot that hast been forgotten; make sweet melody, sing many songs, that thou mayest be remembered.*

she will be brought low. Though her inhabitants will "pass over to Chittim," the island of Cyprus, they will not find peace there, v. 12.

Isaiah now reveals the instrument used to defeat Tyre. Verse 13 reads better, "Behold the land of the Chaldeans! This is the people. It was not the Assyrians who established her for the wild beasts. They [i.e., the Babylonians] set up their siege towers; they laid bare her fortresses; he [a collective singular] has made it for a ruin."[11] At the time that Isaiah writes, Assyria was the dominant power in that part of the world. Isaiah, however, makes it clear that Assyria is not God's instrument to defeat Tyre. The Babylonians under Nebuchadnezzar besieged Tyre thirteen years, ca. 598–585 B.C. There is virtually no historical evidence to tell us the results of this siege. From the passage here, we can conclude that he took and sacked the coastal city, gaining no great spoil for his efforts; cf. Ezekiel 29:17–18. Apparently, the island portion of Tyre escaped Nebuchadnezzar's threat, v. 13.[12] The ships of Tarshish lament (cf. v. 1) the economic deprivation due to the loss of their homeport, v. 14.

2. Restoration of Tyre 23:15–18

15–16 The "seventy years" corresponds to Judah's Babylonian captivity, 605–536 B.C.[13] During this period, Judah no longer traded with Phoenicia,

---

[11]The translation and interpretation of the verse varies widely. The NASB translates, "Behold, the land of the Chaldeans—this is the people which was not. Assyria appointed it for desert creatures—they erected their siege towers, they stripped its palaces, they made it ruin." The NIV gives, "Look at the land of the Babylonians, this people that is now of no account! The Assyrians have made it a place for desert creatures; they raised up their siege towers, they stripped its fortresses bare and turned it into a ruin." The NEB renders, "Look at this land, the destined home of ships! The Chaldeans erected their siege-towers, dismantled its palaces and laid it in ruins."

[12]Motyer, *The Prophecy of Isaiah,* p. 192, takes a different approach. He understands the reference to Chaldea as urging the people to look at the devastation brought about in Mesopotamia by Sargon. The view is possible; however, the view requires a strained interpretation of the phrase "this people was not, till the Assyrian founded it. . . ." Motyer makes this refer to a "non-existent people" who have disappeared due to the savagery of Assyria. Babylon, though, did not disappear at the time of Sargon's conquest.

[13]Brueggemann, *Isaiah 1–39,* p. 186, considers "seventy" as a lifespan. Those who see the destruction will not live to see the rebirth. Kaiser, *Isaiah 13–39,* p. 170, considers the

17 *And it shall come to pass after the end of seventy years, that the Lord will visit Tyre, and she shall turn to her hire, and shall commit fornication with all the kingdoms of the world upon the face of the earth.*

18 *And her merchandise and her hire shall be holiness to the Lord: it shall not be treasured nor laid up; for her merchandise shall be for them that dwell before the Lord, to eat sufficiently, and for durable clothing.*

which was a serious blow to her economy. The time is like "the days of one king," an unchanging period of time when the conditions remain the same.[14] At the end of this time, Tyre will "sing as an harlot [*zanâ*]."[15] The phrase poetically describes how Tyre seeks the favor of the nations again, v. 15. Isaiah picturesquely describes a ruined harlot who strolls the streets. As she walks, she plays a harp to attract attention. In like manner, Tyre will seek to attract potential customers for her trade, v. 16.

17–18 The Lord will let Tyre rebuild her commerce after the captivity ends. She will do this, however, from the wrong motivation. Rather than serving God, she will serve mammon. She prostitutes herself with the nations for the sake of gain. John borrows the language from the verse to describe Babylon, Revelation 17:2, v. 17. Despite this, the Lord will use Tyre for His own purposes. Her wealth will be "holiness to the Lord," used in the Lord's work rather than stored in treasure houses. Most

---

number "an awkward attempt to resolve the differences in content and chronology between vv. 15–16 and 17–18." Watts, *Isaiah 1–33*, p. 308, treats it as a round number. He weakens this by referring to Tyre's ability to withstand Nebuchadnezzar's siege of 13 years, then her continued activity for 240 years. Grogan, p. 147, follows Erlandsson, p. 102, in making this refer to the years 700–630, "when Assyria did not permit Tyre to engage in any business activity." Tyre was strong enough to join Taharqo of Ethiopia in rebelling against Assyria, 673 B.C. and 663 B.C. For this reason, it is debatable how much limitation Assyria placed on Tyre.

[14]There are a wide variety of interpretations of the phrase. Kelley, p. 259, makes the reference to a king represent a normal lifespan. Slotki, p. 109, suggests the possibility that it refers to the life of a specific king, e.g., David. Fausset, p. 636, refers the phrase to a dynasty. Barnes, I, 386, makes it specific, the length of the Babylonian kingdom. Motyer, *The Prophecy of Isaiah,* p. 193, thinks it indicates a precise rather than symbolic time. Young, II, 137, suggests that it refers to the reign of a king. Then, admitting that seventy years is a long time to rule, he suggests that "the point is that it is wiser to make the reckoning too high than too low, in order to show that for a very long time Tyre will be forgotten." Grogan, pp. 148–49, tentatively proposes that the king is God "who has so decreed matters." Because of its similarity to 21:16, I lean to the view described above.

[15]The word *zanâ* occurs here and in vv. 16, 17. The term regularly indicates spiritual prostitution.

likely, this refers to Tyre's help in the rebuilding of the temple after Judah's return from captivity; cf. Ezra 3:7. While we do not know the background, a Christian church developed later at Tyre, Acts 21:3–4. At some point, Tyre provides food and "durable [ʿatîq][16] clothing" for God's people, an act not recorded in either the Bible or history, v. 18.

Practical Applications from Chapter 23

1. The Danger of Departing from Godliness. As mentioned in the introduction to the chapter, Tyre had every opportunity to worship Israel's God. When they turned away from Him to their own false gods, they made themselves worthy of judgment. The chapter describes the results of their actions.

2. God's Control of Human History.

   a. The fall of Tyre, vv. 1–14. The Lord describes the judgment of Tyre in great detail. Those who rely upon her ships for trade will weep over their loss. The Lord will bring Babylon upon Tyre to judge them for their wickedness.

   b. The restoration of Tyre, vv. 15–18. The Lord has a plan for Tyre. He will let her go through economic deprivation. Eventually, however, He will let her rebuild her commerce. The restored Tyre will serve the Lord in different ways.

---

[16]Among others, Von Orelli, p. 137; Watts, *Isaiah 1–33,* pp. 302–3; and Näglesbach, p. 264, refer this to choice or splendid clothing. The word ʿatîq probably relates to an Arabic cognate, "to grow old." A variant spelling occurs in I Chron. 4:22, "ancient." The idea of quality is interpretive. The biblical use supports more directly the idea of age.

1 Behold, the Lord maketh the earth empty, and maketh it waste, and turneth it upside down, and scattereth abroad the inhabitants thereof.
2 And it shall be, as with the people, so with the priest; as with the servant, so with his master; as with the maid, so with her mistress; as with the buyer, so with the seller; as with the lender, so with the borrower; as with the taker of usury, so with the giver of usury to him.
3 The land shall be utterly emptied, and utterly spoiled: for the Lord hath spoken this word.
4 The earth mourneth and fadeth away, the world languisheth and fadeth away, the haughty people of the earth do languish.

ISAIAH 24

With c. 24–27, Isaiah develops a wider focus. In c. 1–12, he has centered his message on Judah and Jerusalem. In c. 13–23, he deals with many of the nations of the biblical world. Now he broadens again the scope of his words. Chapters 24–27 are sometimes called the "Little Apocalypse." The section is little only by comparison with the book of Revelation, the greater Apocalypse. Isaiah turns here to eschatological events that will involve the whole world. There is a logical arrangement to the material. Chapter 24 takes up the Tribulation. Chapter 25 introduces the millennial kingdom of Christ. Chapter 26 describes the resurrection of the saints not previously raised from the dead. Chapter 27 tells of the final triumph of Christ over the nations of the earth. While there are individual verses that stray from this pattern, this is the general structure of the passage.

III. Prophecies of the End Times 24:1–27:13

While the phrase "day of the Lord" does not occur in this section, it is nonetheless the subject of c. 24–27.

A. Tribulation Judgments 24:1–23
1. Upon Individuals 24:1–12

1–4 Isaiah introduces this section with the word "behold" (*hinneh*). The prophet uses the word *hinneh* more than ninety times. The word always calls attention to something and normally indicates something future, e.g., 7:14; 13:9; 52:6.

Isaiah begins by describing the Tribulation judgments. He predicts calamity that engulfs the whole "earth" (ʾereṣ).[1] God makes it "empty" (bôqeq) and "waste" (bôlᵉqah). The phrase "turneth it upside down" comes from the idea of turning a vessel over to shake out its contents. In shaking the earth, He scatters its inhabitants, v. 1. Isaiah names six representative classes of people. Each class includes a person and his natural counterpart: (1) the common person and his "priest," the spiritual guide; (2) the servant and his master; (3) the maid and her mistress; (4) the buyer and seller; (5) the lender and borrower; and (6) the one receiving "usury" (nošeh, or "creditor") and the payer of "usury" (nošeʾ, or "debtor"). In each case, the destiny is the same. God's judgment cuts across all human divisions, v. 2. The judgment of the "land" (ʾereṣ, better "earth") will be complete. Isaiah emphasizes the completeness by repeating the descriptive words hibbôq tibbôq, "utterly emptied," and hibbôz tibbôz, "utterly spoiled." These phrases are the first of six times in the chapter that Isaiah uses an infinitive absolute to intensify the thought of the verbal root.[2] The Lord has decreed that these things will come to pass, v. 3. There will be sorrow throughout the earth. The earth "mourneth" (ʾablâ) and "fadeth away" (nablâ, or "withers").[3] The "world" (tebel, here "inhabited world") "languisheth" (or "grows feeble") and "fadeth away" (again, "withers"). The "haughty" (mᵉrôm, or "high"), the leaders of the earth, "languish" (again "grow feeble") under the pressures they face, v. 4.

---

[1]Watts, *Isaiah 1–33*, pp. 315–16, understands ʾereṣ as Palestine, including Israel, Phoenicia, and Syria. Alexander, I, 404, refers it to the Babylonian conquest of Judah. It is true that ʾereṣ often refers to Israel and the surrounding nations. It is also true, however, that ʾereṣ often refers to the whole earth, e.g., 6:3; 8:9; 12:5; 14:9, 16; 49:13. In addition, the word *tebel*, v. 4, and the context of v. 21, argue that the passage refers to the whole earth. Applying ʾereṣ this way gives us a natural conclusion to c. 1–23 in which Isaiah has broadened his message. He no longer focuses on his nation or the biblical world. He now includes a wider group of people.

[2]See also vv. 19, 20.

[3]The passage in vv. 1–4 is remarkable for its assonance: bôqeq . . . bôlᵉqah, v. 1; nošeh . . . nošeʾ, v. 2; hibbôq tibbôq . . . hibbôz tibbôz, v. 3; ʾablâ nablâ, v. 4. This is characteristic of Isaiah's style of writing. The many occurrences of this style throughout the book argue strongly for a single author. See also vv. 16, 17.

5   *The earth also is defiled under the inhabitants thereof; because they*
    have transgressed the laws, changed the ordinance, broken the ever-
    lasting covenant.
6   *Therefore hath the curse devoured the earth, and they that dwell*
    therein are desolate: therefore the inhabitants of the earth are
    burned, and few men left.
7   *The new wine mourneth, the vine languisheth, all the merryhearted*
    do sigh.
8   *The mirth of tabrets ceaseth, the noise of them that rejoice endeth,*
    the joy of the harp ceaseth.
9   *They shall not drink wine with a song; strong drink shall be bitter to*
    them that drink it.

5–9 Mankind's sin has caused the earth to be "defiled" (or "polluted"). The people have broken and changed God's "laws" (*tôrâ*, see
1:10) and have violated the "everlasting covenant." This refers to the
Noachic covenant, the only continuing covenant that set down standards
by which mankind should live.[4] Since God made this covenant before the

---

[4]Pentecost, pp. 69, 118, identifies this as the "New Covenant." The New Covenant, however, deals with the promise of salvation. Placing faith in Jesus Christ as Savior fulfills it,
not the keeping of specified standards. Motyer, *The Prophecy of Isaiah,* p. 199, relates the
covenant here to the everlasting aspects of all the covenants: the Noachic covenant, the
promise to Abraham, the Sabbath within the Mosaic covenant, and the Davidic promise.
The passage, however, refers to one covenant, not several. Rawlinson, I, 384, suggests that
this is the covenant "between God and man, in virtue of the nature wherewith God has en-
dowed man, and of the laws which he has impressed upon man's conscience." The Bible
does not describe any such covenant. Donald C. Polaski, "Reflections on a Mosaic
Covenant: The Eternal Covenant (Isaiah 24:5) and Intertextuality," *JSOT* 77:55–73, concludes that Isaiah refers to the Mosaic covenant. Whitehouse, I, 271, likewise makes this
the Law, which "had been long codified and was regarded with reverence and awe." The
NT, however, sets the Law of the Mosaic covenant aside as a means of grace. Alexander,
I, 406, refers this to "divine law generally." He explains that "law," "stature," and "covenant"
are synonymous, "being continually interchanged." The descriptive phrase "everlasting
covenant" seems to refer rather to a specific covenant. Young, II, 158, refers the covenant
to the laws given by God to Adam and, through Adam, to all mankind. The problem with
this view is that the Bible records only one law given to Adam, the requirement that he
not eat of the fruit of the tree of the knowledge of good and evil, Gen. 2:16–17. Unless we
accept the idea of some unstated laws given to Adam, it is difficult to see how this can be
the everlasting covenant. The Edenic covenant (Gen. 1:28) did not apply to man in general. The Adamic covenant (Gen. 3:15) promised only ultimate victory over Satan. The
Abrahamic covenant (Gen. 12:2–3; 15:18) dealt with God's choice of Abraham and the
gift of Palestine to his descendants. The Mosaic covenant (Exod. 20–34) gave Israel a law
that Christ fulfilled. The NT specifically sets this aside as a means of salvation, Gal. 2:16.
The Davidic covenant (II Sam. 7:12–16) promised a Savior who would come through
David's descendants. While these covenants are "everlasting," never having been set aside,
they do not set out standards by which man must live.

10 *The city of confusion is broken down: every house is shut up, that no man may come in.*
11 *There is a crying for wine in the streets; all joy is darkened, the mirth of the land is gone.*
12 *In the city is left desolation, and the gate is smitten with destruction.*

division of the peoples into different language groups, it included the whole human race. The requirements of God's covenant with Noah were simple. Mankind was not to eat blood or to illegally take man's life. In turn, God promised never to judge the earth with a worldwide flood and to establish the rainbow as the sign of the covenant, v. 5. Because man has broken this covenant, judgment will fall on the earth. Isaiah states this in the past tense because it is certain in the mind of God. Those who dwell in the earth are "desolate" (better "guilty"). The people will be "burned" (*ḥarû*).[5] While this may be a poetical description of the judgment, such passages as Revelation 8:7–8; 9:17–18; 16:8–9; and 20:9 show that a literal fire will judge men on earth during the Tribulation. Only a "few men [*ʾenôš*, see 2:11]" will be left, cf. Revelation 6:8; 8:9; 9:18, v. 6.

Beginning with v. 7, a poetic lament continues through v. 12. Wine, associated with joy in the OT, will not be available to mankind. The "vine," the source of wine, will "languish" (again "grow feeble") as it brings forth fewer grapes. Men will stop their merriment, v. 7. They will no longer enjoy the music of instruments. The "tabrets" were small drums struck with the hand. The "harp" was a ten-stringed lyre made from the small intestine of a sheep, v. 8. Those who survive will drink their "wine" (*yayin*, see 5:11) without the accompanying sounds of joyful music. Their "strong drink" (*šekar*, see 5:11), wine made from a source other than grapes, will be bitter to them, bringing no joy, v. 9.

10–12 The "city of confusion" (*qiryaṭ-tohû*, or "wasted city")[6] will be "broken down" (*šabar*, see 14:5). Piles of rubble block the entrance into the houses. We cannot identify the city with certainty. It likely is left

---

[5]Alfred Guillaume, "Some Readings in the Dead Sea Scroll of Isaiah," *JBL* 76:42, notes that 1QIsa*ᵃ* reads *ḥwrw*. On this basis, he relates the word to the Arabic cognate *ḥarā*, "decreased in number." This has the advantage of paralleling the last phrase "few men are left." It is debatable, however, if we should exchange one *hapax legomenon* for another. The MT is satisfactory with its a:b::a:b parallelism.

[6]The word *tohû* occurs widely with the meanings of "confusion, waste, empty, or nothing." In each case, the context must guide the sense used. Here, the context of judgment argues for the sense "waste" or "chaos."

13 *When thus it shall be in the midst of the land among the people,
there shall be as the shaking of an olive tree, and as the gleaning
grapes when the vintage is done.*

14 *They shall lift up their voice, they shall sing for the majesty of the
Lord, they shall cry aloud from the sea.*

15 *Wherefore glorify ye the Lord in the fires, even the name of the Lord
God of Israel in the isles of the sea.*

16 *From the uttermost part of the earth have we heard songs, even
glory to the righteous. But I said, My leanness, my leanness, woe
unto me! the treacherous dealers have dealt treacherously; yea, the
treacherous dealers have dealt very treacherously.*

unidentified to represent all cities that God will judge in that day, v. 10.[7]
The survivors grieve. Their "crying for wine [*yayin*]" is a poetical statement that they lack the joy pictured by the wine. The word "streets"
(*ḥûṣ*)[8] is lit. "without." When used of a city, it normally refers to the
"streets." The "joy" of the people is "darkened" (or "turns to gloom").
There is no more "mirth," v. 11. The city lies in "desolation" (*šammâ*,
see 5:9). Its gate, the means of controlling access, crashes in ruins, v. 12.

2. Upon the Earth 24:13–20

13–16 The subject of v. 13 is the same as in the preceding verses. The
Hebrew, however, sets vv. 8–12 apart from v. 13. Once more, the word
"land" (*ʾereṣ*), cf. v. 3, is better "earth." Isaiah compares the judgment to
the fruit left after the beating of olive branches or the gleaning of grape
vines at the time of the "vintage," the grape harvest, v. 13.

The survivors of this devastation will sing praise to the Lord. They
have experienced both the holiness of God that demands punishment of
sin and the power of God that is able to bring the judgment. They sing
their songs of praise "from the sea," an idiomatic expression better rendered "from the west," v. 14. This anticipates the next phrase in which
the people "glorify" (*kabed*, see 3:5) God "in the fires" (*baʾurîm*),[9] idi-

---

[7]Wright, p. 65; Alexander, I, 407; and Barnes, I, 391, identify the city as Jerusalem.
Von Orelli, p. 141, makes it Babylon. Fausset, p. 638, calls it the "apostate church," spiritual Babylon. Wade, p. 159, tentatively suggests Shushan. Most authors recognize the
impossibility of identifying the city.

[8]Delitzsch, I, 429, refers *ḥûṣ* to the "fields." While this is possible, the normal way of
understanding it is of the "streets."

[9]The plural *ʾurîm*, written with the *qibbuṣ*, occurs only here. The related plural, *ʾûrîm*,
"Urim," written with the *šureq*, occurs seven times. The word describes the fiery appearance of the Urim, worn in the priest's breastplate. The plural there is apparently intensive

omatic for "in the east.[10] "From the west to the east, embracing both Gentiles and Jews, mankind sings praise to the Lord. As usual, the "isles" (*ʾiyê*, see 11:11) refer to the coastal areas of the Mediterranean. Those who dwell here also praise the Lord, v. 15. From the ends of the earth, songs of praise rise to the "righteous" (better "righteous one," the Lord).[11]

Isaiah, however, does not join in this chorus of praise. He expresses his grief over the continuing sin that will bring further judgment. The phrase "My leanness [*razî-lî*], my leanness [*razî-lî*]" (or "my wasting, my wasting") expresses his feelings of losing his strength.[12] The repetition of the phrase lends emphasis to the expression. The Hebrew of 16*b* is also repetitive: *bogᵉdîm bagadû ûbeged bôgᵉdîm bagadû*. This emphasizes the cause of his weakness: wicked men continue to work wickedness. They deal "treacherously," deceitfully carrying out their sin. Isaiah repeats the thought again to stress the treachery of the wicked, v. 16.

---

rather than numerical. Variant spellings also occur several times in personal names. The singular *ʾûr*, written with the *šûreq*, occurs in Ezek. 5:2 and Isa. 31:9; 44:16; 47:14; 50:11. In all but 50:11, the context supports the meaning "fire." In 50:11, the use in a phrase causes the word to revert to its root meaning, "light." The use of *ʾûrîm* in personal names argues against the meaning "lands (or regions) of light." The word here is defectively written. The plural of local extension is appropriate when thinking of the light that springs from the fiery sun.

[10]Rawlinson, I, 385, understands the phrase to refer to the "fiery trials" through which the faithful go. The parallelism with "the sea" argues for an idiomatic sense of direction. Henry, p. 130, makes the "fires" those of affliction through which the righteous have come. This also ignores the parallelism. Barnes, I, 393, makes the lights the aurora borealis, which he then takes as representing the east. The aurora borealis, however, is a northern phenomenon and thus not a good symbol of the east. Kaiser, *Isaiah 13–39*, p. 186, and Delitzsch, I, 430, argue for the meaning "lands of light," contrasting with "islands of the sea." They then, however, explain "lands of lights" as the east, where the sun first rises. It is better to refer the idiom directly to the east rather than to a phrase that must be explained.

[11]Among others, Gray, I, 418; Hailey, p. 201; and Von Orelli, p. 142, refer this to those faithful people who have held to their faith in the Lord. Would the people sing praise to themselves? In addition, the context directs the praise to the Lord. It is better to translate "righteous one."

[12]The word *razî* occurs only here. Kaiser, *Isaiah 13–39*, p. 189, relates it to the Aramaic *raz*, "secret." The Vulgate supports this with its *secretum meum*, "my secret." The following phrase, "Woe unto me," indicates that Isaiah states his personal reaction. The form *razî* occurs only here but the root is not rare. The verb *razâ*, "to grow lean," and other related forms occur several times, including 10:16 and 17:4, with the sense supporting "leanness" here. Delitzsch, I, 431, interprets *razî* as "ruin," a possible sense.

17 Fear, and the pit, and the snare, are upon thee, O inhabitant of the earth.

18 And it shall come to pass, that he who fleeth from the noise of the fear shall fall into the pit; and he that cometh up out of the midst of the pit shall be taken in the snare: for the windows from on high are open, and the foundations of the earth do shake.

19 The earth is utterly broken down, the earth is clean dissolved, the earth is moved exceedingly.

20 The earth shall reel to and fro like a drunkard, and shall be removed like a cottage; and the transgression thereof shall be heavy upon it; and it shall fall, and not rise again.

17–20 Isaiah describes the coming judgment with three descriptive words. "Fear" (*paḥad*, better "terror," see 2:10) will come upon man. He will fall into the "pit" (*paḥat*, a hole, never the grave) or, escaping that, into a "snare" (*paḥ*, a trap, often poetic for calamity). The Hebrew uses paronomasia to express the judgment, *paḥad*, *paḥat*, and *paḥ*. This play on words is characteristic of Isaiah's style of writing. The idea is that the people cannot escape the consequences of God's punishment, v. 17. If a man escapes the "noise," the report, of the "fear" (*paḥad*), he will fall into the "pit" (*paḥat*). If he escapes the "pit" (*paḥat*), the "snare" (*paḥ*) will catch him. God has opened "the windows [*ᵃrubâ*] from on high," an idiom picturing the pouring out of His judgment from heaven. The word *ᵃrubâ* refers to an opening. The phrase "windows from on high" idiomatically refers to the opening of the skies through which God pours His judgment. The thought here includes heavenly sources of judgment, e.g., flooding, hail, storms (including tornados and hurricanes), lightning, and meteorites. The shaking of the "foundations of the earth" suggests that earthquakes will bring devastation, v. 18. These cataclysmic judgments will mark the end of the world as we know it. It will become "broken down" (*roᶜâ hitroᶜaᶜâ*, better "totally shattered," see 11:9), "clean dissolved" (*pôr hitpôrᵉrâ*, better "thoroughly broken"), and "moved exceedingly" (*môṭ hitmôṭᵉṭâ*, better "violently shaken").[13] With each of the three descriptive phrases, an infinitive absolute repeats the verbal root to emphasize the thought (cf. v. 3). The earth is not just shattered, broken, and shaken; it is totally shattered, thoroughly broken, and violently shaken, v. 19. The earth will "reel to and fro" (*nôaᶜ tanûaᶜ*, better "greatly stagger") in the same way that a drunkard staggers as he

---

[13]The word *môṭ* indicates "totter, shake, slip." It normally occurs in a poetic sense.

21 *And it shall come to pass in that day, that the Lord shall punish the host of the high ones that are on high, and the kings of the earth upon the earth.*

22 *And they shall be gathered together, as prisoners are gathered in the pit, and shall be shut up in the prison, and after many days shall they be visited.*

23 *Then the moon shall be confounded, and the sun ashamed, when the Lord of hosts shall reign in mount Zion, and in Jerusalem, and before his ancients gloriously.*

walks. Once more, an infinitive absolute intensifies the verbal idea. Isaiah adds here the word picture "like a drunkard" to complete the illustration. The earth will be "removed like a cottage" (or "sway like a hut"). The thought is of an old shack that is about to fall down. The "transgressions" (understanding *peša*ᶜ as a collective singular) of the earth are "heavy" (*kabed*, see 3:5) upon it.[14] The word *peša*ᶜ refers to rebellion of one party against another. God's judgment will cause it to fall. It will never rise again as the same world system.

The judgment is the judgment of the world at the end of the Tribulation. The Lord will follow this with His kingdom reign over the earth; cf. 25:6–8; 26:1–2; 27:6, 13. This act will end the Tribulation time. The millennial kingdom, the rule of Christ over the earth, will begin. Chapter 24 stresses the Tribulation judgments. Chapters 25–27 place their emphasis on the kingdom, v. 20.

3. Upon the Rulers 24:21–23

21–23 Isaiah now singles out the two groups of ungodly leaders who are largely responsible for man's departure from God. The "host of the high ones" are the ungodly angels, who followed Satan in his rebellion against God and now serve him.[15] Cf. Job 4:18; II Peter 2:4 (Jude 6). The

---

[14]The noun *peša*ᶜ is masculine singular. See the discussion of the grammar of a collective singular in c. 16, note 2.

[15]Gray, I, 422, uses a rather puzzling expression to explain "host of the high ones." He calls them "superhuman beings," then has the term include the "sun, moon, and stars," worshiped by men, and the "patron angels . . . of the nations." Mauchline, p. 187, also includes the "sun, moon and stars." Smith, p. 418, includes only the stars. While it is true that men have worshiped the heavenly bodies, the passage here does not include them as "prisoners" in the "pit," nor will they be "visited" later. Kissane, I, 283, refers the term to "pagan gods." A paragraph later, he makes them include the "monsters," i.e., the gods described in *Enuma Elish*, the Babylonian creation epic. The view is impossible since these gods do not exist. Slotki, p. 114, mentions a trivial view, that an eclipse takes

"kings of the earth" are the rulers of the world system at the time Christ returns; cf. Daniel 7:24. The Lord will "punish" (*paqad*, see 10:12)[16] these two groups who have opposed Him, v. 21.

The Lord will place these in bondage just as prisoners would be placed in a "pit" (*bôr*, see 14:15), a dungeon. Then, "after many days," they will be "visited" (*paqad*, or "punished"). The "many days" here refer to the thousand-year reign of Christ. At the end of that time, man will unleash his final rebellion against the Lord (Rev. 20:7–9). Satan and, presumably, his angels (Jude 6) will be judged (Rev. 20:10). Wicked mankind will stand before the Great White Throne judgment (Rev. 20:11–15), v. 22.

At that time, the "moon" (*lᵉbanâ*, "white," used poetically of the moon) will "be confounded" and the "sun" (*ḥammâ*, "hot," used poetically of the sun) will be "ashamed." Both terms refer to the diminishing of these heavenly bodies as they pale before the light of Christ in His reign; cf. 60:19–20; Revelation 21:23; 22:5. He will rule from Jerusalem, the New Jerusalem, Revelation 21:1–2, 23; 22:5. The glory of the Lord will be visible to the "ancients."[17] These are the human leaders who live with Christ in His eternal kingdom, v. 23.[18]

---

place before the coming of Messiah. He also mentions the view that these are the angels of the nations. Delitzsch, I, 434, also takes this position, a possible view. Alexander, I, 410; Cowles, p. 177; and Barnes, I, 396–97, make the phrase refer only to ecclesiastical leaders. The view is possible. The emphasis of "high ones" being "on high" refers rather to angels. Henry, p. 132, refers to earthly kings. The phrase "host of the high ones that are on high" complements "kings of the earth" rather than duplicates it.

[16]The word *paqad* is translated by such words as "number," "want," "punish," "visit," etc. The basic sense of the word seems to be an inspection of something with a view toward making some decision. Sometimes the decision is simply numbering, sometimes a judgment, sometimes to exercising care. The broad semantic range of the word leads to uncertainty in many passages. The idea here is that of punishment.

[17]Young, II, 182, understands the glory as the glory of the church. Connecting the final phrase with the rule of the Lord just set forth, the glory here is that belonging to the Lord. The saints see this glory.

[18]Because the verse introduces the reign of Christ, Watts, *Isaiah 1–33*, p. 327, joins v. 23 to c. 25. The verse makes the transition between the chapters. It concludes c. 24 as much as it introduces c. 25. Since c. 25 begins with a song, it is appropriate to leave v. 23 with c. 24.

Practical Applications from Chapter 24

1. When God's judgment falls, it touches all who sin, v. 2.

   a. The common person and the priest

   b. The servant and the master

   c. The maid and her mistress

   d. The buyer and the seller

   e. The lender and the borrower

   f. The one receiving usury and the one paying usury

   While this listing of the groups falling under judgment is only representative, it illustrates the fact that all will answer to God. Be sure your sin will find you out.

2. The End-time Events

   a. The Tribulation judgments, vv. 14–22

   The events of this world are not random. In God's time, His wrath will fall upon the world. The wicked may carry on their wickedness for a time, v. 16. When the judgment falls, however, the wicked person will know "fear." He will fall into a "pit" from which he can escape only with difficulty. If he escapes, he will find that a "snare" awaits him, vv. 17–18a. Both calamities from heaven and earthly trials will come upon mankind, v. 18b. The world system will become completely broken, v. 19. It will stagger from the judgment and fall, never to rise again, v. 20. No one will escape. The Lord will punish the ungodly angels who have led man astray and the leaders of mankind who have led the world's system, v. 21. They will be shut up during the Millennium before being released to engage in their final rebellion against God.

   b. The final judgment, v. 22

   God will visit the wicked with their eternal punishment, v. 22.

   c. The eternal kingdom

   The sun and moon will pale into insignificance before the glory of the Lord as He sets up His eternal rule, v. 23.

1 *O Lord, thou art my God; I will exalt thee, I will praise thy name;*
for thou hast done wonderful things; thy counsels of old are faithful-
ness and truth.
2 *For thou hast made of a city an heap; of a defenced city a ruin: a*
palace of strangers to be no city; it shall never be built.
3 *Therefore shall the strong people glorify thee, the city of the terrible*
nations shall fear thee.

ISAIAH 25

The millennial kingdom is both a time of righteousness and a time of freedom from wickedness. Isaiah here develops both of these ideas. He opens with a note of praise to the Lord for judging the wicked, vv. 1–5. He then summarizes the blessings of the kingdom. Not only will the saints feast with the Lord but they will also enjoy a lack of sorrow and death, vv. 6–8. Finally, Isaiah describes the judgment that falls upon Moab, an illustration of the righteousness that He will establish through-out the earth. The Lord will trample the wicked and break down their cities as He sets up His rule, vv. 9–12.

B. Kingdom Blessing 25:1–12
1. The Praise of the Lord 25:1–5

1–3 In view of the omnipotence of the Lord, just seen in c. 24 in His judgment of the wicked, He is worthy of praise. Isaiah praises Him for His work in putting down the wicked and defending the nation.[1] Isaiah exalts the Lord and praises His "name." The "name" of the Lord here is equivalent to His nature, those qualities and attributes by which He has revealed Himself to man. The Lord has worked wonderfully in carrying out His will on the earth. As is customary in the book, Isaiah uses the past tense. These future events are so certain to God that the prophet speaks of them as already accomplished. His ancient "counsels," here in-dicating God's plans, are "faithfulness [*ᵉmûnâ*, see 11:5] and truth [*ᵒomen*]." They have been faithfully carried out. The coordination of the feminine *ᵉmûnâ* with the masculine *ᵒomen* shows the nature of His faithful work, "utmost faithfulness" (cf. 3:1), v. 1.[2]

---

[1] Leupold, I, 393, thinks that Israel is the speaker. Vine, p. 56, and Price, p. 110, iden-tify the singer as the godly in Israel. It is entirely possible that the redeemed remnant speaks. There is, however, no clear indication in the verse that this is the case.

[2] The alternation of the masculine and feminine forms of the same root sometimes ex-presses entirety. See note 1, c. 3.

4 *For thou hast been a strength to the poor, a strength to the needy in his distress, a refuge from the storm, a shadow from the heat, when the blast of the terrible ones is as a storm against the wall.*
5 *Thou shalt bring down the noise of strangers, as the heat in a dry place; even the heat with the shadow of a cloud: the branch of the terrible ones shall be brought low.*

The Lord will reduce the godless cities to a "heap" of stones. The fortified city will become a "ruin." As in 24:10, Isaiah does not identify the city.[3] This lets the city represent all cities that oppose God. It stands for all the cities destroyed by the Lord at the close of the Tribulation. The "palace of strangers [*zar*, see 1:7]," i.e., the place from which foreigners rule, becomes "no city," completely devastated, never again to be built, v. 2. Because God judges the wicked, the "strong people" give glory to Him. The parallelism between 2*a* and 2*b* makes it clear that the "strong people" are Gentile nations. Formerly opposed to God, they now "glorify" (*kabed*, see 3:5) Him. The word "city" (*qiryat*) is a collective representing all the cities of the Gentiles.[4] They "fear," i.e., reverence, and honor Him, v. 3.

4–5 This deliverance has helped the oppressed, the "poor" (*dal*, see 10:2) and "needy" (*ʾebyôn*, see 14:30). The Lord is their "strength" (*maʿôz*, the participle indicating a place of safety, a stronghold). The figures of the "storm" and the "heat" portray the attacks of the heathen on God's people. The Lord provides "refuge" and shade, protecting His own. The attack becomes no more than a storm beating against a wall. God shelters His people safely inside the wall, v. 4. He will "bring down" (or "subdue") the "noise" of the "strangers" (*zar*, see 1:7), the tumultuous approach of the heathen. As the heat of a "dry place," a drought, is ended, so the Lord will end the threat of the heathen. Like the heat that cools with the shade of a "cloud" (*ʿab*, normally a "rain cloud," see 5:6) as it passes by, so the "branch" (lit. "song") of the oppressors will be

---

[3]Kraeling, p. 112, gives several reasons for identifying the city as Samaria. The basic reason stems from his effort to make this history rather than prophecy. As in 24:10, Fausset, p. 640, makes the city spiritual Babylon. Vine, p. 56; Cowles, p. 179; and Barnes, I, 399, refer the city to literal Babylon. On the basis of the collective singular in v. 3, Mauchline, p. 188, makes the word a collective, "cities." Verse 3, however, results from the action described in v. 2. There is no way to be certain of the city. Leaving it unnamed makes a satisfactory application.

[4]While collective singulars are generally masculine, certain feminine nouns may also serve as collectives. G.K. 122 *s*; Waltke and O'Connor 6.4.2c; Williams 2.2.27.

> 6 *And in this mountain shall the Lord of hosts make unto all people a feast of fat things, a feast of wines on the lees, of fat things full of marrow, of wines on the lees well refined.*
> 7 *And he will destroy in this mountain the face of the covering cast over all people, and the vail that is spread over all nations.*
> 8 *He will swallow up death in victory; and the Lord God will wipe away tears from off all faces; and the rebuke of his people shall he take away from off all the earth: for the Lord hath spoken it.*

"brought low" (or "answered"). The idea is that the Lord will silence the songs of His enemies, v. 5.[5]

2. The Blessing of the Saints 25:6–8

6 The mountain is Mt. Zion, the center of Messiah's rule; cf. 24:23. The Lord will invite the nations to feast with Him. In the Bible, feasting is a common figure of fellowship; cf. 55:1–2; Psalm 22:29; Proverbs 9:5. The feast includes "fat things," the choicest part of the animal; cf. Genesis 45:18; Nehemiah 8:10. It involves "wines on the lees," wine that has been allowed to stand upon that which settles out. The wine is well aged and thus full flavored. The fatty meat was mixed with "marrow," the soft inner part of the hollow bones of the animals. This was considered a delicacy; cf. Psalm 63:5. The second reference to wine notes that it is "refined," poured off from the lees and thus pure.

This feast is the marriage supper of the Lord and the saints; cf. Revelation 19:9. The millennial context supports this association. Only believers enjoy this banquet, Luke 12:37. The picture represents the continuing fellowship of the saints with the Lord during the kingdom, v. 6.

7–8 Isaiah lists blessings that will come to God's people. The Lord will "destroy" (*bala^c*, or "swallow up," see 3:12) the "covering . . . and the veil." This pictures the removal of sorrow from the people. The veil was worn in times of grief; cf. Leviticus 13:45; II Samuel 15:30; Jeremiah 14:3–4.[6] The "face" of the covering is the surface of the veil that

---

[5]Pentecost, p. 334, includes the "branch" in a list of names given by Arthur Pink for Antichrist. Although this is an eschatological context, there is nothing here that justifies applying the verse to Antichrist. In His deliverance of the world, the Lord will end the rejoicing of the wicked.

[6]On the basis of II Cor. 3:15, Leupold, I, 397; Näglesbach, p. 280; and Hailey, p. 206, make the veil symbolize the spiritual blindness of the people. Watts, *Isaiah 1–33*, p. 331, makes it represent the "curse of the broken covenant." Slotki, p. 116, suggests that the veil is the protection enjoyed by wicked nations. Removing it makes them subject to punishment from God. Kelley, p. 264, relates it to the "tyranny and oppression to which

9 *And it shall be said in that day, Lo, this is our God; we have waited for him, and he will save us: this is the Lord; we have waited for him, we will be glad and rejoice in his salvation.*

10 *For in this mountain shall the hand of the Lord rest, and Moab shall be trodden down under him, even as straw is trodden down for the dunghill.*

11 *And he shall spread forth his hands in the midst of them, as he that swimmeth spreadeth forth his hands to swim: and he shall bring down their pride together with the spoils of their hands.*

12 *And the fortress of the high fort of thy walls shall he bring down, lay low, and bring to the ground, even to the dust.*

another person sees, v. 7.[7] Verse 8 defines the nature of the covering as the grief that envelops the earth. The Lord God will "swallow up" (*balaᶜ*, see 3:12) death, taking it away; cf. Hosea 13:14. Paul quotes the verse in I Corinthians 15:54. This indicates the Lord's final victory over sin. There will be no more tears; cf. Revelation 7:17; 21:4. Further, the world will no longer reproach God's people. The rule of the Lord over the earth reveals that the worship of Christ is indeed right: the Lord has decreed these things, v. 8.

3. The Judgment of the Ungodly 25:9–12

9–10a Verse 9 continues the theme of vv. 1–5. Isaiah looks forward to that time when the people will rejoice in the Lord. In "that day," the day of the kingdom, the people will acknowledge Him as their God. They have "waited" (*qawâ*, see 5:2) for His deliverance from their trials. They are confident that He will "save" (*yašaᶜ*, see 17:10) them, deliver them from the opposition that they have faced. They anticipate rejoicing in the time of His kingdom rule, v. 9. His "hand," the instrument of His power, cf. Exodus 15:6; 32:11; I Chronicles 29:12; Micah 2:1, will rest in favor on Mt. Zion, v. 10a.

10b–12 As an illustration of God's protection, Isaiah singles out Moab as a representative nation that the Lord will tread down. He

---

Israel and other small nations were periodically subjected." While these are possible views, the context of v. 6 and the parallelism with v. 8 suggest that the veil represents the grief removed by the Lord. In v. 6 the Lord restores joy. In v. 8 He removes grief. Verse 7 logically connects these two thoughts.

[7]The "face of . . ." something is often idiomatic for the thing itself. The "face of the old man" (Lev. 19:32) is the man himself. The "face of the earth" (e.g., Num. 12:3) is the earth itself. The "face of the child" (II Kings 4:31) is the child himself. The "face of the Lord" (Ps. 34:16) is the Lord Himself. The "face" generally refers to the surface, the visible part, while the qualifying phrase identifies the subject.

illustrates this with the figure of straw that is "trodden down for the dunghill" (*matben b^emô madmenâ*).[8] The noun *madmenâ* occurs only here. There is an Arabic cognate that means "dung." A related noun *domen*, "dung," occurs several times. Straw was mixed with manure to make fertilizer. In the same way, the Lord will trample Moab into a position of humiliation, v. 10*b*. Moab will try to swim from this position to escape.[9] Despite their efforts, God will bring them low. He will overcome their proud self-evaluation and the "spoils [*'arbôt* better 'trickery'] of their hands," v. 11.[10] Isaiah changes the figure to that of a "fortress" (*mibṣar*, see 17:3), a well-protected city. He perhaps thinks of Ar or Kir-Moab (Kir-Hareseth), major cities of Moab; cf. 15:1. The Lord will break down the walls. He will "bring down, lay low, and bring to the ground, even to the dust." The repetition of descriptive terms points to the completeness of God's victory over Moab, v. 12.

---

[8]The AV reads the *q^erê b^emô*, "for (the water of)," for the *k^etîb b^emê*, "in the waters." There is textual evidence in favor of this. The Septuagint, Vulgate, and Syriac all support *b^emô*. The next verse introduces swimming that presupposes water in the dung pit. The Isaiah Scroll, however, supports the *k^etîb*.

[9]Barnes, I, 403–4, and Henry, p. 136, understand the Lord as the one who stretches out His hands over Moab. The view is possible. In my judgment, the natural thought is of Moab trying to escape the dung pit of their humiliation. The picture of God spreading His hands as a swimmer would be unusual.

[10]While *'arbôt* occurs only here, other forms of the root *'arab*, "to lie in wait, ambush," occur widely. The sense of *'arbôt* is "deceit, trickery."

Practical Applications from Chapter 25

1. Praising the Lord, vv. 1–5

   a. Isaiah determines to praise the Lord, v. 1a. The prophet makes a conscious decision to offer praise to the Lord his God. He purposes to "exalt" Him, to lift Him up high where others can know of Him.

   b. The nature of the Lord is worthy of praise, v. 1b. When we consider the power of God, the wisdom of God, the eternity of God, the grace of God, the love of God, and many other attributes, He deserves praise.

   c. The plans of the Lord are worthy of praise, v. 1c. Recognizing the purposes of God on behalf of His own, how can we do anything other than give Him our praise? He is faithful to accomplish His work. Verses 2–5 describe how the Lord overcomes His enemies as He protects His own. The millennial context of the chapter relates this to the end-time when the Lord sets up His kingdom. At that time, the Gentile nations will honor the Lord.

2. The Hope of the Believer, vv. 6–8

   a. The fellowship with the Lord, v. 6. We will feast with the Lord as we enjoy the finest of food and drink.

   b. The removal of sorrow, vv. 7–8. The Lord will take away death, tears, and the reproach of His people.

3. The Judgment of the Wicked, vv. 9–12

   a. Confidence of believers, vv. 9–10a

   b. Destruction of unbelievers, vv. 10b–12

      (1) Trampling under foot, v. 10b

      (2) Overcoming pride and trickery, v. 11

      (3) Treading down the cities, v. 12

   God's victory is complete.

1 In that day shall this song be sung in the land of Judah; We have a strong city; salvation will God appoint for walls and bulwarks.

2 Open ye the gates, that the righteous nation which keepeth the truth may enter in.

3 Thou wilt keep him in perfect peace, whose mind is stayed on thee: because he trusteth in thee.

ISAIAH 26

In view of what the Lord has described in c. 25, a note of praise is appropriate. Judah now rejoices in the Lord. They praise Him for what He has done for them, vv. 1–4, and for what He has done to their enemies, vv. 5–6. The godly will walk in the ways of the Lord, vv. 7–9. The wicked, however, will not adopt righteous ways, vv. 10–11. It is the Lord who will bring peace to His people, v. 12. Israel will worship Him and will forget past oppression by the heathen, vv. 13–14. He will enlarge the nation, v. 15. In the past, they have not gained deliverance, vv. 16–18, but there is hope for the future. The believing dead will live again, v. 19. The Lord will shield them from His judgments on the earth, vv. 20–21.

C. Millennial Song 26:1–21
1. Rejoicing of the People 26:1–12[1]

1–3 In the day of the Lord's reign, Judah will praise the Lord for His deliverance. She has a "strong city," made strong by the "salvation" provided by God.[2] The "bulwarks" (better "ramparts") are earthen works outside the city wall. This gave greater protection to the people. In the kingdom, the salvation provided by the Lord serves as the "walls and ramparts" of the city, v. 1. The gates of the city are open so that "the righteous nation which keepeth the truth," the people of God, may enter.[3]

---

[1]Rawlinson, I, 414, makes the chapter apply to the church. While the church will undoubtedly praise God in the kingdom, the OT does not develop that aspect. There is no reason to make "the land of Judah" here refer to anything more than the Jewish people.

[2]The verse is ambiguous. Are the "walls and bulwarks" the security of the city? Does "salvation" serve as a defense? Among others, Skinner, *Isaiah I–XXXIX*, p. 192; Gray, p. 438; and Whitehouse, I, 280, adopt the first view. Among others, Von Orelli, p. 145; Herbert, *Isaiah 1–39*, p. 155; and Rawlinson, I, 414, adopt the second. In view of the millennial context of the chapter, I feel the Lord's protection is the more natural of the two positions. The care of the Lord becomes the "walls and bulwarks" of Jerusalem.

[3]Delitzsch, I, 443, makes the cry to open the gate go forth to the angels of heaven. Barnes, I, 405, sees this as the return of the Jews from captivity in Babylon. There is no

4 *Trust ye in the Lord for ever: for in the Lord Jehovah is everlasting strength:*
5 *For he bringeth down them that dwell on high; the lofty city, he layeth it low; he layeth it low, even to the ground; he bringeth it even to the dust.*
6 *The foot shall tread it down, even the feet of the poor, and the steps of the needy.*

The open gates picture the invitation that God extends to all people to enter His kingdom, v. 2. Those who trust the Lord experience "perfect peace." The word "mind" (or "purpose") comes from *yeṣer*, "pottery" and, by extension, something formed. Here, it is formed in the mind, thus "purpose, plan." This is "stayed on thee," relying on the Lord. Literally, the Lord gives this person "peace, peace" (*šalôm šalôm*, see 9:6), rightly translated as "perfect peace" to convey the intensive nature of God's peace, v. 3.[4]

4–6 Isaiah urges others to trust the Lord. The name "Lord Jehovah" (*yah yᵉhwah*), is a doubled name, lit. "the Lord, the Lord." This combination occurs only here and at 12:2. In Him is "everlasting strength." Literally, this phrase is "a rock of ages," an everlasting foundation that will never fail. The term "rock" is often applied to the Lord in the OT, cf. Psalm 18:2, 46; 95:1, v. 4.[5] To illustrate His power, Isaiah recalls how God has overcome His enemies. He has brought down the "lofty city," that city that was once thought invincible.[6] Once again, Isaiah emphasizes the thought by repeating the verb *šapal*, "He layeth it low, He layeth it low." The Lord humbles the city, bringing it down to the ground, v. 5. Those who formerly were oppressed, the "poor" (*ʿanî*, see 3:14) and "needy" (*dal*, see 10:2), will be elevated in the kingdom. They now

---

need to restrict the cry to angels or returning Jews. The context places this in the kingdom. Jerusalem will be open to all believers who come to worship the Lord during the Millennium.

[4]Whitehouse, I, 280, and Kaiser, *Isaiah 13–39*, p. 205, delete the second *šalôm* and translate simply "peace." Doubling a word or phrase, however, is characteristic of Isaiah. He often repeats a thought to convey emphasis, e.g., 12:2; 22:17; 24:16; and 57:19 (where the same construction *šalôm šalôm* occurs again). See also v. 5, "He layeth it low," and v. 15, "Thou hast increased the nation."

[5]In addition to v. 4, Isaiah refers to God as the "rock" in 8:14; 17:10; 30:29; and 44:8. See 30:29 for a summary.

[6]Barnes, I, 400, and Fausset, p. 642, identify the city as Babylon. Henry, p. 138, and Motyer, *The Prophecy of Isaiah*, p. 214, suggest Babylon or Nineveh. It is best to leave the city unidentified, a general representative of every city that raises itself against God.

7 *The way of the just is uprightness: thou, most upright, dost weigh the path of the just.*

8 *Yea, in the way of thy judgments, O Lord, have we waited for thee; the desire of our soul is to thy name, and to the remembrance of thee.*

9 *With my soul have I desired thee in the night; yea, with my spirit within me will I seek thee early: for when thy judgments are in the earth, the inhabitants of the world will learn righteousness.*

10 *Let favour be shewed to the wicked, yet will he not learn righteousness: in the land of uprightness will he deal unjustly, and will not behold the majesty of the Lord.*

11 *Lord, when thy hand is lifted up, they will not see: but they shall see, and be ashamed for their envy at the people; yea, the fire of thine enemies shall devour them.*

12 *Lord, thou wilt ordain peace for us: for thou also hast wrought all our works in us.*

"tread it down" as they walk freely through the city that God has humbled, v. 6.[7]

7–12 Isaiah now looks at the way of the godly. Their way is "uprightness" (*yašar*). The root idea of *yašar* is that of something being "straight." From this comes the ethical meaning of "uprightness" or "justice." The Lord "dost weigh" (*tepalles*) the path. The context of a straight way of life suggests that *palas* refers to making the path "level," directing it past those temptations that would draw the person away from God, cf. Proverbs 15:19, v. 7. The righteous have "waited" (*qawâ*, see 5:2) for the "judgments" (*mišpaṭ*, see 1:17) of God to fall upon the wicked.[8] They hope to see His "name" and His "remembrance" lifted up, v. 8. Isaiah joins with the godly, the righteous ones of the end times. He himself has also sought the Lord's appearance. Isaiah knows that the "judgments" (*mišpaṭ*) of the Lord will bring "righteousness" (*ṣedeq*, see 1:21) to the world, v. 9.

---

[7]Stacey, p. 156, calls the reference to the poor "hardly a realistic detail." He makes the picture "an ideal one" in which the humble "trample over the ruins of . . . proud achievements." Stacey misunderstands the passage as history rather than an eschatological picture of the kingdom. The righteous poor in this life will prosper then. While correctly giving the passage an eschatological sense, Slotki, p. 118, goes too far in identifying the "poor" as the Messiah.

[8]The NEB and NIV translate *mišpaṭ* as "laws," a possible translation. I have opted for "judgments" because v. 9 picks up this thought. The judgments of the Lord will teach the people righteousness.

13 *O Lord our God, other lords beside thee have had dominion over us: but by thee only will we make mention of thy name.*
14 *They are dead, they shall not live; they are deceased, they shall not rise: therefore hast thou visited and destroyed them, and made all their memory to perish.*
15 *Thou hast increased the nation, O Lord, thou hast increased the nation: thou art glorified: thou hadst removed it far unto all the ends of the earth.*

Despite this divine favor that the Lord will give to the world, the wicked will not learn "righteousness" (*ṣedeq*).[9] They will continue to live in an unjust manner. They will not "behold," i.e., "perceive," the majestic power of God, v. 10. Though the Lord will lift His hand over His people to protect them, the wicked will not see Him.[10] Only when God unlooses His judgment will they recognize His work. They will then "be ashamed [*bôš*, see 1:29] for their envy at the people" (better "at the zeal for the people"), i.e., God's zeal on behalf of His own. His "fire," i.e., His judgment, will devour His enemies, v. 11. Isaiah expresses his hope for the future and confidently states his desire that God will bring "peace" (*šalôm*, see 9:6) to His people. This is a natural hope in view of God's past work "in us" (better "for us"), i.e., on Isaiah's people. Whatever good has been accomplished, God has done it, v. 12.

2. Resurrection of the Saints 26:13–21

13–15 In the past, other "lords," human kings, have ruled Israel. Now, however, through the Lord's help, the Jews will praise His name, v. 13.[11] The past oppressors are "deceased" (*rᵉpaʾîm*, refers to those in

---

[9]Näglesbach, p. 285, considers the divine favor here to be the withholding of judgment from the wicked. While this is a possible view, I feel that the preceding verses suggest the general favor of God showed to the world. The wicked will not respond to this.

[10]Leupold, I, 409, and Näglesbach, p. 287, understand the lifting of God's hand as the preparation to deliver a blow of judgment. Elsewhere in the OT, however, the lifting of the Lord's hand is equivalent to taking an oath or to His working on behalf of mankind, e.g., 49:22; Psalm 10:12. It never refers directly to a preparatory work of judgment.

[11]Rawlinson, I, 415, includes false gods among the "lords" and has the prayer come from the saints in the New Jerusalem. Fausset, p. 643, includes false gods and evil passions. He specifically mentions "Antichrist" as one of the lords. The application is too broad. The thought of death in v. 14 naturally limits the lords to human rulers. While Antichrist is one of these, it is too much to find him here. It is also unlikely that this refers to the New Jerusalem. The resurrected saints occupy the eternal city. The context here speaks of victory over the wicked, v. 5; of learning righteousness, v. 9; of the wicked, v. 10; of people resisting the Lord, v. 11; of enemies, v. 18; and of the raptured saints,

16 Lord, in trouble have they visited thee, they poured out a prayer
   when thy chastening was upon them.
17 Like as a woman with child, that draweth near the time of her delivery, is in pain, and crieth out in her pangs; so have we been in thy
   sight, O Lord.
18 We have been with child, we have been in pain, we have as it were
   brought forth wind; we have not wrought any deliverance in the
   earth; neither have the inhabitants of the world fallen.

sheol). They "shall not rise" in the resurrection to oppose God's people
again. God has "visited" (paqad, see 10:12) and destroyed them. Israel
will no longer remember their oppression, v. 14. Israel, however, has received God's blessing. He has "increased the nation [gôy]," [12] the repetition giving emphasis to God's working on their behalf. The Lord will be
"glorified" (kabed, see 3:5) for His work. He has "removed it far unto all
the ends of the earth" (better "extended all the borders of the land"). The
statement looks forward to the kingdom, when Israel will possess far
more territory than in the OT times, cf. 33:17, v. 15. [13]

16–18 Israel's troubles have led them to turn to the Lord. They have
"visited" (paqad, see 10:12) Him in whispered "prayer" (lahaš, see 3:3). [14]
Israel's trials have been painful. Isaiah compares the nation to a woman
in travail with her child, v. 17. They have been in travail, yet they have
not brought forth a child. Despite the pangs of their tribulation, they
have brought forth only "wind," here representing the lack of substance.
They have not gained deliverance from their oppression. Their enemies
have not "fallen" (yippᵉlû), v. 18. [15]

---

v. 20. These are not the saints coming out of the Tribulation into the New Jerusalem.
While the New Jerusalem exists during the Kingdom, the description here is of life on
earth.

[12]Watts, Isaiah 1–33, p. 341, argues that gôy naturally refers to "someone other than Israel." He suggests Assyria, a nation that has grown large. It is true that gôy usually refers
to Gentile nations. It also, however, refers frequently to Israel, e.g., Gen. 12:2; Deut.
4:6–7; Ps. 83:4; Jer. 31:36 and, especially, Isa. 1:4; 9:3; 26:2; 58:2; 66:8.

[13]Skinner, Isaiah I–XXXIX, p. 195, and Whitehouse, I, 283, wrongly make the passage
historical rather than prophetic. The wider context of c. 25–27 argues that this relates to
the kingdom age of Christ.

[14]Whitehouse, I, 283, expresses his doubt that lahaš can be translated "prayer" because
of its normal use as a magical incantation. The word, however, can mean "whisper" with
no sense of an incantation, II Sam. 12:19; Ps. 41:7. The whispered words here are those
of prayer.

[15]Arguing that the noun nepel refers to "birth by miscarriage," Job 3:16; Eccles. 6:3,
Motyer, The Prophecy of Isaiah, p. 218, makes yippᵉlû mean "to be born." This lies

19 *Thy dead men shall live, together with my dead body shall they arise. Awake and sing, ye that dwell in dust: for thy dew is as the dew of herbs, and the earth shall cast out the dead.*

20 *Come, my people, enter thou into thy chambers, and shut thy doors about thee: hide thyself as it were for a little moment, until the indignation be overpast.*

21 *For, behold, the Lord cometh out of his place to punish the inhabitants of the earth for their iniquity: the earth also shall disclose her blood, and shall no more cover her slain.*

19–21 Isaiah suddenly states an eschatological solution to the dilemma. Despite past failure, there is hope for the future. Omitting the supplied words and unnecessary subject, v. 19a reads: "Thy dead shall live, my dead body [*nᵉbelatî*, better 'bodies'] shall arise."[16] This prophesies the coming resurrection of believing Jews. Those who now dwell in the dust of the grave will "awake and sing" praise to God. Their "dew" is like "the dew of herbs [*ʾôrot*, lit. 'light,' best taken here as the 'dew of the dawn']," giving nourishment.[17] With this sense, "dew" here is a symbol of life-giving power. The earth will give up the dead that have been buried in it. The following verses indicate that the prophecy relates to the resurrection of the saints at the Lord's first return, I Corinthians 15:52; I Thessalonians 4:16–17, v. 19. Until the passing of the "indignation," the Tribulation, the saints will enter into their "chambers." They will stay there for "a little moment" until the ending of the "indignation." The picture is of the saints, sheltered in heaven during the tribulation on earth, v. 20.[18] During that time, the Lord will "punish" (*paqad,*

---

behind the NIV translation "we . . . have not given birth to people of the world." The NASB is similar. Skinner, *Isaiah I–XXXIX,* p. 196, argues similarly based on an Arabic cognate. Whitehouse, I, 284, bases a similar argument on the LXX. While the meaning "miscarriage" for the noun *nepel* comes from the verb "to fall," the meaning of birth does not occur elsewhere. Since the verb *napal* occurs more than four hundred times, the OT firmly establishes its root sense of "fall." For this reason, I prefer the traditional rendering of the AV.

[16]While *nᵉbelatî* is a singular noun, the plural verb *yᵉqûmûn,* "they shall rise," gives the noun a collective sense, "bodies."

[17]Whitehouse, I, 285, thinks that the "dew of lights" is dew from the "uppermost heavenly regions where Yahweh, Lord of Life, dwells." He cites Ps. 104:2 and Dan. 2:22 in support of his view. While the view is possible, it is rather esoteric. Assigning the dew to the morning dawn is more natural.

[18]A common interpretation of "chambers" refers it simply to safe places on earth, e.g., Delitzsch, I, 453; Barnes, I, 412; Fausset, p. 644. In my judgment, the context argues for something more than this. There will be few safe places on earth during the Tribulation.

see 10:12) the earth for its wickedness. Blood shed on the earth will now come forth to witness of its "iniquity" (ʿawon, see 1:4). Those who have been slain will similarly stand up as witness to earth's sins, v. 21.

Practical Applications from Chapter 26

1. The Peace of God, vv. 3–4. This comes from
   a. Trust in the Lord, v. 3. The chapter gives several reasons to trust the Lord. His justice will bring righteousness to the earth, v. 9. He has worked on behalf of His people, v. 12. He will enlarge the nation, v. 15. The works of the people have failed, v. 18.
   b. Strength of the Lord, v. 4. He overcomes the wicked, vv. 5–6, 13–14, 21, and raises the dead, v. 19. Such a God is surely able to bring "perfect peace" to His own.
2. The Resurrection of Believers, vv. 19–21
   a. Resurrection to new life, v. 19; cf. John 11:25–26a; Philippians 3:10–11; Hebrews 11:35; Revelation 20:6.
   b. Shelter from divine wrath, v. 20; cf. I Corinthians 15:51–52; Colossians 3:4; I Thessalonians 1:10; James 5:8; Revelation 3:10.
   c. Devastation of wicked mankind, v. 21; cf. 24:17–20; Jeremiah 30:7; Daniel 9:27; Revelation 6:16–17; 14:19–20; 15:1, 7; 16:1.

1 In that day the Lord with his sore and great and strong sword shall punish leviathan the piercing serpent, even leviathan that crooked serpent; and he shall slay the dragon that is in the sea.

ISAIAH 27

This closing chapter of the section (24:1–27:13) focuses on the final triumph of the Lord over the nations of the world. He will destroy His enemies, v. 1. Israel sings in response to the work of the Lord on their behalf, vv. 2–5. The Lord will gather His people back in the land where they will influence the entire world, v. 6. The Lord has not smitten them as He has smitten the heathen, v. 7. He has punished them in measure, v. 8, in order to turn them from their sin, v. 9. Jerusalem will be desolate for a time, vv. 10–11. The Lord, however, will work on their behalf. He will gather His people back into the land, v. 12, where they will worship Him, v. 13.

D. Final Triumph 27:1–13
1. Destruction and Regeneration 27:1–9

1 Isaiah introduces the chapter with the phrase "in that day." This phrase occurs over forty times in the book and seven times in c. 24–27. It locates the action here in the end times. Isaiah anticipates an eschatological victory of the Lord over the rebellious nations of the earth.[1]

The Lord raises His "sore [*qašâ*, i.e., 'cruel']² and great and strong sword" to "punish" (*paqad,* see 10:12) His enemies. The "dragon" is a "serpent" or "sea creature" of some kind. It represents Egypt, called a "dragon" elsewhere, 51:9; Ezekiel 29:3.³ The use of a "dragon" to represent Egypt suggests that the three serpents mentioned here all represent world powers. The word "leviathan" transliterates the Hebrew *liwyatan.* The word comes from a root meaning "twist, coil." This leads to the idea

---

[1]Watts, *Isaiah 1–33*, p. 349, makes the chapter historical. He sees it as belonging to the "day at the end of the seventy years," i.e., of captivity; cf. 23:17. The overall context of c. 24–27 suggests that the chapter is eschatological rather than historical.

²The word *qašâ* means "hard." Metaphorically, it refers to that which is "cruel," e.g., 19:4; Exod. 6:9; Song of Sol. 8:6. Price, p. 115, suggests "well-tempered," but *qašâ* nowhere else has this sense.

³Leslie, p. 270, says that the author "enters into the sphere of Semitic mythology" with the use of these names. Isaiah is poetic here in his choice of language, much the same as we might call someone a "devil" or a "beast." The use of animals to represent nations occurs elsewhere in the OT, e.g., Dan. 7:3–7. There is no need to make this mythological.

of some reptile or animal that moves by a writhing motion. In Job 3:8 ("mourning") and 41:1, it may indicate a crocodile. In Psalm 104:26, it refers to some sea creature, possibly the whale. In Psalm 74:14, the word refers to the crocodile, native to Egypt and thus a proper symbol of Egypt. Since "leviathan" occurs twice here, it is reasonable that the emblems have something in common. Assyria and Babylon satisfy this condition. The word "piercing" (or "fleeing") suggests the Tigris River with its swift current. The word "crooked" describes the meandering Euphrates River. Nineveh, the capital of Assyria, lay on the Tigris River. The Euphrates River ran through the city of Babylon. The Lord will destroy these nations. It is significant that Assyria, Babylon, and Egypt occupy those regions of the world that today most oppose Israel. In the end times, God will overcome that opposition to Himself and to His people, v. 1.[4]

---

[4]There is widespread disagreement on the symbolism of v. 1. Leslie, p. 270, makes the first serpent represent Persia and the second serpent, leviathan, Greece. Herbert, *Isaiah 1–39*, p. 157, makes the symbolism that of the Lord crushing "all disorder in the life of mankind and bring[ing] about the good order of the Kingdom of God." Price, p. 116, sees here "three types of godless world powers: the raider, the besieger, and the deporter." Allegorically, however, these represent Satan and his kingdom. Gray, I, 450–52, refers the symbols to "war in heaven" in which the Lord overcomes those who oppose Him. Skinner, *Isaiah I–XXXIX*, p. 199, relates the symbols to Egypt and to either Assyria and Babylon or Babylon and Persia or Persia and Greece, depending on the date of the passage. Whitehouse, I, 270, sees the Parthians, Syrians, and Egyptians. Later, p. 286, he sees only two nations, Egypt and Greece. Motyer, *The Prophecy of Isaiah,* p. 222, argues that the "piercing" (or "'gliding") serpent suggests a power of the air. The "crooked" (or "coiling") serpent is a power on the ground. The dragon in the sea is a marine power. Together, they show that the Lord will destroy evil powers in the whole creation. Slotki, p. 122, sees them as Assyria, Edom or Rome, and Egypt. Rawlinson, I, 433, associates the creatures with the Devil, the Beast, and the False Prophet. Kaiser, *Isaiah 13–39*, p. 222, understands the beasts as "three parallel synonyms" representing "a single being described in different ways." Cowles, p. 194, makes leviathan represent Babylon in both places. Barnes, I, 414–15, makes all three creatures refer to Babylon. Young, II, 235, equates the creatures with whatever power opposes God. Hailey, p. 219, relates them to "all the powers which serve Satan's efforts to defeat God's purpose." He identifies them as the "beast out of the sea," the "beast out of the earth," and "the harlot" (Rev. 13:1, 11; 17:1). Birks, p. 135, and Henry, p. 144, regard all the symbols as representing Satan. Watts, *Isaiah 1–33*, p. 348, thinks the symbols all stand for Tyre. This sampling shows the disagreement. I have argued my view above.

2 *In that day sing ye unto her, A vineyard of red wine.*
3 *I the Lord do keep it; I will water it every moment: lest any hurt it, I will keep it night and day.*
4 *Fury is not in me: who would set the briers and thorns against me in battle? I would go through them, I would burn them together.*
5 *Or let him take hold of my strength, that he may make peace with me; and he shall make peace with me.*

2–5 In view of God's protection of His people, it is appropriate that Israel "sing" (*ᶜanâ*) a song praising Him.[5] Verse 2 is better translated as an exclamation: "In that day, a vineyard of red wine, sing of it!" The "vineyard" is Israel; cf. 5:1–5; Psalm 80:8; Jeremiah 2:21. It is a vineyard "of red wine," (*ḥemer*, better "of wine"), indicating its fruitfulness.[6] In view of what the Lord has done for the nation, they should praise Him, v. 2.

The Lord cares for the nation. He gives it an abundant supply of water. He waters it "every moment" so that it never lacks moisture. In addition, He watches it "night and day" so that no enemy can "hurt" (*paqad,* see

---

[5]Young, II, 237, relies on the discussion of *ᶜanâ* in Alexander, I, 453–57, to justify the translation "afflict." Young makes the command one given to Israel's enemies. Though they do their worst, God will protect His own. Young summarizes the following arguments: (1) There is no clear ending to the song. Young himself, however, notes the change at v. 6, where there is a clear change of thought from a vine to a tree. (2) Nothing distinguishes the next verses as a song. Hebrew songs do not fit the pattern of modern songs. The meter varies here from verse to verse but other songs in the OT have similar variation. It is much like the metric variation in 5:1–7, a parallel song of the vineyard. (3) The people would not sing a song beginning with the words "I Jehovah keep it." In 5:1–7, however, acknowledged by both Young and Alexander as a song, the Lord also speaks in the first person. We should recognize the OT "song" is more "poetry." It is appropriate to quote the words of the Lord in this. (4) In 5:1–7, the verb "sing" and the cognate noun "song" appear; here there is no cognate noun. We cannot force all songs to follow the same pattern. (5) Of the fifty-six times in which the *piᶜel* of *ᶜanâ* occurs, only three times is the sense of "singing" appropriate, one of which is in this verse. BDB, p. 777, lists *ᶜanâ* IV, "sing," occurring fifteen times in the *qal* and two times in the *piᶜel*. KB, II, 854, lists the word fourteen times in the *qal* and three times in the *piᶜel*. Clearly, the thought of singing is well within the semantic range of the verb. (6) The meaning "afflict" is appropriate here. The interpretation, however, requires the command to go to an unnamed enemy.

[6]There is widespread disagreement as to whether v. 2 uses *ḥemer*, "wine," or *ḥemed*, "desirable, pleasant." The LXX and several Hebrew mss support *ḥemed*. The Isaiah Scroll and Vulgate support *ḥemer*. Motyer, *The Prophecy of Isaiah*, p. 222; Fausset, p. 645; and Alexander, p. 437, accept the MT. Watts, *Isaiah 1–33*, p. 345; Skinner, *Isaiah I–XXXIX*, p. 200; and Leupold, I, 421, adopt the variant reading. While this is not a major change in the meaning, I see no compelling reason to leave the MT, which has the weight of tradition behind it.

6 *He shall cause them that come of Jacob to take root: Israel shall blossom and bud, and fill the face of the world with fruit.*

7 *Hath he smitten him, as he smote those that smote him? or is he slain according to the slaughter of them that are slain by him?*

8 *In measure, when it shooteth forth, thou wilt debate with it: he stayeth his rough wind in the day of the east wind.*

9 *By this therefore shall the iniquity of Jacob be purged; and this is all the fruit to take away his sin; when he maketh all the stones of the altar as chalkstones that are beaten in sunder, the groves and images shall not stand up.*

10:12) it or rob it of its fruit, v. 3. He has no "fury" toward it. Rhetorically, He asks if "briers and thorns," emblems of His enemies, will come against the vineyard of Israel. If so, He will overcome them. He will "go through them" (or "march against them") and burn them, v. 4. He invites His enemies to become His friends. They may accept His "strength" (better "place of strength," i.e., "fortress, refuge"), the protection He gives His own. They may make "peace" (*šalôm,* see 9:6) with Him, v. 5.

6 The Lord will once again plant Israel in the land. He compares them to a tree. He causes them to take root in the land, to blossom and bud, then to bear fruit. The poetic picture here speaks of spiritual fruit. Israel's testimony will be such that they will influence the whole world. The "face of the world" refers to the world itself, everywhere mankind dwells, cf. 23:17, v. 6.

7–9 The questions of v. 7 are rhetorical. Has the Lord smitten "him," Israel, as He has smitten their enemies? Has Israel been slain to the same degree as their enemies? In both cases, the answer is no. Israel's sin has caused the Lord to punish them, but the punishment has been in measure, limited in comparison to that given to the heathen, v. 7. Verse 8 describes God's dealings. It should read, "In measure [*b^esa^ʾs^eʾâ*],[7] by

---

[7]The word *b^esa^ʾs^eʾâ* occurs only here. Older commentators, e.g., Birks, Delitzsch, Näglesbach, derive *b^esa^ʾs^eʾâ* from *s^eʾâ,* "measure," and read *bisʾâ seʾâ,* "by measure and measure" or simply "in measure." Several of the versions (Σ, Θ, Targum, Vulgate) support this. Young, II, 244, mentions the possibility that the doubling of the root expresses progress from one to another, a gradual measure, not all at once. Barnes, I, 417, suggests the meaning "moderation." He draws this from the fact that a *s^eʾâ* is only the third part of an ephah, a relatively small amount, less than one-fourth of a bushel. Some newer authors, e.g., *OTTP,* p. 144, and Kaiser, *Isaiah 13–39,* p. 226, relate the word to an Arabic term, *sa sa,* shouted by goat or donkey drivers as they hurry animals along. From this comes the meaning "move on, drive." KB, II, 738, refers to *sʾsʾ* as "a shout to gather small cattle" but admits it is a hypothetical form. BDB, p. 684, also supports this sense. There is also an Arabic cognate, "push away, drive away," which the NASB follows. The

10 *Yet the defenced city shall be desolate, and the habitation forsaken, and left like a wilderness: there shall the calf feed, and there shall he lie down, and consume the branches thereof.*

11 *When the boughs thereof are withered, they shall be broken off: the women come, and set them on fire: for it is a people of no under-standing: therefore he that made them will not have mercy on them, and he that formed them will shew them no favour.*

sending her out [*bᵉšallᵉḥah*],[8] you pleaded [*rîb*, see 1:17] with her; he drove [*hagâ*] her out by his fierce wind in the day of the east wind." The verse speaks of God's judgment of Israel, sending them into captivity to punish them for their sins. He does this "in measure," giving them the just portion of punishment for their sins. In the second half, the verb *hagâ* means "to drive out," not "to stay." Rather than withholding His judgment, the Lord sends it. He sends the fierce wind to sweep the people away into captivity. The "east wind" comes from the desert into Palestine and is hot and normally a strong wind. It serves elsewhere as a figure of judgment, e.g., Genesis 41:6; Job 27:21; Ezekiel 17:10, v. 8. By means of this judgment, the Lord intends to turn Jacob from its "in-iquity" (*ᶜawon*, see 1:4) and "sin" (*ḥaṭṭaᵓat*, see 3:9). This is the "fruit," i.e., the result, expected by God when He puts away its sin. Israel should turn from idolatry. They should make the "stones of the altar" as pulver-ized "chalkstones." The "groves," i.e., idols erected in worship of the goddess Asherah, and the "images" (or "incense altars," *hammanîm*, see 17:8) should be overthrown. Historically, the captivity did accomplish this. While Israel still engaged in many sins, especially legalism in their interpretation of Scripture, idolatry was not as serious a problem after the return from captivity, v. 9.

2. Desolation and Restoration 27:10–13

10–11 The "defenced city," Jerusalem, will be desolate. That region will be "forsaken," alone, no longer interacting with the world. It will become a grazing area for flocks, v. 10.[9] Shrubbery, probably overgrowing

---

LXX, followed by the NIV, translated this with μαχόμενος, "warfare." With an uncer-tain word, however, the LXX is not a final authority. The translators likewise wrestled with the problem. We can guess at the meaning from the context.

[8]Young, II, 244, explains the feminine suffix on *bᵉšallᵉḥah* as referring to Israel as the wife of God. He sends His faithless wife away. While this is possible, nations are cus-tomarily considered feminine. The use of the feminine suffix is normal.

[9]On the basis of the language in vv. 10–11, Leupold, I, 427; Brueggemann, *Isaiah 1–39*, p. 215; and Stacey, p. 165, refer the city to Samaria. Barnes, I, 419, makes the city

12 *And it shall come to pass in that day, that the Lord shall beat off
from the channel of the river unto the stream of Egypt, and ye shall
be gathered one by one, O ye children of Israel.*

13 *And it shall come to pass in that day, that the great trumpet shall be
blown, and they shall come which were ready to perish in the land of
Assyria, and the outcasts in the land of Egypt, and shall worship the
Lord in the holy mount at Jerusalem.*

the ruins, will wither in the city. The women who live in the surrounding
area will break off branches to use for fuel. People with no spiritual understanding now live in the city. The Creator God will not show mercy
toward them, v. 11.

12–13 Isaiah now turns to the restoration of Israel.[10] From his description, however, it seems that this goes beyond the mere return from
the Babylonian captivity. The Lord will "beat off" (or "thresh") from
"the river unto the stream of Egypt." The "river" often refers to the
Euphrates, e.g., 7:20; 8:7; II Samuel 10:16; I Kings 4:21, 24. The
"stream [*naḥal*, see 7:19] of Egypt" is now called the Wadi el-'Arish.
Elsewhere, it is called the "river of Egypt," e.g., Genesis 15:18; Numbers
34:5. It flowed during the rainy season from the Wilderness of Paran into
the Mediterranean. It formed the southwestern border of Judah. From
this area, He will gather the people as His harvest, v. 12. The "trumpet"
(*šôpar*, see 18:3) will sound an assembly. The *šôpar* was the Jubilee
trumpet of Leviticus 25:9–10, calling the people back to their possessions. Israel will respond and will leave Assyria and Egypt to worship
the Lord again at Jerusalem. Assyria and Egypt are representative here.
They stand for the nations of the world to which Israel has been dispersed. The people return to offer sincere worship to the Lord at
Jerusalem, v. 13.[11]

Babylon. Näglesbach, p. 297, also denies that the city is Jerusalem. He identifies it as
any worldly city that rejects God. The context, however, deals with the captivity of
Judah. It is unlikely that Isaiah would now focus his thoughts on another nation.

[10]Herbert, *Isaiah 1–39*, pp. 159–60, and Motyer, *The Prophecy of Isaiah,* p. 225, divide
vv. 12–13 into two oracles. The first refers to gathering the people within the Promised
Land. The second is a worldwide gathering of Israel. While the view is possible, it seems
to me that the verses are a unit, describing the same harvest. The Lord threshes the people
in v. 12, separating them from the heathen. In v. 13, He describes the process as the
trumpet blast calling the people to assemble.

[11]Watts, *Isaiah 1–33*, p. 351; Henry, pp. 148–49; and Price, p. 118, refer the regathering
to Israel's return from captivity. The phrase "in that day," however, is normally eschatological, e.g., 2:11, 17; 4:2. The reference to the "trumpet" also indicates end-time events;

Practical Applications from Chapter 27

1. The Song of the Vineyard. The song sharply contrasts with the earlier song of the vineyard, 5:1–7. There, it grew stinking grapes, 5:4; here, it is a source of wine, v. 2. There, the Lord laid it waste, 5:5–6*a;* here, He carefully tends it, v. 3. There, the "briers and thorns" grew freely, 5:6*b;* here, the Lord protects it from "briers and thorns," v. 4. There, no rain fell on the vineyard, 5:6*c;* here, the Lord waters it freely, v. 3*b.* There, judgment fell, 5:5–6; here, the Lord blesses it, v. 5. Truly, this is a fruitful vineyard with the favor of the Lord resting on it.

2. God's Care for His Own. The Lord defeats the enemies of His people, v. 1. He will once more reestablish the nation in their land, v. 6. His chastisement of Israel has been limited, vv. 7–8. Through this, He has tried to turn them from their sins, v. 9. The city of Jerusalem has been allowed to fall into ruin, vv. 10–11. Now, however, the Lord will gather His people as a harvest, v. 12. He will call them back into the land. They will leave the lands in which they were held captive and will worship the Lord at Jerusalem, v. 13.

---

cf. Matt. 24:31; I Cor. 15:52; I Thess. 4:6. Young, II, 251, argues that the blowing of the trumpet is figurative. The NT emphasis argues that it is literal.

1 Woe to the crown of pride, to the drunkards of Ephraim, whose
   glorious beauty is a fading flower, which are on the head of the
   fat valleys of them that are overcome with wine!
2 Behold, the Lord hath a mighty and strong one, which as a tempest
   of hail and a destroying storm, as a flood of mighty waters overflowing, shall cast down to the earth with the hand.
3 The crown of pride, the drunkards of Ephraim, shall be trodden
   under feet:
4 And the glorious beauty, which is on the head of the fat valley, shall
   be a fading flower, and as the hasty fruit before the summer; which
   when he that looketh upon it seeth, while it is yet in his hand he
   eateth it up.

ISAIAH 28

In this new section of the book, Isaiah returns to the theme of judgment. This is an appropriate place to take up the matter. He has just
prophesied Israel's glorious future (c. 25–27). This thought might make
the people of Judah arrogant. It might lead them to think that their Jewish ancestry was all that was demanded. They could possibly turn away
from the temple worship and their obedience to the Law. To prevent such
action, Isaiah warns the nation that God will judge sin. In c. 28–31, he
deals with this prospect. Then, having warned against sin, Isaiah turns
back again to happier themes. Chapters 32–35 focus on eschatological
matters and on the prospect of deliverance from Israel's enemies.

IV. Prophecies Instructing God's People 28:1–35:10
A. Warning Against Israel's Sin 28:1–29
1. Pronouncement of Woe 28:1–13
a. Condemnation of the People 28:1–8

1–4 Isaiah begins by pronouncing a "woe" (*hôy,* see 1:4) upon Israel.
He condemns drunken Israel for its "crown of pride," its capital of
Samaria.[1] The city stood on a hill about three hundred feet above its
surroundings.[2] This gave a view of the Mediterranean Sea, twenty-three

---

[1]Wade, p. 177, and Kaiser, *Isaiah 13–39*, p. 239, understand the phrase "crown of
pride" as a wreath of flowers, worn by drunken men of the times. This is not likely. We
have no evidence from the OT that drunken Israelites adorned themselves with flowers.

[2]Young, II, 264, understands the word "crown" topologically as referring to the hill
upon which Samaria stood. It is possible that the shape of the hill suggested the idea of a
crown. Without supporting evidence, however, the idea is forced.

miles away. A double wall protected the city, and cisterns inside the wall furnished water. It was thought invincible. In fact, the city did withstand sieges by Ben-hadad in 863 B.C. (I Kings 20:1) and 850 B.C. (II Kings 6:24–7:16). The "drunkards of Ephraim" glory in it. The mention of drunkenness notes one major sin of the people; cf. v. 3. Amos 6:3–6 gives an expanded description of the Israelites. With their reason hindered by alcohol, they placed their faith in the security given them by their city.

King Omri purchased the hill of Shemer for two talents of silver. He named the city for the former owner of the hill, I Kings 16:24. In all likelihood, the hill had acquired that name and Omri simply kept the name by which people normally referred to it. It is at the head of "fat valleys" (or "a valley of fatnesses [*š^emanîm*]" of those "that are over-come with wine [*yayin,* see 5:11]!"[3] The plural *š^emanîm* indicates the richness of the valley. It slopes away from Samaria to the Mediterranean. That valley and the surrounding mountains have been an abundant source of grain, olives, and figs.

To the Lord, Samaria is a "fading flower" that will soon fall, v. 1. He has prepared "a mighty and strong one," the Assyrian king Sargon, who will come "as a tempest of hail and a destroying storm, as a flood of mighty waters overflowing." The city will be "cast down to the earth." The Lord does this "with the hand." The Lord's "hand" often represents His power, cf. 1:25; 8:11, v. 2. Then, lit., "the crown of pride of the drunkards of Ephraim" will be "trodden" (or "trampled") underfoot. From the repetition in v. 1 and the context, the crown in which the

---

[3]The Hebrew does not connect the phrase "of them that are overcome with wine" to "fat valleys." The passage lit. states, "the valley of fatnesses, those who have been smit-ten by wine." The construction is variously understood. Delitzsch, II, 3, and Young, II, 264–65, suggest that the second phrase is in a genitive relationship to the first: "The valleys of the fatnesses of those smitten down with wine." Delitzsch says, "the logical relationship [overrules] the syntactical usage." Young gives Ezek. 6:11; 45:16, 46:19; II Chron. 15:8; Josh. 8:11 as examples to show that a genitive may follow a noun in the absolute. Watts, *Isaiah 1–33,* p. 359, supplies the copulative. He translates, "[those] who (were) at the head of a fertile valley (are now) those struck down by wine." Motyer, *The Prophecy of Isaiah,* p. 229, takes the second phrase as an independent "exclamation of disgust." He translates, "laid low by wine!" referring the phrase back to the "drunkards of Ephraim." Leupold, I, 414–15, translates the phrase as a genitive but explains the sec-ond phrase as referring to the city: "a city of those 'overcome with wine.'" The grammar is difficult. The context, however, virtually demands that the second phrase modify "the drunkards who are in Ephraim." The translation has the sense ". . . which is upon the head of the rich valley belonging to those drunkards overcome with wine."

> 5 *In that day shall the Lord of hosts be for a crown of glory, and for a*
> *diadem of beauty, unto the residue of his people,*
> 6 *And for a spirit of judgment to him that sitteth in judgment, and for*
> *strength to them that turn the battle to the gate.*
> 7 *But they also have erred through wine, and through strong drink are*
> *out of the way; the priest and the prophet have erred through strong*
> *drink, they are swallowed up of wine, they are out of the way*
> *through strong drink; they err in vision, they stumble in judgment.*
> 8 *For all tables are full of vomit and filthiness, so that there is no*
> *place clean.*

drunkards take pride is Samaria, v. 3.[4] The city will be as "a fading
flower" and "as the hasty fruit" (lit. "the first-ripe fig"). Figs normally
are ready to harvest in August. The first-ripe figs mature early in June
and are eagerly eaten when they appear; cf. Jeremiah 24:2; Hosea 9:10;
Micah 7:1; Nahum 3:12. In the same way, the Assyrians "eateth" (*balaᶜ*,
see 3:12) spoil, eagerly taking it from the city, v. 4.

5–6 After the fall of the earthly hope, some of the people will realize
their misplaced hope. The "residue" (or "remnant") will begin to look to
the "Lord of hosts," the ruler of heavenly and earthly powers; they will
glory in Him. Notice the poetic nature of this change. Before, they had
looked to Samaria as a "crown" and "glorious beauty." Now, it is the
Lord who becomes their "crown of glory" and "diadem of beauty," v. 5.
He will give "a spirit of judgment [*mišpaṭ*, better 'justice,' see 1:17]" to
those who sit in "judgment" (*mišpaṭ*) of disputes.[5] He will give strength
to those who defend the city against attack. The promise points to the return from the captivity. "In that day" (v. 5), as long as the people remain
faithful to the Lord, the nation will know justice and safety, v. 6.[6]

7–8 The words "they also" indicate that Isaiah condemns Judah as
well; cf. v. 14. They also have been drunk, letting "wine" (*yayin*, see
5:11) and "strong drink" (*šekar*, see 5:11) control them. This has caused
them to go "out of the way" (or "go astray"). The priests (cf. Lev. 10:9)

---

[4]Rawlinson, I, 447, understands the crown as "the self-complacent and boastful spirit
of the Israelite people." He is, however, inconsistent. He makes the "crown" of v. 1 and
the "fading flower" in vv. 1, 4, represent Samaria. There is no reason to abruptly go away
from that image here.

[5]Virtually all that mention the *ʾatnaḥ* move it to *hammišpaṭ*. Without this, the second
part of the verse is incomplete. Young, II, 270, agrees with the Massoretic punctuation
although he translates the verse as if he moves the *ʾatnaḥ*.

[6]Wade, p. 178; Skinner, *Isaiah I–XXXIX*, p. 208; and Slotki, p. 127, make the paragraph
messianic. While it is true that the phrase "in that day" often introduces a messianic passage, it is not always true, e.g., 2:20; 3:7; 4:1. In this case, the need to defend against

9 Whom shall he teach knowledge? and whom shall he make to under-
stand doctrine? them that are weaned from the milk, and drawn from
the breasts.

10 For precept must be upon precept, precept upon precept; line upon
line, line upon line; here a little, and there a little:

and prophets (cf. Mic. 2:11), the spiritual leaders of the nation, have
been given to wine and strong drink. They are "swallowed up" (*balaᶜ*,
see 3:12) by the wine. They also are "out of the way" (again, "go
astray") in their decisions and advice. The prophets "err" (or "reel")
from drunkenness while having a "vision" (*ro²eh*).[7] The priests make
wrong "judgment" (*pᵉlîlîyâ*),[8] v. 7. Their drunkenness is so great that
they cover the tables with their "vomit and filthiness" (better "filthy
vomit").[9] The result is that there is "no place," i.e., no clean place, v. 8.

b. Contempt of the People 28:9–13

9–10 The drunken scoffers respond. Whom is Isaiah trying to teach?
Whom is he making "to understand [*bîn*, see 1:3] doctrine [or 'a

---

attack suggests another fulfillment. Rawlinson, I, 447–48, and Barnes, I, 424, assume that
the remnant is primarily the kingdom of Judah. The fulfillment, then, occurs in the reign of
Hezekiah. The period of Hezekiah's rule, however, was not a time that Judah had strength
to overcome its enemies. Only the power of the Lord gave them victory over Assyria.

[7]Driver, "'Another Little Drink'—Isaiah 28:1–22," *Words and Meanings*, 1968, p. 52,
understands *ro²eh* as a variant noun from *rwh*, "to drink one's fill." William Henry Irwin,
Isaiah 28–33: Translation with Philological Notes, 1977, p. 18, makes *ro²eh* "a substantive
from the root *r²h* 'drink one's fill', a by-root of *rwh*." Watts, p. 361, follows this, translating
the phrase "they reeled with drink." The masculine singular active participle *ro²eh* appears
only here without the article. That is understandable since when it occurs elsewhere a specific individual is in view. Isaiah also uses the masculine plural active participle in 30:10
without the article to refer to a group of seers. Despite the single occurrence of *ro²eh* here,
there is no need to look for an alternative meaning. The verb *ra²â* occurs widely with the
sense "to see." The related sense of "vision" is appropriate here.

[8]The word *pᵉlîlîyâ* is a *hapax legomenon*. Irwin, p. 19, sees the root *pll* equivalent to the
Arabic *bll*. He understands "soddenness, moisture," i.e., alcohol. Watts, *Isaiah 1–33*,
p. 361, follows this and translates, "booze." Driver, *Words and Meanings*, p. 53, translates,
"collapse" or "hiccough." This again relates the word to the drunken condition. While the
word *pᵉlîlîyâ* occurs only here, the root *pll* occurs widely in the OT. The verb *palal* elsewhere refers to judging, mediation, intervention, and prayer. The context determines the
sense. The noun forms *palîl* and *palîlâ* consistently refer to judges. The verse makes this a
function of priests and prophets. The prophets see visions while the priests render decisions
of judgment.

[9]Watts, *Isaiah 1–33*, p. 361, moves the *²atnaḥ* from the *ṣo²â* so that "filth" and "vomit"
are separated. He translates, "For all the tables were full of vomit, filth, with no clean
place." While this does not change the sense, I see *qî² ṣo²â* as a simple noun-adjective
combination, "filthy vomit."

*11 For with stammering lips and another tongue will he speak to this
people.*
*12 To whom he said, This is the rest wherewith ye may cause the weary
to rest; and this is the refreshing: yet they would not hear.*
*13 But the word of the Lord was unto them precept upon precept, pre-
cept upon precept; line upon line, line upon line; here a little, and
there a little; that they might go, and fall backward, and be broken,
and snared, and taken.*

message']"? They accuse Isaiah of treating them as recently weaned children, v. 9. They sarcastically describe his teaching as *ṣaw laṣaw ṣaw laṣaw
qaw laqaw qaw laqaw $z^ec\hat{e}r$ šam $z^ec\hat{e}r$ šam*. The word *ṣaw* occurs only at
vv. 10, 13, and Hosea 5:11. It is related to *miṣwâ*, "commandment." The
parallel word *qaw* occurs frequently to indicate a measuring line. The
remaining key words, $z^ec\hat{e}r$ *šam*, are idiomatic, "a little here and a little
there."[10] The translation is something like "rule after rule, rule after rule,
line after line, line after line, a little here, a little there." The repetitious
sounds are meant to ridicule Isaiah's teaching. It is as though Isaiah
teaches them with simple words that a child can understand, v. 10.[11]

11–13 Isaiah responds in an apt manner. God will speak to the people
with "stammering lips and another tongue," i.e., the tongue of their foreign conquerors, v. 11.[12] He had offered "rest" and "refreshing" to them

---

[10]Kaiser, *Isaiah 13–39*, p. 243, follows contorted reasoning to obtain the translation
"Boy, be careful boy, be careful" here and in v. 13. He understands $z^ec\hat{e}r$ as "little one,"
thus equal to "Boy." He then emends *šam* to *šîm*, "to put, place," which he interprets as
"pay attention."

[11]Delitzsch, II, 7, makes this the "babbling language of the drunken scoffers." Irwin,
p. 22, calls v. 10 "a drunken burlesque of Isaiah's 'infantile' style." Whitehouse, I, 295,
makes the line "a nurse's child-prattle." These are possible views. Kaiser, *Isaiah 13–39*,
p. 245, suggests the mocking words are those of a teacher helping his class learn the letters of the alphabet by repeating them over and over. Driver, *Words and Meanings*," p. 54,
asks why they would pick two letters from the middle of the alphabet? Also, v. 9 indicates
that Isaiah treats them as babes, too young to read. Kraeling, p. 120, makes the Hebrew a
magical incantation. Isaiah's "opponents . . . express their reliance on the magic practices."
The view is clearly wrong. Karel van der Toorn, "Echoes of Judaean Necromancy in Isaiah
28, 7–22," *ZAW* 100:209, understands the phrase as "a transcript of the sounds produced
during the necromantic seances." He suggests that these "reproduce bird-like twitterings
and groans." He concludes that v. 11 "does not predict the coming of the Assyrian invaders, with their barbarian tongue." Van der Toorn's view has difficulty fitting into Paul's
use of the verse in I Cor. 14:21.

[12]Paul quotes the verse in I Cor. 14:21 to show that "tongues" are a sign of judgment.
Since Israel refused to hear the prophet who spoke their own language, God would give
them to a people whose language they would not understand. In this way, tongues (foreign languages) are a sign to unbelievers, showing God's presence to them.

14 *Wherefore hear the word of the Lord, ye scornful men, that rule this people which is in Jerusalem.*

15 *Because ye have said, We have made a covenant with death, and with hell are we at agreement; when the overflowing scourge shall pass through, it shall not come unto us: for we have made lies our refuge, and under falsehood have we hid ourselves:*

but they had rejected His offer, v. 12. They had considered "the word of the Lord" a trivial matter. Isaiah repeats the phrasing of v. 10, *ṣaw laṣaw ṣaw laṣaw qaw laqaw qaw laqaw* $z^e{}^c\hat{e}r$ *šam* $z^e{}^c\hat{e}r$ *šam*.[13] Their rejection will bring judgment upon them. Isaiah picturesquely describes this. They will "fall" (or "stagger") backward. They will "be broken" (*šabar*, see 14:5). They will be trapped and taken captive, v. 13.

2. Prospect of Judgment 28:14–22

14–15 Isaiah addresses the "scornful" (*ʾanšê laṣôn*) that "rule" (*mašal*)[14] Jerusalem. The phrase *ʾanšê laṣôn* refers to those who hardened themselves against spiritual truth, who think of themselves as the final authorities. God, however, thinks of these people as weak "men" (*ʾenôš*, see 2:11). Isaiah urges them to hear God's Word, v. 14. They relied on a covenant they had made with Egypt. This was a "covenant of death [*mawet*]," one that would protect them against death from invaders.[15] It

---

[13]A. van Selms, "Isaiah 28 9–13: An Attempt to Give a New Interpretation," *ZAW* 85:332–39, makes the phrase *ṣaw laṣaw ṣaw laṣaw qaw laqaw qaw laqaw* $z^e{}^c\hat{e}r$ *šam* $z^e{}^c\hat{e}r$ *šam* a Hebrew transliteration of an Assyrian original. He makes several assumptions to develop the translation: "Go out! Let him go out! Go out! Let him go out! Wait! Let him wait! Wait! Let him wait! Servant, listen! Servant, listen!" While van Selms view is novel, it involves too many suppositions, all of which must be correct in order for his view to be accepted. This is unlikely.

[14]Von Orelli, p. 158, and Kaiser, *Isaiah 13–39*, p. 248, draw on an alternative meaning of *mašal* and translate, "proverb-makers of this people." While the word *mašal* can mean "proverb," it only infrequently means "to speak in proverbs." The context of v. 15, making covenants to protect them, argues that these are leaders of the city rather than proverb makers.

[15]Driver, *Words and Meanings*, p. 57, personifies death as "the god of death ruling in Sheol." The problem with his view is that there is no god ruling in sheol. Despite what heathen mythology might claim, there is only one God, who rules over all. Herbert, *Isaiah 1–39*, p. 164, suggests that *mawet* is a play on words suggesting "both death and the Canaanite deity môt." It is as though Isaiah accuses them of allying themselves with a dead god instead of the living God. He will therefore bring them to sheol, the place of the dead. This is a vivid interpretation but it is not what the text says. The "agreement with sheol" parallels the "covenant of death." Both describe the misplaced reliance on Egypt. To reinforce this, the parallelism occurs again in v. 18.

16 *Therefore thus saith the Lord God, Behold, I lay in Zion for a foundation a stone, a tried stone, a precious corner stone, a sure foundation: he that believeth shall not make haste.*

gave them an "agreement" with "hell" (*šeʾôl*, here "grave," see 5:14), i.e., security against death.[16] They had no fear of "the overflowing scourge [*šôṭ šôṭep*]."[17] This pictures the Assyrian attack as it sweeps over the land.[18] Isaiah quotes their words but adds clarity to them. They had based their covenant on "lies" (*kazab*) and "falsehood" (*šeqer*, see 9:15).[19] The agreement upon which they rested was false: Egypt would not give them security, v. 15.

16 Only a new agreement will give the people security. God will "lay" (*yissad*)[20] a new "foundation" in the land. This is a "tried [*boḥan*, or 'tested']"[21] stone" that will not crumble under pressure. It is a "precious [or 'valuable'] corner stone" that gives direction to the building. It is a

---

[16]Kraeling, p. 121, suggests that "death" and "sheol" are representative of Egypt and Ethiopia, "whose location in the far south gives them an 'underneath' position." The idea is far-fetched. Nowhere else does death or sheol represent nations. The parallelism here suggests that sheol represents simply the grave, not the realm of the dead.

[17]We should read the *qerê*, *šôt*, as in v. 18, instead of the *ketîb*, *šayiṭ*. In either case, the phrase is another example of the assonance that so often marks Isaiah's writing.

[18]Young, II, 283, 290, thinks that the phrase "overflowing scourge" mixes metaphors. He says that a whip cannot overflow. The word *šôṭep*, however, does not always represent water. In 8:8 and 10:22, the word stands apart from water. The idea here is of the Assyrian army as it engulfs the land.

[19]There is not much difference between *kazab* and *šeqer*. The word *kazab* occurs less frequently. It occurs only in Judges, Psalms, Proverbs, and the Prophets. The word *šeqer* occurs more widely in the OT. Both words refer to that which has no basis in fact.

[20]The verb *yissad* is a *piʿel* perfect 3ms. The LXX reads this as ἐμβαλῶ, a future form. The Targum and 1QIsa[a] support a participle form. The change of person in Isaiah is not rare, however. If we retain the MT, the passage is a prophetic perfect, stating as an accomplished fact what the Lord will do in the future.

[21]The form *boḥan* occurs only here. There are, however, related forms that occur often elsewhere, so the meaning is not in doubt. The word normally has a spiritual sense, often connected with testing character. Young, II, 287, refers the testing to men. The stone is a "stone of testing," revealing men's "attitude toward Him." This is a possible view. Näglesbach, p. 308, makes the expression ambiguous with the possibility of either meaning. Driver, *Words and Meanings*, pp. 59–60, argues that the stone cannot be a figure for the Lord "because it is the Lord who is laying the foundation." He concludes that the picture comes from the recollection of the stones at Solomon's temple. Driver does not see that God the Father is able to make His Son a foundation stone for His people. The phrase describes the stone, showing its adequacy to be the "corner stone." Those who rely on this will not be disappointed.

17 Judgment also will I lay to the line, and righteousness to the plummet: and the hail shall sweep away the refuge of lies, and the waters shall overflow the hiding place.

18 And your covenant with death shall be disannulled, and your agreement with hell shall not stand; when the overflowing scourge shall pass through, then ye shall be trodden down by it.

19 From the time that it goeth forth it shall take you: for morning by morning shall it pass over, by day and by night: and it shall be a vexation only to understand the report.

"sure foundation" (*mûsad mûsad*, or "established foundation") that will never fail. The doubling of the word gives emphasis to the nature of the stone. Romans 9:33; 10:11; and I Peter 2:6 make it clear that this is the Lord Jesus Christ Himself.[22] He is the stone that will not crumble, that has value, and that gives direction to His church. The one who places his faith in this foundation will "not make haste [*yaḥîš*]." The word *yaḥîš*, "to hurry," has the idea here that the believer will have no need to flee. He will stand firm against all opposition.[23] The NT interprets this phrase as καταισκυνθήσεται, "to be disappointed," Romans 9:33; 10:11. This is a messianic promise. While the unbelieving Jews of the OT may fall before their enemies, the believer in Christ will never fail, v. 16.

17–19 The Lord will establish standards by which to measure His work. The new measuring line will be "judgment" (*mišpaṭ*, better "justice," see 1:17). The new "plummet" (*mišqelet*, better "plumb line")[24] will be "righteousness." Returning to the thought of v. 15, Isaiah states that Israel's refuge based on deceitfulness will perish. God's judgment will

---

[22]There is wide disagreement as to the identity of the "stone." Price, p. 122, makes it represent "the divine and indestructible purpose of God." Slotki, p. 130, mentions the possibility that it is Hezekiah (so David Kimchi). Kraeling, p. 121, identifies it as "the remnant who have the quoted words for their slogan." Watts, *Isaiah 1–33*, p. 367, finds the fulfillment in Zion. Kaiser, *Isaiah 13–39*, p. 254, views it as "the faith which gives a refuge as safe as the foundation stones which neither hail nor floods can damage." The Targum and the NT references support the identification of the stone with Christ.

[23]Motyer, *The Prophecy of Isaiah*, p. 233, understands the haste as that of "rushing hither and yon" in contrast with the rest that God wants His children to enjoy.

[24]BDB, p. 1054, understands *mišqelet* as a "leveling instrument, level." Delitzsch, II, 10; Mauchline, p. 200; and Young, II, 288, adopt this sense. While this does not change the interpretation significantly, *mišqelet* is better understood as a "plumb line." The root *šaqal*, "to weigh," suggests a weight of some kind. In the only other use, II Kings 21:13, the meaning of "plumb line" fits nicely.

20 *For the bed is shorter than that a man can stretch himself on it: and the covering narrower than that he can wrap himself in it.*

21 *For the Lord shall rise up as in mount Perazim, he shall be wroth as in the valley of Gibeon, that he may do his work, his strange work; and bring to pass his act, his strange act.*

22 *Now therefore be ye not mockers, lest your bands be made strong: for I have heard from the Lord God of hosts a consumption, even determined upon the whole earth.*

come as a storm of "hail" to "sweep away" ($ya^c\hat{a}$)[25] their "lies" (*kazab*, see v. 15). The "waters" of judgment will overflow their "hiding place," a metaphorical picture of the covenant they relied on, v. 17. Their "covenant with death" and their "agreement with hell ['sheol,' see 5:14]" will be done away with. The "overflowing scourge" of the Assyrian troops will sweep across the land to trample it, v. 18.[26] From the beginning that "it goeth forth," the Assyrian invasion, it will be unstoppable. The attack will come "morning by morning" and "by day and by night," giving the people no rest. The report of this invasion will bring "vexation" ($z^ewa^c\hat{a}$). The word $z^ewa^c\hat{a}$ is stronger than suggested by "vexation." It is better "horror" or "terror," v. 19.

20–22 Isaiah compares Judah's condition to that of a man on a short bed or under a narrow cover. He cannot stretch out without his feet hanging off the end, an uncomfortable position. He cannot curl up without exposing part of his body outside the blanket.[27] Nothing will satisfy them, v. 20. The Lord will come on the scene as in old times. God guided David to overcome the Philistines at Perazim, II Samuel 5:19–21 (I Chron. 14:9–16). The Lord miraculously helped Joshua overcome the

---

[25]The verb $ya^c\hat{a}$ occurs only here. The related noun, ya^c, "shovel," occurs several times, so the meaning is not in doubt. The parallelism supports the meaning "to sweep away, carry away."

[26]Pentecost, pp. 351, 353, understands the "covenant with death" and the "agreement with hell" as the covenant made by Israel with Antichrist. The judgment pictured here, then, is that of the last half of the Tribulation. While there are similarities, there is nothing in the context here to make the passage eschatological. It more logically applies to Judah's reliance on Egypt.

[27]The phrase "wrap himself in it" (*hitkannes*) occurs only here in the *hitpa^cel*. The verb occurs several times in the *qal* with the sense "to gather, collect." The normal reflexive sense of the *hitpa^cel* gives the meaning of gathering oneself together, i.e., curling up in a ball, rather than wrapping oneself with a blanket.

23 Give ye ear, and hear my voice; hearken, and hear my speech.
24 Doth the plowman plow all day to sow? doth he open and break the
*   clods of his ground?*
25 When he hath made plain the face thereof, doth he not cast abroad
*   the fitches, and scatter the cummin, and cast in the principal wheat*
*   and the appointed barley and the rie in their place?*
26 For his God doth instruct him to discretion, and doth teach him.

coalition of Canaanite kings at Gibeon, Joshua 10:6–11.[28] This time, however, the Lord will do a "strange work" and a "strange act," overcoming His own people, v. 21. Israel should turn from its mocking attitude toward spiritual things. Otherwise, their "bands," the binding restrictions placed on them by Assyria, will "be made strong." The Lord has determined "a consumption" (or "complete destruction") on "the whole earth" (*kol⁻haʾareṣ*). The phrase *kol⁻haʾareṣ* is lit. "all the earth" and is ambiguous. Should it refer to Palestine, Israel's "earth," or to the whole world? Isaiah uses *haʾareṣ* in both senses, e.g., a specific region, 1:7, 19; 7:18; 9:1; 28:2; and the world, 2:19, 21; 4:2; 6:3. The context must guide the interpretation. The context here suggests that Isaiah predicts judgment on Palestine for the sins of His people, v. 22.[29]

3. Parables of Encouragement 28:23–29

23–26 Isaiah calls the people to hear his words. The verse introduces two parables that are meant to encourage the people, v. 23. In the first, Isaiah asks rhetorically if the farmer plows continuously after the ground is prepared? Does he continue to break up the ground until the last clod of dirt is broken up, v. 24? The answer is no. When the ground is ready, he makes "plain the face thereof," leveling it. Then he sows "fitches" (*qeṣaḥ*), "cummin" (*kammon*), "principal wheat," "appointed barley," and "rie." The word *qeṣaḥ* occurs only here and in v. 27. It refers to the seeds

---

[28]Among others, Rawlinson, I, 150; Irwin, p. 36; Wade, p. 182; and Alexander, I, 456–57, refer both Perizim and Gibeon to David's conquest of Philistia; cf. the mention of "Geba," i.e., Gibeon, II Sam. 5:25; I Chron. 14:16. The view is possible. I lean toward including Joshua's victory only because the OT emphasizes it more. There are details given to it that the OT does not mention in the account of David's victory over Philistia.

[29]Vine, p. 62, and Leupold, I, 446, understand *haʾareṣ* as judgment upon the whole earth. While it is possible that the punishment of Judah is typical of the Tribulation judgments upon the earth, nothing in the context suggests this.

27 *For the fitches are not threshed with a threshing instrument, neither is a cart wheel turned about upon the cummin; but the fitches are beaten out with a staff, and the cummin with a rod.*

28 *Bread corn is bruised; because he will not ever be threshing it, nor break it with the wheel of his cart, nor bruise it with his horsemen.*

of *Nigella sativa,* a plant that grows throughout the Mediterranean region. These small black seeds are ground for use as a condiment. The word *kammon* also occurs only here and in v. 27. It refers to the aromatic seeds of the herb *Cuminum cyminum,* which also serve as a condiment. It was used in baking, in cooking stews, and as a natural medicine to relieve gas pains. The "principal [*śôrâ*][30] wheat" refers to "row wheat," the principal source of flour in Israel. The "appointed [*nisman*][31] barley" is barley planted in a specially designated place. Barley served as food for animals in OT times and as a source of cheap flour for making bread. The "rie in their place" is spelt sown lit. "in its border," probably a bordering field. Spelt was also used as animal fodder or as a source of cheap flour for making bread, v. 25.[32] The farmer carries out his work with the "discretion" (*mišpaṭ,* see 1:17) given him by God. The word *mišpaṭ* has a nonlegal sense here, the judgment of a man who considers the situation as he farms, v. 26.

27–28 The second parable focuses on the threshing process. The farmer does not thresh the "fitches" (*qeṣaḥ*) and "cummin" (*kammon*) harshly. Rather, he beats the grains out with a flail of some kind. Threshing of other grains often involved a yoke of oxen driven round the threshing floor. As they passed over the grain, their hoofs broke off the

---

[30]The word *śôrâ* occurs only here. There seems to be a contrast in the verse. The fitch and cummin are scattered. The remaining grains are planted carefully. The verb *śûm,* "cast in," has the sense of placing or appointing something. The signal of care guides the translation of the remaining words. Here, the meaning of *śôrâ* comes from related forms: "depart," Hos. 9:12; "cut" (rip apart), I Chron. 20:3; "ruled" (set apart), Judg. 9:22; possibly "appointed" (set apart), Hos. 8:4; and "had power" (apart from another's strength), Hos. 12:4. This sense of being apart gives rise to the meaning "in rows."

[31]The word *nisman* is also a *hapax legomenon.* The meaning "in its place" comes from the parallelism: *ḥiṭṭâ śôrâ,* "wheat in its row," *śᵉᶜorâ nisman,* "barley?" and *kussemet gᵉbulatô,* "rie in its border." The word is unclear, but the parallelism forces a meaning something like "in its place."

[32]Among others, Kissane, I, 319; Kaiser, *Isaiah 13–39,* p. 260; and Barnes, p. 433, refer this to the edges of the field with the spelt bordering the field of wheat. While this is possible, there is no good reason that this should be done. It would also violate Lev. 19:19, the prohibition against sowing different grains in the same field.

29 This also cometh forth from the Lord of hosts, which is wonderful in counsel, and excellent in working.

husks. The oxen might also drag a grinding stone over the grain or drag a board studded with stones or metal teeth over the grain. These methods were too harsh for the lighter seeds. They were spread out, probably on a flat rock, and beaten with a rod or club to thresh them, v. 27. On the other hand, "bread corn" (or "grain for bread") is threshed more normally. It is "bruised" (better "crushed"). The threshing, however, is in measure. The farmer does not continually thresh with the "wheel of his cart" or "horsemen" (better "horses," sometimes used to pull the threshing sledge) lest they damage the grain, v. 28. This practice is from the Lord, who has given wise counsel to the farmer.

29 The point of both parables is to show that God's chastening is in measure. God makes His counsel wonderful. He makes His "working" (*tûšîyâ*) great. The word *tûšîyâ* occurs only here in Isaiah although it occurs eleven times elsewhere in the OT. It has a sense of soundness or competence associated with it. The OT normally translates *tûšîyâ* "wisdom" or "sound wisdom." The Lord shows His counsel and wisdom as He works with His people. He punishes them in order to bring them to the point at which He may bless them. The farmer does not plow continually. There comes a time when he plants and receives a harvest. Likewise, the farmer does not overthresh his crops. He uses the appropriate method in order to gain the grain. In the same way, God will work wonderfully to bring His people to the point of blessing, v. 29.

Practical Applications from Chapter 28

1. Condemnation of Sin
   a. Pride ("crown of pride"), vv. 1, 3
   b. Drunkenness, vv. 1, 3, 7–8
   c. Scorning God's Word, vv. 9–10, 14 ("scornful")
   d. Trusting in man's resources, v. 15

   These sins are representative. They serve to show God's condemnation of all sins.

2. Two Parables to Encourage, vv. 23–29
   a. The sowing of a crop, vv. 23–26. The farmer prepares the soil, v. 24. Then he levels the ground and plants his seed, v. 25. God gives him wisdom for his work, v. 26.
   b. The threshing of a crop, vv. 27–28. The farmer threshes his crops appropriately. He beats the lighter seeds from their husks, v. 27, and crushes the husks of the heavier grain. He does this in measure to keep from damaging the grain, v. 28.
   c. The application of the parables, v. 29. God gives wisdom for these practices. His counsel is wonderful and His wisdom is great. Just as the farmer carries out his sowing and threshing in measure, so God works in measure as He chastens his people. He works to bring His people to the point of blessing; cf. Hebrews 12:11.

1 Woe to Ariel, to Ariel, the city where David dwelt! add ye year to year; let them kill sacrifices.

2 Yet I will distress Ariel, and there shall be heaviness and sorrow: and it shall be unto me as Ariel.

ISAIAH 29

The application of the passage often made is to the Assyrian siege under Sennacherib. Isaiah describes this in some detail later in c. 36–37. Verse 6, however, creates a problem for this approach. In order to apply the passage to Assyria, one must understand v. 6 poetically. The Lord did not overcome Assyria with a storm, earthquake, and fire. In order to apply the passage to Assyria, one must understand these as symbols of God's power.[1] It is possible, however, to take v. 6 literally as a prophecy of the Tribulation. This period will include storms (Rev. 8:7; 16:8–9), earthquake (Isa. 2:19; Rev. 6:12; 8:5; 11:19), and fire (Rev. 8:7, 8; 9:17–18). The application to Assyria, then, does not fully exhaust the sense of the passage.

B. Prospect of National Judgment 29:1–24
1. Rewards of Wickedness 29:1–12
a. Siege of Jerusalem 29:1–4

1–2 Isaiah condemns "Ariel" ($^{\jmath a}r\hat{\imath}^{\jmath}el$, "the hearth of God").[2] The name refers to the fires of God that will burn in judgment at

---

[1] Among others, Leupold, I, 436; Price, p. 126; and Barnes, I, 439, adopt this view. Price, p. 126, makes the judgment sudden "like a clap of thunder, and earthquake, a whirlwind, or a tempest." He omits fire, which is rarely a sudden judgment. Motyer, *The Prophecy of Isaiah,* p. 238, understands these as "a motif of power." Barnes, I, 440, agrees with this but also suggests "that all the agents here referred to may have been employed in the destruction of the Assyrian host, though they are not particularly specified in the history." Since the record of Assyria's defeat occurs in II Kings, II Chronicles, and Isaiah, it is unlikely that such significant detail would have been left out.

[2] There is no denying the difficulty of $^{\jmath a}r\hat{\imath}^{\jmath}el$. Strictly speaking, the word is a compound, $^{\jmath}ar\hat{\imath}$ $^{\jmath}el$, "the lion of God." The word occurs elsewhere as a proper name, Ezra 8:16, where the name readily means "lion of God." It occurs in I Chron. 11:22 (with a variant spelling in II Sam. 23:20), probably best made idiomatic of two valiant warriors from Moab. This also supports the basic meaning "lion of God." A related word, $^{\jmath}er^{\jmath}el$, "valiant ones," occurs in Isa. 33:7. Again, this supports the meaning of "lion of God." The word also occurs in Ezek. 43:15, where it indicates the "hearth" of the altar. In addition, the word $^{\jmath}r^{\jmath}l$ occurs in line 12 of the Moabite inscription to refer to a "hearth." Both "lion" and "hearth" can readily be derived from the verb $^{\jmath}ar\hat{a}$, "to pluck, gather." The lion gathers his food; the hearth gathers its fuel into the fire. Commentators divide on the meaning. Some give the meaning "lion of God," e.g., Henry, Rawlinson, Price. Others accept "hearth of God," e.g., Motyer, *The Prophecy of Isaiah,* Cowles, Skinner. Young, p. 305, tentatively suggests "belonging to God." This meaning rests on cognates and requires an interpretive step. I opt for the sense "hearth of God" primarily because of the sense of v. 2, "it shall be unto me as Ariel."

> 3 *And I will camp against thee round about, and will lay siege against thee with a mount, and I will raise forts against thee.*
> 4 *And thou shalt be brought down, and shalt speak out of the ground, and thy speech shall be low out of the dust, and thy voice shall be, as of one that hath a familiar spirit, out of the ground, and thy speech shall whisper out of the dust.*

Jerusalem.[3] To further identify the city, he calls it "the city where David dwelt" (*ḥanâ*, lit. "camped"). The word *ḥanâ* occurs again in v. 3, where the Lord promises to "camp" about the city. The parallelism suggests that Isaiah refers here to David's camp at the time he conquered Jerusalem, II Samuel 5:6–9.

Isaiah tells the people to "add ye year to year." The following phrase explains this: "let them kill sacrifices" (better "let them complete the feasts"). The thought refers to completing the yearly cycle of feasts. Although the people add one year to another as time passes with the killing of sacrifices, v. 1, God will still punish the nation. He will distress the city with "heaviness" (or "grief") and "sorrow" (or "mourning").[4] It will become as "Ariel," again "the hearth of God," undergoing the fires of judgment. The emphasis in both v. 1 and v. 2 is on Jerusalem. The Lord pronounces a "woe" on them, and will "distress" them. In v. 3, He camps against them and besieges them. In v. 4, the people are "brought down." The passage consistently refers the judgment to Jerusalem, v. 2.

3–4 Just as David had camped against the city, so the Lord will camp against the city. This will be "round about," on all sides of the city. He will besiege them. This will be "with a mount" (*muṣṣab*),[5] a siege-mound raised by the enemy. It will also include "forts" (or "strongholds"), places of

---

[3]Even those who understand *ᵃrîᵓel* as "hearth of God" explain it differently. Leupold, I, 452, views it as "the place where God's home, or hearth-fire, is among his people." Delitzsch, II, 17, understands it to refer to the place where God will consume "the foes like a furnace." Kelley, p. 374, applies it to the presence of the altar in the temple at Jerusalem. Cundall, *Proverbs—Isaiah 39*, p. 85, refers it to "the whole city . . . as a place of sacrifice, the offering being the citizens themselves." The Talmud suggests that the word refers to the shape of the temple altar, "narrow behind and broad in front" (*Middoth* iv.7).

[4]Isaiah poetically uses assonance here, *taᵓᵃnîyâ waᵓᵃnîyâ*, that is difficult to capture in the translation. Translations offer such phrases as "moaning and bemoaning," "groaning and moaning," "mourning and moaning," "sadness and sorrow," and others. The poetic repetition of sounds emphasizes the sorrow that will come upon the people.

[5]The word *muṣṣab* occurs only here. The verb *naṣab*, however, occurs often with the sense "to stand, take an upright position." The word *muṣṣab*, then, refers to the siege-mounds, or entrenchments, placed against the city.

5 *Moreover the multitude of thy strangers shall be like small dust, and the multitude of the terrible ones shall be as chaff that passeth away: yea, it shall be at an instant suddenly.*
6 *Thou shalt be visited of the Lord of hosts with thunder, and with earthquake, and great noise, with storm and tempest, and the flame of devouring fire.*

safety for the enemy made possible by the siege-mounds. Notice that it is the Lord who does these things. Although He works through the enemy, it is the Lord who is in control, v. 3. The people will be "brought down," i.e., humbled. They will no longer speak in a haughty manner. They will "speak out of the ground" and "out of the dust." This pictures the nation in a weakened condition, lying on the ground from where they whisper their words. The voice is that of one through whom a "familiar spirit" speaks. The term "familiar spirit" refers to a demonic spirit who spoke with ethereal tones through a possessed person.[6] The person would "whisper" while lying in the dust. The muttering sounds indicate his exhausted condition; cf. 8:19.[7] Verses 1–4 refer to the Assyrian siege of Jerusalem, v. 4.

b. Suppression of Enemies 29:5–8

5–6 Isaiah abruptly changes his thought. While keeping the thought of Assyria's destruction in mind, he also leaps forward in time to picture the Tribulation judgment of Judah's enemies.[8] The destruction of Assyria pictures the future judgments of the end time. The "strangers" (*zar* see 1:7) who invade the land will become as "small [*daq*] dust."[9] These foreigners here will become as "chaff," the husk of the grain that has no value. This

---

[6]Watts, *Isaiah 1–33*, p. 382, makes this literal. The city "descends into the land of the dead, becoming like a ghost." This seems extreme. It would be unusual for an entire city to die as the result of a siege.

[7]Price, p. 126, understands the sounds of the verse as the "voice of the dying victim as it bleeds slowly to death alongside the brazen altar." The verse, however, relates this to the people of Jerusalem rather than to the sacrifices at the altar.

[8]Cundall, *Proverbs–Isaiah 39*, p. 85; Watts, pp. 378, 383; and Kaiser, *Isaiah 13–39*, pp. 267–68, understand vv. 5–8 as continuing the description of nations coming against Jerusalem. Verses 7–8 rather describe the passing of the threat to Jerusalem and not the conclusion of a bad dream when the threat is over.

[9]The word *daq* occurs elsewhere to refer to the white layer of frost on the ground (Exod. 16:14) and incense that has been ground into powder (Lev. 16:12). Moses ground the golden calf into powder (Exod. 32:20), which he then mixed with water and made the people drink. Josiah ground pagan altars into powder, which he had sprinkled on the graves of their followers (II Chron. 34:4). The grinding here, then, is to a fine powder. This pictures the extent of God's judgment.

7 *And the multitude of all the nations that fight against Ariel, even all that fight against her and her munition, and that distress her, shall be as a dream of a night vision.*

8 *It shall even be as when an hungry man dreameth, and, behold, he eateth; but he awaketh, and his soul is empty: or as when a thirsty man dreameth, and, behold, he drinketh; but he awaketh, and, behold, he is faint, and his soul hath appetite: so shall the multitude of all the nations be, that fight against mount Zion.*

judgment will take place rapidly, "at an instant suddenly," v. 5. They will be "visited" (*paqad*, see 10:12) with great forces of nature. Isaiah mentions "thunder," "earthquake," "great noise," "storm" (or "whirlwind"), "tempest," and "the flame of devouring fire." The picture is awesome. God moves nature to overwhelm the enemies of His people, v. 6.

7–8 The Lord once more identifies Jerusalem as Ariel. Now she is the hearth upon which the fire of God burns His enemies. The enemy fights against Jerusalem and her "munition" (*meṣodatah*, better "stronghold").[10] The deliverance of the city makes the threats by the enemy seem as a dream. The dream is terribly real while it lasts but has no substance when the dreamer awakes, v. 7. Isaiah illustrates the thought. The hungry man dreams of food but when he wakes he is still hungry. The thirsty man dreams of drinking cool water but when he wakes he is faint from his thirst. He still has an "appetite," a desire for water. In the same way, the enemies that fight against Mt. Zion will vanish. Their plans of conquest are only a dream without substance, v. 8.

The defeat of Sennacherib's army, 37:36–38 (II Kings 19:35–37), only partially fulfills the prophecy. While the suddenness of his defeat parallels Isaiah's words, there are also elements of the prediction that differ. The description of nature's fight against the enemies differs from the conquest of Sennacherib's army. For this reason, it is better to find the complete fulfillment in the end-time events when God delivers His people from Antichrist. At that time the Lord will unleash nature against those who oppose Him; cf. Matthew 24:29; Revelation 6:12–14; 8:7–12.

---

[10]Watts, *Isaiah 1–33*, p. 380, understands *meṣodatah* as "siegeworks" raised against Jerusalem by the enemy. Kaiser, *Isaiah 13–39*, p. 264, recognizes that the word is a substantive but translates as a verb, "besiege her" (so NIV). Delitzsch, II, 19, refers the word to the mountain of Zion mentioned in v. 8. Young, II, 312, makes it the temple, God's dwelling place. The form of *meṣodatah* argues against translating it as a verb. I take it generally, not referring to a specific part of Jerusalem but rather a parallel word describing the defenses of the city.

9 *Stay yourselves, and wonder; cry ye out, and cry: they are drunken, but not with wine; they stagger, but not with strong drink.*

10 *For the Lord hath poured out upon you the spirit of deep sleep, and hath closed your eyes: the prophets and your rulers, the seers hath he covered.*

11 *And the vision of all is become unto you as the words of a book that is sealed, which men deliver to one that is learned, saying, Read this, I pray thee: and he saith, I cannot; for it is sealed:*

12 *And the book is delivered to him that is not learned, saying, Read this, I pray thee: and he saith, I am not learned.*

c. Sleep of the People 29:9–12

9–10 Isaiah notes the stupor of the people. They should "stay . . . and wonder" (or "be astonished"), be dumbfounded at the things that he says. The phrase "cry ye out [$hišta^ca\check{s}^c\hat{u}$], and cry [$\check{s}o^c\hat{u}$]" is better "blind yourselves and be blind."[11] Isaiah refers to spiritual blindness, the result of Judah's failure to accept God's commands. He expands the thought by comparing the people to those who stagger as though drunk when they have had no "wine" or "strong drink," cf. 5:11, v. 9. Because of their lack of concern over their sin, the Lord has given them "the spirit of deep sleep [$tardem\hat{a}$]." The word $tardem\hat{a}$ occurs seven times in the OT,[12] each time denoting unusually deep sleep or spiritual torpor. The idea here is of spiritual insensitivity. The parallelism of the text indicates that the "eyes" are the prophets and the "rulers" (or "heads") are the seers. The translation is better "The Lord . . . has closed your eyes, the prophets, and your heads, the seers, He has covered." The idea is that the spiritual leaders are insensitive to truth, v. 10.

11–12 Isaiah illustrates the insensitivity of the people by speaking of a sealed book. They do not understand the "vision of all," i.e., the entire vision. They relate this to the "learned," likely one of the prophets or seers of the previous verse. He cannot understand it because it is sealed, i.e., the meaning is hid from him. While he may understand the words,

---

[11]Watts, *Isaiah 1–33*, p. 384, understands $hišta^ca\check{s}^c\hat{u}$ from $\check{s}a^ca^c$, "to delight," but derives $\check{s}o^c\hat{u}$ from $\check{s}a^c\hat{a}$, "to gaze at." While "delight" is an alternate meaning of $\check{s}a^ca^c$, the thought of delight is not a good parallel to the first clause, "stay. . . ." The NEB gives the first imperative the alternative meaning "enjoy yourselves" but uses the traditional meaning for the second imperative, "be blinded." This is unlikely. Kaiser, *Isaiah 13–39*, p. 269, translates, "stare at each other and stare." This derives both verbs from $\check{s}a^c\hat{a}$, "to gaze," probably not the source.

[12]Here and Gen. 2:21; 15:12; I Sam. 26:12; Job 4:13; 33:15; Prov. 19:15.

13 *Wherefore the Lord said, Forasmuch as this people draw near me with their mouth, and with their lips do honour me, but have removed their heart far from me, and their fear toward me is taught by the precept of men:*

14 *Therefore, behold, I will proceed to do a marvellous work among this people, even a marvellous work and a wonder: for the wisdom of their wise men shall perish, and the understanding of their prudent men shall be hid.*

15 *Woe unto them that seek deep to hide their counsel from the Lord, and their works are in the dark, and they say, Who seeth us? and who knoweth us?*

16 *Surely your turning of things upside down shall be esteemed as the potter's clay: for shall the work say of him that made it, He made me not? or shall the thing framed say of him that framed it, He had no understanding?*

he cannot understand the message, v. 11. They then give the vision to an unlearned man. He also cannot explain it. This is a sad picture: from the leaders to the common people, there is no spiritual understanding, v. 12.

2. Results of Wisdom 29:13–24
a. Condemnation of Man's Way 29:13–16

13–14 The Lord condemns the people for their ritualistic worship. They carry out the worship service. In all likelihood, this relates to the service commanded by Hezekiah when he forbade idolatry, II Chronicles 31:1, and reestablished the worship ritual at the temple, II Chronicles 29:20–36; 31:2–3. The people worship but their worship is hypocritical. They "honour" (*kabed*, see 3:5) God with their speech but their "heart" is far from Him. Their "fear," or reverence, was that which had been taught by "men" (*ᵉnôš*, see 2:11), not God. The statement is the basis for the Lord's condemnation of the scribes and Pharisees, Matthew 15:7–9 (Mark 7:6–7), v. 13. Because of the hypocrisy, the Lord promises to send a "marvellous work" of judgment. He will bring the Assyrian army upon them. This judgment will cause the leadership of Judah's "wise men . . . prudent men" to perish, proving it worthless. Paul draws on this to illustrate the inability of men to understand spiritual truth, I Corinthians 1:19, v. 14.[13]

15–16 Isaiah condemns the attempt to make a secret alliance with Egypt. They work in the dark, hiding from the open light of public

---

[13]The form of the verse is typical of Isaiah. He uses the root *plᵓ* three times, "marvellous work . . . marvellous work . . . a wonder." In addition, he doubles the roots in 14*b*: "the wisdom [*ḥkm*] of their wise men [*ḥkm*]" and "the understanding [*bîn*] of their prudent men [*bîn*]."

*17 Is it not yet a very little while, and Lebanon shall be turned into a
fruitful field, and the fruitful field shall be esteemed as a forest?
18 And in that day shall the deaf hear the words of the book, and the
eyes of the blind shall see out of obscurity, and out of darkness.
19 The meek also shall increase their joy in the Lord, and the poor
among men shall rejoice in the Holy One of Israel.*

awareness and possible rebuke from prophetic voices. They act as
though their plans are hid from the Lord, as if He does not see them or
know of their efforts, v. 15. Verse 16a " is better "O your perversity!
Should the potter be esteemed as the clay?" Clearly the answer is no!
The work does not have the right to criticize the workman. The work
cannot deny the workman's craft. It should not accuse the workman of
lacking "understanding" (*bîn*, see 1:3). The statement bluntly condemns
Judah for rejecting God and His plans for them. Paul relies on this verse
in Romans 9:20, v. 16.

b. Consummation of God's Plan 29:17–24

17–19 The Lord has a glorious plan for the land. In a "little while,"
little from the perspective of eternity, God will bless the land. The mountainous region, the Lebanon mountain range that runs through the land,
will become a "fruitful field." The "fruitful field" in turn will become a
bountiful forest. The statement apparently is proverbial, indicating that
things will be blessed in the kingdom, v. 17.[14] Verses 18–21 illustrate this
idea. The deaf will hear the words of lit. "a book" being read. The blind

---

[14]Näglesbach, p. 322, and Leupold, I, 461, make Lebanon a symbol of Assyria and the
"fruitful field" represent Israel. Assyria, under Sennacherib, will be brought low. Judah
will be exalted. Such symbolism is unique, seen nowhere else in Scripture. Since the
context does not require this, it is better to understand the passage as above. Von Orelli,
p. 166, rejects the idea of "an exalting of the low and a humbling of the high." He sees
this as a "metamorphosis of the sacred land." Lebanon becomes a "fruit-bearing garden,
while that which is now called garden is counted common wood, in consequence of the
higher standard of fertility then applied." While this is possible, it is not likely. This approach sets the verse apart from its context. The following verses describe the reversal of
roles introduced by the proverb of v. 17. The NEB translates v. 17 as though it finishes
the statement of judgment: "The time is but short before Lebanon goes back to grassland
and the grassland is no better than scrub." The translation is remarkably free. It requires
interpretive meanings to be assigned to well-known words. The term *karmel*, "fruitful
field," occurs in 10:18; 16:10; 32:15, 16, where it cannot be mere "grassland." Likewise,
ya'ar occurs several times in the book where the context requires "forest," not "scrub,"
7:2; 9:18; 10:18, 19, 34; 32:15; 37:24; 44:14, 23.

20　*For the terrible one is brought to nought, and the scorner is consumed, and all that watch for iniquity are cut off:*

21　*That make a man an offender for a word, and lay a snare for him that reproveth in the gate, and turn aside the just for a thing of nought.*

22　*Therefore thus saith the Lord, who redeemed Abraham, concerning the house of Jacob, Jacob shall not now be ashamed, neither shall his face now wax pale.*

23　*But when he seeth his children, the work of mine hands, in the midst of him, they shall sanctify my name, and sanctify the Holy One of Jacob, and shall fear the God of Israel.*

24　*They also that erred in spirit shall come to understanding, and they that murmured shall learn doctrine.*

will see what formerly was hidden from their sight, v. 18.[15] The meek will rejoice in the Lord. The "poor" (*ʾebyôn*, see 14:30) will likewise rejoice because he now possesses the greatest of all possessions, the Lord Himself, v. 19.

20–21 The converse will also be true. The "terrible one," the oppressor of others, will fail.[16] The one who scorns God and godliness will be consumed. Those who "watch for iniquity," seeking the chance to do evil, will be cut off in judgment, v. 20. Isaiah takes up those who offend legally. Those who "make a man an offender for a word" are perjurers, whose false words cause another to be considered an "offender," guilty of some wrong. The perjurer will now receive punishment. The one who "reproveth [*môkîaḥ*, see 1:18] in the gate" is a judge.[17] Some set a trap for him in order to cast doubt on his credibility. They will now receive judgment. Those who make an unjust accusation, "a thing of nought [*tohû*, see 24:20]," trying to "turn aside the just," will be condemned, v. 21.

22–24 In that day, the kingdom, Israel's relationship with God will no longer be a problem. The God who "redeemed" (*padâ*, see 1:27) Abraham now says of "the house of Jacob," Israel, that they need not "be ashamed"

---

[15]Skinner, *Isaiah I–XXXIX*, p. 222, and Young, II, 325–26, consider "deaf" and "blind" to be "metaphors for the spiritual obtuseness which at present characterizes the nation." While this is true, it is also true that the Lord will heal physical handicaps in the kingdom. If "meek," "poor," "terrible one," "scorner," and "all that watch for iniquity" are literal, it is likely that "deaf" and "blind" are literal as well.

[16]Vine, p. 64, goes too far when he calls the "terrible one" the "Man of Sin." The context simply makes the oppressor one of several evil ones cut off by the Lord.

[17]Motyer, *The Prophecy of Isaiah*, p. 242, refers this to the witness against wrong. Barnes, I, 446, and Young, II, 329, think this is someone seeking justice in the court. Watts, *Isaiah 1–33*, p. 388, makes this the lawyer who argues for right. These are

(*bôš*, see 1:29).[18] Their faces will no longer "wax pale," showing fear of their enemies. God called Abraham from a heathen background; cf. Joshua 24:2.[19] He established His covenant with Abraham and his descendants, Genesis 12:2–3. In that day when the Lord completes His preparation, Israel will be vindicated. There will be no reason for them to be ashamed because of their faith or to fear their enemies. There is no longer any question of their position, v. 22. When the people see their children, evidence of God's blessing upon them, they will "sanctify" His name[20] by setting it apart as worthy of special honor. They will "sanctify" the "Holy One of Jacob," setting Him above all other gods that have been worshiped in the past. They will "fear" (*ʿaraṣ*, see 8:12) Him. The verb *ʿaraṣ* in the *hipʿîl* better means "regard with awe." This is a proper attitude for the God who has put down wickedness and established His rule over the earth, v. 23. Those who once "erred in spirit," opposing the Lord, will now understand His position and authority. Those who opposed Him will now learn His teachings, v. 24.

---

possible ways to understand *môkîaḥ*. I take *môkîaḥ* in its judicial sense; cf. Gen. 31:37; Isa. 1:18; 11:3. Fausset, p. 654, includes the prophet, the judge, and the plaintiff, probably too broad an application.

[18]The construction is awkward. The verse lit. reads, "Therefore thus says the Lord to the house of Jacob, He who redeemed Abraham, Jacob shall now not be ashamed nor shall his face turn pale." Watts, *Isaiah 1–33*, p. 387, and the NEB point *ʾl* with *ṣerê* rather than *sᵉgol* and translate, "the God of the house of Jacob," rather than, "concerning [or 'to'] the house of Jacob." While this solves an awkward grammatical construction, there is no textual evidence to support the change. The LXX interprets *padâ*, "redeem," as "set apart," whom "He set apart from Abraham." The verb *padâ*, however, never has this sense elsewhere. The AV follows the same approach as the Vulgate and the Targum by reversing the second and third phrases.

[19]Herbert, *Isaiah 1–39*, p. 171, asserts that "no incident occurs in Genesis with which this reference could reasonably be associated." The call, however, out of a pagan background certainly satisfies the statement. Wright, p. 71, wrongly says that "reference to the first of the patriarchs is very rare in the prophets and appears elsewhere in the Isaiah literature only in 63:16." Isaiah, however, mentions Abraham also in 41:8 and 51:2. In addition, the phrase "first father," 43:27, likely refers to Abraham. Jeremiah and Ezekiel each refer once to Abraham.

[20]Among others, Von Orelli, p. 167; Näglesbach, p. 320; and Delitzsch, II, 25, translate, "For when he, when his children see the work of my hands. . . . " Leupold, I, 460, translates, "For when his children see what my hands have done. . . ." This attempts to smooth the statement. It is better, however, to place "his children" in apposition to "the work of mine hands" as in the AV, NASB, and NIV.

Practical Applications from Chapter 29

1. God's Care for His Own Children, vv. 1–8

  a. Correction of their sin, vv. 1–4

    (1) Judgment falls on the people who live where David once camped. Your descent from a godly individual does not keep you from your individual responsibility.

    (2) Although the people of the city go through the ritual of offering sacrifices, the judgment will still come. It is not religion but a personal relationship to God that gives deliverance from the judgment, v. 1.

    (3) God's judgment is thorough. His punishment brings "heaviness and sorrow." The city is as a hearth upon which God kindles His fire, v. 2. He camps against the people, besieges the city, and sets up strongholds against it. All of these insure that no one will escape His penalty for their sin, v. 3. He humbles the people, bringing them to such a weakened state that they lie on the ground barely able to speak, v. 4.

  b. Protection of the people, vv. 5–8

    (1) God will grind the enemy into small dust. He will do this "at an instant," suddenly, a vivid display of His power, v. 5.

    (2) God will send cataclysmic forces of nature against His enemies. These include thunder, earthquake, great noises, whirlwind, tempest, and flames of fire. These continue to display the power of God over this world, v. 6.

    (3) The nations that opposed God's people now vanish, becoming as a dream that vanishes, v. 7. Just as the hungry man dreams of eating but is still hungry when he wakes or the thirsty man dreams of drinking but is still thirsty when he wakes, so the threat from the enemies of God's people has no substance. It is gone, v. 8.

  c. Application of the prophecy

    (1) The near application. The defeat of the Assyrian army partially fulfills the prophecy, 37:36–38 (II Kings 19:35–37). The Lord allowed the Assyrians to oppress the nation as punishment for their sins. At the same time, He gave ultimate deliverance so that the nation could continue to carry out His will for the future.

(2) The final application. The Tribulation judgments will again place Israel in a position of punishment for their sins. They will turn to Him, finally seeing Jesus Christ as the Savior. The Lord will deliver them from the hosts of Antichrist as He takes the steps that will end in His rule over the earth.

2. Causes of God's Judgment, vv. 9–16

a. Spiritual blindness. The people should be amazed at Isaiah's condemnation, v. 9. God judges spiritual blindness with more spiritual blindness. He allows wicked men to give spiritual leadership, v. 10. None can understand spiritual truths, vv. 11–12.

b. Ritualistic worship. The people worship God outwardly but their heart is far from Him. They follow the teachings of men, v. 13.

c. Trusting human resources. The people attempt to make an alliance with Egypt. They work in secret as though God cannot see them, v. 15. The clay has no right to criticize the potter. The work has no right to criticize the worker. In the same way, the people of God have no right to criticize God and His plans for them, v. 16.

3. Blessings of the Kingdom, vv. 17–24

a. Blessings on the land, v. 17

b. Blessings on the people, vv. 18–21

(1) The deaf will hear, the blind will see, v. 18, the meek will rejoice in the Lord, and the poor will rejoice in their knowledge of the Lord, v. 19.

(2) Conversely, the Lord will bring judgment upon the wicked. The oppressor of others will come to nothing. The one who scorned God and godliness will be consumed. Those who looked for opportunities to do evil will be cut off, v. 20. Perjurers, those who seek to ruin the reputation of judges, and those who falsely accuse others will receive judgment, v. 21.

c. Blessings on Israel, vv. 22–24

The nation no longer needs to be ashamed or fear their enemies, v. 22. God will give them children to show His blessing on them. They will sanctify Him, setting Him apart for special honor, v. 23. Although they once rejected the Lord, they will now understand who He is and what honor He deserves, v. 24.

1 Woe to the rebellious children, saith the Lord, that take counsel, but not of me; and that cover with a covering, but not of my spirit, that they may add sin to sin:

2 That walk to go down into Egypt, and have not asked at my mouth; to strengthen themselves in the strength of Pharaoh, and to trust in the shadow of Egypt!

ISAIAH 30

The chapter begins to rebuke Judah for relying on Egypt rather than on the Lord; chapter 31 continues the rebuke. Isaiah weaves an eschatological prophecy into the passage. While Egypt will fail the nation, the Lord will sustain them. He will punish them for their sin of turning from Him. He will afterwards show them mercy. The promise assumes a change in the attitude of the people. When they come to a position of placing their faith in the Lord, He will bestow His blessing upon them. He Himself will dwell with them. He will protect them by judging their enemies. The chapter ends by returning to the OT experience of the nation. The Lord will judge the Assyrian oppressors of Judah.

C. Condemnation of the Egyptian Alliance 30:1–31:9
1. Alliance with Egypt 30:1–17
a. Futility of the Alliance 30:1–5

1–2 The Lord bluntly condemns Judah for relying on Egypt. The people of Judah "take counsel [*ʿeṣâ*]"[1] but not from Him. They "cover with a covering" (*linsok massekâ*) lit. "weave a covering," i.e., make an alliance by plaiting together various matters.[2] The Holy Spirit does not lead them in this. This act causes them to "add sin to sin," multiplying

---

[1]Mitchell Dahood, "Accusative *ʿeṣāh*, 'Wood', in Isaiah 30,1b," *Biblica* 50:57–58, understands "*ʿeṣāh*" as "wood," i.e., wooden idols. This leads him to translate *massekâ* as molten images. While these translations are possible, vv. 2–4 develop the idea of political intrigue. It is more consistent to accept the alternate translations given above.

[2]Young, II, 336; Grogan, p. 200; and Kaiser, *Isaiah 13–39*, p. 282, treat *linsok massekâ* as "pour a libation," an action marking the making of a covenant. Israel, however, did not use a drink offering in making covenants. The ceremonial action mentioned often in the OT in connection with a covenant is that of a blood sacrifice, e.g., Gen. 15:9–10; Exod. 24:5–6; cf. Heb. 9:18–22. Sometimes there was also a ceremonial meal, Gen. 26:30; 31:54; II Sam. 3:12, 20. Isaiah uses *nasak* with the sense of weaving in 25:7. The idea of making a covenant directly parallels the taking of counsel.

3 *Therefore shall the strength of Pharaoh be your shame, and the trust in the shadow of Egypt your confusion.*
4 *For his princes were at Zoan, and his ambassadors came to Hanes.*
5 *They were all ashamed of a people that could not profit them, nor be an help nor profit, but a shame, and also a reproach.*

their "sin" (*ḥaṭṭaʾt*, see 3:9) in turning from the Lord, v. 1.[3] He directly states the nature of their sin. The people have gone to Egypt for help, not asking the Lord to guide them. They have relied on Pharaoh's "strength" (or "means of safety"), probably referring to the army. They have placed themselves under the covering shade cast by Egypt, a metaphor drawn from the protection given by the shade of a tree, v. 2.

3–5 Egypt will prove to be weak. The failure of Egypt's army to defend them will cause Judah to know "shame" (*bôš*, see 1:29). Judah's "trust" (or "shelter") in Egypt's protection will be their "confusion" (*kalam*, or "disgrace"),[4] v. 3. Judah's ("his") princes have traveled to Zoan, on a branch of the Nile in the eastern delta.[5] They have gone to Hanes, mentioned only here and not clearly identified. It must have been an important Egyptian city, v. 4.[6] They "were [lit. 'will be,'] all ashamed [(*hobîš*)]"[7] when they find that Egypt cannot help them in their time of trouble. Rather than helping, their tie to Egypt will bring them shame and reproach, v. 5.

---

[3]Vine, p. 65; Goldingay, p. 165; and Barnes, I, 448, consider the first sin that of failing to trust the Lord. The second sin, added to the first, is that of the foreign alliance with Egypt. This is a possible view.

[4]The word *kalam* often occurs in parallel with *bôš*. In this construction, there is no significant difference between the words. When *kalam* stands by itself, it may have the sense of public humiliation. Occasionally, this sense may occur when the word parallels *bôš*. The context must guide in understanding the sense.

[5]The text does not clearly identify the suffixes. Either they resume the actions of Judah in vv. 1–2 or refer to Pharaoh in v. 3. Skinner, *Isaiah I–XXXIX*, p. 226; Whitehouse, I, 314; and Motyer, *The Prophecy of Isaiah*, p. 246, understand them as referring to Pharaoh. If this is so, however, the antecedent of v. 5 must go back to vv. 1–2. In addition, v. 6 refers to men from Judah going to Egypt. For these reasons, I relate the "his" to Judah in both places.

[6]Many identify Hanes as Heracleopolis, fifty miles north of Cairo, e.g., Delitzsch, II, 28, Von Orelli, p. 171, and Leupold, I, 469. M. G. Kyle, *International Standard Bible Encyclopedia*, II, 1335, suggests it is a city located in the delta nearer Jerusalem. Barnes, I, 440, identifies it as Anusis, biblical Tahpanhes, which he locates in the eastern delta. Most consider Anusis another name for Heracleopolis.

[7]The AV correctly reads the *qᵉrê hobîš*, "shame," rather than the *kᵉtîb hibʾîš*, "stink."

6 *The burden of the beasts of the south: into the land of trouble and anguish, from whence come the young and old lion, the viper and fiery flying serpent, they will carry their riches upon the shoulders of young asses, and their treasures upon the bunches of camels, to a people that shall not profit them.*

7 *For the Egyptians shall help in vain, and to no purpose: therefore have I cried concerning this, Their strength is to sit still.*

8 *Now go, write it before them in a table, and note it in a book, that it may be for the time to come for ever and ever:*

b. Results of the Alliance 30:6–17

6–8 Isaiah now gives additional details to the theme introduced in v. 1. He writes of "the burden [*maśśaʾ*, or 'oracle,' cf. 13:1] of the beasts of the south." The word "beasts" (*bahᵃmôt*, see 18:6) refers to domestic or wild animals. It here embraces the animals mentioned later in the verse.[8] These animals are in the "south" (better "Negeb"), the wilderness area between Judah and Egypt. This is a "land of trouble and anguish," a land of danger for those passing through it. The "young and old lion" (better "lioness and lion") live in this region. The "viper," an unidentified serpent, probably poisonous, and the "flying serpent," again an unidentified poisonous serpent, also live there.[9] The representatives of Judah will bring "riches" and "treasures," no doubt meant to purchase Egypt's help. They carry these on the "shoulders" (or "sides") of donkeys and on the "bunches" (*dabbešet*, or "humps")[10] of camels. Egypt, however, will fail

---

[8]Von Orelli, p. 171; Delitzsch, II, 29; and Leupold, I, 470, refer *bahᵃmôt* to the hippopotamus. Von Orelli, p. 171, calls it a "huge, sluggish beast" that is "an expressive emblem of the empire on the Nile." Henry, p. 165, relates the word to "horses fetched from Egypt," brought by the Jews to carry their payment to Egypt. Kraeling, p. 127, takes the plural *bahᵃmôt* as a plural of "majesty" and translates as "beast," a symbol of Egypt. More reasonably, *bahᵃmôt* refers simply to the animals in the verse.

[9]Kaiser, *Isaiah 13–39*, p. 289, thinks that the author refers to a route filled "not only with real animals but also with imaginary beasts." The problem rests primarily with "fiery flying serpent," *śarap mᵉʿôpep*. The verb *ʿûp*, "to fly," occurs elsewhere, however, to refer not only to literal flight but also in a more general sense. The sparks "fly" up, Job 5:7. David longed to "fly" away from his enemies, Ps. 55:6. Man flies away into death, Ps. 90:10. Wealth flies away from us, Prov. 23:5. Isaiah refers to flying across the boundary leading to Philistia, 11:14. He mentions an aroused serpent, 14:29. It is appropriate to understand the participle here as in 14:29, an aroused or possibly a darting serpent.

[10]The word *dabbešet* occurs only here and at Josh. 19:11, where it is a place name. Harold Cohen, *Biblical Hapax Legomena in the Light of Akkadian and Ugaritic*, p. 132, relates it to a Ugaritic cognate and gives "hump" as the meaning. This is generally accepted since the context requires something of this sort.

9 *That this is a rebellious people, lying children, children that will not hear the law of the Lord:*
10 *Which say to the seers, See not; and to the prophets, Prophesy not unto us right things, speak unto us smooth things, prophesy deceits:*
11 *Get you out of the way, turn aside out of the path, cause the Holy One of Israel to cease from before us.*
12 *Wherefore thus saith the Holy One of Israel, Because ye despise this word, and trust in oppression and perverseness, and stay thereon:*
13 *Therefore this iniquity shall be to you as a breach ready to fall, swelling out in a high wall, whose breaking cometh suddenly at an instant.*
14 *And he shall break it as the breaking of the potters' vessel that is broken in pieces; he shall not spare: so that there shall not be found in the bursting of it a sherd to take fire from the hearth, or to take water withal out of the pit.*

the Jews, v. 6. Because of Egypt's vain pledge, the Lord has cried concerning them, "Their strength is to sit still" (*rahab hem šabet*). The phrase *rahab hem šabet* is better "A proud one are they who sit still." This sarcastically refers to Egypt's words without deeds. The OT elsewhere represents Egypt with the word "Rahab" (*rahab*), 51:9; Psalm 87:4; 89:10.[11] The word means "pride, arrogance" and so is an appropriate name for Egypt. She proudly proclaims her strength but does not use it to defend Judah, v. 7. The Lord commands Isaiah to record these things as a permanent reminder to Israel of her failure to trust Him, v. 8.[12]

9–14 Isaiah begins by noting the sin of the people. They are rebellious. They lie concerning God's ability to deliver them, and they refuse

---

[11]Commentators widely refer to Rahab as a mythical monster, often a dragon, that creates chaos, e.g., Herbert, *Isaiah 1–39*, p. 173; Skinner, *Isaiah I–XXXIX*, p. 227; Kraeling, p. 127; Wright, p. 72. Kaiser, *Isaiah 13–39*, p. 290, relates an elaborate tale in which Rahab personifies the primeval sea. Upon its rebellion against the Lord, He destroys it and those who helped in the rebellion. Whitehouse, I, 316, makes Rahab correspond to Tiamat, the dragon of chaos in Babylonian myth. He wrongly states that Isaiah is the first to apply the name Rahab to Egypt. Cf. Ps. 87:4; 89:10, both written several hundred years before Isaiah. The word *rahab*, however, occurs several times as a substantive, "proud," e.g., Job 26:12; Ps. 40:4; 89:10. There is no hint in Scripture of a mythological being.

[12]Motyer, *The Prophecy of Isaiah,* p. 247, suggests that the references to a tablet ("table") and a scroll ("book") indicate a "public and a private record." While this is possible, there is nothing in the text to suggest this. The parallel commands, "write . . . note . . ." are normal. Kaiser, *Isaiah 13–39*, pp. 293–94, argues that the use of *ḥaqaq*, "note" (better "inscribe"), carving the message into some hard material, means that the message must have been short. He concludes that vv. 8–17 are an expansion by a later editor. The verb *ḥaqaq*, however, may refer to writing in general. Job 19:23 refers to printing (*ḥaqaq*)

15 *For thus saith the Lord God, the Holy One of Israel; In returning and rest shall ye be saved; in quietness and in confidence shall be your strength: and ye would not.*

16 *But ye said, No; for we will flee upon horses; therefore shall ye flee: and, We will ride upon the swift; therefore shall they that pursue you be swift.*

17 *One thousand shall flee at the rebuke of one; at the rebuke of five shall ye flee: till ye be left as a beacon upon the top of a mountain, and as an ensign on an hill.*

to hear His "law" (*tôrâ*, see 1:10), v. 9. They forbid the "seers" (*roʾîm*) and the "prophets" (*hozîm*) to speak the truth. The words *roʾîm* and *hozîm* both emphasize the visions by which the prophets received revelation.[13] The people wanted to hear only "smooth things," deceitful words that agreed with what they wanted, v. 10. The people rejected the prophets. They tell them to "get you out of the way," i.e., to abandon their strictly moral standards. They want them to "turn aside" from their righteous path. In this way, the people reject the Lord Himself, v. 11.

The Lord takes note of Judah's rejection of His Word, given through Isaiah. Instead, they "stay thereon" (or "trust in") "oppression and perverseness [or 'deviousness']," v. 12. For this reason, their "iniquity" (*ʿawon*, see 1:4) will bring sudden judgment. He compares this to a retaining wall that unexpectedly breaks. The wall swells to indicate its weakness, then suddenly breaks. The swelling is a warning; the break is irreversible. The implied thought is that God now warns Israel. If they do not change, sudden judgment will fall on them, v. 13. The Lord will "break" (*šabar*, see 14:5) them completely. Isaiah illustrates this with a clay jar. When it breaks, not even a "sherd," a fragment of the pot, remains to dip ashes from a fire or water from a "pit," a cistern. The vivid picture is of a judgment that devastates the nation, v. 14.

15–17 Verse 15 is one of the most devotional texts of the book. It is at the same time practical as it points to the way of safety yet sad as it

---

in a book. Prov. 8:15 mentions a just "decree" (*haqaq*) and Isa. 10:1 an unjust "decree." Ezek. 23:14 speaks of images "pourtrayed" (*haqâ*) with "vermilion," a reddish color. While *haqaq* often refers to an inscription, it also has other components of meaning. Since it parallels "write" (*katab*), it best refers here to writing. The word *haqaq* is appropriate since the record is permanent.

[13]This is the only place that the AV translates *hozîm* as "prophets." Elsewhere it is generally translated "seer," e.g., 29:10. There is no significant difference between the two words for seer in the verse. The word *roʾîm* is the older word but both occur in the later books of the OT.

18 *And therefore will the Lord wait, that he may be gracious unto you,*
and therefore will he be exalted, that he may have mercy upon you:
for the Lord is a God of judgment: blessed are all they that wait for
him.

notes the refusal of the people. Isaiah parallels two phrases. In each, the
first part describes the action of the people. The second part describes
the result that accompanies the action. The Lord holds out hope for His
own. If they return to Him and rest in His protection rather than in that
of Egypt, they will "be saved" (*yašaʿ*, see 17:10), find deliverance. Their
"quietness" (*šaqaṭ*, see 7:4) and confidence in the Lord will give them
strength to overcome the enemy. Judah, however, will not do this, v. 15.
Isaiah poetically describes their flight. They had thought to "flee" (*nûs*)
on horses to escape the Assyrian threat. They will indeed flee before
them. They had thought to ride swift animals to evade the enemy. They
will find that Assyria pursues them on swift animals, v. 16.[14] Their fear
will be such that a great number will flee before a small number of the
enemy. Their numbers will be so depleted that they will seem a lone
"beacon" (or "pole") on the mountaintop. They will be as an "ensign"
(or "pole") standing on a hill, v. 17.

2. Association with God 30:18–31:9
a. Blessing of God 30:18–26

18 The prophecy now takes on an eschatological aspect. Isaiah promises that the Lord will wait until the judgment has had its effect on the
people. At that time He will be gracious to them. He will be exalted in
showing mercy to the people. God is a God of "judgment" (*mišpaṭ*, or
"justice," see 1:17). Those who wait for His mercy will be "blessed"
(*ʾašʿrê*).[15] The verse introduces vv. 19–26 in which Isaiah describes characteristics of the kingdom, v. 18.

---

[14]Eitan, pp. 72–73, relates *nûs* to an Arabic cognate "to swing." He translates, "No, for
we will swing upon horses." Aside from the question of what swinging on horses means,
the word *nûs* occurs widely in the OT with the regular meaning of "flee, escape." There
is no need to abandon that idea here. Leupold, I, 475, and Näglesbach, p. 332, understand the verse as a planned attack that turns into a rout. The view is possible but the
grammar suggests rather the view given above. The people do not "fly against" an unnamed foe. Rather, "upon horses they will flee."

[15]The word *ʾašʿrê* is plural each of the three times it occurs in the book, here, 32:20,
and 56:2. The plural intensifies the sense of the blessing received from God as the consequence of right behavior. The word is often translated or explained as "happy" (so Slotki,

19 For the people shall dwell in Zion at Jerusalem: thou shalt weep no more: he will be very gracious unto thee at the voice of thy cry; when he shall hear it, he will answer thee.
20 And though the Lord give you the bread of adversity, and the water of affliction, yet shall not thy teachers be removed into a corner any more, but thine eyes shall see thy teachers:
21 And thine ears shall hear a word behind thee, saying, This is the way, walk ye in it, when ye turn to the right hand, and when ye turn to the left.
22 Ye shall defile also the covering of thy graven images of silver, and the ornament of thy molten images of gold: thou shalt cast them away as a menstruous cloth; thou shalt say unto it, Get thee hence.

19–22 The first phrase reads better, "the people in Zion dwelling in Jerusalem." The people of Judah's main city will have their sorrow removed. Jerusalem here stands poetically for the nation. God will extend grace to the people when they cry out to Him in repentance. He will hear their plea and answer them, v. 19. Although the people will experience "the bread of adversity, and the water of affliction" during the Tribulation judgments, their "teachers" will be with them.[16] In both cases, the word "teachers" (*môreyka*) is plural but the only verb is singular. The question is whether the verse refers to a group of teachers in Judah or whether it refers to Messiah, accepted by His people to give them guidance. The priests held the responsibility of teaching the law to the people. From time to time, the prophets also taught the people. We know nothing of any other group of teachers. It is appropriate to understand *môreyka* as a plural of majesty referring to the Lord.[17] He will no longer "be removed into a corner" (*loʾ yikkanep*).[18] This interesting

---

p. 143; Von Orelli, p. 173; NEB), but this does not convey the true sense of the word. The word *ʾašᵉrê* has the sense "to experience blessings or praise." This normally comes in response to some action worthy of reward.

[16]Fausset, p. 658, and Grogan, p. 197, refer the passage to the deliverance from the exile in Babylon. Slotki, p. 144, and Skinner, *Isaiah I–XXXIX*, p. 231, see the deliverance from the Assyrian threat to Jerusalem. The context, however, calls for an eschatological application.

[17]Understandably, many commentators refer *môreyka* to the priests or prophets in their role as teachers. Among these are Motyer, *The Prophecy of Isaiah,* p. 250; Young, II, 356–57; and Grogan, p. 200. The versions differ, the LXX opting for "teachers" and the Vulgate keeping the singular. The Targum understands this as a messianic reference. In my judgment, the continued thought in v. 21 suggests divine guidance from a "teacher." The overall kingdom context likewise supports this view.

[18]While the noun *kanap,* "wing, extremity, corner," occurs over one hundred times, this is the only place that the MT uses the verb. The obvious meaning is something like "to be off to the side, put in a corner." From this we interpret the sense of being hidden.

23 Then shall he give the rain of thy seed, that thou shalt sow the
    ground withal; and bread of the increase of the earth, and it shall be
    fat and plenteous: in that day shall thy cattle feed in large pastures.
24 The oxen likewise and the young asses that ear the ground shall eat
    clean provender, which hath been winnowed with the shovel and with
    the fan.
25 And there shall be upon every high mountain, and upon every high
    hill, rivers and streams of waters in the day of the great slaughter,
    when the towers fall.
26 Moreover the light of the moon shall be as the light of the sun, and
    the light of the sun shall be sevenfold, as the light of seven days, in
    the day that the Lord bindeth up the breach of his people, and
    healeth the stroke of their wound.

phrase notes that the Teacher will no longer hide Himself. The people
will see Him, v. 20. He will direct their walk, showing them the way and
telling them when and in what direction to turn, v. 21. The people, in
turn, will put away their idols. They will "defile" their idols that have
been silver or gold plated, pronouncing them unclean. They will dispose
of them as they would an unclean "menstruous cloth" (dawâ, better "impure thing"), v. 22.[19]

23–26 The Lord will send "the rain of thy seed," the early rain of the
fall. In Palestine, the summer is generally a time of drought. In October
and mid-November, there is a time of heavy rain. These are the early
rains since they come before the planting season. During the winter
months of December, January, and February, there are frequent light
rains. In March and April, the rains increase in intensity. These are the
latter rains that fill out the fruit of the harvest. The Lord gives rain now
as a sign of His blessing. This causes the seed to spring up and gives the
land an abundant harvest and lush pastures for the animals, v. 23. Those
animals that "ear" (or "till") the land will receive a choice mixture of
"clean provender" (beliil hamîṣ). This is "soured fodder," fermented fodder, that has been winnowed from the harvest.[20] The grain in Palestine

---

[19]While dawâ may refer to the menstrual period, the verb simply means "to be sick."
The adjectival form here has the more general meaning "sick," i.e., an impure thing to be
cast away. The word "cloth" does not occur in the text.

[20]Among others, Von Orelli, p. 173; Price, p. 131; and Hailey, p. 258, explain beliil
hamîṣ as "salted fodder." BDB, p. 330, likewise gives this sense. The word hamîṣ occurs
only here. The related word hameṣ, however, refers to something leavened or fermented,
e.g., Exod. 12:15; Lev. 2:11. The sense of "sour" occurs also in the related word homeṣ,
Prov. 10:26; 25:20, "vinegar."

27 *Behold, the name of the Lord cometh from far, burning with his anger, and the burden thereof is heavy: his lips are full of indignation, and his tongue as a devouring fire:*

28 *And his breath, as an overflowing stream, shall reach to the midst of the neck, to sift the nations with the sieve of vanity: and there shall be a bridle in the jaws of the people, causing them to err.*

was heaped on a threshing floor. The farmer threshed the lighter grains such as vetch or cummin by beating them with a flail; cf. 28:27. He threshed the heavier wheat by driving an ox cart around the floor. Sometimes the oxen dragged a heavy board studded with rock or metal. The farmer then used a long-handled winnowing "shovel" or "fan" (better "fork") to separate the grain from the husks and stalks. While the heavier grain fell, the wind would blow the chaff to the side of the floor. Repeated over and over, this gave a relatively pure grain, v. 24. There will be an abundant supply of water. All of this will come at the "day of the great slaughter." This is the great battle at the end of the Tribulation, when the fortified towers of God's enemies fall before His power, v. 25. Isaiah now gives a brief glimpse into the Millennium. The glory of nature will be enhanced. The brightness of the moon and sun will increase. The moon will shine brightly as the sun. The sun's light will increase sevenfold. The description is poetic. The Lord will remove the hindrances to nature's fulness that cause it to "groan and travail," Romans 8:22. At that time, the Lord cares for His own. He binds "the breach of his people" and heals "the stroke of their wound." Both expressions refer to the effects that remain upon the land from the Tribulation battles, v. 26.

b. Victory of God 30:27–33

27–28 The phrase "the name of the Lord" always indicates the full revelation of God to men. He comes with burning wrath and "the burden thereof is heavy" (or "a dense cloud" as in the smoke that billows from a fire). The description poetically describes the judgment of His enemies. His lips are filled with indignation as He pronounces judgment upon those who have opposed Him. Isaiah pictures this judgment with different images. The Lord will come (1) as a fire billowing smoke. He speaks words of indignation as He charges His enemies with sin. His words are as a burning fire that consumes all before it, v. 27. The Lord also comes (2) as an "overflowing stream [*nahal*, see 7:19]," a torrent of water causing flooding to "reach to" (*hasâ*) the neck of a man. This is an interest-

29 Ye shall have a song, as in the night when a holy solemnity is kept; and gladness of heart, as when one goeth with a pipe to come into the mountain of the Lord, to the mighty One of Israel.

ing word picture. The verb *haṣâ* means "to divide." The description here is of a divided man with his head above water and the rest of his body below water. We see again man's helplessness before the Lord's judgment. The Lord is (3) as a "sieve of vanity [*šawʾ,* or 'worthlessness,' see 1:13]." This is a sieve (*napat*) to "sift" (*nûp*) out that which has no value.[21] Finally, He is (4) as a "bridle" to lead His enemies away from the path they have chosen. They seek to be free; He leads them to destruction, v. 28.

29 Israel will rejoice in that time as they rejoiced at the "holy solemnity," the Passover Feast. This was the only Jewish festival celebrated at night (Exod. 12:6–8; Deut. 16:4; Matt. 26:19–20).[22] At the Passover, the lamb was killed lit. "between the two evenings" (Exod. 12:6). Their joy will be like the joy of one who goes to Mt. Zion to worship "the mighty One of Israel" (lit. "the Rock of Israel"). Isaiah uses the image of a mighty rock several times to picture the stable foundation that we have in God, cf. 8:14; 17:10; 26:4; and, negatively, 44:8, v. 29.

The Rock of Israel

a. Eternity of the Rock 26:4

b. Uniqueness of the Rock 44:8

c. Rejoicing in the Rock 30:29

d. Forgetting the Rock 17:10

e. Judgment from the Rock 8:14

---

[21]The word *napat* is a *hapax legomenon.* The verb *nûp,* "to lift, wave, shake," however, occurs several times. Joining the verb with a derived noun is typical of Isaiah's style of writing. The *napat* is something shaken, a "sieve."

[22]Whitehouse, I, 322, suggests that this refers to the Feast of Tabernacles, also a feast marked with joy. He cites several passages in the OT, none of which mention the evening. The Jews celebrated only the Passover Feast at night.

30 *And the Lord shall cause his glorious voice to be heard, and shall shew the lighting down of his arm, with the indignation of his anger, and with the flame of a devouring fire, with scattering, and tempest, and hailstones.*

31 *For through the voice of the Lord shall the Assyrian be beaten down, which smote with a rod.*

32 *And in every place where the grounded staff shall pass, which the Lord shall lay upon him, it shall be with tabrets and harps: and in battles of shaking will he fight with it.*

33 *For Tophet is ordained of old; yea, for the king it is prepared; he hath made it deep and large: the pile thereof is fire and much wood; the breath of the Lord, like a stream of brimstone, doth kindle it.*

30–33 Isaiah describes a fierce storm to illustrate God's power in the judgment. The Lord's "glorious voice," the thunder of the storm, will resound throughout the land. The "lighting down [*naḥat*, or 'descent'] of his arm," the symbol of strength, strikes His enemies.[23] He strikes with "the indignation of his anger" (or "raging anger"). He sends a fire to consume His enemies. There is "scattering" (*nepeṣ*, or "breaking up" as when the cloud pours out rain). There is a "tempest," a downpour, and "hailstones," cf. Exod. 9:18–23; Josh. 10:11, v. 30.[24] Moving away from the general statement of judgment, Isaiah proceeds to a specific description of Assyria's judgment. The Lord will strike Assyria with His voice, here the word of His power. The Assyrian will "be beaten down" (*ḥatat*, better "be dismayed," see 7:8). The phrase "which smote with a rod" is better "when He strikes with the rod," v. 31.[25] Israel rejoices at the blows of judgment from the "grounded staff" (or "appointed staff," the rod appointed by God to strike the blows of judgment). The people play

---

[23]The noun *naḥat*, "lighting down," is a *hapax legomenon*. The verb *naḥet*, however, and a related adjective *naḥet* occur several times. There is no doubt of the meaning "descent."

[24]Vine, p. 67, understands vv. 30–32 as a description of Armageddon, the end-time battle between the Lord and Antichrist. Pentecost, pp. 326, 352–53, 355, also refers this to Antichrist and the northern confederacy. To do this, however, we must take "the Assyrian" as a poetic reference to Antichrist. Since Isaiah regularly alternates between contemporary comment, foretelling the near future, and eschatological prophecy, it is not clear that this is an end-time prophecy.

[25]Motyer, *The Prophecy of Isaiah,* p. 253, translates idiomatically, "who, as [the Lord's] rod, was smiting." This applies the verse to Assyria as the rod of God's punishment for Israel. This leads to the translation of a simple phrase, *baššebeṭ yakkeh,* as "with his scepter he will strike them down." While the translation is possible, nothing here suggests that the rod is the Lord's "sceptre." The rod here merely represents the unspecified means of judgment, not the "sceptre" of the Lord as in the NIV.

"tabrets" (better "tambourines," small hand drums used to beat out a rhythm). They use "harps" (or "lyres") made by cutting strings from the small intestine of a sheep and stretching them across a sounding board. Playing consisted of plucking the strings with the fingers or drawing a plectrum across the strings. The scene suggests a time for celebrating the Lord's victory over Assyria.[26] The Lord fights with "battles of shaking" (*milḥᵃmôt tᵉnapâ*), i.e., brandishing His weapons as He comes against Assyria, v. 32.[27]

The Lord has prepared "Tophet" (*topteh*) for Assyria's punishment. The word *topteh*, "place of burning," refers to the southeastern part of the valley of the Son of Hinnom, Jeremiah 7:31. It was a heathen worship center, Jeremiah 32:35. Josiah "defiled Topheth," II Kings 23:10, to keep the Jews from worshiping the false gods there. After the return from Babylon, the Jews made the valley of Hinnom the city's garbage dump. Fire perpetually burned the refuse, making the place a picture of hell. The Lord has prepared it for the "king." The description of the event in 37:36–38 (II Kings 19:35–37) makes it clear that Sennacherib did not die in the defeat. He here stands as a representative of his army.[28] Although the OT does not discuss this, Judah apparently burned the Assyrian corpses to cleanse the land. The "breath of the Lord," representing His Word by metonymy, is like a "stream [*naḥal*, see 7:19] of brimstone." It will kindle the fires of judgment, v. 33.

---

[26]Näglesbach, p. 338, and Delitzsch, II, 42, understand the music as Israel's accompaniment of the Lord's destruction of Assyria. Delitzsch says, "every stroke of the punishing rod falls . . . with an accompaniment of drums and guitars." Driver, *JSS* 13:51, similarly states, "the strokes laid on the victim keep time with the beats of musical instruments." The view goes counter to the biblical description. The Lord struck Assyria at night while Israel slept. Only in the morning did Israel learn that the Lord had devastated Assyria; cf. 37:36.

[27]Irwin, p. 103, translates *milḥᵃmôt* as "war dances." The translation is speculative and not to be taken seriously. The word *milḥᵃmôt* occurs widely with the meaning "battle" and by extension, "weapons" or "battlefield."

[28]Barnes, I, 464, makes the "king" Hezekiah. He prepares a place for the burning of the corpses. The view is possible. Watts, *Isaiah 1–33*, pp. 405–6, and Delitzsch, II, 43, wrongly refer to the death and cremation of the Assyrian king.

Practical Applications from Chapter 30

1. The Futility of Relying on Man, vv. 1–17

    a. A blunt condemnation, vv. 1–5. The Lord rebukes Judah for relying on Egypt while turning away from Him, v. 1. They have entered into an agreement with Egypt without asking the Lord to guide them, v. 2. Egypt's failure will bring shame and disgrace to them, v. 3. Although Judah's representatives have traveled to Egypt, v. 4, they will be shamed over Egypt's inability to help them, v. 5.

    b. A certain failure, vv. 6–17.

        (1) Statement of the failure, vv. 6–8. Isaiah declares an oracle involving the animals in the Negeb. In this region occupied by wild animals and serpents, the representatives of Judah will load their beasts of burden as they bring gifts to "a people that shall not profit them," v. 6. The Egyptians will not help Judah, v. 7. Isaiah should record these things as a reminder to Judah that she has failed to trust the Lord, v. 8.

        (2) Cause of the failure, vv. 9–14. The people rebel against God. They lie concerning His ability to help them. They do not trust His Word, v. 9. They refuse the message of the prophets but they delight in deceitful words, v. 10. They want the true prophets of God to turn from their righteous ways, v. 11. For this reason, v. 12, judgment will suddenly come on them, v. 13. The Lord will break the nation completely, v. 14.

        (3) Result of the failure, vv. 15–17. The Lord offered deliverance. Judah, however, rejected the offer, v. 15. They thought to flee to safety; the Lord will cause them to flee. They thought to ride swift animals to safety; their enemy will pursue them on swift animals, v. 16. Their fear will be such that a single soldier will cause a thousand of them to flee. A handful of enemy soldiers will cause the nation to flee. Only a few will survive, v. 17.

        While the passage deals directly with the Egyptians' failure to help Judah and Judah's subsequent flight from the Assyrians, it does give us principles that apply broadly. No believer should make human resources his source of strength. Our trust should be in the Lord.

2. The Coming Kingdom, vv. 18–26. The Lord promises that He will have mercy upon His people. He is a just God and those who wait for Him will be blessed, v. 18.

   a. The blessing of the people, vv. 19–22. The Lord will hear when the people cry out to Him in repentance, v. 19. Even though the people will undergo cataclysmic judgments during the Tribulation, there will be a time when Messiah will come to teach them, v. 20. He will direct them in the way they should go, v. 21. This will cause them to get rid of their idols, v. 22.

   b. The blessing of the Land, vv. 23–26. The Lord will send rain to bring forth an abundant harvest, v. 23. The farmer will feed his animals with choice fodder, v. 24. There will be an abundant supply of water. This will be so even in the "day of the great slaughter," the Battle of Armageddon, which ends the Tribulation. The glory of nature will be enhanced. The Lord will care for His own as He heals the land after its sufferings in the Tribulation, v. 25.

3. The Victory of God, vv. 27–33. The final paragraph of the chapter is historical. It looks back to the defeat of the Assyrians by God.

   a. The revelation of the Lord, vv. 27–28. The Lord appears to execute His wrath on the enemies of His people. He will be as a burning fire toward His enemies, v. 27. He will be as a torrent of water, as a sieve to sift out that which has no value, and as a bridle to lead His enemies away from their chosen path, v. 28.

   b. The rejoicing of the people, v. 29. At that time, the people will rejoice as they earlier rejoiced at the time of the Passover and at times of worshiping the Rock of Israel, v. 29.

   c. The rejection of the enemy, vv. 30–33. The Lord illustrates His judgments with several natural calamities, v. 30. He will beat down the Assyrian enemy, v. 31. The people will celebrate the fall of the Assyrians, v. 32. The enemies will be burned in the fires of Tophet, v. 33.

1 *Woe to them that go down to Egypt for help; and stay on horses, and trust in chariots, because they are many; and in horsemen, because they are very strong; but they look not unto the Holy One of Israel, neither seek the Lord!*

2 *Yet he also is wise, and will bring evil, and will not call back his words: but will arise against the house of the evildoers, and against the help of them that work iniquity.*

3 *Now the Egyptians are men, and not God; and their horses flesh, and not spirit. When the Lord shall stretch out his hand, both he that helpeth shall fall, and he that is holpen shall fall down, and they all shall fail together.*

ISAIAH 31

Isaiah now concludes the rebuke begun in c. 30. Judah had trusted in Egypt but had failed to trust in the Lord. The horses, chariots, and horsemen of Egypt impressed them, v. 1. The Lord will therefore judge both Judah and Egypt, v. 2. They will not stand against Him, v. 3. The Lord will fight against His people, v. 4. Then, having judged them, He will show mercy and deliver them from their enemy, v. 5. Isaiah appeals to the people to turn back to their God, v. 6. In the day when He delivers them, they will despise the idols they had formerly worshiped, v. 7. The Lord will destroy the Assyrian oppressor, v. 8. They will flee from the Lord who sends forth His wrath from Jerusalem, v. 9.

c. Defense of God 31:1–9

1–3 Isaiah again condemns Judah for trusting in Egypt; cf. 19:11–15; 30:1–7. They "stay" (or "rely") on horses and chariots and horsemen. Egypt was Judah's source for horses, I Kings 10:28; II Chronicles 1:16; 9:28; chariots and horsemen, II Kings 18:24 (Isa. 36:9). They look to these for strength. At the same time, they reject the Lord as a source of strength, v. 1. Though the nation rejects Him, the Lord is still the wise one. The words imply that the people should have consulted Him. Since they have not turned to Him, He will bring "evil" (*ra*ᶜ, better "calamity, disaster," see 3:9) as He judges the people. He will not "call back" (better "retract") His words of judgment; cf. Numbers 23:19. He will come against Judah, "the house of the evildoers [*ra*ᶜ*a*ᶜ, see 1:4]," who has rejected Him in favor of Egypt. He will likewise move against Egypt, "the help of them that work iniquity," v. 2. Judah has rejected His divine aid in favor of a human resource. The Egyptians are only men and have no

4 *For thus hath the Lord spoken unto me, Like as the lion and the young lion roaring on his prey, when a multitude of shepherds is called forth against him, he will not be afraid of their voice, nor abase himself for the noise of them: so shall the Lord of hosts come down to fight for mount Zion, and for the hill thereof.*
5 *As birds flying, so will the Lord of hosts defend Jerusalem; defending also he will deliver it; and passing over he will preserve it.*

power to withstand God. Their horses are only "flesh" and not "spirit." The phrase directly parallels 3*a*, "the Egyptians are men, and not God." The parallelism suggests that "spirit" here refers to the Holy Spirit.[1] The Egyptians have only weak resources to oppose divine power. When the Lord stretches out His hand in judgment, both Egypt, "he that helpeth," and Judah, "he that is holpen," will fall, v. 3.

4–5 Like a lion or young lion "roaring" (or "growling") at a threat by shepherds who try to take his prey, the Lord will not let others take Jerusalem from Him.[2] He will not "be afraid" (*ḥatat*, or "be dismayed," see 7:8) at "their voice," the voice of the Egyptians. He will not "abase himself" (*ᶜanâ*, or "be humbled")[3] at their "noise" (better "multitude"). The "Lord of hosts," cf. 1:9, will "fight for" (*liṣboᵓ ᶜal*, better "fight

---

[1]Barnes, I, 465, understands flesh as physical strength while spirit represents wisdom and intelligence. Von Orelli, p. 178, views the flesh as a contrast with God, who is spirit. Skinner, *Isaiah I–XXXIX*, p. 237, identifies spirit as the "indestructible element in the universe, by which all life is sustained." He sees this as "the moral purpose of Jehovah." The spiritual is supreme over the material. Motyer, *The Prophecy of Isaiah,* p. 255, contrasts flesh and spirit as that which "needs life and possesses none, and the life-principle itself." Herbert, *Isaiah 1–39*, p. 180, contrasts the weakness of flesh with the unlimited energy of God. Kelley, p. 281, sees the difference as "the brute strength of men and horses" and the "spiritual power . . . that belongs exclusively to God." Leupold, I, 488, sees the distinction as between that which is frail and that which has power. Slotki, p. 148, contrasts that which is "mortal and frail" with "what is enduring." These views are possible. I rely on the parallel with the first phrase to relate "spirit" to the Holy Spirit.

[2]The lion, young lion, and shepherd are not symbols of countries. Mauchline, p. 214; Von Orelli, p. 178; and Kelley, p. 281, make the lions represent Assyria and the shepherds Egypt. On the other hand, Stacey, p. 194, understands Yahweh as the lion, Jerusalem as the prey, and the shepherds as the Assyrians. Motyer, *The Prophecy of Isaiah,* p. 255, views the lion as the Lord and the shepherds as Egypt. Smith, p. 243, sees the lion as the Lord and the shepherds as the political leaders of Judah. These animals are not symbols but rather an illustration of the truth that the Lord fights for His prey.

[3]The word *ᶜanâ* most often indicates "affliction." It also, however, has a strong component of "humbling" in its meaning, e.g., Prov. 3:34; 16:19 (both "lowly"). This is the idea seen here.

6 Turn ye unto him from whom the children of Israel have deeply revolted.

7 For in that day every man shall cast away his idols of silver, and his idols of gold, which your own hands have made unto you for a sin.

8 Then shall the Assyrian fall with the sword, not of a mighty man; and the sword, not of a mean man, shall devour him: but he shall flee from the sword, and his young men shall be discomfited.

9 And he shall pass over to his strong hold for fear, and his princes shall be afraid of the ensign, saith the Lord, whose fire is in Zion, and his furnace in Jerusalem.

against")[4] His temple, "mount Zion," and His city, "the hill thereof." In their time of trouble, Judah has failed to turn to Him. He will therefore show them that Egypt is weak, not able to save them from the Assyrian threat, v. 4.[5]

Having given Judah a vivid illustration of Egypt's weakness, the Lord now works on their behalf. Like birds fluttering over their nests to guard their young, so the Lord will protect His people. He will defend and deliver them. "Passing over" (*pasoaḥ*) them, He will rescue them from their enemies. The use of *pasah* reminds the people of His earlier deliverance from Egypt. At that time, He "passed over" (*pasah*) those houses that had the sacrificial blood applied to their doorposts (Exod. 12:13, 23, 27). Israel had trusted Him then and He had delivered them. When they trust Him now, he will likewise deliver them, v. 5.

6–9 In light of the coming judgment on their enemies, the Lord appeals to the people to "turn" (*šûb*, see 1:27) to the one against whom they had formerly revolted, v. 6. In "that day," the day in which the Lord delivers His people, men will turn from the idols that they had made. They will see that their worship of silver and gold idols is sin. This will

---

[4]The phrase *liṣboʾ ʿal* is at the heart of the interpretation here. The preposition *ʿal* may be translated "upon" (so Brueggemann, *Isaiah 1–39*, Rawlinson, Slotki), "for" (so Cowles, Birks), or "against" (so Näglesbach, Kraeling, Childs). If we translate "for" or "upon," v. 5 continues the thought of the Lord's protection for His own. If we translate "against," v. 4 continues the thought of v. 3, the Lord's judgment of Judah and Egypt. The grammar favors "against." Everywhere else that the verb *ṣabaʾ* followed by *ʿal* occurs (Num. 31:7; Isa. 29:7, 8; Zech. 14:12), the idea is of fighting against an enemy. The Lord, then, will not allow Egypt to deliver Judah. He will rather bring judgment upon Judah because it failed to trust Him for deliverance.

[5]Pentecost, p. 497, applies 31:4–9 to the Millennium. While the text shows the power of the Lord over His enemies, one of the enemies here is Judah, His own people. It is better to delay the kingdom application to c. 32, in which the text clearly looks to the reign of Christ over the world.

cause them to "cast away" (better "despise") the "idols" (*ᵉlîlîm*, see
2:8), v. 7. The Assyrians will fall from the "sword" of God's judgment.
This will not be the sword of a "mighty man" (*îš*, see 2:9); nor will it be
the sword of a "mean man" (*ʾadam*, see 2:9). The implied thought is that
it is the Lord's sword that causes Assyria to flee; cf. II Kings 19:35. His
youth will become "discomfited" (better "forced laborers"). This did not
happen at the defeat of Sennacherib. The statement looks into the future,
when Assyria falls to Babylon and their men become slaves, v. 8. The
phrase "he shall pass over to his strong hold" is lit. "his rock will pass
away." The Assyrian king, the "rock" supporting the nation, will prove to
be weak in the Lord's presence.[6] Second Kings 19:36 tells of the Assyrian retreat after the slaughter of their army by the Lord. They flee in
"fear" (*magôr*), a word that indicates extreme fear, terror, or panic. The
"princes" of the army are "afraid" (*ḥatat*, or "dismayed," see 7:8) to remain near the "ensign," the standard of the Assyrian army. All of this
rests upon the work of the Lord, whose fiery presence and furnace of
judgment are in Jerusalem, v. 9.[7]

---

[6]There are many views on the symbolism of the rock. Young, II, 382, considers it the
Assyrian fortress, the place he finds protection. Fausset, p. 661, and Kraeling, p. 132,
refer it to the Assyrian army. Skinner, *Isaiah I–XXXIX*, p. 239, and Barnes, I, 467, make
it his refuge, the place he hides in fear of his enemy. Without being specific, Alexander,
I, 492, sees it as the Assyrian strength. Driver, *JSS* 13:52; Leslie, p. 81; and Mauchline,
p. 214, view it as the officers of the Assyrian army. Watts, *Isaiah 1–33*, p. 408; Herbert,
Isaiah 1–39, p. 162; and Irwin, p. 116, consider it the god in which Assyria trusts. This
is doubtful since the Assyrians worshiped many gods. The other views are possible. I
have opted to equate the rock with the Assyrian king as being most nearly parallel to the
"princes," who flee from the standard of their army.

[7]Vine, p. 67, makes the destruction of Assyria foreshadow the end-time destruction of
Antichrist. While it is true that the Lord's victory over Assyria shows His power to vanquish His enemies, it is doubtful that this passage hints at the destruction of Antichrist.

Practical Application from Chapter 31

The Sure Defense of the Lord

1. The Weakness of Man's Resources, vv. 1–4. Isaiah condemns those who trust in Egypt to deliver them from the Assyrian threat. They fail to trust the Lord, v. 1. The Lord will judge both Judah and Egypt, v. 2. The Egyptians have only weak resources to withstand the power of God, v. 3. The Lord will not be turned aside from His purpose to chasten His people, v. 4.

2. The Power of God's Resources, vv. 5–9. Having chastened His people, the Lord now promises to deliver them, v. 5. He urges the people to turn to Him, v. 6. When the Lord delivers His people, they will despise the idols that they had made. They will see them as sinful, v. 7. The Assyrian will fall but not because men have defeated him. The Lord Himself will destroy him, v. 8. The Assyrians will flee to their homes in panic as the Lord directs the fires of His judgment toward them, v. 9.

3. The Application of the Passage. The narrative serves to illustrate a basic principle. God's people should not place their trust in human resources at the expense of forgetting Him. God will judge those who trust in the lesser things of this life. We need rather to turn to Him in every area of life.

1 *Behold, a king shall reign in righteousness, and princes shall rule in judgment.*
2 *And a man shall be as an hiding place from the wind, and a covert from the tempest; as rivers of water in a dry place, as the shadow of a great rock in a weary land.*
3 *And the eyes of them that see shall not be dim, and the ears of them that hear shall hearken.*
4 *The heart also of the rash shall understand knowledge, and the tongue of the stammerers shall be ready to speak plainly.*

ISAIAH 32

In contrast with the weakness of heathen nations and idols discussed in c. 30–31, the Lord will rule righteously over the earth. Isaiah devotes the next two chapters to describing this millennial reign. This rule will provide shelter and refreshment to the world, vv. 1–2. Mankind will possess spiritual understanding, vv. 3–4. Both wicked and noble men will be known for what they are, vv. 5–8. Careless women will undergo judgment, vv. 9–12. The land will come under judgment, vv. 13–14. The Lord will once more bring blessing to the land, v. 15. The people will dwell in righteousness and peace, vv. 16–18. The Lord will put down His enemies, v. 19, and bless the land again, v. 20.

D. Promise of Messiah's Rule 32:1–20
1. Reign of the Messiah 32:1–8

1–4 Isaiah looks at the future reign of Christ during the Millennium.[1] The "king," Messiah, will reign in "righteousness" (*ṣedeq*, see 1:21) together with His "princes," who rule in "judgment" (*mišpaṭ*, or "justice," see 1:17).[2] From elsewhere, we conclude that these princes are the

---

[1]Kissane, I, 362, understands the particle *hen* as conditional, "if." Verses 1–4 then become a protasis, "if a king should reign in righteousness. . . ." The apodosis follows in v. 5. Men would become known for what they are. The normal use of *hen* as a conditional particle argues against the view. When *hen* is conditional, the *waw* apodosis always follows it (G.K. 159 *w*). Verse 5 lacks this.

[2]A *lamed* preposition introduces both *ṣedeq* and *mišpaṭ*. In this context, the *lamed* indicates "according to." The king and the princes render judgments according to the standards of God's Word. J. W. Olley, "Notes on Isaiah XXXII 1, XLV 19, 23 and LXIII 1," *VT* 33:446–49, concludes that the *lamed* indicates purpose. The king and the princes rule in order "to bring about righteousness, and . . . judgement." The view rests upon other occurrences of *lamed* with *ṣedeq* and *mišpaṭ*. The view is possible although the occurrences of *lamed* elsewhere have a variety of uses.

saints.[3] Such passages as Daniel 7:22, 27; I Corinthians 6:2; Revelation 1:6; 5:10; and 22:5 make it clear that the Lord will involve the saints in governing the millennial kingdom, v. 1. In that time, "a man" (*'îš*) will be a refuge from the storms that often buffet men in life. While *'îš* normally refers to "man," it may also be translated "each," e.g., Genesis 10:5; 40:5; Exodus 12:3; Jeremiah 12:15. Here, *'îš* refers back to v. 1, both Messiah and His saints giving protection to the world.[4] As Isaiah often does, he multiplies the metaphors to illustrate the idea of protection. These righteous rulers, the King and His saints, provide a shelter from the wind, a haven in the storm, refreshing water in the desert, and shade in a "weary land," i.e., a land that is parched, v. 2.

Mankind will no longer see dimly or hear with difficulty, v. 3. Verse 4 gives this word picture a spiritual sense. The "heart," here referring to the mind, of the "rash," those that once spoke hastily, will now "understand" (*bîn*, see 1:3) spiritual truth. The "stammerers," those who at one time had difficulty expressing spiritual truth, now will speak clearly. This expresses the spiritual understanding given by the Lord to His people, contra. 6:10; 29:10, v. 4.

---

[3]Leslie, p. 103, and Kraeling, p. 132, reject any messianic application. Alexander, II, 1, and Kelley, p. 282, make the passage general, describing the ideal righteous rule of any king. Barnes, I, 469, and Ibn Ezra, p. 148, relate the verse to Hezekiah. The "princes" are various officers of his kingdom. Watts, *Isaiah 1–33*, pp. 410–11, translates the opening word *hen* as "suppose." He then makes the passage a dialogue between a teacher and his students. The teacher poses a situation and the students recite the results. Leupold, I, 497, denies that this is Messiah. He understands the verse to describe a time "contemporary with the prophet" and makes this symbolic of messianic rule. While this view winds up at the right place, it is unnecessarily complicated. To all of these views, the context naturally suggests a directly messianic application. The king rules in righteousness. The saints rule with Him to provide justice throughout the world. The world receives protection from buffetings. All have spiritual understanding. The true character of man becomes public. In addition, vv. 15–20 return to the messianic emphasis.

[4]Näglesbach, p. 345, refers to various kings who before oppressed God's people. Now, they protect them. Mauchline, p. 215, views this as the members of the community, each helping one another. Alexander, II, 2, identifies *'îš* as the Messiah alone. Barnes, I, 469, identifies the king as Hezekiah. In general, the interpretation of *'îš* follows the view held of v. 1.

5 *The vile person shall be no more called liberal, nor the churl said to be bountiful.*
6 *For the vile person will speak villany, and his heart will work iniquity, to practise hypocrisy, and to utter error against the Lord, to make empty the soul of the hungry, and he will cause the drink of the thirsty to fail.*
7 *The instruments also of the churl are evil: he deviseth wicked devices to destroy the poor with lying words, even when the needy speaketh right.*
8 *But the liberal deviseth liberal things; and by liberal things shall he stand.*
9 *Rise up, ye women that are at ease; hear my voice, ye careless daughters; give ear unto my speech.*
10 *Many days and years shall ye be troubled, ye careless women: for the vintage shall fail, the gathering shall not come.*
11 *Tremble, ye women that are at ease; be troubled, ye careless ones: strip you, and make you bare, and gird sackcloth upon your loins.*
12 *They shall lament for the teats, for the pleasant fields, for the fruitful vine.*

5–8 Men will know the true character of others. The "vile person" (lit. "fool") will not be called "liberal" (lit. "noble"). The "churl" (lit. "scoundrel") will not be called "bountiful" (or "generous"), v. 5. The wicked man will be seen for what he is. The "vile person," again "fool," will speak of "villany" (lit. "folly"). His mind will devise "iniquity," thinking of wicked actions. He will practice "hypocrisy" (better "godlessness"). He will speak heretically against the Lord. It is no wonder that he fails to meet the needs of others. He makes them hunger and thirst as he seeks gain for himself, v. 6. The "churl" (again "scoundrel") uses "evil" (*ra͑*, see 3:9) against others. He plans his attack to destroy the "poor" (*͑anî*, see 3:14) with "lying [*šeqer*, see 9:15] words" even when the "needy" (*͗ebyôn*, see 14:30) person has spoken "right" (*mišpaṭ*, or "justly," see 1:17), v. 7. In sharp contrast, the "liberal" (again "noble") lives in accord with his noble character: he makes noble plans and stands on noble principles, v. 8.

2. Warning of the Judgment 32:9–14

9–12 Isaiah warns the women to turn from being "at ease," complacent toward spiritual matters. They should stop their "careless" (*baṭaḥ*) ways. The verb *baṭaḥ* normally refers to those who "trust" in something. Here, the trust of the women has led to a careless attitude toward spiritual matters. Judgment is about to come upon the land. The women should therefore listen to Isaiah's words, v. 9. The phrase "many days and years" is lit. "days upon a year," i.e., in a little more than a year.[5] The "careless" (again "trusting") women should forsake their indifference to spiritual matters since the judgment is about to fall. The "vintage," the grape harvest, will fail. The "gathering" of the crops will not take place, v. 10. Those women who are at ease now with no cares to disturb them should "tremble" with fear. The "careless ['trusting'] ones," secure in their complacency, should be "troubled." They should strip themselves and put on "sackcloth."[6] While the word "sackcloth" does not occur here, it is certain that this is Isaiah's meaning. The wearing of sackcloth as an outward sign of inward grief is common in the OT, e.g., 3:24; 15:3; Genesis 37:34, v. 11.

Verse 12 is difficult only because of the idiom used. Literally, the verse reads something like this: "Upon the breasts are lamentings [sopᵉdîm][7] concerning the pleasant fields, concerning the fruitful vine." The first phrase refers to beatings upon the breasts, a picturesque way of showing grief.[8] Isaiah now gives the cause of the sorrow. The people lament the loss of their fields and vines, v. 12.

---

[5]The expression "many days and years" is an idiom. Rawlinson, I, 523, understands it as something less than two years. Slotki, p. 152, takes it as "at the time of the next year's harvest." Watts, *Isaiah 1–33*, p. 415, thinks that it means a few days less than a year. Irwin, p. 128, interprets the phrase as "next year." Delitzsch, II, 51, explains it as "an undefined number of days, at the most a year from the present time." The preposition ʿal normally means "above, over." This suggests that the time will be days over a year, i.e., a bit more than a year.

[6]Kaiser, *Isaiah 13–39*, p. 330, understands the stripping as the baring of the breast by the women. There are archaeological signs to indicate that this was a heathen custom of sorrowing women. There is no hint of this in the OT. Israelites showed their grief by wearing sackcloth, by beating upon their breasts, or by weeping. They tore their clothes, wore black, sat in ashes, or sprinkled ashes on their head. They removed jewelry, shaved their head, or cut their hair. They fasted, plucked out the hair on the head or in the beard, or refrained from sacrificial food. They were silent, bowed the head, or lifted up their hands to God in prayer. Nakedness or partial nakedness, however, is associated more with shame than grief.

[7]The form sopᵉdîm is masculine and thus creates a problem of interpretation since men do not have prominent breasts. Nothing, however, prevents men from showing their grief in the same way as women. The Isaiah Scroll changes the form to a feminine imperative, "beat upon your breasts." The MT, however, is the more difficult reading because of the gender. In addition, while women have been in view before the verse, the following verses enlarge the thought to include all "people." The only other passage to mention beating upon the breast as a way of showing grief is Nah. 2:7. We simply do not know enough to limit this to women.

[8]Barnes, I, 473, understands the "teats," the breasts, to represent "that which nourishes or sustains life." He makes this synonymous with the "fruitful fields." Young, II, 395–96,

13 Upon the land of my people shall come up thorns and briers; yea, upon all the houses of joy in the joyous city:
14 Because the palaces shall be forsaken; the multitude of the city shall be left; the forts and towers shall be for dens for ever, a joy of wild asses, a pasture of flocks;
15 Until the spirit be poured upon us from on high, and the wilderness be a fruitful field, and the fruitful field be counted for a forest.
16 Then judgment shall dwell in the wilderness, and righteousness remain in the fruitful field.
17 And the work of righteousness shall be peace; and the effect of righteousness quietness and assurance for ever.
18 And my people shall dwell in a peaceable habitation, and in sure dwellings, and in quiet resting places;

13–14 The judgment will let "thorns and briers" grow over the land. They will cover even the "houses of joy," the places in which great rejoicing occurred. These were in "the joyous city," most likely Jerusalem, v. 13. Jerusalem will be desolate. They will abandon the "palaces" (singular, thus "palace"). This is the seat of government. The "multitude of the city," i.e., the populated city, will be forsaken. The "forts," lit. "Ophel," refer to the southeastern hill of the city. The "towers" (*baḥan,* or "watchtower")[9] refer to a spur off Mt. Moriah from which the shepherds watched their flocks. These will become "dens" (*mᵉᶜarôt*),[10] the homes of wild animals, and grazing areas for wild asses and sheep, v. 14.

3. Promise of the Spirit 32:15–20

15–18 Isaiah suddenly changes his thought. The Holy Spirit will bring blessing to the land.[11] This refers to the millennial kingdom, when

---

likewise adopts this position. While the view is possible, the "breasts" nowhere else represent fruitful fields.

[9]The noun *baḥan* occurs only here with this sense. The verb *baḥan,* "to examine," however, occurs frequently. The noun is a place for examination, i.e., a watchtower.

[10]The word *mᵉᶜarôt* normally indicates caves. It apparently refers here to the home of wild animals, i.e., their dens.

[11]Herbert, *Isaiah 1–39,* p. 185, calls the word "Spirit" misleading. He says, "What is meant is that divine power that is able to transform, recreate and bring new life." The traditional view is that the Spirit here is the Holy Spirit. The OT elsewhere credits the Spirit with working in the original Creation, Gen. 1:2; Job 26:13; 33:4. It is not surprising that He works as well in the re-creation of the earth.

19 When it shall hail, coming down on the forest; and the city shall be low in a low place.

20 Blessed are ye that sow beside all waters, that send forth thither the feet of the ox and the ass.

God pours out His blessing upon the people in Palestine once more.[12] The wilderness region will become fruitful while the fruitful fields will become forests. As in 29:17, the statement is proverbial, pointing to the changes in the kingdom. Crops will become abundant. The unproductive areas will bring forth fruit. The areas that are now productive will bring forth forests, v. 15. At that time, "judgment" (mišpaṭ, better "justice," see 1:17) and "righteousness" will prevail throughout the land (cf. v. 1), v. 16. Righteousness will work to produce "peace" (šalôm, see 9:6). Isaiah expresses this here by paralleling it with "quietness [šaqaṭ, see 7:4] and "assurance [beṭaḥ, see 14:30] for ever," v. 17. The people will dwell securely, in a "peaceable" (šalôm) place. There will be no trouble from external threats. Their homes will be "sure" (or "secure") and "quiet" (or "undisturbed"). The picture is of a nation at peace with itself and with other nations, v. 18.

19–20 The opening phrase is better "And it will hail when the forest comes down." Isaiah has used "hail" (barad)[13] earlier as a symbol of God's judgment, 30:30. He has used the "forest" before to refer to Assyria's judgment; cf. 10:34. He likewise has mentioned the "city" when referring to Nineveh or Babylon, major Assyrian cities, 25:2–3; 26:5.[14] He now returns to this symbolism. Assyria, representing Israel's enemies, must fall before God's people can rise, v. 19.

At that time, God's blessing will come upon His people. The word "blessed" (ʾašᵉrê, see 30:18) is a plural construct, "blessednesses." This

---

[12]Hailey, p. 274, finds the fulfillment of this at Pentecost. This forces him to understand the passage symbolically with the fruitful field being "spiritual blessings." The view ignores the eschatological context of the chapter.

[13]The verb barad occurs only here but there is no doubt of the meaning. The related noun barad, "hail," occurs over twenty times.

[14]Among others, Motyer, *The Prophecy of Isaiah,* p. 261; Von Orelli, p. 181; and Delitzsch, II, 54, understand the "forest" as Assyria and the "city" as Jerusalem. Hailey, pp. 275–76, makes the forest represent military powers and the city "desolated world-cities." Kaiser, *Isaiah 13–39*, p. 335, makes the "forest" the enemy army. The "city" is the "world capital which is the source of all hostility towards the people of God and the city of God." These views are inconsistent. The parallelism suggests that both "forest" and "city" refer to the same people.

gives it an intensive sense, "O the blessing!" or "How blessed!" Those who sow the crops also send forth their animals to graze. The fields will bring forth such an abundant harvest that the ox and ass will be allowed to wander freely. No one will care what damage they might do to the crops, v. 20.

Practical Applications from Chapter 32

1. Blessings of the Kingdom, vv. 1–8, 15–20

   a. The righteous rule of Christ and the saints will bring justice to the earth, v. 1. This will give protection to mankind, v. 2.

   b. Mankind will possess increased spiritual understanding, vv. 3–4.

   c. The true character of others will appear. Men will not be able to portray themselves for what they are not, v. 5. Their wickedness will be seen in what they do, v. 6. The wicked will be wicked, v. 7, but the noble person will be noble, v. 8.

   d. The Holy Spirit will work to cause the land to bring forth abundantly, v. 15.

   e. There will be justice and righteousness throughout the world, v. 16. This will bring peace and satisfaction, v. 17. Mankind will dwell securely without fear of attack, v. 18.

   f. The Lord will destroy His enemies, v. 19. His blessing will be on those who belong to Him, v. 20.

In view of the blessings that the Lord has planned for His kingdom, believers today may have confidence that we are on the winning side. There is no reason to follow the ways of this world. We should instead follow the Lord.

2. Chastisement of God's People, vv. 9–14

   a. Warning of the judgment. Isaiah singles out the women of the land and rebukes them for their indifference to spiritual matters, vv. 9–10a. Judgment will therefore affect the crops, v. 10b. The women should tremble in fear. They should put on sackcloth to show their inward grief, v. 11. The men should show outward signs of grief over the destruction of the crops, v. 12.

   b. Description of the judgment. Thorns and briers will overcome the land. They will grow even on the houses that once were places of rejoicing, v. 13. The place of government will be forsaken. The people will leave the city. Places in the city that once were populated will become the homes of wild animals. Animals will graze there, v. 14.

c. Application of the judgment. As with other pictures of judgment, this illustrates the wrath of God toward sin. Rather than passively submitting to sin, we should actively fight against it. Only then will we gain God's favor.

1 Woe to thee that spoilest, and thou wast not spoiled; and dealest treacherously, and they dealt not treacherously with thee! when thou shalt cease to spoil, thou shalt be spoiled; and when thou shalt make an end to deal treacherously, they shall deal treacherously with thee.

ISAIAH 33

Isaiah returns once more to the miraculous deliverance of Judah from the Assyrian invasion. He has brought up the topic before, 14:24–27; 18:3–6; 29:1–4; 30:30–33, and he will develop it further in 36:1–21 and 37:1–13, 21–38. The dramatic defeat of the Assyrians as the Lord rescues His people is a vivid illustration of God's control of human history. Isaiah develops the theme here as an encouragement to the nation. It serves to introduce the future rule of the Lord over the earth.

E. Deliverance from Assyrian Might 33:1–24
1. Assurance of Victory 33:1–6

1 Isaiah pronounces a "woe" (*hôy*, cf. 1:4)[1] upon Assyria. The use of the interjection *hôy* is characteristic of Isaiah. Almost half of its total occurrences in the OT are in this book, e.g., 5:8, 11, 18, 20, 21, 22; 17:12; 28:1; 45:9, 10. Isaiah refers to a nation that took spoil and practiced treachery on other nations. She herself, however, has never been spoiled or been the object of treachery. The nation in view is undoubtedly Assyria. When she shall "make an end" (*kanneloteka*)[2] in oppressing others, she herself will be the object of oppression, v. 1.

---

[1] The use of *hôy* in the opening verse connects the chapter to the previous chapters of this section that also use the word (28:1; 29:1, 15; 30:1; 31:1). The chapter has the repetition of a verb and its noun (*ʾasap*), v. 4. There are repeated words beginning phrases (*ʿattâ . . . ʿattâ . . . ʿattâ*, v. 10; *mî yagûr lanû . . . mî yagûr lanû*, v. 14; *ʾayyeh . . . ʾayyeh . . . ʾayyeh*, v. 18; *yehwah . . . yehwah . . . yehwah*, v. 22). The chapter uses symbols (caterpillar, locusts, v. 4; chaff, stubble, v. 11; tabernacle, stakes, cords, v. 20; elements of a ship, v. 23). Much of the vocabulary occurs elsewhere in the book. The emphasis on eschatology is familiar. These are all elements of Isaiah's writing style.

[2] The word *kanneloteka* occurs only here. BDB, p. 649, locates it as the *hipʿîl* infinitive from the unused root *nlh*. It suggests, however, that the reading should be *kekalloteka*, the *piʿel* infinitive from *kalâ*, "to end." The Isaiah Scroll supports this suggestion. Young, II, 405, relates the MT reading to an Arabic cognate *nāla*, "to complete." Either approach gives the same result.

2 *O Lord, be gracious unto us; we have waited for thee: be thou their arm every morning, our salvation also in the time of trouble.*
3 *At the noise of the tumult the people fled; at the lifting up of thyself the nations were scattered.*
4 *And your spoil shall be gathered like the gathering of the caterpiller: as the running to and fro of locusts shall he run upon them.*
5 *The Lord is exalted; for he dwelleth on high: he hath filled Zion with judgment and righteousness.*
6 *And wisdom and knowledge shall be the stability of thy times, and strength of salvation: the fear of the Lord is his treasure.*

2–4 The thought of Assyria's defeat causes Isaiah to pray spontaneously. The people have "waited" (*qawâ*, see 5:2) for God to intervene. He asks the Lord to be Israel's "arm," a natural symbol of strength; cf. 30:30; 51:9; 52:10; 53:1. The phrase "every morning" refers to the need for daily strength. Isaiah identifies himself with the people in his request that the Lord will be "our salvation." The word "salvation" here has the sense of deliverance from enemies "in the time of trouble," v. 2. The Lord immediately gives Isaiah a vision to show him the answer to his prayer. At the "noise of the tumult," the thundering voice of God, the Assyrians flee. As God is "lifted up," exalted, the nations scatter before Him, v. 3. Israel gathers spoil from their enemies like the "gathering of the caterpiller." The caterpillar is a form of locust; cf. Psalm 78:46; Joel 1:4; 2:25. Like a swarm of locusts "shall he [Judah] run upon them [Assyria]." Isaiah looks forward to the time that Judah will swarm over the Assyrian camp, v. 4.[3]

5–6 The people now recognize the exalted position of the Lord. He dwells above the nations of this world; cf. Psalm 113:4–6. His gracious work on behalf of the people causes "judgment" (*mišpaṭ*, better "justice," see 1:17) and righteousness to fill the land, v. 5. The first half of v. 6 is better "And He [i.e., the Lord] will be the stability [*ʾemûnâ*, see 11:5] of your times, a wealth of salvation, wisdom, and knowledge." The word

---

[3]Young, II, 407, suggests that the phrase "gathering of locusts" (i.e., caterpillars) is an objective genitive. In the Near East, the people often gather the locusts for the purpose of destroying them. The thought here, then, is that the spoil taken from the Assyrians will be taken away so that nothing remains. His view, however, suffers from the fact that it does not parallel the second half of the verse. Even Young admits that "the second half of the verse refers to the running about of swarms of insects." This pictures the swarming of Judah over the enemy camp. For this reason, it is best to understand the first phrase as a subjective genitive, "the gathering that locusts make." Both phrases describe the descent of Judah on the enemy camp to gather spoil.

7 *Behold, their valiant ones shall cry without: the ambassadors of peace shall weep bitterly.*

8 *The highways lie waste, the wayfaring man ceaseth: he hath broken the covenant, he hath despised the cities, he regardeth no man.*

9 *The earth mourneth and languisheth: Lebanon is ashamed and hewn down: Sharon is like a wilderness; and Bashan and Carmel shake off their fruits.*

ᵊmûnâ conveys the idea here of reliableness. We may trust the Lord to sustain us. The word "wealth" governs "salvation, wisdom, and knowledge." The Lord gives these in abundance. The word "salvation" is plural with an intensive sense. It refers to the fullness of salvation that God provides. In context, "wisdom" and "knowledge" relate to spiritual matters. In addition, the "fear of the Lord," a reverential attitude toward God, is "his treasure." This is Israel's treasure, a precious possession given to those who belong to the Lord, v. 6.[4]

2. Intervention of God 33:7–12

7–9 The "valiant ones" (*ʾerʾellam*) and the "ambassadors" are parallel.[5] Both terms refer to the Jewish negotiators who try to make

---

[4]Since the verse does not mention Zion or Judah, Motyer, *The Prophecy of Isaiah,* p. 264, reasons that the pronoun "his" refers to the Lord. The "fear of the Lord" is the treasure that God has in store for His people. The view is possible but doubtful. The phrase "fear of the Lord" occurs twenty-nine times in the OT, primarily in Proverbs (fourteen times) and Isaiah (six times). It normally refers to an attitude either possessed by the people or urged upon the people. Watts, *Isaiah 1–33*, p. 420, makes "Lord" govern all four construct nouns (salvation, wisdom, knowledge, fear): "the abundance of salvation, wisdom, knowledge, and fear of Yahweh—that is his treasure." This ignores the *ʾatnaḥ*, the verse division. G.K. 130 *b* explains these forms before the copulative as "an intentional reversion to the old feminine ending *ath*" for the purpose of avoiding the *â wa* sound.

[5]The word *ʾerʾellam* is difficult. BDB, p. 72, says it is "wholly dubious." KB, I, 82, suggests that the word is corrupted. KB proposes *ʾarʾelîm*, "heroes," or *ʾariʾelîm*, "priests" or "inhabitants of Jerusalem." Siegfried J. Schwantes, "A Historical Approach to the *ʾrʾlm* of Is 33:7," *Andrews University Seminary Studies* 3:158–66, relates the word to *ʾarʾelî*, a member of Gad, in Gen. 46:16; Num. 26:17. He suggests that *ʾerʾellam* here are "members of the royal bodyguard who traced their ancestry back to אראל־י of the tribe of Gad." The mere coincidence of names is a tenuous basis on which to assume descent. Scott, p. 350, refers to 29:1 in translating "priests of the altar." He apparently reasons that the altar must imply "priests." Kissane, I, 374, derives the word from the name Ariel, cf. 29:1, 2, 7. He concludes that the word here means "Arielites." From the parallelism, we can relate the word to *ʾᵃrîʾel*, II Sam. 23:20 (see also I Chron. 11:22). The word combines *ʾarî*, "lion," and *ʾel*, "God." The "lion of God" indicates "warriors." Kelley, p. 285, translates, "the men of Ariel" and understands Ariel as naming Jerusalem, cf. 29:1, 2, 7.

peace with Assyria. Second Kings 18:14–16 records Hezekiah's attempt to buy off Assyria by paying tribute. Sennacherib, the Assyrian king, accepted the tribute but then continued his invasion of Judah. This caused the envoys to "cry" and "weep bitterly" when they realized Assyria's intentions, v. 7.[6] Normal movement within the land ceases for fear of the Assyrian invaders. Sennacherib refuses to honor the covenant with Judah. He continues his conquest of the "cities" (ʿarîm).[7] He shows no fear of "man" (ʾenôš, see 2:11), v. 8. The whole land mourns the prospect of defeat. In the north, the Lebanon Mountains are "ashamed and hewn down" (better "shamed and withered"). The fertile Plain of Sharon between Mt. Carmel and Joppa is now like a "wilderness" (ʿarabâ). The ʿarabâ was the name given to the wilderness region to the south of Judah (see 21:13). Sharon was normally well watered and therefore fertile. The Assyrian armies have trampled the crops of Sharon so that it now resembles a wilderness. The rich area of Bashan lay across the Jordan between Gilead and Mt. Hermon. It was specially a place for the raising of cattle, Deuteronomy 32:14; Ezekiel 39:18. Mt. Carmel was on the coast of the Mediterranean in northern Palestine. The name "Carmel" means "fruitful" or "garden." These places now lie waste, no longer yielding their fruit to the people, v. 9.

Young, II, 410, understands ʾerʾellam as the Assyrian soldiers who cry out as they approach the city. He draws a contrast between the halves of the verse. While these views are possible, the parallelism suggests men who have something to do with gaining peace with Assyria. While the form is difficult, we can adopt a meaning with a fair amount of confidence.

[6]Vine, p. 69, makes vv. 9–13 refer to Israel's state under Antichrist. There is, however, no context to support this. It is better to limit the passage to Judah and Assyria.

[7]Among others, Stacey, p. 202; Leslie, p. 275; and OTTP, p. 146, emend ʿarîm to ʿedîm, "witnesses." The Isaiah Scroll supports the change. This has the advantage of parallelling "covenant." The verse, however, has three clauses, not two. There is a sequence rather than parallel thoughts. It is likely that 1QIsaᵃ confused the rêš and the dalet. Delbert R. Hillers, "A Hebrew Cognate of unuššu/ʾunṭ in Is. 33:8," HTR 64:257–59, recognizes the three phrases. He argues from Ugaritic that ʾenôš means "land-tax." It is unlikely that we should adopt such a novel meaning for this well-known word.

10 *Now will I rise, saith the Lord; now will I be exalted; now will I lift up myself.*

11 *Ye shall conceive chaff, ye shall bring forth stubble: your breath, as fire, shall devour you.*

12 *And the people shall be as the burnings of lime: as thorns cut up shall they be burned in the fire.*

13 *Hear, ye that are far off, what I have done; and, ye that are near, acknowledge my might.*

14 *The sinners in Zion are afraid; fearfulness hath surprised the hypocrites. Who among us shall dwell with the devouring fire? who among us shall dwell with everlasting burnings?*

15 *He that walketh righteously, and speaketh uprightly; he that despiseth the gain of oppressions, that shaketh his hands from holding of bribes, that stoppeth his ears from hearing of blood, and shutteth his eyes from seeing evil;*

16 *He shall dwell on high: his place of defence shall be the munitions of rocks: bread shall be given him; his waters shall be sure.*

10–12 In response to the plight of His people, the Lord now states His intention to intervene. He will "rise" against Assyria. He will "be exalted" as He acts on behalf of Judah. He will "lift up" Himself against their enemies, v. 10. Assyria will "conceive chaff" and "bring forth stubble." The husks of the grain, "chaff," and the dried stalks of the grain, "stubble," picture the worthlessness of Assyria's invasion. Their "breath," the vain threats made against the people, cf. 36:4–10, 12–20, will be as a fire consuming them, v. 11. Their "people" lit. "will be as the burnings of lime" (or "will be burned to lime"). The burning of bones, mainly calcium carbonate, results in calcium oxide, a dehydrated form of lime. The word "people" is plural. It refers to the various nations that contributed troops to the Assyrian army.[8] The enemy will be as the burning of thorns that have been cut up and thrown into the fire. Both word pictures illustrate the complete destruction of the Assyrian army, v. 12.

3. Deliverance of Judah 33:13–24

13–16 The Lord first addresses far-off nations, then those that are near. He tells them to note His power in what He has done, v. 13. Not only the heathen but also the chosen people react to His works. The

---

[8]Alexander, II, 10, thinks that the plural word includes all the "nations that incur the wrath of God." It is true that the passage does not name Assyria. The wider context of c. 28–31, however, gives prominence to Assyria.

"sinners in Zion," Jews who have failed to abide by His Word, are "afraid" (*pahad* see 2:10), a strong sense of fear, "dread, terror." The "hypocrites" (*hanep*, see 9:17) experience "fearfulness" (better "trembling"). Rhetorically, the Lord asks who can withstand the everlasting fire of His judgment, v. 14. Only the godly man will be able to stand. The Lord describes the godly. He first focuses on the godly man's own actions, then on his actions relating to others. He walks through this life in righteousness. His speech is upright, straight, and therefore trustworthy. He "despiseth" (or "rejects") gain that comes from "oppression" (or "extortion"), taking advantage of others who have no power to withstand his pressure. He shakes his hands, showing them empty, not taking bribes offered to him. He will not listen to plans that may lead to murder. He refuses to look favorably at that which is "evil" (*ra*ᶜ, see 3:9), v. 15.

Marks of Godliness, v. 15
Positively
  1. Living righteously
  2. Speaking reliably
Negatively
  3. Avoiding extortion
  4. Rejecting bribes
  5. Refusing brutality
  6. Scorning evil

---

16 The Lord promises to bless the righteous man. He describes him metaphorically as living in a refuge high in the mountains. His place of defense is "the munitions of rocks" (or "the rocky stronghold"),[9] well stocked with food and water. At a time when the nation faces what seems to be certain defeat, the Lord promises security to those who are godly. The stark contrast promotes the value of godliness, v. 16.

---

[9]Irwin, p. 152, understands the rocky fortress as the heavenly dwelling place of the saints. I would not go this far. It is rather a metaphorical picture of safety.

17 Thine eyes shall see the king in his beauty: they shall behold the
    land that is very far off.
18 Thine heart shall meditate terror. Where is the scribe? where is the
    receiver? where is he that counted the towers?
19 Thou shalt not see a fierce people, a people of a deeper speech than
    thou canst perceive; of a stammering tongue, that thou canst not
    understand.

17–19 Verse 17 makes a transition to messianic prophecy. The scope
of the blessing described in vv. 17–22 goes beyond any temporal blessing experienced in the OT. It is a preview of the millennial kingdom. The
godly man will see "the king in his beauty," a picturesque description of
the Messiah Himself.[10] He will see "the land that is very far off [ʾereṣ
marḥaqqîm]."[11] This is an enlarged land that has undergone physical
changes so that distant places now are visible, cf. 26:15, v. 17. His
"heart," here referring to his mind, will think of the previous "terror"
(ʾêmâ).[12] Where are the Assyrian leaders? Where is the "scribe" who as-
sesses the tribute? Where is the "receiver" (better "weigher") who totals
the wealth received? Where is "he that counted the towers," the one who
considers Judah's defenses and plans the attack; cf. Psalm 48:12–13?[13]
The questions imply that all are gone, v. 18. Judah will no longer see the
"fierce people" with different speech. The Assyrian soldiers spoke with
a "deeper" (or "unintelligible") speech that could not be understood.
They used a "stammering [laʿag]"[14] tongue" that the Jews could not comprehend, v. 19.

---

[10]Among others, Herbert, *Isaiah 1–39*, p. 190; Delitzsch, II, 63; and Watts, *Isaiah
1–33*, p. 428, view the king as a Judean king. Brueggemann, *Isaiah 1–39*, p. 265, and
Leupold, I, 519, specifically reject the Messiah in favor of God the Father. Barnes, I,
484, refers this to Hezekiah. The eschatological context supports the view that the king is
Messiah.

[11]Irwin, p. 154, understands ʾereṣ marḥaqqîm as "distant city" and applies it to the heavenly Jerusalem. His argument is weak. The word ʾereṣ occurs widely and its meaning of
"land" is not in doubt.

[12]Irwin, p. 155, translates ʾêmâ as "awe." He then explains the remainder of the verse
as a statement of Jerusalem's magnificence. Who is able to measure its magnificence?
The word ʾêmâ, however, occurs elsewhere sixteen times, always with a sense of "terror."

[13]Driver, *JSS* 13:53, understands the "towers" as "heaps, piles (of coins)," cf. Song of
Sol. 5:13, "sweet flowers" (lit. "towers of spices"). The view is possible although it requires an unusual interpretation of migdalîm, "towers."

[14]While the word laʿag may refer to mocking speech, it is more likely here that it refers
to speech that cannot be understood, stammering speech; cf. 28:11.

20 *Look upon Zion, the city of our solemnities: thine eyes shall see Jerusalem a quiet habitation, a tabernacle that shall not be taken down; not one of the stakes thereof shall ever be removed, neither shall any of the cords thereof be broken.*

21 *But there the glorious Lord will be unto us a place of broad rivers and streams; wherein shall go no galley with oars, neither shall gallant ship pass thereby.*

22 *For the Lord is our judge, the Lord is our lawgiver, the Lord is our king; he will save us.*

20–22 The Lord urges godly men to look on Jerusalem, the city of "solemnities," i.e., the appointed feasts carried out year by year. These undoubtedly are memorial feasts. In OT times they look forward to the work of Christ. In the kingdom, they will look backward to His finished work. In both eras, the feasts remind us of the Lord's sacrifice and of our need for total dedication to Him.

The city is now a "quiet" (or "secure") place to live. It is a "tabernacle" (or "tent," the dwelling of nomads) that will not "be taken down" (*ṣaᶜan*, better "loaded," as for moving to a new place).[15] The tent stakes will not be pulled up and the tent cords "broken" (or "snapped"), a real possibility with continual wear, v. 20. The majestic Lord will defend His people. He will be as a place with rivers and "streams" (or "wide canals"). No enemy ship will row on these watercourses that surround the city. The metaphor comes from those large cities such as Babylon or No-Amon that relied on surrounding moats or rivers to protect them. In the same way, the Lord will protect His own, v. 21. He will rule His people: He will act as their judge, lawgiver, and king, to "save" (*yašaᶜ*, see 17:10) them from their enemies.

The passage clearly goes beyond any local fulfillment. The immediate deliverance of Judah from the Assyrians foreshadows the greater deliverance of God's people during the kingdom. Antichrist and his hosts will fail as the Lord first delivers His people, and then establishes His own rule over the earth, v. 22.

---

[15]This is the only place that *ṣaᶜan* occurs. Related cognates (Akkadian *ṣênu*, "to load, ship," Aramaic *ṭaᶜan*, "to load," cf. Gen. 45:17) support the idea of "loading" in preparation for moving to a new place.

23 *Thy tacklings are loosed; they could not well strengthen their mast,*
they could not spread the sail: then is the prey of a great spoil di-
vided; the lame take the prey.
24 *And the inhabitant shall not say, I am sick: the people that dwell*
therein shall be forgiven their iniquity.

23–24 Jerusalem in Isaiah's time is as a ship not ready for battle.[16]
Her "tacklings" (or "cords," the rigging of the ship) are loose and cannot
hold the mainmast in place. The sailors cannot spread the "sail" (*nes*) for
fear that the mast will fall. Yet, when the Lord delivers them, they will
take a "great spoil" from their enemies. The plunder will be so great that
even the "lame" will collect spoil, v. 23. The joy will be great enough to
heal the sick. In a startling statement, Isaiah notes that God will forgive
the "iniquity" (ᶜ*awon*, see 1:4) of the people. Once more, this has an eschatological sense. It looks forward to Israel's conversion during the
Tribulation, cf. Zechariah 13:1, v. 24.

Practical Applications from Chapter 33

1. The Assurance of Victory, vv. 1–16

   a. The prophecy of Assyria's defeat. Isaiah describes the doom of
   the mighty Assyrian enemy, v. 1. Isaiah impulsively prays that the
   Lord will be Israel's strength and deliverer from their enemy, v. 2.
   The Lord responds, giving the prophet a vision to show how He
   will answer his prayer, vv. 3–4.

   b. The exaltation of Israel's God. The people recognize the exalted
   position held by the Lord. He dwells above the nations of the
   world. He brings justice and righteousness to the land, v. 5. He
   sustains the nation with a fullness of salvation. He gives an

---

[16]Henry, p. 488; Alexander, II, 17; Fausett, p. 666; and Barnes, I, 488, understand the
ship as a symbol of Assyria. Without being specific, Slotki, p. 158, makes the ship a
symbol of Israel's "enemy." Watts, *Isaiah 1–33*, p. 425, does not see a nautical motif
here. He understands *nes* as "flag." The Assyrians cannot defend it. These views go contrary to the context. The verses both before and after v. 23 refer to the Lord's blessings
upon the Jews. In addition, seeing the ship as Assyria requires a change of subject in the
middle of the verse. The last part clearly refers to Israel spoiling their enemies. For this
reason, I relate the ship to Jerusalem. Kissane, pp. 378–79, argues that the figure is not a
ship. He notes that *nes* never has the meaning of "sail" elsewhere. He visualizes a pole
set on a hill from which a "signal" flies. The view is possible; however, the symbolism
remains the same.

abundance of wisdom and knowledge in spiritual matters. He gives His people a reverential attitude toward Him, v. 6.

c. The description of God's intervention. The Jewish representatives will fail in their effort to make peace with Assyria, v. 7. Normal movement in the land will cease because of Assyria's oppression, v. 8. The land itself suffers, v. 9. With this bleak situation, the Lord now intervenes on behalf of His people. He will rise against the enemy, v. 10. He will overwhelm them, v. 11. Their army will be burned as the result of their complete destruction, v. 12.

d. The deliverance of the Lord's people. The Lord calls on the nations of the world to hear what He has done, v. 13. The wicked will realize that no one can stand against Him, v. 14. Only the godly, v. 15, will find safety, v. 16.

2. Marks of the Millennium, vv. 17–22

a. Scenes to encourage. The godly will see the "king in His beauty," the Lord Himself. The godly will as well see the land, now enlarged in the kingdom, v. 17. Their enemies, however, will no longer be in view, vv. 18–19.

b. Worship of the Lord. The people in Jerusalem will carry out the feasts of worship year by year, v. 20a.

c. Defense by the Lord. Jerusalem will now be a safe place in which to dwell, v. 20b. The Lord Himself will protect the city, v. 21.

d. Rule of the Lord. He will rule the people, acting as judge, lawgiver, and king to give them deliverance from their enemies, v. 22.

e. Forgiveness of sins. In Isaiah's day, the people are weak. The Lord, however, will still use them to gather spoil from the Assyrian camp, v. 23. This serves as a picture of Israel during the kingdom. They will not be sick because their sins have been forgiven and they have no need of God's chastening, v. 24.

1 *Come near, ye nations, to hear; and hearken, ye people: let the earth hear, and all that is therein; the world, and all things that come forth of it.*

2 *For the indignation of the Lord is upon all nations, and his fury upon all their armies: he hath utterly destroyed them, he hath delivered them to the slaughter.*

3 *Their slain also shall be cast out, and their stink shall come up out of their carcases, and the mountains shall be melted with their blood.*

ISAIAH 34

With few exceptions, there is general agreement that c. 34 and c. 35 are one prophecy. Chapter 34 describes the end-time judgments of the world. Chapter 35 follows with the description of the millennial kingdom. This pattern of judgment followed by blessing is a mark of OT prophecy. It occurs frequently elsewhere in Isaiah, e.g., 2:6–4:1, 4:2–6; 19:1–15, 16–25; 24:1–23, 25:1–12. These two chapters climax the first part of Isaiah. Chapters 36–39 are a historical interlude. Chapters 40–66 stress Babylon and prophetic themes.

F. Destruction of God's Enemies 34:1–17[1]
1. Judgment of the World 34:1–4

1–3 The Lord calls all nations to hear His Word.[2] The repetition, "hear . . . hearken . . . hear," lends emphasis to the call, which goes to all nations because the judgment about to be announced will affect them, v. 1. The Lord is about to judge the world. The statement "he hath utterly destroyed [*heḥerîm*, see 11:15] them . . ." is a prophetic perfect, an act so certain in the mind of God that it is stated as an accomplished fact. The Lord must completely destroy this world system before He can set up His own kingdom, v. 2. He pictures the slaughter of the nations. So many die that the dead are "cast out," left unburied on the ground. Their carcasses rot. The torrents of blood that come from the dead cause the

---

[1] Many authors attribute these chapters to late editors. There is, of course, no textual material to support the idea that they are late. The nature of the material is Isaianic. We can find the same eschatological emphasis elsewhere in Isaiah, e.g., 34:4; cf. 13:10; 35:1; cf. 32:15–16. There are intentional plays on the sounds of words: *namassû . . . namaqqû*, 34:3b, 4a; *parîm . . . ᶜaparam*, 34:7. There are repeated verbs: *yibbôl . . . kinᵉbol . . . ûknobelet*, 34:4; *wᵉtiprah . . tiprah*, 35:1b, 2a; and nouns, *lᵉneṣaḥ nᵉṣaḥîm*, 34:10d. Repeated words begin phrases: *ᶜal⁻kol . . . ᶜal⁻kol*, 34:2; *ʾaz . . . ʾaz*, 35:5, 6. These similarities to Isaiah's style of writing give us confidence that the material belongs to Isaiah.

[2] The practice of calling the nations of the world as witnesses of God's work is characteristic of Isaiah, e.g., 18:3; 33:13; 43:9; 49:1; 52:10.

4 *And all the host of heaven shall be dissolved, and the heavens shall be rolled together as a scroll: and all their host shall fall down, as the leaf falleth off from the vine, and as a falling fig from the fig tree.*
5 *For my sword shall be bathed in heaven: behold, it shall come down upon Idumea, and upon the people of my curse, to judgment.*
6 *The sword of the Lord is filled with blood, it is made fat with fatness, and with the blood of lambs and goats, with the fat of the kidneys of rams: for the Lord hath a sacrifice in Bozrah, and a great slaughter in the land of Idumea.*
7 *And the unicorns shall come down with them, and the bullocks with the bulls; and their land shall be soaked with blood, and their dust made fat with fatness.*
8 *For it is the day of the Lord's vengeance, and the year of recompences for the controversy of Zion.*

mountains to "be melted," i.e., eroded. The picture is of the Tribulation judgments that occur at the end of this age. Although the description involves hyperbole, it gives us a picture of the end-time judgments, v. 3.

4 The heavens themselves suffer in that day. The "host of heaven," the heavenly bodies themselves, will "be dissolved" (*maqaq*), disappear from sight.[3] The "heavens," a parallel reference to the "host of heaven," the heavenly bodies, will be rolled up like a scroll, also to disappear; cf. Revelation 6:13–14. The heavenly "host" will "fall down" (*nabel*, better "fade away, wither") just as the leaf fades on the vine or the "falling fig" (or "withering," probably referring to the leaves) of the fig tree, v. 4.[4]

The picture given here is dramatic. This is no localized conquest of a nation. This is the future cataclysmic destruction of the heavens. Other passages such as Psalm 102:26 and Joel 3:15 repeat the prophecy. The NT draws on this picture in such passages as Matthew 24:29; Mark 13:24–25; II Peter 3:7–10; and Revelation 8:12. We have here the final judgment of the world in preparation for the kingdom ruled by the Lord.

2. Judgment of Edom 34:5–17

5–8 The Lord now turns from the future judgment to a more immediate judgment. Edom was Israel's perpetual enemy in OT times, Ezekiel 35:5.

---

[3]The verb *maqaq* means "to pine away, rot away." Coupled with the verb *nabel*, "to fade," it gives the sense that the heavens will gradually disappear; cf. 65:17; 66:22; II Pet. 3:13; Rev. 21:1. The Lord prolongs the disappearance over the course of the Tribulation. This heightens the fear created in men. Throughout history, men have worshiped the heavenly bodies. The Lord now shows their weakness.

[4]Whitehouse, I, 342, thinks that the ancients regarded the stars as spirits. While this may have been true of the heathen, there is no evidence that the Jews held this position.

As such, she represents all nations that will be overthrown by God. While the judgment described here is past, it represents the Tribulation judgments that are yet future. The Lord has "bathed" (*riwwᵉtâ*, or "satiated")[5] His sword, drinking its fill in the destruction of the heavens.[6] Now it descends to Idumea (lit. "Edom"). This is a nation under God's "curse" (*ḥerem*, see 11:15), which will suffer "judgment" (*mišpaṭ*, see 1:17), v. 5. Animals as well will die in the destruction. Their death fills the Lord's sword of judgment with fat, an important part of OT sacrifices; cf. Leviticus 3:3, 9. The blood of lambs and goats will be shed as a sacrifice to the Lord. The "fat of the kidneys of rams" is as well a sacrifice to the Lord; cf. Exodus 29:22. The judgment that falls upon Bozrah and Edom results in this "sacrifice" (*zebaḥ*, see 1:11). Bozrah, a large city in northern Edom, was located on an oasis about twenty-five miles southeast of the Dead Sea, v. 6. The "unicorns" (*rᵉʾemîm*) are thought to be wild oxen.[7] The *rᵉʾem* was strong, Numbers 23:22; untamed, Job 39:9–11; and had two horns, Deuteronomy 33:17; Psalm 22:21. The grouping with bullocks and bulls suggests a larger animal. The greatness of the devastation causes the land to be "soaked" (or "saturated") with blood. The dust will be filled with the fat of the animals, v. 7.[8] This is the

---

[5]With support from the Isaiah Scroll, the NEB emends *riwwᵉtâ* to *tirʾâ* and translates, "the sword of the Lord appears in heaven." Driver, *JSS* 13:55, and Watts, *Isaiah 34–66*, p. 5, adopt this position. There is textual support for both views. The Vulgate translates *inebriatus*, "drunken," and the LXX translates ἐμεθύσθη, "drunken," while the Isaiah Scroll and the Targum support "appear." The similar thought in v. 6*a* favors the MT.

[6]There are a variety of other interpretations of the verse. Näglesbach, p. 364, and Slotki, p. 160, refer the work of the sword to the slaughter of the heavenly beings that stand against the Lord. Henry, p. 190, alludes to a custom of dipping the sword in some liquid to harden or brighten it. The Lord bathes His sword "in his counsel and decree, in his justice and power" in preparation for His judgment of man. Price, p. 142, varies this slightly. He refers to tempering the steel of the sword by dipping it "in heavenly waters" to prepare it. He does not explain what the "heavenly waters" are. Fausset, p. 667, makes the "sword" a "knife" for sacrifice. God forms His purpose in heaven for His work on earth. The most widely held view is that God's sword is drunken with wrath. It rushes from heaven as drunken to bring judgment on Edom. So Barnes, I, 493; Young, II, 432; and Hailey, p. 288. I see the phrase as finishing the thought of v. 4. The sword finishes the destruction of the heavenly bodies. It as well falls in judgment on mankind.

[7]Price, p. 142, suggests that *rᵉʾem* refers to the rhinoceros. Von Orelli, p. 190, gives the buffalo. Birks, p. 169, understands the antelope. There is no evidence that these animals were widespread in Palestine. In addition, the Akkadian cognate *rîmu*, "wild ox," supports the view given above.

[8]Henry, p. 191, and Vine, p. 71, understand vv. 6–7 as figurative. The animals represent the leaders of the armies that oppose the Lord. The reference to "sacrifice" in v. 6 makes this view unlikely.

9 *And the streams thereof shall be turned into pitch, and the dust thereof into brimstone, and the land thereof shall become burning pitch.*
10 *It shall not be quenched night nor day; the smoke thereof shall go up for ever: from generation to generation it shall lie waste; none shall pass through it for ever and ever.*

"day of the Lord's vengeance," cf. 61:2; 63:4; Jeremiah 46:10, and the "year of recompences." The words "day" and "year" poetically refer to a period of time. There is no emphasis here on one period being short and the other long. The Lord will take vengeance on those who have opposed Him. His holy nature requires Him to punish those who have refused Him; He will recompense them for their sin. The intensive plural "recompences" gives additional emphasis to the judgment. The phrases refer to the Tribulation judgments introduced earlier in vv. 1–3, v. 8.

9–10 Volcanic judgments come on Edom, a judgment similar to that which fell on Sodom and Gomorrah, Genesis 19:24; cf. Jeremiah 49:18. The "streams" (or "ravines," *nahal*, see 7:19) now fill with molten pitch. "Brimstone," burning stone, replaces the "dust," loose dirt. "Burning pitch" fills the land. Once again, the Lord uses hyperbole to heighten the description of the Tribulation judgments, v. 9. The fires burn night and day and from generation to generation. Men will not pass through Edom "for ever and ever." The land will be a vivid illustration of God's wrath toward sin.

We normally think of the kingdom age as a time of perfection. There are, however, hints in the Bible that reminders of the Lord's judgment on sin continue through the kingdom. The existence of the salty marshes, Ezekiel 47:11, suggests that parts of the earth remain under the effects of sin. The existence of sin in the kingdom, requiring judges, Isaiah 1:26; an "iron rod" rule by the Lord, Psalm 2:9; and the rebellion of mankind, Revelation 20:7–9, show us that man himself will continue to be a sinful creature. The everlasting smoke of "Babylon," Revelation 19:3, continues to tell man that God judges sin, v. 10.

11 *But the cormorant and the bittern shall possess it; the owl also and the raven shall dwell in it: and he shall stretch out upon it the line of confusion, and the stones of emptiness.*

12 *They shall call the nobles thereof to the kingdom, but none shall be there, and all her princes shall be nothing.*

13 *And thorns shall come up in her palaces, nettles and brambles in the fortresses thereof: and it shall be an habitation of dragons, and a court for owls.*

14 *The wild beasts of the desert shall also meet with the wild beasts of the island, and the satyr shall cry to his fellow; the screech owl also shall rest there, and find for herself a place of rest.*

15 *There shall the great owl make her nest, and lay, and hatch, and gather under her shadow: there shall the vultures also be gathered, every one with her mate.*

11–15 Wildlife will possess the land. The "cormorant" (*qaʾat*) is an unknown bird. It is unclean and therefore not to be eaten, Leviticus 11:18 ("pelican"); Deuteronomy 14:17. It dwells alone in the wilderness, Psalm 102:6. The word is often translated "pelican." That, however, is a bird that lives near water and is not appropriate here. The *qaʾat* can dwell in a high place, Zephaniah 2:14. We can only speculate on its identity.[9] The identity of the "bittern" (*qippôd*, see 14:23) is unclear as well.[10] The "owl" is an unclean bird, Leviticus 11:17; Deuteronomy 14:16. Its name, *yanšôp*, comes from a root meaning "twilight." From this, it is thought to be an evening bird, perhaps some kind of owl.[11] The "raven" is the only one of these birds about which there is general agreement. All of the birds will dwell there since the land is emptied of its inhabitants. The Lord stretches a line over the land to measure the "confusion" (*tohû*, better "waste," see 24:10). The "stones," weights used with plumb lines, measure the degree of emptiness in the land, cf. 28:17, v. 11.

---

[9]Kaiser, *Isaiah 13–39*, p. 352, suggests "owl." Leupold, I, 529, gives "jackdaw." The RSV gives "hawk." The NEB gives "horned owl." The NIV gives "desert owl." The LXX translates ὄρνεα, "bird." The wide diversity of suggestions comes from the unknown identity of the bird.

[10]The NIV gives "screech owl." The NEB gives "bustard." "Porcupine" and "hedgehog" are widely suggested but the context here calls for a bird of some kind.

[11]The NIV renders *yanšôp* as "desert owl." The NEB gives "screech owl." Delitzsch, II, 72, suggests "eared owl." Leupold, I, 529, gives "longeared owl." Leslie, p. 133, gives "great owl." Kaiser, *Isaiah 13–39*, p. 352, offers "hornbill." Young, II, 437, gives "crane." The LXX translates ἴβεις, "ibises." Once more, we can only guess at the meaning.

Verse 12*a* is better "Its nobles they seek, and there are none there they call royalty [*mᵉlûkâ*]."¹² Edom's princes are "nothing" (*ᵓepes*). The word *ᵓepes* has to do with something that "ends." The princes here have "ceased to be." They either have been killed or have gone into captivity. They are no longer able to provide leadership for the land, v. 12. Thorns, nettles, and "brambles" (or "thistles") overgrow the "palaces" (or "citadels") and "fortresses" (*mibṣar*, see 17:3). The land becomes the dwelling place of "dragons" (or "serpents") and "owls" (*bᵉnôt yaᶜᵃnâ*, lit. "daughters of the owls," unidentified birds, cf. 13:21), v. 13. The "wild beasts of the desert" (better "desert creatures") join the "wild beasts of the island" (better "jackals" or "wolves"). The "satyr" (*śaᶜîr*, better "goats," see 13:21) will cry out and the "screech owl" (*lîlît*, "night creature," an unidentified nocturnal bird or animal) will rest there, v. 14.¹³ The "great owl" (*qippôz*, uncertain, possibly the "dart snake" or "arrow snake") makes her nest there.¹⁴ She lays her eggs, hatches them, and gathers her brood in the shade of her body. The "vultures" (*dayyôt*, an unknown "bird of prey")¹⁵ are unclean birds, Deuteronomy 14:13. They gather there with their mates. The paragraph illustrates the result of the judgment on Edom, the representative of all heathen nations. The great variety of birds, snakes, and animals given here show the state of the land. It has returned to a natural state, uninhabited by man but filled with wildlife, v. 15.

---

¹²Leupold, I, 529, translates *mᵉlûkâ* "kingdom" and understands the verse as saying that no kingdom exists for the nobles to rule. While this is true, the word *mᵉlûkâ* refers to "kingship" or "royalty" rather than the physical kingdom. In addition, the parallelism suggests that there are no nobles left to assume a leadership role.

¹³The word *lîlît* occurs only here. Many authors understand it to represent Lilith, a female demon in Babylonian demonology. The rabbis taught that Lilith flew in the form of an owl, stealing or strangling children at night; see Ludwig Blau, "Lilith," *Jewish Encyclopedia*, VIII, 88. Among others, Kraeling, p. 139; Cohen, p. 133; Wade, p. 219; and Watts, *Isaiah 34–66*, p. 13, accept this as referring to Lilith. There is no reason, however, to impose a pagan myth upon the text here. The context argues for a nocturnal bird or animal.

¹⁴The word *qippôz* occurs only here. As with the birds in v. 11, there are numerous suggestions for the identity here. The NASB gives "snake." The NIV offers "owl." The NEB suggests "sand-partridge." Childs, p. 251, gives "arrow-snake." Kaiser, *Isaiah 13–39*, p. 352, renders the word "viper." The LXX read *qippôd*, as in v. 11, and translated ἐχῖνος, "hedgehog."

¹⁵The word *dayyôt* occurs only here and in Deut. 14:13. While many follow the AV's "vultures," there are also other suggestions. The NASB gives "hawks." The NIV offers "falcons." The NEB and RSV give "kites." The NRSV gives "buzzards." Leslie, p. 134, translates "owl." Von Orelli, p. 191, suggests "eagles."

16 *Seek ye out of the book of the Lord, and read: no one of these shall fail, none shall want her mate: for my mouth it hath commanded, and his spirit it hath gathered them.*

17 *And he hath cast the lot for them, and his hand hath divided it unto them by line: they shall possess it for ever, from generation to generation shall they dwell therein.*

16–17 Isaiah urges the people to seek the promises found in the "book of the Lord."[16] He refers here to words of the Lord. These were spoken by "my mouth" (lit. "His mouth") and gathered by God's "Spirit." For this reason, none of the animals he has mentioned will fail to dwell in the land. They will have their "mate" so all can perpetuate themselves, v. 16. The Lord has indeed cast His lot on Edom, selecting it for judgment. He will measure the region and divide it into dwellings for the birds and animals. They will dwell there forever, v. 17.

---

[16]Mauchline, p. 226, identifies the book as the "book of life," the record of every man's destiny. It is difficult, however, to see how the Jews could seek out this heavenly book to read it. Kelley, p. 288, suggests that the book refers to a treaty made between Judah and Edom. We know of no such treaty. Even if it existed, the people would not have had access to such a treaty. Slotki, p. 163, gives a Jewish view. The book is the Book of Genesis, which was written "at the command of the Lord." The fact that none will be missing refers to the entrance of all of the animals into the ark of Noah. If none of these were missing, "how much more would His judgment and decree cause none of the animals to abstain from coming to Edom where there would be an abundant supply of flesh and fat!" The view is fanciful and without contextual support.

Practical Applications from Chapter 34

1. The Tribulation Judgments

    a. Judgment of nature. The Lord will destroy the heavenly bodies, vv. 4–5a. As His judgment falls on the earth, the animals will also die. The blood of lambs, goats, and rams is a sacrifice to the Lord, v. 6. Wild oxen, bullocks, and bulls will fall, v. 7. Volcanic eruptions will take place, v. 9, with the fires burning night and day. The land will be desolate forever with no one passing through it, v. 10. Birds will dwell there with the land lying under the judgment of God, v. 11. Thorns and briers will overgrow the buildings. Serpents and birds will make it their home, v. 13. Wild animals and birds will live there, v. 14–15. The Lord has decreed the judgment and it will come to pass. The wild birds and animals will perpetuate themselves in the land, v. 16. The Lord has divided the land into dwellings for them, v. 17.

    b. Judgment of the nations. The Lord calls the nations of the world to hear His decree, v. 1. He will unleash His wrath upon the nations and their armies, v. 2. Their dead will lie unburied with their carcasses rotting. Torrents of blood will erode the mountains, v. 3. He will destroy Edom, representing the nations, v. 5b. He will take vengeance on those who have opposed Him, v. 8. The leaders of the nations will fall, v. 12.

2. The Word of God, v. 16 ("the book of the Lord")

    a. A reliable witness 34:16; 45:23

    b. A permanent record 30:8; 40:8; 59:21

    c. A kingdom guide 2:3

    d. A fruitful message 55:11

1 The wilderness and the solitary place shall be glad for them; and
   the desert shall rejoice, and blossom as the rose.
2 It shall blossom abundantly, and rejoice even with joy and singing:
   the glory of Lebanon shall be given unto it, the excellency of Carmel
   and Sharon, they shall see the glory of the Lord, and the excellency
   of our God.

ISAIAH 35

Chapter 35 logically follows c. 34. There the prophet describes the
Tribulation judgments of God upon the world. He now follows with a
brief description of the millennial kingdom. Both the earth and mankind
reflect the influence of righteousness. The land brings forth abundantly,
vv. 1–2. There is renewed water to nourish the desert, vv. 6–7. Man grows
stronger, v. 3, and no longer fears, v. 4. The Lord will heal physical infirmities, v. 5. The godly will travel safely in the land, vv. 8–9. The redeemed
will travel to Jerusalem, rejoicing as they go and not feeling any sorrow,
v. 10. The picture is that of the ideal earth, the earth created for man but
lost by man's sin. The Lord now brings this ideal into being once more.

G. Blessing of the Millennial Kingdom 35:1–10

1–2 The earth responds to the kingdom rule of the Lord. The entire
land will become fruitful.[1] The wilderness and the "solitary place" (bet-
ter "parched land") will "be glad ($y^e\acute{s}u\acute{s}\hat{u}m$)[2] for them" (better "rejoice"

---

[1]Hailey, p. 294, spiritualizes the passage. He refers the "wilderness" to the barren religious life of the people. The new life of the desert pictures the spiritual life that now
flourishes. The context, however, of v. 7 and 32:15–16 supports the literal fruitfulness of
the land. John Kleinig, "The Holy Way: An Exegetical Study of Isaiah 35:1–10,"
Lutheran Theological Journal 17:115–20, takes the passage "literally and metaphorically." He makes the blind, deaf, lame, and dumb of vv. 5–6 metaphors for spiritual
weakness. Water in vv. 6b–7 represents the Holy Spirit. The lion in v. 9 poetically portrays human predators. As with all spiritualizing, the interpreter becomes the authority
since the symbols mean whatever he wishes them to mean. There is no need here to go
beyond the literal sense.

[2]The *mêm* in $y^e\acute{s}u\acute{s}\hat{u}m$ is variously explained. Since there is no antecedent, it is puzzling. Fausset, p. 669, and Barnes, I, 502, understand it poetically to refer to the blessings that follow. This is unusual, however, and unlikely. Intransitive verbs do not
normally have objects. Watts, p. 6, argues that the suffix is reflexive. He translates,
"rouse themselves in gladness." This, again, is highly unusual. G.K. 47 *n* and BDB,
p. 965, call it a dittography. Kaiser, *Isaiah 13–39*, p. 360, adopts this approach. KB, IV,
1314, gives a more conservative explanation. This considers the paragogic *nûn* of $y^e\acute{s}u\acute{s}an$
to have assimilated to the following *mêm*. Delitzsch, II, 76; Näglesbach, p. 369; and
Von Orelli, p. 191, follow this approach.

3 *Strengthen ye the weak hands, and confirm the feeble knees.*
4 *Say to them that are of a fearful heart, Be strong, fear not: behold, your God will come with vengeance, even God with a recompence; he will come and save you.*
5 *Then the eyes of the blind shall be opened, and the ears of the deaf shall be unstopped.*
6 *Then shall the lame man leap as an hart, and the tongue of the dumb sing: for in the wilderness shall waters break out, and streams in the desert.*

with no prepositional phrase following). The expression poetically pictures the flourishing of the barren land. The "desert" (better "Arabah"), the valley running south of the Dead Sea to the Gulf of Aqabah, will blossom like the "rose" (*ḥᵃbaṣṣelet*, uncertain, thought to be the "crocus" or "meadow saffron"), cf. 51:3, v. 1.[3] The barren land will "blossom abundantly" (*paroaḥ tipraḥ*), the repetition of the root conveying intensity. Metaphorically, Isaiah pictures the land with great rejoicing and "singing" (or "shout of joy"). The Lord gives to the barren areas the "glory of Lebanon," famed for its cedars, Psalm 104:16. He also gives it the fruitfulness of Carmel and Sharon. The name "Carmel" means "fruitful field"; cf. 10:18; 29:17; 32:15–16. Jutting out into the Mediterranean Sea, it received abundant rain each year and was heavily wooded, Micah 7:14. The Plain of Sharon extended south from Mt. Carmel to Joppa. It was noted for its flowers, Song of Solomon 2:1, and was a place for grazing flocks, 65:10; I Chronicles 27:29. The barren regions of Palestine will see the "glory" and "excellency" of God in His blessings upon them, v. 2.[4]

3–6 There is reason to encourage the discouraged. There is hope for those who hear the promises of the kingdom. The NT draws upon this

---

[3]Because *ḥᵃbaṣṣelet* occurs only here and Song of Sol. 2:1, it is open to a variety of interpretations. Mauchline, p. 226, suggests "asphodel." Slotki, p. 165, understands it as "rose." Leslie, p. 135, gives "narcissus." The LXX translates it as κρίνον, "lily." Näglesbach, p. 370, argues from the fact that the final three radicals, *bṣl*, mean "onion." He concludes that the quadrilateral root here must be a bulbous plant. He suggests "fire lily." Näglesbach also rejects the meadow saffron because of its poisonous roots. Delitzsch, II, 77, argues similarly but ends up with "crocus." The point here, however, comes from the beauty of the flower, not the effect of its roots. In addition, the seeds of the meadow saffron have medicinal use.

[4]Leupold, I, 537, refers the pronoun "they" to the people of Judah, mentioned in the previous chapter. While this is possible, the barren areas mentioned in v. 1 are the more immediate antecedent.

image of encouragement in Hebrews 12:12. The author there notes that those who respond to discipline have reason to hope. Rather than giving in to discouragement, they should be strong, v. 3. Those who have a "fearful heart" (or "hurried heart," one that beats rapidly with fear and is therefore anxious) will receive strength from knowing that the Lord will right the wrongs of this life. He will come with "vengeance" and a "recompense" to punish their enemies.[5] He will "save" (*yaša*ᶜ, see 17:10) them, delivering them from the enemy's attack, v. 4.[6]

The Lord will heal physical ailments. The blind will see and the deaf will hear. While Matthew 11:5 and Luke 7:22 draw on this verse, they do not give the final fulfillment of the verse. The Lord's ministry of healing was only a foretaste of greater blessings to come. The kingdom will be a time of good health for all, cf. 29:18, v. 5. The lame will leap like the "hart" (or "stag"). The "dumb," those not able to speak, will sing. The Lord will also heal the land. Springs of water will break out in the wilderness and "streams" (or "ravines," *nahal*, see 7:19) filled with water will flow in the "desert" (again, Arabah, cf. v. 1), cf. 41:17–20, v. 6.[7]

---

[5]Kleinig, p. 117, understands "vengeance" (*naqam*) and "recompense" (*gᵉmûl*) as "synonyms for salvation." While these bring deliverance to God's people, the words themselves are not synonyms of salvation. In this context, both *naqam* and *gᵉmûl* refer to actions by which God delivers His people.

[6]Barnes, I, 503, distinguishes between God and Messiah. He understands the verse to say that God destroys the enemies to prepare the way for the coming of Messiah. In opposition to this, the Bible teaches that the Lord will judge the nations, Matt. 25:31–46; John 5:22; Rev. 20:11–15.

[7]Henry, p. 196, spiritualizes the passage. He makes the "waters" and "streams" represent the outpouring of the Holy Spirit on the Gentiles. The "parched ground" and "thirsty land" in v. 7 are those without forgiveness of their sins. The "pool" and "spring of water" in v. 7 are the gospel as it goes forth to the unsaved. The "habitations of dragons," v. 7, are Gentile cities. The establishment of Christian churches turns these into productive areas, "grass with reeds and rushes." The interpretation is highly subjective, depending only on the imagination of the author. There is nothing here to suggest anything but a literal understanding of the passage.

7 *And the parched ground shall become a pool, and the thirsty land springs of water: in the habitation of dragons, where each lay, shall be grass with reeds and rushes.*

8 *And an highway shall be there, and a way, and it shall be called The way of holiness; the unclean shall not pass over it; but it shall be for those: the wayfaring men, though fools, shall not err therein.*

9 *No lion shall be there, nor any ravenous beast shall go up thereon, it shall not be found there; but the redeemed shall walk there:*

10 *And the ransomed of the Lord shall return, and come to Zion with songs and everlasting joy upon their heads: they shall obtain joy and gladness, and sorrow and sighing shall flee away.*

7–10 The "parched ground" (*šarab*) will become a pool of water.[8] The "thirsty land" will become a source of springs. In the desolate regions where "dragons" (or "serpents") make their lair, the grass will become "reeds and rushes."[9] The phrase "reeds and rushes" is significant because these grow along rivers. The picture is of an abundant supply of water to the former wilderness, v. 7.

The Lord will make a "highway" (*maslûl*)[10] in the land for the use of His people alone. The name "way of holiness" indicates that only the holy people use the road. The "unclean" (*ṭameʾ*, see 6:5) cannot travel along it; cf. 11:16; 19:23; 40:3–4. Here *ṭameʾ* describes wicked individuals; cf. 64:6. The rest of the verse reads better, "it shall be for those who walk upon the way. Fools will not wander on it." The "fools" (*ʾewîlîm*, see 19:11) are morally wicked people who have turned from God; cf. Proverbs 1:7.[11] They are among the "unclean" already mentioned and

---

[8]Smith, I, 441; Skinner, *Isaiah I–XXXIX*, pp. 259–60; and Cowles, p. 264, take *šarab* as "mirage." Skinner says, "the illusion which mocks the thirsty caravan shall become a reality." The problem with this view is that *šarab* occurs only here and in 49:10. In neither case does the context support "mirage." The parallelism argues for "parched ground" here. The word also occurs in Ecclus. 43:22 modifying *dšn*, giving the phrase "parched grass."

[9]Young, II, 452, translates "green grass for reed and rush." While the *lamed* preposition has broad uses, the sense "in place of" is rare. The more normal sense expresses result. In addition, all through vv. 5–7, Isaiah speaks of undesirable things becoming more desirable. Here grass, which may grow in barren places, becomes reeds and rushes, which require abundant water.

[10]The word *maslûl* is a *hapax legomenon*. The verb, however, and numerous related words occur so that the meaning is not in doubt. The word *maslûl* seems to be a variant spelling of *mesillâ*, also "highway," a word that occurs several times, e.g., 7:3; 11:16; 19:23; 40:3; 49:11.

[11]Delitzsch, II, 79, refers the "fools" to "simple ones." He comments that the road is so clear "that even an idiot could not miss it." Barnes, I, 507; Rawlinson, I, 569; and Vine,

therefore will not be allowed to travel the road, v. 8. The road will be safe; no dangerous beasts will travel it.[12] This will let the "redeemed" (g^e'ûlîm)[13] walk safely. Because of the conditions placed upon the Kinsman-Redeemer in Leviticus, where the OT develops the concept, the go'el is an important type of Christ. The go'el relationship involved five elements:

(1) an impoverished condition, Leviticus 25:47, picturing man's spiritual condition apart from Jesus Christ;

(2) a kinsman relationship, Leviticus 25:48–49, established by the Lord through His birth as the son of Mary;

(3) the willingness of the redeemer, Leviticus 25:25, shown by Christ in coming into this world;

(4) the ability of the redeemer, Leviticus 25:50–52, seen in Christ's successful resistance of Satan's temptations; and

(5) the resulting relationship of the redeemed, Leviticus 25:53, acquired by believers when they place their faith in Jesus Christ as Savior.

This is an important theological concept with the go'el regularly suggesting the redemptive work of Christ, v. 9. Those who have been "ransomed" (padâ, see 1:27) from their sin by the blood of Christ will travel to "Zion," Jerusalem. They will rejoice as they go, singing and with a sense of lasting joy.[14] There will be no sorrow to torment them. With minor changes, the verse occurs again in 51:11, v. 10.

---

p. 72, adopt this view. Leupold, I, 541, makes this refer to the "inexperienced," those who have not used the road before. The noun 'ᵉwîlîm, however, does not refer to a simple or inexperienced person. It regularly denotes a morally wicked man with no fear of God. It retains this meaning here.

[12]Continuing his allegorical interpretation of the chapter, Henry, p. 196, makes the "lion" represent Satan. The "ravenous beast" is one "from an untoward generation." "Zion" is first the "gospel church," then "the heavenly Zion." This approach ignores basic principles of Bible interpretation.

[13]This is the first of twenty-four appearances in Isaiah. The root g'l also occurs at 41:14; 43:1, 14; 44:6, 22, 23, 24; 47:4; 48:17, 20; 49:7, 26; 51:10; 52:3, 9; 54:5, 8; 59:20; 60:16; 62:12; 63:4, 9, 16.

[14]McKenzie, p. 10, considers the "joy upon their heads" a metaphor of joy. This has a basis in "a cultic practice . . . of wearing wreaths or garlands to symbolize rejoicing." It is difficult to see, however, how we can ascribe a cultic practice to believers. It is also difficult to see how a short-lived wreath of flowers or plants can represent "everlasting joy."

Practical Application from Chapter 35

The Glorious Future
1. Renewal of the Land. The barren land of Palestine will flourish with plants and flowers, v. 1. It will be like the heavily forested Lebanon mountains and the fruitful regions of Mt. Carmel and the Plain of Sharon, v. 2. There will be abundant water, v. 6*b.* Places that formerly had no water will become sources of water. The dens of snakes will grow "reeds and rushes" along the now flowing rivers, v. 7.

2. Restoration of the People. The weak become strong, v. 3. God Himself will come to defend them, v. 4. The blind will see, the deaf will hear, v. 5, the lame will leap, and the dumb will sing, v. 6*a.* There will be safety in the land. Travelers need not fear the actions of the wicked, v. 8, nor the attack of wild beasts, v. 9. The redeemed will come with rejoicing to Zion. There will be no need to grieve, v. 10.

ISAIAH 36

V. Historical Interlude 36:1–39:8

Chapters 36–39 parallel in large part II Kings 18:13–20:19. There are differences, however. The author of Kings adds some details, e.g., Sennacherib's false agreement, II Kings 18:14–16, and omits some minor details, e.g., Hezekiah's recovery, 39:1; cf. II Kings 20:12. Isaiah likewise adds some details, e.g., Hezekiah's psalm of praise, 38:9–20, and omits minor details, e.g., Tartan and Rabsaris, 36:2; cf. II Kings 18:17. In general, Isaiah's account is shorter. The question naturally arises, "Who is the original author?" Did the author of Kings borrow from Isaiah, or did Isaiah borrow from the author of Kings?[1] Did both the authors of Kings and Isaiah borrow from a third source?[2]

In my judgment, both draw on an unknown source. If either narrative had only deletions, it would be easy to make the fuller narrative the original. With the narratives having both additions and deletions, it is more likely that both drew from a third source. In addition, if the record in Kings is made the original, the passage in Isaiah must reflect the work of a late editor. Without any compelling evidence in favor of this, I cannot accept this approach to Isaiah.

The historical section introduces Babylon as the new enemy of the Jews. Up to this point, Isaiah's prophecies have often discussed Judah's relationship with Assyria. Over and over, he has foretold the supernatural deliverance from Sennacherib's invasion. Beginning with c. 40, however, he begins to focus on Babylon as the primary threat to Judah. The historical section makes this transition. Chapters 36–37 conclude the emphasis on Assyria. Chapter 38 relates a personal incident involving Hezekiah. This serves as motivation for the Babylonian ruler to contact

---

[1]The parallel passage in II Chron. 32:1–21 is later than either the Kings narrative or Isaiah's record. Traditionally, Ezra wrote the Book of Chronicles ca. 400 B.C.

[2]Among others, Leupold, I, 546; Näglesbach, p. 372; and Mauchline, p. 229, make the author of Kings the original and Isaiah the copy. Among others, Fausset, p. 671; Barnes, II, 2; and Alexander, II, 44, make Isaiah the original and Kings the copy. Among others, Rawlinson, II, 1; Cowles, p. 267; and Motyer, *The Prophecy of Isaiah,* p. 286, think that both accounts come from a third source. As noted in the introduction, Isaiah acted as the court historian, II Chron. 26:22; 32:32. For this reason, Cowles suggests that Isaiah had written an earlier account of the Assyrian invasion, then borrowed from it to write these chapters. The view is possible but cannot be proven.

1 *Now it came to pass in the fourteenth year of king Hezekiah, that Sennacherib king of Assyria came up against all the defenced cities of Judah, and took them.*
2 *And the king of Assyria sent Rabshakeh from Lachish to Jerusalem unto king Hezekiah with a great army. And he stood by the conduit of the upper pool in the highway of the fuller's field.*
3 *Then came forth unto him Eliakim, Hilkiah's son, which was over the house, and Shebna the scribe, and Joah, Asaph's son, the recorder.*

Hezekiah in c. 39. The visit introduces Babylon, later to become Judah's primary enemy.

A. Assyria's Oppression 36:1–21

According to II Kings 18:14–16, Hezekiah paid Sennacherib a tribute of three hundred talents of silver and thirty talents of gold. Instead of turning back from Judah, the Assyrian king continued his conquest. Undoubtedly, he felt that there was sufficient wealth in Judah to justify his continued invasion. Isaiah omits the record of II Kings 18:14–16, possibly not wanting to refer to the king's lapse of faith in failing to trust the Lord. He records instead this continued invasion by the Assyrian army.

1–3 (II Kings 18:13, 17–18) Hezekiah ruled Judah ca. 715–687 B.C.[3] The invasion in his "fourteenth year" took place ca. 701 B.C. The Assyrian records of Sennacherib describe his third campaign: "Hezekiah the Jew who did not bow down to my yoke, forty-six of his strong cities, walled forts, and numberless small cities which were in their vicinity by

---

[3]The chronology of Hezekiah is difficult. We know from the Assyrian records that Sennacherib invaded Judah in 701 B.C. The record here, then, indicates that Hezekiah's accession to the throne took place in 715 B.C. Second Kings 18:1–2 tells us that Hezekiah was twenty-five years old at the beginning of his rule, which was the third year of Hoshea's reign in Israel. According to vv. 9–10, Shalmaneser began his siege of Samaria four years later and conquered the city in Hezekiah's sixth year. We know that Samaria fell in 721 B.C. This places Hezekiah's rule as beginning ca. 727 B.C. Different attempts have been made to reconcile these numbers. Price, p. 150; Von Orelli, p. 197; and Näglesbach, p. 377, suggest that the reference to Hezekiah's fourteenth year relates more to the fourteenth year after his sickness rather than to his reign. This disagrees with II Kings 18:9–10. Wright, p. 76, suggests that there were two campaigns of Sennacherib against Jerusalem, one in 701 B.C. and another in 690 B.C. Isaiah 36–37 refer to the second campaign. The Assyrian annals do not support the idea of two campaigns. Rawlinson, II, 1, says, "there is an irreconcilable difference between this note of time . . . and the Assyrian inscriptions." If we assume a period of coregency between Hezekiah and his father, Ahaz, we can harmonize the dates. The passage in Kings refers to Hezekiah as coregent with Ahaz, ca. 727 B.C. The passage in Isaiah refers to him when he is the sole ruler. This explanation does not solve all of the problems of Hezekiah's chronology, but it at least harmonizes II Kings 18 with Isaiah 36.

4 *And Rabshakeh said unto them, Say ye now to Hezekiah, Thus saith
the great king, the king of Assyria, What confidence is this wherein
thou trustest?*

5 *I say, sayest thou, (but they are but vain words) I have counsel and
strength for war: now on whom dost thou trust, that thou rebellest
against me?*

6 *Lo, thou trustest in the staff of this broken reed, on Egypt; whereon
if a man lean, it will go into his hand, and pierce it: so is Pharaoh
king of Egypt to all that trust in him.*

means of well-stamped embankments and bringing near battering rams,
assaulting by foot soldiers, breaches, tunnels and ladders, I besieged, I
conquered. 200,150 people, young and old, male and female, horses,
mules, asses, camels, oxen and sheep which were numberless I drove out
from among them and counted as booty. Himself, like a bird in a cage,
within Jerusalem, his royal residence, I shut up. I cast up siege walls
around him. . . ."[4] This record supports the statement here that Assyria
"came against all the defenced cities of Judah, and took them," v. 1.

Sennacherib sends the "Rabshakeh," a title indicating the "chief officer," to negotiate with Hezekiah. Second Kings 18:17 tells us that "Tartan" and "Rabsaris" accompany him. These are also titles. The "Tartan"
commands the Assyrian troops; cf. 20:1. The "Rabshakeh" was likely the
second-in-command under the "Tartan." The "Rabsaris" was the chief
eunuch, possibly the head of the servants to the king and his nobles.
Leading his army, the Rabshakeh comes from Lachish, about twenty-five
miles southwest of Jerusalem. The Assyrian records tell us that Lachish
was the center of the Assyrian army's operations. This officer meets with
the aides of Hezekiah to negotiate. The meeting place, "the conduit of
the upper pool in the highway of the fuller's field," lies west of the Jaffa
gate in the Valley of Hinnom; cf. 7:3. It was close enough to the wall
that the Jews could hear the talking (cf. v. 11), v. 2.

Three Jewish leaders meet with the Assyrians. Eliakim, the son of
Hilkiah, previously mentioned in 22:15–25, is now "over the house," the
steward. Shebna, formerly the steward but now the "scribe," cf.
22:15–19, records notes of the meeting. Joah, the son of Asaph, is the
"recorder," keeping the historical and legal records of the land. Because
of their high positions, the three represent Hezekiah in the meeting, v. 3.

4–6 (II Kings 18:19–21) The Assyrian leader speaks to the Jews.
They are on his own level of authority, so he assumes they will repeat

---

[4]Adapted from *ANET*, p. 288.

7 But if thou say to me, We trust in the Lord our God: is it not he, whose high places and whose altars Hezekiah hath taken away, and said to Judah and to Jerusalem, Ye shall worship before this altar?

accurately his words to Hezekiah. He begins by criticizing the Jews: "What confidence is this wherein thou trusteth?" In other words, why do you rely on Egypt, v. 4? Hezekiah may say he has "counsel and strength for war" but these are "vain words" ($d^e bar\text{-}s^e patayim$).[5] Who could Hezekiah trust that would let him rebel against "me," Assyria, v. 5? He is trusting in a "broken reed." The reed is an appropriate symbol of Egypt since the Nile River was lined with reeds; cf. 19:6. The picture is of leaning on a reed when it suddenly breaks. Part of the reed pierces the body as it falls. In the same way, if Hezekiah continues to lean on Egypt, it will hurt him, v. 6.

7 (II Kings 18:22) The Rabshakeh's second criticism is of Hezekiah's reforms. To purify the worship of the nation, the king had stopped the people from worshiping at "high places." He had cut down the wooden pillars erected in worship of Asherah. He had broken into pieces the bronze serpent made by Moses; cf. II Kings 18:4; II Chronicles 30:14; 31:1. All of these reforms carried out commands previously given by the Lord, Deuteronomy 12:2–3, 5–6, 13–14. In some way, the news of these radical changes has come to Assyria. The Assyrian leader shows his ignorance of God's Word by criticizing the changes. He accuses Hezekiah of offending Israel's gods, v. 7.

---

[5]The phrase $d^e bar\text{-}s^e patayim$, "words of the lips," is idiomatic for "vain words"; cf. Prov. 14:23. This supports the reading *ʾamarta*, "you say," as in II Kings 18:20, rather than the $k^e t\hat{i}b$ *ʾamartî*, "I say." If we retain the $k^e t\hat{i}b$, as in the AV, we must add something to the verse if it is Hezekiah speaking. About twenty Hebrew mss, including 1QIsaᵃ, along with the Vulgate, support the change. Leupold, I, 549, follows the MT. He understands the expression as saying that the "strategy and might for war . . . amount to mere words." Delitzsch, II, 87, relates the "counsel and strength for war" as the promises of help from Egypt. These are "mere boasting." Slotki, p. 167, alternates speakers. Hezekiah calls Sennacherib's assertion in v. 4 "vain words." The Assyrian replies that Hezekiah has no counsel or strength for war. This approach is not natural. In view of the close parallel to II Kings 18, I would adopt the $q^e r\hat{e}$.

8 Now therefore give pledges, I pray thee, to my master the king of Assyria, and I will give thee two thousand horses, if thou be able on
thy part to set riders upon them.

9 How then wilt thou turn away the face of one captain of the least of
my master's servants, and put thy trust on Egypt for chariots and for
horsemen?

10 And am I now come up without the Lord against this land to destroy
it? the Lord said unto me, Go up against this land, and destroy it.

8–9 (II Kings 18:23–24) The Assyrian officer appeals to the Jews to
"give pledges" (better "make a bargain"). He wants them to pledge loyalty to Sennacherib. In turn, he will give them two thousand horses to
ride if they can find riders for them. The statement is sarcastic. The Jews
had depended on Egypt for horses, 31:1, but they had not supplied them.
The suggestion that Judah does not have two thousand riders points out
their weakness, v. 8. With this weakness, how will they resist one of the
lesser Assyrian "captain[s]" (*paḥat*)?[6] Why does Hezekiah continue to
trust in Egypt, v. 9?

10 (II Kings 18:25) The Assyrian again shows his ignorance of God.
He claims to have a divine commission to destroy Judah. Since many of
the Jewish cities have fallen to the Assyrian army, he assumes that Israel's God is angry with them. He translates this into a commission to
punish Judah. He hopes by this to frighten the Jews into submission. The
claim is false, proved by Assyria's failure to destroy the land. The Rabshakeh, however, states his divine commission in the effort of frighten-
ing the Jews, v. 10.

---

[6]Slotki, p. 167, understands *paḥat* as "the governor of a province." It is true that the
word can denote a governor, e.g., I Kings 10:15; Ezra 8:36; Neh. 2:7. The context here,
however, calls for a military leader, a commander of troops as in I Kings 20:24; Jer.
51:23, 28, 57.

11　Then said Eliakim and Shebna and Joah unto Rabshakeh, Speak, I
　　pray thee, unto thy servants in the Syrian language; for we under-
　　stand it: and speak not to us in the Jews' language, in the ears of the
　　people that are on the wall.
12　But Rabshakeh said, Hath my master sent me to thy master and to
　　thee to speak these words? hath he not sent me to the men that sit
　　upon the wall, that they may eat their own dung, and drink their own
　　piss with you?
13　Then Rabshakeh stood, and cried with a loud voice in the Jews' lan-
　　guage, and said, Hear ye the words of the great king, the king of
　　Assyria.
14　Thus saith the king, Let not Hezekiah deceive you: for he shall not
　　be able to deliver you.
15　Neither let Hezekiah make you trust in the Lord, saying, The Lord
　　will surely deliver us: this city shall not be delivered into the hand of
　　the king of Assyria.
16　Hearken not to Hezekiah: for thus saith the king of Assyria, Make an
　　agreement with me by a present, and come out to me: and eat ye
　　every one of his vine, and every one of his fig tree, and drink ye
　　every one the waters of his own cistern;
17　Until I come and take you away to a land like your own land, a land
　　of corn and wine, a land of bread and vineyards.

11–17 (II Kings 18:26–32) The Jewish delegation urges the Assyrian
officer to speak in Aramaic. At this time, Aramaic was the trade language of the biblical world. While Aramaic and Hebrew are closely related, there are many differences. The common people would not have
been familiar with these. Eliakim, Shebna, and Joah want to keep the ne-
gotiations away from the people, v. 11. The Assyrian, however, responds
with a rhetorical question. Has he been sent only to Hezekiah and his
representatives? Has he not been sent to the weak "men" (ʾᵉnôš, see
2:11) seated on the wall where they can hear? They are the ones who
will eat their own waste products when famine sets in due to the siege,
v. 12. He cries directly to the people, urging them to hear Sennacherib's
message, v. 13. He warns them not to let Hezekiah deceive them with
false promises of hope. He will not be able to deliver them from the
Assyrian army, v. 14. They should not believe that the Lord will deliver
them. They should reject Hezekiah's statements of divine help, v. 15.
Sennacherib has made them a generous offer. If they will "make an
agreement with me by a present" (bᵉrakâ, better "make a blessing")[7]

---

[7]The word bᵉrakâ does not occur again with this sense. Cowles, p. 273, understands
bᵉrakâ in its more usual sense of "blessing." The Rabshakeh hopes to persuade them to

18 *Beware lest Hezekiah persuade you, saying, The Lord will deliver us. Hath any of the gods of the nations delivered his land out of the hand of the king of Assyria?*
19 *Where are the gods of Hamath and Arphad? where are the gods of Sepharvaim? and have they delivered Samaria out of my hand?*
20 *Who are they among all the gods of these lands, that have delivered their land out of my hand, that the Lord should deliver Jerusalem out of my hand?*
21 *But they held their peace, and answered him not a word: for the king's commandment was, saying, Answer him not.*

with him, they can return to their dwellings. The sequence of imperatives here indicates that making a blessing is the condition. The certain consequence is coming to the Assyrian king, then enjoying the fruit of their vines, eating figs, and drinking water from their wells. Making a blessing is idiomatic for entering into an agreement that will bring blessing to both parties. Each one can eat the food he has grown and drink the water from his own "cistern" (or "well"), v. 16.[8] At some future time, the Assyrian king will settle them in another land. To reassure the people, he promises that it will be "a land of corn and wine, a land of bread and vineyards." The resettlement of captive nations was a custom of the Assyrians; cf. II Kings 17:6, 24; 18:11. This was meant to destroy ties to the old nation. It separated the people from their gods, thought to be localized deities, and made it more likely that they would adopt the gods of their conquerors. Finally, it minimized the chances of revolt, v. 17.

18–21 (II Kings 18:33–36) The Rabshakeh again warns the people against letting Hezekiah "persuade" (or "mislead") them. He considers Hezekiah's trust in the Lord a vain hope and therefore misleading. He asks rhetorically if any of the gods of other nations have delivered their people from Assyria, v. 18. To illustrate his point, he mentions several

---

yield to him and gain the blessing of peace for themselves. Kaiser, *Isaiah 13–39*, p. 382, considers b*e*rakâ a euphemism for making peace. Näglesbach, p. 379, makes it a "treaty" by metonymy, the blessing standing for the agreement. Alexander, II, 50, understands the word as referring to a greeting, entering into "amicable intercourse." A. Murtonen, "The Use and Meaning of the Words l*e*bârek and b*e*råkå*h* in the Old Testament," *VT* 9:174, understands that "both parties 'bless' each other, i.e., work for the benefit of one another." All of these views wind up at the same place, entering into an agreement with Assyria that will bring blessing to them.

[8]Technically, a cistern (*bôr*) is a reservoir of some kind. In Palestine, the people used these to collect rainwater for future use. The word *bôr*, however, is broader than this. It may also refer to a well, Deut. 6:11; I Sam. 19:22, or fountain, Jer. 6:7. All of these sources of water are in view here.

> 22 *Then came Eliakim, the son of Hilkiah, that was over the household,*
> *and Shebna the scribe, and Joah, the son of Asaph, the recorder, to*
> *Hezekiah with their clothes rent, and told him the words of Rab-*
> *shakeh.*

cities recently defeated by Assyria. Hamath, a Syrian city located on the
Orontes River, had fallen to Assyria, ca. 720 B.C. Arphad (better
"Arpad"), also a Syrian city, was about one hundred miles north of
Hamath. Assyria conquered Arpad several times, including its defeat by
Sargon, ca. 720 B.C. Sepharvaim is always mentioned in connection with
Hamath. This leads to making it a Syrian city also, probably located close
by. Its location is not known although some identify it with Sibraim, a
city conquered ca. 727 B.C. by Shalmaneser V. Samaria was the capital of
Israel, the northern ten tribes. It fell to Assyria ca. 721 B.C., v. 19. Who of
the gods of these cities have delivered their people? These gods have not
withstood the Assyrian power. Neither will the God of Jerusalem deliver
it. Hezekiah has commanded the people not to respond to the Assyrians.
They remain quiet at the Rabshakeh's words, v. 21.

B. Hezekiah's Response 36:22–37:38
1. Hezekiah's Plea and Isaiah's Response 36:22–37:7

22 (II Kings 18:37) Hezekiah's delegates return to him with their
clothes torn, an outward sign of their inward grief; cf. Genesis 37:34;
II Kings 5:7–8. They repeat to Hezekiah the words of the Assyrian
leader, v. 22.

Practical Applications from Chapter 36

1. The Lack of Spiritual Understanding by the Heathen

   a. Pride in their accomplishments. The Assyrian leader cannot believe that Judah would fight against "me," Assyria, v. 5. He re-
   cites for the people the past conquests of other cities (note "my
   . . . my . . . my"), vv. 18-20.

   b. Criticism of Hezekiah's reforms. Hezekiah has stopped the
   people from idolatry and from worshiping at altars scattered
   through the land. The Rabshakeh does not realize that these steps
   followed the commands of God. He thinks of them as offending
   Judah's God, v. 7.

   c. Claim to a divine commission. The Assyrian commander justifies
   the attack on Judah by relating it to Judah's God. He claims

falsely that the Lord Himself has sent him to destroy the nation, v. 10.

d. Misunderstanding of God's being

(1) The Rabshakeh fails to recognize the power of Judah's God. He claims that the Lord will not be able to deliver Judah. Although Hezekiah may try to persuade the people that their God is powerful, He cannot defeat the Assyrians, v. 15.

(2) The Assyrian military commander also fails to recognize the uniqueness of God. He compares Him to the gods of heathen cities that have not delivered their people from Assyria. Judah's "God," however, is not like the "gods" of the heathen. He is the only true God, vv. 18-20.

2. God's Punishment of Sin in His People. The Lord allows the Assyrian army to come "against all the defenced cities of Judah," v. 1. We know from the historical records of Assyria that Sennacherib did indeed defeat many cities within Judah. He came away with substantial spoil including both people and wealth. Had the Rabshakeh limited his claim to a divine commission, v. 10, he would have been correct. The Lord did use Assyria as a rod to punish the sin in Judah; cf. 10:5-6. The incident well illustrates God's efforts to purify His people by punishing their sin; cf. Job 5:17; Psalm 94:12; Proverbs 3:11-12; Hebrews 12:5-6; Revelation 3:19.

1 *And it came to pass, when king Hezekiah heard it, that he rent his clothes, and covered himself with sackcloth, and went into the house of the Lord.*

2 *And he sent Eliakim, who was over the household, and Shebna the scribe, and the elders of the priests covered with sackcloth, unto Isaiah the prophet the son of Amoz.*

3 *And they said unto him, Thus saith Hezekiah, This day is a day of trouble, and of rebuke, and of blasphemy: for the children are come to the birth, and there is not strength to bring forth.*

4 *It may be the Lord thy God will hear the words of Rabshakeh, whom the king of Assyria his master hath sent to reproach the living God, and will reprove the words which the Lord thy God hath heard: wherefore lift up thy prayer for the remnant that is left.*

5 *So the servants of king Hezekiah came to Isaiah.*

6 *And Isaiah said unto them, Thus shall ye say unto your master, Thus saith the Lord, Be not afraid of the words that thou hast heard, wherewith the servants of the king of Assyria have blasphemed me.*

7 *Behold, I will send a blast upon him, and he shall hear a rumour, and return to his own land; and I will cause him to fall by the sword in his own land.*

ISAIAH 37

Isaiah continues his narrative giving the account of the Assyrian siege of Jerusalem. While c. 36 has focused on the Assyrian threat, c. 37 tells of Hezekiah's response to the threat. There is no question of trusting in help that might come from Egypt. The king shows by his actions that he looks only to the Lord for deliverance from the Assyrian army. The Lord responds to Hezekiah's faith. He first sends Isaiah to assure the king of Jerusalem's safety. Then, in a brief account (vv. 36–38), the record tells of the Assyrian defeat.

1–2 (II Kings 19:1–2) At the news from Eliakim, Shebna, and Joah, Hezekiah himself tears his clothes and dons sackcloth. These outward actions show his grief at the threat to the city; cf. II Samuel 3:31. He then goes to the temple, the place of prayer in times of national emergency, v. 1. He also sends Eliakim and Shebna to lead a delegation to Isaiah; cf. 36:3. The group also includes the "elders of the priests," the leading priests. These also put on "sackcloth" to show their grief over the Assyrian threat, v. 2.

3–7 (II Kings 19:3–7) The delegation gives the news to Isaiah. They tell him of Hezekiah's reaction, speaking of the day as one of "trouble, and of rebuke, and of blasphemy [$n^{e\jmath}a\d{s}\^a$, or 'contempt'].["][1] Using the figure of childbirth, in which the mother has no strength to bear her child, Hezekiah has pictured a life-threatening situation. Apparently, this was a proverbial expression (see Hos. 13:13), v. 3. The delegation expresses their hope that God will hear the disdainful words spoken against Him by the Rabshakeh. His master has sent him to "reproach the living God." God "may" ($^\jmath\^ulay$) "reprove" ($yaka\d{h}$, see 1:18) Assyria for their speech against Him. The use of $^\jmath\^ulay$, "may, perhaps," recognizes that Judah has no claim on God at this point. Their sins made them deserving of punishment. The delegation urges Isaiah to pray for the "remnant," the Jews shut up in the city, cf. II Kings 19:4, v. 4. Verse 5 recaps vv. 2–4, the visit of the Jews to their prophet, v. 5.

Isaiah responds. They should tell Hezekiah not to fear the threats made by the "servants" (na^car) of the Assyrian king. Isaiah's words may be satirical. The word na^car means "boy, youth, child." The meaning "servant" comes from the age at which so many began their service. In using the term, Isaiah does not stress age so much as immaturity. They speak words without knowing the consequences of their speech.

The threats from Assyria have "blasphemed" God by denying His power to deliver His own, v. 6. The Lord will "send a blast" (lit. "give a spirit") that will cause Sennacherib to listen to a "rumour" (better "report"). Verse 9 suggests that the "rumour" is the report of Tirhakah's arrival.[2] The spirit of fear will cause him to abandon his attempt at conquest. He will return to his homeland. The Lord will cause him to die in his own land, v. 7.

---

[1]Rawlinson, II, 17, understands $n^{e\jmath}a\d{s}\^a$ as "blasphemy" since this is its meaning in other places. The meaning of "contempt," however, fits as well in the passages that he cites. Alexander, II, 53, interprets $n^{e\jmath}a\d{s}\^a$ as "blasphemy." He states, "the oral expression of contempt for God is blasphemy." This is interpretation. Skinner, *Isaiah I–XXXIX*, p. 267, argues that $n^{e\jmath}a\d{s}\^a$ here means "rejection" since the word differs in its pointing from Neh. 9:18, 26; Ezek. 35:12. The pointing there is $ne^\jmath a\d{s}\^ot$. The view is possible.

[2]Henry, p. 200, makes the rumor the news of the slaughter of the Assyrian army. From the description here, this cannot be correct. The slaughtered army is Sennacherib's own army. Verse 33 makes it clear that the army does not approach Jerusalem. Among others, Mauchline, p. 231; Wade, p. 231; and Whitehouse, pp. 41, 359, suggest that the rumor involved a rebellion in Babylon. We do not have enough evidence to be dogmatic about the cause.

8 So Rabshakeh returned, and found the king of Assyria warring against Libnah: for he had heard that he was departed from Lachish.

9 And he heard say concerning Tirhakah king of Ethiopia, He is come forth to make war with thee. And when he heard it, he sent messengers to Hezekiah, saying,

10 Thus shall ye speak to Hezekiah king of Judah, saying, Let not thy God, in whom thou trustest, deceive thee, saying, Jerusalem shall not be given into the hand of the king of Assyria.

11 Behold, thou hast heard what the kings of Assyria have done to all lands by destroying them utterly; and shalt thou be delivered?

12 Have the gods of the nations delivered them which my fathers have destroyed, as Gozan, and Haran, and Rezeph, and the children of Eden which were in Telassar?

13 Where is the king of Hamath, and the king of Arphad, and the king of the city of Sepharvaim, Hena, and Ivah?

2. Sennacherib's Strategy and Rabshakeh's Threat 37:8–13

8–9a (II Kings 19:8–9a) Since the Rabshakeh's initial effort to gain Judah's surrender has failed, he returns to Sennacherib, probably to get further instructions. Word comes to him that the king is at Libnah, about ten miles due north of Lachish, v. 8. The king has heard that Tirhakah, the king of Ethiopia, is coming with reinforcements, v. 9a.[3]

9b–13 (II Kings 19:9b–13) After hearing "it," the Rabshakeh's report, he sends messengers back to Hezekiah. Apparently, he hopes to bring

---

[3]The reference to Tirhakah is controversial. Kaiser, *Isaiah 13–39*, p. 375, is typical when he says, "in the year 701, Tirhakah was not king, and, in view of his youth, was probably not in a position to be in command of the Egyptian army. He did not ascend the throne until the year 690/89." Motyer, *The Prophecy of Isaiah*, p. 280, rebuts this: "It is now known . . . that he was a young man of twenty or so in 701 B.C. . . . He may have been accorded the title of king proleptically, since he did not accede to Egypt's throne until 690." Tirhakah was the third king of the twenty-fifth dynasty in Egypt. Piankhi, king of Ethiopia, conquered most of Egypt, ca. 725 B.C. His younger brother, Shabako, defeated the Egyptian ruler Bochoris to end the twenty-fourth dynasty. He became pharaoh, ruling from Thebes. His nephew Shabitko followed him as pharaoh. Shabitko's brother Tirhakah followed him on the throne, ca. 690 B.C. The reference to his being a "king" at this time is explained differently: (1) Isaiah wrote the biblical record later, after Tirhakah became king. The reference to Sennacherib's death ca. 681 B.C., v. 37, supports this view. (2) Tirhakah may have been coregent with his brother and uncle at this time. This is probably not the case since Tirhakah was only nine or ten years old at this time. (3) Tirhakah was a "king" in the sense of being a highly placed military leader of royal blood. We do not have enough information to be certain. It is, however, reasonable to refer to him as "king." Kenneth A. Kitchen, *Ancient Orient and Old Testament* (Chicago: Inter-Varsity Press, 1966), pp. 82–84, discusses the chronology of Tirhakah.

14 And Hezekiah received the letter from the hand of the messengers, and read it: and Hezekiah went up unto the house of the Lord, and spread it before the Lord.

about a last-minute surrender before Tirhakah arrives, v. 9*b*. The messengers are to tell Hezekiah not to rely on his God for deliverance, v. 10. The Assyrian kings have destroyed other lands "utterly" (*haḥerîm*, see 11:15). Why should Hezekiah think he will be any different, v. 11? He asks rhetorically, "Have the gods of the nations delivered them?" The question reflects the ancient belief that every nation had its own gods. Sennacherib's question shows his belief that the gods of Assyria were stronger than the gods of other nations. His "fathers" have destroyed these gods. The title "fathers" refers to earlier Assyrian emperors, not to actual ancestors. His father, Sargon, had been a general in the army, who usurped the throne after the death of Shalmaneser. Sennacherib was only the second king in his dynasty.

The king gives several examples of Assyria's power. Gozan, about one hundred miles east of Carchemish, on the Habor River in Mesopotamia, a tributary of the Euphrates River, had fallen earlier to Assyria. Haran was a trading center on the Balikh River in northern Mesopotamia, also a tributary of the Euphrates River. The Assyrians earlier had controlled Haran. Rezeph is present-day Rusafah, south of the Euphrates on the way to Tadmor, an important oasis about 140 miles northeast of Damascus. It was also under the control of the Assyrians. The "children of Eden" may refer to the merchants of Ezekiel 27:23 (see also Amos 1:5), who lived in Telassar (Thelasar, II Kings 19:12). We cannot locate this accurately. All of these cities had fallen to Assyria, v. 12. Hamath, Arphad, and Sepharvaim have been mentioned in 36:19. Hena and Ivah are unknown locations. Other than placing their defeats prior to 701 B.C., we do not know when they fell to Assyria, v. 13.

3. Hezekiah's Repentance and Further Prayer 37:14–20

14 (II Kings 19:14) Second Chronicles 32:17 mentions "letters" written by Sennacherib to Hezekiah. Hezekiah receives the "letter" (lit. "letters"). The plural probably indicates the several pages of the single scroll.[4] Although most lengthy documents were written on a scroll, the

---

[4]Slotki, p. 172, suggests that Sennacherib sent Hezekiah several letters. While this is possible, there is no reason that more than one letter should have been necessary.

15 *And Hezekiah prayed unto the Lord, saying,*
16 *O Lord of hosts, God of Israel, that dwellest between the cherubims, thou art the God, even thou alone, of all the kingdoms of the earth: thou hast made heaven and earth.*
17 *Incline thine ear, O Lord, and hear; open thine eyes, O Lord, and see: and hear all the words of Sennacherib, which hath sent to reproach the living God.*
18 *Of a truth, Lord, the kings of Assyria have laid waste all the nations, and their countries,*
19 *And have cast their gods into the fire: for they were no gods, but the work of men's hands, wood and stone: therefore they have destroyed them.*
20 *Now therefore, O Lord our God, save us from his hand, that all the kingdoms of the earth may know that thou art the Lord, even thou only.*

scroll included individual pages. It is not clear here whether the messengers read the letter orally before giving it to Hezekiah or whether the letter summarized the orally given message. In either case, Hezekiah takes the letter to the temple. He spreads the letter out before the Lord, a symbolic act calling God's attention to the threat. There is no longer any trust in Egypt. Hezekiah goes directly to the Lord for his help, v. 14.

15–20 (II Kings 19:15–19) The king begins to pray, v. 15. He addresses God as the "Lord of hosts," cf. 1:9, the ruler of the hosts of heaven and earth. In addition, He is the "God of Israel," who has chosen the nation as His own. He dwells "between the cherubims" (*yošeb hakkᵉrubîm*). The phrase refers to God's position in the temple between the cherubs that looked down on the mercy seat, Exodus 37:7–9.[5] Hezekiah praises God as the one who is over all the kingdoms of the earth. This view goes radically against the prevailing view of the time since the heathen generally looked on the gods as localized, limited to their own nations; cf. v. 12. Hezekiah has a correct view of God as King. In addition, He is the Creator of heaven and earth, a powerful God and, therefore, able to defeat Assyria, v. 16. Having set forth his belief that

---

[5] Among others, Delitzsch, II, 98; Kaiser, *Isaiah 13–39*, p. 393; and Leslie, p. 93, understand *yošeb hakkᵉrubîm* as "enthroned above the cherubim." They interpret this as referring to God's exalted position above the heavenly beings. While it is true that God has an exalted position, the verb *yašab* normally means "to sit, dwell." It does not have a sense of enthronement. In particular, when used with *hakkᵉrubîm* (I Sam. 4:4; II Sam. 6:2; II Kings 19:15; I Chron. 13:6; Ps. 80:1), the idea of dwelling with the cherubs in the temple makes sense. In I Sam. 4:4; II Sam. 6:2; and I Chron. 13:6, the context specifically mentions the ark of the covenant.

21 *Then Isaiah the son of Amoz sent unto Hezekiah, saying, Thus saith the Lord God of Israel, Whereas thou hast prayed to me against Sennacherib king of Assyria:*

22 *This is the word which the Lord hath spoken concerning him; The virgin, the daughter of Zion, hath despised thee, and laughed thee to scorn; the daughter of Jerusalem hath shaken her head at thee.*

God is mighty, Hezekiah asks Him to hear and see the words of Sennacherib, which have disparaged His ability to deliver Judah, v. 17. He acknowledges that the Assyrians have conquered "all the nations, and their countries" (lit. "all the lands [kol‾ha²ᵃraṣot] and their land").[6] The statement embraces both the defeat of other lands and the oppression of their own land. Hezekiah probably refers to the burdens of taxation and enforced service in the Assyrian army, v. 18. To further establish their conquests, the Assyrians have burned the gods of the nations. These were weak gods, made of wood and stone by craftsmen. The Assyrians therefore have destroyed them, v. 19. Now they intend to do the same to Judah and to Judah's God. Hezekiah therefore begs God to intervene. The deliverance of Judah will show the nations that the Lord is the only true God. Hezekiah's prayer shows a repentant spirit. He no longer depends on Egypt. Hezekiah wants God to receive glory, v. 20.

4. Jehovah's Answer and Isaiah's Prophecy 37:21–35

21–22 (II Kings 19:20–21) Moved by the Holy Spirit to answer Hezekiah's prayer, Isaiah sends an answer to him. The Lord acknowledges his prayer against Sennacherib, v. 21. The Lord describes how Judah will react to Assyria. He speaks of the nation as "the virgin," referring to the fact that the Assyrian has not yet ravished her; cf. 23:12. The "daughter of Zion," the population of Jerusalem, has "despised" (bazâ)[7] Assyria. They have "laughed thee to scorn" (la°ag, or "mocked thee," see 33:19). They have shaken their head at them, a gesture of contempt (cf. Ps. 22:7; 44:14; 109:25; Jer.18:16; Lam. 2:15), v. 22.

---

[6]The idea of the Assyrians oppressing their own land has caused several authors to follow the reading in II Kings 19:17, ²et‾haggôyim, "the nations," rather than kol‾ha²ᵃraṣot, "all the lands." Among others, Delitzsch, II, 99, and Näglesbach, p 384, accept the reading from Kings here. The textual evidence for this change is weak. In view of Isaiah's willingness to edit his source for the historical record, a change here is not surprising. There are numerous differences from the narrative in Kings.

[7]The word bazâ refers to something contemptible, worthy to be disdained or despised. It includes here feelings of scorn.

23 Whom hast thou reproached and blasphemed? and against whom hast thou exalted thy voice, and lifted up thine eyes on high? even against the Holy One of Israel.

24 By thy servants hast thou reproached the Lord, and hast said, By the multitude of my chariots am I come up to the height of the mountains, to the sides of Lebanon; and I will cut down the tall cedars thereof, and the choice fir trees thereof: and I will enter into the height of his border, and the forest of his Carmel.

25 I have digged, and drunk water; and with the sole of my feet have I dried up all the rivers of the besieged places.

23–25 (II Kings 19:22–24) Rhetorically, the Lord asks whom Sennacherib has blasphemed. Clearly, he has spoken against the Lord Himself, v. 23. He has boasted of what he has done. The pronouns "I" and "my" occur seven times in vv. 24–25. He has come to the heights of the Lebanon Mountains, to the "sides" (*yarkâ*, or "extreme parts," see 14:13) of the mountains in the northern part of Palestine. Sennacherib's boast is that nothing has stopped him. He has conquered the heights of Lebanon; he has mastered the remote areas in the mountains. He has cut down the tall cedar trees and choice fir (or "cypress") trees of the mountains. He plans to enter the "height of his border" (*merôm qiṣṣô*) and the "forest of his Carmel" (*ya῾ar karmillô*). The phrase *merôm qiṣṣô* is lit. the "height of his end." It refers to the remote heights of the land. The companion phrase *ya῾ar karmillô* is lit. the "forest of his fruitful field." This likely refers to the fruitful region of Carmel in the north. These boastful statements recap Sennacherib's conquest of the northern part of the land. Syria, Phoenicia, and Israel have fallen to him, v. 24. He has crossed barren lands, digging wells as he needed them and drinking the water. His army is so vast that merely crossing the "rivers of the besieged places [*maṣôr*]," i.e., Egypt, dries them up.[8] This boastful statement describes the cutting off of waters flowing into besieged cities. He pictures the conquest of Egypt as past, confident in his ability to overcome the nation, v. 25.

---

[8]Among others, Leupold, I, 570; Slotki, p. 175; and Young, II, 491, translate *maṣôr* as "Egypt." This is then a boastful statement that the army is so vast that it would dry up the arms of the Nile River in crossing them. The word *maṣôr*, "defence," occurs at 19:6 referring to Egypt.

26 *Hast thou not heard long ago, how I have done it; and of ancient times, that I have formed it? now have I brought it to pass, that thou shouldest be to lay waste defenced cities into ruinous heaps.*

27 *Therefore their inhabitants were of small power, they were dismayed and confounded: they were as the grass of the field, and as the green herb, as the grass on the housetops, and as corn blasted before it be grown up.*

28 *But I know thy abode, and thy going out, and thy coming in, and thy rage against me.*

29 *Because thy rage against me, and thy tumult, is come up into mine ears, therefore will I put my hook in thy nose, and my bridle in thy lips, and I will turn thee back by the way by which thou camest.*

26–29 (II Kings 19:25–28) The Lord now speaks. The phrase "I have done it" indicates that all of these things have been done according to God's plan. He has "formed it" in the sense of planning these circumstances. He has "brought it to pass" for the purpose of humbling Israel. In vv. 24–25 Sennacherib has boasted of what He has done. The Lord now answers with the truths of what He has done. From "long ago," He had "done it," decreed that the Assyrian victories should take place. He has "formed [or 'planned'] it," the conquests of the Assyrians. He now brings to pass the invasion of Assyria into Judah. The statement in vv. 24–25 is one of pride; the statement in v. 26 is one of fact. God has brought Sennacherib into the land for His purposes. The "defenced cities" have been turned into "ruinous heaps," v. 26. The Jews were weak, "of small power." The phrase is idiomatic, lit. "short of hand." This indicates the limitation that kept them from accomplishing what they wished; cf. 50:2; 59:1; Numbers 11:23. They were "dismayed [ḥatat, see 7:8] and confounded" (bôš, or "put to shame," see 1:29). He compares the people to vegetation scorched under the blazing sun. The phrase "grass on the housetops" refers to the sod placed as insulation on the flat-roofed Palestinian houses. The grass growing there would have shallow roots and a lack of water. It would soon die from the heat. The phrase "corn blasted before it be grown up" is better "the fields before the standing grain." The picture is of a barren field before it springs to life with the crops.[9] Once more, the phrase refers to Judah, v. 27.

---

[9]Second Kings 19:26 uses the word šᵉdepâ, "blasted," instead of šᵉdemâ, "field." The AV translates the verse with Kings. There is, however, no reason to abandon the MT at this point. Isaiah regularly shows his individuality in the description. He differs at several places from the author of Kings.

30 *And this shall be a sign unto thee, Ye shall eat this year such as groweth of itself; and the second year that which springeth of the same: and in the third year sow ye, and reap, and plant vineyards, and eat the fruit thereof.*

31 *And the remnant that is escaped of the house of Judah shall again take root downward, and bear fruit upward:*

32 *For out of Jerusalem shall go forth a remnant, and they that escape out of mount Zion: the zeal of the Lord of hosts shall do this.*

The Lord knows the "abode" (or "sitting down") of the Assyrian king. He knows when he goes out and when he comes in. He knows the "rage" of the king against "me," the Lord, v. 28. Because this rage and "tumult" (better "arrogance") have come to God's notice, He will judge the king. He will put a "hook" in his nose and a bridle in his mouth to turn him back to Assyria. The picture of a hook in the nose becomes more vivid from an Assyrian relief in Senjirli, which shows the Ethiopian king Tirhakah with a hook through his lips and tied with a rope to another captive king. While the Lord does not mean the term literally here, it still vividly describes turning Sennacherib around to send him back to Assyria, v. 29.

30–32 (II Kings 19:29–31) The Assyrian troops had prevented the sowing of crops. Although the Lord would turn them away from Judah, it would be some time before the people could raise crops. They would need to acquire livestock and seed, plow the land, sow their seed, raise the crops, and harvest them. For this reason, the people would not sow and reap until the third year. In the meantime, they would eat that which had sprung up naturally. Some crops for them to eat would grow the first year. It was too late to sow the fields, so they would need to eat grain the next year that "springeth of the same [*šaḥîs*],"[10] i.e., came up naturally. They would sow their seed and plant their vineyards the third year and reap the fruit from their labors. This sequence of events would be a "sign" (*ʾôt*, see 7:11) to them of the Lord's control. He will deliver them, v. 30.[11] The mention of crops leads naturally into the next element. The

---

[10] The word *šaḥîs* here and the parallel word *saḥîs* in II Kings 19:29 are *hapax legomena*. It is not possible to tell which form is original or if both forms are original. From the context, the words must parallel *sapîaḥ*, "such as groweth of itself," in meaning.

[11] Henry, p. 203, suggests that the second year was a sabbatic year, Exod. 23:10–11; Lev. 25:2–7. There is, however, no indication in the text of this. Moreover, it would have violated Lev. 25:5 to eat that which grew naturally during a sabbatic year.

33 *Therefore thus saith the Lord concerning the king of Assyria, He shall not come into this city, nor shoot an arrow there, nor come before it with shields, nor cast a bank against it.*
34 *By the way that he came, by the same shall he return, and shall not come into this city, saith the Lord.*
35 *For I will defend this city to save it for mine own sake, and for my servant David's sake.*
36 *Then the angel of the Lord went forth, and smote in the camp of the Assyrians a hundred and fourscore and five thousand: and when they arose early in the morning, behold, they were all dead corpses.*
37 *So Sennacherib king of Assyria departed, and went and returned, and dwelt at Nineveh.*
38 *And it came to pass, as he was worshipping in the house of Nisroch his god, that Adrammelech and Sharezer his sons smote him with the sword; and they escaped into the land of Armenia: and Esarhaddon his son reigned in his stead.*

remnant that had escaped the Assyrians will flourish in the land. The oppression from Assyria was meant to purge the nation of its dross. Now, the nation will take deeper root and bring forth abundantly. They will no longer be a "remnant." Rather, they will multiply to reflect God's blessings, v. 31. From Jerusalem, where the Assyrians had shut them up, the remnant will spread over the land. The "zeal" (*qinʾâ*, see 9:7) of the Lord will accomplish this blessing, v. 32.

33–35 (II Kings 19:32–34) Sennacherib will not enter Jerusalem. He will not even conduct military operations against it. His army will not shoot arrows into the city or come against it with their shields. He will not "cast a bank against it," i.e., raise a siege mound of dirt. The deliverance will be complete, v. 33. Sennacherib will return to Assyria by the same route that he had followed in coming. He will not enter Jerusalem, v. 34. The Lord Himself will "save" (*yašaʿ*, see 17:10) the city. He will do this for "mine own sake," the sake of maintaining His honor. He will uphold His covenant with David to continue the line of David ruling the nation, v. 35.

5. Assyria's Fall and Sennacherib's Death 37:36–38

36–38 (II Kings 19:35–37) In fulfillment of the prophecy, the "angel of the Lord" strikes 185,000 Assyrian soldiers dead. Second Chronicles 32:21 adds that the dead include "all the mighty men of valour, and the leaders and captains in the camp of the king of Assyria." The narrative in

II Kings places the destruction in "that night," immediately following the prophecy of deliverance.[12] The phrase "angel of the Lord" normally refers to the Lord Himself, e.g., Genesis 16:7–11; Exodus 3:2; Psalm 34:7. The phrase occurs more than fifty times in the OT. This is its only occurrence in Isaiah. When the survivors among the Assyrians rise in the morning, they find that the bulk of the army has died.[13] From v. 33, we conclude that the disaster overtakes Sennacherib's army, not the detachment at Jerusalem, v. 36.[14] In terror, prompted by the threat of Egyptian reinforcements, v. 9, and by the devastation of his army, Sennacherib returns to Assyria, v. 37.

About twenty years later, Sennacherib worships in the temple of Nisroch. We know nothing of this god outside of this verse and its parallel in II Kings 19.[15] "Adrammelech and Sharezer," two of his sons, are apparently jealous that he prefers a younger son, Esar-haddon, to them. While Esar-haddon is away on a military campaign, the brothers assassinate their father. They temporarily escape to "Armenia" (lit. "Ararat"), north of Mesopotamia between the Black and Caspian Seas. Assyrian records relate that Esar-haddon's son Ashurbanipal later captures the surviving members of the plot and puts them to death, v. 38.

---

[12]The Talmud, *Berakoth* 10*b*, gives a fanciful account of the Rabshakeh's death. Supposedly, Hezekiah's daughter gave birth to Manasseh and the Rabshakeh. "One day [Hezekiah] carried them on his shoulder to the Synagogue . . . and one of them said, 'Father's bald head is good for breaking nuts on', while the other said 'it is good for roasting fish on.'" Hezekiah then threw them both on the ground. Rabshakeh died while Manasseh lived.

[13]It is often assumed that some sort of pestilence came upon the Assyrian camp to cause the death of the soldiers. So Wade, p. 237; Leslie, p. 96; Leupold, I, 575; Wright, p. 82. Isa. 33:1, 4, however, tell us that the Jews took spoil from the Assyrian camp. It is unlikely that they would have done this if a pestilence caused the deaths.

[14]Josephus, *Antiquities* 10.1.4–5, has Sennacherib in Egypt conducting a siege of Pelusium. Upon hearing of Tirhaqah's approach, he returns to Judah. He hears there of the pestilence that has overtaken the army at Jerusalem and therefore takes the remainder of his army back to Assyria. Josephus relied to some extent on the flawed histories of Herodotus and Berossus. The biblical account has Sennacherib fighting against Libnah and in constant communication with the Rabshakeh. It is more likely that the destruction strikes Sennacherib's own army. Delitzsch, II, 108, makes the phrase "that night," II Kings 19:35, refer to the night in which Sennacherib begins his siege of Jerusalem. It does not mean the night following Isaiah's prophecy. Verse 33, however, excludes the possibility of Sennacherib besieging Jerusalem.

[15]Delitzsch, II, 110, suggests that Nisroch is a god of marriage. Näglesbach, p. 393, refers to an inscription from Ashur-banipal in which he mentions "the month of Nisroch, the Lord of humanity." Others, however, note that the name Nisroch does not occur outside of the OT.

Practical Applications from Chapter 37

1. The Prayer of Faith. In response to the prompting of his servants, v. 4, Hezekiah goes to the Lord in prayer. He first goes to the temple, the dwelling of God among His people, v. 14. He then begins his prayer, v. 15.

   a. The praises of God. Hezekiah praises the Lord for who He is. He is the only God "of all the kingdoms of the earth." He is the Creator God, v. 16.

   b. The plea to God. Hezekiah asks the Lord to see and hear the words of the Assyrian king, who has reproached God, v. 17. The Assyrians are powerful: they have defeated other nations and oppressed their own people, v. 18. They have destroyed the false gods of these heathen nations, v. 19. In view of Assyria's power and their treatment of the gods, Hezekiah asks the Lord to deliver Judah. This alone will let the nations of the world know the power of Israel's God, v. 20.

   c. The power of God. In view of Hezekiah's prayer, v. 21, the Lord predicts Judah's rejoicing over the Assyrian defeat, v. 22. Assyria has sinned. They have blasphemed God, v. 23. They have given themselves credit for what God has done, vv. 24–26. They will therefore have no power to stand against the Lord. He will turn them back to their own land, vv. 27–29. They will not lift their weapons against Jerusalem, v. 33. They will return to their own city, v. 34. The Lord Himself will defend His people, v. 35. The answer comes as the Lord has predicted. The angel of the Lord strikes 185,000 Assyrian troops dead, v. 36. Sennacherib is forced to return to Nineveh, v. 37.

2. The Danger of Pride, vv. 24–25. The Assyrian king tries to usurp the place of God. He attributes his accomplishments to his own power. Verses 24–25 read, "my . . . I . . . I . . . I . . . I . . . my . . . I." In each case, he fails to give God the credit for what has happened under his leadership. Verse 26 reads, "I . . . I . . . I." The Lord makes it clear that He is the one who has given the Assyrians power to accomplish what they have done. The incident shows the danger of taking credit for what God does. Believers should always humbly give credit to the Lord for what He accomplishes through them.

1 *In those days was Hezekiah sick unto death. And Isaiah the prophet
the son of Amoz came unto him, and said unto him, Thus saith the
Lord, Set thine house in order: for thou shalt die, and not live.*
2 *Then Hezekiah turned his face toward the wall, and prayed unto
the Lord,*
3 *And said, Remember now, O Lord, I beseech thee, how I have
walked before thee in truth and with a perfect heart, and have done
that which is good in thy sight. And Hezekiah wept sore.*

ISAIAH 38

The material in c. 38–39 parallels the record in II Kings 20:1–21. As
with c. 36–37, there is evidence that both Isaiah and the author of Kings
borrowed from a third source. There are additions in Kings and additions
in Isaiah as well as omissions in both books. The order of Isaiah differs
from the order in Kings. The account in Isaiah is generally shorter than
that in Kings.

This chapter relates a personal incident, a serious illness and the anticipation of death, in Hezekiah's life. The Lord, however, miraculously
restores him to health. This serves as the basis for a visit from Babylonian representatives in c. 39. This prepares for the prophecies involving
Babylon in the latter part of the book.

C. Hezekiah's Illness 38:1–22
1. Hezekiah's Problem 38:1–3

1–3 (II Kings 20:1–3) From 36:1; 38:5; and II Kings 18:2, we can
date Hezekiah's illness at 701 B.C. or a little before. Merodach-baladan,
mentioned in 39:1, ruled Babylon on two occasions. The final rule lasted
only nine months in 702 B.C. This is likely the time of Hezekiah's sickness and recovery. This date puts the events of c. 38 at the time of the
Assyrian threat. From v. 6, the events of the chapter take place before
c. 36–37.[1]

From v. 21, we see that the illness involved a "boil" (*šᵉḥîn*), an inflam-
mation or eruption of some unknown kind. The use of *šᵉḥîn* elsewhere
shows its seriousness. It was one of the plagues of Egypt. The magicians

---

[1]Slotki, p. 178, relates Jewish tradition that places Hezekiah's illness three days before
Sennacherib's fall. Supposedly, Hezekiah went to the temple to pray on the third day,
II Kings 20:5, 8. This was the first day of the Passover celebration. While it is an inter-
esting tradition, there is no biblical evidence to place these events at Passover.

of Pharaoh could not stand because of $\check{s}^e\hbar\hat{i}n$, Exodus 9:11. In some cases, it was incurable, Deuteronomy 28:35 ("botch"). This was apparently the case with Hezekiah.

Isaiah tells the king to set his affairs in order as he prepares for his death, v. 1. Hezekiah, however, goes to the Lord in prayer, v. 2.[2] He reminds the Lord of his faithfulness in serving Him. He has carried out the "truth" of God's Word. This no doubt included previously written revelation.[3] It would also include the on-going guidance given by Isaiah. Hezekiah has lived with a "perfect heart" (better "whole heart"), one completely yielded to God. He has done "good in [God's] sight." He "wept sore" (or "wept bitterly") as he agonized over the prospect of death.

There are several possible reasons for Hezekiah's obvious grief at the thought of death. (1) It is natural to fight death, particularly for one who was so young. Hezekiah began his reign when he was twenty-five, II Kings 18:2. Sennacherib invaded Judah in his fourteenth year, Isaiah 36:1. At this time, then, the king was only thirty-nine years old. (2) Hezekiah did not have an heir. Manasseh began his reign when he was just twelve years old, II Kings 21:1. He must have been born during the additional fifteen years of life given Hezekiah. Had the king died, this would have broken the line of descent from David, v. 3.[4] (3) He may have been concerned about the threat from Assyria. His death would have left the nation without a leader.

---

[2]Slotki, p. 178, makes the prayer one of confession. The Talmud also mentions this in *Berakoth* 10a. Hezekiah realizes that he has sinned by failing to marry and have children to continue the Davidic line. There is no biblical support for the view. The biblical record of the prayer stresses the king's faithfulness, not his sin.

[3]Hezekiah would have known of past revelation from the Lord. The priests kept the writings of Moses, Joshua, and the other earlier authors. Such passages as Deut. 17:18; 31:9, 24–26; II Kings 22:8 (II Chron. 34:14–15); Dan. 9:13; Mal. 4:4 show that this was done.

[4]Josephus, *Antiquities* 10.2.1, gives this as the reason for Hezekiah's prayer. The emphasis in v. 5 on the Lord as being "the God of David" may suggest that Hezekiah had been most concerned about the lack of an heir. Verse 6, however, suggests that Hezekiah was concerned over the threat to his people from Assyria.

4 Then came the word of the Lord to Isaiah, saying,
5 Go, and say to Hezekiah, Thus saith the Lord, the God of David thy
   father, I have heard thy prayer, I have seen thy tears: behold, I will
   add unto thy days fifteen years.
6 And I will deliver thee and this city out of the hand of the king of
   Assyria: and I will defend this city.
7 And this shall be a sign unto thee from the Lord, that the Lord will
   do this thing that he hath spoken;
8 Behold, I will bring again the shadow of the degrees, which is gone
   down in the sun dial of Ahaz, ten degrees backward. So the sun returned ten degrees, by which degrees it was gone down.

2. Hezekiah's Deliverance 38:4–8

4–8 (II Kings 20:4–6, 9–10) The Lord speaks to Isaiah. The account
in II Kings 20:4 adds the detail that the Lord spoke to Isaiah before he
came to the "middle court" (or "midst of the city"), v. 4.[5] He tells him to
return to Hezekiah. He is to assure the king that the Lord has heard his
prayer and seen his grief and will extend his life by fifteen years. Second
Kings adds that he will worship in the temple in three days, v. 5. The
Lord will deliver Hezekiah and the city from the Assyrians, v. 6. A
"sign" (*'ôt*, see 7:11), referred to in v. 22, assures the king that the Lord
will do what He has said, v. 7. He will bring the shadow of the "degrees"
(*ma'alôt*) moving along the "sun dial" (*ma'alôt*) backward. Second
Kings 20:9–11 relates that Isaiah offered Hezekiah the choice of having
the shadow move forward or backward. Knowing that moving forward
was the natural motion, Hezekiah asked that the shadow move backward.
As the Lord had offered, the shadow moved backward ten "degrees"
(*ma'alôt*). The word *ma'alôt* nowhere else refers to the divisions of a
sundial. The word often refers to "steps," e.g., I Kings 10:19–20; Ezekiel
40:22–49; or "stairs," e.g., II Kings 9:13; Nehemiah 3:15; 12:37. There
is division over how to understand *ma'alôt* here.[6] I understand *ma'alôt* as

---

[5]The MT in II Kings 20:4 reads *ha'îr*, "city." The *q'rê* reading, followed by the AV, is
haser, "court," some court in the palace. The LXX, Vulgate, and several mss support the
q'rê. C. F. Keil, *Second Book of the Kings*, in *Commentary on the Old Testament*, III,
trans. James Martin (Grand Rapids, Mich.: William B. Eerdmans Publishing Company,
rpt. 1978), p. 462, defends the MT. Most authors, however, adopt the *q'rê*. There is no
great change in the sense with either reading.

[6]Among others, Cowles, p. 291; Von Orelli, p. 205; and Barnes, II, 33, understand
ma'alôt as the degrees of a sundial. On the other hand, Kaiser, *Isaiah 13–39*, p. 398; Leupold, I, 581; and Stacey, p. 228, consider *ma'alôt* as steps. I accept the latter view on the
basis of the sense of the word elsewhere in the OT. The traditional view, however, fits

9 The writing of Hezekiah king of Judah, when he had been sick, and was recovered of his sickness:
10 I said in the cutting off of my days, I shall go to the gates of the grave: I am deprived of the residue of my years.
11 I said, I shall not see the Lord, even the Lord, in the land of the living: I shall behold man no more with the inhabitants of the world.

"steps." The shadow along the steps, apparently built during the time of Ahaz, moved backward ten steps.

There is a well-known myth in Christian circles that asserts that a day has been lost in time. Supposedly, military computers have traced it to the sun's motion backward. The myth relates it to the loss of "about a whole day," Joshua 10:13, and the return of the sun ten degrees here, equivalent to forty minutes.[7] There are several problems with the story. It assumes that the sun moved backward. If this happened, the folklore of ancient nations would have recorded it. We have no indication of this. If an eclipse had happened, a computer analysis could confirm it. No such confirmation exists. In order to have such a computer study of solar motion, we would need an accurate position of the sun and stars before Joshua's time. No such record exists. The Lord may just as well have caused a miraculous refraction of the sun's light in Jerusalem.

There is no need for Christians to create stories to confirm the biblical record. A miracle occurred. It does not need confirmation. Believers need to accept it simply on the basis of the inspired account in Isaiah, cf. II Kings 20:8–11, v. 8. The record of Hezekiah's deliverance continues in vv. 21–22.

3. Hezekiah's Psalm 38:9–20

9–11 The king writes a song to commemorate his healing. The psalm is unique to Isaiah, not recorded in either II Kings 20 or II Chronicles 32. Second Chronicles 29:25–30 records Hezekiah's restoration of the temple

---

naturally into the narrative. According to Herodotus (ii.109), the Babylonians invented the sundial. It would likely have passed to the Syrians and Assyrians from them. Ahaz may well have brought back the design for a sundial at the same time that he brought back the pattern of the heathen altar he had made for the temple, II Kings 16:10. Since v. 8 refers to the *ma^{ca}lôt* as the "sun dial of Ahaz," it may be that this was something unusual, not merely a staircase. It may, however, refer simply to a staircase built in the reign of Ahaz.

[7]For example, Harry Rimmer, *Modern Science and the Long Day of Joshua* (Los Angeles: Glendale Publishers, 1927), pp. 1–26, discusses the view favorably.

music. Proverbs 25:1 shows his interest in preserving the writings of Solomon. Verse 20 speaks of other songs written by the king. There is ample evidence of his musical interest and ability.

After his sickness, Hezekiah records some of his feelings, v. 9.[8] At first, he had been shocked with the realization that death would come "in the cutting off [$d^om\hat{\imath}$] of my days" (lit. "in the rest [or 'quietness, silence'] of my days"). The word $d^om\hat{\imath}$ refers to the time of normal health, the time when Hezekiah was proceeding naturally through life.[9] At this time, he learned that he was to enter "the gates of the grave [$\check{s}^e{}^{\jmath}ol$, see 5:14]." The noun $\check{s}^e{}^{\jmath}ol$ has a normal meaning of grave. Hezekiah uses the phrase to indicate that the grave was but the entry to the afterworld. This would deprive him of the normal life span that he had anticipated, v. 10. Hezekiah laments the fact that he will no more see the Lord's gracious work among men. In repeating the name "Lord [yah], even the Lord [yah],"[10] Hezekiah stresses the loss that he anticipates. He will not see "the Lord Himself" in the "land of the living," simply life itself. He

---

[8]Among others, Wade, p. 241; Kaiser, *Isaiah 13–39*, p. 398; and Delitzsch, II, 116, emend "writing" (*miktab*) to Michtam (*miktam*), a change that the LXX supports. This same heading occurs at Pss. 16, 56–60. The word has an uncertain meaning. Kaiser suggests "atoning poem." Wade renders it "a golden (i.e., choice) poem." Herbert, *Isaiah 1–39*, p. 212, supports "poem." Watts, *Isaiah 34–66*, p. 54, gives "psalm." The textual evidence for the change is not strong. We gain nothing by exchanging a word with a known meaning for one with an uncertain sense.

[9]Birks, p. 189; Skinner, *Isaiah I–XXXIX*, p. 279; and Wade, p. 241, translate $d^om\hat{\imath}$ as "noontide." Noon is a metaphor for the middle of the day, i.e., a time of rest, as when the sun seems to stand still in the sky, or as the midpoint of life. While interpretive, the view does rest on the common meaning of *damam*. Kaiser, *Isaiah 13–39*, p. 398, takes the word from *dmm* II, "lament," and translates, "misery [of my days]." Dahood, *CBQ* 22:400–404, argues similarly based on Akkadian and Ugaritic cognates. The word $d^om\hat{\imath}$ occurs elsewhere at 62:6, 7; and Ps. 83:1. In each case, it must mean something like "silence." Stacey, p. 229, suggests that the word refers to the period when corruption destroys the corpse in the grave. It is as though the "rest of my days" is the "remainder of my days," when the corpse is still recognizable. This view is not likely.

[10]The name *yah* is an abbreviated form of *yahweh*. The word occurs fifty times in all parts of the OT but primarily in Psalms. It occurs in Isaiah here and at 12:2 and 26:4. This is the only place that the repeated *yah yah* occurs. Mitchell Dahood, "חֲדֵל 'Cessation' in Isaiah 38,11," *Biblica* 52:215–16, groups the second *yah* with 11*b*. This gives seven syllables in 11*a* and 11*b*. Dahood translates "I said, I shall not enjoy, O Yah, O Yah, the land of the living." This goes contrary to the Hebrew accents. In addition, Isaiah varies the syllable count widely in this section, e.g., v. 9, 12:9; v. 10, 12:10:10, v. 12, 14:16:11. This is prose, not poetry. There is no reason to expect parallel syllabification.

*12 Mine age is departed, and is removed from me as a shepherd's tent:
I have cut off like a weaver my life: he will cut me off with pining
sickness: from day even to night wilt thou make an end of me.*

*13 I reckoned till morning, that, as a lion, so will he break all my
bones: from day even to night wilt thou make an end of me.*

*14 Like a crane or a swallow, so did I chatter: I did mourn as a dove:
mine eyes fail with looking upward: O Lord, I am oppressed; undertake for me.*

would not be able to enjoy fellowship with "man" (*ʾadam*, see 2:9), others who are also passing from this "world" (*ḥadel*),[11] v. 11.

12–14 The phrase "mine age [*dôr*]" is best understood as "my
dwelling." The root has the sense of "circle." It normally refers to the
"circle" of life, i.e., one generation following another generation (as in
13:20; 34:10, 17). Here, however, the meaning of "dwelling" comes
from the nature of a tent as surrounding the living area. Hezekiah compares his dwelling to a "shepherd's tent." It is "departed" (lit. "pulled
up"), taken down and moved to another place. His life has been "cut
off" (lit. "rolled up") like the weaver's cloth. The Lord will "cut me off
with pining sickness" (*dallâ*, better "from the loom"). Strictly speaking,
the *dallâ* is the thrum, a fringe of warp threads left on the upper part of
the loom after the weaver cuts the warp to free the cloth. Hezekiah uses
this to illustrate how his own life has been cut off. Just as the day passes
into night, so the Lord is ending the day of his life and sending him into
the night of the grave, v. 12.

After the initial shock, Hezekiah "reckoned" (better "composed myself") till the morning came. He found, however, that his pain continued.
He illustrates this with the figure of a lion pouncing upon his victim and
breaking its bones. Once more, cf. v. 12, he illustrates his fate with the
figure of day passing into night, v. 13. His prayers are like the twittering
of a bird, "a crane or a swallow." The AV inverts the order of the MT:
"swallow or crane." He "mourn[s]" like a dove as he cries out to the

---

[11]If *ḥadel* is correct, this is the only occurrence of the form. The verb *ḥadal*, "to cease,
stop," however, occurs widely in the OT. This leads to the meaning "cessation." The
phrase, then, refers to the dwellers of this life that are passing away. Many, including the
AV, emend to *ḥeled*, the enduring "world." This more directly parallels the land of the living" in the first half of the verse. 1QIsaᵃ supports the MT but other mss support *ḥeled*.
The LXX omits the word but the Vulgate supports the change. We cannot be certain
since the textual evidence is not conclusive.

15 *What shall I say? he hath both spoken unto me, and himself hath done it: I shall go softly all my years in the bitterness of my soul.*

16 *O Lord, by these things men live, and in all these things is the life of my spirit: so wilt thou recover me, and make me to live.*

17 *Behold, for peace I had great bitterness: but thou hast in love to my soul delivered it from the pit of corruption: for thou hast cast all my sins behind thy back.*

18 *For the grave cannot praise thee, death can not celebrate thee: they that go down into the pit cannot hope for thy truth.*

19 *The living, the living, he shall praise thee, as I do this day: the father to the children shall make known thy truth.*

20 *The Lord was ready to save me: therefore we will sing my songs to the stringed instruments all the days of our life in the house of the Lord.*

Lord.[12] His eyes "fail" (or "look weakly") upward to God. Hezekiah summarizes his prayer: "O Lord, I am oppressed; undertake for me." The last phrase is better "be surety for me." It is as though Hezekiah views death as a creditor demanding payment for the debt of sin. He pleads with the Lord to be His security, v. 14.

15–20 The tone of Hezekiah's psalm changes at this point. He has recalled his feelings when anticipating his early death. Now he thanks the Lord for delivering him. He asks, "What shall I say?" The question acknowledges his inability to adequately describe God's goodness. The Lord has both promised deliverance from death and accomplished it. In response, Hezekiah pledges to "go softly" (or "walk deliberately") for the rest of his life. This is a poetic expression of the humility he feels. The phrase "in [ʿal] the bitterness of my soul" refers to the bitterness from which God has delivered him. In view of this, he can pledge to live only in a way that pleases the Lord, v. 15.[13] The phrase "these things" refers back to v. 15, to the pledge and work of God in extending his life. It is by the promise of God that men live and by the accomplishments of God that Hezekiah himself has been renewed. He expresses his confi-

---

[12]Young, II, 521; Kaiser, *Isaiah 13–39*, p. 405; and Barnes, II, 39, consider the twittering and mourning the sounds of grief as Hezekiah describes his pain. From the next phrase in the verse, however, it is more likely that these are the sounds of prayer as Hezekiah feebly expresses his desires to the Lord.

[13]Delitzsch, II, 120, understands the preposition ʿal, translated "in" by the AV, as "in addition to." He refers this to all the years that follow the king's bitter sickness. The view is possible although a causal sense for ʿal is more common.

dence that God will "recover me" (better "restore me to health") and make him live, v. 16.

Hezekiah acknowledges that "for peace" (*šalôm*, see 9:6) he had felt "great bitterness" (*mar̄lî mar*). The AV correctly catches the sense of the repeated *mar* with "great bitterness." The Lord had given him the experience for his good.[14] The Lord has shown His love by delivering him physically, "from the pit of corruption." He has also delivered him spiritually, casting "all my sins behind thy back," where they cannot be seen, cf. 43:25; Micah 7:19, v. 17.

> The verse has been called the John 3:16 of the Old Testament. Matthew Henry well notes that when we cast our sins behind our back, taking no notice of them, God sets them before His face, ready to judge them. When, however, we set our sins before our face, confessing them to God, He casts them behind His back, where they will not be seen.

Those who are in the "grave" (*šeʾôl*, see 5:14), here best taken as sheol, the abode of the dead, cannot praise the Lord on earth. Those who have died cannot praise Him; cf. Psalm 6:5; 115:17. Those who are in the "pit" (*bôr*, see 14:15) of condemnation, cf. 14:15, have no hope for the future, v. 18. Only the living can praise God as Hezekiah himself is doing. As is so characteristic of Isaiah, he repeats the word "living," *ḥay ḥay*, "the living himself." This emphasizes the source of the praise that should come to the Lord. Anticipating the birth of children that God will give to him, Hezekiah pledges to make known God's truth to them, v. 19. Because the Lord is ready to "save" (*yašaʿ*, see 17:10) the king from his sickness, he will sing "my songs," songs of praise that he has written, accompanied by "stringed instruments" (*neginôt*)[15] for the rest of his life. He will do this publicly as he worships in the temple, v. 20.

---

[14]Barnes, II, 40; Slotki, p. 181; and Henry, p. 208, understand the first phrase, "instead of the peace I expected, You brought me through a bitter experience." While this is possible, the rest of the verse explains the first phrase rather than contrasts with it. God had given Hezekiah "peace," great personal good, by delivering him from the threat of death.

[15]The titles of psalms transliterate *neginôt* as Neginoth in Pss. 4, 6, 54, 55, 61, 67, 76. The word refers to "stringed instruments."

21 For Isaiah had said, Let them take a lump of figs, and lay it for a plaister upon the boil, and he shall recover.
22 Hezekiah also had said, What is the sign that I shall go up to the house of the Lord?

4. Hezekiah's Deliverance (continued from vv. 4–8) 38:21–22[16]

21–22 (II Kings 20:7–8) As a medicinal aid, Isaiah had instructed the servants to prepare a "lump" (lit. "cake") of figs. They should "lay it for a plaister" (lit. "rub it") on the boil. Apparently, the dried figs were mixed with some liquid and then spread over the "boil" (šᵉḥîn, see v. 1) to draw the poison out. While this is a simple medical procedure, the effect it produces is miraculous, something that would not have happened save in response to Hezekiah's prayer, cf. II Kings 20:7, v. 21. Encouraged by the promise of life, Hezekiah asks for a "sign" (ʾôt, see 7:11) to confirm the miracle. Nothing here hints that Hezekiah's request shows a lack of faith.[17] Second Kings 20:5 tells us that Isaiah responds with the promise that he will go to the temple to worship in three days, cf. II Kings 20:8, v. 22.[18]

Practical Applications from Chapter 38

1. The Power of Prayer. After hearing that his sickness will end with his death, v. 1, the king begins to pray, v. 2. He reminds the Lord of his godly life. With faint effort, he expresses his prayer. He asks the Lord to undertake in this experience, v. 3. The Lord responds and

---

[16]Among others, Delitzsch, II, 113; Von Orelli, p. 205; and Mauchline, pp. 233–34, move vv. 21–22 to follow v. 6. While this brings the text into agreement with II Kings, Isaiah has shown on several occasions that he does not slavishly follow some other account of Hezekiah's healing. By placing the passage here, he makes a smooth transition to c. 39.

[17]Motyer, *The Prophecy of Isaiah,* p. 295, suggests that Hezekiah's question stems from his lack of faith in God's promise of healing. There is, however, no condemnation of the king, either here or in II Kings 20:5. In contrast with wicked Ahaz, who refused to ask for a sign, 7:12, Hezekiah gives the Lord an additional way to prove His faithfulness.

[18]Vicki Hoffer, "An Exegesis of Isaiah 38:21," *JSOT* 56:75–83, relates the sickness and healing to the nation. The sickness suggests the Assyrian threat. The pronouncement of healing is a guarantee of success in facing Assyria. The additional fifteen years of life represent the additional years of life given to the nation. This will end in the Babylonian conquest, ending in the years of exile in Babylon. The visit by the king to the temple represents Israel's return and worship at the rebuilt temple. While Hoffer's view is more conservative than that of many who reject the entire account as an editorial addition, it lacks credibility. Hoffer is the sole authority for spiritualizing the passage.

calls Isaiah, v. 4, to return to Hezekiah. God has heard his prayer and sees the grief in his heart. He will have fifteen additional years of life, v. 5.

2. The Illustration of Salvation, v. 17

   a. God orders the circumstances for Hezekiah's good, v. 17*a*.

   b. God delivers Hezekiah from the "pit of corruption," v. 17*b*.

   c. God remembers Hezekiah's sins no more, v. 17*c*.

3. Verses 18–19 illustrate the need for evangelism.

To Speak of Him

Who alone can praise thy name,
   Can show the world redeeming power,
   Can give them truth in darkened hour?
Who alone can spread the fame
Of He who glory left and flesh became?

Can the grave that barren lies
   Cause sin to yield its binding sway,
   Teach men to know the Saviour's way?
Shall that lifeless corpse arise
To sing redemption's song with joyful cries?

Shall death's voice know golden dawn,
   Awake the world the truth to know,
   Help men to see the crimson flow?
Will death yield in glad song
To praise the Master's name 'til time has gone?

Nay, all these in vain are raised,
   Death can never give men their choice,
   For truth demands a living voice.
In needy hours, darkened days,
The living, the living, he shall give praise.

1 At that time Merodach-baladan, the son of Baladan, king of Babylon, sent letters and a present to Hezekiah: for he had heard that he had been sick, and was recovered.

2 And Hezekiah was glad of them, and shewed them the house of his precious things, the silver, and the gold, and the spices, and the precious ointment, and all the house of his armour, and all that was found in his treasures: there was nothing in his house, nor in all his dominion, that Hezekiah shewed them not.

ISAIAH 39

The chapter makes a transition: Babylon, not Assyria, has become Judah's main enemy. Merodach-Baladan was an early tribal leader in Babylon. By his Akkadian name Marduk-apal-idinna, "Marduk has given a son," he served as the chief of the *bit-yakin,* one of the tribes in southern Babylon.[1] The text here describes him as the "son of Baladan." Assyrian records call him the "son of Yakin." This may simply identify him as a descendant of Yakin, or it may make him a member of the *bit-yakin* tribe. There is an Assyrian record of him paying tribute as he submits to their control, ca. 729 B.C.

After the death of Shalmaneser, Merodach-Baladan rebelled against Assyria. After conquering the city of Babylon ca. 721 B.C., he was considered the leader of the united Babylonian tribal groups. He ruled for about twelve years until the Assyrians under Sargon II defeated his army. He then fled into the south. About 702 B.C., after Sennacherib came to power in Assyria, Merodach-Baladan again claimed power. It is "at that time" when he sends an embassy to congratulate Hezekiah on recovering from his life-threatening illness. While the text does not say what was in his "letters," it is widely thought that Merodach-Baladan was exploring the possibility of a joint rebellion against Assyria. His name occurs elsewhere in the OT only in the parallel passage in II Kings 20:12, where the *mem* has been replaced with *beth.*

D. Hezekiah's Pride 39:1–8

1–2 (II Kings 20:12–13) The messengers of Merodach-Baladan bring "letters and a present" to Hezekiah. The plural "letters" likely reflects

---

[1]There are other personal names compounded with Marduk in the OT: Evil-Merodach, II Kings 25:27; Jer. 52:31; Mordecai, Ezra 2:2 (Neh. 7:7) and over fifty times in Esther. Jer. 50:2 mentions the god Merodach by name.

3 *Then came Isaiah the prophet unto king Hezekiah, and said unto*
   him, What said these men? and from whence came they unto thee?
   And Hezekiah said, They are come from a far country unto me, even
   from Babylon.
4 *Then said he, What have they seen in thine house? And Hezekiah*
   answered, All that is in mine house have they seen: there is nothing
   among my treasures that I have not shewed them.

the several pages within the single scroll; cf. 37:14. The "present" was undoubtedly the gift customary at the meeting of representatives from two countries. The stated purpose of the visit is to bring the news that the Babylonians have heard of Hezekiah's miraculous recovery. From Isaiah's reaction in vv. 3–7, it is likely that the visit was an attempt to arrange an alliance with Judah against Assyria, v. 1.[2]

Hezekiah is eager to impress the messengers with his strength. He shows them "the house of his precious things," a storehouse in which he kept valuables. He displays his wealth, the "house of his armour [$k^e l\hat{i}$, see 10:28]," and his treasures. From the fact that $k^e l\hat{i}$ is surrounded by references to wealth and treasures, it is likely that it means something similar here. The gloss "jewels" is appropriate.[3]

The key to this event is Hezekiah's use of the personal pronoun. The word "his" occurs five times in v. 2. He uses the pronoun "me" once in v. 3. The pronouns "my," "mine," and "I" all occur in v. 4. Hezekiah lets pride control him as he tries to impress the Babylonians with his wealth, v. 2.

3–4 (II Kings 20:14–15) Isaiah questions Hezekiah about the messengers. What have they said? Where are they from? The king responds to the second question only. It is possible that he tries to cover the suggestion of an alliance. He tells Isaiah that the men are from Babylon, v. 3. Isaiah asks a third question, "What have they seen in thine house?" The

---

[2]Because of the reference to Hezekiah's riches, v. 2, Delitzsch, II, 124, and Leupold, p. 592, place the visit of the Babylonians before the Assyrian threat. Supposedly, Hezekiah's payment of tribute, II Kings 18:14–16, must come after v. 2. This, however, runs into conflict with 38:6, which places Hezekiah's illness at the time of the Assyrian siege. It is highly unlikely that Hezekiah would have been left with no wealth to show to the Babylonians. He may have been hurt financially by the tribute paid to Sennacherib, but his level of financial difficulty would not have been on the same level as the average person's financial problems.

[3]Others suggest that the "house of his armour" is the same as the "house of the forest," cf. 22:8, his armory. So, among others, Rawlinson, II, 57; Näglesbach, p. 408; and Alexander, II, 89. Because $k^e l\hat{i}$ is so varied in its meaning, we cannot be certain.

> 5 Then said Isaiah to Hezekiah, Hear the word of the Lord of hosts:
> 6 Behold, the days come, that all that is in thine house, and that which thy fathers have laid up in store until this day, shall be carried to Babylon: nothing shall be left, saith the Lord.
> 7 And of thy sons that shall issue from thee, which thou shalt beget, shall they take away; and they shall be eunuchs in the palace of the king of Babylon.
> 8 Then said Hezekiah to Isaiah, Good is the word of the Lord which thou hast spoken. He said moreover, For there shall be peace and truth in my days.

king answers that they have seen all; He has not withheld anything from them, v. 4.

5–8 (II Kings 20:16–19) The prophet gives the king a message from "the Lord of hosts," see 1:9. The name is significant. Hezekiah had emphasized human resources rather than divine strength, v. 5. The days will come in which the Babylonians will take to Babylon all of the wealth of which Hezekiah had boasted.[4] Nothing will be left, v. 6. Hezekiah's "sons" will go into captivity. The most notable example of this is Manasseh, II Chronicles 33:11. In addition, since the word "son" often means "descendant," the prophecy also includes the captivities of Jehoiakim, II Chronicles 36:5–6; Jehoiachin, II Chronicles 36:9–10; and Zedekiah, II Kings 25:7. Babylon as well put other unnamed royal descendants in captivity, Daniel 1:3. They will become "eunuchs" (better "officials") in the Babylonian court. This is the first prophecy of Babylonian captivity. This theme comes up again many times in the remaining chapters of the book, v. 7.

Hezekiah responds well: "Good is the word of the Lord. . . ." We must read the statement in light of II Chronicles 32:26. Hezekiah has a repentant spirit: he humbles himself, turning from the pride that had led him to boast of his wealth, and he accepts God's will in the matter. The

---

[4]Herbert, *Isaiah 1–39*, p. 214, suggests that the prophecy originally had Nineveh in view. Later, after the fall of Jerusalem in 586 B.C., a scribe substituted Babylon. Kaiser, *Isaiah 13–39*, pp. 408–10, makes the passage an explanation of the plundering of Judah's treasury by Nebuchadnezzar as well as the later deportation of Judah's kings. The scribe traces this back to Hezekiah's actions. He dates it after the fall of Jerusalem. Stacey, pp. 230–31, dates the narrative "much later" than the fall of Jerusalem. These efforts to attribute the passage to a later scribe rest on the refusal to admit the possibility of prophecy. Supposedly, Isaiah could not have known of Babylon's power since that lay more than a century in the future. When we recognize the guidance of the Holy Spirit in Isaiah's words, the difficulty vanishes.

phrase "there shall be peace and truth in my days" notes the fact that the kingdom will continue normally for a time. Hezekiah finds comfort in this, v. 8.[5]

Practical Applications from Chapter 39

1. The Danger of Pride. Hezekiah uses a personal pronoun nine times in vv. 2–4. Pride is the same sin found in the heathen king, 37:24–25. Satan and his representatives try to make us trust ourselves rather than God; cf. II Chronicles 32:25; I Timothy 3:6; I John 2:16.

2. The Illustration of Judgment. Sin very rarely affects only the individual. We see here that God's judgment also affected the descendants of Hezekiah. Manasseh, Jehoiakim, Jehoiachin, and other unnamed descendants all went into captivity in Babylon, vv. 6–7.

---

[5]Brueggemann, *Isaiah 1–39*, p. 313, interprets Hezekiah's statement as "a cynical, self-satisfied response." He accepts God's will because it will not come during his life. Janet Edwards, "Prophetic Paradox: Isaiah 6:9–10," *Studia Biblica et Theologica* 6:52, likewise misunderstands the passage. She states: "the words of Isaiah are utterly misinterpreted by the king, and seem to foster a complacency and confidence that drives Hezekiah closer to Babylon instead of away from alliance." These views go contrary to the record of Hezekiah's humbling himself in II Chron. 32:26.

1 Comfort ye, comfort ye my people, saith your God.
2 Speak ye comfortably to Jerusalem, and cry unto her, that her
warfare is accomplished, that her iniquity is pardoned: for she
hath received of the Lord's hand double for all her sins.

ISAIAH 40

This chapter introduces the part of the book that commonly has the title Deutero-Isaiah. This name is wrong since it suggests a second author. The style of writing, the historical acceptance by the Jews, and the NT use of Isaiah give ample proof of a single author. I have summarized the arguments for the unity of the book in the Introduction and have adopted this view in the remaining parts of the book.

Isaiah turns in this chapter to prophecies of comfort that rest upon the power of Israel's God. The nation has been punished for its sins. This clears the way for the Lord to come to rule over the people and to care for them, vv. 1–11. The remainder of the chapter, vv. 12–31, lays stress on the power of God. He is omnipotent, v. 12; omniscient; vv. 13–14; transcendent, vv. 15–17, 18–20, 25–26; loving, v. 27; and He has revealed Himself to the nation, v. 28. He is sufficient to meet their every need, vv. 29–31.

VI. Prophecies of Redemption and Restoration 40:1–55:13[1]
A. Promise of Israel's Restoration 40:1–41:29
1. Comfort of God 40:1–11

1–2 God commands an unidentified group to "comfort ye" (*naham*, see 1:24) His people.[2] The repetition of the *pi'el* masculine plural impera-

---

[1]There is debate over the date and authorship of c. 40–55. Leslie, p. 138, assigns them to "an unnamed and unknown poet-prophet who is designated . . . as Deutero-Isaiah." He dates it ca. 540 B.C. Kelley, pp. 160, 297, dates it at roughly the same time but makes the authors disciples of Isaiah. McKenzie, p. xviii, places the author in the Babylonian exile. C. C. Torrey, *The Second Isaiah*, pp. 53, 109, dates the work ca. 400 B.C. and puts the author in Palestine. As I have argued in the Introduction, there is no need to reject the eighth century authorship of Isaiah for the entire book.

[2]Kelley, p. 297, notes that "this is the only time in the Scriptures that the prophets are commanded to comfort . . . ordinarily they are sent not to comfort but to condemn." This is an overstatement. While there is no other command to a prophet to comfort, there are many places that the prophet's message brings comfort, e.g., 41:10; 49:13; 51:3, 12; 61:2; 66:13. There is a balance in the message of the prophets. Much of it condemns and much of it comforts.

tive lends emphasis to the command.[3] We cannot deny that a group receives the command. The plural imperative occurs twice more in v. 3. In v. 6, however, the imperative is a masculine singular. Putting this together, it is reasonable that the command goes generally to the prophets. Isaiah, however, is the primary spokesman. The prophets should repeat their words of comfort over and over as they encourage the people.[4] This is the major theme of the second half of the book. Even the form of the command encourages. Isaiah is to comfort "my people." The command comes from "your God." The personal pronouns emphasize the relationship between God and Israel. While God may have punished Judah for their sins, they are still God's people and He is still their God, v. 1.

Jerusalem, the capital of the nation, serves to represent the people. Isaiah is to "speak ye comfortably," lit. "concerning the heart." This idiomatic expression indicates that the prophet should speak in a kindly manner, encouraging the hearts of the Jews. There are three reasons for this. In the first place, their "warfare" ($s^eba^{\flat}$) is ended. In addition to meanings connected with war, the word $s^eba^{\flat}$ may also mean "service" or "work," e.g., Numbers 4:23, 30, 35. It may as well refer to a time of difficulty, e.g., Job 7:1; 14:14. The context in the next verses relates this to the coming kingdom of Christ. The punishment of Judah is over and the Lord comes to rule over them.

In the second place, God has "pardoned" (*raṣâ*) the "iniquity" (*ᶜawon*, see 1:4) of the nation. The verb *raṣâ* has the root idea "to be pleased

---

[3]There is little agreement as to the identity of the spokesman. Delitzsch, II, 139, and Kelley, p. 297, make the prophets the ones receiving the command. Kraeling, p. 151, follows the LXX in understanding the priests as the ones receiving the command. Barnes, II, 52, combines these views. He directs the command to priests or prophets. Leupold, II, 21, and Näglesbach, p. 421, understand that anyone receiving the message that God comforts His people should spread the news. These views are all possible. Frank M. Cross Jr., "The Council of Yahweh in Second Isaiah," *JNES* 12:274–77, and Motyer, *The Prophecy of Isaiah*, p. 299, make a "heavenly court" the object of the command. Although I Kings 22:19–22 describes a heavenly court, there is no record of such a court giving words of encouragement to God's people. Watts, *Isaiah 34–66*, p. 80, sees the recipients as the "exiles in Mesopotamia." This view requires a late date for the passage. I have discussed my view above.

[4]The use of epanadiplosis, repeating a word for the sake of emphasis, is characteristic of Isaiah, e.g., 6:3; 26:3; 29:1; 38:11, 19; 51:9, 17; 52:1, 11; 57:14; 62:10. In addition, he quite often repeats a phrase for emphasis, e.g., 24:16; 28:10, 13. Isaiah makes use of repetition in all parts of the book. This characteristic of his style argues for a single author of the book.

with." It expresses here the idea that Judah's iniquity has been satisfied, i.e., her punishment has satisfied the Lord. The statement implies that Judah has confessed her sins and received God's gracious forgiveness. The past punishment of God's people has prepared them for His further work on their behalf.[5]

Finally, she has received "double" (*kepel*) punishment for her "sins" (*ḥaṭṭaʾtâ*, see 3:9). The idea of double punishment cannot be pressed too far. It would be unworthy of God to say that He punished twice as much as the people deserved.[6] It is more that the idea of double punishment is idiomatic for a full measure of punishment. The thought occurs elsewhere in Job 11:6 and Ezekiel 21:14. It also occurs in Isaiah 61:7; Jeremiah 16:18; 17:18, where the authors use *mišneh* rather than *kepel*. This is also the case with the reward of God's people in Zechariah 9:12.

The prophecy looks to the future. The statements here are prophetic perfects. They are so certain to God that He states them as past facts. The Jews will complete their suffering, then turn to the Lord. The complete fulfillment will take place in the millennial kingdom, when Christ rules the earth from Jerusalem, v. 2.

---

[5]August Pieper, *Isaiah II,* 1979, p. 78, points the verse to the death of Christ at Calvary. While possible, the view is probably too specific. It is enough to leave the verse as a general statement of future blessing.

[6]Barnes, II, 54, suggests that the doubling was twice "that which had been usually inflicted on rebellious nations, or on the nation before for its sins." This calls into question the fairness of the punishment. Fausset, p. 685, refers it to the "two-fold captivity—the Assyrian or Babylonian and the Roman." Rome, however, did not put Israel into captivity. She conquered the nation and placed a king over the land to rule it. Alexander, II, 95, suggests that double refers "not to punishment, but to favour after suffering." This disagrees with the parallelism of the last three phrases in the verse. These are all introduced with *kî*. This argues that all the phrases refer in some way to Israel's sin. Scott, p. 425, understands "double"punishment as "Oriental exaggeration." Torrey, p. 305, similarly calls it "rhetorical exaggeration." Although their explanation is similar to that above, there is a significant difference between an idiom and an exaggeration. McKenzie, p. 17, notes that double damages were assessed in the Law, Exod. 22:4, 7, 9, and that God restored to Job double wealth and years, Job 42:12–16; cf. 1:3; Ps. 90:10. The Law, however, came before any punishment. The people knew the penalty in advance. That is not the case here. Anthony Phillips, "Double for All Her Sins," *ZAW* 94:130–32, explains the doubling as in duration. "Whereas one generation properly experienced the destruction of Jerusalem and consequent exile, its duration has extended to another 'innocent' generation as well." This limits the focus to the exile and the return to Palestine. Israel has suffered for well over 2,600 years, which is far more than a second generation.

3 *The voice of him that crieth in the wilderness, Prepare ye the way of*
the Lord, make straight in the desert a highway for our God.
4 *Every valley shall be exalted, and every mountain and hill shall be*
made low: and the crooked shall be made straight, and the rough
places plain:
5 *And the glory of the Lord shall be revealed, and all flesh shall see it*
together: for the mouth of the Lord hath spoken it.

3–5 An unidentified voice cries that the way should be prepared for
the Lord's coming. In ancient times, the king's servants would go before
him to insure that no obstacles blocked the king's travels; cf. Malachi
3:1.[7] The NT makes clear that John the Baptist fulfilled this role for the
Lord (Matt. 3:3; Mark 1:3; Luke 1:76; 3:4; John 1:23).

The accents group the first two Hebrew words without saying where
the call comes from: "A voice is calling." The remaining two phrases are
parallel: "In the wilderness make clear the way of the Lord, make
straight in the desert a highway for our God." The NT paraphrases the
statement. The Gospel writers picture John as a voice crying in the
wilderness, then give his message as "Prepare ye the way of the Lord,
make his paths straight" (Matt. 3:3; Mark 1:3; Luke 3:4–5; John 1:23).[8]

Judah was to "prepare" (better "make clear") the way that the Lord
would travel. They should "make straight" (or "make smooth") His path-
way. This command pictures removing every obstacle that would prevent
the Lord from coming to them, v. 3.[9] Verse 4 picturesquely shows the results of this preparation. Deep valleys are lifted up, mountains are made
low, "crooked" (or "rough") places become "straight" (better "smooth"),
and "rough [*harkasîm*, or "rugged"] places" become a "plain" (*biqʻâ*).[10]

---

[7]Josephus, *Antiquities* 7.4.187, tells of how Solomon paved the road that led to
Jerusalem with black stones. This action made travel easier to his royal city.

[8]James D. Smart, *History and Theology in Second Isaiah*, 1965, p. 47, makes the desert
"symbolic of what man's life has become and must ever become when he is without
God." While devotional in nature, the statement ignores the NT development in which
John prepares for the coming of the Lord.

[9]Among others, Skinner, *Isaiah XL–LXVI*, p. 4; Wade, p. 250; and North, p. 39, make
the wilderness and desert the barren region between Babylon and Palestine. The voice
prepares for the return from captivity to Jerusalem. The problem with this view lies in
the fact that Judah did not travel through the wilderness in the return from captivity. For
this reason, it is better to find the fulfillment in the future than in the past.

[10]The word *harkasîm* occurs only here. The verb *rakes*, "to bind," occurs only in Exod.
28:28; 39:21. There is also an Akkadian root *rakasu* that refers to building earthworks,
bridges, or fortresses. The idea is that of hills or peaks bound together. The thought here

6 *The voice said, Cry. And he said, What shall I cry? All flesh is grass,*
   and all the goodliness thereof is as the flower of the field:
7 *The grass withereth, the flower fadeth: because the spirit of the Lord*
   bloweth upon it: surely the people is grass.
8 *The grass withereth, the flower fadeth: but the word of our God*
   shall stand for ever.

There will be physical changes in the kingdom, 2:2. The "living waters"
flow from Jerusalem to the Dead Sea and to the Mediterranean Sea
(Zech. 14:8). The land around Jerusalem will be lifted up (Zech. 14:10).
The primary thought, however, is metaphorical. Every barrier will be removed that keeps the Lord from coming to His own. The Jews will repent of their sins and will accept Jesus Christ as the Messiah, v. 4. He
will then reveal His glory and all will see Him, Titus 2:13; Revelation
1:7. The promise is certain since God Himself has spoken it, v. 5.[11]

6–8 Another voice speaks, telling an unidentified messenger to "cry."
When the messenger questions this, the voice specifically commands
that he should compare "all flesh" with grass and all of man's "goodliness" (ḥesed, or "loyal love," see 16:5)[12] with flowers in the fields. Peter
uses this same illustration to show the transitory nature of life, I Peter
1:24–25, v. 6.[13] These quickly wither and die in the summer heat. The
phrase "the spirit of the Lord bloweth on it" is better "the wind of the
Lord bloweth on it." As with all the forces of nature, the wind is under
the control of the Lord. The people are like the grass, v. 7. The vegeta-

---

of "rugged places" is adequate. By contrast, it must be the opposite of *biqʿâ*. The word
biqʿâ refers to a broad valley as opposed to a mountain, e.g., Deut. 8:7; 11:11. It may
also refer to a plain, e.g., Gen. 11:2; Ezek. 3:22, 23; Zech. 12:11. The context here supports the meaning of "plain."

[11]The phrase "the mouth of the Lord hath spoken it" occurs here and in 1:20 and
58:14. Putting this another way, the phrase occurs once in each of the three major parts
of the book. Since no other OT writer uses the phrase, this supports Isaiah's authorship
of the whole book.

[12]L. J. Kuyper, "The Meaning of חסד Isa. XL 6," *VT* 13:489–92, argues that ḥesed has
the meaning of "strength" here. In support, he cites several other references in which the
word can be translated "strength." In each case, the translation "loyal love" or "loyalty"
is also suitable. There is no reason to abandon that sense here.

[13]Among others, North, p. 40; Herbert, *Isaiah 40–66*, p. 19; and Westermann, p. 40,
read *waʾomar*, "I say," rather than *weʾamar*, "he said." The LXX, Vulgate, and 1QIsaᵃ all
support this. If we accept the change, this becomes the only place that Isaiah speaks directly of himself. Delitzsch, II, 143, gets around this by having Isaiah refer to an "ideal
person, whom he has before him in visionary objectiveness." The change can be explained as an effort to clarify this unknown person. There is less of a problem leaving the
speaker unidentified than in making him Isaiah and creating a unique situation.

9 *O Zion, that bringest good tidings, get thee up into the high moun-*
   tain; O Jerusalem, that bringest good tidings, lift up thy voice with
   strength; lift it up, be not afraid; say unto the cities of Judah, Behold
   your God!
10 *Behold, the Lord God will come with strong hand, and his arm shall*
   rule for him: behold, his reward is with him, and his work before him.
11 *He shall feed his flock like a shepherd: he shall gather the lambs*
   with his arm, and carry them in his bosom, and shall gently lead
   those that are with young.

tion dies and the flower fades. Only God's Word endures forever. Comparing man to vegetation is common in the OT, e.g., 37:27; Psalm 90:5–6; 92:7; 102:11; 103:15–16. James 1:10–11 refers to it. First Peter 1:24–25 quotes the passage to show that the gospel will endure forever, cf. Matthew 5:18; 24:35, v. 8.

9–11 The unknown speaker urges the Jews to proclaim the coming of the Lord.[14] Jerusalem, as the capital, appropriately leads the way for the nation. To enhance the proclamation, they should go to the top of the highest mountain. They should shout the message with all of their strength. The whole nation should hear of the Lord's coming, v. 9. He will come with a "strong hand" (better "with strength"). His "arm," a natural symbol of strength, represents His power as He rules; cf. 33:2; 51:5. He brings His "reward" and His "work" (*pe*ᶜ*ullâ*, or "recompense") for the faithful. The word *pe*ᶜ*ullâ* has a broad meaning. It refers both to work and to the wages of work. Most often, however, it has the sense of "recompense," a meaning also seen elsewhere in Isaiah (cf. 62:11).[15] The parallelism suggests that the "reward" and the "recompense" refer to the same thing. When the word "recompense" has this sense elsewhere, e.g., 49:4, it always has the sense of a recompense "belonging to" someone rather than "paid to" another. This suggests that the reward and recompense here refer to the faithful who belong to the Lord. These come with

---

[14]Among others, Wade, p. 252; Skinner, *Isaiah XL–LXVI*, p. 6; and Rawlinson, II, 67, translate, "O thou that tellest good tidings to Zion . . . to Jerusalem." Isaiah 41:27 and 52:7 support this translation. Those references occur in different contexts and are not conclusive. Grammatically, we may translate the verse this way or with the AV. In both cases, the participle "that bringest good tidings" (*me*ᵇ*basseret*) is feminine. This agrees better with Zion and Jerusalem as subjects rather than objects.

[15]Delitzsch, II, 146; Näglesbach, p. 425; and Vine, p. 81, understand the "reward" as that given to the faithful. The "work" (or "recompense") is the punishment given to the Lord's enemies. While the view is possible, the parallelism argues against it. Further, nothing in the context mentions the punishment of enemies.

12 Who hath measured the waters in the hollow of his hand, and meted out heaven with the span, and comprehended the dust of the earth in a measure, and weighed the mountains in scales, and the hills in a balance?

13 Who hath directed the Spirit of the Lord, or being his counsellor hath taught him?

14 With whom took he counsel, and who instructed him, and taught him in the path of judgment, and taught him knowledge, and shewed to him the way of understanding?

Him as He returns to the land, v. 10.[16] Like a shepherd, He will care for His own. In the OT, the "shepherd" is always either one who cares for sheep or a civil leader of some kind. The Lord will be king, ruling over His people. He will carry out His responsibilities as a shepherd. He will "feed" (or "pasture") them, gather them with his arm, carry them close to His "bosom" (*ḥêq*). The word *ḥêq* refers to a depression or hollow. It often refers to the hollow at the breasts but can as well refer to the depression formed at the fold of a garment; cf. Proverbs 6:27; 16:33; 17:23. The Lord will lead "those that are with young" (*ᶜalôt*). The word *ᶜalôt* refers to nursing ewes, those still giving milk to their young. This is a picture of the tender care of His people given by the Lord, v. 11.

2. Power of God 40:12–31

12–14 The Lord asks a series of rhetorical questions. The questions come in groups: vv. 12*a–b–c–d–e*, 13–14, 18*a–b*, 21*a–b–c–d*, 25*a–b*, 27*a–b*, 28*a–b*. They emphatically introduce new thoughts. The initial group of questions shows the omnipotence of God. Who can measure the waters of the world in the palm of his hand?[17] Who can measure the heavens with the span of his hand? Who can calculate the dust of the earth with a "measure" (*šališ*)?[18] Who can weigh the mountains in a scale and the hills in a balance? Clearly, the answer to these questions is "no one." God alone is omnipotent. Isaiah illustrates this thought elsewhere in the chapter as he points to the creative work of God, vv. 21, 26, 28, v. 12.

---

[16]Pentecost, p. 535, and Barnes, II, 63, understand the recompense as that given to the faithful. While this is possible, the view requires that we understand "recompense" differently than in other places of the OT.

[17]Herbert, *Isaiah 40–66*, p. 23, makes these "the waters of chaos"; cf. Gen. 1:6–10. Nothing here requires that we limit the "waters" to those before the completed Creation.

[18]The word *šališ* properly means "a third." This leads to the question "a third of what?" The word occurs again only at Ps. 80:5 ("measure"), in which it is also indeterminate. The quantity "a third of an ephah," about a fourth of a bushel, is most often suggested;

15 *Behold, the nations are as a drop of a bucket, and are counted as the small dust of the balance: behold, he taketh up the isles as a very little thing.*
16 *And Lebanon is not sufficient to burn, nor the beasts thereof sufficient for a burnt offering.*
17 *All nations before him are as nothing; and they are counted to him less than nothing, and vanity.*

The next set of questions brings out the omniscience of the Lord. Who gave direction to the Spirit of the Lord or, serving as His counselor, taught Him?[19] The apostle Paul quotes the verse twice, Romans 11:34; I Corinthians 2:16, v. 13. Who gave the Spirit counsel and "instructed him" (*bîn*, better "made Him understand," see 1:3), teaching Him "judgment" (*mišpaṭ*, better "justice," see 1:17), "knowledge," and "understanding"? Once more, the answer is "no one," v. 14.

15–17 Isaiah pauses in the middle of the questions to show God's greatness. In comparison with Him, the nations of the world are as "a drop [*mar*] of [better 'from'] a bucket [*delî*]."[20] The picture is of a drop hanging from a bucket from which water has been poured. It is an insignificant amount. The nations are like the "small dust [*šaḥaq*] of the balance." The word *šaḥaq* normally refers to a cloud, a collection of fine droplets of water. Here it refers to a collection of fine dust particles. These would settle on the scale from the air and would not measurably affect the scales. The Lord would so consider the "isles" (*ʾî*, see 11:11), the coastal regions of the Mediterranean Sea, as a small thing to pick up,

---

cf. 5:10. H. Porter, "Measure," *International Standard Bible Encyclopedia*, III, p. 2016, suggests "threefold, large measure." Gill, p. 225, notes that the Vulgate translates, "with three fingers." On this basis, he concludes "that the dust of the earth, or the earth itself, which is but dust, is no more with the Lord than so much earth or dust as a man can hold between his thumb and two fingers." Childs, p. 305, speculates "basket," a suggestion with little to commend it. While we do not know the exact amount of a *šališ*, we do know that man cannot measure "the dust of the earth."

[19]North, p. 44, understands "Spirit" as "spirit," not the Holy Spirit. He notes that Paul uses the term "mind" as he quotes from the LXX. Paul does this deliberately because of his conclusion. Believers have the "mind of Christ." This "mind," however, comes to us by the indwelling Holy Spirit. There is no reason to abandon that thought here.

[20]The word *mar* occurs only here. It apparently comes from *marar*, unused in Hebrew but "to pass by, flow," in Arabic. The context, something from a bucket and obviously very small, supports the meaning "drop." Price, p. 168, translates *delî* as "rain-cloud." The picture of a single drop amid all of the drops in a storm is correct, but there is little support for the translation. The word *delî* occurs elsewhere only as a dual in Num. 24:7, in which the translation "rain cloud" will not stand. The root *dalâ*, "to draw [water]" occurs in Exod. 2:16, 19, in which it clearly refers to drawing water from a well.

18 *To whom then will ye liken God? or what likeness will ye compare unto him?*

19 *The workman melteth a graven image, and the goldsmith spreadeth it over with gold, and casteth silver chains.*

20 *He that is so impoverished that he hath no oblation chooseth a tree that will not rot; he seeketh unto him a cunning workman to prepare a graven image, that shall not be moved.*

v. 15. The Lebanon Mountains, heavily forested in biblical times, cf. 37:24; 60:13, could not furnish enough wood for a worthy sacrifice. All of the animals living in the mountains would not be adequate for a worthy burnt offering to the Lord, v. 16. All the nations taken together are as nothing before Him. They are regarded as "less than nothing [*me'epes*, see 34:12][21] and vanity [*tohû*, see 24:10, 'confusion']." The word *tohû* indicates "emptiness." Isaiah heaps the descriptive terms together to show the relative nothingness of the nations in comparison with God, v. 17.

18–20 Isaiah now asks two more questions to continue the thought of God's incomparableness. To whom will men compare God? What likeness can men compare to God? None are like God, cf. v. 25, v. 18.[22] The following two verses expand the thought to show that Isaiah has idols in mind. The "workman" (or "craftsman") "melteth" (or "casts") a "graven image" (*pesel*). While *pesel* elsewhere may be an idol of wood, metal, or stone, the fact of casting it shows that Isaiah thinks of a metal idol. The "goldsmith" (*ṣorep*, or "smith")[23] plates it with gold and casts silver "chains" (*r^etuqôt*)[24] to decorate the idol, v. 19.

---

[21]Von Orelli, p. 223; Skinner, *Isaiah XL–LXVI*, p. 10; and Whitehouse, II, 57, understand the *min*-preposition as partitive. The nations are from nothingness. It is better, in my judgment, to understand the *min* as comparative rather than partitive. See Waltke and O'Connor, 14.4d, note 22. They are "less than nothing." The idiom shows that the nations of the world do not impress God with their wealth, power, and accomplishments.

[22]Tryggve N. D. Mettinger, "The Elimination of a Crux? A Syntactic and Semantic Study of Isaiah XL 18–20," in *VTS*, XXVI, 1974, p. 79, follows the Vulgate and LXX in understanding the *ha* in *happesel*, "image," v. 19, and in *hamsukkan*, "image," v. 20, as interrogative particles. He translates, "Maybe an idol . . . maybe an image. . . ." While the translation does not change the sense, it would be unusual for the *ha* to have a full vowel before a nongutteral. The poetical nature of the passage also argues against making this an interrogative.

[23]When used of metal, the word *ṣorep* occurs most often in connection with the working of silver. It also refers to the working of gold or simply refining or melting metal. The sense of "smith" embraces all of these ideas.

[24]Watts, *Isaiah 34–66*, p. 87, argues that *r^etuqôt* refers to a "fastener" to hold the idol to its wooden base. While *r^etuqôt* is a *hapax legomenon*, related forms meaning "chain" occur at I Kings 6:21 and Ezek. 7:23. It is still possible that the chain is for the purpose

21 *Have ye not known? have ye not heard? hath it not been told you
from the beginning? have ye not understood from the foundations of
the earth?*

22 *It is he that sitteth upon the circle of the earth, and the inhabitants
thereof are as grasshoppers; that stretcheth out the heavens as a
curtain, and spreadeth them out as a tent to dwell in:*

23 *That bringeth the princes to nothing; he maketh the judges of the
earth as vanity.*

24 *Yea, they shall not be planted; yea, they shall not be sown: yea, their
stock shall not take root in the earth: and he shall also blow upon
them, and they shall wither, and the whirlwind shall take them away
as stubble.*

One who is too "impoverished" (*hamsukkan*)[25] to bring an offering
still makes an idol. Although he cannot afford to cast an expensive idol,
he chooses a hard wood that will not decay.[26] He hires a wise craftsman
to make the "graven image" (*pesel*), a carved idol that "shall not be
moved," i.e., overthrown on its base, v. 20.

21–24 Returning to His earlier approach, the Lord asks four more
questions. With these questions, the expected answer is yes. Judah did
know. They had heard. These truths had been told them. They did understand. Only with the last question does Isaiah reveal the focus of the
questions. Does Judah understand the earth's creation? The final "from"
is not in the text and should be omitted. Has Judah "understood [*bîn*, see
1:3] the foundations of the earth"? In other words, have they not under-

---

of holding the idol to its base. It is also possible that it is for ornamentation. Since a
"goldsmith" makes the chain from "silver," I have opted for ornamentation. Merely
securing the idol in an upright position would not have required silver.

[25]The word *mᵉsukkan* is a *hapax legomenon*. In form, it is the *puᶜal* participle of *sakan*,
"to be poor," an unused root. This has led to various interpretations. Nägelsbach, p. 429,
relates it to *šakan*, "to dwell," then contorts the meaning to indicate a person who has
been made to sit still, brought down, thus poor. Delitzsch, II, 151, appeals to Deut. 8:9
(*miskenut*, "scarceness") to support the meaning of "poor." McKenzie, p. 21, interprets
mᵉsukkan as a type of tree, lit. "a tree of consecration." Mettinger, pp. 81–82, relates the
hapax to a denominative Ugaritic verb *skn*, "to make a statue or an image." He then lets
tᵉrûmâ modify *hamsukkan* and translates, "an image which is a sacred contribution."
H. G. M. Williamson, "Isaiah 40,20—A Case of Not Seeing the Wood for the Trees,"
Biblica 67:14–19, follows Mettinger in seeing the interrogative particle in *hamsukkan*.
He relates *mᵉsukkan* to an Akkadian word for wood from the sissoo tree. Other efforts
as well have been made to make sense of a difficult phrase.

[26]Price, p. 169, understands the tree as the mulberry, better known for its fruit than its
hard wood. The text does not let us identify the wood.

stood that it is God who established the earth, cf. Proverbs 3:19, v. 21? It is the Lord who sits "upon" (or "above") the "circle" (*ḥûg*) of the earth. The *ḥûg* of the earth is its heavenly surrounding, as in Job 22:14.[27] The Lord sits above His creation. The thought is of God seated on His heavenly throne; cf. 6:1; I Kings 22:19. From that exalted position, the people of the earth are as grasshoppers. The contrast is not between height and depth. God is well able to see man from any height. The contrast is rather between significance and insignificance. In an eternal light, man has little significance. The Lord stretches the heavens out like a "curtain" (*doq*) to veil himself. The word *doq* occurs only here. It is from *daqaq*, "to crush," and thus to make something fine or thin. The noun form probably indicates a thin curtain or veil. He "spreadeth" (*matah*)[28] the heavens like a tent in which He dwells. The verb *matah* is also a *hapax legomenon*. From the parallelism with "stretcheth out," it must mean something like "spreads," v. 22. In comparison to Him, the leaders of the earth are as nothing. The "princes" of this life pass off the scene and become "nothing." The "judges" of the earth likewise become as "vanity" (*tohû*, see 24:10), without value, v. 23. These leaders are not like strong trees with deep roots, able to resist the buffetings of this life. They are scarcely (*bal*) planted, scarcely (*bal*) sown in the earth, and their stock scarcely (*bal*) allowed to grow roots.[29] The Lord then blows on them and His breath takes them away in judgment. They "wither" before the heat of His anger. They are as stubble blown by the "whirlwind" (or "storm"), v. 24.

25–27 In the next pair of questions, the Lord once more brings out His transcendence. Is there anyone like the Lord? Is anyone equal to

---

[27]Prov. 8:27 ("compass") refers to the circular appearance of the horizon. Job 26:10 uses the verb form *hag* to describe the encirclement of the waters. Among others, Grogan, p. 246; Young, III, 57; and Pieper, p. 127, understand the "circle" as the horizon. This is a natural sense, in view of what man sees when he looks over the horizon. I have chosen to make the "circle" the heavens above the earth since the verse emphasizes God's dwelling above the heavens rather than the disk of the earth; cf. Ps. 113:5–6.

[28]The noun *ʾamtahat*, "sack," from the same root, occurs twelve times, all in Genesis, e.g., 42:27, 28; 44:2, 12. The connection lies in the stretching of the sack as it is filled.

[29]The negative *bal* normally is "no" or "not." The context here forces the meaning of "scarcely" or "hardly." The leaders do come into their earthly positions. They have no permanence, however. They pass off the scene in a short time.

25 *To whom then will ye liken me, or shall I be equal? saith the Holy One.*
26 *Lift up your eyes on high, and behold who hath created these things, that bringeth out their host by number: he calleth them all by names by the greatness of his might, for that he is strong in power; not one faileth.*
27 *Why sayest thou, O Jacob, and speakest, O Israel, My way is hid from the Lord, and my judgment is passed over from my God?*
28 *Hast thou not known? hast thou not heard, that the everlasting God, the Lord, the Creator of the ends of the earth, fainteth not, neither is weary? there is no searching of his understanding.*
29 *He giveth power to the faint; and to them that have no might he increaseth strength.*
30 *Even the youths shall faint and be weary, and the young men shall utterly fall:*
31 *But they that wait upon the Lord shall renew their strength; they shall mount up with wings as eagles; they shall run, and not be weary; and they shall walk, and not faint.*

Him? The expected answer is no (cf. v. 18), v. 25. As an illustration of His power, Isaiah returns to creation. God created the heavenly bodies and brings them out each night "by number," all of them taking their place each night. He names them all.[30] His greatness is such that His power keeps the stars. None of them "faileth" (or "is lacking"), v. 26.

Only one interrogative marks the next set of questions. In view of God's care for the universe, how can Judah say that God does not know the problems that faced them? Was their way hid from God? Had He ignored their need of "judgment" (*mišpaṭ*, better "justice," see 1:17)? The expected answer is a resounding no! God was fully aware of their needs, v. 27.

28–31 The final pair of questions confront Judah with past revelation to them. Have they not known? Yes, they have known. Have they not heard? Yes, they have heard. The Lord is the "everlasting God." He is the "Lord," the redemptive name of God. He is the Creator God. The Lord does not faint or grow tired. No one comprehends His understanding, v. 28. He supplies power to the weak, cf. II Corinthians 12:9, v. 29. By comparison with those whom the Lord sustains, youths will grow weary and young men will "utterly fall" (*kašôl yikkašelû*). The repeated root

---

[30]While this is not a major teaching, the verse incidentally confirms the finite nature of the universe. Every star has a name. The stars may be innumerable to man but they are counted and named by God.

kašal is correctly intensified "utterly fall," v. 30.[31] Those, however, who "wait" (*qawâ*, see 5:2) upon the Lord will find that He renews their strength. They will "mount up with wings as eagles," a picture of their ability to overcome obstacles before them; cf. Psalm 103:5. They will run without becoming weary. They will walk without fainting. The application is more than physical. It refers to the spiritual power given by God to those who trust Him, cf. II Corinthians 12:10*b*, v. 31.

Practical Applications from Chapter 40

1. The Shepherding Role of Our Lord, v. 11
   a. The need of a Shepherd, Matthew 9:36 (Mark 6:34)
   b. The goodness of the Shepherd, John 10:11, 14
   c. The greatness of the Shepherd, Hebrews 13:20
   d. The uniqueness of the Shepherd, John 10:16
   e. The position of the Shepherd, I Peter 5:4
2. The Nature of God
   a. His omnipotence, v. 12 (illustrated by Creation, v. 21)
   b. His omniscience, vv. 13–14
   c. His transcendence, vv. 15–17, 18, 20, 25–26
   d. His love, v. 27
   e. His self-revelation, v. 28
   f. His sufficiency, vv. 29–31

---

[31]Young, III, 68, and Leupold, II, 39, make the comparison to God Himself. Youth, in all their vigor and strength, will grow faint in comparison to God. Verse 31, however, shows that the comparison is with those who draw their strength from the Lord.

1 *Keep silence before me, O islands; and let the people renew their strength: let them come near; then let them speak: let us come near together to judgment.*

2 *Who raised up the righteous man from the east, called him to his foot, gave the nations before him, and made him rule over kings? he gave them as the dust to his sword, and as driven stubble to his bow.*

3 *He pursued them, and passed safely; even by the way that he had not gone with his feet.*

4 *Who hath wrought and done it, calling the generations from the beginning? I the Lord, the first, and with the last; I am he.*

ISAIAH 41

The chapter makes an important transition by introducing Cyrus, a major character in this part of the book. He was a younger son of Cambyses, the king of Persia, and Mandane, daughter of Astyages, the king of Media. He became ruler of Anshan, a province of Elam to the south of Shushan, ca. 559 B.C. Upon the death of his brother Cyaxares, he became the king of Persia. Seeking to expand his kingdom, he defeated his father-in-law Astyages, ca. 550 B.C., and united the Medes and the Persians. He defeated Croesus, king of Lydia, in 546 B.C. In 539 B.C., his army under the leadership of Darius defeated Babylon. He died in battle ca. 530 B.C. His tomb still stands at Pasargadae, in modern Iraq. The Lord raises up this heathen king to restore captive Judah to their land.

3. Triumph of God 41:1–29

1–4 God commands the "islands" (*ʾiyîm*, "coastlands," see 11:11) to be quiet before Him. The term specially includes the areas around the Mediterranean.[1] These people should renew their strength in preparation for "judgment" (*mišpaṭ*, see 1:17). In this context, the Lord invites them to a trial in which He will judge their actions, v. 1. The reason for this appearance before God now appears. The Lord rhetorically asks who has raised up "the righteous man from the east [*mizraḥ*, see 43:5]." The verse reads better "Who has stirred up one from the east, He calls him in righteousness [*ṣedeq*, see 1:21] to His feet [*regel*]."[2] The question refers to

---

[1] Wright, p. 100, understands *ʾiyîm* here as "all peoples of the world." The view is unlikely. The biblical teachings focus on the biblical world.

[2] Several authors make *ṣedek* a personification. Pieper, p. 143, calls it "the personified covenant-faith" that calls Cyrus forth. Motyer, *The Prophecy of Isaiah*, p. 310, makes it personify the Lord, who calls Cyrus. Cowles, p. 319, considers it as personifying "justice." While it is possible to make *ṣedek* the subject, there is no clear indication of what it

Cyrus II, also known as Cyrus the Great, a major character in c. 41, 45, 46, and 48.[3] As is common in the book, the verbs are prophetic perfects, referring to certain future events as though they are accomplished facts. The call is "in righteousness" in that it is for a righteous purpose. God calls Cyrus "to his foot." This expression indicates that Cyrus is subject to Him.[4] The Lord makes him a victorious ruler over "the nations." Other kings are as "dust" to his sword and as "driven stubble," i.e., stubble driven by the wind, to his bow. They are weak, not able to stand against him, v. 2.

Cyrus successfully defeats his foes. He goes "safely" (šalôm, see 9:6) "by the way that he had not gone with his feet" as he enters new territories to conquer. This brief statement sums up the history of Cyrus, v. 3. Once more, the Lord asks who has done this. Answering the question, He states that He has raised up the "generations" of man from "the beginning" of time. From the "first" of time, He is the Lord. With the "last" generations, He is still God.[5] He is the eternal God, who alone has the perspective to bring the generations into being, v. 4.

---

personifies. Leupold, II, 42, understands ṣedek as "victory." He translates, "one whom victory attends at every step." The translation, however, requires rare meanings for both ṣedek and regel. Watts, Isaiah 34–66, p. 102, argues that ṣedek here means "salvation," in the sense of "success." It is debatable if ṣedek has this sense. Literally, the text reads "righteous(ness) he calls him to his feet." I understand ṣedek to describe the call as having a righteous goal.

[3]Since the passage does not name Cyrus, other persons have been suggested. Gill, p. 231, suggests the apostle Paul. Henry, pp. 220–21, applies the call to Abraham's call from Ur of the Chaldees. The Isaiah Targum also gives Abraham although it makes him a "paradigm of Israel." The Talmud, Shabbath 156b, applies the verse to Abraham. Kissane, II, 22–23, follows the traditional Jewish view. Baba Bathra 15a has the curious view that it is Abraham who is the same as Ethan the Ezrahite, I Kings 4:31; Ps. 89 title.

[4]Kissane, p. 29, argues that the phrase "to his feet" always means "behind him." On this basis, he translates, "called him to follow." The joining of the lamed preposition with regel, however, may also indicate direction towards, Exod. 4:25; Job 18:11. The singular "foot" suggests the position to which the Lord calls Cyrus.

[5]Isaiah is the only OT author to describe God as the "first . . . last." The expression "first . . . last" occurs also at 44:6 and 48:12. The phrasing here, however, is unusual. Only here does Isaiah express "last" as a plural. The change gives a different emphasis from 44:6 and 48:12. There, the focus is on God in time. Here, the focus begins with time, then shifts to mankind. God is from the beginning. He is still God with the latter generations.

5 *The isles saw it, and feared; the ends of the earth were afraid, drew near, and came.*

6 *They helped every one his neighbour; and every one said to his brother, Be of good courage.*

7 *So the carpenter encouraged the goldsmith, and he that smootheth with the hammer him that smote the anvil, saying, It is ready for the sodering: and he fastened it with nails, that it should not be moved.*

8 *But thou, Israel, art my servant, Jacob whom I have chosen, the seed of Abraham my friend.*

9 *Thou whom I have taken from the ends of the earth, and called thee from the chief men thereof, and said unto thee, Thou art my servant; I have chosen thee, and not cast thee away.*

10 *Fear thou not; for I am with thee: be not dismayed; for I am thy God: I will strengthen thee; yea, I will help thee; yea, I will uphold thee with the right hand of my righteousness.*

5–7 The "isles," the people in the coastal areas of the Mediterranean (cf. v. 1), fear the exploits of Cyrus. They "drew near, and came," joining together to meet the challenge, v. 5. They help one another. Each one encourages the next to be brave, v. 6. The "carpenter" (or "craftsman") encourages the "goldsmith" (*ṣorep*, or "smith," see 40:19) as they make new idols to help them meet the challenge. The one "that smootheth with the hammer [*paṭṭîš*]"[6] describes the smith as he prepares the gold leaf that will cover the idol. He encourages the smith that strikes the "anvil," possibly making the nails he will use. The phrase "saying, It is ready for the soldering" is better "saying of the soldering, 'It is good.'" The smith fastens the idols with nails so that they will not be overthrown, v. 7.

8–10 The Lord reminds Israel that she is His "servant." She is "Jacob," the one chosen by God to be the progenitor of the twelve tribes; cf. Genesis 28:13–15; 35:9–12. She is the "seed of Abraham," the "friend of God," II Chronicles 20:7; James 2:23, the one with whom God had established His covenant, Genesis 12:2–3. The stress on the relationship of the nation with Jacob and Abraham suggests that she has no need to fear. The heathen may fear the exploits of Cyrus but Israel has no need of this, v. 8.[7] The Lord has chosen Israel "from the ends of the

---

[6]Skinner, *Isaiah XL–LXVI*, p. 20, understands *paṭṭîš* as a "sledge-hammer." It is difficult to see how a sledgehammer fits here with "smoothing" something. In the only other occurrences of the word, Jer. 23:29; 50:23, the hammer is a powerful weapon. The word, however, may well describe a generic hammer with the context suggesting the size.

[7]Pentecost, p. 489, applies vv. 8–14 to the millennial kingdom as a promise of supernatural protection. The context, however, does not support an eschatological application

11 *Behold, all they that were incensed against thee shall be ashamed and confounded: they shall be as nothing; and they that strive with thee shall perish.*

12 *Thou shalt seek them, and shalt not find them, even them that contended with thee: they that war against thee shall be as nothing, and as a thing of nought.*

13 *For I the Lord thy God will hold thy right hand, saying unto thee, Fear not; I will help thee.*

earth" when Abraham was still in Ur, Genesis 11:31.[8] He has called her "from the chief men" (*ʾaṣîlîm*, better "remote parts"). The word *ʾaṣîlîm* is better "sides, extremities," or "remote areas."[9] The parallelism with the phrase "ends of the earth" suggests that the calling comes while they are still in the distant regions. He has chosen them to be His servant and He will not reject them, v. 9. For this reason, the people have no reason to fear. The Lord will be with them. He will be their "God," the name expressing His omnipotence. He will strengthen, help, and uphold them with the "right hand of my righteousness" (*ṣedeq*, or "My righteous right hand," see 1:21). The "right hand" is an emblem of God's power, (cf. 48:13; 62:8). He extends it now to meet Israel's needs. It is "righteous" since God limits its use to righteous causes, here the defense of His people. There is a progression in God's relationship with His people: (1) He first strengthens them, enabling them to use their abilities and resources. (2) Then, He joins with them, giving them help where they are weak. (3) Finally, He upholds them so that the enemy's attacks will fail. The rest of the chapter expands the promise, giving details of the Lord's work on Israel's behalf, v. 10.

11–13 Israel's enemies will be "ashamed [*bôš*, see 1:29] and confounded [*kalam* see 30:3]." "They" (*ʾenôš*, see 2:11) who fight against the nation will be as "nothing." The parallelism with "perish" and the further development in v. 12 indicate that those who oppose Israel will

---

at this point. The passage is a simple statement expressing Israel's relationship with God. The following passage, vv. 17–20, develops the eschatological aspect.

[8]Von Orelli, p. 230, refers the "ends of the earth" to Israel's call out of Egypt. His view is possible.

[9]Rawlinson, II, 97, argues that *ʾaṣîlîm* has the meaning "chief men" since this is its sense in the only other place it occurs, Exod. 24:11. The word comes from the root *ʾaṣal*, "to withdraw, set apart." The word in Exod. 24:11 refers to a "noble," one set apart from others. The idea of apartness, i.e., remoteness, is best here, where the phrase parallels "ends of the earth."

14 Fear not, thou worm Jacob, and ye men of Israel; I will help thee, saith the Lord, and thy redeemer, the Holy One of Israel.

15 Behold, I will make thee a new sharp threshing instrument having teeth: thou shalt thresh the mountains, and beat them small, and shalt make the hills as chaff.

16 Thou shalt fan them, and the wind shall carry them away, and the whirlwind shall scatter them: and thou shalt rejoice in the Lord, and shalt glory in the Holy One of Israel.

disappear, v. 11. If Israel seeks their enemies, they will not find "them" (*ʾenôš*, see 2:11). They will become as nothing, no longer existing. They will become "a thing of nought" (*ʾepes*, or "nonexistent," see 34:12), v. 12. The Lord will hold Israel's "right hand." This again refers to the hand of strength.[10] The promise is that God will strengthen Israel's power. They do not need to fear since He will help them, v. 13.

14–16 The Lord addresses Israel as a "worm." This is an emblem of weakness; cf. Job 25:6; Psalm 22:6. To clarify the subject, He calls them "men [*mat*] of Israel."[11] The Lord will help them. He identifies Himself as their "redeemer" (*goʾel*, see 35:9). The word *goʾel* is often understood as a "kinsman-redeemer." It occurs here and twenty-two additional times in the remainder of the book. It occurs in the first part of Isaiah only at 35:9, v. 14.

The Lord will make Israel as a "threshing instrument" (or "threshing sledge"). This was a heavy sled with teeth of metal or stone set in the planks. The oxen dragged the sledge over the grain to break the husks; cf. 28:27. This allowed the winnowing to take place. Israel would thresh "mountains" and "hills." This figurative expression shows the greatness

---

[10]Herbert, *Isaiah 40–66,* p. 33, wrongly relates the taking of the right hand to the pagan ceremony in which the Babylonian kings "took the right hand of Marduk." The view ignores the widespread symbolic use of the right hand as the hand of blessing and honor, e.g., Gen. 48:13–18; I Kings 2:19; Ps. 16:11, or the hand of strength, e.g., Job 40:14; Ps. 17:7; 63:8.

[11]Leupold, II, 49, understands *mat* as suggesting that there are not many men in the nation. The idea of a small number appears elsewhere, e.g., Gen. 34:30; Deut. 4:27. There are also occurrences in which the thought of a small number does not appear, e.g., Job 22:15; Ps. 17:14. The connotation of number, then, is secondary. Normally, a context is necessary to draw the conclusion of a small number. Watts, *Isaiah 34–66,* p. 100, relates the word to the Akkadian *mutu,* "cornworm." He translates "caterpillar," parallel to "worm" in the first phrase. This would be an exceptional use of *mat.* The word is not rare but regularly occurs with the general meaning of "man." Only with a context can we expand the translation to describe the man in some way, e.g., lying ("vain") men, Job 11:11; wicked men, Job 22:15.

17 *When the poor and needy seek water, and there is none, and their*
tongue faileth for thirst, I the Lord will hear them, I the God of Is-
rael will not forsake them.
18 *I will open rivers in high places, and fountains in the midst of the*
valleys: I will make the wilderness a pool of water, and the dry land
springs of water.
19 *I will plant in the wilderness the cedar, the shittah tree, and the myr-*
tle, and the oil tree; I will set in the desert the fir tree, and the pine,
and the box tree together:
20 *That they may see, and know, and consider, and understand together,*
that the hand of the Lord hath done this, and the Holy One of Israel
hath created it.

of Israel's victory over her enemies, v. 15.[12] They will "fan" (or "win-
now") them. The wind will "carry them away" and the whirlwind will
"scatter them." The word picture comes from the winnowing of grain.
The farmer would thresh the grain by dragging a threshing sledge over it
to separate the grain from the husks. Using the winnowing fan, he would
toss the mixture of grain, straw, and chaff into the air. The wind blowing
across the threshing floor would blow the lighter material to the side
while the heavier grain would fall in the center. In the same way, Israel's
enemies will be carried away. The picture shows the completeness of Israel's victory over their foes. In turn, Israel will rejoice in the Lord, who
has blessed them, v. 16.

17–20 The Lord will supply the needs of the people. Isaiah gives the
example of the "poor [ʿanî, or 'afflicted,' see 3:14] and needy [ʾebyôn, see
14:30]" seeking water in the wilderness. Their tongue "faileth for thirst."
They cry to the Lord for help and He hears their plea. From the context,
the example is figurative, illustrating God's care for His own, v. 17.[13] He
opens rivers in the "high places" (šᵉpayîm).[14] The šᵉpayîm are the barren

---

[12]Slotki, p. 195, mentions the idea that the mountains and hills represent "mighty
worldly forces that obstruct the development and spread of the moral and spiritual ideas
which Israel upholds." McKenzie, pp. 30–31, suggests that they stand for "loftiness and
pride and power." Barnes, II, 89, sees the mountains and hills as picturing large and small
kingdoms. Brueggemann, *Isaiah 40–66*, p. 35, specifically relates them to Babylon.
Alexander, II, 124, rejects "states or governments." He understands the weak worm of
v. 14 that grinds down the hills as picturing weak Israel overcoming "the most dispropor-
tionate obstacles." There is room for some variation in understanding the symbolism here.

[13]Pieper, p. 162; Rawlinson, II, 98, and Leupold, II, 51, understand this as a change in
Israel's condition. The "poor and needy" are those suffering from spiritual poverty. Nothing here, however, requires more than an illustration of blessing.

[14]Among others, Henry, p. 224; Barnes, II, 89; and Kraeling, p. 157, relate this to the
return from Babylonian captivity. Ezra 1–2, however, which gives us the most detailed

21 *Produce your cause, saith the Lord; bring forth your strong reasons, saith the King of Jacob.*

22 *Let them bring them forth, and shew us what shall happen: let them shew the former things, what they be, that we may consider them, and know the latter end of them; or declare us things for to come.*

23 *Shew the things that are to come hereafter, that we may know that ye are gods: yea, do good, or do evil, that we may be dismayed, and behold it together.*

24 *Behold, ye are of nothing, and your work of nought: an abomination is he that chooseth you.*

heights of the mountains. These become the source of rivers of water to meet the needs of the people. God will cause fountains of water to spring forth in the "valleys" (*biqᶜâ*, see 40:4). Enough sources of water appear in the wilderness that it is as a pool of water. The "dry" (or "parched") land will become springs of water, v. 18. Trees will flourish in previously barren places. The "cedar" is an unidentified species. The "shittah" is probably the acacia, a hardwood tree. The "myrtle" is an evergreen shrub with white berries and edible blue black berries. The "oil tree" is not identified clearly. It is possibly a wild olive tree. The "fir" is most likely the cypress tree. The "pine" is possibly the boxwood tree but cannot be identified certainly. The "box tree" is also an unidentified tree. All these, named as representative trees, will grow "in the wilderness" areas of the land. The growth illustrates the abundant supply of water in what was formerly a dry wilderness, v. 19. All mankind will know that the Lord has blessed His people. They will reflect on the power of the Lord that does these things. He has created these new conditions.

The fulfillment of vv. 17–20 is yet future. When the Lord returns to set up His kingdom on the earth, the wilderness areas will bring forth abundant vegetation; cf. 35:1–2, 6–7. The land now bears the marks of a sin-cursed world, but the Lord will remove the curse and give the land His blessing, v. 20.

21–24 The Lord returns to the trial setting introduced earlier in v. 1. He invites the heathen to produce evidence in support of their gods. The title "King of Jacob" is only a variation of "King of Israel." This is the

---

record of the return, says nothing of such a miracle. The way along which Israel would normally have come was not a wilderness. The nation would have crossed several rivers along the way. In addition to the above view, Grogan, p. 251, mentions two more possible fulfillments: (1) figurative, God supplying all the needs of Israel; and (2) symbolic, the fulfillment of every spiritual need in Christ.

25 *I have raised up one from the north, and he shall come: from the rising of the sun shall he call upon my name: and he shall come upon princes as upon morter, and as the potter treadeth clay.*
26 *Who hath declared from the beginning, that we may know? and beforetime, that we may say, He is righteous? yea, there is none that sheweth, yea, there is none that declareth, yea, there is none that heareth your words.*
27 *The first shall say to Zion, Behold, behold them: and I will give to Jerusalem one that bringeth good tidings.*
28 *For I beheld, and there was no man; even among them, and there was no counsellor, that, when I asked of them, could answer a word.*
29 *Behold, they are all vanity; their works are nothing: their molten images are wind and confusion.*

only time this title appears in the OT, but the Lord's position as king over Israel appears often in the book, e.g., 6:5; 32:1; 33:17; 43:15; 44:6, v. 21. Let these gods predict the future. Let them tell of the "former things," earlier predictions that now have been fulfilled. This will let God's people reflect on these matters. Again, He challenges the heathen gods to predict the future, v. 22. Let these gods predict the future in order to prove their deity. The phrase "do good, or do evil" is equivalent to saying, "do something" to show that you exist. This will cause Israel to be "dismayed" (or "look anxiously about") and to "behold [*nira²*] it together," i.e., see the results, v. 23.[15]

There is an implied pause between v. 23 and v. 24. It need not be long, simply sufficient for the gods to respond to the challenge. When they fail, the Lord concludes that they are "of nothing," nonexistent. Moreover, their work is "of nought" (*²apaᶜ*),[16] worthless. Anyone who chooses to follow these gods is an "abomination" to God, v. 24.

25–29 In sharp contrast with the idols, the Lord predicts His future work. He has "raised up" Cyrus, such a certain event that He states it as an accomplished event. Cyrus comes from the "north" and from "the ris-

---

[15]Watts, *Isaiah 34–66*, p. 112, follows the *qᵉrê* and locates *nir²eh* from *yara²*, "to fear." Kraeling, p. 158, and Kelley, p. 305, also translate similarly. In form, however, *nira²* is closer to the *nipᶜal* of *ra²â*, "to see." G.K. 48 *g*, note 1, locates the word as a shortened cohortative form from *ra²â*.

[16]The word *²apaᶜ* is a *hapax legomenon*. BDB, p. 67, suggests that this is a textual error for *²apes*, from *²apas*, "ceasing," and therefore "nought." Childs, p. 315; Wade, p. 266; and Westerlund, p. 82, follow this view. There is, however, only weak evidence for calling this an error in copying. Pieper, p. 168, overstates his argument by claiming that verbs beginning with *p* and ending with a guttural "are imitative of blowing." He relates *paᶜâ*, to "breath, wind, nothing" and concludes that *²apaᶜ* means "nothing." There are,

ing of the sun," the east.[17] Both Media and Persia lie to the east of Palestine. Because of the wilderness east of Palestine, the Medo-Persian invasion came from the north.[18] Cyrus calls upon "my name," God's name. There is no problem with this when we recognize that calling on the Lord's name does not mean accepting the Lord as his God. We know from archaeology that Cyrus recognized many gods. The emperor called on God in his proclamation to release the Jews from captivity; cf. Ezra 1:2.[19] The Cylinder of Cyrus is an archaeological record describing the conquest of Babylon and the freeing of those who have been held captive in Babylon. In this, the king addresses Bel, Nabu, and Marduk as his chief gods. He asks the lesser gods to pray to them on his behalf. He no doubt considered Israel's God to be one of these gods. He tramples the kings of other nations under his feet as though they were mortar or clay, easily moldable substances, v. 25.

Who but God has predicted this so that His people may know the future? As the result, they may say, "He is righteous [or 'right']," i.e., His words are accurate and therefore trustworthy. There is no one who has predicted these things. There is no one who has heard "your words," the words of the false gods, v. 26. The interpretation of v. 27 turns on the understanding of the word "first" (*ri'šôn*).[20] The phrase has a variety of interpretations. In addition, the first phrase has no verb. We must either

---

however, several *p*-verbs ending with gutturals that have nothing to do with blowing or breathing, e.g., *pala'*, *pasaḥ*, *pašaᶜ*. Delitzsch, II, 169, derives the word from *paᶜâ*, "to breathe," which he interprets as a synonym of *'awen*, "weariness," *hebel*, "vapor, breath," and *ruaḥ*, "wind, breath." He concludes that *'apaᶜ* means "nothing." This seems to be the best derivation.

[17]Kissane, II, 34, makes the "north" refer to Haran and "the rising of the sun" to Ur of the Chaldees. This leads him to make the "one" speak of Abraham, who came first from Ur, then from Haran. Abraham, however, does not fit the description of v. 2. He did not rule over nations. Smart, pp. 77–78, understands the "one" as "restored and transformed Israel." It is difficult, however, to fit this into the picture of historical Israel. The wider context of c. 44, 45, 46, and 48 supports the identification of Cyrus with the "one" raised up by the Lord.

[18]Several authors, e.g., Smith, Pieper, Von Orelli, understand the directions to refer to Persia, to the east of Babylon, and Media, to the north of Babylon. While this is true, it is more natural to refer the verse to Palestine and to understand the directions as above.

[19]Leupold, II, 55, translates *yiqra'*, "proclaim" rather than "call." While the translation is possible, the sense of "proclaiming" is distinctly minor in comparison to that of "calling."

[20]Näglesbach, p. 446; Pieper, p. 171; and Skinner, *Isaiah XL–LXVI*, p. 27, refer *ri'šôn* to Cyrus, the beginner of Israel's redemption. Cowles, p. 327, and Young, III, 103, understands *ri'šôn* as a substantive referring to the Lord. The bringer of good news is Isaiah

supply a verb or reach forward in the verse to "I will give." Verse 27 continues the thought of v. 26. This leads to supplying the verb ʾamartî, "I have said," and understanding riʾšôn as an adverb. This gives the translation "I formerly said to Zion, Behold, Behold them!" He refers to the "good tidings" (mᵉbaśśer) He has given them. The idols had not foretold the future but the Lord had done so. Verse 27b moves on to say that He will give them one to bring good news to them. This bringer of good news is Cyrus, the one who lets them return from the captivity to Jerusalem, v. 27. Among the heathen, there has been no one who could give such guidance. The Lord had searched in vain for a "counsellor" who could give wise guidance to the people. If He should ask, no one can return an answer, v. 28. They are all "vanity" (or "wickedness"). Their works are "nothing" (or "ended," ʾepes, cf. 34:12), having no lasting value. Their "images" (nesek)[21] are as wind and "confusion" (tohû, see 24:10, better "emptiness"), v. 29.

---

himself. Delitzsch, II, 172, takes riʾšôn as a reference to time, the Lord being the first to speak of Zion's redemption. He takes mᵉbaśśer as a plural, the "prophets" who declared the nation's deliverance from Babylon. The verse is difficult.

[21]The nesek is an image made from molten metal.

Practical Applications from Chapter 41

1. Forsaking Fear
    a. Commanded by God, 7:4; 35:4; 51:7
    b. Different from the world, 8:11–12
        (1) Redeemed by the Lord from our sins, 43:1
        (2) Created by God for His purposes, 44:2
        (3) Protected by the Lord from the enemy, 54:14
    c. Help of the Lord, 41:10, 13, 14; 43:15
        (1) No other god, 44:8
        (2) No future shame, 54:4
2. God's Control of History
    a. The challenge to the heathen. God invites them to a trial, v. 1. They may give evidence to show the power of their gods, v. 21. Let them predict the future, v. 22. Let them do anything, v. 23. If they fail, it is because they do not exist, v. 24.
    b. The call of Cyrus. The Lord uses this heathen king for a righteous purpose, v. 2. To this end, He makes him a victorious ruler, v. 2. It is the Lord who raises up the generations of man, v. 4. God has raised up Cyrus, v. 25. He has predicted this so that Israel may trust Him, v. 26. He has predicted the future, v. 27, a distinct contrast with the heathen gods, v. 28. They are nothing, v. 29.
    c. The conquests of Cyrus. He defeats new territories, v. 3. The nations fear him, v. 5, and encourage one another to be brave, v. 6. They will, however, be defeated, vv. 11–12.
    d. The confidence of Israel. Israel does not need to fear Cyrus, v. 8. The Lord has chosen them for Himself, v. 9, and He will sustain them, vv. 10, 13. He will be their Kinsman-Redeemer, v. 14, and give them victory over their enemies, vv. 15–16. The Lord will supply their needs, vv. 17–19, and all will know of God's blessing on them, v. 20.

ISAIAH 42

The chapter introduces the first of several anonymous "servant" passages.[1] The immediate question that we face here is the identification of the servant. Earlier, the book refers to different servants of the Lord: Isaiah (20:3), Eliakim (22:20), David (37:35), and faithful Israel (41:8). To this, we may add unfaithful Israel (42:19) and several more references to Israel or Jacob (e.g., 44:1, 2, 21). When we look at the NT references to the Servant passages in c. 42, 49, 50, and 53, however, we find a messianic application added to the other mentions of the servant. Matthew 12:18–20 applies the current passage to Christ. Other NT passages refer as well to the Servant passages.[2] For this reason, we must identify the anonymous "servant" of Isaiah as Jesus Christ.[3]

---

[1]I include 42:1–9; 49:1–13; 50:4–11; and 52:13–53:12 as Servant passages. The excursus at the end of this chapter summarizes the teaching of these passages. J. Barton Payne, *The Theology of the Older Testament* (Grand Rapids, Mich.: Zondervan Publishing House, 1962), p. 254, adds 61:1–3 as a fifth Servant passage. Most authors, however, accept only four Servant songs although there is variation in the verses included in each song.

[2]Acts 13:47; cf. 49:6; II Cor. 6:2; cf. 49:8; Rev. 7:16; cf. 49:10; Rom. 15:21; cf. 52:15; John 12:38; Rom. 10:16; cf. 53:1; I Pet. 2:24; cf. 53:5; Matt. 8:16–17; cf. 53:4; Acts 8:32–35; cf. 53:7–8; Mark 15:28; Luke 22:37; cf. 53:12. In addition, there are many NT allusions that seem to point to these passages. Nestle's Greek NT gives three quotations and allusions to 42:1–4; nine to 49:1–13; two to 50:4–11; and fifteen to 52:13–53:12.

[3]There are a variety of other interpretations. The LXX identified the "servant" as Israel by translating v. 1*a* Ἰακώβ ὁ παῖς μου ("Jacob my servant") and expanding the next phrase with Ἰσραήλ ὁ ἐκλεκτός μου ("Israel my chosen"). Among modern authors, Brueggemann, *Isaiah 40–66*, p. 42; Childs, p. 325; and Kelley, p. 326, accept this view. The interpretation faces the problem of bringing justice to the Gentiles, something Israel has never done. Further, the character of the Servant in v. 2 is not the character of Israel. Recognizing these problems, some have made the Servant "idealized Israel." Skinner, *Isaiah XL–LXVI*, p. 28; Whitehouse, II, 18–19; and McKenzie, p. xliv, are among those who hold this view. This position faces the difficulty that the Servant has a ministry to Israel, 49:5–6; 53:8. It is awkward to have Israel ministering to Israel. An older view that is rarely held today is that the Servant is Cyrus. Watts, *Isaiah 34–66*, p. 114, suggests this position. The view rests on the mention of Cyrus in 44:28; 45:1, not Servant passages. It faces several difficulties. The character of the Servant in v. 2 does not fit that of Cyrus. Further, it is not reasonable to say that the Holy Spirit filled Cyrus; cf. v. 1. Orlinsky, pp. 75–96, identifies the Servant as Second Isaiah. The view, of course, rests on the faulty attribution of the book to several authors. Snaith, p. 175, equates the Servant with the Jewish exiles in Babylon. It is difficult, however, to accept his conclusion that c. 53 has nothing "to do with ideas of atonement." He understands the chapter as explaining "away the sufferings of the Servant, to show that they ought not to have been his at all," p. 204. This does not agree with the NT use of the passage.

1 Behold my servant, whom I uphold; mine elect, in whom my soul delighteth; I have put my spirit upon him: he shall bring forth judgment to the Gentiles.
2 He shall not cry, nor lift up, nor cause his voice to be heard in the street.
3 A bruised reed shall he not break, and the smoking flax shall he not quench: he shall bring forth judgment unto truth.
4 He shall not fail nor be discouraged, till he have set judgment in the earth: and the isles shall wait for his law.

It is clear that the term "servant" can refer to different people or groups. There is a sense, however, in which a relationship exists between these. The broadest group fulfilling the term is Israel. From within the set of people in Israel, various individuals stand out as "servants of the Lord." The most prominent of these in the final chapters of Isaiah is the Messiah, the Lord Jesus Christ. Because of the theological importance of the Servant, an excursus at the end of this chapter summarizes the teaching concerning Him.

B. Description of God's Servants 42:1–25
1. Servant of the Lord 42:1–9[4]

1–4 The chapter opens with the words of the Father. The initial "Behold" connects the passage with c. 41. There, vv. 24, 29, the Lord had shown the weakness of false gods. Now, He contrasts the work of His Servant. The Lord introduces the Servant as "my servant." The pronoun emphasizes the total yieldedness of the Servant to the Father. The Father "uphold[s]" (or "support[s]") the Servant. He is the Father's "elect" (or "chosen") as He carries out the Father's work. The Father "delighteth" (*raṣâ*, see 40:2) in Him. This expression of delight is the basis for Mark 1:11, in which Mark combines Psalm 2:7 and Isaiah 42:1. Matthew 12:18–21 also quotes the description given in vv. 1–4.

The Father gives Him the Holy Spirit.[5] This power allows Him to bring "judgment" (*mišpaṭ*, better "justice," see 1:17) to the "Gentiles" (or

---

[4]Allan A. McRae, "The Servant of the Lord in Isaiah," *Bibliotheca Sacra* 121:128, limits the Servant passage to vv. 1–7. North, p. 60; Herbert, *Isaiah 40–66*, p. 40; and Kelley, p. 306, limit it to vv. 1–4. Rawlinson, II, 116, includes vv. 1–8 in the passage. This variation rests on the individual understanding of the passage.

[5]Wright, p. 105, understands *rûaḥ* as "breath, wind." He takes this as a metaphor for God's "breathing into" people, i.e., inspiring them to do His work. While this is a possible meaning elsewhere, mere inspired work is not adequate to bring about justice on the earth. This is a supernatural work and requires the supernatural Spirit of God.

"nations").[6] While this is not the main teaching here, it is still worth noting that the fulfillment of this promise lies in the future. Justice is a mark of the Millennium, when the Lord rules the earth and all receive just treatment. Another incidental teaching relates to the nature of God. The verse mentions the Trinity, "my servant . . . I . . . spirit," v. 1.[7]

The Servant possesses a meek spirit. In contrast with normal rulers, He works in a gentle fashion. He does not "cry" (ṣaʿaq),[8] calling attention to Himself by His manner; cf. Zechariah 9:9; Matthew 11:29. He is not ostentatious, attracting the notice of others, by "lift[ing]" His voice in the streets, v. 2. He does not break the "bruised reed" or quench the "smoking flax" (or "dimly burning wick"). The "reed" was the cane that grew in marshy places, often beside a river; cf. 36:6. The fibers from the bark of "flax" could be twisted into a wick; cf. 1:31. The reed could be broken and the wick could be snuffed out. The two figures represent those who are lowly in this life; cf. 57:15; 61:1. The Servant treats them fairly. He brings "judgment" (mišpaṭ, better "justice," see 1:17) forth "unto truth" (leʾemet, or "according to truth").[9] The infallible standard of truth is the basis upon which He renders justice to mankind, v. 3. He does not fail in His work. He does not become discouraged over the failure of mankind to eagerly embrace His Word. He will continue until He establishes "judgment" (mišpaṭ, or "justice") throughout the world. The "isles" (ʾiyîm, cf. 11:11) are the coastal areas and, by metonymy, the Mediterranean region. The word here occurs in poetic variation with "the earth," the inhabited world. The people eagerly "wait" (yaḥal) for His "law" (tôrâ, see 1:10), the teaching that brings peace to mankind. The

---

[6]Pieper, p. 179, makes mišpaṭ "the Gospel of grace in Christ." This is an unwarranted extension of the meaning of the word. The normal sense of "justice" is appropriate here.

[7]This is one of several references in the book that mention all three members of the Godhead. See also 11:2; 48:16; 59:19–21; 61:1; 63:7–14.

[8]Kelley, p. 307, understands the verb ṣaʿaq as the cry of a weak person to a stronger. He therefore takes this as the statement of relief "forever banishing from his lips the cry of distress." The view stems from Kelley's identification of the Servant as Israel. When we see the Servant as the Messiah, the view is not appropriate. Fausset, p. 694, makes the cry that of an altercation in a house, loud enough to be heard outside. The view limits the normal sense of κραυγάζω in Matt. 12:19. Cf. John 19:15 and Acts 22:23, where we cannot sustain this sense.

[9]The lamed preposition is variously understood. Among others, Leupold, II, 62; Kelley, p. 305; and Kraeling, p. 160, translate leʾemet as an adverb, "faithfully," describing the manner in which the Lord brings forth justice. While this is possible, I prefer to retain the force of the preposition by translating "according to." This leads nicely into the explanation of v. 4.

5 *Thus saith God the Lord, he that created the heavens, and stretched them out; he that spread forth the earth, and that which cometh out of it; he that giveth breath unto the people upon it, and spirit to them that walk therein:*

6 *I the Lord have called thee in righteousness, and will hold thine hand, and will keep thee, and give thee for a covenant of the people, for a light of the Gentiles;*

7 *To open the blind eyes, to bring out the prisoners from the prison, and them that sit in darkness out of the prison house.*

8 *I am the Lord: that is my name: and my glory will I not give to another, neither my praise to graven images.*

9 *Behold, the former things are come to pass, and new things do I declare: before they spring forth I tell you of them.*

verb *yaḥal* has a sense of confidence associated with it. The people anticipate the Lord coming to bring His teaching to them, v. 4.[10]

5–9 The omnipotent God now speaks. To establish His right to act, He presents Himself as the Creator of the heavens and the earth. He has brought into being all that "cometh out of" the earth, the vegetation. His crowning work in Creation has been human life, v. 5. He addresses the Servant directly.[11] He has called Him "in righteousness" (*ṣedeq*, see 1:21), for a righteous purpose. He will hold His hand, implying the giving of both strength and guidance. He will "keep" (or "guard") Him from satanic attacks that would turn Him aside from God's work. He will give Him as a "covenant of the people." This is the New Covenant spoken of in 54:10; cf. Jeremiah 31:31–34. The Servant is the Covenant in that He is the means by which the covenant comes into being. To receive Jesus Christ is to receive the covenant that God has made with man.[12] In addition, He is "a light" of the nations, the only means by which unsaved

---

[10]Delitzsch, II, 177, refers the teaching to the gospel, which I would include but broaden to include other principles of Christianity as well. When followed, these bring personal and community peace.

[11]Cundall, *Isaiah 40—Jeremiah,* p. 6, makes the Father speak to Cyrus in vv. 5–9. Westermann, p. 99, directs the speech to Israel. It is difficult, however, to ignore the context of vv. 1–4, where even Cundall sees the Messiah and Westerlund sees an individual. In addition, Cyrus was not a "covenant" for the Jews, and he did not bring spiritual "light" to the Gentiles.

[12]Delitzsch, II, 179, asserts that the word *ʿam,* "people," in contrast with *gôy,* "Gentiles," always refers to Israel. Such verses as 2:4; 10:6; 13:4; and 33:3 show that this is not the case. The words *ʿam* and *gôy* poetically vary the designation of the nations of the world. In the case here, this would include Israel and the heathen. The Lord offers salvation to all that place their faith in Jesus Christ as the Savior from God's wrath against sin.

10 Sing unto the Lord a new song, and his praise from the end of the earth, ye that go down to the sea, and all that is therein; the isles, and the inhabitants thereof.
11 Let the wilderness and the cities thereof lift up their voice, the villages that Kedar doth inhabit: let the inhabitants of the rock sing, let them shout from the top of the mountains.
12 Let them give glory unto the Lord, and declare his praise in the islands.

man can see spiritual truth; cf. John 1:4, 9; 8:12. The apostles Paul and Barnabas refer to this in their contact with the Gentiles in Antioch of Pisidia, Acts 13:47. Acts 26:23 may also draw on the thought, v. 6. He gives sight to the blind and releases the prisoners from their bondage. While the Lord did heal the blind, e.g., Matthew 9:27–29; 12:22; 15:30–31, the thought here is of giving spiritual sight and of releasing those who are in bondage to sin, cf. 48:8–9, v. 7.

Verse 8 continues the words of the Father. He is "the Lord" (y^{e}hwah). This is the name that God uses to show His redemptive nature. It is the covenant name by which God enters into a relationship with man. This is a worthy name, one that He defends. He will not let others take His glory, nor will He let idols receive the "praise" (t^{e}hillâ)[13] that is rightly due to Him. The implied thought is that the work of the Servant honors the Father, v. 8. The "former things," the prophecies given earlier, have now been fulfilled.[14] He now tells them "new things" before they come to pass. From the context, the "new things" relate to the Servant, v. 9.

2. Victory over Enemies 42:10–25

10–12 The prospect of these "new things" being fulfilled causes Isaiah to write the first song of the second part of the book.[15] The Lord

---

[13]The word t^{e}hillâ indicates the praiseworthiness of a person or thing. It regularly refers to the Lord because of His work on behalf of His own.

[14]Henry, p 229, relates the promises to the church. The view that makes Israel represent the church is not possible in the OT. Among others, Skinner, *Isaiah XL–LXVI*, p. 33; Motyer, *The Prophecy of Isaiah*, p. 322; and Delitzsch, II, 181, refer the "former things" to the prophecies concerning Cyrus. To accept this, we would have to accept the Deutero-Isaiah authorship of the passage or treat the statement as a prophetic perfect. I have already argued against multiple authors in the book. The context of the next phrase makes it unlikely that this is a prophetic perfect.

[15]Isaiah refers to singing in every major part of the book, e.g., 5:1; 12:2, 5; 14:7; 24:14, 16; 27:2; 30:29; 35:2, 6, 10; 38:20; 44:23; 48:20–22; 49:13; 51:11; 52:8–10; 54:1; 55:12; 65:14.

*13 The Lord shall go forth as a mighty man, he shall stir up jealousy
like a man of war: he shall cry, yea, roar; he shall prevail against
his enemies.*
*14 I have long time holden my peace; I have been still, and refrained
myself: now will I cry like a travailing woman; I will destroy and devour at once.*
*15 I will make waste mountains and hills, and dry up all their herbs;
and I will make the rivers islands, and I will dry up the pools.*
*16 And I will bring the blind by a way that they knew not; I will lead
them in paths that they have not known: I will make darkness light
before them, and crooked things straight. These things will I do unto
them, and not forsake them.*
*17 They shall be turned back, they shall be greatly ashamed, that trust
in graven images, that say to the molten images, Ye are our gods.*

commands the whole earth to sing a "new song" of "praise" (*t*ᵉ*hillâ*, see
v. 8) to God. Those who "go down to the sea," sailors, and "all that is
therein," all that live in the waters, shall praise the Lord. All that live in
the "isles" (*ʾîyîm*, see 11:11), the Mediterranean region, cf. v. 4, shall
likewise praise God. The use of these diverse groups represents by
synecdoche all parts of the earth. This note of praise is appropriate at the
beginning of a passage that describes the millennial kingdom. Verses
10–17 find their fulfillment in the reign of the Lord over the earth, v. 10.
The "wilderness" and the "cities" join in the song. The "villages" (or
"settlements") of "Kedar," located in the northern Arabian desert, represent the wilderness region. The people of "the rock" (*selaᶜ*, lit. "Sela,"
capital of Edom, known later as "Petra") represent the cities.[16] All join
together in praising God. Shouting from the "top of the mountains" is
open praise, done in full view of others, v. 11. They declare God's
"glory" (*kabôd*, see 3:5) and "praise" (*t*ᵉ*hillâ*, see v. 8) throughout the
"islands," again the Mediterranean world and the representative of the
inhabited world (cf. v. 4), v. 12.

   13–17 The Lord will go forth against His enemies. He will go out as
a "mighty man" (*gibbôr*, see 3:2), often a valiant person or a warrior. He
will stir up His "jealousy" (better "zeal") as He goes into battle. He will

---

[16]Among others, Wade, p. 223; Cowles, p. 335; and Henry, p. 230, understand *selaᶜ* as
"rocky." The phrase then refers to Arabia Petræa, the stony northwestern part of Arabia.
This parallels the last phrase, "shout from the top of the mountains." The view is possible. I prefer to have the two phrases parallel the "wilderness" and "cities" mentioned at
the first of the verse.

"cry" and "roar." Quite possibly, this is the "sharp sword" that comes from the Lord's mouth to command the destruction of His enemies, Revelation 19:15.[17] He will "prevail" (or "show Himself mighty") against His enemies.

There is no conflict with the meekness of the Lord stated in v. 2. The two passages describe different aspects of His work: Verse 2 describes the character of the ruler, and vv. 13–14 picture the climactic battle against His enemies, v. 13.

He has held His peace in the past. Now He utters His war cry against His enemies. The strength of the "cry" (*paʿâ*, or "groan")[18] is like that of a woman "travailing" as she brings forth her child. He will "destroy and devour" (*ʾeššom weʾešʾap*, better "gasp and pant").[19] The image again comes from the woman giving birth as she strains to deliver the child. The illustration portrays the Lord's intensity to vanquish His enemies. The woman brings new life into the world. In the same way, the Lord anticipates bringing a new relationship between Him and mankind into the world, v. 14.[20]

Looking into the future, the Lord describes the drought that will take place in the land. The only fulfillment of this that we know of comes in Revelation 16:8–9 during the Tribulation judgments, v. 15. At the same time, He will lead the spiritually blind in a new way. He will turn their darkness into light and their crooked paths into straight ones. This is the

---

[17]Others, e.g., Barnes, II, 106; Von Orelli, p. 237; and Wright, p. 106, see this as the battle cry of a warrior. This is a possible view.

[18]The word *paʿâ* occurs only here. The context of a travailing woman as well as Aramaic and Arabic cognate words meaning "bleat" support the sense "groan" here.

[19]The word *ʾeššom* occurs only here. The related noun *nešamâ*, "breath," however, occurs several times. This supports the meaning "to breathe." The context forces us to give this a sense of "panting." The parallel word, *ʾešʾap*, "to gasp, pant," likewise supports this sense.

[20]Katheryn Pfisterer Darr, "Like Warrior, like Woman: Destruction and Deliverance in Isaiah 42:10–17," *CBQ* 49:560–71, argues that the simile of a travailing woman pictures the behavior of those who are not actually giving birth. Rather, they are in circumstances that lead to responses of pain and anguish like that of a woman in childbirth. This cannot be true of God. She therefore finds the significance in "what proceeds from the throat of God." God's breath elsewhere is destructive, e.g., Ps. 18:15; Isa. 30:33; 40:7, 24. She rejects any metaphor here of Yahweh giving birth. She finds instead a picture of His "power and might" over His enemies. Her view is possible. I would note, however, that Isaiah uses the verb *yalad* to refer to bringing forth the nation, 49:21; 51:18; 66:8–9. God's breath is regularly associated with life, e.g., Gen. 2:7; Job 33:4. Since equating a travailing woman with a powerful warrior is not seen elsewhere, I prefer to see a birth context here. The newness seen in vv. 16–17 supports this.

18 *Hear, ye deaf; and look, ye blind, that ye may see.*
19 *Who is blind, but my servant? or deaf, as my messenger that I sent?*
    who is blind as he that is perfect, and blind as the Lord's servant?
20 *Seeing many things, but thou observest not; opening the ears, but he*
    heareth not.
21 *The Lord is well pleased for his righteousness' sake; he will magnify*
    the law, and make it honourable.
22 *But this is a people robbed and spoiled; they are all of them snared*
    in holes, and they are hid in prison houses: they are for a prey, and
    none delivereth; for a spoil, and none saith, Restore.

conversion of Israel during the Tribulation; cf. 29:24; Zechariah 13:1. He repeats the promise, giving emphasis to the statement of His work on behalf of His people, v. 16. They will be "ashamed" (*bôš*, see 1:29) of the idols they had formerly worshiped. They will reject both the "graven images" (*pesel*, see 40:19) and molten idols, v. 17.

18–20 The Lord commands the spiritually "deaf" and "blind," v. 18. These terms refer to Israel, God's "servant" and "messenger." They had been "perfect" (*mᵉšullam*, better "in a covenant of peace"),[21] perfectly content to claim a relationship with God without obeying Him. They had been called to be God's servant, yet they had failed to serve Him. The service of Israel stands in stark contrast with the service of the Servant described earlier, v. 19. They had seen many things—the past works of God—but had not seen God's working in these. They had heard many things—the many voices of prophecy—but had not heard God's voice in these, v. 20.

21–22 The Lord was "well pleased," satisfied. His work on behalf of Israel was for the sake of His "righteousness" (*ṣedeq*, see 1:21), having a redemptive purpose. He will cause His "law" (*tôrâ*, cf. 1:10) to become great and "honourable" (better "glorious"). The *tôrâ* embraces all of the moral teachings of the OT, v. 21. Because Israel has refused to respond, God had judged them. They were "robbed and spoiled" by other nations. They were "snared [*peaḥ*] in holes [*baḥûrîm*]," in captivity with no one

---

[21]The word *mᵉšullam* is variously understood. Westermann, p. 110, says, "the sense is quite uncertain." North, p. 69, similarly says, "the meaning is wholly dubious and the text uncertain." Whitehouse, II, 88, suggests repointing the word to *mošlam* and translating, "devoted one," i.e., devoted to God's service. This, however, does not agree with the context of one who is spiritually blind and deaf. The Vulgate apparently read *mošlam*, "their ruler" but this makes little sense unless the "servant" here becomes Israel's king. By form, *mᵉšullam* is a *puᶜal* participle with the sense "be in a covenant of peace." Israel had this relationship to God but failed to live in a way that agreed with their position.

23 Who among you will give ear to this? who will hearken and hear for
the time to come?
24 Who gave Jacob for a spoil, and Israel to the robbers? did not the
Lord, he against whom we have sinned? for they would not walk in
his ways, neither were they obedient unto his law.
25 Therefore he hath poured upon him the fury of his anger, and the
strength of battle: and it hath set him on fire round about, yet he
knew not; and it burned him, yet he laid it not to heart.

to deliver them.[22] They were a "prey" for others and none could deliver
them. They were a "spoil" that would not be restored to them, v. 22.

23–25 The Lord rhetorically asks the people to listen to this rebuke.
The rhetorical questions suggest that no one will listen, v. 23. He asks
another rhetorical question, then answers the question. The Lord has
given His people to their enemies because of their sin. "They" did not
walk in His ways, neither did "they" obey His "law" (*tôrâ*, see 1:10). In
both cases, the pronoun "they" refers to Israel, v. 24. This has caused
God to pour out the "fury" (or "heat") of His wrath on them. He has
brought them to know "the strength of battle." The results have "set [Is-
rael] on fire" and "burned" the nation, yet the people did not recognize
their condition before God, v. 25.

---

[22]The word *peah* is a *hapax legomenon*. The related form *pah* occurs several times with
the meaning of "trap," e.g., Ps. 124:7; Amos 3:5. A meaning of "snare, trap" is not in
doubt. The word *bahûrîm* is lit. "young men," a meaning that has no sense here. We may
revocalize the word to *behorîm*, "in holes," or understand *bahûrîm* as exceptional due to
the influence of the *be*-preposition and the article.

Practical Applications from Chapter 42

1. The Ministry of Christ, vv. 1–4
   a. Filling of the Spirit, v. 1*a, b*
   b. Meekness of Christ, vv. 2–3*a*
   c. Confidence of the Lord, v. 4*a*
   d. Justice in the world, vv. 1*c*, 4*a*
   e. Establishment of His law, v. 4*b*

2. Plan of God, vv. 5–9
   a. The Creator of heaven and earth, including mankind, has the right to act, v. 5.
   b. The Lord calls the Servant for a righteous purpose. He guides and guards Him from anything that would turn Him aside from this end. He brings the New Covenant into being through Him. He becomes a spiritual "light" to the nations, v. 6, giving them spiritual sight and freedom from sin, v. 7.
   c. God is the redemptive one. He will defend His name, not letting others take His glory or give praise to idols, v. 8. He has fulfilled earlier prophecies. He now tells the "new things" that relate to His Son, v. 9.

3. Victory over the Enemies of God, vv. 10–25
   a. Judgment of the Lord. He commands Israel, His spiritually deaf and blind servants, vv. 18–19. They had seen and heard God's works and teaching but had not responded, v. 20. He will now exalt His Word, v. 21, as He judges His people, v. 22. They, however, will not respond to His work, vv. 23–24. They will undergo additional judgment without seeing their need to turn to God, v. 25.
   b. Victory of the Lord. The Lord goes forth in battle against His enemies, v. 13. He has held His peace but He now goes to war, v. 14. His judgment will bring drought to the land during the Tribulation judgments, v. 15. Those who were spiritually blind will now turn to Him for His guidance, v. 16. They will be ashamed that they had formerly worshiped idols, v. 17.
   c. Praise to the Lord. The whole earth sings its praise to God, vv. 10–12.

EXCURSUS: THE SERVANT

The Preparation of the Servant

In the comments on 42:1–4, I have identified the Servant with Jesus Christ. Chapter 42 introduces His character and work. The Father empowers the Servant with His Holy Spirit, 42:1. He gives Him effective speech so that He can comfort those weighed down with cares, 50:4a. He guides the Servant through each day, 50:4b. The Servant does not rebel against this guidance, 50:5, but acts wisely, 52:13a.

He has a humble beginning, 53:2a. Nothing about His appearance attracts others to Him, 53:2b. Others despise and reject Him, 53:3a. He anguishes over the sins of mankind, 53:3b. The Servant restrains Himself. He does not cry out loudly to draw attention to Himself. The fact that Isaiah develops this with the parallel phrases "nor lift up [His voice], nor cause His voice to be heard in the streets" emphasizes His manner, 42:2.

The Servant Himself speaks. He urges the nations of the world to hear His voice, 49:1a. God the Father has called Him before birth, 49:1b. He has given Him speech that will cut to the heart, 49:2a, c. At the same time, He has protected Him, apparently from satanic opposition, 49:2b, d.

Initially, the Servant's work does not accomplish much, 49:4a. Others reject Him, 53:1. Rather than ceasing His work, He leaves the judgment of it with the Father, 49:4b. The Father responds. He has called the Servant to gather Israel back to Himself. This will bring honor to the Servant. He will continue to draw strength from God, 49:5.

The Suffering of the Servant

The first hint that the Servant will suffer comes in 50:6. Others will beat Him and pluck the hair from His cheeks. They will publicly humiliate Him by spitting in His face. Others will be astonished at His suffering, 52:14a. His appearance will be disfigured extremely and His shape distorted, 52:14b. Men will turn from Him, despising Him, 53:3c. They see only the shameful death by crucifixion and fail to esteem Him for His sacrificial work on Calvary, 53:3d. They consider that God Himself has judged Him, 53:4b. They do not reflect on the purpose of His death, 53:8a.

The Servant bears the burdens of mankind, 53:4a. His death is not for His own sins. He has done nothing worthy of death, 53:9cd. He is pierced for the sins of others, 53:5a. He bears the emotional burden of judgment for sin in our place, 53:5b. He bears chastening to secure our peace with God, 53:5c. His scourging brings spiritual healing, 53:5d. All have strayed from the ways of God and have gone their own way. The Father, however, has laid our sins on the Servant as He voluntarily atones for the sins of mankind, 53:6. He suffers without complaint, 53:7a. Like a docile lamb being sheared, He quietly accepts the burden, 53:7b. He accepts His death for the transgressions of God's chosen people, 53:8b. He bears the sins of many, 53:11c. He will sprinkle His blood upon mankind to redeem them from their sin, 52:15a. The kings of the earth will not comment on this since it is a new work, never seen before. They will diligently consider His work, 52:15b. He is buried with other wicked men, 53:9a, although His grave is in the tomb of a wealthy man, 53:9b.

The sacrificial death of the Servant pleases the Father, 53:10a. He sends Him to this death, 53:10b. The trespass offering of His soul brings the Father's blessings. He gains a spiritual seed and eternal life, 53:10c. He carries out that which pleases the Father, 53:10d. Because the Servant has suffered for sin, He is satisfied with the results, 53:11a. By His knowledge of the Father's will, the Servant justifies many, 53:11b.

The Servant will not turn away from this, 50:6. Instead, He will maintain His trust in God. He is confident that these actions will not disgrace Him, 50:7. The one who vindicates Him is near. He willingly appears in court with others that may accuse Him, 50:8. The Father will help Him. His enemies will therefore fail in their attempts to condemn Him, 50:9.

The Servant has poured out His soul as a sacrificial offering, 53:12b. He was counted with other transgressors at Calvary, v. 53:12c. He has borne the sins of others, 53:12d. He now intercedes with the Father on behalf of those whom He has redeemed, 53:12e.

The Reign of the Servant

The Father, who will reward the Servant for His atoning death, will graciously divide His reward between the Servant and those who fight against the wicked, 53:12a. The Father recognizes Him as Israel's leader and will glorify Himself through Him, 49:3. He will exalt the Servant, 52:13b.

Merely restoring Israel to God is not a great task. The Father also charges Him to bring the Gentiles to Him. This will extend the salvation of man throughout the whole earth, 49:6. He executes justice upon the heathen nations, 42:1. He treats the lowly with fairness, 42:3*a*. He renders justice according to truth, 42:3*b*. He will not fail or become discouraged in this until the world accepts His Word, 42:4. Biblical teaching elsewhere sets this in the kingdom, when the Lord rules over the earth, Joel 3:1–2; Matthew 25:40, 45; Jude 14–15; cf. Isaiah 32:1.

The Father is Israel's Redeemer. He is also the Holy One, wholly trustworthy. He speaks to the Servant, the one rejected by mankind, considered but a lowly servant, 49:7*a*. The days will come, in the kingdom, when heathen leaders will accept Him: they will worship Him because they see that God has chosen Him, 49:7*b*.

The Father speaks again. He has heard the Servant's prayers. He has protected Him from satanic attacks. He will continue to work through Him. He gives Him "for a covenant of the people." He will restore the land of Palestine to a place of kingdom blessing, 49:8. The Servant will free those who have been imprisoned in the nations. They will return to Palestine, finding food to sustain them as they go, 49:9. The Lord will protect them from the flaming sun and give them water, 49:10. He will make paths for the people through the mountains, 49:11. The people will come to Palestine from all over the world, 49:12. In spontaneous praise, Isaiah calls for the heavens and the earth to sing to the Lord. He has comforted and given mercy to His people, 49:13.

In view of this protection of His Servant, the Father now speaks to the faithful. Those who obey the Lord and His Servant—even though sin still marks their lives—should fully trust the Lord, 50:10. Those who walk in the light of their own way will suffer punishment, 50:11.

1 But now thus saith the Lord that created thee, O Jacob, and he that
  formed thee, O Israel, Fear not: for I have redeemed thee, I have
  called thee by thy name; thou art mine.
2 When thou passest through the waters, I will be with thee; and
  through the rivers, they shall not overflow thee: when thou walkest
  through the fire, thou shalt not be burned; neither shall the flame
  kindle upon thee.
3 For I am the Lord thy God, the Holy One of Israel, thy Saviour: I
  gave Egypt for thy ransom, Ethiopia and Seba for thee.
4 Since thou wast precious in my sight, thou hast been honourable,
  and I have loved thee: therefore will I give men for thee, and people
  for thy life.

ISAIAH 43

In a very typical manner, Isaiah follows the rebuke of c. 42 with
promises of comfort. The Lord will draw Israel back to Himself. He will
gather them from the nations, vv. 1–9, and charge them to serve as His
witnesses to others, vv. 10–15. He has delivered them with miracles in
the past; He will now do a new thing for them as He blesses the land
during the kingdom, vv. 16–21. Israel spurns this commission. They
have failed to worship Him properly in the past, vv. 22–24. Yet He has
chosen them for Himself. He therefore invites them to show Him their
good works and righteousness. They cannot respond. They have sinned
from the beginning, bringing punishment upon themselves, vv. 25–28.

C. Protection of God's People 43:1–45:25
1. Blessing of the Faithful 43:1–44:5
a. Gathering of the Nation 43:1–9

1–4 The adversative "But now" sets this section off in contrast with
the previous section. Verses 18–25 in c. 42 speak of rebuke and judgment for sin. The Lord now begins to speak of blessing. He has "created" (bara⁾) the nation, bringing them into existence. He has "formed"
(yaṣar) them. The verb yaṣar differs from bara⁾ although it often parallels
it. The action of bara⁾ is more that of bringing something into existence
that did not exist before. It occurs in the qal only with God as its subject.
The verb yaṣar, however, has to do with shaping. It occurs appropriately
to describe the potter who molds the clay, e.g., 29:16; 64:8.

The people need not fear since the Lord has "redeemed" (ga⁾al, verb
form of go⁾el, see 35:9) them. He has called them by their name. The

371

phrase describes God's choice of Israel to be His own people; cf. 45:4. They belong to Him, v. 1. The Lord shows His care for His people. The "waters . . . rivers . . . fire . . . flame" are all metaphors of danger.[1] Bridges were not common in OT times. Crossing over a lake or passing a river could bring the threat of harm, e.g., Exodus 14:27–28; Jonah 1:4. Likewise, a fire of any kind presents possible danger, e.g., Genesis 19:24; Daniel 3:22. Regardless of the jeopardy they may face, the Lord will protect them. The promise refers to faithful Israel, not to the entire nation. When Israel sinned, the Lord brought them into judgment, v. 2. The Lord is their God. Isaiah multiplies names as He refers to the relationship between the Lord and His people. He is the "Holy One of Israel." The name stresses God's character as holy and thus not violating His Word to Israel. He is their "Saviour" (yašaᶜ, see 17:10), the one who has redeemed them from bondage and from sin.

He will give other nations as a "ransom" (koper) for them. The word koper often refers to atonement by means of a substitutionary offering. It normally involved the sacrifice of an innocent animal. It elsewhere refers to the sin offering, a picture of the atoning work of the Lord in offering Himself as a sacrifice for mankind's sin, e.g., Leviticus 4:20, 26, 31, 35. Here, however, the Lord limits the usage to national deliverance. This was fulfilled in the Persian Empire. Ethiopia lay south of Egypt above the first cataract of the Nile River. Seba, also called Meroë in history, was a province of Ethiopia. Its location is uncertain although it is often located near the confluence of the White and Blue Nile, in the southern part of Ethiopia.[2] Cambyses, son of Cyrus the Great, conquered Egypt and Ethiopia ca. 525 B.C. While these nations became tributaries

---

[1]Brueggemann, *Isaiah 40–66*, p. 53, is doubly wrong when he makes water a picture of "baptism, a sacrament of relationship whereby we are inducted into the protective and sure care of Yahweh." The water does not picture baptism here, and baptism is not the means by which people come into the care of the Lord. Ibn Ezra, p. 193, makes the "waters" and "fire" represent "the armies of Persia and Media . . . that were to conquer Babylon." The passage, however, refers generally to God's care of Israel. It does not refer to any specific time of deliverance.

[2]So Josephus, *Antiquities* 1.6.2, cited by Barry J. Beitgel, *The Moody Atlas of Bible Lands* (Chicago; Moody Press, 1985), p. 77. Seba is sometimes confused with Sheba, in southwest Arabia, e.g., "Seba," "Sabeans." *Unger's Bible Dictionary* (Chicago: Moody Press, 1957), pp. 941, 990. Herbert, *Isaiah 40–66*, p. 49, understands the reference to Ethiopia and Seba as idiomatic for "the farthest parts of the world." While this is possible, nothing in the passage indicates that it is anything other than literal.

5 *Fear not: for I am with thee: I will bring thy seed from the east, and gather thee from the west;*
6 *I will say to the north, Give up; and to the south, Keep not back: bring my sons from far, and my daughters from the ends of the earth;*
7 *Even every one that is called by my name: for I have created him for my glory, I have formed him; yea, I have made him.*

of Persia, Israel received her freedom, v. 3.[3] The Lord did this "since" (*me²ašer*) she was "precious" (*yaqar*, see 13:12) and "honourable" (*kabed*, better "honored," see 3:5) in His sight.[4] Her freedom comes from God's love for the nation. He will let "men" (*²adam*), mankind, i.e., other nations, suffer judgment while giving Israel her freedom, v. 4.

5–7 Israel need not fear. The Lord will restore her people from across the earth. From everywhere they have been scattered, He will bring them back. They will come from the east, the west, the north, and the south.[5] Following the fall of Judah to Babylon, the people scattered throughout the world.[6] They are His "sons" and "daughters," and He will gather them from "the ends of the earth," vv. 5–6.[7] These are the ones who have been "called by my name." The phrase indicates the nation's position as God's people. Israel has been "created" (*bara²*, see v. 1) for God's glory.

---

[3]Motyer, *The Prophecy of Isaiah,* p. 331, interprets the promise of giving Egypt, Ethiopia, and Seba the divine judgment inflicted on Egypt at the Exodus. The passage, however, touches on the same idea as 45:14. The Exodus does not fulfill the details given there.

[4]The NEB repoints *me²ašer* to *me²ašer,* "Assyria," and *²adam* to *²edom,* "Edom." Kari Maalstad, "Einige Erwägungen zu Jes. XLIII 4," *VT* 16:512–14, earlier argued this same change. Isa1Q^a supports the MT. The LXX translates ἀφ' οὗ . . . ἀνθρώπους πολλούς, "since . . . many men." The Vulgate gives *ex quo . . . homines,* "since . . . men." This is strong support for the MT.

[5]While the Hebrew for "north" and "south" is straightforward, the words for "east" and "west" are a bit more unusual. The "east" is *mizraḥ,* the "place of rising," i.e., the east. The "west" is *ma²arab,* the "place of darkness," i.e., where the sun sets in the west.

[6]E.g., Assyria, Pathros (upper Egypt), Cush (Ethiopia), Elam (east of Babylon), Shinar (ancient Babylon), Hamath (Syria), Isa. 11:11; Sinim (uncertain, see 49:12, note 15); Egypt, Assyria (Zech. 10:10); and the NT, which shows the Jews scattered throughout the Mediterranean.

[7]Cowles, p. 342, wrongly broadens the promise. He understands this to refer to the calling of both Gentiles and Jews, "all who are really God's people." Verse 1 refers to the redemption of Jacob and Israel. Verse 3 mentions the giving of other nations as payment for the freedom given to Judah. Verse 5 speaks of the "seed" of Israel. While the Gentiles will know God's blessings in the kingdom, the passage here does not mention them.

8 *Bring forth the blind people that have eyes, and the deaf that have ears.*

9 *Let all the nations be gathered together, and let the people be assembled: who among them can declare this, and shew us former things? let them bring forth their witnesses, that they may be justified: or let them hear, and say, It is truth.*

10 *Ye are my witnesses, saith the Lord, and my servant whom I have chosen: that ye may know and believe me, and understand that I am he: before me there was no God formed, neither shall there be after me.*

11 *I, even I, am the Lord; and beside me there is no saviour.*

12 *I have declared, and have saved, and I have shewed, when there was no strange god among you: therefore ye are my witnesses, saith the Lord, that I am God.*

13 *Yea, before the day was I am he; and there is none that can deliver out of my hand: I will work, and who shall let it?*

He has "formed" (*yaṣar*, see v. 1) them and "made" (*ʿaśâ*)[8] the nation. Because of this, He will bring them back to the land, v. 7.

8–9 The Lord challenges the spiritually "blind" and "deaf" in Israel; cf. 42:18–19. They have eyes to see the works of God, yet they are spiritually blind. They have ears to hear of the works of God, yet they are deaf, not having heard with understanding, v. 8.[9] Let the nations of the world also gather together. Who among them can tell of prophecies by their gods? Let them bring forth witnesses to prove the power of their gods. Let them "be justified," shown reliable in what they say. Let them declare the "truth" of what their gods have said. There is an implied silence to this invitation from the Lord, v. 9.

b. Commissioning of the People 43:10–15

10–13 The Lord now turns to the faithful in Israel. They will serve as His witnesses. They are His "servant." He has chosen them for a three-fold purpose: to "know" (*yadaʿ*, see 1:3) Him, to "believe" (*hipʿîl* of *ʾaman*, see 7:9) Him, and to "understand" (*bîn*, see 1:3) that He alone is God. The verb *yadaʿ* refers to knowledge that comes from observation and thinking and, especially, to experiential knowledge. Israel gained this

---

[8]The word *ʿaśâ* is the most widely used word to describe the making of something. It refers generally to "doing" or "making" with no special emphasis on the process or the results.

[9]Barnes, II, 117, makes the spiritually blind and deaf the Gentile nations. While this is possible, it is rather that God calls both Jews, v. 8, and Gentiles, v. 9, giving them the opportunity to witness His works. When this fails, He turns to faithful Israel, v. 10.

14 Thus saith the Lord, your redeemer, the Holy One of Israel; For your sake I have sent to Babylon, and have brought down all their nobles, and the Chaldeans, whose cry is in the ships.
15 I am the Lord, your Holy One, the creator of Israel, your King.

by their involvement with the works of God. When one has experiential knowledge of God, certain belief (*ʾaman*) follows. The verb *bîn* refers to the ability to distinguish between opposites. Here, the people understand that God alone is God. This logically follows the knowledge of His works and belief in His ways.

There is no other God (*ʾel*, the name that reflects God's power and greatness) before or after Him, v. 10. He is the Lord (*yᵉhwah*, the redemptive name of God, see 42:8). The repeated use of the pronoun "I" lends emphasis to the statement: "I, even I myself!" There is no "saviour" (*yašaᶜ*, see 17:10) other than Him, v. 11. He has openly declared the future. He has "saved" (*yašaᶜ*), delivering His people from their trials. He has "shewed," proclaiming His truth. No "strange [*zar*, see 1:7] god" has done this. The word *zar* refers to something outside of the normal class in Israel. Here, the *zar* is a god other than the true God of Israel. Israel was witness that He alone is God, v. 12. The phrase "before the day was," i.e., since the dawn of time, indicates the Lord is still the same God.[10] There is no one who takes the people from Him. No one will "let" (better "hinder") His work, v. 13.

14–15 Again, as in v. 3, the Lord multiplies His names. He is the "Lord," the name used of God in His redemptive work. He is the "redeemer" (*goʾel*, see 35:9). He is the "Holy One of Israel," as in v. 3 emphasizing His faithfulness to His Word. With these names bringing out the character of God, it is certain that He will perform His promise. It is certain; therefore, He states it as an accomplished fact though it lies more than a hundred years in the future. For Israel's sake, the Lord will bring down Babylon. He will bring down their "nobles" (better "fugitives") and the Chaldeans whose "cry is in the ships." Chaldea was a part of Babylon, southeast of the city at the mouth of the Euphrates

---

[10]The opening phrase, *gam-mîyôm*, is subject to differing interpretations. Delitzsch, II, 194, understands it as "from this time forth." Barnes, II, 119, considers it to say, "before the beginning of time; from eternity." Fausset, p. 669, takes it as "from the time of the first existence of day." The early versions support this last view. The LXX translates ἔτι ἀπ᾽ ἀρχῆς, "even from the beginning." The Vulgate reads *ab initio*, "from the beginning." All of the views agree that there is no one like God. Since v. 12 refers to God's work in past time, it is reasonable to so understand v. 13.

16 *Thus saith the Lord, which maketh a way in the sea, and a path in the mighty waters;*

17 *Which bringeth forth the chariot and horse, the army and the power; they shall lie down together, they shall not rise: they are extinct, they are quenched as tow.*

18 *Remember ye not the former things, neither consider the things of old.*

19 *Behold, I will do a new thing; now it shall spring forth; shall ye not know it? I will even make a way in the wilderness, and rivers in the desert.*

20 *The beast of the field shall honour me, the dragons and the owls: because I give waters in the wilderness, and rivers in the desert, to give drink to my people, my chosen.*

21 *This people have I formed for myself; they shall shew forth my praise.*

River. Nabopolassar, Nebuchadnezzar's father and founder of the new Babylonian empire, was a Chaldean. The phrase "whose cry [*rinnâ*][11] is in their ships" indicates that the Chaldeans gloried in the ships by means of which they carried on trade with other nations. Herodotus refers to Babylonian ships discharging their cargo in the city, v. 14.[12] By conquering Babylon, the Lord will show Himself to be what He is. (1) He is the "Lord," the redemptive one, and deserving of their gratitude. (2) He is Israel's "Holy One," faithful to His Word, and deserving of their worship. (3) He is the Creator of the nation and therefore deserving of their reverence. (4) He is their King and therefore deserving of their obedience, v. 15.

c. Work of God 43:16–21

16–17 The Lord recalls how He had delivered Israel. He had made "a way" through the "sea" and "mighty waters." These terms are parallel, both referring to the Red Sea, v. 16. He overcame Pharaoh's army, including the "chariot and horse, the army and the power [ʿ*izzûz*, or 'powerful man']." All "lie down together" in the sea. They "shall not rise." They are "extinct" (or "extinguished"). He has "quenched" them as if they were "tow" (or "a wick"), v. 17.

18–21 Israel, however, should not dwell on the miracles of the past. The implied thought is that the past is past. They need to look to the

---

[11]Wade, p. 280, suggests that the cry was "the call by which the rowers were made to keep time." Rawlinson, II, 139, makes the cry one of wailing as the fugitives flee. The word *rinnâ* refers to a cry of rejoicing or singing, not a cadence for rowers or a lament, e.g., 14:7; 35:10; 48:20.

[12]*The Histories* i.194.

22 *But thou hast not called upon me, O Jacob; but thou hast been weary of me, O Israel.*
23 *Thou hast not brought me the small cattle of thy burnt offerings; neither hast thou honoured me with thy sacrifices. I have not caused thee to serve with an offering, nor wearied thee with incense.*
24 *Thou hast bought me no sweet cane with money, neither hast thou filled me with the fat of thy sacrifices: but thou hast made me to serve with thy sins, thou hast wearied me with thine iniquities.*

present and future needs of the nation, v. 18. God is going to do a "new thing" for them. The description of this event takes it beyond the mere deliverance of the Jews from their captivity in Babylon. The Lord will "make a way in the wilderness"; cf. 11:16; 19:23; 35:8; 40:3; 41:18–19. He will cause rivers to break out in the desert; cf. 41:18. The promise looks forward to the kingdom, when all the land will receive God's blessing, v. 19.[13] The "beast of the field," the wild animal, will "honour" Him. The "dragons" (better "serpents") and "owls" (*b^enôt ya^canâ*, "daughters of the owls," cf. 13:21), an unidentified unclean bird, will "honour" (*kabed*, see 3:5) God as they enjoy His provision. In providing water for His people, God also provides the water that the animals need. Their response honors Him, v. 20. God has made Israel for Himself. They will therefore "praise" (*t^ehillâ*, see 42:8) Him as they experience His blessing during the kingdom, v. 21.

d. Failure of the People 43:22–28

22–24 Israel has failed to sincerely worship God. They have not prayed. They have tired of the ritual worship required by God, v. 22. They have not "honoured" (*kabed*, see 3:5) Him with sacrifices of "small cattle" for burnt offerings. The "small cattle" are lit. "members of a flock." In the OT, this refers to lambs or sheep. God had not commanded them to bring "an offering" (or "meal offering") or "incense" (better "frankincense"), a gum resin that was burned in the tabernacle worship, Exodus 30:34. These were freewill offerings and should not have "wearied" the people, v. 23. They have not bought "sweet cane," calamus, an aromatic reed that formed part of the holy anointing oil, Exodus 30:23.

---

[13] Among others, Leupold, II, 89; Näglesbach, p. 470; and Motyer, *The Prophecy of Isaiah*, p. 337, refer the "new thing" to the deliverance of Israel from Babylon. The context, however, refers to rivers springing up in the wilderness. Something this remarkable would be mentioned in Ezra or Nehemiah. It is not. For this reason it is better to refer the passage to the kingdom, when the Lord will indeed do new things for the land.

25 *I, even I, am he that blotteth out thy transgressions for mine own sake, and will not remember thy sins.*
26 *Put me in remembrance: let us plead together: declare thou, that thou mayest be justified.*
27 *Thy first father hath sinned, and thy teachers have transgressed against me.*
28 *Therefore I have profaned the princes of the sanctuary, and have given Jacob to the curse, and Israel to reproaches.*

It was imported, Jeremiah 6:20, perhaps from Tyre, where it was sold in the markets, Ezekiel 27:19. They have not brought the "fat of thy sacrifices," the choicest part of the animal and so to be given in sacrifice, Leviticus 3:16. God had not burdened them. Instead, they had burdened Him by making Him "serve with [their] sins" (*ḥaṭṭaʾt*, see 3:9) as He carried out His work toward them though they continued to violate His Word. They had tired Him with their "iniquities" (*ʿawon*, see 1:4), v. 24.

25–28 The Lord reminds the people of His grace toward them. The repetition of the pronoun again (cf. v. 11) emphasizes His gracious acts toward them. He had blotted out their "transgressions [*pešaʿ*, see 24:20] for mine own sake," a sovereign act not based on their works; cf. Ephesians 2:8–9; Titus 3:5. He "will not remember [their] sins." The idea is not that God forgave their sins with no repentance on their part. Rather, this was His sovereign decision to choose Israel for Himself, a decision not based on their works. It was a gracious choice, v. 25. In view of this grace, He again (cf. v. 8) invites the nation to justify itself by showing its good works. They should "put me in remembrance" by listing their obedience and good actions. They should "plead" (better "argue") their case with Him. They should "declare" their righteousness, recounting the evidences that would prove them right. The lack of an answer implies Israel's silence. They had no good works to warrant His gracious choice, v. 26. From the very beginning, they had sinned against God. The phrase "first father" best refers to Abraham; cf. Matthew 3:9; Romans 4:1.[14] Their "teachers" (or "interpreters"), the priests who taught God's law to

---

[14]Kelley, p. 313; Von Orelli, p. 246; and Kraeling, p. 166, refer the phrase to Jacob rather than Abraham. Alexander, II, 159; Henry, p. 240; and Cowles, p. 349, relate it to Adam, the father of the human race. Fausset, p. 700, understands the phrase as a collective, referring to the ancestors of the Jews. Kissane, II, 59, makes it "the people of Israel of the period between David and the Exile." Without being dogmatic, Motyer, *Isaiah,* p. 274, suggests several possibilities including Aaron as the "first father." Barnes, II, 125, sees it as designating the high priests of the nation. Ibn Ezra, p. 198, refers this to Jeroboam, the first king of the northern confederation of tribes. Arguments can be made

the people, had also sinned, v. 27. God had therefore carried the "princes [*śar*, or 'rulers'] of the sanctuary," the priests, into captivity; cf. II Kings 17:27; Ezra 2:36, 70.[15] This "profaned" (*ḥalal*, see 23:9) them in placing them in positions that made them ritually unclean. God has given the nation as well to the "curse" (*ḥerem*, or "destruction," see 11:15). The word *ḥerem* normally describes something devoted to God and not for man. It often refers to something that was to be destroyed. The Lord would also give the nation to "reproaches." The plural here most likely intensifies the nature of the reproach that comes on the people in judgment for their sin, v. 28.

---

for and against each of these views. Based on the NT references to Abraham as Israel's "father," I accept the view given above. The identification of the "first father" is not critical. The point of the verse is that sin has marked Israel from its beginning.

[15]North, p. 78, understands "princes of the sanctuary" as "holy princes," kings "who were sacramentally anointed for their high office." The phrase occurs again only in I Chron. 24:5, in which it refers to priests. McKenzie, p. 60, limits the phrase to the heads of the priestly families. While this is possible, the mention of the sanctuary more likely refers to the priests who ruled over the temple worship.

Practical Applications from Chapter 43

1. No Other God, vv. 10, 12
   a. He is the Creator, 45:18.
   b. He is the only God, 43:10, 12; 45:5, 6, 14; 46:9.
   c. He is the only Rock, i.e., the solid foundation, 44:8.
   d. He is the Eternal One, 44:6.
   e. He is the only Savior, 43:11; 45:21, 22.

2. Chosen by God, v. 10
   a. So that we may "know" Him, gaining an understanding of the Lord by learning His Word, meditating on Him, and putting Him to the test. To know Him is to love Him—for what He has done in salvation; for what He is doing in life; and for what He will do in gaining victory over this sinful world.
   b. So that we may "believe" Him, gaining confidence in His ability to lead, to empower, and to protect. To know Him is to trust Him—for all that we need both personally and in our ministries.
   c. So that we may "understand" Him, growing in the ability to discern good from bad, the better from the best, the will of God from the will of man. To understand Him is to accept His Word for its direction in our lives—setting the standards by which we live, giving the orders that we obey, and describing the future for which we long.

3. Who Is the Lord, v. 15?
   a. The Redemptive One—we should thank Him.
   b. The Holy One—we should worship Him.
   c. The Creator—we should reverence Him.
   d. The King—we should obey Him.

1 Yet now hear, O Jacob my servant; and Israel, whom I have chosen:
2 Thus saith the Lord that made thee, and formed thee from the womb, which will help thee; Fear not, O Jacob, my servant; and thou, Jesurun, whom I have chosen.
3 For I will pour water upon him that is thirsty, and floods upon the dry ground: I will pour my spirit upon thy seed, and my blessing upon thine offspring:
4 And they shall spring up as among the grass, as willows by the water courses.
5 One shall say, I am the Lord's; and another shall call himself by the name of Jacob; and another shall subscribe with his hand unto the Lord, and surname himself by the name of Israel.

ISAIAH 44

In contrast to the rebuke of Israel given at the end of c. 43, the Lord now promises blessing to His people. With this, the chapter concludes the thought introduced earlier. He has chosen Israel for Himself. Though they have sinned, He will bring them to a position in which He may extend His favor to them. He will give them His Spirit, vv. 1–5. No idol can do what He does, vv. 6–20. It is the Lord alone who will do these things, vv. 21–27. As an illustration, the Lord introduces Cyrus the Great, the one through whom He will bring about Israel's restoration from captivity, v. 28. Chapter 45 develops this work of Cyrus more fully.

e. Promise of the Spirit 44:1–5

1–5 Jacob is God's "servant." The Lord calls Israel to hear the message He is about to give. He has chosen them for Himself, v. 1. He emphasizes again His right to choose the nation. He is their Creator; He formed them "from the womb." The idiomatic expression brings out the fact that God worked in human history even before bringing Israel into existence. He prepared the way for the nation. He first chose Abraham and brought him to Canaan. He continued His covenant with Isaac and Jacob. He sent Jacob's son Joseph into Egypt, where he assumed a position of power. From that position, he brought his family into the land and settled them in Goshen. There, shielded from the sin of Egypt and from the sin of Canaan, the nation grew into a mighty people. Since He has chosen them for Himself, the nation need not fear the future. They are His "servant." The name "Jesurun" (better "Jeshurun") occurs again only in Deuteronomy 32:15; 33:5, 26. It is a poetic name for Israel meaning "upright one." Applied to Israel, the name describes what God wanted for the nation, v. 2.

The Lord promises to bless the people. He will pour water on "him that is thirsty" (ṣameʾ, or "the thirsty land").[1] In addition, He will give the Holy Spirit without measure to His people; cf. Joel 2:28–29. The parallelism requires "blessing" to be another name for the Holy Spirit. This promise of a refreshed land and the fulness of God's Spirit looks forward to the millennial kingdom of Christ, v. 3. The nation will then prosper. Isaiah uses the figures of an unnamed plant springing "among the grass" (bᵉbên ḥaṣîr)[2] and "willows" (ʿarab, or "poplars") growing by the streams.[3] These figures portray the growth of the nation, v. 4. This blessing will cause the heathen to come to the Lord as proselytes. One will say he belongs to the Lord. Another will become a Jewish proselyte, calling himself by the name of Jacob. Still another will "subscribe with his hand" (or "write with his hand") that he belongs to the Lord.[4]

---

[1] The adjective ṣameʾ means "thirsty." The text does not say whether a "thirsty land" or a "thirsty man" is in view. Young, III, 167; Delitzsch, II, 203; and Rawlinson, II, 155, understand this as water poured out for those who thirst. Barnes, II, 128; Leupold, II, 99; and Slotki, p. 212, take it as water coming to the desert. Either view is possible, but the parallelism best supports "thirsty land" opposite "dry ground." Brueggemann, *Isaiah 40–66*, p. 65; Kelley, p. 314; and Fausset, p. 701, make ṣameʾ mean "thirsty land" but then understand it as a figure of Israel thirsting after righteousness. It is just as valid to make the statement a promise of blessing for the land.

[2] J. M. Allegro, "The Meaning of בין in Isaiah XLIV, 4," *JTS* 13:154–56, relates bên to the ben tree, a tall tree with intense green leaves and seed pods. This grows in the biblical world. He understands ḥaṣîr as an adjective and translates, "he shall spring up as the green ben tree." A. Guillaume, "A Note on the Meaning of בין," *ZAW* 63:109–10, relates bên to an Arabic cognate meaning "region, tract, area, a piece of land extending as far as the eye can reach." He translates, "They shall spring up like a field of grass." The ordinary meaning of the MT is clear.

[3] We cannot identify the ʿarab with certainty. The willow and poplar are most often suggested. It must have been a tree with darker wood since ʿarab also means "evening, dark." Both the willow and poplar grow by sources of water.

[4] The construction is awkward. The phrase reads "and another, he will write, his hand, to the Lord." This forces the translator to decide whether "hand" is the object of the action, "write on his hand," or the subject of the action, "his hand will write." Leupold, II, 100; Wade, p. 285; and Westerlund, p. 237, take the phrase to mean "tattooing the hand with the name of the Lord." Tattoos violated the Mosaic Law, Lev. 19:28. The heathen, however, would not know this. They would perceive it as a religious act that would be of help to them. This view, however, requires that we supply the preposition ʿal, "upon." Vine, p. 108; Delitzsch, II, 205; and Young, III, 168–69, understand the phrase as writing with the hand. This is a simpler view that agrees with the OT law on tattoos.

6 *Thus saith the Lord the King of Israel, and his redeemer the Lord of hosts; I am the first, and I am the last; and beside me there is no God.*

7 *And who, as I, shall call, and shall declare it, and set it in order for me, since I appointed the ancient people? and the things that are coming, and shall come, let them shew unto them.*

8 *Fear ye not, neither be afraid: have not I told thee from that time, and have declared it? ye are even my witnesses. Is there a God beside me? yea, there is no God; I know not any.*

Another will "surname himself" (*kanâ*, or "title himself") with the name of Israel, v. 5.[5]

2. Weakness of False Idols 44:6–28
a. Sovereignty of the Lord 44:6–11

6–8 The Lord declares His uniqueness. The cumulative effect of the five divine names is to establish His nature. He is "the Lord" (*yᵉhwah*, see 42:8), the one who interacts with mankind. He is "the King of Israel," the ruler of the nation. He is "his redeemer" (*goʾel*, see 35:9), who has made provision for forgiveness of sins. He is "the Lord of hosts," ruling the hosts of heaven and earth and thus powerful; cf. 1:9. He is "the first . . . the last," the one who has existed throughout eternity; cf. 41:4; 48:12.[6] There is truly no other god "beside me," on the same level as God, v. 6. Who else has predicted the future? Since God's creation of the "ancient people," the human race, no one has successfully predicted the future, v. 7.[7] For this reason, there is no need for Israel to "fear" (*paḥad*, see 2:10) or to "be afraid" (*tirhû*)[8] of the heathen gods. God has

---

[5]The verb *kanâ* here is a *piᶜel* imperfect. This is not normally reflexive. Here, however, the phrase demands a reflexive sense. The Arabic cognate may be reflexive. The Hebrew word apparently has this same sense here, where the context virtually requires it.

[6]Only Isaiah uses the phrase "first . . . last" of the Lord. The phrase "the first and the last" also occurs in the NT three times, all referring to Jesus Christ. See Rev. 1:17; 2:8; 22:13.

[7]Barnes, II, 131–32; Fausset, p. 702; and Näglesbach, p. 480, apply the phrase to Israel. While this is a possible view, it limits the statement of the verse. The Lord does not say, "Who has prophesied since the beginning of Israel?" Rather, He says, "Who has prophesied since the beginning of mankind?"

[8]The root *rahâ* is unknown. The AV conjectures the meaning "be afraid" for *tirhû*. The Vulgate gives *conturbemini*, "be troubled." The LXX omits the word. KB, II, 437, suggests a root *yrh*, "to be paralyzed with fear." 1QIsaᵃ reads *tîrʾû*, "fear," quite possibly correct. The parallelism requires something that harmonizes with *paḥad*.

9 *They that make a graven image are all of them vanity; and their de-*
lectable things shall not profit; and they are their own witnesses;
they see not, nor know; that they may be ashamed.

10 *Who hath formed a god, or molten a graven image that is profitable*
for nothing?

11 *Behold, all his fellows shall be ashamed: and the workmen, they are*
of men: let them all be gathered together, let them stand up; yet they
shall fear, and they shall be ashamed together.

told them "from that time" (or "from time past") that they need not fear
the heathen, e.g., Deuteronomy 1:21; 31:6, 8. They are witnesses that
there is "no God" other than their God. This is lit. "no Rock"; cf. 26:4;
30:29. He is the solid foundation upon which we may build our lives,
v. 8.[9]

9–11 Those who make "a graven image" (*pesel*, see 40:19) are "vanity" (*tohû*, or "futile," see 24:10). Their "delectable things" (or "precious
things") will not profit them. The last half of the verse is better "their
witnesses themselves [*ᶜedêhem hemmâ*] will not see and will not know."[10]
Retaining the *hemmâ*, the witnesses are the blind and ignorant idols. The
result is that "they," those who have made the idols, are "ashamed" (*bôš*,
see 1:29) of their actions, v. 9. Isaiah rhetorically asks who has done
such an unprofitable thing? The implied answer is that all who make "a
graven image" (*pesel*, see 40:19) have done this, v. 10. They will be
"ashamed" (*bôš*). Those who make the idols are mere men. Though all
who worship idols should gather together, though they should stand up
in defiance of God, it will not help. They will "fear" (*paḥad*, "dread," cf.
2:10) and will be "ashamed" (*bôš*), v. 11.

---

[9]Watts, *Isaiah 34–66,* p. 145, sees the Rock as "a sure place of refuge." Kelly, p. 314,
sees it as a "shield and defense." Slotki, p. 214, describes the Rock as a "fortress and
shelter." Motyer, *The Prophecy of Isaiah,* p. 345, makes it "a symbol of refuge . . . trust-
worthiness, changeless integrity . . . and reality." While the Lord is all of these and more,
the terms do not adequately describe the Rock. He is a foundation, a support, the basis
upon which our salvation rests; cf. 17:10.

[10]The rabbis suspected *hemmâ* as a dittography of the preceding suffix *hem.* They
therefore pointed it with the *puncta extraordinaria,* one of only fifteen such in the OT, to
call attention to it. The Isaiah Scroll writes the word above the line. The word appears in
the LXX. The construction is unusual but not impossible. The repetition of the pronoun
gives emphasis, "they are witnesses themselves. . . ."

12 The smith with the tongs both worketh in the coals, and fashioneth it with hammers, and worketh it with the strength of his arms: yea, he is hungry, and his strength faileth: he drinketh no water, and is faint.

13 The carpenter stretcheth out his rule; he marketh it out with a line; he fitteth it with planes, and he marketh it out with the compass, and maketh it after the figure of a man, according to the beauty of a man; that it may remain in the house.

14 He heweth him down cedars, and taketh the cypress and the oak, which he strengtheneth for himself among the trees of the forest: he planteth an ash, and the rain doth nourish it.

15 Then shall it be for a man to burn: for he will take thereof, and warm himself; yea, he kindleth it, and baketh bread; yea, he maketh a god, and worshippeth it; he maketh it a graven image, and falleth down thereto.

16 He burneth part thereof in the fire; with part thereof he eateth flesh; he roasteth roast, and is satisfied: yea, he warmeth himself, and saith, Aha, I am warm, I have seen the fire:

17 And the residue thereof he maketh a god, even his graven image: he falleth down unto it, and worshippeth it, and prayeth unto it, and saith, Deliver me; for thou art my god.

b. Structure of the Idols 44:12–20

12–17 Isaiah begins here to describe the construction of an idol. The passage is satirical, holding the process up to ridicule. The initial phrase is better "the craftsman [*haraš*] shapes iron with a cutting tool [*ma^ᶜašad*]."[11] He works with the metal in the coals and fashions "it," the idol, with his hammer. The difficulty of the work leaves him hungry and weak. He is thirsty and faint. The description lays stress on the insubstantial source of the metal idol. It comes from the skill of a frail workman, v. 12. The "carpenter" (*haraš*) as well prepares an idol.[12] He stretches out his "rule" (better "line") and marks the image with his "line" (*śered*, or "stylus").[13] He "fitteth [or 'works'] it with planes." He makes the wooden image in

---

[11]The word *ma^ᶜašad* occurs only here and Jer. 10:3. The differing context in these verses gives us no help in determining the sense. Perhaps the general meaning of "tool" is appropriate.

[12]The word *haraš*, "carpenter," is best translated "craftsman" in v. 12. The context in v. 13 involves working with wood while the worker in v. 12 uses metal.

[13]The word *śered* occurs only here with this sense. From the context, it is some sort of marker, either a tool or chalk. Commentators differ over the meaning. Young, III, 175; McKenzie, p. 66; and Näglesbach, p. 482, suggest "red chalk." Watts, *Isaiah 34–66*, p. 138; Slotki, p. 215; and Delitzsch, II, 228, give "pencil." KB, III, 1354, and BDB, p. 975, suggest "stylus." I have adopted this since it is doubtful that pencils existed in biblical times.

the shape of a man (ʾîš). At the same time, it has the "beauty of a man [ʾadam]."[14] This is a frame over which metal will be plated; cf. 40:19. He prepares the image before placing it in its "house," the shrine in which it will rest. It is ludicrous that the god needs protection, v. 13. Some unknown man, "he," not the craftsman of the previous verse, goes into the forest to cut down trees to use. He cuts down cedar, cypress, and oak trees. Several varieties of cedar grow in Palestine. Most often, the OT refers to the "cedar of Lebanon," which grew in the mountainous regions of Palestine. The trunk was up to fourteen feet in diameter and the tree grew up to one hundred feet high. The "cypress" (tirzâ) is tentatively suggested to be the holm oak. The word tirzâ occurs only here, so it is not possible to identify the tree certainly. Since the carpenter cuts this into an idol, it must be some sort of hardwood tree. The grouping with the cedar and oak tree also supports this. If the holm oak is correct, it is a hardwood tree in Palestine that grows up to forty feet high. The "oak" cannot be made any more specific. There are several different kinds of oak growing in Palestine, any one of which may be satisfactory for the making of an idol.

The man "strengtheneth for himself" the tree in the sense of raising it until it becomes strong. He plants an "ash" (ʾoren), an unknown tree. The word ʾoren occurs only here. It is possibly a cedar tree.[15] The context suggests some type of hardwood. The rain feeds it, v. 14. When it has grown, the man cuts it down and burns part of it for warmth, uses part for baking bread, and makes part of it into a god to worship. He carves it into a "graven image" (pesel, see 40:19) and then falls before it in worship, v. 15. To stress his satire, Isaiah repeats himself. The workman burns "part" (ḥeṣyô) of the wood.[16] With another "part" (ḥeṣyô), he cooks

---

[14]The word ʾîš refers to man at his best, a man of "high degree." The figure has, however, the beauty of an ʾadam (see 2:9), man in his lowest form. Man at his best is not much! The Targum understands "the beauty of a man" to refer to a female figure. It is more likely, however, that the expression is ironic. As low as he is, man cannot conceive of anything higher than himself.

[15]The word ʾoren is uncertain. Childs, pp. 339–40, translates as "laurel" but also suggests that it may be a corruption of ʾerez. The scribal use of the literae minusculae suggests uncertainty with the word. The Akkadian cognate erinu is "cedar," equivalent to the Hebrew ʾerez, "cedar." Näglesbach, p. 481, and Cohen, p. 45, suggest "cedar." Slotki, p. 216, gives "bay-tree." Skinner, Isaiah XL–LXVI, p. 57, translates "fir-tree." Westermann, p. 145, offers "spruce." Delitzsch, II, 210, renders the word "fig." The Vulgate translates pinum, "pine," an interpretive view.

[16]The word ḥeṣyô is lit. "half." This creates a minor problem. How can the workman burn half, cook with half, and still have a "residue," v. 17, from which to make an idol?

18 *They have not known nor understood: for he hath shut their eyes,*
   that they cannot see; and their hearts, that they cannot understand.
19 *And none considereth in his heart, neither is there knowledge nor*
   understanding to say, I have burned part of it in the fire; yea, also I
   have baked bread upon the coals thereof; I have roasted flesh, and
   eaten it: and shall I make the residue thereof an abomination? shall
   I fall down to the stock of a tree?
20 *He feedeth on ashes: a deceived heart hath turned him aside, that he*
   cannot deliver his soul, nor say, Is there not a lie in my right hand?

meat and satisfies his hunger. He warms himself, recognizing that he has
a good fire, v. 16. From the "residue" (or "remainder"), he carves a
"graven image" (*pesel*, see 40:19). He falls before it, offers worship,
prays to it, and seeks from it deliverance from his trials, v. 17.

18–20 Those who worship idols have not "understood" (*bîn*, see 1:3)
the stupidity of their actions.[17] God ("he") has "shut [*ṭaḥ*] their eyes."
The verb *ṭaḥ* means "to smear." It is as though God has smeared something over their spiritual eyes to blind their spiritual insight. They are
spiritually blind and lack understanding, v. 18. No one "considereth in"
(or "turns," *šûb*, see 1:27) his heart back to the truth. They lack spiritual
knowledge and understanding to recognize what they have done. They
burn "part" (*ḥeṣyô*) of the wood while baking bread and roasting meat to
eat and make the rest into an idol. The final phrase of the verse is a simple statement rather than a question: "I fall down to a block [*bûl*] of
wood," v. 19.[18] Isaiah describes the idolater with a proverb: "He feedeth
on ashes"; cf. Psalm 102:9. There is a sharp contrast between the idolater who feeds on ashes and the believer who feeds on the Bread of Life,
John 6:35. The idolater's deception has turned him away from the truth.

Westerlund, p. 145, and Wade, p. 288, suggest different emendations to avoid the second
ḥeṣyô. There is, however, no need to emend the verse. We may solve the conflict in two
ways. The fact that Isaiah speaks satirically may cause him to exaggerate consciously as
he ridicules those who make the idols. Isaiah may also use *ḥeṣyô* twice in referring to the
same half. The workman may use the same half for warmth and cooking. Verse 19 supports this view when it mentions the *ḥeṣyô* used for burning and cooking. The "residue"
is left for an idol.

[17]Several authors, e.g., Wade, Kraeling, Wright, mention that the heathen do not actually consider idols to be gods. Rather, they are only symbols of the gods. Isaiah supposedly fails to take this into consideration. This misunderstands the nature of Isaiah's
diatribe against idolatry. In speaking satirically, the prophet uses conscious exaggeration
to make his point.

[18]The word *bul* occurs only here and at Job 40:20. The word apparently refers to the
product of a tree; here it is wood and in Job it is fruit.

21 *Remember these, O Jacob and Israel; for thou art my servant: I have formed thee; thou art my servant: O Israel, thou shalt not be forgotten of me.*

22 *I have blotted out, as a thick cloud, thy transgressions, and, as a cloud, thy sins: return unto me; for I have redeemed thee.*

23 *Sing, O ye heavens; for the Lord hath done it: shout, ye lower parts of the earth: break forth into singing, ye mountains, O forest, and every tree therein: for the Lord hath redeemed Jacob, and glorified himself in Israel.*

His soul is bound by sin. He cannot see that the idol he holds in his right hand is a "lie" (*šeqer*, see 9:15) that has deceived him, v. 20.

c. Superiority of the Lord 44:21–28

21–23 The Lord urges His people to "remember [*zᵉkar*] these," the words just spoken.[19] The nation is His servant because He has created it. He will not forget the nation, v. 21. As a thick fog blocks the view, so the Lord has blocked Israel's "transgressions" (*pešaᶜ*, see 24:20) from His view. As the morning haze dissipates with the warmth of the day, so their "sins" (*ḥaṭṭaʾt*, see 3:9) have gone from before the Lord. They should "return" (*šûb*, see 1:27) to Him because He has "redeemed [*gaʾal*, the verb form of *goʾel*, cf. 35:9] them." The promise here rests on the future atoning work of Christ at Calvary. Israel will accept Christ as their Messiah and the nation will be "redeemed." The Lord states it as a past event because it is certain in His mind, v. 22. Both heaven and earth sing praise to God for this deliverance. The phrase "lower parts of the earth" speaks of the earth as being beneath the heavens.[20] The mountains and trees of the forest sing praise to the Lord. He has "redeemed" (*gaʾal*, see 35:9) His people. His redemptive work has "glorified" (*paʾar*) Himself, v. 23.[21]

---

[19]Pieper, p. 256, and Young, III, 182, refer the word "these" to that which is about to be spoken. Normally, however, the imperative *zᵉkar* looks backward in time. In particular, in the rare occasions when *zᵉkar* occurs with the demonstrative pronoun, as here, Ps. 74:18; Isa. 46:8, it looks backward rather than forward.

[20]Delitzsch, II, 214, refers the phrase to "the interior of the earth, with its caves, its pits, and its deep abysses." It is not necessary to be this specific. All of the earth is low in comparison to the heavens.

[21]The *hitpaʾel* verb *paʾar* occurs seven times (Exod. 8:9; Judg. 7:2; Isa. 10:15; 44:23; 49:3; 60:21; 61:3), always with a reflexive sense, "I will glorify myself." This is not a boastful statement but rather a statement of fact. God is deserving of glory. He glorifies Himself in one way through His redemptive work.

24 Thus saith the Lord, thy redeemer, and he that formed thee from the womb, I am the Lord that maketh all things; that stretcheth forth the heavens alone; that spreadeth abroad the earth by myself;

25 That frustrateth the tokens of the liars, and maketh diviners mad; that turneth wise men backward, and maketh their knowledge foolish;

26 That confirmeth the word of his servant, and performeth the counsel of his messengers; that saith to Jerusalem, Thou shalt be inhabited; and to the cities of Judah, Ye shall be built, and I will raise up the decayed places thereof:

27 That saith to the deep, Be dry, and I will dry up thy rivers:

28 That saith of Cyrus, He is my shepherd, and shall perform all my pleasure: even saying to Jerusalem, Thou shalt be built; and to the temple, Thy foundation shall be laid.

24–28 The Lord speaks again. He is Israel's "redeemer" (*go'el*, cf. 35:9) and the one who brought the nation into being. He alone is the omnipotent Creator of the heavens and the earth. No one else helped Him do this, v. 24. He is the one who frustrates the "tokens" (*'ôt*, better "omens," see 7:11) of the "liars." The false prophets often relied on omens in their predictions. The Lord calls them "liars," false, because they claim knowledge of the future. He makes the "diviners" of the future "mad" (better "fools"). He turns the wise men "backward," making their so-called knowledge foolish, v. 25. At the same time, He confirms the words of His "servant," the faithful prophet. He brings to pass the prophecies that the Jews will live in Jerusalem again and that the cities of Judah will be rebuilt. He will cause her "decayed places" (or "ruins") to be built again, v. 26. He as well prophesies that the "deep" (*ṣulâ*), the Euphrates River and its tributaries, will become dry; cf. Jeremiah 51:36.[22] The conquest of Babylon by Cyrus about two hundred years later fulfills this prophecy. The Greek historian Herodotus tells us that a large area had been prepared to reduce the speed of the Euphrates so that an enemy sailing it would be exposed to prolonged attack. Cyrus

---

[22]The word *ṣulâ* is a *hapax legomenon*. There are, however, related words elsewhere so that the meaning "ocean deep, watery deep" is not in doubt. Herbert, *Isaiah 40–66,* p. 65, refers the "deep" to the "waters of the abyss around and under the earth." He does not expand this but apparently means it of one source of the floodwaters, Gen. 7:11. Price, p. 190; Grogan, p. 269; and Alexander, II, 174, understand drying up the "deep" as a reference to parting the Red Sea. While we cannot be certain, referring the "deep" to the Euphrates River makes a natural transition to Cyrus in v. 28. See the discussion of Cyrus at 41:3.

supposedly turned the river into this marsh area and entered Babylon when the river became fordable, v. 27.[23] The Lord identifies Cyrus as His "shepherd." In the OT, the "shepherd" represents a king or other civil ruler. Cyrus will do all of the Lord's "pleasure" (*ḥepeṣ*). The word *ḥepeṣ* has a strong emotional component, thus "delight" or "good pleasure" is appropriate. Cyrus fulfilled this prediction by giving permission to re-build both Jerusalem and the temple; cf. Ezra 1:1–4. Josephus said, "When Cyrus read this, and admired the divine power, an earnest desire and ambition seized upon him to fulfill what was so written," v. 28.[24]

Practical Applications from Chapter 44

1. The Nature of God, v. 6
   a. He is "the Lord," the name of the God who interacts with mankind. In particular, this is the name used in connection with the sacrifices, the redemptive name of God.
   b. He is "the King," the Ruler of mankind and the one to whom we owe our obedience.
   c. He is the "Redeemer" who became a man in order to redeem mankind. See 35:9.
   d. He is the "Lord of Hosts," the Ruler of heaven and earth. See 1:9.
   e. He is "the first, and . . . the last," the eternal God who does not change.
      With v. 6, we may confidently say, "there is no God" beside our God.

2. The Folly of Worshiping Idols
   a. Idols are man-made gods, vv. 12–17.
   b. Worshiping idols shows a lack of spiritual understanding, vv. 18–19.
   c. Idols deceive the worshiper, v. 20.
   d. Idols have no profit, vv. 9–10.

---

[23] *The Histories* 1.185, 191.
[24] *Antiquities* 11.1.2.

1 Thus saith the Lord to his anointed, to Cyrus, whose right hand I have holden, to subdue nations before him; and I will loose the loins of kings, to open before him the two leaved gates; and the gates shall not be shut;

2 I will go before thee, and make the crooked places straight: I will break in pieces the gates of brass, and cut in sunder the bars of iron:

3 And I will give thee the treasures of darkness, and hidden riches of secret places, that thou mayest know that I, the Lord, which call thee by thy name, am the God of Israel.

ISAIAH 45

The chapter continues the thought of Cyrus introduced in c. 44. Chapter 45 is unique in that it is the only place in the Bible in which God directly addresses a heathen king. He addresses David directly, e.g., I Samuel 23:2, 4, 11. He speaks to other kings through prophets, dreams, and visions. Cyrus is such a pivotal character in Israel's history that the Lord directs these words to him in an unmistakable way.

3. Deliverance of Israel 45:1–25
a. Coming of Cyrus 45:1–8

1–3 The Lord speaks to Cyrus. Not only does the Lord speak directly to Cyrus, but He also calls him His "anointed" (*mašîah*).[1] In the OT, the word *mašîah*, more commonly transliterated as messiah, refers to several individuals. It applies not only to Christ (Ps. 2:2; Dan. 9:25–26) but also to the patriarchs (Ps. 105:15), priests (Lev. 4:3, 5, 16), kings (I Sam. 24:6; II Sam. 1:14, 16), and prophets (I Kings 19:16).[2] The word comes from the practice of anointing a person with oil in setting him apart to a task, e.g., Exodus 28:41; 29:7; I Samuel 15:1. In this case, Cyrus is set apart for the task of restoring the Jews to their land. He is God's "anointed" in the sense of being chosen to accomplish His will with regard to the Jews.

---

[1]Price, pp. 190–92, understands *mašîah* as a prophecy of Messiah. He wrongly argues that the name "Cyrus" (*kôreš*) means "shepherd." If we relate the name to the noun *kareś*, the word means "belly." The Akkadian cognate *karašu* also means "belly." Price explains the phrase "though thou hast not known me," vv. 4–5, as intimating "the dawning messianic consciousness of Jesus." The only reference to the childhood of Jesus, Luke 2:41–50, indicates that he was fully conscious of His deity at the age of twelve.

[2]Several authors, e.g., Leupold, II, 118; Kelley, p. 318; and North, p. 87, mistakenly state that the name Messiah does not occur in OT prophecy of Jesus Christ. It is true that the name Messiah does not refer frequently to Christ. It is also true, however, that Acts 4:26 quotes Ps. 2:2 and applies it directly to the Lord. Dan. 9:25–26 applies the name Messiah to Christ. Rawlinson, II, 175, is also wrong in stating that the "anointed" always refers to an Israelite king or to Messiah. As seen above, it may also refer to priests, prophets, or to the patriarchs.

4 For Jacob my servant's sake, and Israel mine elect, I have even called thee by thy name: I have surnamed thee, though thou hast not known me.
5 I am the Lord, and there is none else, there is no God beside me: I girded thee, though thou hast not known me:
6 That they may know from the rising of the sun, and from the west, that there is none beside me. I am the Lord, and there is none else.
7 I form the light, and create darkness: I make peace, and create evil: I the Lord do all these things.

The Lord holds the "right hand" of Cyrus. This suggests that the Lord guides him to accomplish His will. He subdues nations before Cyrus. He looses "the loins of kings." This pictures the untying of the belt that held the robe in place. It is the opposite of "girding up the loins," Exodus 12:11; I Kings 18:46, a picture of preparing for vigorous activity.[3] Here, then, the Lord hinders the preparations of kings to face Cyrus. The Lord will open the "two leaved gates" before Cyrus. The statement generally refers to the gates of the cities conquered by Cyrus. It may as well be a specific reference to the gates of Babylon, conquered by Cyrus in 539 B.C., v. 1.

The Lord speaks directly to Cyrus. He will make the "crooked places" (*hᵃdûrîm*, or "mountains") "straight" (or "level") before Cyrus,[4] a picture of removing obstacles that would hinder him. He breaks down for Cyrus the gates of cities and the bars that lock the gates. Herodotus said of Babylon, "The wall contains a hundred gates in the circuit of the wall, all of bronze, with posts and lintels of the same," v. 2.[5] The Lord gives Cyrus the "treasures of darkness," wealth that has been hidden away in dark vaults, and riches from other "secret places." He intends to do these things so that Cyrus will experientially "know" (*yadaᶜ*, cf. 1:3) that Israel's God is the one who has called him, v. 3.

4–7 Because of the Jewish people, God has called Cyrus by name in this prophecy. He has "surnamed" Cyrus, applying titles of honor to him, even though Cyrus has "not known me." This last phrase refers to

---

[3]This is the only place that this idiom occurs. Ezek. 21:6 and 29:7 are similar in portraying the weakening of the loins. Several passages, e.g., Isa. 20:2; 32:11, refer to wearing sackcloth on the loins as a show of grief.

[4]The word *hᵃdûrîm* normally means "honor" or "adorn." Motyer, *The Prophecy of Isaiah,* p. 358, derives the sense of "mountains" by understanding *hadar* as "to swell." He makes *hᵃdûrîm* a *qal* passive participle, something "upraised," i.e., mountains. The root takes this sense nowhere else. The LXX and the Isaiah Scroll support the reading *hᵃrarîm,* "mountains."

[5]*The Histories* i.179.

8 *Drop down, ye heavens, from above, and let the skies pour down righteousness: let the earth open, and let them bring forth salvation, and let righteousness spring up together; I the Lord have created it.*

God's call of Cyrus while he was still a heathen with no knowledge of the true God, v. 4.[6] There is no God beside the Lord who could do such things. Isaiah repeats this thought to give it emphasis. The Lord has "girded" Cyrus, preparing him for his work, though Cyrus did not know God as his God. The repetition that Cyrus did not experientially "know" (*yadaᶜ*, see 1:3) God lays stress on the thought. The Lord is using a heathen king to carry out His will for Israel, v. 5. From the "rising of the sun," the east, and from the "west" (*maᶜᵃrabâ*, see 43:5), others will know of God's uniqueness. He alone is the Lord, v. 6.[7] He controls the "light" and "darkness," both most likely used symbolically here of good and evil. He makes "peace" (*šalôm*, see 9:6) and creates "evil" (*raᶜ*). The word *raᶜ* has a broad range of meanings and includes physical, emotional, and spiritual evil. It occurs here in contrast with "peace" and perhaps is best "calamity," v. 7.

8 In view of what the Lord intends to accomplish through Cyrus, He now speaks idealistically of the result of this work. There is no object of the verb "drop down" (*harᶜîpû*). From the continuation of the thought and the parallelism in 8*b,* it is clear that spiritual blessings are in view. The verb *harᶜîpû* occurs only here in the *hipᶜîl*. In this context, it has the normal causative sense. The heavens bring forth abundant rain. The Lord commands "salvation" (*yešaᶜ*, see 17:10) and "righteousness" (*ṣedaqâ*, see 1:21) to abound in His creation. It is the Lord who has created such an abundance of goodness in the earth, v. 8.[8]

---

[6]Among others, Pieper, p. 268; Delitzsch, II, 220; and Rawlinson, II, 174, understand the phrase "hast not known me" to refer to the call of Cyrus given before his birth; cf. Jer. 1:5. This is a possible view. I prefer the view above since it gives a more direct contrast with "Jacob," the servant of God, and "Israel," the elect of God.

[7]Brueggemann, *Isaiah 40–66,* p. 76, notes that God may use an unsaved person for His purposes. He then draws the conclusion that "Marx and Freud may be prophets in their time and place." His choice of words is poor. While God undoubtedly uses the unsaved for His purposes, He does not call them as "prophets" of His Word.

[8]North, p. 89, raises a straw man that he then knocks down: "The predictions in these verses were not fulfilled in the way the Prophet expected. Babylon was not entered forcibly, nor was it destroyed. Cyrus . . . did not become a convert to Judaism." Isaiah, however, does not predict a forcible entry into Babylon or the destruction of the city. He does not predict the conversion of Cyrus. North misinterprets the passage.

9 Woe unto him that striveth with his Maker! Let the potsherd strive with the potsherds of the earth. Shall the clay say to him that fashioneth it, What makest thou? or thy work, He hath no hands?

10 Woe unto him that saith unto his father, What begettest thou? or to the woman, What hast thou brought forth?

11 Thus saith the Lord, the Holy One of Israel, and his Maker, Ask me of things to come concerning my sons, and concerning the work of my hands command ye me.

12 I have made the earth, and created man upon it: I, even my hands, have stretched out the heavens, and all their host have I commanded.

13 I have raised him up in righteousness, and I will direct all his ways: he shall build my city, and he shall let go my captives, not for price nor reward, saith the Lord of hosts.

b. Complaint of Israel 45:9–13

9–10 There are some who apparently think it is wrong to use a king like Cyrus, who does not know God, to perform God's work. Isaiah rebukes these, pronouncing a woe upon them for contending with God. They are, better, "a potsherd among the potsherds of the ground." A potsherd was a fragment of a broken pot. It represents something weak or of a lowly nature. Should the pot criticize its maker? Should the work say, "he hath no hands," using hyperbole to express his lack of skill?[9] Paul draws on this argument in Romans 9:20–21, when he reproves those who question God's work, v. 9? Woe to the one who would criticize his parents for what he himself is, v. 10.

11–13 If Israel has questions about the future, she should ask the Lord directly. The Lord describes Himself as "holy" and therefore trustworthy. Further, He has brought the nation into existence. The people are His "sons," implying a fatherly love for them. The phrase "command ye me" communicates clearly the right to ask, v. 11. He is the Creator, the one who has made the earth and stretched out the heavens. He has placed "man" (ʾadam, see 2:9) on it. His "hands," the emblems of His power, have done this. He commands (or "appoints") the heavenly bodies, putting each one in its proper place, v. 12. He has raised up "him," Cyrus, "in righteousness" (ṣedeq, see 1:21), for a righteous purpose. Cyrus will rebuild Jerusalem; cf. Ezra 1:1–4.[10] He will return the cap-

---

[9]Slotki, p. 222, makes vv. 9–13 directed toward Habakkuk. While Habakkuk questioned God (Hab. 1:2–4; 1:13–17), it is highly unlikely that Isaiah wrote for him. There is no example in the OT of one prophet writing for another prophet.

[10]Whitehouse, pp. 124–25, implies the inaccuracy of the passage since Jerusalem was not rebuilt during the reign of Cyrus. Nothing in the passage, however, states that the

14 *Thus saith the Lord, The labour of Egypt, and merchandise of*
Ethiopia and of the Sabeans, men of stature, shall come over unto
thee, and they shall be thine: they shall come after thee; in chains
they shall come over, and they shall fall down unto thee, they shall
make supplication unto thee, saying, Surely God is in thee; and there
is none else, there is no God.

15 *Verily thou art a God that hidest thyself, O God of Israel, the Saviour.*

16 *They shall be ashamed, and also confounded, all of them: they shall*
go to confusion together that are makers of idols.

17 *But Israel shall be saved in the Lord with an everlasting salvation:*
ye shall not be ashamed nor confounded world without end.

tives freely, "not for price nor reward." The decree of Cyrus will come in response to the leading of God's Spirit, not as the result of a payment of money to the king, cf. 43:3–4, v. 13.[11]

c. Conversion of the Gentiles 45:14–25

14–17 Egypt, Ethiopia, south of Egypt, and the Sabeans, from Meroë, a province of Ethiopia, bring their tribute.[12] The Sabeans are further identified as "men [$^{\circ e}nôš$, see 2:11] of stature."[13] The pronoun "thee" refers to Israel.[14] The act of falling down shows the Sabeans' submission. They

---

rebuilding of Jerusalem was finished while Cyrus lived. He was responsible for the first return of the Jews from the captivity, Ezra 1:1–4. Almost fifty thousand Jews returned, Ezra 2:64–65. Although the OT states nothing about where these lived, it is reasonable to assume that they built or renovated homes. The altar was set up in the city and worship begun, Ezra 3:1–6. The Jews hired workers to bring cedar for the building, Ezra 3:7. The temple foundation was laid, Ezra 3:10. It is fair to say that Cyrus was responsible for the rebuilding of Jerusalem even though additional building was completed later.

[11]Smart, p. 130, wants to omit Cyrus as the creation of a later editor. He thinks such interpretation shows "remarkable inconsistency regarding v. 13, emphasizing the generosity of Cyrus in his liberation of the Babylonian Jews without receiving any 'price or reward,' but forgetting that they have already pictured Cyrus in vs. 1–3 as being richly rewarded by God." Smart misunderstands the chapter. It is true that God rewarded him with "treasures," v. 3. It is likewise true that the Jews paid him nothing, v. 13. There is no conflict between v. 3 and v. 13.

[12]Numerous authors refer the Sabeans to a people in southwest Arabia descended from Sheba, Gen. 10:28. The best-known history of the nation involves the visit of its queen to see Solomon, I Kings 10:1–13. The grouping of the people here with Ethiopia and Egypt makes it more likely that this is the Seba in Ethiopia. See note 2, c. 43.

[13]Herodotus, *The Histories* iii.20, 114, said: "those Ethiopians . . . are said to be the tallest and fairest of all men. . . . the men are the tallest and fairest and longest-living *of all men.*"

[14]Among others, North, p. 91; Kraeling, p. 172; and Watts, *Isaiah 34–66,* p. 161, make these nations bring their tribute to Cyrus. The pronoun "thee," however, is feminine. This

come "in chains," a picture of their submission to the people of God. They acknowledge the presence of God in Israel. The fulfillment of this submission is yet future. In the millennial kingdom the Gentile nations will seek the favor of Israel, cf. 2:2–3; 49:22, v. 14.[15] Overwhelmed with what he has seen, Isaiah spontaneously prays.[16] He acknowledges that God is a God who hides Himself, i.e., His ways are beyond man's ability to comprehend. He is Israel's "Saviour." From the context of vv. 21–25, the deliverance in view here is from Israel's sins, v. 15. The heathen will be "ashamed" (*bôš*, see 1:29) of their ways and will be "confounded" (*kalam*, or "disgraced," see 30:3). Those who have made idols will experience "confusion" (*kalam*, or "disgrace"), v. 16. Israel, however, will be saved with "an everlasting salvation." This is not merely a temporary deliverance from some trial; this is eternal life. This reflects a new relationship between Israel and God. They will never be "ashamed" (*bôš*) or "confounded" (*kalam*, again "disgraced"). By using the same verb roots in vv. 16–17, Isaiah heightens the contrast. The heathen, who have worshiped gods made with their own hands, will be ashamed and dishonored. Israel, who now worships the only God, will not be ashamed or dishonored, v. 17.

---

reflects the early belief that the verse referred to Israel. Those who apply the verse to Cyrus must repoint the verse. In addition, the affirmation that "there is none else, there is no God" can hardly be attributed to Cyrus. While He acknowledged God as Israel's God, Ezra 1:2–3, He did not accept God as the only God. The Cylinder of Cyrus, an archaeological record, proves otherwise.

[15]Westerlund, p. 169, thinks this prophecy "strange" since "it visualizes a state of well-being for Israel still lying in the future, a thing which occurs nowhere else in the prophet's work." He admits, however, that 60:13–14 describe the same future blessing of Israel. He concludes that v. 14 was originally a part of c. 60 that somehow became separated to its present place. This illustrates circular reasoning. He assumes the conclusion, then argues his way to it.

[16]Among others, Näglesbach, p. 496; Skinner, *Isaiah XL–LXVI*, p. 71; and Slotki, p. 223, make the redeemed heathen of v. 14 the speaker here. The view is possible. The change in thought between v. 14 and v. 15 is so drastic that it seems to me that there is a new speaker.

18 *For thus saith the Lord that created the heavens; God himself that formed the earth and made it; he hath established it, he created it not in vain, he formed it to be inhabited: I am the Lord; and there is none else.*

19 *I have not spoken in secret, in a dark place of the earth: I said not unto the seed of Jacob, Seek ye me in vain: I the Lord speak righteousness, I declare things that are right.*

20 *Assemble yourselves and come; draw near together, ye that are escaped of the nations: they have no knowledge that set up the wood of their graven image, and pray unto a god that cannot save.*

21 *Tell ye, and bring them near; yea, let them take counsel together: who hath declared this from ancient time? who hath told it from that time? have not I the Lord? and there is no God else beside me; a just God and a Saviour; there is none beside me.*

18–21 To illustrate His power to accomplish His purposes, God portrays Himself as the Creator of the heavens and earth. He did not form the earth "in vain" (*tohû,* or "empty," see 24:10).[17] No, He made it to be inhabited. He is the Lord "and there is none else." He will therefore accomplish His purposes for this world, v. 18. To this end, He has not spoken "in secret" or "in a dark place." These phrases contrast the words of God with the words of the heathen oracles. It is thought that the words of an oracle often came from a dark cave in which the oracle supposedly lived. We do not have detailed descriptions of oracles in the Bible. Second Kings 1:2 refers to consulting a heathen oracle. God did not tell the offspring of Jacob to seek him "in vain" (*tohû,* again "empty," thus, without purpose). No, He speaks in righteousness. He says things that are right. The implied thought is that the people should seek the Lord sincerely, v. 19.

The Lord urges those who have escaped Cyrus's conquests to come together to test the truth. Those who "set up" (better "carry") their "graven image" (*pesel,* see 40:19), their carved wooden idol, and pray to a god without power to deliver them, have no knowledge, v. 20. Let them present their arguments. Who among them has predicted the future? Only the Lord has done this. There is no other God beside Him. He is a "just" (or "righteous") God and a "Saviour." In view of the context of

---

[17]Brueggemann, *Isaiah 40–66,* p. 83, notes that God did create the earth *tohû,* Gen. 1:2. He therefore limits the verse to the Babylonian captivity or to idol makers (called *tohû,* 44:9) or to the idols themselves that bring *tohû,* 41:29. It is not necessary to limit the verse. The use of *tohû* in Gen. 1:2 does not bear on God's overall purpose in the creation. The creation was not finished at that point.

22 *Look unto me, and be ye saved, all the ends of the earth: for I am God, and there is none else.*
23 *I have sworn by myself, the word is gone out of my mouth in right-eousness, and shall not return, That unto me every knee shall bow, every tongue shall swear.*
24 *Surely, shall one say, in the Lord have I righteousness and strength: even to him shall men come; and all that are incensed against him shall be ashamed.*
25 *In the Lord shall all the seed of Israel be justified, and shall glory.*

vv. 22–25, the thought here includes more than mere redemption from captivity. God is a Savior who redeems people from their spiritual bondage, v. 21.

22–25 The Lord invites men from "all the ends of the earth" to receive the salvation that He offers. He is God and there is no other god who can offer this salvation. The thought anticipates the fuller development of salvation in the NT, e.g., Romans 10:13; II Peter 3:9, v. 22. He has "sworn by myself" that He will perform His Word. This is one of seven times that God swears by Himself. Men often swear an oath by God. The idea is that we swear in the presence of a higher power that what we say is correct. Since God cannot take an oath by a higher power, He swears by Himself, the highest power that is. A time will come when all will bow before God, a proper position of humility in the presence of deity, and "swear," i.e., acknowledge that He is God. The apostle Paul develops this thought further, Romans 14:11; Philippians 2:10–11. The unsaved will acknowledge Him, but it will be too late to accept Him as their Savior. The saved, however, will joyfully acknowledge Him as their Savior, v. 23.

Men will acknowledge that "righteousness" and "strength" are in the Lord. The plural "righteousness" is intensive. It refers to absolute righteousness. From the parallelism to "righteousness," the "strength" spoken of is spiritual strength. Men will come to Him. Those who have been "incensed" (or "angry") at God will be "ashamed" (*bôš*, see 1:29), v. 24. Israel will also turn to Him. They will be "justified," declared righteous by God. They will glory in their position. The thought here is of righteous Israel, not merely those who are Jews by birth. Only those who accept Jesus Christ as their Redeemer will enjoy the blessing of an eternal relationship with the Father, v. 25.

Practical Applications from Chapter 45

1. The Oaths of God

   a. All will acknowledge God, Isaiah 45:23.

   b. He will judge those who reject His Word, Jeremiah 22:5.

   c. He will judge the heathen, Jeremiah 49:13; 51:14.

   d. He will judge the Jews, Amos 6:8.

   e. He will bless the faithful, Genesis 22:16; Hebrews 6:13–14.

2. The Power of God

   a. He controls the events of history so that He accomplishes His will through them. His call of Cyrus illustrates this, vv. 1–4, 5*b*, 13. He controls good and evil, making peace and allowing calamity, v. 7.

   b. He is the unique God. No other God exists, v. 5*a*, 6, 21*b*.

   c. He is the Creator of heaven and earth, vv. 12, 18.

   d. He will establish His kingdom on the earth. All will acknowledge Him as the Lord, v. 23*b*. Israel will enter into a new relationship with Him, vv. 17, 25. The heathen nations will acknowledge Israel as the Lord's own people, v. 14. They will be ashamed that they had ever been angry with Him, v. 24*b*.

   e. His ways are beyond man's comprehension, v. 15.

   f. He openly declares His will, v. 19, and brings salvation and righteousness to the earth, v. 8. Men should forsake their false worship, v. 20, and turn to the Lord, who alone gives salvation, v. 22. Only in Him is righteousness and spiritual strength, v. 24*a*.

   In view of God's power and gracious offer of salvation, men should turn to Him now for deliverance from their sins.

1 *Bel boweth down, Nebo stoopeth, their idols were upon the beasts,*
   and upon the cattle: your carriages were heavy loaden; they are a
   burden to the weary beast.
2 *They stoop, they bow down together; they could not deliver the bur-*
   den, but themselves are gone into captivity.

ISAIAH 46

Chapter 46 naturally continues the development of c. 44–45. The Lord has introduced Cyrus there as the one responsible for building Jerusalem, 44:28, and giving freedom to the captives, 45:13*b*. He is the one before whom the gates of cities will open, 45:1. He is the one who will receive treasures now hidden away in darkness, 45:3. He is the one girded by the Lord for his work, 45:5. He is the one raised up by the Lord for a righteous purpose, 45:13*a*. The Lord now develops this theme by showing that Babylon will fall to Cyrus. In c. 46 He focuses on the fall of Babylon's gods. With the fall of the false gods, Isaiah introduces the rise of the true God, who will rule the earth.

D. Fall of Wicked Babylon 46:1–47:15
1. Destruction of Idols 46:1–13

1–2 Isaiah describes the failure of the heathen gods. The god "Bel," a variant of Baal ("Lord"), was head of the Babylonian pantheon of gods. Bel was a title. The word appears elsewhere in the OT only in compound names.[1] The god also had the name "Marduk" (Merodach, Jer. 50:2). The god "Nebo," the son of Bel, was the god of wisdom and learning. The name also appears in the OT only in compound names.[2] Both of these names appear in history in the names of the Babylonian kings Belshazzar, Nabopolassar, Nebuchadnezzar, and Nabonidus. These idols bow down (*kara^c*) and stoop (*qores*) in the sense of idols laid as a heavy "burden" (*maśśa^ɔ*, see 13:1) on an animal to carry. The word "carriages" refers to baggage carried on the animals, v. 1.[3] The idols remain stooped (*qaras*) and bowed down (*kara^c*). They have no power to deliver the

---

[1]Belteshazzar (Daniel), e.g., Dan. 1:7; 2:26; 4:8, 9, 18, 19; King Belshazzar, e.g., Dan. 5:1, 2, 9, 22, 29, 30.

[2]Nebuchadnezzar (or Nebuchadrezzar), e.g., Jer. 21:2, 7; 22:25; 24:1; Dan. 1:1, 18; Nebuzar-adan, e.g., II Kings 25:8, 11, 20; Jer. 39:9, 10, 11, 13; Nebushasban, Jer. 39:13.

[3]The verb *qaras* occurs only in 46:1, 2. The parallelism with *kara^c* argues for the sense "bow down." The related noun *qeres*, "hook," can be thought of as something bent.

3 *Hearken unto me, O house of Jacob, and all the remnant of the house of Israel, which are borne by me from the belly, which are carried from the womb:*

4 *And even to your old age I am he; and even to hoar hairs will I carry you: I have made, and I will bear; even I will carry, and will deliver you.*

5 *To whom will ye liken me, and make me equal, and compare me, that we may be like?*

6 *They lavish gold out of the bag, and weigh silver in the balance, and hire a goldsmith; and he maketh it a god: they fall down, yea, they worship.*

7 *They bear him upon the shoulder, they carry him, and set him in his place, and he standeth; from his place shall he not remove: yea, one shall cry unto him, yet can he not answer, nor save him out of his trouble.*

"burden" (*maśśaʾ*, see 13:1) carried by the animal. Rather, they themselves will go into captivity as spoil taken by the enemy, v. 2.

3–4 The Lord urges the "house of Jacob" and the "house of Israel" to listen to Him. These phrases occur here in poetic variation. Both refer simply to the nation.[4] He has carried them "from the belly" and "from the womb," i.e., from their birth as a nation; cf. Deuteronomy 32:11–12. Note the contrast with the heathen gods. The animals carried them. God, however, carries His people, v. 3. He will continue to carry them through the trials they face. He will carry them "even to your old age . . . even to hoar [or 'gray'] hairs," i.e., to their old age as a nation. He has made the nation and He will therefore sustain them. The fivefold repetition of the personal pronoun *ʾanî* gives emphasis to the statement: "I myself am He, I myself will carry, I myself have made, I myself will bear, I myself will carry and will deliver," v. 4.

5–7 The rhetorical question makes the point that no one is like the Lord. No other god equals Him in power and wisdom. No other god compares to Him in His attributes, v. 5. For the fourth time, the Lord satirically describes the making of an idol; cf. also 40:19–20; 41:6–7; 44:12–19 (see also 37:19, "they were no gods, but the work of men's

---

[4]Delitzsch, II, 233, makes the "house of Jacob" refer to Judah and the "house of Israel" refer to the northern ten tribes. Nothing in the parallelism or context supports this view. God has carried the nation from its beginning. He will carry them into old age. They should therefore remember that He alone is God, v. 9.

8 *Remember this, and shew yourselves men: bring it again to mind, O ye transgressors.*

9 *Remember the former things of old: for I am God, and there is none else; I am God, and there is none like me,*

10 *Declaring the end from the beginning, and from ancient times the things that are not yet done, saying, My counsel shall stand, and I will do all my pleasure:*

11 *Calling a ravenous bird from the east, the man that executeth my counsel from a far country: yea, I have spoken it, I will also bring it to pass; I have purposed it, I will also do it.*

hands, wood and stone"). The heathen "lavish" (*zûl*)[5] gold from their moneybag and weigh out some silver. They hire a "goldsmith" (*ṣôrep*, or "smith," see 40:19) to make a god. From the fact that gold idols could be burned, Exodus 32:20, it seems that a wood frame was first made, then gold plating applied. Earlier, Isaiah has spoken of adding silver chains to an idol, 40:19. The ridicule reaches a new height with the reference to a "god" (*ʾel*). The word *ʾel* has the sense of a mighty one. This "mighty one," however, has no might. Nonetheless, the heathen fall down in worship before their god, v. 6. They bear the idol on their shoulders. They carry it and set it in "his place," the shrine made for the idol. The image stands there with no power to move about. Although people cry out in prayer to it, it cannot answer or deliver them from their trials, v. 7.

8–11 Israel should remember "this" (*zoʾt*), the powerlessness of idols.[6] The phrase "shew yourselves men" (*hitʾošašû*) is better "establish yourselves," i.e., stand fast.[7] In calling them "transgressors," the Lord re-

---

[5]The word *zûl* occurs only here. It comes from an unused root meaning "to depart, remove." This underlies the related word *zûlâ*, found often as "except, besides." Here, *zûl* parallels the weighing out of silver. This leads to the sense of "meting out" the gold in preparation for the making of an idol.

[6]Pieper, p. 299, argues that *zoʾt* points to something new, not what has been mentioned. He finds the subject in v. 9, the works of God in the past. His interpretation is possible. The demonstrative pronoun *zoʾt*, however, may point backward, e.g., 5:25; 9:12; 41:20; 42:23. In calling the people "transgressors," the Lord joins them to the idols that He has just called them to "remember." They had worshiped that which had no power.

[7]The verb *hitʾošašû* is a *hapax legomenon*. It comes from the unused root *ʾašaš*, cognate to Akkadian and Arabic verbs meaning "to found, establish." This parallels the other imperatives in the verse. So KB, BDB. Henk Leene, "Isaiah 46.8—Summons to Be Human?" *JSOT* 30:111–21, argues that the meaning "be firm" does not fit here. He derives the word from *ʾîš*, "to be human." Isaiah exhorts Israel to "behave as human beings, i.e., to move away from idol-making." The AV derives it from the same root *ʾîš* but gives it the sense of "be a man." Delitzsch, II, 235, derives it from the unused root *ʾašâ*, "to be

12 *Hearken unto me, ye stouthearted, that are far from righteousness:*
13 *I bring near my righteousness; it shall not be far off, and my salva-*
tion shall not tarry: and I will place salvation in Zion for Israel my
glory.

minds the people that they had not always been faithful in this matter, v. 8. They should remember "the former things of old," God's works in the past. He is the only true God. There is no other God beside Him. The repetition of this thought makes it emphatic, v. 9. He declares the "end" from the "beginning." The "end" here refers to the future events centered on the coming of Cyrus. The "beginning" and "ancient times" refer to earlier times in the nation's history; cf. 37:26; 40:21. He pledges that His counsel will persist and that He will carry out His "pleasure" (*ḥepeṣ*, see 44:28), v. 10. He has called Cyrus like "a ravenous bird" (*ʿayiṭ*, better "a bird of prey")[8] from the "east" (*mizraḥ*, see 43:5) of Palestine.[9] He will carry out God's counsels from "a far country," Persia. The Lord has "spoken" this, decreeing its accomplishment. He will see that this is done. The repetition of the conjunction lays emphasis on the work of God in this: "I also have spoken . . . I will also bring it to pass . . . I also have purposed . . . I will also do it," v. 11.

12–13 The Lord speaks to the "stouthearted" (*ʾabbîrê leb*, or "strong of heart," see 10:13), those who have hardened themselves against God and are "far from righteousness." The word *ʾabbîr* refers to a bull. It poetically pictures strength. The Lord directs His words to rebellious Jews, v. 12. The next verse stresses what He plans for Israel. He will bring His "righteousness" to the nation. He will wait no longer to bring the nation into a new relationship with Him in which they keep His Word. He will

---

firm, strong." This has some support from related nouns in the OT. The Vulgate reads *confundamini*, "be confused," which requires an unlikely change to *hitbošašû*. The LXX reads στενάξατε, "groan," which assumes an even more unlikely derivation from *ʾanaḥ* or *ʾanaq*. Various emendations have been suggested but none have greater likelihood than the derivation from *ʾašaš*.

[8]The *ʿayiṭ* is not any one bird. The root verb *ʿayaṭ* means "to scream," I Sam. 25:14. This naturally leads to the shriek of a bird. Watts, p. 166, makes *ʿayiṭ* specific, an "eagle." This is too restrictive. Slotki, p. 228, and Fausset, p. 711, suggest that the emblem reflects the rapidity of Cyrus's movements. Alexander, II, 194, finds the connection in "rapacity and fierceness." The bird of prey will suit either of these views.

[9]Snaith, p. 164, understands the "ravenous bird" as "triumphant Israel, swooping down in victory." This does not explain how the bird could come "from a far country." Certainly, Israel returning from Babylon could not be pictured as "victorious."

bring His "salvation" to them, delivering them from the trials that have plagued the nation throughout its existence. The final phrase is better "I will grant salvation in Zion and my glory to Israel." The nation thus will not only gain its freedom but the Lord will also exalt it before the other nations of the world. The final fulfillment of this promise will take place during the millennial kingdom, when Israel worships the Lord as Savior. They will then walk in fellowship with Him, enjoying peace and seen by the nations as the people uniquely blessed by God, v. 13.

Practical Application from Chapter 46

False and True Worship
1. The Weakness of False Gods. The false gods will fail, v. 1. They have no power to deliver, v. 2. The heathen make their gods, then worship what they have made, v. 6. This "god" has no power to move or to answer prayer, v. 7.
2. The Power of the True God. It is God who has created the nation, v. 3. He will continue to sustain them, v. 4. No other god equals Him in power and wisdom, v. 5. The people should remember the weakness of their idols, v. 8, and the power of the true God, v. 9. He knows the future, v. 10. The coming of Cyrus illustrates this truth, v. 11. The Lord invites the rebellious, v. 12, to enter into a new relationship with Him. He will then openly exalt this nation before other nations. The people will then walk in fellowship with Him, v. 13.

1 Come down, and sit in the dust, O virgin daughter of Babylon, sit on
   the ground: there is no throne, O daughter of the Chaldeans: for
   thou shalt no more be called tender and delicate.
2 Take the millstones, and grind meal: uncover thy locks, make bare
   the leg, uncover the thigh, pass over the rivers.
3 Thy nakedness shall be uncovered, yea, thy shame shall be seen: I
   will take vengeance, and I will not meet thee as a man.
4 As for our redeemer, the Lord of hosts is his name, the Holy One of
   Israel.
5 Sit thou silent, and get thee into darkness, O daughter of the
   Chaldeans: for thou shalt no more be called, The lady of kingdoms.

ISAIAH 47

Chapter 47 continues to develop the work of Cyrus in his conquest of
Babylon. In the previous chapter, the Lord has described the weakness of
Babylon's gods. He now describes the loss of Babylon's power. Cyrus
has been called to free Israel from captivity, 45:13*b*. This will let them
rebuild Jerusalem, 44:28; 45:13*a*. Cyrus will make this possible by his
defeat of Babylon. Babylon had showed the Jews no mercy. The Lord
will now show her no mercy. He will humble and shame her by the conquest of Cyrus.

2. Destruction of Babylon 47:1–15

1–5 The Lord describes the humbling of Babylon. The "virgin daughter of Babylon" refers to the people of Babylon. The Lord pictures them
as pure, not yet dishonored by defeat.[1] The woman, representing Babylon,
will no longer rule the nations. She now sits on the ground rather than
being elevated on a throne. Treated as a slave, she will no longer be
called "tender and delicate," v. 1. Isaiah continues to use the figure of a
woman to represent the nation. She will do the work of grinding the
meal. The dual word "millstones" (*reḥayim*) refers to the upper and lower
millstones used in the handmill. This used two circular stones up to two
feet in diameter. The lower stone was slightly convex while the upper
stone was concave. A hole in the center of the upper stone allowed grain
to be fed between the stones. A handle near the edge of the upper stone

---

[1]The picture of a people as a "virgin" is common in the OT, especially in the writings
of Jeremiah. Cf. II Kings 19:21; Isa. 23:12; 37:22; Jer. 14:17; 18:13; 31:4, 21; 46:11;
Lam. 1:15; 2:13; Amos 5:2. Isaiah uses the word "virgin" three times to refer to a nation,
here and in 23:12; 37:22. In each case, the term describes a nation not yet conquered by
its enemy. It is, for a time, pure. It is, however, about to be ravished.

let it turn about a shaft rising from the center of the lower stone. Either the wife, Job 31:10, or a servant, Exodus 11:5; Lamentations 5:13, prepared the grain. A cloth gathered the grain as it dropped from between the stones.

She will "uncover thy locks" (better "remove your veil"), exposing herself to public view. She will "make bare the leg [*šobel*]"[2] (better "strip off the skirt") in order to cross the rivers. She will "uncover the thigh" as she crosses streams to travel to her new home.[3] She will "pass over the rivers" as she travels to her place of service as a slave, v. 2.

Babylon will be exposed to open shame. She will be seen as naked with her "shame" revealed. The "shame" here is her public humiliation.[4] The Lord will take vengeance on her and not "meet [*pagaᶜ*] thee as a man." The verb *pagaᶜ* in the *qal* normally refers to meeting someone. There is no need for a specialized meaning here.[5] The Lord will not meet Babylon as one man meets another but will overwhelm her, giving her no opportunity to resist His judgment, v. 3. The "Lord of hosts," ruler of the hosts of heaven and earth, is the "redeemer" (*goʾel*, see 35:9) of the nation. He is the "Holy One of Israel" and therefore His promises are reliable, v. 4. The "daughter of the Chaldeans," cf. v. 1, the Babylonians, will sit in silence as they grieve over their fate.[6] They will go into dark-

---

[2]While the noun *šobel* occurs only here, related words refer to the flowing of a stream and to the stretching out of a path. This leads to the idea of a flowing garment, a "skirt."

[3]Alexander, II, 198, understands this as habitual exposure, a mark of lower-class women. He argues that there is no evidence of Cyrus deporting the Babylonians. The next phrase, however, speaks of crossing rivers. This supports the idea of a forced departure from the city and would be a natural time for lifting the robe.

[4]Leupold, II, 149, understands "shame" to refer to the woman's "genitalia." The woman, however, represents Babylon, v. 1, rather than an actual woman. I prefer to make her shame the humiliation that the nation receives as she falls to the Medo-Persian alliance.

[5]Delitzsch, II, 237, and the NASB translate, "spare no man." This is interpretive. The verb *pagaᶜ* does not have this meaning elsewhere. Cowles, p. 376, extends the thought of "meet" to "strike" as in "striking hands," making an agreement, or "striking against," falling upon the nation without opposition. The end result in both views is total destruction. He has the right idea although he gives *pagaᶜ* a sense it does not have.

[6]Pieper, p. 309, suggests that sitting in silence and darkness refers to consigning Babylon to sheol. He supports the view from 14:9–11, 15, in which the king of Babylon goes into sheol, and Ps. 115:17, in which the dead go into silence. The verse in Psalms has nothing to do with sheol, and c. 14 in Isaiah deals with the king as a type of Satan. From the earlier context, Babylon goes into captivity here rather than into sheol.

[7]Leupold, II, 150, makes the "darkness" a symbol of Babylon's "relative obscurity." While this symbolism is possible, the normal use of darkness as a symbol is of gloom or depression, e.g., II Sam. 22:29; Ps. 18:28; 88:18; Lam. 3:2.

6 *I was wroth with my people, I have polluted mine inheritance, and given them into thine hand: thou didst shew them no mercy; upon the ancient hast thou very heavily laid thy yoke.*

7 *And thou saidst, I shall be a lady for ever: so that thou didst not lay these things to thy heart, neither didst remember the latter end of it.*

8 *Therefore hear now this, thou that art given to pleasures, that dwellest carelessly, that sayest in thine heart, I am, and none else beside me; I shall not sit as a widow, neither shall I know the loss of children:*

9 *But these two things shall come to thee in a moment in one day, the loss of children, and widowhood: they shall come upon thee in their perfection for the multitude of thy sorceries, and for the great abundance of thine enchantments.*

10 *For thou hast trusted in thy wickedness: thou hast said, None seeth me. Thy wisdom and thy knowledge, it hath perverted thee; and thou hast said in thine heart, I am, and none else beside me.*

11 *Therefore shall evil come upon thee; thou shalt not know from whence it riseth: and mischief shall fall upon thee; thou shalt not be able to put it off: and desolation shall come upon thee suddenly, which thou shalt not know.*

ness, a symbol of their sorrow.[7] The nation will no longer be considered the "lady [g^{e}beret] of kingdoms." The word g^{e}beret is the feminine form of geber, which often has the sense of "mighty man." The feminine form refers to a "mighty lady," i.e., a queen among kingdoms, v. 5.

6–7 One reason for Babylon's fall is her treatment of the Jews. God had been "wroth" (qaṣap, see 8:21) with His people because of their sin. He had "polluted" (ḥalal, see 23:9) the nation by placing them in Babylon, an unclean nation. Babylon, however, had showed them no mercy. She had even "laid thy yoke" on the "ancient" (or "aged"), forcing them into demanding work, v. 6.[8] She proudly thought of herself as continuing as a "lady" (g^{e}baret, again a "mighty lady, a queen," see v. 5) among the nations forever. For this reason, she gave no thought to her treatment of Israel or to "the latter end of it," the time when she would answer to God, v. 7.

8–11 The phrase "thou that art given to pleasures" is better "O voluptuous one" or "O sensual one." The Lord addresses her as though she has overfeasted on spoils. She has lived "carelessly," with no thought of

---

[8]Westermann, p. 191, states that "the treatment meted out to the exiles in Babylon was not particularly cruel." Other Scripture, however, also mentions the treatment of the elderly in Babylon. Deut. 28:50 prophesies this. Lam. 1:19; 2:21; and 5:12 refer to harsh treatment of the elderly. Westermann states that "these certainly must represent isolated cases." He gives, however, no evidence to support the view. The fact that people are driven from their homes into captivity certainly sounds oppressive.

danger. She has arrogantly thought that no other nation compared to her. She would never become a "widow," losing her king. She would never lose her "children," the inhabitants of the city. In effect, Babylon's attitude amounted to self-deification, determining her own fate. John draws on this picture in Revelation 18:7–8, where he describes the final judgment of spiritual Babylon, v. 8. The Lord will judge her. In a single day, the two things will happen that she had thought would never happen. She will lose her "children" and shall become a "widow." Babylon lost her "children" when her soldiers died in the defeat by Cyrus and others were put to death. She became a "widow" when the Persians put Belshazzar, her king, to death. The judgment will come in "perfection" (better "fulness") because of her reliance on various forms of spiritism. She has trusted "sorceries," demon-controlled divination, and "enchantments," various spells meant to influence others, v. 9. She has trusted in her own "wickedness" (*ra^c*, see 3:9). She thought that no one knew of what she had done. Her wisdom and knowledge had "perverted" (or "enticed") the nation. She considered no other nation her equal, v. 10. The Lord will bring "evil" (*ra^c*), sudden judgment, upon her. She will not "know from whence it riseth [*šahrah*, or 'know its dawn,' see 8:20]," its beginning. The Babylonians will not look for the judgment to come on them.[9] The "mischief" (or "disaster") will come and they will not be able to "put it off." The "desolation" (or "destruction"), which they will not experientially know about (*yada^c*, see 1:3), will suddenly come on them, v. 11.

The Mistakes of Babylon, v. 8
1. Focusing on pleasures
2. Ignoring the future
3. Exalting herself

---

[9]Because of the parallelism with *kapp^{e}rah*, *šahrah* is often taken as a *pi^{c}el* infinitive. The awkward translation, "you shall not know to seek it," has led some to seek an alternative meaning. Among others, Von Orelli, p. 265; McKenzie, p. 91; and Näglesbach, p. 516, follow an Arabic cognate and translate, "charm away," "exorcise," or "conjure." Leupold, II, 152, translates, "know how to control." These translations have no support from the meaning of *šahar* elsewhere. Fausset, p. 713, and Cowles, p. 379, treat *šahar* as a noun and translate "dawn." Both make this the light after the judgment. Isaiah uses the word in 8:20 in this way. Motyer, *The Prophecy of Isaiah,* p. 374, and Barnes, II, 180, also translate as "dawn" but understand this as the beginning of the judgment. I have followed this view above.

12 *Stand now with thine enchantments, and with the multitude of thy*
sorceries, wherein thou hast laboured from thy youth; if so be thou
shalt be able to profit, if so be thou mayest prevail.
13 *Thou art wearied in the multitude of thy counsels. Let now the as-*
trologers, the stargazers, the monthly prognosticators, stand up, and
save thee from these things that shall come upon thee.
14 *Behold, they shall be as stubble; the fire shall burn them; they shall*
not deliver themselves from the power of the flame: there shall not
be a coal to warm at, nor fire to sit before it.
15 *Thus shall they be unto thee with whom thou hast laboured, even thy*
merchants, from thy youth: they shall wander every one to his quar-
ter; none shall save thee.

12–15 Isaiah challenges Babylon to bring forth her evil practices. She
should stand with her "enchantments" (or "spells"; cf. v. 9). She should
rely upon her many "sorceries," her divination; cf. v. 9. They have spent
many hours in developing these practices. Perhaps they will profit from
them and "thou mayest prevail" (lit. "cause trembling" to their enemies),
v. 12. They have spent many hours in study, wearying themselves with
this preparation. Let them now use their skills to predict the future. The
"astrologers" (*hobrê šamayim*)[10] are those who base their predictions on
divisions of the heavens. The "stargazers" (*haḥozîm bakkôkabîm*)[11] are
those who predict the future by the stars. The "monthly prognosticators"
are those who declare the future at the coming of each new moon. The
three expressions refer to the same practice of prophesying by means of
the heavenly bodies. Isaiah challenges these to deliver the people "from
these things that shall come upon thee," v. 13.[12] They will not be able to

---

[10]The phrase *hobrê šamayim* depends on the meaning assigned to the *hapax legomenon*
habar. There is an Arabic cognate that means "to cut." Reading the *qᵉrê hobrê* gives the
sense "divider of the heavens," i.e., interpreting the movements of the constellations.
Young, III, 242, mentions the Ugaritic cognate *hbr*, "to bow down," and tentatively suggests that the phrase refers to those who bow down to the heavens. He retains, however,
"dividers of the heavens" in the commentary. The Isaiah Scroll reads *ḥôbrê*, "charmers
[or joiners] of the heavens," probably an erroneous reading.

[11]The phrase *haḥozîm bakkôkabîm* is lit. "those who view the stars." In context, these
are those who prophesy from the positions of the stars. There is no clear distinction between *haḥozîm bakkôkabîm* and *hobrê šamayim*.

[12]Because the verse separates the verb "save" from the clause "from these things that
shall come upon thee," Young, III, 243, connects the clause with the "monthly prognosticators." He translates, "who cause thee to know with respect to the months (new moons)
from those things that are coming against thee." The view is possible. However, the view
expressed above is equally natural. Isaiah places the verb early in the verse to give it emphasis: "Let them save—the astrologers, stargazers, and those who make monthly predictions—from that which comes upon you." This gives the *min* preposition a natural
partitive sense. Verse 14 speaks of the inability of the seers to give deliverance.

do it but will be as "stubble" burned in the fire of judgment. This will not be merely a coal to warm someone or a small fire to sit before. The poetical statement implies that this will be a fiery storm of judgment, v. 14. Isaiah introduces a new thought to show the hopelessness of the city. "They . . . with whom thou hast laboured" are the "merchants" (or "traders")[13] who have carried on their business from Babylon's "youth," the early days of its history. These might be thought of as a powerful resource to help the city stand against its enemies. They will fail in this. Instead, they will "wander" to their "quarter" (or "other side"), i.e., across the river away from the enemy. None will deliver the city, v. 15.

Practical Application from Chapter 47

The Illustration of Judgment

1. Shame of the Judgment, vv. 1–5

   Mighty Babylon experiences shame, v. 1, grinding meal at a mill. She will shamefully expose herself as she goes into captivity, v. 2. The Lord's conquest of Babylon publicly humiliates her, v. 3. Israel's powerful God promises this, v. 4. Babylon will lose her position among the nations, v. 5.

2. Reason for the Judgment, vv. 6–11

   Babylon had oppressed God's people, v. 6. Because of her pride in her position, she gave no thought to answering to God for her actions, v. 7. She was proud, v. 8, and will therefore come into divine judgment, v. 9. She trusted herself, v. 10, but will not avoid God's wrath, v. 11.

3. Certainty of the Judgment, vv. 12–15

   Babylon may bring forth her spells and her sorceries, v. 12. Let those who predict the future by means of the heavenly bodies give her deliverance, v. 13. These will fail, v. 14. Her merchants will fail her, v. 15.

   Just as God judged wicked Babylon, so He will judge sinners today. The only escape lies in receiving the salvation that He offers through Jesus Christ.

---

[13] Among others, Henry, p. 267; Pieper, p. 318; and Whitehouse, I, 208, identify the traders as the astrologers, etc., who have sold their services. The view is possible.

1 Hear ye this, O house of Jacob, which are called by the name of Israel, and are come forth out of the waters of Judah, which swear by the name of the Lord, and make mention of the God of Israel, but not in truth, nor in righteousness.
2 For they call themselves of the holy city, and stay themselves upon the God of Israel; The Lord of hosts is his name.

ISAIAH 48

This is the final chapter devoted to the fall of Babylon. Initially, the Lord contrasts His work with that of the false gods. He knows the wickedness of His people, vv. 1–4, 8. To keep them from giving false gods the credit, He tells the future before it happens, vv. 5–7. He will not, however, unleash His full wrath against Israel, v. 9. He will work to draw them back to Himself, vv. 10–11. He reminds them of His eternity and power, vv. 12–13. He will cause Babylon to fall, vv. 14–15. He invites the nation to turn to Him, v. 16. They will receive their freedom from the captivity, v. 20. He will bless them with prosperity, v. 17; peace, v. 18; progeny, v. 19; and protection, v. 21. Peace, however, will not come to the wicked, v. 22.

E. Deliverance by the Faithful God 48:1–22
1. Demonstration of God's Power 48:1–11

1–2 The Lord speaks to the "house of Jacob." Although He calls them "Israel," the parallel phrase "waters of Judah" limits this to the remnant from Judah. They are from the "waters of Judah" in that this is the source: the remnant flows out from the river. Only Isaiah uses the word picture "waters of Judah" to describe the source of the nation. The similar phrase "fountain of . . ." occurs more often to denote a source, e.g., Psalm 36:9; Proverbs 13:14; 14:27; Jeremiah 2:13; 17:13.

The Lord now condemns the people. Although they took oaths in His name and spoke openly of God, they were not sincere. They did not do this in truth or with righteousness, v. 1. They claimed the "holy city," Jerusalem, as their worship center. They claimed to "stay themselves," to trust, in God who is the "Lord of hosts," the ruler of the hosts of

3 *I have declared the former things from the beginning; and they went forth out of my mouth, and I shewed them; I did them suddenly, and they came to pass.*

4 *Because I knew that thou art obstinate, and thy neck is an iron sinew, and thy brow brass;*

5 *I have even from the beginning declared it to thee; before it came to pass I shewed it thee: lest thou shouldest say, Mine idol hath done them, and my graven image, and my molten image, hath commanded them.*

heaven and earth. There is an implied thought of hypocrisy in this profession, v. 2.

3–5 By His prophecies of the future, the Lord has showed Himself to be God. He proclaimed the "former things" and they came to pass; cf. 41:22; 42:9; 43:9; 46:9. He is not specific as to what these "former things" include. By leaving it as a general term, it embraces all of the prophecies of God's blessings on the nation that have been fulfilled to this time, e.g., Genesis 12:2–3; 46:3–4; II Kings 19:32–34. The Lord predicted these blessings and He brought them to pass. He worked suddenly to bring them about, v. 3.[1] Israel, however, remained obstinate. Their neck was an "iron sinew," stiff-necked, hardened against God. Their forehead was "brass" (better "bronze"), hardened against spiritual things. The "neck" occurs elsewhere as a symbol of obstinacy, e.g., Deuteronomy 9:6; 10:16; Psalm 75:5; Proverbs 29:1. The "forehead" also has this symbolism; cf. –Jeremiah 3:3; Ezekiel 3:7–9, v. 4. The Lord has foretold the end from the beginning so that Israel could not credit His blessings to her idols. The term "idol" (*ʿoṣeb*) refers to the work that man puts into making an idol. The "graven image" (*pesel*, see 40:19) here is a carved wooden idol. The "molten image" (*nesek*, see 41:29) is a cast metal idol, v. 5.

---

[1] Skinner, *Isaiah XL–LXVI*, p. 89, refers the "former things" to the prediction of Cyrus's appearance. This cannot be, however, since the predictions relating to Cyrus have not yet been fulfilled at this time. Young, III, 247; Price, p. 202; and Henry, p. 268, include both prophecies of blessing and judgment for the nation. Since v. 5 implies that blessings are in view, this idea is unlikely. The Lord has predicted these in advance to keep the people from giving credit to their false gods.

6 *Thou hast heard, see all this; and will not ye declare it? I have shewed thee new things from this time, even hidden things, and thou didst not know them.*

7 *They are created now, and not from the beginning; even before the day when thou heardest them not; lest thou shouldest say, Behold, I knew them.*

8 *Yea, thou heardest not; yea, thou knewest not; yea, from that time that thine ear was not opened: for I knew that thou wouldest deal very treacherously, and wast called a transgressor from the womb.*

9 *For my name's sake will I defer mine anger, and for my praise will I refrain for thee, that I cut thee not off.*

10 *Behold, I have refined thee, but not with silver; I have chosen thee in the furnace of affliction.*

11 *For mine own sake, even for mine own sake, will I do it: for how should my name be polluted? and I will not give my glory unto another.*

6–8 Israel has "heard" these prophecies. The Lord commands them to "see" the fulfillments and speak of them to others. The Lord will now reveal other new things, things that have been "hidden" (*naṣar*)[2] in the past that Israel had not experienced, v. 6. The Lord creates them now, i.e., brings them into being as He controls history. He does this now, not "from the beginning," in time past. He does this before Israel has heard of them so that she will not claim prior knowledge, v. 7.[3] The Lord again emphasizes Israel's failure to know in advance of His works: "yea, thou heardest not; yea, thou knewest not; yea, from that time that thine ear was not opened." The adverb *gam*, "yea," introduces each phrase to lend additional emphasis. The final phrase is better "yea, from old time your ear was not open." The Lord has kept this knowledge from Israel because He knew that she would be treacherous, claiming prior knowledge or attributing the works to other gods. Israel has been a "transgressor" (or "rebel") from her birth as a nation, v. 8.

9–11 The Lord will defer the full intensity of His anger against Israel "for my name's sake," His reputation. Should He annihilate them, the

---

[2]The participle form of *naṣar* refers to something that is watched or guarded. Here, the word refers to things that had been "hidden," i.e., guarded, from Israel's knowledge in the past.

[3]The final three phrases are parallel: "not from the beginning" (or "not from old times"), "even before the day" (or "not before today"), and "thou heardest them not" (or "you have not heard them"). There is no need to introduce "when" into the sequence. A *waw* conjunction introduces each phrase, "and . . . and . . . and. . . ." The repetition simply emphasizes that these prophecies had occurred in the past, when Israel could not

heathen would think that He were weak, not able to protect His own. This would detract from God's "praise" ($t^ehillâ$, see 42:8). From the parallelism, "praise" here equals God's reputation. For this reason, He will "refrain [$hatam$][4] for them, that I cut thee not off," v. 9. He has "refined" the nation but not "with [or 'for'] silver," i.e., not receiving profit from the nation.[5] The refining of silver is a natural metaphor for purifying something. Elsewhere, the OT uses the refining of silver to illustrate God's work of purifying His people, e.g., Psalm 66:10; Ezekiel 22:22; Zechariah 13:9; Malachi 3:3. God has prepared the nation. He has chosen them in the "furnace of affliction," the trials through which they had passed. Since the OT elsewhere calls Egypt a "furnace" (Deut. 4:20; I Kings 8:51; Jer. 11:4), Israel's captivity there may well be in view here. The Lord had worked through the trials in Egypt to bring the nation into being. They were still not purified from sin and were therefore not profitable to Him, v. 10. By repeating the phrase "for mine own sake," He gives emphasis to the promise "I will do it." This picks up the thought of v. 9, in which the Lord had said that He would not cut the nation off. He will not allow His name to be "polluted" ($halal$, see 23:9) by others who

---

know of their fulfillment. Smith, pp. 206, 209, translates the final two phrases "and before to-day thou hast not heard them." He interprets this to mean, "there are some things . . . He does not foretell before they come to pass." Specifically, God did not reveal the name of Cyrus until he moved against Babylon. This view assumes the authorship of Isaiah II in the time of Cyrus. If we accept a single author, Smith's view is not possible.

[4]The verb $hatam$ occurs only here. There is, however, support for the meaning "restrain." An Arabic cognate refers to a nose ring that allows camels to be restrained. The Vulgate translates as *infrenabo*, "I will restrain."

[5]Commentators and translations understand the b^e-preposition in various ways. Leupold, II, 166, translates as a verb, "and not found you to be silver," not a possible translation although the interpretation is possible. Delitzsch, II, 249–50, understands the b^e to introduce an accusative predicate, "not in the manner of silver" but more severely. In contrast, Motyer, *The Prophecy of Isaiah,* p. 379, makes the refining less severe. God has not refined the nation as He would refine silver. The nation is all dross and such refining would reduce them to nothing. I cannot see this view since there were those in the nation who served the Lord. Young, III, 253, translates, "not with silver." This implies that the result of the refining process is not silver, i.e., the nation is not pure. Näglesbach, p. 521, understands "not as silver," i.e., in the same way that silver is refined. God has placed Israel in the "furnace of affliction" to punish rather than to purify them. Whitehouse, I, 140, makes the phrase describe Israel. God has not refined them as silver but as "some base metal or unworthy substance." Ibn Ezra, p. 219, considers that God purifies the nation in the "furnace of affliction," not in the "silver refinery." These latter views are all possible. There is not enough information given to be certain about the interpretation.

12 Hearken unto me, O Jacob and Israel, my called; I am he; I am the first, I also am the last.

13 Mine hand also hath laid the foundation of the earth, and my right hand hath spanned the heavens: when I call unto them, they stand up together.

14 All ye, assemble yourselves, and hear; which among them hath declared these things? The Lord hath loved him: he will do his pleasure on Babylon, and his arm shall be on the Chaldeans.

15 I, even I, have spoken; yea, I have called him: I have brought him, and he shall make his way prosperous.

16 Come ye near unto me, hear ye this; I have not spoken in secret from the beginning; from the time that it was, there am I: and now the Lord God, and his Spirit, hath sent me.

consider Him too weak to protect Israel. He will not give the glory due Him to another god, v. 11.

2. Deliverance by God's Power 48:12–22

12–16 The Lord pleads with Israel to listen to Him. The phrase "I am he" reminds them that He is the true God. He is as well "the first" and "the last," the eternal God, cf. 41:4; 44:6, v. 12. He is the Creator, who has made the earth and "spanned" (better "spread out") the heavens. He has absolute authority over the creation. When He calls, the earth and heavens "stand up together," come into being, v. 13.[6]

He calls the heathen to assemble. Who among "them," their idols, has declared such things as the Lord? The Lord loves "him." The pronoun refers to Cyrus, the character who has been so much in evidence in the previous chapters (45:1–13; 46:11; 47:1, 3–5).[7] God's "love" here is not saving love. It is rather pleasure in this one who does what God wants him to do. In particular, Cyrus will "do his pleasure [*ḥepeṣ*, see 44:28]," carry out His plans, by judging the Chaldeans. God will overcome Babylon with His "arm." Isaiah often uses the arm as a symbol of strength, cf. 30:30; 40:10; 51:9; 52:10, v. 14. Again making an emphatic statement, the Lord speaks of His call to Cyrus. He has brought him to Babylon. For this reason, Cyrus will prosper as he carries out his plans, v. 15.

---

[6]Among others, Cowles, p. 385; Brueggemann, *Isaiah 40–66,* p. 105; and Rawlinson, II, 216, understand the phrase "stand up together" as a continuing response throughout history to the directions of the Lord. While this is possible, the parallelism with the first half of the verse supports better the statement of creation.

[7]Although Henry, p. 271, relates the pronoun to Cyrus, he goes too far in making Cyrus a "type" of Christ. An unsaved king cannot be a type of the perfect Son of God.

17 *Thus saith the Lord, thy Redeemer, the Holy One of Israel; I am the Lord thy God which teacheth thee to profit, which leadeth thee by the way that thou shouldest go.*

18 *O that thou hadst hearkened to my commandments! then had thy peace been as a river, and thy righteousness as the waves of the sea:*

19 *Thy seed also had been as the sand, and the offspring of thy bowels like the gravel thereof; his name should not have been cut off nor destroyed from before me.*

The Lord urges Israel to draw near to Him. He has not spoken secretly. No, from the beginning He has been there. God the Father has now sent "me." The identification of the spokesman rests on the use of the first person pronoun throughout the previous verses. Beginning with v. 3, the first person pronoun refers to God, with only the obvious exceptions in vv. 5, 7. In v. 17, the Lord again speaks. Verse 16, however, distinguishes between God, the Spirit, and the spokesman. This leaves no doubt that the personal pronouns throughout the chapter refer to God the Son.[8] This is one of only a few OT verses to clearly distinguish between God the Father, God the Son, and God the Spirit.[9] Elsewhere, 61:1; John 3:34; 17:3 also refer to the Father sending the Son. The order of the words in the verse supports the translation, "And now, the Lord God has sent Me and His Spirit." The Holy Spirit empowers the Son for His work, v. 16.

17–19 The Lord identifies Himself as the "Redeemer" (*goʾel*, see 35:9) of Israel, the Holy One of the nation, and the Lord their God. He then reveals His reason for His work on behalf of the nation. He teaches them the way that will benefit them, the way in which they should go. This illustrates the teaching found in Hebrews 12:11. One of God's purposes in refining His people is to show them the path that will bring His blessing, v. 17. If Israel had listened to His commands, they would have enjoyed abundant "peace" (*šalôm*, see 9:6) and righteousness (*ṣedeq*, see 1:21). The mighty river with its unending flow of water illustrates the peace He wanted them to enjoy. The repetitive motion of the waves illus-

---

[8]Snaith, p. 188, and Von Orelli, p. 268, identify the speaker as Israel. Delitzsch, II, 253, and Childs, p. 378, identify him as the Servant of c. 49. Unfortunately, both misidentify the Servant as Israel. The excursus following c. 42 discusses the Servant. Among others, Barnes, II, 192; North, p. 105; and Kelley, p. 327, identify the spokesman as Isaiah. Among others, Watts, *Isaiah 34–66,* p. 178; McKenzie, p. 99; and Pieper, p. 336, make Cyrus the speaker. These views require a sudden change of spokesman at v. 16. The context, however, does not indicate a change. The fact that Isaiah speaks of the Lord should not be surprising; cf. 2:2–4; 6:1; 7:14; 9:6–7; 52:13–53:12.

[9]Six passages in Isaiah mention the Trinity. See also 11:2; 42:1; 59:19–21; 61:1; 63:7–14.

20 *Go ye forth of Babylon, flee ye from the Chaldeans, with a voice of*
singing declare ye, tell this, utter it even to the end of the earth; say
ye, The Lord hath redeemed his servant Jacob.
21 *And they thirsted not when he led them through the deserts: he*
caused the waters to flow out of the rock for them: he clave the rock
also, and the waters gushed out.
22 *There is no peace, saith the Lord, unto the wicked.*

trates the "righteousness" (*ṣᵉdaqâ*) they would have practiced. The combination of righteousness producing peace is always God's desire for His
people, cf. 32:17; 60:17; 62:1, v. 18.[10] The nation would also have multiplied in number. The Lord illustrates this by comparing their children to
"sand" and the "offspring of their bowels [*maᶜâ*]" to "gravel thereof"
(better "grains of it," i.e., of sand).[11] They would never have been "cut
off" or "destroyed" as a nation, v. 19.

20–22 The Lord urges His people to leave Babylon. They are to sing
praises to God for delivering them from the captivity. They are to tell
"the end of the earth" that the Lord has "redeemed" (*gaʾal*, see 35:9)
them, v. 20. As an illustration of the provision they will enjoy, Isaiah recalls how God sustained the people through their wanderings in the
wilderness. God had provided abundant water for them from the rock
(Exod. 17:6; Num. 20:11), v. 21. In contrast with the peace they will
enjoy with God's favor, Isaiah reminds the people that God has decreed
that there is no "peace" (*šalôm*) for the wicked. The obvious contrast
with v. 18 suggests that the wicked are those who disobey God. There
will be an eternal judgment resulting in the lack of peace for these who
have rejected God's Word. With the substitution of *yᵉhwah* for *ʾelohîm*,
the verse is identical to 57:21, v. 22.[12]

---

[10]Young, III, 261, understands "righteousness" as a "comprehensive term for salvation." The word *ṣᵉdaqâ*, see 1:21, indicates conformity to an ethical or moral standard.
There is no reason to change that thought here.

[11]The word *maᶜâ*, "grains," occurs only here. It is related to *meᶜeh*, "bowels" or "inward
parts." The inward parts of sand are the individual grains. Several authors, however, prefer to translate *maᶜâ* as "bowels" or "inward parts." They refer this to the wealth of life
within the sea with v. 18 furnishing the antecedent. Among others, Cowles, p. 389;
Barnes, II, 194; and Fausset, p. 716, adopt this position. It is, however, awkward to reach
past "sand" to find "sea" as the antecedent. The Targum, LXX, and Vulgate support the
translation "grains."

[12]Motyer, *The Prophecy of Isaiah*, p. 382, explains v. 22 as a warning to the nation.
Changing merely their location will not change their character. Coming back to Canaan
will not bring them peace. His view is possible although, in my judgment, it does not
support the idea of rejoicing that God commands in v. 20.

Practical Applications from Chapter 48

1. Attributes of God. There is an unusual emphasis on God's attributes. He shows His omniscience by His knowledge of the future, vv. 3, 5, 6, 8. He shows His omnipotence in His role as the Creator, v. 13. He shows His eternality with His claim, "I am the first, I also am the last," v. 12. The Trinity appears with the mention of all three members of the Godhead, v. 16. He shows His mercy with His promises to redeemed Israel, vv. 17–18, 21. He shows His holiness with the implied statement of eternal judgment, v. 22.

2. Contrasts in Peace. Those who obey the Lord's commands have abundant peace, v. 18. The wicked, however, who refuse God's commands, have no peace, v. 22.

1 Listen, O isles, unto me; and hearken, ye people, from far; The Lord hath called me from the womb; from the bowels of my mother hath he made mention of my name.
2 And he hath made my mouth like a sharp sword; in the shadow of his hand hath he hid me, and made me a polished shaft; in his quiver hath he hid me;
3 And said unto me, Thou art my servant, O Israel, in whom I will be glorified.
4 Then I said, I have laboured in vain, I have spent my strength for nought, and in vain: yet surely my judgment is with the Lord, and my work with my God.
5 And now, saith the Lord that formed me from the womb to be his servant, to bring Jacob again to him, Though Israel be not gathered, yet shall I be glorious in the eyes of the Lord, and my God shall be my strength.
6 And he said, It is a light thing that thou shouldest be my servant to raise up the tribes of Jacob, and to restore the preserved of Israel: I will also give thee for a light to the Gentiles, that thou mayest be my salvation unto the end of the earth.

ISAIAH 49

The chapter introduces a major part of the book. Chapters 49–55 develop the Servant of the Lord, introduced earlier in 42:1–9. This section has three of the four widely recognized Servant passages, 49:1–13; 50:4–11; and 52:13–53:12.[1] In addition, other clear messianic and kingdom prophecies occur, e.g., 49:16–18; 51:4–6, 22–23; 55:3–5. The present chapter describes the calling and ministry of the Servant, vv. 1–7. This will climax in the deliverance of Israel and the establishment of the millennial kingdom, vv. 8–13. The thought of the nation's freedom from captivity and persecution leads the Lord to answer several complaints of His people. The coming kingdom rule of the Servant will solve these problems, vv. 14–26.

F. Work of God's Servant 49:1–50:11
1. The Servant's Call 49:1–13[2]

1–6 The opening paragraphs of the chapter give the second of the four Servant passages in Isaiah. In 42:1–9, God the Father had spoken to

---

[1]An excursus following c. 42 summarizes the teaching of Isaiah on the Servant of the Lord.

[2]Leupold, II, 59, limits the Servant passage here to vv. 1–7. McKenzie, p. 104; Westermann, p. 206; and Whitehouse, II, 152, consider vv. 1–6 the Servant song. The passage is open to individual interpretation.

the Servant. Here, the Servant Himself speaks. He urges the "isles" (or "coastlands," *îyîm*, see 11:11), the Mediterranean region, and far-off people to listen to His message. The message thus goes to Gentiles as well as Jews.

The Lord has called the Servant from before birth. When we identify the Servant as Jesus Christ, the fulfillment of this comes in the Annunciation, Luke 1:26–38, and conception of Jesus, Matthew 1:20–24. As with 42:1–9, the NT applies the current passage to the Lord (Acts 13:47; cf. v. 6), v. 1.[3] He has made His mouth "a sharp sword." The "mouth" by metonymy represents the Servant's speech; cf. Ephesians 6:17; Revelation 19:15. The "polished shaft," an arrow, is one cleansed from anything that might deflect it in flight. The arrow speaks also of piercing words; cf. Psalm 57:4; 64:3; Proverbs 25:18; Jeremiah 9:8. His speech will cut deep into the hearts of men; cf. Jeremiah 23:29; Hebrews 4:12.

The Father has hidden Him in "the shadow of his hand." Throughout the book, Isaiah uses a "shadow" as an image of protection, e.g., 4:6; 16:3; 51:16. Here also, the Father protects the Servant with a "shadow."[4] He has as well hidden Him in His quiver, again speaking of protection. The thought is of protection from satanic attacks, e.g., Luke 4:28–30; John 8:59; 10:31, 39. Although men may carry out these attacks, the underlying direction and power comes from Satan, v. 2.

Elsewhere, Isaiah calls "Israel" His servant, e.g., 41:8; 44:21. He cannot, however, refer to the nation here since vv. 5–6 portray the Servant as ministering to the nation. God calls the Servant "Israel" (*yiśra'el*) here since He is Israel's head.[5] The Father will "be glorified" (better "glorify

---

[3]Others identify the Servant differently. Smart, p. 151, and Smith, p. 265, equate the Servant with ideal Israel. Whitehouse, II, 156, sees the Servant as the "personification of a community," Israel. Goldingay, p. 281, identifies the Servant as Isaiah. Watts, *Isaiah 34–66*, pp. 185–86, sees two Servants here. Verses 1–4 refer to Israel, and vv. 5–12 to Darius, the successor to Cambyses, the son of Cyrus. Delitzsch, II, 258–59, sees the child of a "virgin," some maiden in the royal household, growing up during the Assyrian captivity.

[4]Barnes, II, 199, understands this as the shadow of the Father's hand falling on the handle of a sword about to be drawn in defense of the Servant. While this is picturesque, the verse does not mention a sword used for defense of the Servant.

[5]Pieper, p. 354, makes "Israel" a predicate nominative parallel to "Servant." He translates, "You are my Servant, you are Israel . . . ," i.e., the Servant is the one who truly strives with God. It is highly unlikely that *yiśra'el* is a predicate nominative. The *'atnaḥ* separates it from the verb, indicating it is not part of the thought in the first phrase. Further, the name "Israel" reflects the physical wrestling of Jacob with God as he sought God's blessing. The Servant, walking in perfect fellowship with the Father, does not need

Himself," *paʾar*, see 44:23) through the Servant.[6] As the Servant redeems the nation, brings the Gentile nations to worship the Father, overcomes sin in the world, and a host of other things, the Father glorifies Himself. He has conceived this plan and all men will worship Him, v. 3. At the first, the Servant's work bears little fruit. The statement "I have laboured in vain, I have spent my strength for naught, and in vain" does not show a depressed spirit.[7] It states the facts of his life. He acknowledges the lack of significant results. At the same time, He leaves His "judgment" (*mišpaṭ*, see 1:17) and His "work" (or "recompense," *peʿullâ*, see 40:10) with the Father, v. 4.

The Father, the one who called the Servant before birth to "bring" (*šûb*, see 1:27) Israel back to Himself, speaks.[8] The phrase "though Israel

---

to strive with God to gain His blessing. Barnes, II, 201, correctly makes "Israel" a vocative. He then misapplies it as Pieper, making Messiah strive with God. Wade, p. 315, understands *yiśraʾel* as a predicate nominative but makes "Israel" mean that God strives with His people. This turns around the thought expressed in Gen. 32:28. God did not strive with Jacob to get him to accept His will. Jacob strove with God to gain His blessing. Henry, p. 275, follows the popular sense of Israel: "Thou art Israel . . . *the prince with God.*" He then introduces the thought of wrestling with God. The outcome is misleading since it leaves the false impression that "Israel" means "prince with God." Motyer, *The Prophecy of Isaiah*, p. 386, observes that the nation Israel is not capable of "living up to what it means to be Israel." God is faced with a choice: the failure of His plans or finding a true Israel. But if God abandons the original plan, this is the same as failure, an unthinkable act. Alexander, II, 226, understands the Servant as including both Messiah and the nation, "the body with its head." This faces the difficulty of reconciling it with vv. 5–6 in which the Servant ministers to Israel. Both the context and the description of the Servant argue that it is an individual.

[6]Among others, Delitzsch, II, 261; Brueggemann, *Isaiah 40–66,* p. 11; and Price, p. 206, understand the verb as a passive: "I will be glorified." The translation is possible although the *hitpaʿel* is not normally passive. The reflexive sense for the verb is more common. Making it a passive changes the sense so that the Father receives glory rather than glorifying Himself. It is not boastful for the Father to glorify Himself. It is rather a statement of fact, a declaration of what He does through His works.

[7]Motyer, *The Prophecy of Isaiah,* p. 387, views the statement as expressing despondency. He admits that there is no single moment in the Lord's life that we can point to as lying behind this. He looks at Israel's rejection of the Lord, their unbelief, prejudice, etc., and then concludes, "What was diffused throughout the Lord's whole earthly course, Isaiah compresses into a single moment." Pieper, p. 355, sees this as expressing the Lord's "days on earth as a weak human being, with no confidence in Himself, vividly conscious of His own weakness and infirmity." Leupold, II, 178, describes this as "voicing his inner pain over his apparent lack of success." These views do not recognize that such depression is sin. The Lord came to give victory over all sin, including the sin of the depression that comes from failing to trust God. He did not give in to this evil emotion.

[8]Allan A. MacRae, *The Gospel of Isaiah,* p. 106; Delitzsch, II, 259; and Young, III, 267–68, understand the forming of the Servant "from the womb" as alluding to the Virgin

> 7 *Thus saith the Lord, the Redeemer of Israel, and his Holy One, to him whom man despiseth, to him whom the nation abhorreth, to a servant of rulers, Kings shall see and arise, princes also shall worship, because of the Lord that is faithful, and the Holy One of Israel, and he shall choose thee.*

be not [*loʾ*] gathered" is better "that Israel be gathered to Him [*lô*]."[9] As the result of His faithful work, the Servant will be "glorious" (*kabed*, better "honored," see 3:5) in the Father's sight. In turn, He will continue to draw strength from the Father, v. 5. The Father gives the Servant an additional charge. In light of God's total plan, it is a relatively minor thing to bring the "tribes of Jacob" and the "preserved [*neṣîrê*][10] of Israel" back to God. The Servant shall also light the path of the Gentiles to bring them to God; cf. John 8:12. In this sense, He is the Father's "salvation" throughout the earth. Simeon, in Luke 2:29–32, applied these words to the baby Jesus. The apostle Paul also based his evangelism of the Gentiles on this verse; cf. Acts 13:47; 26:23. The preponderance of Gentiles in the church partially fulfills the prophecy. The greater fulfillment, however, lies in the future, in the millennium, when the whole earth recognizes the salvation that Jesus Christ alone can give, v. 6.

7 God now speaks to the Servant, the first of two brief speeches (see also vv. 8–13). The Father here describes Himself as Israel's "Redeemer" (*goʾel*, see 35:9), appropriate in view of His relationship to the nation. He is the "Holy One." He is therefore thoroughly trustworthy. He speaks to the Servant, the one "whom man despiseth." He is the one abhorred by the "nation" (*gôy*, better "people," including the Gentiles as well as the Jews). He is the one who is but a lowly servant to the Jewish leaders and the Roman emperor. Nevertheless, the time will come when the relation-

---

Birth. While this is possible, the OT also speaks of the Lord as forming Job and Jeremiah in the womb (Job 31:15; Jer. 1:5). It is probably too much to see the Virgin Birth here.

[9]There is widespread agreement that the *qerê lô*, "to him," is correct. The Vulgate followed the *ketîb loʾ*, "not," but the LXX, Targum, and 1QIsa[a] accept the *qerê*. The *qerê* best supports the parallelism in the verse.

[10]The form *neṣîrê* does not occur again. The *qerê neṣûrê* is the qal passive participle of *naṣar*, "to guard." We can explain the *ketîb* as miswriting the *yôd* for the *šûreq*. The LXX reads διασποράν, understanding some form of *pazar* or *pûṣ*, "dispersed of Israel," an unlikely change. The NEB assumes *niṣrê*, "descendants." While this is possible, the noun form of *naṣar* occurs only four other times in the OT (including Isa. 11:1; 14:19; 60:21). If we accept the *ketîb*, as in 1QIsa[a], we must explain *neṣîrê* as a variant adjectival form derived from *naṣar*. The *qerê* gives the same sense.

8 *Thus saith the Lord, In an acceptable time have I heard thee, and in a day of salvation have I helped thee: and I will preserve thee, and give thee for a covenant of the people, to establish the earth, to cause to inherit the desolate heritages;*

9 *That thou mayest say to the prisoners, Go forth; to them that are in darkness, Shew yourselves. They shall feed in the ways, and their pastures shall be in all high places.*

10 *They shall not hunger nor thirst; neither shall the heat nor sun smite them: for he that hath mercy on them shall lead them, even by the springs of water shall he guide them.*

11 *And I will make all my mountains a way, and my highways shall be exalted.*

12 *Behold, these shall come from far: and, lo, these from the north and from the west; and these from the land of Sinim.*

13 *Sing, O heavens; and be joyful, O earth; and break forth into singing, O mountains: for the Lord hath comforted his people, and will have mercy upon his afflicted.*

ship will change. Gentile "kings" and "princes" will reverence Him. They will do this because of the Father "that is faithful and the Holy One of Israel" (better "who is faithful, the Holy One of Israel"). The final phrase continues this, "who has chosen You," i.e., the Servant. Once again, the fulfillment of this is in the kingdom, when the Lord rules the earth, v. 7.[11]

8–13 The Father has heard the prayers of the Servant. While the text does not give these prayers, the use of "heard" (or "answered") shows that the Father has responded to the requests. These have come "in an acceptable time" (or "a time of favor") and in "a day of salvation." Both phrases refer to the time suitable for extending God's forgiveness to mankind. Paul quotes the verse in II Corinthians 6:2 to show that God has heard those who have called on Him for salvation. They ought therefore to live for Him.

The focus here is on God's answers to the Servant's prayer. These take place in the time that God extends salvation to mankind. It is likely that these refer to the continuing strengthening of the Lord against satanic attacks; cf. v. 2. The Father will give Him "for a covenant of the people." In this role, He will "establish" (or "raise up") the "earth," the land of

---

[11]We may dismiss the suggestion of Watts, *Isaiah 34–66,* p. 187, that God addresses Darius in the verse. There is no evidence that Darius was despised and abhorred by the Gentile nations. To call him a "servant of rulers" understates his position as general of the Medo-Persian army.

Palestine, restoring it to a place with God's blessing upon it.[12] He will cause the people to inherit the "desolate heritages," the land of Palestine formerly under the judgment of God. As before, the passage looks forward to the millennial reign of Christ, when God removes His curse from the land, v. 8.[13]

The Servant will free the "prisoners" from their captivity in the nations.[14] He will prosper them. He pictures them as sheep, feeding "in the ways" (or "by the paths") and in the "high places" (*šepayîm*, or "barren hills," see 41:18). The idea is that God now blesses the land. Places that formerly furnished no grazing will now provide food, v. 9. He will keep them from hunger and thirst. He will shelter them from the "heat" (*šarab*)[15] of the blazing sun. He will "lead them" (*yenahagem*) and "guide them" (*yenahalem*) to springs of water.[16] The apostle John borrows this thought to describe a heavenly scene in Revelation 7:16–17, v. 10. He will make paths for them through the mountains. His highways will "be exalted" (or "raised up"), letting them travel through the mountainous regions, v. 11. From all over the world, His people will come to Palestine. The "north" represents the countries of Asia. The "west" is better the "sea," the direction in which the lands of Europe lie. We cannot identify the "land of Sinim" with certainty. From the context, it apparently is a land far from Palestine. Since the "north" and "sea" have been mentioned, it is likely that Sinim lay to the south or east of Palestine. There are a variety of suggested locations. We cannot do more, however, than

---

[12]Fausset, p. 718, spiritualizes the passage. He makes the "land" include the "heavenly land forfeited by man's sin." The heavenly goal of the believer occurs elsewhere, e.g., I Cor. 15:49; II Cor. 5:1. There is no reason, however, to see anything other than the literal meaning here. Isaiah teaches the renewal of the land in other passages, e.g., 35:1–2; 51:3.

[13]Brueggemann, *Isaiah 40–66,* p. 114; Smith, p. 315; and Watts, *Isaiah 34–66,* p. 188, refer the promise to the return of Israel from Babylon. Young, III, 278, refers it to the time of Christ's coming into the world. In light of vv. 6, 12, this must be something more than these limited occupations of Palestine. This involves the Jewish people from around the world.

[14]Among others, Rawlinson, II, 232; Henry, p. 277; and Young, III, 279, spiritualize the "prisoners" as those who are bound by sin. The mention of physical locations in v. 12 argues that these are prisoners in the more common sense of the word.

[15]The word *šarab* occurs only here and in 35:7, where I have argued for the meaning "parched ground." Here, the combination with "sun" suggests a hendiadys, the "heat of the sun."

[16]The wordplay with *yenahagem* and *yenahalem* is normal with Isaiah. Wordplay marks his writings in every part of the book.

*14 But Zion said, The Lord hath forsaken me, and my Lord hath forgot-
ten me.*

*15 Can a woman forget her sucking child, that she should not have
compassion on the son of her womb? yea, they may forget, yet will I
not forget thee.*

*16 Behold, I have graven thee upon the palms of my hands; thy walls
are continually before me.*

*17 Thy children shall make haste; thy destroyers and they that made
thee waste shall go forth of thee.*

*18 Lift up thine eyes round about, and behold: all these gather them-
selves together, and come to thee. As I live, saith the Lord, thou shalt
surely clothe thee with them all, as with an ornament, and bind them
on thee, as a bride doeth.*

to say that it represents a far-off place, v. 12.[17] Isaiah spontaneously
bursts into a song of praise. He calls for heaven and earth to praise the
Lord for His goodness to His people. He has "comforted" (*naḥam*, see
1:24) and extended mercy to His "afflicted" (*ʿanî*, see 3:14) people, v. 13.

2. The Lord's Faithfulness 49:14–50:11
a. Reassurance of Israel 49:14–26

14–18 The thought of the Lord's deliverance reminds the Lord of
Israel's complaints. They have faced three problems. The Lord answers
the first of these in vv. 14–18, the second in vv. 19–23, and the last in
vv. 24–26. In the first problem, Israel expresses their feeling that God no
longer remembers them. The "Lord" (*yᵉhwah*), the merciful God who

---

[17]The LXX interpreted Sinim as περσῶν, "Persia." The Isaiah Scroll reads *swnyym*. On
the supposition that this should be pointed *sᵉweneh*, some refer it to Syene, modern
Aswan, in Egypt. Wright, p. 123; Herbert, *Isaiah 40–66*, p. 90; and Kelley, p. 330, follow this although 1QIsaᵃ was likely interpretive. The Targum and Vulgate indicate a
"south country." Price, p. 207; Vine, p. 129; and Faussett, p. 719, suggest China on the
basis of an early Tsin dynasty. This dynasty, however, did not come to power until several
hundred years after Isaiah. Skinner, *Isaiah XL–LXVI*, p. 104 mentions the view that this
refers to the Sinites of Gen. 10:17. This, however, is thought to lie north of Palestine.
Slotki, p. 242, proposes Pelusium, an Egyptian city in the delta of the Nile, called "Sin"
in Ezek. 30:15–16. This, however, is not far from Palestine. Rawlinson, II, 232, relies on
Ps. 107:3, in which "sea" refers to the south. He then makes "Sinim" refer to the west
and interprets it as Phoenicia. This also is too close to fit the pattern of the verse. Pieper,
p. 369, understands "far" as the "east." The land of "Sinim" then refers to the west. He
does not identify this other than as "a western, Mediterranean land." Henry, p. 278, suggests that it is a province of Babylon. With this variety of suggestions to choose from,
there is no sure identification. Isaiah and his readers knew "Sinim," but its location has
been lost to history.

interacts with His people, has forsaken them. The "Lord" (*ʾadonay*), the mighty God who rules Israel, has forgotten them, v. 14. The Lord answers this with a beautiful metaphor. He speaks of a nursing mother, filled with love for her child. The woman might forget her child but the Lord will never forget Israel, v. 15. He has engraved the nation upon the palms of His hands so that He continually sees the walls of Jerusalem. The city here by synechdoche represents the nation. The statement suggests the wounds of Christ at the Crucifixion, a continuing reminder of His death on behalf of His people, v. 16.[18] Her "children" (*banayik*, better "sons")[19] return from their captivity to occupy the city. The "destroyer" (or "those who have torn down") and those who have laid the city waste have fled from the city, v. 17. The Lord urges the people to look at the returnees. Just as a bride dresses and adorns herself on her wedding day, so Palestine will put on the returning people. The Lord swears by Himself, "as I live," that this will come to pass. The fulfillment lies in the Millennium. While there have been partial fulfillments in history, the description here suggests an abundance of people, as in the kingdom age, v. 18.

---

[18]Von Orelli, p. 273, translates *ḥaqaq* as "scratched," a meaning not found elsewhere. He understands this as an allusion to "printing figures or symbolical signs on the hands or arms." The references he uses to support this, Deut. 6:8 and 11:18, do not refer to printing. Deut. 6:8 speaks of binding a phylactery with portions of Scripture in it on the wrist or forehead. Deut. 11:18 refers to placing a mezuzah with Scripture passages on the right-hand doorpost of the house. North, p. 111, suggests that the Lord tattoos a plan of the rebuilt city on His hands. Without citing evidence, Vine, p. 130, states that the "Jews had a custom of marking on their hands . . . a delineation of the city and the temple, as a sign of their devotion to, and perpetual remembrance of, them." Young, III, 285, curiously speaks of God engraving the name of Zion on His hands. He recognizes that the OT prohibited tattooing but cites Pieper favorably that "forbidding the practice does not prohibit the use of the figure." These views face the problem that the OT forbad tattooing, Lev. 19:28; 21:5. Using a forbidden practice to portray a wholesome image is not appropriate.

[19]The LXX, Targum, Vulgate, and 1QIsa*ᵃ* adopt the reading *bonayik*, "builders," while the MT reads *banayik*, "sons." This involves a change in the vowel pointing only. The context will support either reading. Motyer, *The Prophecy of Isaiah,* p. 394; Young, III, 286; and Delitzsch, II, 269, accept *banayik*. McKenzie, p. 110; North, p. 111; and Brueggemann, *Isaiah 40–66,* p. 116, accept *bonayik*. The contrast with v. 17*b* supports *bonayik* as the correct reading. Verses 18–21, however, focus on the individuals, *banayik*, rather than their work. The root *ben* occurs again in vv. 15, 20, 22, and 25. In addition, "sons" makes an acceptable contrast with v. 17*b*. For these reasons, I accept the MT. Islwyn Blythin, "A Note on Isaiah XLIX 16–17," *VT* 16:230, well says, "The sons *are* also the builders . . . and the stones . . . but they are living stones and the builders of the people of God into an integrated, vital and purposeful community."

19 *For thy waste and thy desolate places, and the land of thy destruc-*
    tion, shall even now be too narrow by reason of the inhabitants, and
    they that swallowed thee up shall be far away.
20 *The children which thou shalt have, after thou hast lost the other,*
    shall say again in thine ears, The place is too strait for me: give
    place to me that I may dwell.
21 *Then shalt thou say in thine heart, Who hath begotten me these, see-*
    ing I have lost my children, and am desolate, a captive, and remov-
    ing to and fro? and who hath brought up these? Behold, I was left
    alone; these, where had they been?
22 *Thus saith the Lord God, Behold, I will lift up mine hand to the Gen-*
    tiles, and set up my standard to the people: and they shall bring thy
    sons in their arms, and thy daughters shall be carried upon their
    shoulders.
23 *And kings shall be thy nursing fathers, and their queens thy nursing*
    mothers: they shall bow down to thee with their face toward the
    earth, and lick up the dust of thy feet; and thou shalt know that I am
    the Lord: for they shall not be ashamed that wait for me.

19–23 The second problem faced by Israel was that of the crowded
land. Because of its "waste" parts and its "desolate places," the land in
which Israel faced "destruction" will be too "narrow" (or "cramped") to
hold the returning people. Moreover, the people that "swallowed" (*bala*ᶜ,
see 3:12) them will be far away, no longer a threat to them. There will no
longer be any threat to keep more people from coming to the land, v. 19.
The phrase "the children which thou shalt have, after thou hast lost the
other" is better "the sons of your bereavement." These are the children
born to the nation after its dispersion throughout the nations. They will
complain of the cramped quarters. They need more land to dwell in,
v. 20. Israel will be amazed at the number of people. She will wonder
where they have come from. She has been bereaved of her people and
has been desolate. She has been "a captive" (or "an exile") and "removing to and fro" (or "turned aside") from her homeland. Where have these
people come from? Those who are "alone" in Palestine are amazed at
the number of exiles who return to the land, v. 21.

The Lord answers these questions. He will lift up His hand to the heathen, which signals to them that they are to assist the Jews in returning
to Palestine. He has "set up [a] standard," a marker to rally His people to
return. They will bring their sons in the "arms" (or "bosom") and carry
their daughters on their shoulders as they return. The picture is of a parent who carries his child over some obstacle. In like manner, the Gentile

24 *Shall the prey be taken from the mighty, or the lawful captive deliv-*
ered?
25 *But thus saith the Lord, Even the captives of the mighty shall be taken*
away, and the prey of the terrible shall be delivered: for I will contend
with him that contendeth with thee, and I will save thy children.
26 *And I will feed them that oppress thee with their own flesh; and they*
shall be drunken with their own blood, as with sweet wine: and all
flesh shall know that I the Lord am thy Saviour and thy Redeemer,
the mighty One of Jacob.

nations will help the Jews overcome the obstacles that keep them from
Palestine. This implies that the heathen will no longer persecute the
Jews. They will rather help them in every way possible. This is clearly a
millennial promise. Notice that the Gentile nations will carry out the
Lord's will during the reign of Christ, v. 22. Heathen kings and queens
who once ruled Israel will now nurse the people, giving them spoil to
sustain them as they return; cf. 60:16. Whereas Israel once bowed down
to them, they will now bow down to Israel as they submit to the nation.
The phrase "lick up the dust of thy feet" portrays the humbling of these
who at one time have ruled over the people; cf. Genesis 3:14; Psalm
72:9. They will now know that the Lord is God. Those who "wait"
(*qawâ*, or "look eagerly," see 5:2) for the Lord will not be "ashamed"
(*bôš*, see 1:29).

The Lord does not answer the main question except by implication.
The Jews have called attention to the lack of land to support those who
come to Palestine. The Lord states that He will work to bring more
people. He implies by this that the land will no longer be arid. We know
from elsewhere that the Lord will return the land to its former productive
condition. Originally, it was a "land of milk and honey" (Exod. 3:8, 17;
Josh. 5:6). He will renew the land's ability to support the people, v. 23.

24–26 The final problem faced by Israel lay in its captivity. The word
"mighty" (*gibbôr*, see 3:2) refers to warriors. The phrase "lawful captive"
(*šebî ṣaddîq*) is better *šebî ʿarîṣ*, "captives of a tyrant."[20] The rhetorical
question asks, "Do captives generally receive freedom?" The expected
answer is no, v. 24. The Lord, however, will bring this to pass. He will

---

[20]The Isaiah Scroll reads ʿariṣ, "tyrant," for ṣaddîq, "righteous." The LXX and Vulgate
support this as does v. 25. Pieper, p. 382; Motyer, *The Prophecy of Isaiah,* p. 396; and
Goldingay, p. 288, follow the MT, but Young, III, 292; Leupold, II, 187; and Wright,
p. 124, accept the emendation. In my judgment, the parallelism of the verse and the
support of v. 25 favor reading ʿariṣ.

free the "captives of the mighty [*gibbôr*, see 3:2]." He will contend with the one who has contended with Israel, and He will "save" (*yaša*ᶜ, see 17:10) the people from their captivity, v. 25. He will feed those who have oppressed Israel "with their own flesh." This refers to Armageddon, at the end of the Tribulation. The enemies of Israel see their own flesh and blood fall before the power of the Lord.[21] The supernatural deliverance of His people will cause all to know that the Lord is Israel's "Saviour" (*yaša*ᶜ, see 17:10), their "Redeemer" (*goʾel*, see 35:9). He is "the mighty One of Jacob," referring to the nation, v. 26.

Practical Applications from Chapter 49

1. The Promised Reign of Christ, vv. 8–13
   a. Renewal of the land, v. 8
   b. Restoration of the prisoners, vv. 9, 11–12
   c. Provision of the people, v. 10
   d. Praise to the Savior, v. 13
2. Faithfulness of the Lord
   a. The Lord remembers His people, vv. 14–18. In the same way, the Lord remembers those who are His own today.
   b. The Lord will renew the land, vv. 19–23. In the same way, the Lord renews life for His people today. "Old things pass away; all things become new!"
   c. The Lord will free the captives, vv. 24–26. In the same way, the Lord frees those who are presently bound by sin,

---

[21] Among others, Kelley, p. 332; Leupold, II, 188; and Barnes, II, 216, see this as the result of civil war among Israel's enemies. Rawlinson, II, 234, relates this specifically to the desertion of Babylonian troops. These go over to Persia to fight against their own people. Price, p. 208, and McKenzie, p. 112, understand it as war between the nations that fight against Israel. Näglesbach, p. 539, refers the passage to the last judgment of "fleshly Israel." Young, III, 293, suggests that Israel's enemies engage in cannibalism. Dahood, *CBQ* 22:404, views this as a metaphor representing the reduction of Israel's enemies "to the last extremity." This is the only view that lets the passage happen swiftly. The Lord does not prolong the end-time destruction of Israel's enemies.

*1 Thus saith the Lord, Where is the bill of your mother's divorcement,
whom I have put away? or which of my creditors is it to whom I
have sold you? Behold, for your iniquities have ye sold yourselves,
and for your transgressions is your mother put away.*

ISAIAH 50

This chapter presents the third of the Servant passages.[1] Verses 1–3
state Israel's problem and show God's power to deliver them. Verses 4–9
introduce the suffering Servant. Through His sufferings, He makes possible complete victory over sin and man's alienation from God. Verses
10–11 present a choice to Israel. They can follow the Servant by trusting
the Lord (v. 10). They can walk through life following their own will and
receive judgment from God (v. 11).

b. Deliverance of Israel 50:1–11

1 The Lord asks two questions to bring out Judah's feelings that God
had rejected her. Did the nation have a certificate showing that God had
divorced her? The question alludes to Deuteronomy 24:1 in which a man
would write out a formal statement of the divorce. The Lord also asks
whether He has sold them to settle a debt that He owed, an allusion to
such passages as Exodus 21:7 and Leviticus 25:39. It was possible for a
poor person to sell himself or his children into servitude to pay his debt;
II Kings 4:1; Nehemiah 5:5; and Matthew 18:25 illustrate the practice.
Had this happened to Israel? To both questions, the answer is no! They
had no certificate of divorce nor had God sold them into captivity. Because of their "iniquities" (*ᶜawon*, see 1:4), they had "sold [them]selves"
(*nimkartem*)[2] into captivity. Her own "transgressions" (*pešaᶜ*, see 24:20)
have caused the "mother," the nation, to be "put away," temporarily separated from God as though she no longer belonged to Him, v. 1.

---

[1]See also 42:1–9; 49:1–13; 52:12–53:12. The excursus following c. 42 summarizes Isaiah's teaching about the Servant.

[2]We may translate the *nipᶜal* verb *nimkartem* as a passive, "you were sold," or as a reflexive, "you sold yourselves." Among others, Westermann, p. 223; Watts, *Isaiah 34–66,*
p. 191; and Skinner, *Isaiah XL–LXVI,* p. 111, translate it as a passive. The Lord, however,
has already denied selling Israel. In addition, to sell an Israelite into slavery violated the
Mosaic Law, Exod. 21:16; Deut. 24:7; cf. Amos 2:6. The same verb occurs in 52:3 with
the same sense. For these reasons, I prefer the reflexive translation.

2 *Wherefore, when I came, was there no man? when I called, was
   there none to answer? Is my hand shortened at all, that it cannot redeem? or have I no power to deliver? behold, at my rebuke I dry up
   the sea, I make the rivers a wilderness: their fish stinketh, because
   there is no water, and dieth for thirst.*
3 *I clothe the heavens with blackness, and I make sackcloth their
   covering.*
4 *The Lord God hath given me the tongue of the learned, that I should
   know how to speak a word in season to him that is weary: he wakeneth morning by morning, he wakeneth mine ear to hear as the
   learned.*
5 *The Lord God hath opened mine ear, and I was not rebellious, neither turned away back.*
6 *I gave my back to the smiters, and my cheeks to them that plucked
   off the hair: I hid not my face from shame and spitting.*

2–3 Why had no one responded when He came to the nation through
His prophets? When He called, why did no one answer? Is God's hand
shortened so that He cannot reach His people to redeem them; cf. 59:1?
Has He no power to deliver? To show His power, Isaiah gives several examples from Israel's history. He had dried up the Red Sea, Exodus
14:21–22. He had turned the Jordan River into parched ground. The plural "rivers" is likely a plural of intensity, appropriate with the Jordan in
flood stage at the time, Joshua 3:15.[3] He made the fish die from lack of
water and decay with a stench, Exodus 7:21, v. 2. Verse 3 should also be
set in the past. It continues the illustration from Egypt. He had turned
the heavens dark. Sackcloth, made from dark goat's hair, pictures the
darkness of the skies, Exodus 10:22–23, v. 3.

4–6 The Servant of the Lord appears suddenly. Although the word
"Servant" does not appear until v. 10, the nature of the material here

---

[3]Brueggemann, *Isaiah 40–66,* p. 121, and Motyer, *The Prophecy of Isaiah,* p. 398, relate the drying up of the waters to a part of God's work in Creation. North, p. 111, suggests either Creation or the Exodus and concludes that the passage may refer to both.
Cundall, *Isaiah 40—Jeremiah,* p. 14, suggests either the crossing of the Red Sea or a
"severe drought accompanied by sandstorms," possibly in Babylon. Von Orelli, p. 277,
and Vine, p. 133, refer the drying of the river to God's judgment on Babylon. Barnes, II,
220, makes it the drying of some unknown river. Alexander, II, 249, translates the
phrases relating to water as futures because of the use of the imperfect verb tense. The
imperfect, however, may also express past actions that continued for a short time. Since
the text is not specific, we cannot be certain as to what the Lord refers to here. It is,
however, reasonable that he would give an example from the past to illustrate his power.
This would rule out any reference to Babylon or to an unknown river. Creation is possible although there is no reason to mention the drying up of waters when the whole of
creation demonstrates God's power.

points to the Lord.[4] He is the one through whom the final deliverance will come. The Servant speaks, describing His relationship to God.[5] The Lord gives Him "the tongue of the learned" (*limmûdîm*).[6] Led by the Spirit of God, He is a disciple of the Father. He knows how to "speak [*ʿût*] a word [of encouragement] to him that is weary" (or to "sustain the weary with a word").[7] He wakens the Servant morning after morning to receive direction for His ministry.[8] At the same time, He wakens Him "to hear as the learned" (*limmûdîm*). As before, *limmûdîm* refers to a disciple. He receives new messages from God to guide Him moment by moment, v. 4. He has opened his ear to receive continuing guidance. He did not rebel at this nor did He turn away from the Lord, v. 5. Verse 6 reveals

---

[4]I extend the Servant passage to v. 11. Hailey, p. 416; Kraeling, p. 181; and Rawlinson, II, 248, consider the song to end at v. 9. There is room for variation in applying the passage to the Servant.

[5]As before, authors identify the Servant differently. Skinner, *Isaiah XL–LXVI,* p. 113, thinks that some prophet such as Jeremiah lies behind the description. Westermann, p. 228, suggests Deutero-Isaiah. Ibn Ezra, p. 229; Slotki, p. 247; and Goldingay, p. 289, think it is Isaiah. Brueggemann, *Isaiah 40–66,* p. 122, sees him as a teacher of the exiles in Babylon. Watts, *Isaiah 34–66,* p. 197, makes him "Darius's advocate and defender in Jerusalem." Wade, p. 324, applies the passage to Israel. The NT makes it clear that the passage refers to Christ: v. 6*a,* cf. Matt. 27:26; Mark 15:15; John 19:1; v. 6*b,* cf. Matt. 26:67; Mark 14:65.

[6]The word *limmûdîm* comes from *lamad,* "to teach." The noun form occurs only six times, twice here and in 8:16; 54:13; Jer. 2:24; 13:23. In 8:16, it refers to "disciples." In 54:13, it refers to those "taught" by the Lord, i.e., "disciples" of the Lord. In Jer. 2:24, it describes a donkey who has been taught by the wilderness, in his own way a disciple of the wilderness. In Jer. 13:23, it describes someone "taught" to do evil, again, a disciple of wickedness. There is no reason to change the thought here. The Father gives the Son speech that reflects his discipleship.

[7]The verb *ʿût* is a *hapax legomenon.* There is no clear cognate in other languages. BDB, p. 736, calls the meaning "very dub[ious]." KB, III, 804, gives only a question mark. Westermann, p. 225, reads *laʿⁿnôt,* "answer." This interprets εἰπεῖν in the LXX, which itself was interpretive. Delitzsch, II, 277, relates *ʿût* to an Arabic word, "to help with words." Näglesbach, p. 545, however, gives the Arabic cognate the meaning "sustain." The Vulgate gives *sustentare,* "sustain." Both the NASB and the NIV follow this. The context tells us that the word has to do with speech, either sustaining it or delivering it. His words encourage those who bear heavy burdens; cf. Matt. 11:28–30.

[8]Barnes, II, 221, and Delitzsch, II, 277, understand "morning by morning" as the Father waking the Son early each morning to instruct Him on what He should preach. Delitzsch contrasts this with those prophets who receive revelation by dreams or visions. These views are too literal an interpretation of the phrase. In 28:19, the same phrase refers to continued time, much the same as the phrase "day by day," Exod. 29:38; Ezra 6:9. As the Holy Spirit led the Lord, He received guidance continually, not each morning for the day's activities.

432

7 *For the Lord God will help me; therefore shall I not be confounded: therefore have I set my face like a flint, and I know that I shall not be ashamed.*

8 *He is near that justifieth me; who will contend with me? let us stand together: who is mine adversary? let him come near to me.*

9 *Behold, the Lord God will help me; who is he that shall condemn me? lo, they all shall wax old as a garment; the moth shall eat them up.*

the identity of the Servant as the Son of God. He gave His back to the smiters, Matthew 27:26 (Mark 15:15; John 19:1). He gave His cheeks to those who plucked out the hair, a sign of contempt for Him; cf. I Chronicles 19:4. Although the NT does not record this, we do not doubt that it was done. He did not hide Himself from open "shame" (*kᵉlimmâ*, see 30:3), being publicly displayed as under God's curse (Deut. 21:23) and having men spit upon Him, Matthew 26:67 (Mark 14:65) and Matthew 27:30 (Mark 15:19). The OT makes it clear that this was a gross insult, Numbers 12:14; Deuteronomy 25:9; Job 30:10, v. 6.

7–9 The Servant trusts God to help Him. He knows that He will not "be confounded" (*kalam*, or "humiliated," see 30:3) because of His reliance on God. While the Lord did experience public humiliation, the result of His trust in God will be honor. He has set His face, "like a flint," resolutely setting Himself to follow the Lord; cf. Ezekiel 3:8–9. He knows that He will not be "ashamed" (*bôš*, see 1:29). The statement creates a minor problem since v. 6 has just said that the Servant did not hide from "shame" (*kᵉlimmâ*). The Hebrew has a sense not seen in English. The word *kᵉlimmâ* in v. 6 refers to public humiliation. The Lord did briefly experience this. The word *bôš* in v. 7 refers to the shame that comes as the result of failure, either by oneself or by someone or something in which one trusts. Since the Servant trusts in God, He will not be "ashamed," v. 7.

God, the one who "justifieth me," declaring Him righteous, is near. Who then can "contend" (*rîb*, see 1:17) with Him? Let him come forward and they will "stand together." The phrase suggests a court trial in which the accused and the accuser stand before the judge. Where is His "adversary," lit. the "lord of my judgment [*mišpaṭ*, see 1:17]," i.e., the one who controls the accusation against Him? Let him come near with His charge. Both questions require a negative answer. There is no one who can successfully accuse him of failure. No one can successfully charge Him with wrong, v. 8. The Servant again expresses His confidence in the Father. He will help Him; who, therefore, can successfully

10 Who is among you that feareth the Lord, that obeyeth the voice of his servant, that walketh in darkness, and hath no light? let him trust in the name of the Lord, and stay upon his God.
11 Behold, all ye that kindle a fire, that compass yourselves about with sparks: walk in the light of your fire, and in the sparks that ye have kindled. This shall ye have of mine hand; ye shall lie down in sorrow.

condemn Him? His enemies will wear themselves out, becoming as an old garment that is moth-eaten, cf. Psalm 102:26, v. 9.

10–11 The final two verses logically conclude the chapter. The spokesman is the Servant.[9] He has not turned away from doing the Father's will. Why then should others reject His will? The Father has shown the way of victory to the people. He now challenges them. Are there those who fear the Lord and obey the voice of His Servant and yet walk in darkness?[10] In Isaiah, the fear of the Lord may be a feeling of terror, e.g., 2:10, 19. Here, however, it is a reverence for the Lord. Despite this attitude toward the Lord, sinful actions still mark them. Let them "trust" the Lord completely. Let them "stay" (or "rely") upon God, v. 10.

On the other hand, are there those who care nothing about the Lord? The phrase "kindle a fire" metaphorically pictures those who light their own way through the darkness in life caused by sin. Likewise, those who "compass yourselves about with sparks" (better "clasp firebrands") again illuminate their own path. These have no reverence for God. They walk in the "light of [the] fire" they have kindled, their own will, and they will suffer punishment. The Lord Himself will see that they lie down in "sorrow" (ma‘ăṣebâ). The word ma‘ăṣebâ occurs only here although related forms occur elsewhere. The root is ‘aṣab, "to grieve, vex." It has a strong sense here, "pain" or "torment." This is the end of those who turn their back on the Lord, v. 11.

---

[9]Näglesbach, p. 547; Goldingay, p. 291; and Vine, p. 136, identify the speaker as Jehovah, God the Father. McKenzie, p. 117; Young, III, 303; and Wright, p. 126, identify the speaker as Isaiah. Watts, Isaiah 34–66, p. 197; Cundall, Isaiah 40—Jeremiah, p. 14; and Fausset, p. 722, view the speaker as the Servant although they differ as to his identity. While the person speaking does not change the sense of the verse, the reference to judgment in v. 11 relates best to the Son of God, John 5:22. In Rev. 20:11, it is the Son who sits on the Great White Throne at the final judgment.

[10]Lindsey, p. 93, places the question mark at the end of the first line. He feels that the NIV offers the smoothest sense to the passage: "Who among you fears the Lord and obeys the word of his servant? Let him who walks in the dark, who has no light, trust in the name of the Lord and rely on his God." The relative pronoun ʾăšer and the perfect tense verbs argue against this. While the AV and NASB may not give as smooth a sense, they are truer to the grammar.

Practical Application from Chapter 50

Deliverance of God's People

1. The Problem. The people feel that God has rejected the nation. This, however, is their own fault. They have sold themselves into slavery by their sin, v. 1. God had sent prophets to them but they had not answered. God has the power to deliver them, vv. 2–3. Israel's problem aptly illustrates the plight of the sinner today. He is under the control of sin because he has not responded to God's repeated calls to him.

2. The Solution. God has given His Servant the ability to encourage others. He continually disciples Him, v. 4. The Servant readily receives this direction, v. 5. In the course of His work, He suffers dreadful abuse, v. 6. He continues to rely on God, knowing that He will never suffer the disgrace of failure, v. 7. God is near Him. No one can successfully accuse Him, v. 8. The Father will help Him. His enemies therefore will wear themselves out with their attacks, v. 9. Identifying the Servant as Jesus Christ, we see that He is able to deliver those who come to Him. He suffered that man might be free from his sin.

3. The Choice. The Lord has shown the way to victory. The people must respond. They should trust the Lord completely, v. 10. Those who reject the Lord will continue to walk by the light of their own wisdom. They will suffer the consequences, v. 11. This is the great choice faced by man today: salvation as the result of trusting Christ or suffering as the result of trusting self. It is a choice that everyone must make.

1 Hearken to me, ye that follow after righteousness, ye that seek the Lord: look unto the rock whence ye are hewn, and to the hole of the pit whence ye are digged.
2 Look unto Abraham your father, and unto Sarah that bare you: for I called him alone, and blessed him, and increased him.
3 For the Lord shall comfort Zion: he will comfort all her waste places; and he will make her wilderness like Eden, and her desert like the garden of the Lord; joy and gladness shall be found therein, thanksgiving, and the voice of melody.

ISAIAH 51

As so often occurs in the second part of the book, the chapter takes a message that applies to the people of Isaiah's day and uses it to predict end-time events. The prophet begins by speaking to the faithful of his own time, vv. 1–8. He then appeals to God to move on behalf of His people, vv. 9–11. The Lord responds by speaking of His care for the nation, vv. 12–16. With this assurance, Isaiah calls on the nation to turn from the sins that have brought God's judgment, vv. 17–20. The Lord will judge their enemies and bless them, vv. 21–23. The chapter weaves into this message prophecies of the kingdom, vv. 3, 5, 11, 13–14; the new heavens and new earth, vv. 6, 16; the eternal reward of the righteous, v. 22; and the eternal judgment of the wicked, v. 23.

G. Responsibilities of God's People 51:1–52:12
1. Blessings on the People 51:1–16

1–3 Isaiah, speaking as though identified with the Lord, calls those who walk in "righteousness" (*ṣedeq*, see 1:21) in Israel to look at their beginning.[1] The word "hearken" occurs in vv. 1, 4, and 7. This gives natural points of division in the first part of the chapter. The "rock," a natural picture of a foundation, represents Abraham, Israel's father. The "hole of the pit" (*maqqebet bôr*),[2] a natural picture of the womb, represents

---

[1]Watts, *Isaiah 34–66,* p. 204, makes Darius the speaker. He presents himself to the Jews as a benevolent ruler. The Lord interrupts Darius's speech in vv. 2–3 but Darius speaks again in v. 4. Aside from the fact that Darius would not have known of Israel's history, there is no indication that the first person pronouns in vv. 1, 2, and 4 refer to different speakers.

[2]Among others, Leupold, II, 199; Young, III, 307; and Skinner, *Isaiah XL–LXVI,* p. 118, along with the NASB and NIV, interpret *maqqebet bôr* as "quarry." The phrase refers to a quarry or some other depression from which material has been removed, e.g., a well, mine, a source of peat. The verse gives two metaphors to show the nation's descent from Abraham and Sarah. Israel is like a rock taken from a greater rock or dirt taken out of a pit. Verse 2*a*

Sarah, their mother. Verse 2*a* makes this symbolism clear, vv. 1–2*a*.[3]
God called Abraham "alone" (*ʾeḥad*, better "when he was one").[4] Giving
him His blessing, He multiplied him into a great nation, v. 2*b*.[5] The Lord
promises to "comfort" (*niḥam*, see 1:24)[6] the nation. He will make the
wilderness bloom abundantly; cf. 35:1–2. The comparison to Eden, the
"garden of God," suggests that the phrase looks ahead to the millennial
kingdom.[7] Only at that time will God heal the wilderness. It will then be
a place for giving thanks and singing to God, v. 3.

---

then goes on to develop the metaphor. The view ignores the natural symbolism of the rock
and the pit described above.

[3]Cowles, p. 410, argues that both the "rock" and the "hole of the pit" refer to Abraham.
This ignores the mention of Sarah in v. 2. Alexander, II, 260, also places the emphasis on
Abraham. He thinks that mention of Sarah is for "rhythmical effect" only. Birks, p. 253,
sees the rock as that which resists the mason's tool. The pit is something "mean and low."
These then represent the "Chaldean idolatry" from which Abraham and Sarah came at
God's call. Slotki, p. 250, mentions the view that *maqqebet bôr* should be translated
"hammer of the pit." This rests on the fact that *maqqebet* occurs elsewhere only at Judg.
4:21, where it must be translated "hammer" or "mallet." The root *naqab*, "to pierce," underlies both translations. The hammer is a tool used to cause piercing. The "hole" is the
result, the pierced substance. There is no need to introduce "hammer" here since it adds
nothing to the meaning.

[4]J. Gerald Janzen, "An Echo of the Shema in Isaiah 51:1–3," *JSOT* 43:69–82, understands *ʾeḥad* to refer to the uniqueness of the Lord rather than Abraham. The word *ʾeḥad*
is the antecedent to the three following verbs: "I as one called . . . I as one blessed . . .
I as one made him many." While the translation is grammatically possible, it goes against
the virtually unanimous historical treatment of the verse. The LXX translates ὅτι εἷς ἦν,
"when he was one." The NASB renders the phrase, "when he was one." The NIV reads
"he was but one." Ezek. 33:24 and Heb. 11:12 may well allude to this passage.

[5]Wade, p. 327, understands *ʾeḥad* as indicating that Abraham was "the head of but a
single family." The view is possible although the call in Gen. 12:1 says nothing about his
family. Further, the emphasis in Gen. 18:19 is on Abraham alone.

[6]Pieper, p. 400, thinks that "comfort" is "stiff and mechanical" and therefore does not
fit in this passage. He argues that the "original meaning of *naḥam* is 'to breathe deeply.'"
From this, the conjugations reflect actions "connected with hard breathing." He suggests
that the word here means "to rebuild," i.e., that God will once more build the nation.
Frankly, I cannot see that "rebuild" is less "stiff and mechanical" than "comfort." More
importantly, the OT regularly uses the *piᶜel* verb *niḥam* as "comfort, console."

[7]McKenzie, p. 123, displays his liberal bias when he refers to the "myth of the Garden
of *Eden*." When we consider the promise, the mention of Eden is appropriate. The Lord
will restore the earth to its condition before Adam's sin brought the curse upon it.

4 *Hearken unto me, my people; and give ear unto me, O my nation:*
  for a law shall proceed from me, and I will make my judgment to
  rest for a light of the people.
5 *My righteousness is near; my salvation is gone forth, and mine arms*
  shall judge the people; the isles shall wait upon me, and on mine
  arm shall they trust.
6 *Lift up your eyes to the heavens, and look upon the earth beneath:*
  for the heavens shall vanish away like smoke, and the earth shall
  wax old like a garment, and they that dwell therein shall die in like
  manner: but my salvation shall be for ever, and my righteousness
  shall not be abolished.

4–6 The Lord again calls the nation to listen to Him. He will give His
"law" (*tôrâ*, cf. 1:10) to the people. The word *tôrâ* here is "law" rather than
"instruction." While there is a component of teaching in the meaning of
tôrâ, the context here shows that the instruction of law is in view. If the
people accept this, "judgment" (*mišpaṭ*, better "justice," see 1:17) from the
Lord will enlighten the land, v. 4. The Lord will send forth His "righteousness" (*ṣedeq*, see 1:21) and "salvation" (*yešaᶜ*, see 17:10). As is common in
the book, the Lord states this as an accomplished fact. This is a prophetic
perfect, a future act that is certain in His mind. The ultimate fulfillment
lies in the millennial reign of Christ over the earth. His "arms" (*zᵉroᶜay*),
the symbol of His power, will bring justice to the land.[8] The "isles" (*îyîm*,
see 11:11), the coastal regions, by metonymy represent the nations. These
will "wait" (*qawâ*, see 5:2) for Him and "trust" [*yaḥal*, better "confidently
expect," see 42:4] His "arm." As before, this is the symbol of God's power,
v. 5. The Lord tells the people to look at the heavens and the earth. Although these seem stable, they will perish. The heavens will "vanish" (or
"dissipate") like smoke. The earth will become old. Those who dwell on
the earth will "die in like manner" (*kᵉmô⁻ken yᵉmûtûn*).[9] The thought an-

---

[8]Zöckler, p. 552, notes that *zᵉrôaᶜ* is singular when it has a symbolic sense of protection or support. Because it is plural here, he gives it a physical sense. Motyer, *The
Prophecy of Isaiah,* p. 405, notes that the plural *zᵉroᶜay* may be a "plural of amplitude,
pledging the fulness of divine personal action to the task." It may also recall Deut. 33:27,
the only other place that the plural refers to the Lord while having a symbolic sense. The
word also occurs in the plural to symbolize military power, Dan. 11:15, 22, 31, or man's
strength, e.g., Gen. 49:24; Ps. 37:17.

[9]Among others, Skinner, *Isaiah XL–LXVI,* p. 120; Von Orelli, p. 281; and Brueggemann,
Isaiah 40–66, p. 127, translate *kᵉmô⁻ken yᵉmûtûn,* "die like gnats." The NIV translates "die
like flies." The singular word *ken* never refers to insects. The adverb *ken* often occurs as a
response to *kᵉ,* "like . . . so." The use here with the pleonastically written *kᵉmô* to indicate
"likewise" is unusual, but the sense fits well into the passage.

7 *Hearken unto me, ye that know righteousness, the people in whose heart is my law; fear ye not the reproach of men, neither be ye afraid of their revilings.*

8 *For the moth shall eat them up like a garment, and the worm shall eat them like wool: but my righteousness shall be for ever, and my salvation from generation to generation.*

9 *Awake, awake, put on strength, O arm of the Lord; awake, as in the ancient days, in the generations of old. Art thou not it that hath cut Rahab, and wounded the dragon?*

10 *Art thou not it which hath dried the sea, the waters of the great deep; that hath made the depths of the sea a way for the ransomed to pass over?*

11 *Therefore the redeemed of the Lord shall return, and come with singing unto Zion; and everlasting joy shall be upon their head: they shall obtain gladness and joy; and sorrow and mourning shall flee away.*

ticipates the end-time destruction of the earth. At that time, the Lord will replace this sin-cursed universe with "new heavens and a new earth," II Peter 3:12–13. The Lord's "salvation" and "righteousness" will not "be abolished" (*ḥatat,* or "be broken," see 7:8) but will continue forever, v. 6.

7–8 For the third time in the passage, the Lord commands His people to "hearken" to Him. Those who know "righteousness" (*ṣedeq,* see 1:21) and have God's "law" (*torâ,* see 1:10) in their heart do not need to "be afraid" (*ḥatat,* or "be dismayed," see 7:8) of opposition from frail "men" (*ᵉnôš,* see 2:11); cf. Proverbs 29:25. Before the Lord, all the wicked are *ᵉnôš.* We should not fear what they say as they offer "reproach" or "revilings" to His people, v. 7. Just as the "moth" or the "worm" (*sas*), they will perish. This is the only time the word *sas* occurs in the OT. From the context, it indicates a larval form of some insect.[10] In contrast, the Lord's "righteousness" and "salvation" will continue forever, v. 8.

9–11 In response to the assurance of God's blessing, Isaiah prays on behalf of the nation. The doubled phrase "awake, awake" occurs five times in the OT, three of them in Isaiah.[11] The doubled imperative "awake" is an emphatic plea. He asks the Lord to awaken His "arm," i.e., to move it, to show His power to Israel as in ancient times. He recalls God's victory over "Rahab" (*rahab,* cf. 30:7) and the "dragon" (*tannîn,* cf. 27:1). Both names

---

[10]Skinner, *Isaiah XL–LXVI,* p. 121, and Von Orelli, p. 181, understand *sas* as a species of moth. The LXX translates as σητός, "moth." The Vulgate translates *tinea,* "moth." The Akkadian cognate *sasu* is "moth." The NASB gives "grub." The NIV agrees with the AV, "worm."

[11]Judg. 5:12 (twice); Isa. 51:9, 17; 52:1.

12 I, even I, am he that comforteth you: who art thou, that thou shouldest be afraid of a man that shall die, and of the son of man which shall be made as grass;
13 And forgettest the Lord thy maker, that hath stretched forth the heavens, and laid the foundations of the earth; and hast feared continually every day because of the fury of the oppressor, as if he were ready to destroy? and where is the fury of the oppressor?
14 The captive exile hasteneth that he may be loosed, and that he should not die in the pit, nor that his bread should fail.

represent Egypt, v. 9.[12] Isaiah recalls the deliverance from Egyptian bondage when God led the people through the Red Sea. The drying of the waters made it possible for those He "ransomed" (*ga³al*, cf. 35:9) to escape, v. 10. The "redeemed" (*padâ*, see 1:27) nation will rejoice as they return to Palestine. This joy will be unending. There will be no more grief. Once again, the fulfillment lies in the future, in the kingdom, when the Lord rules the world from Palestine. With only minor differences, the verse repeats 35:10, v. 11.

12–14 The Lord speaks of His comfort of Israel. The doubled "I" makes this emphatic. God Himself "comforteth" (*naham*, see 1:24) His people. Why, then, should they fear mortal man (*^{3e}nôš*, cf. v. 7) or the "son of man," who is like the "grass"? Isaiah speaks of grass in the same way as in 40:7–8, a plant that withers under the sun. In like manner, mankind is weak and not to be feared, v. 12. Why should Israel forget the Creator of the heavens and earth? The fact that He "stretched forth the heavens, and laid the foundations of the earth" shows His power; cf. Jeremiah 32:17. Why have they continually "feared" (or "dreaded," *pahad*, cf. 2:10) their enemy, here generally referring to their end-time enemies? The rhetorical question "where is the fury of the oppressor" looks into the future.[13] Where is the enemy? He no longer exists, v. 13. The "captive exile" (*so^ceh*, or

---

[12]Among others, Kelley, p. 337; Goldingay, pp. 294–95; and Westermann, p. 242, assert that Isaiah's account borrows from the Babylonian creation myth. Both "Rahab" (Pss. 87:4; 89:10) and the "dragon" (Isa. 27:1; Ezek. 29:3; 32:2) occur elsewhere as symbols of Egypt. There is no reason to depart from that symbolism here in favor of a heathen story that widely uses fantasy. In addition, the context of v. 10 supports a reference to Egypt.

[13]Among others, Leupold, II, 206; Barnes, II, 231; and Rawlinson, II, 261, identify the "oppressor" as Babylon. Watts, *Isaiah 34–66*, p. 212, relates the oppression to the Persian civil war of 522 B.C. Julian Morganstern, "'The Oppressor' of Isa 51 13—Who Was He?" *JBL* 81:31–34, makes the "oppressor" Xerxes, the Persian king, defeated by Greece ca. 479 B.C. These views ignore the eschatological context. The return of Israel to Palestine, vv. 11, 13–14, and the new heavens and earth, v. 16, argue for an end-time fulfillment.

15 But I am the Lord thy God, that divided the sea, whose waves
   roared: The Lord of hosts is his name.
16 And I have put my words in thy mouth, and I have covered thee in
   the shadow of mine hand, that I may plant the heavens, and lay the
   foundations of the earth, and say unto Zion, Thou art my people.
17 Awake, awake, stand up, O Jerusalem, which hast drunk at the hand
   of the Lord the cup of his fury; thou hast drunken the dregs of the
   cup of trembling, and wrung them out.
18 There is none to guide her among all the sons whom she hath
   brought forth; neither is there any that taketh her by the hand of all
   the sons that she hath brought up.
19 These two things are come unto thee; who shall be sorry for thee?
   desolation, and destruction, and the famine, and the sword: by
   whom shall I comfort thee?
20 Thy sons have fainted, they lie at the head of all the streets, as a wild
   bull in a net: they are full of the fury of the Lord, the rebuke of thy God.

"one stooping")[14] will soon be free from his bondage. They will not "die in
the pit," in their imprisonment.[15] Their "bread" will not fail them, v. 14.

   15–16 The Lord shows His power by recalling the division of the Red
Sea. Further, He reminds them that He is the "Lord of hosts," the ruler
of the heavenly and earthly hosts, v. 15. He has chosen Israel to give His
message to the world. To this end, He has protected her, covering her
with the shadow of His hand; cf. 49:2. He will "plant the heavens," "lay
the foundations of the earth," and claim Israel as His own.[16] These are all
works of the end time, when the Lord will create new heavens and a new
earth. At that time, Israel will be openly seen as the people of God, v. 16.

2. Charge to the People 51:17–52:12

   17–20 Isaiah again calls on the people to stand up. Before, v. 9, he
had called on the Lord. Here, the *hithpoᶜel* verb is reflexive, "awaken

---

[14]The root *ṣaᶜâ*, "to bend," here refers to one bent over. Poetically, it refers to bending
from the burden of his bondage. The companion word "exile" comes from the context
rather than the Hebrew. Von Orelli, p. 282, understands this as a prisoner bowed from
fetters that do not allow an upright position. It is more likely that the captives in Babylon
had a degree of freedom. When the opportunity came to return, only a small percentage
of them made that choice.

[15]Wade, p. 330, and McKenzie, p. 123, interpret "pit" as sheol, the place of the dead.
While that idea fits *šaḥat* elsewhere, it is not appropriate here. He will gain his freedom
from the pit, something that will never happen to those in sheol.

[16]Slotki, p. 254, mentions the view that the phrases "plant the heavens" and "lay the
foundations of the earth" are figurative of Israel. Since the verse states plainly that Israel

441

yourself!" The repeated call is emphatic, "Awaken yourself, awaken your-self!" The nation should turn from the drunken stupor in which she lies as a result of the Lord's judgment. The "dregs of the cup of trembling" is better the "goblet [*qubbaᶜat*],[17] the cup [*kôs*] of reeling." It pictures the nation as having drunk fully from the cup that brings about uncontrol-lable staggering. They had "wrung them out" (or "drained it"). All this pictures Israel as suffering greatly under God's judgment, v. 17. None of her children, the people of the nation, can guide her away from this judg-ment. Her sons cannot take her hand to lead her away from judgment, v. 18.[18] Rather, two forms of judgment will fall on her. The first rhetorical question in the verse implies that no one will grieve over Judah's fate. She will suffer punishment that comes from inside the nation, "desola-tion" (or "devastation") and "famine." She will also suffer punishment that comes from outside the nation, "destruction" and "sword."[19] The sec-ond rhetorical question implies that the destruction will be so great as to keep even the Lord from giving them "comfort" (*naham*, see 1:24), v. 19. Her men will be faint with hunger. They lie helpless in the streets. They are trapped as a "wild bull" (*teʾô*)[20] in a net. The *teʾô* is an unknown wild

---

is the "people" that belong to God, there is no need to interpret these phrases poetically. A literal understanding fits nicely with what we know of the renovation of the universe in the end time.

[17]The word *qubbaᶜat* occurs only here and in a similar construction in v. 22. An Akkadian cognate, *qabutu*, "bowl," supports the meaning of "cup" or "goblet." It is in construct here to *kôs*, an appositional relationship that clarifies its meaning.

[18]The AV has captured the wordplay in 18*b* and 18*d*, *mikkol⁻banîm yaladâ* and *mikkol⁻banîm giddelâ*, with their translation "all the sons whom she hath brought forth . . . all the sons that she hath brought up." Such wordplay is characteristic of Isaiah's writings throughout the book.

[19]There are differing explanations to the seeming problem of "two things" being fol-lowed by four judgments. Cowles, p. 416, makes the "famine" and "sword" explanatory of "desolation" and "destruction." Slotki, p. 255, is similar except that he relates the "sword" to "desolation" (which he translates as "plunder") and the "famine" to "destruc-tion." Wade, p. 332, understands this as two pairs of things: (1) desolation of the land and destruction of the city, and (2) starvation and slaughter of the people. Motyer, *The Prophecy of Isaiah*, p. 414, makes "desolation" (or "ruin") and "destruction" come on the property while "famine" and "sword" touch the people. Brueggemann, *Isaiah 40–66*, p. 133, views this as a "double word pair," "devastation and destruction" and "famine and sword." These describe "two facets of military invasion and occupation." Rawlinson, II, 262, makes the second pair the cause of the first pair. The famine produces "desola-tion" (which he translates as "wasting") and the sword produces "destruction." There is virtual agreement in grouping the four named judgments into two pairs. The disagree-ment comes in how to arrange the grouping.

[20]Ibn Ezra, p. 235, makes the *teʾô* a bird caught in a net. Deut. 14:4–5, however, refers to it as an animal.

21 *Therefore hear now this, thou afflicted, and drunken, but not with wine:*

22 *Thus saith thy Lord the Lord, and thy God that pleadeth the cause of his people, Behold, I have taken out of thine hand the cup of trembling, even the dregs of the cup of my fury; thou shalt no more drink it again:*

23 *But I will put it into the hand of them that afflict thee; which have said to thy soul, Bow down, that we may go over: and thou hast laid thy body as the ground, and as the street, to them that went over.*

animal, possibly a wild sheep or antelope. The people suffer the wrath of God, v. 20.

21–23 The "afflicted" (*ʿanî*, see 3:14) nation is not drunk with "wine" (*yayin*, see 5:11) but with God's judgment. This should cause them to listen to God's message and to return to Him, cf. Hebrews 12:11; Revelation 3:19, v. 21. The Lord speaks to give hope for the future. The threefold repetition of divine names ("Lord . . . Lord . . . God") coupled with the doubled personal pronoun ("thy") makes the statement emphatic. This is Israel's God who speaks on their behalf. He "pleadeth" (*rîb*, or "contends," see 1:17) for them. He will take the cup of "trembling" (again, "reeling," see v. 17) from them. The statement, phrased as a prophetic perfect, certain in God's mind, anticipates Israel's repentance and acceptance of Christ as her Savior. There will no longer be a need to drink fully from "the dregs of the cup of my fury" (or "the goblet, the cup of my fury," see v. 17). They will suffer no more, a promise of rest in the kingdom, v. 22. God will put "it," the cup of judgment, into the hands of those who have afflicted His people. These have caused Israel's "soul" to "bow down," humbling them. Those who afflict them have made Israel's "body" (better "back") as the ground or a street so that they could walk on them. The picture of walking on Israel's back is probably figurative. We have no knowledge that this actually took place although it may have. Joshua 10:24 and Zechariah 10:5 record similar experiences. In any case, their tormentors will now receive punishment. Isaiah continues to relate the passage to the kingdom: the wicked will go to their eternal punishment while the righteous enter into the glorious reign of Christ, Joel 3:1–2; Matthew 25:31–46, v. 23.

Practical Applications from Chapter 51

1. The Remembering, vv. 1–8
   a. Remember what you were and what you have become, vv. 1–3.
   b. Remember God's Word and what it produces, vv. 4–6.
   c. Remember the Lord and the protection He gives, vv. 7–8.
2. The Awakening, 51:9–52:6
   a. When God wakes up, 51:9–16. Isaiah prays that God will awaken as in the days when He gave Israel victory over Egypt, v. 9, and brought the nation through the Red Sea, v. 10. This will introduce the kingdom, when the nation returns to Palestine, v. 11. The Lord responds to the prayer. He reminds the people of His care for them. They have no need to fear mortal man, v. 12. They should not forget the Lord when oppression comes to them. He is the omnipotent Creator, v. 13. He will give them freedom, v. 14. He showed His power by dividing the waters of the Red Sea. He rules over the hosts of heaven and earth, v. 15. He will protect Israel until the time that He brings them into the new heavens and earth, v. 16.
   b. When man wakes up, 51:17–52:12
      (1) Isaiah calls on the people to awaken to the freedom God will give them, 51:17–23. They have been drinking the cup of the Lord's judgment, v. 17. No one can take the nation away from this divine punishment, v. 18. She will suffer judgment that comes from within the nation and from without the nation, v. 19. Her men will be helpless, v. 20. Isaiah appeals to those suffering God's wrath, v. 21. There is hope for the future. The Lord will remove the punishment (implying repentance from her sins), v. 22, and give it to her enemies, v. 23.
      (2) Isaiah calls on the people to awaken to their responsibility of holiness, 52:1–12. They should wear the garments of salvation, no longer marked by sin, v. 1. They should free themselves from the bondage of the past, v. 2. They have sold themselves into bondage without receiving any payment; the Lord will now redeem them without paying their captors, v. 3. The captivities in Egypt and Assyria illustrate the past bondage, v. 4. This had caused the heathen to blaspheme the Lord as a weak God, v. 5. He will now show His power by redeeming them. Israel will know that it is the Lord who has

done this, v. 6. The messenger that tells of God's deliverance, both from bondage and from sin, is "beautiful," v. 7. The watchmen rejoice at the news, v. 8. The land rejoices at the news, v. 9. The Lord has shown His power by delivering His people, v. 10. The people should return to Jerusalem, cleansing themselves from sin as they go, v. 11. They will travel in peace with the Lord protecting them, v. 12.

1 *Awake, awake; put on thy strength, O Zion; put on thy beautiful garments, O Jerusalem, the holy city: for henceforth there shall no more come into thee the uncircumcised and the unclean.*
2 *Shake thyself from the dust; arise, and sit down, O Jerusalem: loose thyself from the bands of thy neck, O captive daughter of Zion.*

ISAIAH 52

The verbal cue "Awake, awake" signals us that the first part of the chapter belongs to c. 51. The first call to "awake," 51:9, urged the Lord to move on behalf of His people. The second call, 51:17, encouraged the people to turn from the sins that have brought them under judgment. If they will turn to the Lord, He will give them His blessing. The first twelve verses of c. 52 exhort the people to respond with holiness to the Lord's deliverance. The fulfillment of 51:9 to 52:12 lies in the millennial reign of the Lord.

Verses 13–15, the remaining paragraph in the chapter, introduce the fourth and last of the Servant passages and connects with c. 53, in which the fuller development of the Servant's sacrificial work occurs. The Servant's sacrifice reflects His wise actions, v. 13. It causes Him to undergo extreme physical disfigurement, v. 14. The sprinkling of His blood brings salvation, an act that causes awe among the rulers of the world, v. 15.

1–2 As in 51:9, 17, Isaiah calls on Zion with emphasis. His call, "Awake, awake," seeks to rouse her to assume her new position in the kingdom. The judgments of the past are gone. She is now ready to enter into the position of eternal blessing from God. She should lay aside the clothing that reflected grief; cf. 15:3. Instead, she should "put on [better 'clothe yourself with'] thy strength." This strength stands in stark contrast to the past. She has been weak, dominated by the nations of the world. Now she will be strong, the dominant nation exalted over other nations on the earth.[1] Enjoying a new intimate relationship with the Lord, she now has strength to carry out His will.

She should as well "put on [again 'clothe yourself with'] thy beautiful garments." She now will wear the "garments of salvation," 61:10. This clothing is appropriate to Jerusalem as "the holy city" into which no "uncircumcised" or "unclean" will enter; cf. Revelation 21:27. Circum-

---

[1]Others understand the word "strength" differently. Henry, p. 295, refers it to bestirring themselves, to a change in attitude, no longer being despondent. Barnes, II, 238, sees it as boldness and confidence. Skinner, *Isaiah XL–LXVI*, p. 128, parallels the word with "beauty" and makes it equal to "splendour." Kraeling, p. 191, parallels it with "garments" and refers it to putting on "fine raiment." I prefer the common meaning.

3 *For thus saith the Lord, Ye have sold yourselves for nought; and ye shall be redeemed without money.*

4 *For thus saith the Lord God, My people went down aforetime into Egypt to sojourn there; and the Assyrian oppressed them without cause.*

5 *Now therefore, what have I here, saith the Lord, that my people is taken away for nought? they that rule over them make them to howl, saith the Lord; and my name continually every day is blasphemed.*

6 *Therefore my people shall know my name: therefore they shall know in that day that I am he that doth speak: behold, it is I.*

cision was the sign of the covenant between God and His people. The physical act represented the putting away of uncleanness from the person; cf. Deuteronomy 10:16; Jeremiah 4:4. The OT symbolic action finds fulfillment through salvation and the new relationship with Jesus Christ, Romans 2:29; Philippians 3:3; Colossians 2:11. For this reason, the term "uncircumcised" occurs here with its symbolic sense. The parallel word "unclean" (*ṭame²*, see 6:5) makes this thought clear, v. 1.

The people should shake off the "dust" of judgment. They should release themselves from the "bands" (or "chains") that have bound them. The description is general. It covers the history of Israel since their rejection of the Lord.[2] At all times and in all places, they have experienced persecution. This now ends. Jerusalem, the capital and an appropriate symbol for the nation, should rise from its desolation. The phrase "sit down, O Jerusalem" is better "O captive Jerusalem." This parallels the last phrase, "O captive daughter of Zion." Jerusalem is now free from her bondage, v. 2.

3–6 The Lord notes that "ye have sold yourselves for nought" (*nimkartem*, see 50:1 in which the same verb occurs).[3] Historically, Israel has not received anything from the nations in return for their persecution and enslavement. Therefore, the Lord will redeem His people from their bondage without paying the nations anything, v. 3. In Egypt, Israel had been sojourners, guests. Despite this, Pharaoh had oppressed them. Later, the Assyrians oppressed them "without cause." We must

---

[2] Pieper, p. 421, limits the judgment to the Babylonian captivity. There is, however, no reason to restrict the application to Babylon. Verse 4 mentions the bondage in Egypt and the persecution from Assyria and v. 5 refers to Babylon. This application best includes all forms of persecution faced throughout history.

[3] Among others, Von Orelli, p. 285; Wright, p. 128; and Slotki, p. 257, translate *nimkartem* as a passive, "You were sold." The argument for a reflexive translation is the same as at 50:1. The Lord there denies selling His people into captivity. In addition, the Mosaic Law forbade selling Israelites into slavery, Exod. 21:16; Deut. 24:7; Amos 2:6.

7 *How beautiful upon the mountains are the feet of him that bringeth good tidings, that publisheth peace; that bringeth good tidings of good, that publisheth salvation; that saith unto Zion, Thy God reigneth!*

8 *Thy watchmen shall lift up the voice; with the voice together shall they sing: for they shall see eye to eye, when the Lord shall bring again Zion.*

9 *Break forth into joy, sing together, ye waste places of Jerusalem: for the Lord hath comforted his people, he hath redeemed Jerusalem.*

10 *The Lord hath made bare his holy arm in the eyes of all the nations; and all the ends of the earth shall see the salvation of our God.*

understand this phrase from the world's point of view. There was a spiritual cause but Assyria did not know this, v. 4. The Lord again takes note that the nations oppress Israel "for nought," without paying them anything. Those who "rule over them" (*mošlaw*) brutally oppress them, bringing forth a "howl" (*yᵉhêlîlû*) of pain.[4] The heathen have "blasphemed" God's name. This reflects their thinking that He is not powerful enough to care for His people.[5] Paul quotes the last part of the verse in Romans 2:24 to show the impact that the believer's sin has on the unbeliever, v. 5. The Lord will deliver His people. This will let Israel know His "name." Here, as is common, God's "name" represents His nature as a powerful God. In the day of deliverance, they will know that it is God who has spoken the promise of deliverance, v. 6.

7–10 Verse 7 pictures the arrival of a messenger who brings news of national deliverance. The mountains are those about Jerusalem. The phrase "how beautiful [*naʾwû*] are the feet" is idiomatic.[6] It pictures the

---

[4]Westermann, p. 248, translates *mošlaw* as a noun with *yᵉhêlîlû* the verb, "their rulers wail." He then interprets this as the overlords of Israel putting on airs. The word *mošlaw* is the qal active participle of *mašal*, "to rule." The following word *yᵉhêlîlû* is a hipʿîl with its usual causative sense. The translation of the AV is correct. Those who rule over Israel cause howls of grief. This also rules out Näglesbach's view, p. 563, that it is the rulers who howl with glee over their conquest of Israel. Although 1QIsaᵃ and the Vulgate translate the verb as *yᵉhallelû*, "to mock," there is no need to repoint the verb. The LXX translates ὀλολύζετε, "you howl," supporting the MT.

[5]Among others, Whitehouse, II, 188; Rawlinson, II, 279; and Goldingay, p. 298, understand the rulers as Babylon. There is, however, no reason to make the verse specific. The pattern of persecution causing howls of pain in Israel has been true historically. See note 2.

[6]Alexander, II, 278, renders *naʾwû* as "timely." The word occurs only three times, here and at Ps. 93:5 ("becometh") and Song of Sol. 1:10 ("comely"). Rom. 10:15 renders *naʾwû* as ὡραῖοι, which lays the stress on appearance. The NT translators rendered the word "beautiful" all four times it appears (Matt. 23:27; Acts 3:2, 10; Rom. 10:15). In Matt.

11 Depart ye, depart ye, go ye out from thence, touch no unclean thing; go ye out of the midst of her; be ye clean, that bear the vessels of the Lord.
12 For ye shall not go out with haste, nor go by flight: for the Lord will go before you; and the God of Israel will be your rereward.

desirability of the message; cf. Nahum 1:15. It is a good message, one that tells of "peace" and "good" and "salvation" (or "deliverance"). The deliverance proves once more to the people that their God does indeed rule. We should not restrict the message of the OT messenger to national deliverance.[7] The NT use in Romans 10:13–15 shows clearly that the message includes personal salvation in its meaning. Those who proclaim the gospel to others also have a message of "peace" (šalôm, see 9:6). It is a message of deliverance from sin, v. 7.

The "watchmen" on the walls of the city rejoice with singing at the news of deliverance.[8] They see "eye to eye," idiomatic for "near at hand," when "the Lord shall bring again Zion" (bᵉšûb yᵉhwah ṣîyôn, better "when the Lord returns to Zion").[9] The watchmen rejoice in the coming of their Lord to establish His rule from Jerusalem, v. 8. Isaiah commands the land to rejoice at this deliverance of God. It was filled with "wasted places." Now these are fruitful. He has both "comforted" (naḥam, see 1:24) and "redeemed" (gaʾal, see 35:9) the people, v. 9. He has "made bare his holy arm." The figure comes from the warrior who bares his arm in preparation for battle so that nothing will hinder him; cf. Psalm 98:1. He has done this openly so that all may see the deliverance of His people, v. 10.

11–12 As in v. 1, the doubled imperative gives emphasis to the command. There, the people were to awake. Now, they are to return to

---

23:27; Acts 3:2, 10, the word can mean only "beautiful." Rom. 10:15 follows the traditional rendering of Isa. 52:7. The evidence supports the translation "beautiful" here.

[7]It is common to apply the passage to the return of Judah from Babylon. Among others, Brueggemann, *Isaiah 40–66*, p. 138; Watts, *Isaiah 34–66*, pp. 216–17; and Slotki, p. 258, speak about the return from Babylon. There is a kingdom context, however, to the passage. Verse 7 refers to the message of salvation, v. 8 to the Lord's return to Jerusalem, v. 9 to the healing of the land, and v. 10 to a worldwide salvation.

[8]Delitzsch, II, 299, and Kraeling, p. 192, understand the "watchmen" to be the prophets of the nation. Näglesbach, p. 564, considers them spirit-beings. Rawlinson, II, 279, calls them angels. Barnes, II, 243, spiritualizes the meaning to refer the term to "ministers of religion" rejoicing in "the visits of Divine mercy to a church and people." Nothing in the passage, however, suggests a metaphorical sense. It would be natural for the watchmen to rejoice at such news of deliverance.

[9]The meaning of the phrase bᵉšûb yᵉhwah ṣîyôn is open to interpretation, depending on the sense given to the verb šûb. Delitzsch, II, 299, and Vine, p. 144, translate with the AV.

13 *Behold, my servant shall deal prudently, he shall be exalted and ex-*
tolled, and be very high.
14 *As many were astonied at thee; his visage was so marred more than*
any man, and his form more than the sons of men:
15 *So shall he sprinkle many nations; the kings shall shut their mouths*
at him: for that which had not been told them shall they see; and
that which they had not heard shall they consider.

Palestine. The people should purify themselves as they leave the nations, touching no "unclean" (*ṭameʾ*, see 6:5) thing. This ritual purity was especially necessary for those involved with the temple service. There is a requirement of purity for those who carry the temple vessels; cf. Ezra 1:7–11; 5:14–15. Uncleanness would not be compatible with the "beautiful garments" of salvation (v. 1) now worn by the people. The apostle Paul draws on this picture as he commands his readers to be pure, II Corinthians 6:17. The application extends to Christians in all ages, v. 11. The return of the people will be leisurely. This pictures the peaceful conditions under which they travel. The Lord will go before them to provide guidance and protection. He will be their "rereward" (*meʾassip*, better "rear guard") as well, v. 12.[10]

H. Redemption of God's People 52:13–55:13
1. The Servant's Suffering 52:13–53:12

13–15 This paragraph introduces the final Servant passage.[11] Here, the Servant will "deal prudently" (*yaśkîl*, or "act wisely").[12] The result is

---

Among others, however, Leupold, II, 215; Näglesbach, p. 565; and Young, III, 331, understand *šûb* as an infinitive construct and translate "the return of the Lord to Zion" or "when the Lord returns to Zion." This is grammatically easier to defend.

[10]Barnes, II, 246, takes *meʾassip* in its root sense, "to gather." He understands the verse to refer to the Lord's gathering the people from their captivity. The *piˤel* participle form of *ʾasap*, however, is often a substantive. The participle occurs in this way in Num. 10:25; Josh. 6:9, 13, and as a verb in Judg. 19:15, 18; Isa. 62:9; Jer. 9:22. While either view is possible, the thought of the Lord being Israel's rear guard nicely connects with His going before them. He provides complete protection for His people.

[11]See also 42:1–9; 49:1–13; 50:4–11, and the excursus at the end of c. 42. As with the other passages, there are various identities given to the Servant here. Whitehouse, II, 194, makes him "afflicted Israel." McKenzie, pp. lii, 134, and Slotki, p. 260, make him idealized Israel. Brueggemann, pp. 143–44, and Wright, p. 130, accept the collective view that identifies the Servant as both Israel and Jesus Christ. Goldingay, p. 308, sees him as Isaiah. Watts, *Isaiah 34–66,* p. 227, understands the Servant to be Darius. More than the other Servant passages, the NT clearly identifies the Servant of 52:13–53:12 as Jesus Christ: 52:15, cf. Rom. 15:21; 53:1, cf. John 12:38; Rom. 10:16; 53:4, cf. Matt.

that He will be "exalted . . . extolled . . . be very high." The repetition of these terms gives an emphatic statement of His high position, v. 13. There is a brief change of persons in 14*a* as the Father speaks directly to the Servant. He then returns to speaking of Him in the third person. Many will be "astonied" (or "appalled") at Him. From the development of the passage, this is the reaction of His followers at His crucifixion. His "visage" (or "appearance") will be "marred" (*mišhat*) "more" (*meʾîš*)[13] than that of others throughout history; cf. 50:6; Matthew 26:67; 27:29–30. His "form" (or "shape") will be distorted far more than normal, v. 14.

As a result of His sacrifice, He will "sprinkle" (*yazzeh*) many with His blood, shed for their sins. The verb *nazâ* occurs twenty-three other times in the OT. Without exception, it has the meaning "sprinkle."[14] It normally refers to the sprinkling of blood, but it also refers to the sprinkling

---

8:17; 53:5, cf. I Pet. 2:24; 53:6, cf. I Pet. 2:25; 53:7, cf. Acts 8:32; 53:8, cf. Acts 8:33; 53:9, cf. I Pet. 2:22; 53:12, cf. Mark 15:28; Luke 22:37. There is no doubt that the NT writers saw Jesus Christ in this Servant passage.

[12]A large number of authors and translations understand *yaśkîl* as "prosper." Among these are Lindsey, p. 103; Smith, p. 342; and Fausset, p. 728. The debate turns largely on whether the verb parallels 13*b* or whether 13*b* is the result. Either view is possible. I have opted for "act wisely" since this is more common in the OT. There are only a couple of places that the *hipʿîl* imperfect of *śakal* must mean prosper (Josh. 1:8; Prov. 17:8) while there are several places that it must refer to wise actions (Deut. 32:29; Ps. 32:8; 94:8; 101:2; Dan. 9:25).

[13]The partitive *min* in *meʾîš* here indicates that the Lord was outside the class of normal men in His appearance. From the description of His sufferings in the NT, it is understandable that His appearance was startling to those who saw Him. The noun *mišhat*, "marred," occurs only here. The root *šht*, "to go to ruin," however, occurs over fifty times, so the meaning is not in doubt. A related noun, *mašhît*, "ruin, destruction," also occurs frequently.

[14]Pieper, p. 432, argues that *hizzâ* does not have the sense of "sprinkle" with a person as the object. He feels that the context requires something related to "mute astonishment." He understands the *hipʿîl* verb as causative. The nations, "like spattered drops of water, scatter in consternation over the sudden spectacle of the glory of the Servant." While it is true that the verb nowhere has a person or thing as its direct object, it is also true that it rarely has a person in view. In only two places (II Kings 9:33; Isa. 63:3) does it refer to human blood. Elsewhere, it refers to the priestly work of sprinkling the blood or to ritual sprinkling. The work of Christ fulfills this. Watts, *Isaiah 34–66*, II, 225, and McKenzie, p. 129, make *nazâ* a *hapax legomenon* from *naz*, an Arabic cognate meaning "to startle." Among others, Leupold, II, 224; Hailey, p. 436; and North, p. 132, adopt this reading. This requires us to adopt a verb seen nowhere else in the OT. Childs, p. 412, argues that the semantic range of meaning of *nazâ* includes the idea of "startle, surprise." While the meaning fits into the rest of the verse, this ignores the allusions to the verse in Heb. 10:22; 12:24; I Pet. 1:2.

of oil or water. The sprinkling of blood in sacrifice demonstrated the offering of the animal. The obedient action showed the faith of the person in God's Word. That sense fits beautifully here, where the Crucifixion is so clearly in view.[15] Those who receive the sprinkling of the blood are pure before God.

Many rulers will "shut their mouths at him." They do not comment on the Servant's work. This is new to them. No one has ever told them, and they have not heard of anything like the redemptive work of Christ.[16] They will "consider" this, standing in awe of His accomplishments. In Romans 15:21, the apostle Paul refers to this verse to justify his practice of preaching in places no one else had presented Christ to the people, v. 15.

Practical Applications from Chapter 52

1. See Awakening, c. 51
2. The Sacrificial Work of Christ, vv. 13–15

   a. A wise work, resulting in the exaltation of the Servant, v. 13

   b. A suffering work, resulting in the marring of His features, v. 14

   c. A saving work, resulting in the astonishment of kings, v. 15

---

[15]Henry, p. 300, wrongly finds the fulfillment of this in baptism. While baptism portrays salvation, it is not a means of salvation.

[16]R. E. Watts, "The Meaning of *ᶜālāw yiqpᵉṣû mᵉlākîm pîhem* in Isaiah LII 15," *VT* 40:327–35, argues that shutting the mouths of the kings refers to "the kings' subjugation and loss of authority." He considers the expression "a metonymy of effect." The "effect is put for the action that caused it . . . injustice shuts its mouth because it is being or will be judged." He bases the view on passages that refer to the king's command setting some action in motion. A similar idiom occurs in Job 5:16 and Ps. 107:42, in which "iniquity shuts its mouth." Although Watts goes too far in equating the speech with the act of oppression, his view is possible. It is also worth noting that the withholding of speech occurs with different idioms. Job 21:5; 29:8–10; and Mic. 7:16 refer the closing of the mouth to amazement at circumstances. Job 29:21–22 suggests a wait for directions. In Judg. 18:19, the closing of the mouth relates to cooperation rather than confrontation. Both Job 40:4 and Prov. 30:32 connect this with humility and repentance. Any of these idioms are appropriate here. The emphasis in the verse that the work of Christ is new to these kings supports the view that astonishment overtakes them. Understanding the plan of God, they change their attitude toward spiritual matters. Many references state that Gentile kings assist the Jews in their return to Palestine, e.g., 49:7; 60:10. It is clear that the Gentile leaders will seek to please the Lord by helping His chosen people.

1 *Who hath believed our report? and to whom is the arm of the Lord revealed?*

2 *For he shall grow up before him as a tender plant, and as a root out of a dry ground: he hath no form nor comeliness; and when we shall see him, there is no beauty that we should desire him.*

3 *He is despised and rejected of men; a man of sorrows, and acquainted with grief: and we hid as it were our faces from him; he was despised, and we esteemed him not.*

ISAIAH 53

This final Servant passage climaxes the teaching regarding the Servant. From the NT use of the passage, some eleven times (including 52:15), it is clear that the chapter describes the atoning work of Jesus Christ. The passage stands with Psalm 22 as the most detailed description of the sacrifice at Calvary. Perhaps more than any other passage in the book, the chapter justifies Isaiah as *"the Evangelical Prophet."*

1–3 The prophet Isaiah speaks.[1] He asks rhetorically whether anyone has accepted the report concerning Messiah.[2] The expected answer is no! The NT quotes this, John 12:38 and Romans 10:16, in both cases

---

[1] Smith, p. 348, makes Israel the speaker in vv. 1–6. Only at v. 7 does he see Isaiah speaking. Von Orelli, pp. 287–88, likewise considers Israel the speaker in vv. 1–6. He, however, identifies the nation as the "penitent Church." North, p. 133, makes the speaker the converted Gentile nations with Israel being the Servant. Wright, p. 131, understands the speaker as the Gentile kings mentioned in 52:15. Slotki, p. 261, makes the speaker the Babylonians or a representative of Babylon. It is highly unlikely that the chapter reflects Israel's speech. In order to accept the nation as the speaker, we must give them a spiritual maturity that they did not have. The chapter clearly looks forward to the sacrificial work of Christ. Israel did not have this spiritual discernment. For the same reasons, it is difficult to accept Gentiles as the speaker. In Matt. 8:17; John 12:38; and Rom. 10:16, the NT makes "Esaias" the speaker. This refers to the book rather than to the prophet.

[2] Orlinsky, pp. 59–63, 92–96, denies that c. 53 refers to Christ. He calls this "eisegesis," reading NT thought back into the OT. He argues that the person in c. 53 "did not die." He understands the statement that "he shall see his seed," v. 10, to mean that he lived to see his grandchildren. The reference to death, v. 12, is hyperbole. Orlinsky's view comes naturally as the result of rejecting the inspiration of the NT. The view that the chapter refers to the Lord rests on a solid foundation. It describes an individual, not a nation. Not only does it use the singular pronoun but also v. 3 specifically mentions a "man." If we substitute "Israel" for the pronouns "he" and "him," it is awkward to explain the "we" pronoun in vv. 2–6. In vv. 6, 8*b*, the individual suffers for the nation. In vv. 8–9, the passage describes the burial of an individual. In v. 11, the passage describes the Servant as "righteous," a description that could not apply to the nation. Historically, the Jews applied the chapter to the Messiah until the mid-twelfth century. At that time, a reaction against Christianity caused them to adopt other views.

> 4 *Surely he hath borne our griefs, and carried our sorrows: yet we did esteem him stricken, smitten of God, and afflicted.*
> 5 *But he was wounded for our transgressions, he was bruised for our iniquities: the chastisement of our peace was upon him; and with his stripes we are healed.*
> 6 *All we like sheep have gone astray; we have turned every one to his own way; and the Lord hath laid on him the iniquity of us all.*

showing that the rejection of the gospel was foretold, v. 1. He grows up "before him," before God, who is fully aware of His Servant's condition. He is as a "tender plant" (*yôneq*) and as a "root [*šoreš*] out of a dry ground"; cf. 11:1.[3] These phrases suggest His humble beginning. He has no "form" (or "shape") or "comeliness" (better "majesty") to draw attention to Himself. He has no "beauty" (better "appearance") to attract others to Himself, v. 2. Men despise (*bazâ*) and reject (*ḥᵃdal*) Him.[4] He is a "man of sorrows, and acquainted with grief" as he undergoes both physical pain and mental anguish over the sins of men. Men turn their faces from Him. He is despised, not esteemed for His ministry to men. To the Jews, crucifixion marked a person as a heretic and worthy of shame; cf. Deuteronomy 21:22–23. Isaiah sees this attitude extended by the Jews toward the Lord, v. 3.[5]

4–6 The prophet now introduces the redemptive work of Christ. He bore the "griefs" and "sorrows" of mankind. Matthew 8:17 applies this to bearing the burdens of mankind as He cast out the demons that afflicted others. Despite this, the Jews looked upon Him as one "afflicted" (*ᶜanâ*, see 31:4) by God. This verse was the means of bringing the eighteenth-century Scottish pastor and author John Brown of Haddington to

---

[3]The word *yôneq* refers to someone or something that sucks, a "suckling." The word here describes a shoot from a plant that sucks strength from the main plant. The picture is of something small and relatively minor. Likewise, the *šoreš* is a shoot coming from a root in the barren ground. Once more, this is something small, almost trivial.

[4]The words are picturesque. The verb *bazâ* is strong, "to be vile, worthless," and thus "despised." The term *ḥᵃdal* is from the verb meaning "to cease." The derivative occurs three times, here and Ps. 39:4 ("frail," i.e., "short-lived") and Ezek. 3:27 ("he that forbeareth," i.e., "ceases from hearing"). The thought here is that the Servant "ceases from acceptance" by men, i.e., they forsake Him. The NEB translates, "he shrank from the sight of men" but this does not parallel *bazâ*.

[5]Skinner, *Isaiah XL–LXVI*, p. 139, concludes, "leprosy is strongly suggested." Whitehouse, II, 201, likewise states, "The despised and martyred community of exiles is . . . regarded as a leper and outcast." There is no evidence to justify the view. The conclusions follow from misidentifying the Servant.

7 *He was oppressed, and he was afflicted, yet he opened not his mouth: he is brought as a lamb to the slaughter, and as a sheep before her shearers is dumb, so he openeth not his mouth.*

8 *He was taken from prison and from judgment: and who shall declare his generation? for he was cut off out of the land of the living: for the transgression of my people was he stricken.*

9 *And he made his grave with the wicked, and with the rich in his death; because he had done no violence, neither was any deceit in his mouth.*

accept the Lord as his Savior. He saw here, for the first time, what Christ had done for him, v. 4. The Lord's death on the cross was not for His own sins. He was "wounded" (better "pierced") because of man's "transgressions" (*pešaᶜ*, see 24:20); cf. Zechariah 12:10. This points to the nails piercing the Lord's hands and feet and to the spear piercing His side on the cross. He was "bruised" (*dakaʾ*, see 3:15; better "crushed") because of our "iniquities" (*ᶜawon*, see 1:4). This refers to the emotional suffering of the Lord at Calvary as He bore man's sin. He was chastened to bring about our peace with God. By means of His "stripes," most likely referring to the welts raised by the scourging, we receive spiritual healing.[6] Isaiah uses plural pronouns as he identifies himself with other Israelites. Sometimes these are believing (i.e., vv. 5–6) and sometimes unbelieving (i.e., vv. 2–4), v. 5. Sheep are prone to scatter, Ezekiel 34:6. Like sheep that wander from the place of safety, so mankind goes his own way. The Lord, however, has "laid" (*hipᶜil* of *pagaᶜ*)[7] on the Servant "the iniquity [*ᶜawon*, see 1:4] of us all." To make certain that there is no mistake in the application, I Peter 2:24–25 applies the passage to the atoning death of Jesus Christ, v. 6.

7–9 The suffering Servant endures the oppression without speaking of its unfairness, Matthew 27:12, 14. He is "oppressed" (*nagaś*, see 3:5) and "afflicted" (*ᶜanâ* see 31:4) yet He does not complain. Both *nagaś* and *ᶜanâ* suggest severe physical or emotional abuse. Like a dumb sheep brought to the slaughter or to have its wool sheared, so He quietly

---

[6]The "stripes" here serve by metonymy to represent the whole of Christ's substitutionary suffering and death at Calvary.

[7]The basic meaning of *pagaᶜ* is "to meet," see 47:3. In the *hipᶜil*, the verb has a causative sense that leads in different directions, all with the sense of "causing to meet." Here, our iniquities "meet" the Lord in that they are "laid" on Him. In v. 12, the Servant "meets" the Father in prayer, i.e., He intercedes for us.

accepts His fate.[8] It is this passage that prepared the heart of the Ethiopian eunuch to receive Christ, Acts 8:32–33 (LXX), v. 7. He is taken from "prison" (*ᶜoṣer*, or "restraint")[9] and "judgment" (*mišpaṭ*, see 1:17).[10] The verb "taken" here refers to the Servant's death, which takes Him away from the undeserved treatment given Him by the Jews.[11] The quote in Acts turns this thought around: "His judgment was taken away." The evil commanded by the religious leaders lost its force at the death of Christ. Again, however, this expresses the idea of separation between the Lord and judgment.

The phrase "who shall declare [*śîaḥ*] his generation" is better "and as for His generation, who shall consider it?"[12] The verb *śîaḥ* in the *polel* theme occurs elsewhere only at Psalm 143:5, in which it means "meditate." That sense is appropriate here. The rhetorical question suggests that not many of His day will think much about the Servant's death. He is cut off from among the living.

---

[8]The NT develops further the thought of Messiah as the lamb; cf. John 1:29, 36; I Pet. 1:19; Rev. 5:6, 8, 12, 13; 6:1, 16; 7:9, 10, 14, 17; 12:11; 13:8; 14:1, 4, 10; 15:3; 17:14; 19:7, 9; 21:9, 14, 22, 23, 27; 22:1, 3.

[9]The word *ᶜoṣer* is, more appropriately, "restraint." The ideas of "prison" (AV) or "oppression" (NASB, NIV) are interpretive. Delitzsch, II, 324, describes it as "a persecuting treatment which restrains by outward force, such as prison or bonds." The word occurs again at Ps. 107:39 ("oppression," or "constraint") and Prov. 30:16 ("barren," restrained from conception). The general thought of "restraint" is appropriate in referring to the treatment given to the Lord. The Jews restrained Him in taking Him captive, in questioning Him, and in crucifying Him.

[10]A *min* preposition introduces both "restraint" and "judgment." Whitehouse, II, 204, understands the *min* as "on account of." Watts, *Isaiah 34–66*, p. 224, translates, "because of." Brueggemann, *Isaiah 40–66*, p. 147, takes the phrase as "by a perversion of justice." These pronouns suggest the violent treatment received by the Lord and the judgment rendered by the authorities as the cause of His being taken away. While this is possible, the *min* preposition normally indicates separation, not cause. If we render the phrase "He was taken away from restraint and judgment," the verse speaks of death taking the Servant away from the unjust treatment given Him by the Jews.

[11]Henry, VI, 105, discussing Acts 8:33, interprets 53:8 as the hurrying of the Lord "with the utmost violence and precipitation from one judgment-seat to another." In his comments on Isaiah (IV, 306), he understands the verb to refer to the Lord's resurrection. By this means, He was taken from the unjust "judgment" and the "prison" of the grave. The context, "cut off out of the land of the living," relates the verse to the death of Christ rather than His resurrection.

[12]The NIV misses the sense with its translation: "And who can speak of his descendants?" It is meaningless here to speak of the descendants of the Lord.

Because of the "transgression" (*peša^c*, see 24:20) of God's people, "was he stricken" (better "the stroke was upon Him").[13] The verse has the redemptive work of the Lord in view. The NT makes it clear that the passage applies to the Lord, v. 8. He "made" (*natan*) His grave with the "wicked" (*r^eša^cîm*); cf. Luke 23:32–33.[14] He died at the same time as other wicked men and, no doubt, was buried at the same general time as these others. It would have been appropriate to bury the Lord in the sepulchers of the kings (II Chron. 21:20; 24:25; 28:27). Instead, He received a common burial with His body not even anointed fully with spices (Mark 16:1; Luke 24:1). He joins with the "rich" (*^cašîr*)[15] in His death; cf. Matthew 27:57–60.[16] The word "death" is plural, but since multiple

---

[13]The phrase is lit. "from the transgression of my people there was a stroke to him [*l^emô*]." The NASB and NIV marginal readings understand *l^emô* in a plural sense, referring to the nation. Both translate, "for the transgression of my people to whom the stroke was due." This requires them to supply the verb "was due." The word *l^emô* is often singular. If we understand it that way, the translation above is acceptable. It is simpler and more common to supply the copulative.

[14]The sense given *natan* determines the sense given to the verse. Barnes, II, 276; McKenzie, p. 130; and Skinner, *Isaiah XL–LXVI,* p. 145, understand the verb as a passive, "was made" or "was assigned." This suggests that the Jews anticipated burying the Servant with other wicked persons. The verb *natan*, however, occurs elsewhere as a passive in the *nip^cal* or *hop^cal*. There is no reason to translate the *qal* here as a passive. Delitzsch, II, 326; Näglesbach, p. 578; and Von Orelli, p. 289, make the subject of *natan* indefinite and translate, "they made. . . ." The idea again is that the intention was to degrade the Lord by burying Him with the wicked dead. The verb, however, is a 3ms, "he made." These views also suffer in that *natan* governs both clauses. While the Jews may have planned a grave with the wicked, they did not plan one with the rich. The verb *natan* occurs over two thousand times and has a broad semantic range of meaning. While it is normally "give," over one hundred times it has the sense "made." It is appropriate here to follow the AV. While He died and was buried with the wicked, His burial took place in a rich man's tomb.

[15]G. W. Ahlström, "Notes to Isaiah 53:8f," *BZ* 13 (1969): 95–98, calls attention to the play on words in the verse. Isaiah alternates *r^eša^cîm* and *^cašîr*, "wicked" and "rich," changing the order of the consonants. This verbal play marks Isaiah's writings throughout the whole book. It argues for a single author. Ahlström argues that *^cašîr* must be similar to *r^eša^cîm* in meaning because of the play on words. Isaiah, however, sometimes plays on words involving different meanings, e.g., 5:7 (2 times); 19:18; 21:11; 65:12. With a clear NT fulfillment of the prophecy, there is no need to abandon the normal meaning of "rich."

[16]Skinner, *Isaiah XL–LXVI,* p. 145, notes that it was a disgrace not to be buried in the family plot, II Sam. 18:17. It was an ignominious burial to be buried among the "common people," Jer. 26:23. The view is possible although the OT is not clear about this. Whitehouse, II, 205, and Herbert, *Isaiah 40–66,* p. 114, understand this as a burial in Babylon. The view rests on the wrong identification of the Servant. Von Orelli, p. 289, and Kelley, p. 344, make "rich" parallel with "wicked," giving it the same sense. Nothing, however, is inherently wrong with being rich.

10 Yet it pleased the Lord to bruise him; he hath put him to grief: when thou shalt make his soul an offering for sin, he shall see his seed, he shall prolong his days, and the pleasure of the Lord shall prosper in his hand.

11 He shall see of the travail of his soul, and shall be satisfied: by his knowledge shall my righteous servant justify many; for he shall bear their iniquities.

deaths are not possible, it likely refers to the nature of His death, a violent and gruesome end.[17] His death came even though He had done no violence or deceit. The innocent one died for the guilt of mankind. First Peter 2:22 applies this to the Lord, v. 9.

10–11 It pleased the Father to "bruise" (*daka²*, again "crush," indicating the violent nature of His suffering and death, cf. v. 5) the Son. He has put Him to grief. The particle "when" (*²im*) is better conditional, "if."[18] If He offers His soul as "an offering for sin" (better "a trespass offering"), the Servant will receive the Father's blessing. He will gain a spiritual seed and prolonged life; cf. Revelation 1:8. He will carry out the "pleasure" (*ḥepeṣ*, see 44:28) of the Father, v. 10. The phrase "He shall see of the travail of his soul . . ." is better "after the travail of His soul, He shall see. . . ."[19] The Son sees the "travail of His soul [*napšô*]," His suffering for sin, and He is satisfied.[20] By His knowledge of the

---

[17]Delitzsch, II, 328, calls it a "martyr's death." Price, p. 226, speaks of a "tragic death." Motyer, *The Prophecy of Isaiah,* p. 436, considers it a "supreme/magnificent death." These are all possible attempts to explain the plural "deaths." McKenzie, p. 131; Von Orelli, p. 289; and Slotki, p. 263, understand the word as "tomb." This requires repointing *bmtyw* and deriving it from *bamôt.* This word occurs over one hundred times as "high place, mountain, fortress," etc., but never as "tomb" or "grave."

[18]The temporal use of *²im* is rare. In those few passages that a temporal sense is appropriate, the context requires it. That is not the case here.

[19]Rawlinson, II, 298, and Delitzsch, II, 338, interpret the *min* as causative "because of the travail . . . he shall see and be satisfied." This faces the same objection as in v. 8. The preposition *min* is partitive, not causative. I have given it a temporal sense, "away from the travail," i.e., "after the travail." Von Orelli, p. 290, and Fausset, p. 330, understand the phrase as "out of the travail," i.e., the fruit that comes out of the travail. The view is possible. Alexander, II, 304, makes *napšô* refer to the whole life of the Servant. This satisfies the Father. While this is also possible, the context focuses more on the atonement of Christ on the cross. It would be strange to suddenly go away from this for a single clause, then to return to the redemptive work of the Lord.

[20]Young, III, 356, views the two verbs "he shall see" and "he shall be satisfied" as a hendiadys. He translates, "He shall see with abundant satisfaction." It is, however, unusual to take verbs as a hendiadys. Leupold, II, 233, makes the second verb the object, "he shall see satisfaction." This is grammatically wrong. Skinner, *Isaiah XL–LXVI,*

12 Therefore will I divide him a portion with the great, and he shall divide the spoil with the strong; because he hath poured out his soul unto death: and he was numbered with the transgressors; and he bare the sin of many, and made intercession for the transgressors.

Father's will "shall my righteous servant justify many" (better "shall the Righteous One, my servant, justify many"). He does this by bearing their "iniquities" (ʿ*awon*, see 1:4) upon Himself, cf. v. 6, v. 11.

12 The Father rewards Him for His atoning work. He graciously divides the reward between the Servant and those who fight with Him in the battle against the wicked; cf. Revelation 19:14. The passage ends as it began, by emphasizing the Servant's work. He has poured out His soul to death. He was "numbered" (or "counted") with the transgressors when He took our sins at Calvary; cf. Mark 15:28; Luke 22:37. He Himself bore the sins of many; cf. Hebrews 9:28. He continually "makes intercession" (*pagaʿ*, see v. 6) for the transgressors, Romans 8:34; Hebrews 7:25; I John 2:1.

---

p. 147, subordinates the second verb to the first, "he shall see with satisfaction." Slotki, p. 264, is similar: "he shall see to the full." G.K. 120 *b* gives this construction as an illustration of coordination of verbs without the copula. The second verb naturally gives the result of the first. The LXX and 1QIsaᵃ insert ʾ*ôr*, "light," after "he shall see." Numerous translations and commentaries follow this, e.g., Westermann, Brueggemann, McKenzie, NIV, NEB. This leaves unanswered what "light" represents although some interpret as the "light of life."

Practical Applications from Chapter 53

1. The Work of Christ

   a. The triumph of the Servant, 52:13–15. This leads naturally to an explanation.

   b. The rejection of the Servant, 53:1–3. The Jews reject Him. Yet we have

   c. The suffering of the Servant, 53:4–6. His vicarious suffering. This leads to

   d. The atonement of the Servant, 53:7–11. Now we return to where we started

   e. The reward of the Servant, 53:12

2. The New Testament Use of the Fourth Servant Song[21]

   a. The sacrifice of Christ

   (1) Matthew 8:17 (Isa. 53:4) justifies the healing ministry of the Lord. This illustrates His redemptive work in that He heals the effects of sin.

   (2) Acts 8:32 (Isa. 53:7) pictures Him as a sacrificial lamb that does not resist death.

   (3) Acts 8:33 (Isa. 53:8) speaks of His death that takes Him from the unjust judgment pronounced upon him by the Jews.

   (4) Luke 22:37 (Isa. 53:12) warns His disciples of His identification with sinners. Mark 15:28 (also Isa. 53:12) shows that the Cross, when the crucifixion takes place between two sinners, fulfills this prophecy.

   b. The life of the believer

   (1) First Peter 2:20 admonishes believers to "do well." When we suffer for a godly life, this pleases God. Peter then illustrates this challenge with three quotations from Isaiah 53.

   (2) First Peter 2:22 (Isa. 53:9) begins the description of Christ's response to unjust suffering. He "did no sin" nor did He speak deceitfully. The significance of this is that sin often begins with a person's speech; cf. I Peter 2:1; 3:10. Verse 23 gives illustrations of times that the Lord might well have spoken

---

[21]While I have modified his work, Kenneth D. Litwak, in an excellent article, "The Use of Quotations from Isaiah 52:13–53:12 in the New Testament," *JETS* 26:385–94, suggests this topic.

wicked words had He responded in kind to those who mocked Him.

(3) First Peter 2:24 (Isa. 53:5) describes the sacrificial work of Christ. Though it must have been personally distasteful to take our sins upon Himself, He gave Himself for the redemption of sinners. They, in turn, should live in "righteousness."

(4) First Peter 2:25 (Isa. 53:6) describes man's waywardness. The work of Christ, however, brings us to Him. There is an implied command to live suitably.

c. The preaching of the gospel

(1) Romans 15:21 (Isa. 52:15) justifies missionary efforts to take the gospel to those who have never heard. The verse as well justifies soulwinning activities as believers try to reach others who have never effectually heard. Too many believers turn away from missions and too many believers fail to take the gospel anywhere.

(2) Those who hear will often reject the gospel. John 12:38 (Isa. 53:1) describes how the Jews rejected the miracles of Christ as proof of His deity. Romans 10:16 (Isa. 53:1) describes how others rejected the gospel when Paul delivered it. Just as Jesus and Paul persevered in the face of rejection, so should Christians today remain faithful to God's call to win the lost to Him.

1 Sing, O barren, thou that didst not bear; break forth into singing, and cry aloud, thou that didst not travail with child: for more are the children of the desolate than the children of the married wife, saith the Lord.

2 Enlarge the place of thy tent, and let them stretch forth the curtains of thine habitations: spare not, lengthen thy cords, and strengthen thy stakes;

3 For thou shalt break forth on the right hand and on the left; and thy seed shall inherit the Gentiles, and make the desolate cities to be inhabited.

ISAIAH 54

Chapter 54 logically follows c. 53. Isaiah has just finished describing the suffering and atoning work of the Lord. He now turns to the glorious future of the believing nation in the kingdom of the Messiah. The nation will grow in number and occupy a larger amount of territory. She will dominate the Gentiles. She will enjoy a new relationship with her Lord as He gives her peace. She will experience blessing after blessing as she enjoys the eternal relationship with the Lord.

2. The Nation's Security 54:1–17
a. The Increase of Israel 54:1–10

1–3 Isaiah urges the oppressed nation to rejoice over the coming blessings of God.[1] The nation is presently "barren," not bringing forth children. Yet this "desolate" one will have more children than when she was "the married wife."[2] The promise is of millennial blessing. The "deso-

---

[1]Young, III, 360–61, applies c. 54–57 to the church on the basis that the words "Zion" and "Jerusalem" do not occur. Among others, Price, p. 229, and Fausset, p. 733, also refer to the church. There are numerous indications, however, that Isaiah still speaks to Israel. He speaks of inheriting the "Gentiles," 54:3. He refers to the "shame of thy youth," the Egyptian bondage, and the "reproach of thy widowhood," the Babylonian captivity, 54:4. He mentions the temple, the "house," the "walls" of the city, 56:5, and sacrifices on "mine altar," 56:7. He refers to the death of the righteous, naturally taken to refer to the time of Manasseh's persecution of the godly, 57:1. He mentions the practice of idolatry, 57:5, in Israel. It is wrong to neglect Israel in favor of the church. There is a future for believing Israel as well as for believers from other nations.

[2]Barnes, II, 288, understands "desolate" Israel as the nation in Babylonian captivity. It is true that this period illustrates a time of God's judgment on Israel. It is also true, however, that Israel has for a large part of its history been under God's judgment. It is better to see the passage as eschatological. It looks at the end times, when Israel will enjoy God's blessings. Barnes also makes the expression a proverb that promises "a much greater increase than [Israel] had any reason to apprehend." Ibn Ezra, p. 246, understands

4 Fear not; for thou shalt not be ashamed: neither be thou confounded; for thou shalt not be put to shame: for thou shalt forget the shame of thy youth, and shalt not remember the reproach of thy widowhood any more.

late" nation, long under God's judgment, will multiply to a larger size than in OT times, when she was considered the "wife" of God; cf. v. 5, 62:4. Paul develops this thought in Galatians 4:27. The figure of "barren" Israel there comes from Sarah. Israel is to rejoice as God gives her children after she is "desolate." She has more children than she and her "husband" could naturally have been expected to conceive. The spiritual parallel is that restored Israel with her faith in Jesus Christ as her Messiah and Savior will flourish more than Israel under law, v. 1. Her "tent," the dwelling, will grow larger. The "curtains" of her dwelling are the walls of the tent, which God will lengthen. The "cords" holding the tent to the pegs lengthen to hold the increased size of the tent. The longer "stakes" stabilize the dwelling. This metaphorical picture shows the increased size of the nation in the day of God's blessing, v. 2.[3] She extends her national boundaries "on the right hand and on the left." Since the OT references directions to the east, this shows the growth of the nation to the north and south.[4] Gentile nations come under her control. She occupies cities that had formerly been desolate, v. 3.

4–8 Israel should no longer fear. She will not be "ashamed" (*bôš*, see 1:29) or "confounded" (*kalam*, or "dishonored," see 30:3). She will not

---

"the married wife" as Israel when she had a king. Israel in captivity will yet be greater than in her former history. These views miss the eschatological nature of the passage. The married wife of God is the OT Israel. The "barren" and "desolate" wife is Israel under the judgments predicted by Isaiah. This same wife will enjoy God's blessings when she returns to the Lord and enters the kingdom.

[3]Verse 2 has historical significance. It served as the text for William Carey's sermon to the Northampton Baptist Association at Nottingham, England, on May 31, 1792. Carey developed two points from the verse: (1) Expect great things from God, and (2) attempt great things for God. As a result of the message, the pastors formed the Baptist Missionary Society. This organization led the way for the modern missionary movement.

[4]Alexander, II, 310, understands "right" and "left" as "indefinite expressions meaning on all sides or in all directions." Young, III, 362, has this same view. There are, however, passages in the OT that can be understood only by referencing directions to the east, e.g., Gen. 14:15, Hobah on the "left hand of the Damascus," to the north; Exod. 14:22, "a wall . . . on their right hand, and on their left," on the north and south of the people; Josh. 19:27, Cabul, on the "left hand," to the north; and Ezek. 16:46, Samaria, at the "left hand," to the north, and Sodom, at the "right hand," to the south.

5 *For thy Maker is thine husband; the Lord of hosts is his name; and thy Redeemer the Holy One of Israel; The God of the whole earth shall he be called.*

6 *For the Lord hath called thee as a woman forsaken and grieved in spirit, and a wife of youth, when thou wast refused, saith thy God.*

7 *For a small moment have I forsaken thee; but with great mercies will I gather thee.*

8 *In a little wrath I hid my face from thee for a moment; but with everlasting kindness will I have mercy on thee, saith the Lord thy Redeemer.*

be "put to shame" (*ḥaper*, or "be confounded"). There is no significant difference here between *bôš*, *kalam*, and *ḥaper*. The repetition of the thought strengthens the promise. She will put behind her the "shame of thy youth," the Egyptian bondage. She will also forget the "reproach of thy widowhood," the Babylonian captivity, v. 4.

Their "husband" (*bo^{c}alayik*) is their "Maker" (*^{c}ośayik*).[5] He is the "Lord of hosts," the ruler of the heavenly and earthly hosts. Their Redeemer (*go^{ɔ}el*, see 35:9) is the Holy God. He will be recognized as "the God of the whole earth," v. 5. He has called Israel to Himself from their oppression. She is like a forsaken wife with a sad spirit and like the wife of a man's youth, once loved but later rejected, v. 6.[6] He has briefly turned from her. Now He will bring her back to Himself with great "mercies" (better "compassions"), v. 7. The phrase "in a little wrath" is better "with overflowing [*šeṣep*][7] wrath." God has been angry with His people for a short time. Now He will show "mercy" (again "compas-

---

[5]The AV translation reverses the order of the Hebrew. By placing *ba^{c}al* at the first, the text places the emphasis first on the relationship with God, then on His might. The words *bo^{c}alayik* and *^{c}ośayik* are honorific plurals; see Waltke and O'Connor, p. 122. These occur naturally in referring to God.

[6]McKenzie, p. 139, misunderstands the image. He concludes that the phrase "echoes polygamy." The "wife of one's youth" is the first of the wives, who still has a "privileged position." The Bible, however, presents Israel as the only wife of God. While God may have set her aside temporarily because of her sin, He has not taken another wife in her place. When she becomes faithful, she will be restored to her position.

[7]The word *šeṣep* occurs only here. It is a variant spelling of *šetep*, "overflow, flood." The spelling was possibly influenced by the following word *qeṣep*, "wrath." Isaiah often uses assonance, e.g., *k^{e}hereg h^{a}rugayw horag*, 27:7; *w^{e}kelay kelayw*, 32:7; *ûbarad b^{e}redet*, 32:19. The LXX translates μικρῷ, "small, little." The Vulgate translates *momento*, "short." These are both likely interpretive, seeking a contrast with "everlasting."

9 *For this is as the waters of Noah unto me: for as I have sworn that the waters of Noah should no more go over the earth; so have I sworn that I would not be wroth with thee, nor rebuke thee.*
10 *For the mountains shall depart, and the hills be removed; but my kindness shall not depart from thee, neither shall the covenant of my peace be removed, saith the Lord that hath mercy on thee.*

sion") by showing everlasting "kindness" (*ḥesed*, "loyalty," see 16:5) to her. The name "Redeemer" (*goʾel*, cf. 35:9) shows His special relation to the nation, v. 8.

9–10 The Lord's promise is as the "waters of Noah," i.e., the Noachic covenant, to Him; cf. Genesis 9:12–17.[8] In this, the Lord swore never to inundate the earth again. This was an everlasting covenant. So the Lord will never be "wroth" (*qaṣap*, see 8:21) with His redeemed people.[9] This is clearly a kingdom promise, to be fulfilled after the nation returns to Him, v. 9.[10] The mountains, symbols of stability, may move. The hills may "be removed" (*môṭ*, or "shake," see 24:19). In contrast, the Lord will not reject Israel. He will not take His "kindness" (or "loyalty," *ḥesed*, see 16:5) from them. Likewise, His covenant bringing "peace" (*šalôm*, see 9:6) to the nation will not be "removed" (*môṭ*).[11] The use of *môṭ* is deliberate. The Lord contrasts the covenant with the shaking of the hills in an earthquake. God's covenant is steadfast, firm, not something to shake with the times or circumstances, v. 10.

---

[8]Leupold, p. 242; Skinner, p. 154; and Whitehouse, II, 213, understand the phrase "the waters of Noah" as "the days of Noah." The difference is slight, *kᵉmê noaḥ* for *kîmê noaḥ*. The LXX, 1QIsaᵃ, and many Hebrew mss support the MT. The sense of the verse is the same with both readings.

[9]Rawlinson, II, 315, understands this as a promise to the church. God promises not to send His church into captivity. The context, however, wholly deals with Israel. Nothing here argues that we should abandon the nation in favor of an organization that does not appear elsewhere in the OT.

[10]Brueggemann, *Isaiah 40–66,* p. 155, understands the word "this" to refer to the Babylonian captivity. The Exile is like the Flood in being a time of chaos, caused by the Lord but about to end. God promises that He will never again exile His people. Nothing in the context points to the Exile here. The word "this" points to the logical antecedent in v. 7, the compassion that the Lord promises to show to Israel.

[11]While the root *môṭ* refers to tottering or shaking, it most often has a metaphorical sense of insecurity, e.g., Lev. 25:35 ("decay"); Job 41:23; Ps. 10:6; 13:4. Isaiah here makes a play on words. While *môṭ* first refers to a literal shaking of the hills, its second use is poetical. His covenant is not insecure.

11 O thou afflicted, tossed with tempest, and not comforted, behold, I will lay thy stones with fair colours, and lay thy foundations with sapphires.

12 And I will make thy windows of agates, and thy gates of carbuncles, and all thy borders of pleasant stones.

13 And all thy children shall be taught of the Lord; and great shall be the peace of thy children.

14 In righteousness shalt thou be established: thou shalt be far from oppression; for thou shalt not fear: and from terror; for it shall not come near thee.

b. The Protection of Israel 54:11–17

11–12 Isaiah gives a brief description of the New Jerusalem that marks the kingdom. Though Jerusalem is now an "afflicted" (*ʿanî*, see 3:14) city, one not "comforted" (*naham*, see 1:24), God will build it with signs of beauty. He will lay the stones in the walls with "fair colours" (*pûk*, "antimony"),[12] giving a black color to the mortar. He will stud the foundations with "sapphires," blue or bluish purple gemstones, v. 11. He will make the "windows" (or "battlements"), projections on the walls, from "agates," unknown precious stones, possibly rubies. He will make the gates of "carbuncles" (*ʾeqdah*).[13] The "borders," i.e., the outer walls, will be of "pleasant stones." Revelation 21:18–21 develops the passage further, v. 12.[14]

13–14 The Holy Spirit will indwell the "children" (better "sons") of the city so that they are "taught [*limmûd*][15] of the Lord"; cf. Jeremiah 31:31–34. This will produce great "peace" (*šalôm*, see 9:6). The context

---

[12]The word *pûk* occurs here and at II Kings 9:30; I Chron. 29:2; and Jer. 4:30. Although metallic antimony is silvery white (note "glistering stones," I Chron. 29:2), the powdered form contributes to a black substance used by women in coloring their eyebrows and eyelids.

[13]The word *ʾeqdah* is a *hapax legomenon*. The root *qadah* means "to burn, kindle." This has led to several suggestions: "carbuncles" or fiery gemstones such as "beryl" or "crystal." The LXX translates λίθους κρυστάλλου, "crystalline stones." The Vulgate translates *lapides sculptos*, "graven stones." Rev. 21:21 indicates that the gates of heaven are each made of single pearls. The words "pearl" or "pearls," however, do not occur clearly in the OT. This leaves the meaning of *ʾeqdah* tentative.

[14]Henry, IV, 313, and Fausset, p. 735, spiritualize the passage to make it refer to the church. The church on earth will be glorious. There is, however, no reason to depart from a literal sense here, particularly when the NT supports the idea of a beautiful New Jerusalem.

[15]The passive participle "taught" (*limmûd*) may have the force of a noun. For this reason, Alexander, II, 317; Delitzsch, II, 350; and Goldingay, p. 317, understand something like "all your children will be disciples of the Lord." While this is possible, I prefer the verbal sense brought out by the NT, "your sons will be taught by the Lord."

15 *Behold, they shall surely gather together, but not by me: whosoever
    shall gather together against thee shall fall for thy sake.*
16 *Behold, I have created the smith that bloweth the coals in the fire,
    and that bringeth forth an instrument for his work; and I have cre-
    ated the waster to destroy.*
17 *No weapon that is formed against thee shall prosper; and every
    tongue that shall rise against thee in judgment thou shalt condemn.
    This is the heritage of the servants of the Lord, and their righteous-
    ness is of me, saith the Lord.*

here suggests that this is an attitude that embraces both inward and outward peace. The NT quotes from the verse to prove that it is God's
teaching that draws men to Himself, John 6:45, v. 13. Their righteousness will bring God's blessing. He will keep oppression from them. As a
result, they will not fear, nor will "terror" (or "destruction") come on
them, v. 14.

15–17 Others may "gather together" (*gôr yagûr*, or "fiercely attack")[16]
against Israel but this is not from the Lord. No matter who oppose Israel,
they will fail. The final verses of the chapter introduce a new eschatological thought. Israel will face opposition during the kingdom. This
undoubtedly refers to the rebellion of the nations at the end of the millennium, cf. Revelation 20:7–9, v. 15. The Lord has brought the smith
into existence. He "bloweth the coals in the fire" with his bellows to increase the heat. By this means he makes "an instrument" (*kᵉlî*, see 39:2)
for his work. The word *kᵉlî* has a broad range of meaning. The context
here argues that this is a weapon made for use against the Lord and His
people. The Lord has created also the "waster" (or "destroyer") to bring
ruin. This is the soldier who uses the weapons, v. 16. The Lord will control, however, the weapons that others bring against Israel. No weapon
will be successful. Israel will condemn the speech that seeks "judgment"
(*mišpaṭ*, see 1:17), the charges that others make against them. This is
their "heritage" because they are God's servants. The "righteousness" of
the people, now experienced because of their new relation to God
through Jesus Christ, is a gift from the Lord, v. 17.

---

[16]The construction is emphatic. The infinitive followed by the imperfect verb suggests
the certainty of opposition. It is questionable whether the verb is *gûr* I, "to sojourn," i.e.,
"gather together," or *gûr* II, "to stir up strife." Delitzsch, II, 351; Slotki, p. 268; and Vine,
p. 156, understand *gûr* I. Leupold, II, 243; Barnes, II, 294; and Skinner, *Isaiah XL–LXVI,*
p. 156, understand *gûr* II. The hostile context supports *gûr* II, "to attack." If *gûr* I,
"gather," is understood, it must have a hostile sense, gathering to threaten the nation.

Practical Applications from Chapter 54

1. The Blessing of the Lord
   a. The cause for joy, v. 1*a*
   b. The multiplication of the people, v. 1*b*
   c. The enlargement of the land, vv. 2–3
   d. The escape from past sorrows, v. 4
   e. The relationship with the Lord, vv. 5–10
      (1) Recognition of His position, v. 5
      (2) Demonstration of His mercy, vv. 6–8
      (3) Promise of His loyalty, vv. 9–10
2. The Millennial Kingdom, vv. 11–17
   a. The city of God's people, vv. 11–14
      (1) The description of God's city, vv. 11–12
      (2) The peace of God's people, vv. 13–14
   b. The rebellion of Satan's people, vv. 15–17
      (1) The failure of the rebellion, v. 15
      (2) The power of God, v. 16
      (3) The protection of Israel, v. 17

1 *Ho, every one that thirsteth, come ye to the waters, and he that hath*
no money; come ye, buy, and eat; yea, come, buy wine and milk
without money and without price.
2 *Wherefore do ye spend money for that which is not bread? and your*
labour for that which satisfieth not? hearken diligently unto me, and
eat ye that which is good, and let your soul delight itself in fatness.
3 *Incline your ear, and come unto me: hear, and your soul shall live;*
and I will make an everlasting covenant with you, even the sure mer-
cies of David.

ISAIAH 55

To enter the kingdom discussed in c. 54, there must be a new relationship with God. The Lord now develops this thought. He invites the
people to come to Him and freely receive the spiritual gifts that He
gives, v. 1. Why should they waste their resources on that which does not
satisfy, v. 2? He will give them the mercies that are fulfilled in Christ, v.
3. He has given "David," His Son, to lead Israel and to rule the Gentile
nations, vv. 4–5. Isaiah urges the people to turn to the Lord, vv. 6–7. His
thoughts and ways are higher than those of man, vv. 8–9. He will bless
the earth with fruit, v. 10. His Word likewise will bring forth fruit, v. 11.
The people will rejoice in His kingdom, v. 12*a*. The land will flourish to
show God's blessing, a blessing that will be eternal, vv. 12*b*–13.

3. The Lord's Salvation 55:1–13

1–3 The Lord calls everyone who "thirsteth." The verb is here a
metaphorical picture of an intense desire; cf. Matthew 5:6. He invites
these to come to the "waters," again a metaphorical picture, this time of
spiritual blessings.[1] The Lord freely gives water, wine, and milk. Water,
44:3; Ezekiel 36:25; wine, Proverbs 9:2, 5; and milk, Joel 3:18, all occur
elsewhere in a figurative sense, representing spiritual blessings.[2] God
gives these gifts "without price." They are thus available to all, not just
those who can afford them. As Revelation 22:17 says, "whosoever will"
may "take the water of life freely," v. 1.

---

[1]Kraeling, p. 199, understands v. 1 as an invitation to the people to return to Jerusalem,
where they will be able to enjoy the blessings of free food and drink. From the context of
vv. 3–5, speaking of the covenant made with David, v. 1 is rather an invitation to partake in
the spiritual blessings given by God as He fulfills the promises made earlier to the nation.

[2]Slotki, pp. 269–70, understands "water" as a symbol for the Law and "wine" and
"milk" as symbols for learning. This severely limits the symbolism. On the basis of the
figurative use of "water," "wine," and "milk" elsewhere, it is appropriate to make them
general figures of spiritual blessing.

Why should the people "spend money" (better "weigh out silver")? The literal translation is important since "money" did not come into use until the seventh century B.C., about one hundred years after Isaiah. Until that time, buyers would weigh out silver or some other substance; cf. 46:6; Genesis 23:16; I Kings 20:39 ("pay" = "weigh"). The first mention of coins, "drams," in the OT is in the fifth century B.C. books of Chronicles, Ezra, and Nehemiah.

Why should the people purchase that which is "not bread," i.e., that which does not nourish? Why should they work for that which does not satisfy? The Lord again invites them to come to Him for food that is good. If they come, they will "delight . . . in fatness." The word "fatness" occurs elsewhere as a symbol of the rich blessings that God gives, e.g., Psalm 36:8; 63:5; Jeremiah 31:14, v. 2. The Lord commands the people to listen to Him. If they respond, they will "live." In view of the context, this offers them eternal life. The Lord will confirm the everlasting covenant of David with them. This covenant, given in II Samuel 7:12–16, promises Israel the everlasting reign of Jesus Christ. The phrase "even the sure mercies of David" is in apposition to the "everlasting covenant." This describes the covenant as conveying the faithful "mercies" (or "loyalties," *ḥesed*, see 16:5) of God to David. Paul quotes from this verse in his sermon at Antioch in Pisidia, Acts 13:34.[3] The quotation establishes the messianic fulfillment of the prophecy.[4] The greatest example of the "mercies" of God is the gift of His Son as the Savior of mankind, v. 3.

---

[3]Paul's use of v. 3 is inconclusive as to the sense of *ḥesed*. Acts 13:34 lit. reads: "the holy and faithful things of David." The supplied word *things* is understood differently: "blessings" (NASB), "mercies" (AV), "promises" (Stewart Custer, *Witness to Christ: a Commentary on Acts* [Greenville, S.C.: BJU Press, 2000], p. 193); "things" (William Barclay, *The Acts of the Apostles* [Philadelphia: The Westminster Press, 1955], p. 111), etc. I have opted for "loyalties" as being a dominant sense of the word *ḥesed*.

[4]Walter C. Kaiser Jr., "The Unfailing Kindnesses Promised to David: Isaiah 55:3," *JSOT* 45: 95, denies that v. 3 refers to the Messiah. He follows Delitzsch, II, 355, who states, "The directly messianic application of the name 'David' is to be objected to, on the ground that the Messiah is never so called without further remark." This statement ignores the comment in v. 4 that refers to "David" in v. 3. Such passages as Jer. 30:9; Ezek. 34:23–24; 37:24; and Hos. 3:5 illustrate that the OT often calls Messiah by the name of "David." Both Delitzsch and Kaiser refer v. 4 to the historical David and v. 5 to the Messiah. They refer to v. 4 as the type and v. 5 as the antitype. In view of the NT's use of v. 3, the passage must be messianic.

4 *Behold, I have given him for a witness to the people, a leader and*
  commander to the people.
5 *Behold, thou shalt call a nation that thou knowest not, and nations*
  that knew not thee shall run unto thee because of the Lord thy God,
  and for the Holy One of Israel; for he hath glorified thee.
6 *Seek ye the Lord while he may be found, call ye upon him while he*
  is near:
7 *Let the wicked forsake his way, and the unrighteous man his*
  thoughts: and let him return unto the Lord, and he will have mercy
  upon him; and to our God, for he will abundantly pardon.

4–5 The Lord has given "him," the second David, as a "witness" to
the nations. Through His position as "leader and commander to the
people," He will lead Israel to victories over their enemies. As so often
in the book, the statement is a prophetic perfect. The thought is so sure
to God that He states it as an accomplished fact, v. 4.[5] The Lord will call
all nations to Himself. The Gentile nations that formerly did not know
Him as their King will come to Him. God ("he") will be with Him
("thee") to give Him glory in the eyes of all mankind, v. 5.

6–7 The thought of Messiah's future reign leads Isaiah to speak. He
urges the people to seek the Lord during the time that He may be found.
They should call on Him in prayer "while" He is near them. In both
phrases, the b^e-preposition ("while") has a temporal sense. This implies
that there will be a time the Lord may *not* be found, when He is *not* near.
This agrees with teaching elsewhere that urges men to seek the Lord
now, cf. 49:8 (II Cor. 6:2; Prov. 27:1; 29:1; Jer. 29:12–14), v. 6. At the
same time they seek Him, they should abandon their sins and "return"
(*šûb*, see 1:27) to the Lord. They should abandon both their "way," their
wicked practices, and their "thoughts," the evil that they dwell on men-
tally. This will bring God's mercy and abundant pardon to them, v. 7.

---

[5]The only real question with v. 4 is whether the Lord speaks of the historical King
David or whether He refers to the coming King David. Skinner, p. 160, analyzes the problem well although he adopts an intermediate position. He applies v. 4 to King David and
v. 5 to Messiah. Price, p. 233, agrees with this position. The majority of authors make the
pronouns in v. 5 refer to Israel. They conclude that God transfers David's authority and
power to the nation. Among those with this position are Goldingay, p. 313; Kelley, p. 349;
and Herbert, *Isaiah 40–66*, p. 124. Watts, *Isaiah 34–66*, p. 246, stands alone in referring
v. 5 to Darius, but the context of v. 3 and v. 5 is clearly messianic. The antecedent to the
pronoun "him" in v. 4 is in v. 3. In addition, v. 5 points to the future inclusion of the Gentiles in the kingdom. For this reason, I refer the passage, vv. 3–5, to Messiah.

8 For my thoughts are not your thoughts, neither are your ways my ways, saith the Lord.
9 For as the heavens are higher than the earth, so are my ways higher than your ways, and my thoughts than your thoughts.
10 For as the rain cometh down, and the snow from heaven, and returneth not thither, but watereth the earth, and maketh it bring forth and bud, that it may give seed to the sower, and bread to the eater:
11 So shall my word be that goeth forth out of my mouth: it shall not return unto me void, but it shall accomplish that which I please, and it shall prosper in the thing whereto I sent it.

> Those who come to the Lord must leave their sin. No one comes to Christ while intending to continue in his or her sin.

8–11 The Lord's thoughts and ways differ from those of man. The words "thoughts" and "ways" refer back to v. 7. Those who come to the Lord should leave their evil thoughts and ways because these are not His thoughts and ways, v. 8.[6] Isaiah illustrates this truth by contrasting the height of the starry heavens with that of the earth. The earth is our reference point. We stand on it. Even if we should climb the highest mountain, we would still be on the surface of the earth. The heavens, however, extend light-years away from the earth. God's ways and thoughts are indeed "higher," more profound and more noble, than man's ways and thoughts, v. 9.

Isaiah now illustrates the certainty of God's promise to receive those who come to Him. Moisture, "rain" and "snow," comes from the sky to

---

[6]Rawlinson, II, 330; Barnes, II, 302; and Fausset, p. 737, refer vv. 8–9 to the "pardon" mentioned in v. 7. Man finds it difficult to pardon but God's ways are not man's ways. The view is possible. Goldingay, p. 314, refers God's ways and thoughts to "Yahweh's way of running the world and fulfilling a plan for it." He fulfilled this through Cyrus, a way different from what Israel would have developed. Slotki, p. 271, refers the two verses to "the transcendence of God's thoughts and ways." While these views have an element of truth in them, they neglect the context of vv. 6–7. Smart, pp. 225–26, correctly says that the statement "is not an abstract statement of the infinite distance between God and man, but rather, a warning to Israel that its thoughts and ways are not those of a people in covenant with God." Brueggemann, *Isaiah 40–66,* p. 160, refers Israel's ways and thoughts to their desire to remain in Babylon. God, however, planned a "wholly new future in Jerusalem." The view ignores the context.

12 *For ye shall go out with joy, and be led forth with peace: the moun-*
tains and the hills shall break forth before you into singing, and all
the trees of the field shall clap their hands.
13 *Instead of the thorn shall come up the fir tree, and instead of the*
brier shall come up the myrtle tree: and it shall be to the Lord for a
name, for an everlasting sign that shall not be cut off.

water the earth and bring forth fruit. From this we gain seed for future crops and food to sustain life, v. 10. In the same way, God's Word will bring forth fruit. The fruit of God's Word is redemption, drawing men away from their sin to Him. The gospel will not return to the Lord "empty," devoid of consequences. It will bring forth spiritual fruit, prospering in the cause for which the Lord had sent it, v. 11.[7]

12–13 Israel will rejoice in the Lord when He establishes His kingdom.[8] They will know the "peace" (*šalôm*, see 9:6) that He alone can give. In that day, the land will rejoice. The mountains will sing as they experience freedom from the curse that has plagued the earth. The trees will clap their "hands," the branches, as they enjoy abundant fruitfulness during the millennial kingdom. The picture is of branches rubbing against one another because of the luxuriant growth of the tree, v. 12. There will no longer be the "thorn" (*na*ᶜᵃ*ṣûṣ*) and "brier" (*sirpad*), evidence of God's curse on creation.[9] Rather, the "fir tree," probably the

---

[7]This promise puzzles many Christians. They may witness without seeing decisions. Many become discouraged and stop their attempts at evangelism. The problem is that we define "fruit" wrongly. The "fruit" of evangelism comes in different ways. It may leave a person without excuse. He hears the gospel and rejects it. He will stand before God in judgment. The gospel seed may also germinate later into a decision for Christ. The fruit here lies in bringing the unsaved person a step closer to the time he will receive the Lord. The gospel may also result in an immediate decision. All of these are the "fruit" of evangelism. It is the Lord's responsibility to determine the fruit that we bear in evangelism. It is the Christian's responsibility to be faithful.

[8]Among others, Rawlinson, II, 331; Kelley, p. 350; and Slotki, p. 272, view vv. 12–13 as describing the return from the Babylonian captivity. It is difficult to see how this can be an "everlasting sign" that will not be cut off. The passage is better understood as eschatological, referring to the kingdom, when Israel dwells in a land free from the curse of sin.

[9]We must translate the words *na*ᶜᵃ*ṣûṣ* and *sirpad* from the context. The word *na*ᶜᵃ*ṣûṣ* occurs only here and at 7:19, where it is plural. The translation "thorn" or "thorn-bush" is appropriate. The versions deal variously with the *hapax legomenon sirpad*. The LXX renders it κονύζης, "fleabane," probably not correct since this is a desirable plant. The Vulgate gives *urtica*, "nettles." Leslie, p. 202, gives "desert plant." Childs, p. 432, renders it "thistle." Näglesbach, p. 600, suggests "flea-wort," a plant whose seeds have a mild laxative effect. These efforts come from the verse, which requires some kind of undesirable plant.

cypress, and the "myrtle tree," cf. 41:19, will grow. The land, once barren, now flourishes with new plant life. This will serve as a "name," i.e., a "memorial," to the Lord. Everywhere men look there will be evidence of the Lord's gracious blessing. The word "sign" (ʾôt, see 7:11) almost always refers to a religious sign of some kind. The "everlasting sign" here is the permanent blessing of God on the earth. The restored earth will never be "cut off" again by judgment, v. 13.[10]

Practical Application from Chapter 55

The Salvation of Man and Rule over the Earth
1. The Thirsty Man, vv. 1–3
    a. The desire for salvation: "every one that thirsteth," v. 1*a*
    b. The offer of salvation: "come ye, buy, and eat; yea, come . . . hearken diligently," vv. 1*b, 2b*
    c. The missing of salvation: "that which is not bread . . . satisfieth not," v. 2*a*
    d. The gift of salvation: "without money and without price," v. 1*c*
    e. The eternity of salvation: "everlasting covenant," v. 3
2. The Victorious Leader, vv. 4–5
    a. The work of the Savior: "a witness . . . a leader . . . a commander," v. 4
    b. The response to the Savior: "nations that knew not thee shall run unto thee," v. 5
3. The Seeker After God, vv. 6–7
    a. The nearness of the Lord: "may be found . . . near," v. 6
    b. The prayer of the sinner: "seek ye the Lord . . . call ye upon Him," v. 6
    c. The practice of the repentant: "forsake his way, and . . . his thoughts," v. 7*a*
    d. The mercy of God: "he will have mercy . . . he will abundantly pardon," v. 7*b*

---

[10]Henry, p. 321, and Fausset, p. 737, spiritualize the passage. They make it refer to the church as flourishing while the "briers" and "thorns," enemies of the church, are cut off. While it is true that the church will flourish during the kingdom, the passage here is literal. It refers to the removal of the curse on the land so that it brings forth vegetation apart from those plants associated with the curse.

4. The Nature and Work of God, vv. 8–11

    a. The requirement for purity: "my thoughts" and "my ways" are not "your thoughts" and "your ways," v. 8

    b. The contrast with man: "my thoughts" and "my ways" are higher than "your thoughts" and "your ways," v. 9

    c. The provision for man: "seed to the sower, and bread to the eater," v. 10

    d. The fruit of the Word: "it shall accomplish . . . it shall prosper . . . ," v. 11

5. The Kingdom of Christ, vv. 12–13

    a. The rejoicing of His people: "with joy . . . with praise," v. 12*a*

    b. The fruitfulness of the land: "singing . . . clap their hands . . . fir tree . . . myrtle," v. 12*b*, 13*a*

    c. The continuance of His blessing: "everlasting sign that shall not be cut off," v. 13*b*

1 Thus saith the Lord, Keep ye judgment, and do justice: for my salvation is near to come, and my righteousness to be revealed.

2 Blessed is the man that doeth this, and the son of man that layeth hold on it; that keepeth the sabbath from polluting it, and keepeth his hand from doing any evil.

ISAIAH 56

The present chapter continues to emphasize the kingdom age. The people should be holy since the Lord's deliverance is imminent, v. 1. They should keep the Law, v. 2. In the kingdom, no one need be separated from the Lord, v. 3. He will give those who keep His commands a name in His house, vv. 4–5. Proselytes who keep His commands will worship Him, vv. 6–7. He will gather both Jews and Gentiles to Himself, v. 8. He condemns the wicked leaders, however, who fail to oppose sin and instead seek personal gain, vv. 9–12.

VII. Prophecies of Future Glory 56:1–66:24[1]
A. Instruction of the People 56:1–57:21
1. Assurance of the Righteous 56:1–8

1–2 The Lord initially continues His emphasis on eschatology. He urges the people to be holy. They should keep "judgment" (*mišpaṭ*, better "justice," see 1:17) and do "justice" (*ṣᵉdaqâ*, better "righteousness," see 1:21). They should do this in view of the soon return of the Lord. He will bring His "salvation" near and reveal His "righteousness"; cf. I John 2:28; 3:1–3. The consistent view of Scripture is that the Lord's return is imminent, something that can happen at any moment, v.1. As an example of right behavior, Isaiah cites two commandments from the Law. The weak "man" (*ᵉnôš*, see 2:11) who does not "pollute" (*ḥalal*, see 23:9) the Sabbath and avoids evil will be "blessed" (*ʾašᵉrê*, see 30:18). With reference to the Sabbath, *ḥalal* indicates profaning the day by treating it

---

[1]Beginning with c. 56, the style of writing changes from the previous chapters. For this reason, many assume that the author has changed. While the author is often called Trito-Isaiah, the current view is that c. 56–66 are the work of a school of men who followed Isaianic principles. These men supposedly lived in Palestine after the return from the Babylonian captivity. There are no valid reasons that demand that we accept this view. While there are differences in the style and vocabulary, these represent the change of subjects discussed. There are as well similarities in the style and vocabulary that argue for a single author of the book. Among those who argue for multiple authorship of c. 56–66 are Goldingay, p. 315; Westermann, pp. 27–28; and Wright, p. 137. The Introduction summarizes the arguments against multiple authors and for a single author of the book.

3 *Neither let the son of the stranger, that hath joined himself to the Lord, speak, saying, The Lord hath utterly separated me from his people: neither let the eunuch say, Behold, I am a dry tree.*

4 *For thus saith the Lord unto the eunuchs that keep my sabbaths, and choose the things that please me, and take hold of my covenant;*

5 *Even unto them will I give in mine house and within my walls a place and a name better than of sons and of daughters: I will give them an everlasting name, that shall not be cut off.*

6 *Also the sons of the stranger, that join themselves to the Lord, to serve him, and to love the name of the Lord, to be his servants, every one that keepeth the sabbath from polluting it, and taketh hold of my covenant;*

7 *Even them will I bring to my holy mountain, and make them joyful in my house of prayer: their burnt offerings and their sacrifices shall be accepted upon mine altar; for mine house shall be called an house of prayer for all people.*

8 *The Lord God which gathereth the outcasts of Israel saith, Yet will I gather others to him, beside those that are gathered unto him.*

in a common way, making it no different from any other day of the week. The keeping of the Sabbath represents the first part of the Ten Commandments governing man's relationship with God. He should as well avoid "evil" (*ra*ᶜ, see 3:9). This command summarizes the second part of the Ten Commandments, which deal with man's relationship with mankind, v. 2.

3–8 The millennial kingdom will allow worship by all who come to the Lord. The "son of the stranger," a proselyte who has "joined himself" (*hannilwâ*)[2] to Judaism, and the "eunuch," one who has been mutilated so as to allow service in some heathen court, express their concern. Has the Lord separated those with a heathen background from His people? In the OT, the "stranger" could be admitted to full participation in worship if he would accept the requirements of the Law, Exodus 12:48–49. There were restrictions placed on the Ammonites and Moabites, Deuteronomy 23:3; Nehemiah 13:1, and Edomites and Egyptians, Deuteronomy 23:7–8. Is the eunuch a "dry tree," without the potential of bearing fruit? The statement hints at the restriction of

---

[2]The vowel pointing of the verb "joined" (*hannilwâ*) is an irregular 3ms perfect but the sense is clear. If we point it as a *nip*ᶜ*al* participle, *hannilweh*, it is in apposition to the "son of the stranger." This clarifies the position of the proselyte. The reflexive sense of the *nip*ᶜ*al* fits nicely here. Delitzsch, II, 361, and Näglesbach, p. 605, leave the verb pointed as a perfect and explain the *h*ᵉ-prefix as having the force of a relative pronoun, a rare use.

Deuteronomy 23:1, a verse that refers to those who mutilate themselves in order to follow some cultic ritual. Isaiah tells them not to have these concerns, v. 3. The eunuch should live a godly life. As in v. 2, the Lord again mentions the keeping of the Sabbath and doing that which pleases God. In addition, He mentions the need to accept the covenant. He does not develop the idea of the New Covenant here. Such passages as Jeremiah 31:31–34 and Hebrews 8:7–13 give more insight into this. Since this is a kingdom context, the covenant here is that made through placing one's faith in Christ as man's Savior, v. 4. God will give those eunuchs who please Him a "place" (*yad*)[3] and a "name" in His "house." The "house" of God occurs often in the OT to denote God's family, His people, e.g., Numbers 12:7; Psalm 23:6; 36:8. These eunuchs will have their remembrance within the "walls" of God's house. These are more than the walls of the temple or the walls of Jerusalem. The "walls" parallel the "house" and therefore refer to the boundaries of the house of God.[4] God will give "them" (*lô*)[5] a name, i.e., a reputation, better than that that comes from having a family. While some have their name carried on through their families, the faithful eunuch will himself live forever.[6] This is a kingdom promise, v. 5. In the same way, the "sons of the stranger," proselytes, who come to the Lord will worship Him. They serve and love His name, i.e., His nature. Once more, as in vv. 2, 4, not "polluting" (*halal*, see 23:9) the Sabbath and accepting the New

---

[3]The word *yad* normally means "hand." There are, however, two places in which it has a sense of "memorial," I Sam. 15:12 and II Sam. 18:18. Among others, Whitehouse, II, 243; Wright, p. 139; and Leupold, II, 266, understand it in that sense here. Price, p. 238, has a curious view. He understands *yad* literally as if the Lord will "preserve the hand print of such a devout person within his walls." The translation "place," however, occurs regularly elsewhere, e.g., Num. 2:17; Deut. 23:12; Jer. 6:3. This gives the correct sense and does not need to be changed from the AV.

[4]Rawlinson, II, 345; Barnes, II, 307; and Watts, *Isaiah 34–66,* p. 249, understand the "walls" as those of Jerusalem. Wright, p. 139, refers them to the temple. The kingdom context and the parallelism to "house" argue that the walls refer to the family of God.

[5]The final "them" is singular, *lô*, in the MT. The Isaiah Scroll, LXX, and Vulgate read the plural *lahem*. This parallels the first "them" (*lahem*). It is equally possible that *lô* has an indefinite sense, "each one, such a one."

[6]George A. F. Knight, *The New Israel: A Commentary on the Book of Isaiah 56–66,* 1985, p. 8, is extreme. He includes "the homosexual" among others who gain a place in the covenant "even though these folk are unable to form a link in the historical chain of human life." The ability to father children has nothing to do with inclusion under the New Covenant. Only if the homosexual repents of his sin and places his faith in the finished work of Christ can he be included in the covenant.

9 *All ye beasts of the field, come to devour, yea, all ye beasts in the forest.*
10 *His watchmen are blind: they are all ignorant, they are all dumb dogs, they cannot bark; sleeping, lying down, loving to slumber.*
11 *Yea, they are greedy dogs which can never have enough, and they are shepherds that cannot understand: they all look to their own way, every one for his gain, from his quarter.*
12 *Come ye, say they, I will fetch wine, and we will fill ourselves with strong drink; and to morrow shall be as this day, and much more abundant.*

Covenant they show their love for the Lord. Though these are Gentiles, they belong to God's family in the kingdom, v. 6.[7] They will worship at His "holy mountain," the location of the temple. They will rejoice in His "house of prayer"; cf. I Kings 8:41–43 (II Chron. 6:32–33). He will accept their burnt offerings and other animal sacrifices (*zebaḥ*).[8] The Lord again stresses that His house will be a place of prayer for all people in the kingdom. The Lord based His scathing rebuke of the Jews in the temple on this passage, cf. Matthew 21:13 (Mark 11:17; Luke 19:46), v. 7. The Lord God who gathers the "outcasts [or 'dispersed'] of Israel" has also promised to gather "others," Gentiles, to Himself; cf. 19:16–25; 45:14; 49:22; John 10:16. The ultimate fulfillment of the promise lies in the millennial reign of Christ, v. 8.

2. Condemnation of the Wicked 56:9–57:2

9–12 Isaiah now begins to condemn the faithless leaders of Judah. In view of the glorious future that lies ahead, the failure of the nation's leaders is all the worse. When they should have set the example of faithfulness, they instead practiced wickedness. Isaiah compares the wicked leaders of Judah's enemies to "beasts," ready to attack the nation, v. 9.[9]

---

[7]Henry, p. 324, makes the passage refer to the return from Babylon. The Jews should invite their neighbors in Babylon to come with them. They should forsake their gods and begin worshiping Israel's God. The passage, however, relates to the millennial kingdom.

[8]The important teaching in this verse deals with the purpose of sacrifices in the kingdom. The OT sacrifices did not bring forgiveness of sin, Heb. 10:4. That came only through the blood of Christ, Heb. 9:12–14. The sacrifices did, however, let the people show their faith in God. On the basis of this faith, God forgave the sins of the OT saints, Rom. 3:25. There is now no other sacrifice needed, Heb. 10:12. The kingdom sacrifices, then, cannot be for the purpose of securing salvation. They rather are memorials. They look back at the Cross and remind believers of the offering of God's Son on their behalf.

[9]Ibn Ezra, p. 258, understands the "beasts of the field" as "the wicked nations." They come to devour the "beasts of the forest," wicked Israel. I would make the parallelism of

Judah's leaders, their "watchmen," are spiritually blind and ignorant. Isaiah illustrates their condition with three word pictures. (1) They are like dumb dogs that cannot "bark" (*linboaḥ*).[10] Dogs in those times were often kept with the flocks to warn the shepherd of danger, Job 30:1. These, however, are "sleeping" (*hazâ*, or "dreaming"),[11] lazy and so unaware of their danger, v. 10. (2) They are greedy dogs. They have no satisfaction with what they have; they occupy themselves with gaining more. (3) They are self-centered "shepherds" who do not "understand" (*bîn*, see 1:3) that the shepherd cares for the flock.[12] These care only for themselves, seeking personal gain "from his [or 'every'] quarter" (*miqqaṣehû*),[13] i.e., totally, v. 11. As a result of their spiritual blindness, they satisfy their lusts for pleasure. They fill themselves with "wine" and "strong drink"; cf. 5:11. They plan each day to indulge themselves to the same degree or more, v. 12.

---

the two phrases synonymous rather than antithetic. In addition, the context focuses only on the wicked Jewish leaders.

[10]The verb *nabaḥ* is a *hapax legomenon*. Cohen, pp. 114–15, relates it to an Akkadian cognate meaning "to bark." There are also Aramaic and Arabic cognates with this meaning.

[11]The word *hozîm* occurs only here. There is an Arabic cognate meaning "to talk deliriously." This leads to the sense of "raving." Delitzsch, II, 366–67; Slotki, p. 275; and Young, III, 396, adopt this. It refers to someone talking in his sleep. Näglesbach, p. 613, understands "snarling in sleep," the sounds of a sleeping dog. KB, I, 243, suggests "pant," clearly influenced by the "dogs" in the verse. The LXX translates ἐνυπνιαζόμενοι, "dreaming." The Targum offers *nîmîn*, "drowsy, slumbering." The Vulgate gives *videntes vana*, "seeing vain things." The context supports "dreaming."

[12]Kissane, II, 221, understands the shepherds, watchmen, and dogs symbolically. The shepherds are the rulers, the watchmen are the prophets, and the dogs are lesser officials of state. This is unlikely. Dogs nowhere else represent governmental officials. Further, the passage makes these parallel terms. Isaiah calls the watchmen both dogs, v. 10, and shepherds, v. 11.

[13]The word *miqqaṣehû*, lit. "from his end," is difficult to translate. Westermann, p. 316, suggests "one and all." Pieper, p. 501, gives "to his own profit." Skinner, *Isaiah XL–LXVI*, p. 169, renders the word "without exception." Delitzsch, II, 366, goes in a different direction, "throughout his border," to the limit of his influence. The idiom does not translate exactly into English. Some explanatory paraphrase is necessary.

Practical Applications from Chapter 56

1. Whosoever Will May Come
   a. All may worship God. The proselyte need not fear. One formerly dedicated to a system of false worship need not fear, v. 3. Those who keep the Law, illustrated by the fourth commandment, please God, and accept the covenant offered through God's Son, v. 4, will receive recognition among God's people, v. 5.
   b. All may come to God. The proselyte that serves the Lord, those who keep the Law (again illustrated by keeping the Sabbath), and those who accept the New Covenant, v. 6, will worship with joy in the temple. The Lord will accept their sacrifices, and His house will be a place of prayer for them, v. 7. He will gather both Jews and Gentiles to Himself, v. 8.

2. Condemnation of Wicked Leaders
   a. They attack those they should lead, v. 9.
   b. They do not warn of danger, v. 10.
   c. They are greedy, caring only for themselves, v. 11.
   d. They live for pleasure, loving alcohol, v. 12.

1 *The righteous perisheth, and no man layeth it to heart: and merciful men are taken away, none considering that the righteous is taken away from the evil to come.*

2 *He shall enter into peace: they shall rest in their beds, each one walking in his uprightness.*

ISAIAH 57

The chapter continues the theme of instruction for the Jews. In contrast with the wicked who involve themselves with evil, 56:9–12, the righteous escape this through their death, vv. 1–2. Isaiah rebukes the wicked that worship false gods, vv. 3–8, and rely on heathen kings, vv. 9–10. They have turned from the Lord, v. 11. Their false worship will not help them, v. 12. Let them continue to rely on their gods while the righteous rely on God, an eschatological promise, v. 13. He will command a way to be made so that the righteous can come to worship Him, v. 14. The exalted, eternal, and holy God will encourage repentant man, v. 15. He will limit His judgment on mankind, v. 16. Man, however, has continued in his wickedness, v. 17. The Lord will work with him to bring him to Himself, v. 18. He will bless the godly, v. 19, and bring turmoil to the wicked, vv. 20–21.

1–2 The opening verses apparently come from the time of Manasseh; cf. II Kings 21:16. Josephus describes the persecution of the godly: "[Manasseh] was so hardy as to defile the temple of God, and the city, and the whole country . . . for, by setting out from a contempt of God, he barbarously slew all the righteous men that were among the Hebrews; nor would he spare the prophets, for he every day slew some of them, till Jerusalem was overflown with blood."[1] Although the "righteous" are dying at this time, no one "layeth it to heart" (or "sets his heart upon it"); cf. 47:7; 57:11. The "merciful" (or "loyal") die, but no one recognizes that they are being "taken away from the evil [*ra*ᶜ, see 3:9] to come," the national judgment of Israel, v. 1. These martyrs "enter into peace [*šalôm*, see 9:6]" in heaven with God.[2] They "rest in their beds,"

---

[1]*Antiquities* 10.3.1.

[2]Wade, p. 361, equates "peace" with the grave and understands the phrase as completing v. 1. It is difficult, however, to see how the grave is a place of peace. Brueggemann, *Isaiah 40–66*, p. 176, says that "the poetry surely has no notion of life-after-death but only offers an assurance that the righteous are kept peaceably and safely, even though large threats are operative." The word *šalôm* is the direct object of the verb, not an adverb. The righteous enters into "peace." This is the great hope that keeps men faithful in times of adversity.

3 But draw near hither, ye sons of the sorceress, the seed of the adulterer and the whore.
4 Against whom do ye sport yourselves? against whom make ye a wide mouth, and draw out the tongue? are ye not children of transgression, a seed of falsehood,
5 Enflaming yourselves with idols under every green tree, slaying the children in the valleys under the clifts of the rocks?
6 Among the smooth stones of the stream is thy portion; they, they are thy lot: even to them hast thou poured a drink offering, thou hast offered a meat offering. Should I receive comfort in these?
7 Upon a lofty and high mountain hast thou set thy bed: even thither wentest thou up to offer sacrifice.
8 Behind the doors also and the posts hast thou set up thy remembrance: for thou hast discovered thyself to another than me, and art gone up; thou hast enlarged thy bed, and made thee a covenant with them; thou lovedst their bed where thou sawest it.

their graves, "each one walking in his uprightness" (lit. "he who walked in his uprightness"), v. 2.[3]

3. Contention with the Idolaters 57:3–14

3–8 Isaiah calls the wicked to "draw near hither" to listen as he describes them. They are the spiritual descendants of the "sorceress" (or "soothsaying woman"). The term by metonymy stands for the various forms of spiritualism that found a place in Israel. The people are the spiritual seed of the "adulterer" (na'ap) and the "whore," (zanâ, or "prostitute," see 1:21). The description includes both the men and women who worship false gods. Both of these terms often refer to spiritual whoredom as people reject God in favor of false gods, cf. Jeremiah 3:8 (na'ap, "adultery," zanâ, "harlot"), v. 3. They scoff at the righteous. They open their mouths and stick out their tongues in mockery; cf. Psalm 22:7; 35:21. They are the spiritual offspring of "transgression" (pesa', or "rebellion," see 24:20)[4] and of "falsehood" (šeqer, see 9:15), v. 4.

---

[3]Watts, *Isaiah 34–66*, p. 254, explains the variation between singular and plural ("He shall . . . they shall . . . their beds.") by making the plural refer to the wicked "watchmen" in 56:10. This is awkward since the following *qal* masculine singular participle modifies the verb making the subject "walk in his uprightness." There is no need to see anything other than poetic variation in the interchange between singular and plural. The righteous (plural) rest, each one of whom (singular) walked righteously.

[4]The word *pesa'* has a fundamental sense of rebellion connected with it. This results in a break in the relationship between two parties. When referring to man's relationship with God, the word usually indicates some "transgression," which breaks the relationship with God. Only repentance and restoration can prevent punishment from God.

They inflame themselves "with idols" (*ʾelîm*, better "among mighty trees," commonly understood as "oaks")⁵ while practicing sacred prostitution. This takes place among the luxuriant trees of the forests. In addition, they offer their children in the "valleys" (or "ravines," *naḥal*, see 7:19), secluded places where they worship. Child sacrifice was part of the worship of Molech, Leviticus 18:21; II Kings 23:10; and Baal, Jeremiah 19:5; Psalm 106:28, 36, 37. Presumably, the heathen offered their children to other gods as well, v. 5. They set up "smooth stones" (*ḥalaq*)⁶ to their idols in the "streams" (*naḥal*, or "ravines" as in v. 5). They leave drink and "meat" (better "meal") offerings at their site. These stones represent their "portion" (*ḥeleq*),⁷ the only thing they will gain by their worship. The repetition of the pronoun "they" conveys emphasis. "They, they" (*hem hem*, an emphatic statement), the stones themselves, are the portion and lot of the people. Should the Lord receive "comfort" (*naḥam*, see 1:24) from this worship? The rhetorical question demands a "no!" answer, v. 6. They set up their "bed," the site for sacred prostitution in the worship of the gods, on the high mountains. They offer their

---

⁵The word *ʾelîm* may mean "idols"; cf. 45:20 ("god"); 57:5, or "trees"; cf. 61:3. Because of the parallelism with "every green tree," most understand this here as "trees." Barnes, II, 316; Watts, *Isaiah 34–66,* p. 254; and Henry, p. 328, understand "idols." Knight, p. 13, bridges the gap by referring to "sacred oaks."

⁶There is debate as to the source of *hallᵉqê*. Barnes, II, 317, relates it to *halaq* I, "to divide." He considers the word to refer to "the dividings of the valley," i.e., watered portions of the valley set aside for worship. Price, p. 242, follows this view. Skinner, *Isaiah XL–LXVI,* p. 173, relates the word to *halaq* II, "to be smooth, slippery." He considers this a description of the worship of flattering and deceitful false gods. Motyer, *The Prophecy of Isaiah,* p. 472, derives similarly but suggests that it refers to "stones worn by water erosion into shapes suggestive of a resident 'god.'" In a later book, *Isaiah: an Introduction and Commentary,* p. 354, Motyer relates the word to the "duplicity" of "false religion." Kraeling, p. 204, tentatively suggests that Isaiah "consigns [the idolators] to a stony land . . . because they worshiped sacred stones." Näglesbach, p. 617, sees this as a corruption of earlier practices to set up stones as a remembrance of God, e.g., Gen. 28:18; 35:14. W. H. Irwin, "'The, [*sic*] Smooth Stones of the Wady'? Isaiah 57, 6," *CBQ* 29:31–40, argues from Ugaritic for the root *halaq* III, "to die, perish." He translates, "the dead of the Wady" and refers the phrase to child sacrifice and to burial places in "the wady." The Lord here promises retribution to those who have rebelled against Him. Irwin's argument is weakened by the absence of *halaq* III anywhere else in the OT. I have followed the majority view since the pouring of drink offerings and the meal offerings seem more suited to stone idols than to a portion of ground in a wadi.

⁷The combination of *halaq,* "smooth," with *heleq,* "portion," is a play on words, typical of Isaiah's style of writing. He joins *halaq* II, "to be smooth" and *halaq* I, "to divide [into portions]" with both words having the same consonants.

9 *And thou wentest to the king with ointment, and didst increase thy perfumes, and didst send thy messengers far off, and didst debase thyself even unto hell.*

10 *Thou art wearied in the greatness of thy way; yet saidst thou not, There is no hope: thou hast found the life of thine hand; therefore thou wast not grieved.*

sacrifices there, v. 7. The people had set up their "remembrance" in their houses. This likely refers to the household idols that represent the deities they worshiped.[8] The phrase "thou hast discovered thyself to another than me" is better "apart from me you have uncovered yourself." In addition, they had "gone up" and "enlarged" their bed, preparing to enter into spiritual adultery. They had made a covenant with the false gods. They loved the "bed" of these gods. The final phrase, "where thou sawest it," is lit. "you saw the hand [*yad*, see 56:5]."[9] The *yad* may represent a place. Here, it reflects the actions of the people in seeing the place they can commit sacred prostitution. The statement is a harsh rebuke of the people for their worship of false gods, v. 8.

9–10 Rather than trusting the Lord, they sent gifts to the heathen "king" (*melek*)[10] under whom they live; cf. II Kings 16:7–8. They sent

---

[8]Deut. 6:9; 11:20, commands the people to write a portion of God's Word and to place it on the doorpost or gate. Orthodox Jews write Deut. 6:4–9; 11:13–21 on parchment, place it in a case, and affix this to their doorpost. This is called a mezuzah from the Hebrew word meaning "doorpost." Among others, Motyer, *The Prophecy of Isaiah*, p. 473; Leupold, II, 276; and Watts, *Isaiah 34–66*, p. 258, understand the passage here to refer to this. While the view is possible, the context argues more for idolatry. If this refers to the mezuzah, it is an abrupt introduction of the thought.

[9]Herbert, *Isaiah 40–66*, p. 139, states that *yad* is "some sexual representation as a symbol of fertility." Delitzsch, II, 375–76 takes *yad* as "manhood." Leupold, II, 276, refers *yad* to "nakedness" as though Israel "delighted in indecent exposure." *OTTP*, p. 155, takes it as the "male organ." These views accept a highly speculative interpretation, found nowhere else clearly in the OT. Pieper, p. 515, and Young, III, 405, refer *yad* to the "remembrance." Motyer, *The Prophecy of Isaiah*, pp. 473–74, sees this as a vision of lasting fame. Barnes, II, 319, understands it as "place" but makes it a place for idols in the land. These are possible views.

[10]Among others, Leupold, II, 276; Wade, p. 364; and *OTTP*, p. 155, understand *melek* to refer to Molech rather than to a heathen king. Leupold relates the passage to I Kings 11:5, 7. While it is true that Israel worshiped Molech at times, the fact of sending messengers a great distance points to a "king" rather than a false god. Likewise, there is no point to mentioning "messengers" unless a king is in view. The presence of the definite article seems to indicate that a specific king is in view. We do not, however, have enough information to identify him. Barnes, II, 319, however, understands "king" in a collective sense, any of the heathen kings with whom Judah allied themselves.

11 *And of whom hast thou been afraid or feared, that thou hast lied, and hast not remembered me, nor laid it to thy heart? have not I held my peace even of old, and thou fearest me not?*

12 *I will declare thy righteousness, and thy works; for they shall not profit thee.*

13 *When thou criest, let thy companies deliver thee; but the wind shall carry them all away; vanity shall take them: but he that putteth his trust in me shall possess the land, and shall inherit my holy mountain;*

14 *And shall say, Cast ye up, cast ye up, prepare the way, take up the stumblingblock out of the way of my people.*

messengers a great distance for this purpose. Their willingness to enter into agreements with the heathen "debase[d]" (*šapel*)[11] themselves "unto hell" (*šeʾol*, see 5:14). This is hyperbole, showing how far they had abased themselves in trusting the heathen, v. 9. Even though they were weary with the effort involved in making covenants with the heathen, they would not confess a lack of hope. Each new agreement brought them "the life of thine hand," renewed strength. They were therefore not "grieved" (better "faint"), v. 10.

11–14 The Lord asks whom Israel has "been afraid" of (or "been anxious over") and "feared" (or "reverenced") that they have gone from Him? The people have lied, professing to worship God while bowing down to idols. They had not remembered God, not even thinking about Him. He has "held [His] peace" (or "been silent") for many years, the silence of His judgment on the land. Despite this, they did not fear Him, v. 11. He now will "declare" (or "make known") their "righteousness" and their "works." The thought is of their self-righteousness and their idolatrous works,[12] which will not profit them, v. 12. When trials come

---

[11]Kraeling, p. 204, follows the RSV translation "sent down even to Sheol." He suggests that this refers to worship of some netherworld deity, possibly Adonis. Wade, p. 365, suggests the Egyptian god Osiris. McKenzie, p. 158, speaks of "seeking oracular responses from the gods of the underworld." The verb *šapel* occurs in the *hipʿîl* theme twenty-one times. Overwhelmingly, it has the sense of humbling someone. Even in the three times that it refers to bringing something low, there is a sense of humbling connected with it. There is no need to translate *šapel* here as "send down, descend." The context has to do with making agreements with kings, not with false gods.

[12]Kelley, p. 354, understands the verse to speak of the nation's "righteous deeds." This misses the irony of the statement. Alexander, II, 347, interprets the statement, "I will declare . . ." with the sense of seeing if the people are righteous. To do this, God must examine their works. While this is possible, it reads into the text something that the Lord leaves unsaid. Henry, p. 331, and Fausset, p. 741, refer the "works" to evil works in general, not specifically idolatry. This is a possible view although v. 13 refers to idols.

upon them, causing them to cry out for help, let their "companies" of idols deliver them. The statement, of course, is ironic. The idols are so weak that the slightest "wind" of judgment will "carry" (*nasa*)[13] them away. The "vanity" (or "breath") of God's wrath will overtake them. In contrast, those who trust the Lord will possess the land.[14] They will receive the "holy mountain," Mt. Zion, Jerusalem, the capital of the land.[15] The verse makes the transition to a kingdom promise, v. 13.

Verse 14 continues the kingdom theme. The 3ms verb "shall say" better translates "and He shall say." The subject is the Lord.[16] He commands "cast ye up, cast ye up," building the road along which the people return to Palestine; cf. 35:8; 40:3; 62:10.[17] The doubled imperative gives emphasis to the command. The way of God's people is to be straight with hindrances removed. Nothing will hinder them from coming to worship Him, v. 14.

---

[13]Watts, *Isaiah 34–66,* p. 259, translates *nasa* as "lift" and understands the imperfect as a jussive. He translates the phrase "and all of them lift a spirit or take a breath" and refers this to "the séances of spiritualism." While this is technically correct, it requires contorted reasoning to find the thought of a séance here.

[14]Ibn Ezra, p. 263, compares the verse with 56:6 and concludes that the people will show their "trust" by keeping the Sabbath. This is arbitrary. While keeping the Sabbath was one obligation of Israel, there were many others as well. Isaiah 56:6 mentions several of these, not merely the keeping of the Sabbath.

[15]Several authors refer the "holy mountain" to the mountainous land of Palestine, e.g., Wade, p. 366, and Leupold, II, 278. While this is possible, the phrase "holy mountain" customarily refers to Mt. Zion, Jerusalem, although it may also be specific in referring to Mt. Moriah, the location of the temple within Jerusalem.

[16]Delitzsch, II, 379, says that this is not the Lord but "a heavenly cry." Rawlinson, II, 358, states clearly that it is an "angelic" speaker. Leupold, II, 279, avoids identifying the spokesman. He says, "who it is that speaks . . . is unimportant." Cowles, p. 467, and Young, III, 409, also leave the speaker unknown. Watts, *Isaiah 34–66,* p. 261, follows the Vulgate in reading "and I say." He refers this to a "new speaker." These views fail to account for the phrase "my people." This most naturally leads to the Lord as the speaker.

[17]Slotki, p. 280, spiritualizes the "way." He suggests that this refers to removing sin from the heart as the necessary way to approach the Lord. Price, p. 243, likewise spiritualizes this as the removal of sin that would keep the church from revival. Isaiah, however, elsewhere refers to a highway during the kingdom that will connect Mesopotamia, Palestine, and Egypt, e.g. 11:16; 19:23.

15 *For thus saith the high and lofty One that inhabiteth eternity, whose name is Holy; I dwell in the high and holy place, with him also that is of a contrite and humble spirit, to revive the spirit of the humble, and to revive the heart of the contrite ones.*

16 *For I will not contend for ever, neither will I be always wroth: for the spirit should fail before me, and the souls which I have made.*

17 *For the iniquity of his covetousness was I wroth, and smote him: I hid me, and was wroth, and he went on frowardly in the way of his heart.*

18 *I have seen his ways, and will heal him: I will lead him also, and restore comforts unto him and to his mourners.*

4. Promise from the Lord 57:15–21

15–18 The "high and lofty One [or 'exalted One']," the eternal and holy God, reveals His desire. The name "Holy" reflects the character of God as being absolutely free of evil. This God dwells in a "high and holy place," an appropriate description of heaven. Yet, He chooses to dwell with those who have contrite and humble spirits. There is a direct contrast with those spoken of in the previous verses. There, man arrogantly turned away from God to his own way. Here, man humbles himself to accept the ways of God. It is an amazing thought that the infinite God wants the companionship of finite man. To this end, He will "revive" them, encouraging and blessing them. The "contrite ones" (*dakka²*, see 3:15) are those who have been crushed in spirit, humbled before God, v. 15.

God will not "contend" (*rîb*, or "accuse," see 1:17) forever. He will not be "wroth" (*qaṣap*, see 8:21) with man. He will restrain and limit Himself lest man totally fall before Him. This would destroy mankind from the Creation, v. 16. He has smitten man in judgment because of his "iniquity" (*²awon*, see 1:4). He has hidden Himself from man because He was "wroth" (*qaṣap*) with man's sin. Man, however, continued "frowardly" (or "backsliding") in his own way, v. 17. God has seen man's ways. He will work with him to "heal him," forgiving his sin. He will "lead" (*naḥâ*)[18] man, giving him the guidance that he needs. He will

---

[18]McKenzie, p. 160; Wade, p. 368; and Kissane, II, 228–29, revocalize *²anḥehû* and derive it from *nuaḥ*. They translate something like "I will give him comfort." While this does not greatly change the sense of the verse, there is no need for the change. The MT gives a natural progression: healing (i.e., pardoning) . . . guidance (away from error) . . . comfort (of a renewed relationship). John S. Kselman, "A Note on *w²nḥhw* in Isa 57:18," *CBQ* 43:539–42, sees v. 18 as corresponding to v. 17. "I struck him" (v. 17) . . . "I will heal him" (v. 18). "He went wandering" (v. 17) . . . "I will lead him" (v. 18). For this reason, he supports the MT.

19 I create the fruit of the lips; Peace, peace to him that is far off, and to him that is near, saith the Lord; and I will heal him.
20 But the wicked are like the troubled sea, when it cannot rest, whose waters cast up mire and dirt.
21 There is no peace, saith my God, to the wicked.

restore him to blessing by giving comfort to the "mourners" (*?abel*)[19] who grieve over the calamities of life, v. 18.

19–21 Isaiah now gives a summary conclusion to the paragraph. The godly will receive blessing while the ungodly receive dissatisfaction for their life. The Lord gives man new speech, "the fruit of the lips." He does not clearly define this. The following words, "Peace, peace . . . ," give the nature of this new fruit. This message is an incipient gospel. The Lord offers "peace" (*šalôm*, see 9:6) to the "far off" and to the "near," i.e., both to the Gentiles and to the Jews.[20] The doubled *šalôm* gives emphasis. The phrase indicates "perfect peace" as in 26:3. The author of Hebrews alludes to this "fruit of the lips" when he speaks of giving "the sacrifice of praise to God continually," Hebrews 13:15. There is no better way to praise the Lord than by bringing others to know Him as their Savior, v. 19. In contrast, those who refuse God's call are like the "troubled sea," in constant turmoil and without "rest" (*šaqaṭ*, see 7:4). Its waters bring up "mire [*repeš*][21] and dirt [*ṭiṭ*, or 'mud']" by their motion, v. 20. The wicked cannot know *šalôm* since this comes only from God. The "no" (*?ên*) is made emphatic here by its position in the sentence.

---

[19]The word *?abel* does not refer to grief over one's own sin. It most often refers to grief over the death of someone else. It also indicates grief over external circumstances. Barnes, II, 325, refers the mourning to the "long and painful captivity in Babylon." Henry, p. 334, refers the grief to sin but limits it to those in Babylon that sorrowed over sin. Herbert, *Isaiah 40–66*, p. 141, views this as "ritual mourning accompanied by a fast." Vine, p. 114, speaks of "those who mourned by reason of their wanderings." Watts, *Isaiah 34–66*, p. 263, makes the mourners a second group, "those who wish [Israel] well, proselytes and others who fear Yahweh." Ibn Ezra, p. 265, similarly refers the mourners to "friends" who grieve at Israel's calamities. The context argues that this is an eschatological promise. Verse 19 extends the comfort throughout the whole earth.

[20]Slotki, p. 282, references everything to Jerusalem. Those who are "far off" are far from the Holy City. Those who are near are near the city. The Targum relates these terms to sinners who lived far from the Law but have recently repented, and to the righteous who have kept the Law. Among others, Näglesbach, p. 623; Barnes, II, 325; and Cowles, p. 470, refer this to Gentiles and Jews. Paul's use of the words "afar . . . nigh" in Eph. 2:17 seems to be coincidental rather than explanatory of this verse.

[21]The noun *repeš* occurs only here. It is related to *rapas*, "to stamp, tread down," and thus "to foul by stamping." Related words in the *qal* and *nipʿal* themes occur at Prov. 25:26; and Ezek. 32:2; 34:18. The parallelism to *ṭiṭ* suggests a meaning of "mire" or "mud."

There exists no possibility of the wicked man knowing peace. With the substitution of *ᵉlohîm* for *yᵉhwah*, the verse is identical to 48:22, v. 21.

Practical Applications from Chapter 57

1. The Futility of Idolatry
   a. The nature of false worship. Those who worship false gods are the spiritual descendants of spiritualism and immorality, v. 3. They mock the truth and show themselves the spiritual offspring of rebels and liars, v. 4. They practice sacred prostitution and child sacrifice, v. 5. The idols themselves are all that they will receive. Their worship does not please God, v. 6. They worship on the mountains, v. 7, and set up idols in their houses. They have practiced spiritual adultery by worshiping gods other than God Himself, v. 8.
   b. The trust of heathen kings. Rather than trusting the Lord, the people send gifts to the heathen king under whom they live, v. 9. Although the effort of making agreements with the heathen tires them, each new agreement brings new hope, v. 10.
   c. The weakness of false gods. Who has caused Israel to turn from the Lord, v. 11? He will now reveal the self-righteousness and idolatrous works of the people, which lack profit, v. 12. Let the idols deliver them. They are so lacking in power that the slightest judgment will carry them away, v. 13*a*. Those who trust the Lord will receive the land in the kingdom, v. 13*b*. At that time, the Lord will command a road to be built that will give His people access to Jerusalem, v. 14.

2. Contrasts in Peace
   a. The invitation to mankind. The exalted, eternal, and holy God humbles Himself to dwell with repentant sinners. He encourages and blesses them, v. 15. He will not fully display His wrath toward sinful men, which would destroy all mankind, v. 16. Although God has judged man, he has continued to go his own way, v. 17. God, however, will work with man to bring him into the ways of righteousness. He will guide him and comfort those who mourn, v. 18.
   b. The response to God. The Lord will give perfect peace to the godly, v. 19. Those who refuse the Lord will experience constant turmoil, v. 20. It is impossible for them to know peace, v. 21.

1 *Cry aloud, spare not, lift up thy voice like a trumpet, and shew my people their transgression, and the house of Jacob their sins.*

2 *Yet they seek me daily, and delight to know my ways, as a nation that did righteousness, and forsook not the ordinance of their God: they ask of me the ordinances of justice; they take delight in approaching to God.*

3 *Wherefore have we fasted, say they, and thou seest not? wherefore have we afflicted our soul, and thou takest no knowledge? Behold, in the day of your fast ye find pleasure, and exact all your labours.*

4 *Behold, ye fast for strife and debate, and to smite with the fist of wickedness: ye shall not fast as ye do this day, to make your voice to be heard on high.*

5 *Is it such a fast that I have chosen? a day for a man to afflict his soul? is it to bow down his head as a bulrush, and to spread sackcloth and ashes under him? wilt thou call this a fast, and an acceptable day to the Lord?*

ISAIAH 58

Despite their practice of idolatry and other sins, Israel had not abandoned their religion. They continued to carry on a formal worship. They observed the regular festivals and other religious rituals. They did this, however, without a true worship of the Lord. Isaiah now rebukes the ritualism of the people. He urges them to turn from their forms of worship and to receive the blessings that will come from God. He lists these in great variety to show the abundance that flows out of the sincere worship of God.

B. Restoration of the People 58:1–60:22
1. Reformation of Worship 58:1–14

1–5 The Lord commissions Isaiah to warn His people. The word "aloud" is lit. "with throat," i.e., with a full, strong sound. He should not fail to warn them. His voice should be "like a trumpet" (*šôpar*, see 18:3). In the OT, the *šôpar* often warned the people of approaching danger, e.g., I Samuel 13:3; Jeremiah 4:5; Amos 3:6. Isaiah here is to call the "transgression" (*pešaᶜ*, see 24:20) and "sins" (*ḥaṭṭaʾt*, see 3:9) of the people to their attention. The word "transgression" refers to rebellion against God. The "sins" are a falling short of God's standards, v. 1. The people ritualistically keep the laws of God. They "daily" (*yôm yôm*) come to Him, referring to the daily sacrifices made in the temple. The repeated *yôm* indicates a fullness of days. This may be the days of a year, of a life, or, as here, of a day-by-day practice. They profess a delight in His ways. They portray themselves as a nation doing righteousness, not turning away from the "ordinance" (*mišpaṭ*, see 1:17) of God. Because of this, they ask Him for "ordinances [*mišpaṭ*, see 1:17] of justice [*ṣedek*, see 1:21]" (or "righteous judgments"), judgments that accord with their own ideas of justice.[1] The statement "they take delight" does not refer to a sincere worship of God. The people were caught up in ritualism. They delighted in the false sense of security that it gave, v. 2. They wonder why the Lord has not responded to them. They have fasted but it is as though the Lord did not see them. They had "afflicted [their] soul" by fasting but the Lord took no knowledge of them.[2] The phrase "afflicted [*ʿanâ*, see 31:4] our soul" comes from the fact that fasting causes a person to go against his natural desires by withholding food from his hungry body.[3] The Lord responds to the people. They have not changed their ways. In the very "day" that they fast, they "find pleasure" in their activities.[4] Their "pleasure" (*ḥepeṣ*, see 44:28) here involves increasing their

---

[1]Näglesbach, p. 630, understands "ordinances of justice" as "an impartial judicial procedure." This suggests that the Lord has not treated them fairly in bringing judgment upon them. Pieper, p. 434, thinks that this reflects a desire to know the reason that God treats them as He has when they have lived righteously. Wade, p. 369, understands this as a request to clarify "doubtful points of ritual observance." Delitzsch, II, 385, sees this as requests that God judge their enemies. The overall context suggests something that agrees with their perverted sense of righteousness.

[2]God commanded only one fast to Israel, that of the Day of Atonement, Lev. 16:29, 31; 23:27–32; Num. 29:7; cf. Acts 27:9. On occasion, individuals might fast to express their personal sorrow over some calamity, e.g., II Sam. 12:21, 23; Ps. 35:13; Dan. 6:18. Moses fasted during his time on Mt. Sinai to receive the Law, Exod. 34:28. A fast might accompany some civic occasion, e.g., I Kings 21:9, 12, or a time of national prayer, II Chron. 20:3; Ezra 8:21; Esther 4:3. After the exile, the Jews added other fast days, Zech. 8:19. The fast of the fourth month remembered the fall of Jerusalem. That of the fifth month recalled the destruction of the temple. The fast of the seventh month remembered the murder of Gedaliah (Jer. 41:2). The fast of the tenth month commemorated the beginning of Nebuchadnezzar's attack on Jerusalem. The NT refers to ritual fasting of the Pharisees, Matt. 9:14 (Mark 2:18; Luke 5:33); cf. Luke 18:12. They fasted on the second and fifth days of each week. This remembered Moses, who supposedly ascended Mt. Sinai on Thursday, the fifth day of the week, and returned to the people on Monday, the second day of the week. The Lord rebuked the hypocrisy of the Pharisees in their fasts, Matt. 6:16.

[3]The phrase refers to fasting in Isaiah here and at vv. 5, 10. Elsewhere it occurs in Lev. 16:29, 31; 23:27, 29, 32; Num. 29:7; 30:13.

[4]Knight, p. 23, feels that "day" points "to the idea of an eschatological 'moment.'" It is a time with eternal significance. Isaiah, however, deals with historical actions of the people, here and in vv. 4, 5. There is no hint of future significance here.

6 *Is not this the fast that I have chosen? to loose the bands of wicked-*
ness, to undo the heavy burdens, and to let the oppressed go free,
and that ye break every yoke?
7 *Is it not to deal thy bread to the hungry, and that thou bring the poor*
that are cast out to thy house? when thou seest the naked, that thou
cover him; and that thou hide not thyself from thine own flesh?

own wealth.[5] To this end, they "exact [*nagaś*, see 3:5] all your labours" (or "oppress all your laborers"). Their fast day was treated as an ordinary day for work, v. 3. Their fasting makes them irritable. They become involved with "strife and debate," even striking someone with their fist. It is a "fist of wickedness" because the people use it in a wicked practice. This kind of fast will not cause God to hear their prayers, v. 4. The Lord asks rhetorically if this is the kind of fast He has chosen. Is it a day for a person to "afflict his soul"; cf. v. 3? Is it a day for bowing their head like the "bulrush" (or "reed," a plant that grows in marshes) to show their piety? Is it a day for lying in "sackcloth," cf. 3:24, and "ashes," common symbols of grief; cf. Job 2:8; Jeremiah 6:26? Clearly, it is not. Does anyone think that this is the kind of fast day that God wants? Will He accept this? The answer is again no, v. 5.

6–7 The Lord expects godly actions from the one who fasts. He wants him to loosen the "bands of wickedness," the bondage into which others have fallen because of wicked actions. He wants him to undo the "heavy burdens" (or "bands of the yoke"), constraints placed on others by the abuse of power. He wants him to free those whom he has oppressed. He wants him to break the "yoke," i.e., the burdens of servitude that he has placed on others, v. 6.[6] He should show charity to those who have needs. He should "deal" (or "divide") his food with the hungry. He should give shelter in his own home to the "poor [*ʿanî*, see 3:14] that are cast out," the homeless poor. He should provide clothing to the "naked," those who

---

[5]Among others, Westermann, pp. 331, 340; Rawlinson, II, 372, 374; and Von Orelli, p. 312, translate *ḥepeṣ* as "business" here and in v. 13. The word normally has the sense of "delight" or "desire." It is best to keep that thought here and to understand that the pleasure of the people comes from their wealth. Ibn Ezra, p. 266, refers the word to proceeding with a lawsuit against a fellow Israelite. The view is possible although it limits the application of the verse.

[6]The verbs in vv. 5–7 are either infinitives or 2ms verbs. These should be understood as indeterminate, "each one." In v. 6, Isaiah uses the 2mp verb, "you [pl.] break every yoke." This reveals the indeterminate nature of the passage. All who fast must follow the principles laid down in this instruction.

8 Then shall thy light break forth as the morning, and thine health
   shall spring forth speedily: and thy righteousness shall go before
   thee; the glory of the Lord shall be thy rereward.
9 Then shalt thou call, and the Lord shall answer; thou shalt cry, and
   he shall say, Here I am. If thou take away from the midst of thee the
   yoke, the putting forth of the finger, and speaking vanity;
10 And if thou draw out thy soul to the hungry, and satisfy the afflicted
   soul; then shall thy light rise in obscurity, and thy darkness be as the
   noonday:
11 And the Lord shall guide thee continually, and satisfy thy soul in
   drought, and make fat thy bones: and thou shalt be like a watered
   garden, and like a spring of water, whose waters fail not.
12 And they that shall be of thee shall build the old waste places: thou
   shalt raise up the foundations of many generations; and thou shalt be
   called, The repairer of the breach, The restorer of paths to dwell in.

are partially clad. He should not turn away from "thine own flesh," others of the nation. The list is not complete but represents all the charitable works that opportunity brings to God's people, v. 7.

8–12 These changes will lead to God's blessings. Isaiah lists ten distinct examples to show the bounty of God's goodness to those who seek to please Him. In the first place, the people will experience the "light" of His love (rather than the darkness of His wrath). It breaks forth as the "morning" (šaḥar, or "dawn," see 8:20). Next, they will enjoy good "health," recovery from the state into which their sins had brought them. Third, "righteousness" (ṣedeq, see 1:21) will mark their way. Fourth, the "glory of the Lord" will guard their back, protecting them, cf. 52:12, v. 8. Fifth, the Lord will answer their prayers. Sixth, when they call on Him, He will reveal Himself to them. These last two blessings differ. With the answered prayer, the Lord meets the needs of the people. With the revelation of the Lord, He gives them a sense of His presence.

All these blessings rest upon their changed conduct. They should no longer place the "yoke" of oppression on others; cf. v. 6. They should abandon practices such as pointing their finger at others, scornfully mocking those more godly than themselves.[7] They should give up speak-

---

[7]The meaning of pointing with the finger is vague. Prov. 6:13 refers to pointing with the fingers, an attempt at speechless communication. The lack of information about the practice has led to several suggestions here. Pieper, p. 540, sees it as a threatening gesture. Westermann, p. 339, understands it as a derisive gesture. Henry, p. 339, suggests either a "sign of displeasure" with the purpose of correcting behavior or an authoritative gesture given when making "unrighteous sentences." Motyer, *The Prophecy of Isaiah,*

*13 If thou turn away thy foot from the sabbath, from doing thy pleasure
on my holy day; and call the sabbath a delight, the holy of the Lord,
honourable; and shalt honour him, not doing thine own ways, nor
finding thine own pleasure, nor speaking thine own words:*
*14 Then shalt thou delight thyself in the Lord; and I will cause thee to
ride upon the high places of the earth, and feed thee with the heritage of Jacob thy father: for the mouth of the Lord hath spoken it.*

ing of "vanity" (better "wickedness"), a practice that may include several
kinds of sinful speech, v. 9.

The people should show charity to those in need. If they help the
"hungry" and the "afflicted soul," one who does not have food to eat,
then a seventh blessing will come. The "light" of God's blessing will
shine on them. In place of "obscurity" (better "darkness"), metaphorically standing for their oppressed condition, there will be the light of
blessing. In place of the "darkness" (or "gloom") of their position under
judgment will come the bright light of "noon day," again the blessing of
God, v. 10. Eighth, the Lord will give them continual guidance. Ninth,
they will enjoy material prosperity. Isaiah pictures this as refreshing
water in "drought" (better "scorched places") and "mak[ing] fat" (better
"strengthen[ing]") their "bones," equivalent to the body. They will be
like a watered garden and like an unfailing spring of water, v. 11. Tenth,
they will rebuild the wasted ruins of the land. Some of these have lain in
ruins for "many generations." This will lead others to give them new
names, the "repairer of the breach" and the "restorer of the paths [or
'streets'] to dwell in." The names picture the rebuilding of Jerusalem's
walls and streets along which people live, v. 12.

13–14 In addition to the changes summarized in vv. 6–10, the Lord
gives a specific condition for blessing. The people must make the Sabbath into a holy day. They should not make the day into one devoted to
the "pleasure" (ḥepeṣ, see v. 3) that comes from wealth.[8] The phrase
"turn away thy foot" suggests that the Sabbath is holy ground. The

---

p. 482, sees it as "acting by innuendo." Watts, *Isaiah 34–66*, p. 275, thinks it "may refer
to spying or accusing" as one tries to cause fear in someone else. Kissane, p. 237, calls it
"equivalent to sending forth the *hand*." This could be either an attack on another person
or an attempt to seize someone's property. Several authors, e.g., Rawlinson, II, 375;
Slotki, p. 285; and Price, p. 247, refer the gesture to showing scorn.

[8]See n. 5. It is not that God's people cannot do things that bring pleasure on the Sabbath. It is rather that we should not devote the day to the same pursuits of making money
that we follow the other days of the week.

people should not enter into it lightly. They should "call" (*qara*ʾ) it a day of "delight." The phrase "holy of the Lord" refers to the Sabbath. Grammatically, it also follows *qara*ʾ, i.e., they "call" the "holy of the Lord," the Sabbath, an "honourable" (*kabed*, see 3:5) day. The people should avoid turning it into a common day. They "honour" (*kabed*) the Lord by not doing their "own ways," the routine activities of life. They honor Him by not doing their "own pleasure [*hepeṣ*]," the pleasurable activities designed to lead to additional wealth. They honor Him by not speaking their "own words," the idle chatter that occupies much of their speech. This last suggests that at least some of our speech should center on the Lord. In short, the Lord's Day should not be made into a routine day much like the other days of the week, v. 13. Setting this day apart to the Lord will show their delight in Him. He will bless them. They will "ride upon the high places of the earth," a victory procession over the land of Palestine.[9] He will fulfill His promises of inheritance made to Jacob, e.g., Genesis 28:4; Psalm 105:9–10. These promises are sure, spoken by the Lord Himself, v. 14.

Practical Applications from Chapter 58

1. The Blessings of God

    a. The conditions of blessing. When the people begin to show godliness in their lives, the Lord will bless them. They need to unloose the "bands of wickedness," to stop placing burdens on others, to free others from their oppression, and break off the burdens of service that they have placed on others, v. 6. They should show charity to others, giving them food, housing, and clothing. They should not turn away from others with needs, v. 7. They should lift the burden of oppression from others. They should turn from showing scorn of others and no longer speak wickedly, v. 9cd. They should meet the needs of the hungry and afflicted, v. 10a.

    b. The scope of blessing

    (1) Dawning of God's love, v. 8

    (2) Recovery from God's judgment, v. 8

    (3) Righteousness of man's behavior, v. 8

    (4) Protection from man's attack, v. 8

---

[9]See also Deut. 33:29; Amos 4:13; Mic. 1:3.

(5) Answer to man's prayer, v. 9*a*

(6) Revelation of God's presence, v. 9*b*

(7) Presence of God's blessing, v. 10

(8) Guidance of man's actions, v. 11*a*

(9) Supply of man's needs, v. 11*b*

(10) Rebuilding of man's dwellings, v. 12

2. Observing the Sabbath

   a. Avoiding the pleasures that come from making money (also mentioned below), v. 13

   b. Recognizing the holiness of a day devoted to the Lord, v. 13

   c. Delighting in the presence of a day of rest and worship, v. 13

   d. Setting the day apart as an "honourable" day, v. 13

   e. Honoring the Lord, v. 13

      (1) Not doing the routine activities of life, v. 13

      (2) Not engaging in activities designed to produce wealth (already mentioned once; the repetition may indicate a natural tendency to put wealth ahead of the Lord), v. 13

      (3) Not practicing idle chatter in speech, v. 13

   f. Delighting in the Lord of the Sabbath, v. 14

   g. Receiving the promised blessing for those who set this day aside, v. 14

1 Behold, the Lord's hand is not shortened, that it cannot save; neither his ear heavy, that it cannot hear:

2 But your iniquities have separated between you and your God, and your sins have hid his face from you, that he will not hear.

3 For your hands are defiled with blood, and your fingers with iniquity; your lips have spoken lies, your tongue hath muttered perverseness.

4 None calleth for justice, nor any pleadeth for truth: they trust in vanity, and speak lies; they conceive mischief, and bring forth iniquity.

5 They hatch cockatrice' eggs, and weave the spider's web: he that eateth of their eggs dieth, and that which is crushed breaketh out into a viper.

ISAIAH 59

Chapter 59 continues the theme introduced in c. 58. Isaiah had urged moral reformation there. The lack of morality has caused God to turn away from the nation of Israel. He cannot bless a sinful people. Isaiah develops that thought further in c. 59. He urges the people to turn back to the Lord and describes the judgments they have suffered because of their sin. When the people confess their sin and begin to practice godliness, the Lord will intervene on their behalf. He will overcome their enemies and enter into an everlasting covenant with them.

2. Salvation of Israel 59:1–21
a. Cause for Punishment 59:1–8

1–2 Isaiah answers the complaint of those who have accused the Lord of leaving His people. His hand is "not shortened, that it cannot save [*yaša^c*, see 17:10]." This idiomatic expression shows that the Lord has not lost His power to lift the people out of their troubles; cf. 50:2; Numbers 11:23. His ear is not too "heavy" (*kabed*, see 3:5) to hear, another idiomatic expression; cf. 6:10. He is not dull of hearing but is well able to listen to the prayers of the people, v. 1.

Israel's "iniquities" (*^cawon*, see 1:4) and "sins" (*hatta^{>}t*, see 3:9) have caused their separation from God. The "iniquities" (*^cawon*) and "sins" (*hatta^{>}t*) of Judah have, in a sense, erected a wall between them and God. His face is now "hid" from them. This is a frequent word picture throughout the OT showing God's alienation from His people, e.g., 8:17; 54:8; 64:7; Psalm 10:11; 13:1; Jeremiah 16:17. For this reason, He will not answer their prayers, v. 2.

3–8 Isaiah lists the sins of the people. As usual, the list is not complete; it is a representative list meant to show the people their sin. Verse 3

6 *Their webs shall not become garments, neither shall they cover
  themselves with their works: their works are works of iniquity, and
  the act of violence is in their hands.*
7 *Their feet run to evil, and they make haste to shed innocent blood:
  their thoughts are thoughts of iniquity; wasting and destruction are
  in their paths.*
8 *The way of peace they know not; and there is no judgment in their
  goings: they have made them crooked paths: whosoever goeth
  therein shall not know peace.*

is poetic, using members of the body as involved with their sin. They are
guilty of murder, defiling their hands with blood and their fingers with
"iniquity" (*ʿawon*, see 1:4). Their lips speak "lies" (*šeqer*, see 9:15).
Their tongue talks "perverseness" (*ʿawlâ*). The word *ʿawlâ* refers generally to injustice or unrighteousness, v. 3.

The people have no concern for "justice" (*ṣedeq*, see 1:21, better
"righteousness"). No one "pleadeth" (*nipʿal* of *šapaṭ*) for "truth" (*ᵉmûnâ*,
see 11:5). The verb *šapaṭ* is a legal word. The word in the *nipʿal* theme
refers to pleading the case, arguing the facts of a matter. They trust in
"vanity" (*tohû*, or "emptiness," see 24:10), things without substance.
They speak "lies" (*šawᵓ*, see 1:13). There is a difference between *šeqer*
and *šawᵓ*. The noun *šeqer* refers to falsehood, speech without any basis in
fact. The word *šawᵓ*, however, is "empty speech," speech that has no
value. In v. 3, lying refers to untruthfulness with one another. In v. 4, it
refers to untruthfulness in their worship of God.[1]

Isaiah poetically describes the people as conceiving "mischief" (or
"trouble") and giving birth to iniquity, cf. Job 15:35; Psalm 7:14, v. 4.
They hatch "cockatrice' [*ṣepaʿ*] eggs" and weave the "spider's web," both
pictures of their poisonous influence. The *ṣepaʿ* is an unidentified poisonous serpent, possibly the adder. Those who eat their eggs, coming
under their influence, die. The "crushed" (*zûreh*)[2] egg becomes a "viper"
(*ᵓepʿeh*), also an unidentified poisonous serpent, v. 5.

---

[1]Whitehouse, II, 272; Herbert, p. 151; and Leupold, II, 297, refer v. 4 to false testimony
in a law court. Henry, p. 344, includes this along with general "slanders and false accusa-
tions" against others. We should not limit the words *ṣedek* and *ᵉmûnâ*, however, to the court
of law. These words reflect a general apathy of Israelite society toward the Lord Himself.

[2]The word *zûreh* occurs only here. The verb *zûr*, however, "to press," occurs several
times so that the meaning "crushed" or "broken" is not in doubt.

> 9 *Therefore is judgment far from us, neither doth justice overtake us: we wait for light, but behold obscurity; for brightness, but we walk in darkness.*
>
> 10 *We grope for the wall like the blind, and we grope as if we had no eyes: we stumble at noonday as in the night; we are in desolate places as dead men.*
>
> 11 *We roar all like bears, and mourn sore like doves: we look for judgment, but there is none; for salvation, but it is far off from us.*

The webs that the people weave will not become clothing to cover their evil. Their works will not cover them. These are works of iniquity and violence that are open to view. They will not bring blessing, v. 6. Isaiah again summarizes their wickedness. They eagerly do "evil" (*ra*ᶜ, see 3:9). They "shed innocent blood," committing murder. They have wicked thoughts. They produce "wasting" (or "devastation") and "destruction," v. 7. They do not know the way that brings "peace" (*šalôm*, see 9:6); cf. 57:21. Paul draws on vv. 7–8*a* in his catalog of sins in Romans 3:15–17. The people do not bring forth "judgment" (*mišpaṭ*, better "justice," see 1:17) in their "goings," their well-defined ways of life. They walk in "crooked paths," paths of wickedness that do not lead them to peace, v. 8.

b. Confession of Sin 59:9–15*a*

9–11 Some in the land acknowledge their sin. The plural pronoun "us" indicates that this is a group of people. They lament the lack of "judgment" (better "justice") and "justice" (better "righteousness"). They "wait" (*qawâ*, see 5:2) for "light" to guide them but find only "obscurity" (or "darkness"). They seek "brightness," a shining light from some source, but they find only "darkness" (or "gloom"), v. 9. The sins of the people have walled them in to judgment. The people "grope for" (*gašaš*, or "feel")[3] the wall as blind men, seeking in vain a way out. They stumble in the full light of the sun as though it were "night" (or "twilight"). They are "in desolate places" (*ʾašmannîm*, better "among the healthy")[4] as the dead, v. 10. They "roar" (or "growl") like bears with

---

[3]The word *gašaš* occurs only twice, both times in this verse. There are, however, cognate words in several languages that support the meaning "grope, feel."

[4]The noun *ʾašmannîm* is a *hapax legomenon.* It comes from the verb *šaman*, "to be fat," and thus "healthy." The NASB interprets as "vigorous" and the NIV as "strong." The following samples other suggestions: Watts, *Isaiah 34–66*, p. 278, "full vigor"; Pieper, p. 554, "strength of manhood"; Young, III, 434, "stout" or "full strength"; Slotki, p. 289, "lusty." These glosses all give the same basic sense.

*12 For our transgressions are multiplied before thee, and our sins tes-
tify against us: for our transgressions are with us; and as for our
iniquities, we know them;*

*13 In transgressing and lying against the Lord, and departing away
from our God, speaking oppression and revolt, conceiving and utter-
ing from the heart words of falsehood.*

*14 And judgment is turned away backward, and justice standeth afar
off: for truth is fallen in the street, and equity cannot enter.*

*15 Yea, truth faileth; and he that departeth from evil maketh himself a
prey: and the Lord saw it, and it displeased him that there was no
judgment.*

impatience. They moan like doves over their condition. They "look"
(*qawâ*, see 5:2) in vain for "judgment" (better "justice"). They look for
"salvation" (or "deliverance") but it is far away, v. 11.

12–15a This lack of hope leads the people to confess their sin. Their
"transgressions" (*pešaᶜ*, see 24:20), their rebellions against God, are many.
Their "sins" (*hattaʾt*, see 3:9) witness against them. Their "transgressions"
(or "rebellions," *pešaᶜ*) are ever with them. They "know," i.e., acknowledge
(*yadaᶜ*, see 1:3), their "iniquities" (*ᶜawon*, see 1:4). The combination of
pešaᶜ, *hattaʾt*, and *ᶜawon* draws together the various aspects of their sin.
They had rebelled against God ("transgressions"). They had fallen short
of His standards ("sins"). They had twisted and perverted His standards
("iniquities"). The combination stresses the extent of their wickedness.
The sins are not hidden, v. 12. Isaiah now develops their sin in detail. Six
infinitives in v. 13 expand the thought given in v. 12. (1) They are guilty
of "transgressing" (or "rebellion," *pašoaᶜ*) against the Lord.[5] (2) They
practiced "lying against" (or "denying") the Lord. (3) They have gone
away from Him. (4) They have spoken of "oppression and revolt." (5) They
have conceived and (6) spoken "lies" (*šeqer*, see v. 3) from their heart,
v. 13. The result of these sins is that "judgment" ("justice") is "turned
away backward" (or "driven back"). Similarly, "justice" ("righteousness")
is far off. The "truth" has "fallen [or 'stumbled'] in the street [*rᵉhôb*, see
15:3]" no longer revealing herself openly to men. In addition, "equity"
(or "uprightness") cannot enter among the people, v. 14. As well, truth
"faileth" (or "is lacking"). The person who turns away from "evil" (*raᶜ*,
see 3:9) becomes a "prey," a victim, v. 15a.

---

[5]Watts, *Isaiah 34–66*, p. 283, arbitrarily makes *pašoaᶜ* a "political word." He refers this
to rebellion against Persia. Grammatically, however, Judah's "transgressing" parallels her
denial of the Lord. These are both sins against the Lord.

16 *And he saw that there was no man, and wondered that there was no intercessor: therefore his arm brought salvation unto him; and his righteousness, it sustained him.*

17 *For he put on righteousness as a breastplate, and an helmet of salvation upon his head; and he put on the garments of vengeance for clothing, and was clad with zeal as a cloke.*

18 *According to their deeds, accordingly he will repay, fury to his adversaries, recompence to his enemies; to the islands he will repay recompence.*

19 *So shall they fear the name of the Lord from the west, and his glory from the rising of the sun. When the enemy shall come in like a flood, the Spirit of the Lord shall lift up a standard against him.*

20 *And the Redeemer shall come to Zion, and unto them that turn from transgression in Jacob, saith the Lord.*

21 *As for me, this is my covenant with them, saith the Lord; My spirit that is upon thee, and my words which I have put in thy mouth, shall not depart out of thy mouth, nor out of the mouth of thy seed, nor out of the mouth of thy seed's seed, saith the Lord, from henceforth and for ever.*

c. Confirmation of Blessing 59:15*b*–21

15*b*–17 This lack of "judgment" ("justice") displeases the Lord, v. 15*b*. He sees that there is no godly man standing up on behalf of the people and He "wondered" (or "was astounded") that there was no "intercessor" (*pagaᶜ*, see 53:6). He therefore intervenes Himself. His "arm," the symbol of His power, brings "salvation" (*yašaᶜ*, see 17:10) to the people. His "righteousness" sustains Him, keeping Him from failing in His task, v. 16. His righteousness serves as a "breastplate" to protect the body. He puts on the "helmet of salvation" to protect His head. The "garments of vengeance," i.e., garments worn as He exacts vengeance, serve as clothing. The vengeance of the Lord is not mere revenge. It is a natural outgrowth of His holiness as He responds to the sin of mankind. He wraps Himself with "zeal" (*qinʾâ*, see 9:7) as a "cloke" (or "robe"). Paul develops this picture in Ephesians 6:11–17 and in I Thessalonians 5:8, in which he speaks of the Christian's armor. The Lord imparts His armor to believers, v. 17.

18–21 The Lord will judge His enemies according to their works. He will direct anger and recompense to those who have opposed Him. As is normal in Isaiah, the "islands" (*ʾîyîm*, see 11:11) refer to the coastal regions. They stand poetically here for the nations, v. 18. They will then fear the "name" of God, i.e., His nature. This fear will extend from the "west" (*ma^{c}arab*, see 43:5). They will fear His "glory" from "the rising of the sun." As in 41:25 and 45:6, the "rising of the sun" refers to the east. The "glory" of God here parallels the "name" of God. Both terms refer to God's revelation of Himself.

The last half of the verse is difficult. When the enemy of the Lord comes in like a "flood" (better "river"), the Spirit of the Lord will "lift up a standard against him" (better "drive him away"), gaining victory for His people.[6] This refers to the final battle of the Tribulation era. Antichrist will marshal his forces in vain against the Lord, Revelation 19:11–16, 19–21, v. 19.

The Lord will come to His people as the *go°el*, the Kinsman-Redeemer; cf. 35:9. He will come to those in Judah who "turn" (*šûb*, see 1:27) away from their "transgression" (or "rebellion," *peša^c*, see 24:20). Paul draws on this promise in Romans 11:26–27, v. 20. The Lord enters into an everlasting covenant with His people; cf. Jeremiah 31:31–34. The second person masculine singular pronouns that follow in the rest of the verse refer back to Israel as a nation.[7] He will never withdraw His Spirit from them, nor will He take His Word away from them, or their descendants. The ultimate fulfillment of the promise lies in the future. During the Tribulation, Israel will turn to the Lord, Zechariah 12:10; 13:1. From that time on, the Lord will honor the promise that He makes here. Paul quotes generally from vv. 20–21 in Romans 11:26–27 as he discusses the salvation of Israel.

---

[6]The alternative way of taking the verse interprets "enemy" (*ṣar*) as "narrow, strait," an adjective modifying "river," and thus "a pent-up [or 'dammed-up'] stream" that the "wind of the Lord" drives. The whole expression describes the Lord coming on behalf of His people: "when he comes like a torrential stream that the wind of the Lord drives." Kraeling, p. 210; Delitzsch, II, 406; Leupold, II, 302; and Brueggemann, *Isaiah 40–66*, p. 200, are among those who hold the view. While it is technically correct to translate the verse this way, Isaiah normally uses *rûaḥ y^{e}hwah* elsewhere to refer to the "Spirit of the Lord." Only 40:7 is an exception to this and the context there clearly requires "wind" instead of "Spirit." In addition, the meaning of "narrow, strait" for *ṣar* is distinctly a secondary meaning. Finally, the concept of a "pent-up stream" being released from its barricade by a driving wind is an unusual word picture. For these reasons, I understand the verse as discussed above.

[7]Slotki, p. 291, makes the 2ms pronouns refer to Isaiah. The prophet here is a personification of "all faithful Israelites." Goldingay, p. 337, likewise makes the words refer to Isaiah. He in turn represents the people. The change of pronoun is not a problem. Isaiah moves from addressing the nation as a group of individuals to addressing the nation as a unit. The change of pronouns is not rare in Isaiah's writings, e.g., 17:14; 49:15; 51:15; 62:12.

Note that vv. 19–21 mention all three members of the Godhead: "the Spirit of the Lord" and "my spirit," "the Redeemer," and "the Lord" (three times), v. 21.[8]

Practical Applications from Chapter 59

1. Causes for Punishment

    a. Spurning the help of God. He is well able to lift man out of his problems and to hear his cries for help, v. 1. Man's "sins" and "iniquities" separate man from God so that He does not answer man's prayers, v. 2.

    b. Practicing the sins of wickedness

        (1) The poetic picture of sin. Men's "hands" are guilty of murder. Their "fingers" have been involved with iniquity. Their "lips" speak lies; their "tongue" is unrighteous, v. 3. They conceive trouble and give birth to iniquity, v. 4b. They hatch the eggs of a poisonous snake and weave a spider's web to capture their prey. Anyone eating their eggs dies of the poison. An egg that is broken brings forth a poisonous serpent, v. 5. The webs that they weave cannot cover their sin, v. 6a. Their feet run so that they may perform evil, v. 7a.

        (2) The plain description of sin. There is no concern for righteousness. No one argues the case for truth. The people trust in things that do not exist. They are untruthful in their speech, v. 4a. Their works will not cover them since these reveal iniquity and violence that all can see, v. 6bcd. They are eager to murder the innocent. They think thoughts of iniquity. They cause devastation and destruction, v. 7bcd.

        (3) The certain results of sin

           (a) Positively. They are not just in their dealings with others.

           (b) Negatively. The people do not know where to find peace. Their ways are crooked ways that fail to produce peace, v. 8.

2. The Right Response to Sin

    a. The confession by the people

---

[8]This is one of several passages in Isaiah that refer to the Trinity. See also 11:2; 42:1; 48:16; 61:1; and 63:7–14.

(1) The people acknowledge their sin. They recognize the lack of justice and righteousness in the land (mentioned also in v. 14, giving emphasis to the statement). There is only darkness ahead, v. 9. There is no hope, v. 10. They respond with impatience and sorrow. There is no justice or deliverance, v. 11.

(2) They confess their rebellion, their shortcomings, and their going aside from the ways of God, v. 12. They have rebelled against the Lord, denied Him, and gone away from Him. They have spoken of oppressing others and rebelling against the moral standards of God. They have lied, v. 13. There is no justice or righteousness in the land because truth and uprightness have been restrained, v. 14. Truth is lacking. Those who turn from evil become a prey for others, v. 15a.

b. The work by God

(1) The Lord is displeased by the lack of justice in the land, v. 15b. He Himself acts to deliver the people. His own righteousness keeps Him from failing, v. 16. He is protected by righteousness, salvation, vengeance that comes from His holiness, and zeal, v. 17.

(2) The Lord judges His enemies, v. 18. This brings a widespread fear of God. Though enemies oppose God's people, His Spirit will give victory over them, v. 19.

(3) The Lord redeems His people, v. 20, and makes a new covenant with them. He will never again withdraw His Spirit from them or take His Word from them. This establishes an eternal union between God and man, v. 21.

1 Arise, shine; for thy light is come, and the glory of the Lord is risen
   upon thee.
2 For, behold, the darkness shall cover the earth, and gross darkness
   the people: but the Lord shall arise upon thee, and his glory shall be
   seen upon thee.
3 And the Gentiles shall come to thy light, and kings to the brightness
   of thy rising.
4 Lift up thine eyes round about, and see: all they gather themselves
   together, they come to thee: thy sons shall come from far, and thy
   daughters shall be nursed at thy side.

ISAIAH 60

The previous chapter ended with the presence of the Lord and His blessing on Israel. Isaiah now continues this theme. He describes the growth and increased glory of the nation in the first part, vv. 1–9. He then focuses on the blessings that will come to Jerusalem in the kingdom. It will have a position of glory. Gentile nations will bring them tribute. It will be a time of prosperity and peace. Isaiah then moves past the Millennium to the eternal ages. The city will enjoy peace and the eternal blessing of God upon it, vv. 10–22.

3. Exaltation of the Nation 60:1–22
a. Glory of the Nation 60:1–9

1–2 Isaiah calls on Israel to greet the "light" of God's glory that shines on them.[1] From the development of this thought in the remainder of the passage, Isaiah refers to the millennial kingdom.[2] It is during this time that the nation will enjoy such a position of glory as Isaiah describes, v. 1. The world will be in darkness at the end of the Tribulation. Israel, however, will see the brightness of God's glory as He rescues them from the power of Antichrist, v. 2.

3–5 As the world moves into the kingdom reign of Christ, the Gentiles will respond to Israel's glory. Their kings will come to "the bright-

---

[1]The imperatives and suffixes in the verse are all feminine. The question is whether these refer to the nation or to Jerusalem. Among others, Watts, *Isaiah 34–66,* p. 295; Wade, p. 389; and Smith, p. 429, apply the passage to Jerusalem. While the view is possible, I have applied it to the nation because of the reference to "sons" and "daughters" in vv. 4, 9. It is more natural to refer these to the nation.

[2]Cowles, p. 488, relates this to "the true church, God's real children." While Israel will indeed be a part of the true church during the kingdom, she retains a distinctive position. The passage focuses on Israel alone, not Israel as representing the true church.

5 *Then thou shalt see, and flow together, and thine heart shall fear,
and be enlarged; because the abundance of the sea shall be converted unto thee, the forces of the Gentiles shall come unto thee.*
6 *The multitude of camels shall cover thee, the dromedaries of Midian
and Ephah; all they from Sheba shall come: they shall bring gold
and incense; and they shall shew forth the praises of the Lord.*
7 *All the flocks of Kedar shall be gathered together unto thee, the rams
of Nebaioth shall minister unto thee: they shall come up with acceptance on mine altar, and I will glorify the house of my glory.*
8 *Who are these that fly as a cloud, and as the doves to their windows?*
9 *Surely the isles shall wait for me, and the ships of Tarshish first, to
bring thy sons from far, their silver and their gold with them, unto
the name of the Lord thy God, and to the Holy One of Israel, because he hath glorified thee.*

ness of thy rising." The contrast with the darkness at the end of the
Tribulation enhances the glory now seen in the land, v. 3. As Zion looks,
they will see people coming to the land. Those Jews who have been dispersed from Palestine will return. They will come "from far," from
around the world; cf. 11:11–12; 43:5–7. The phrase "daughters shall be
nursed at thy side" is lit. "daughters will be carried upon the side," i.e.,
at the hip. This refers to the oriental way of carrying children, v. 4.[3] Israel will see and "flow together" (*nahar*, better "be radiant"),[4] filled with
joy over these blessings. Their heart will "fear" (*pahad*, see 2:10), having
a dread of doing anything that would limit the blessing of the Lord. At
the same time, it will "be enlarged" (or "swell") with emotion as they
see others coming to the land. The "abundance of the sea," the wealth of
the sea and the islands in it, and the "forces of the Gentiles" (or "wealth
of the nations") as well come to Israel. This reflects the tribute brought
by the Gentiles to Israel as they offer worship to the Lord, v. 5.

6–9 Camels carrying tribute are so numerous as to cover the land.
This poetical picture portrays the prosperity of the nation. The "dromedaries" (better "young camels") come bearing goods. These one-humped
animals are ideal for traveling in that part of the world. Their broad feet
let them walk readily over sand. They can travel well over a hundred

---

[3]Young, III, 446, refers the verse to converted heathen rather than dispersed Israelites.
He does not give a reason for going away from the pronouns in the verse.

[4]There are two verbs, *nahar* I, "to flow," and *nahar* II, "to shine, beam." The parallelism
with the emotions favors *nahar* II. The radiant face accompanies the heart filled with
emotions.

miles in a day while carrying a load. They come from Midian and Ephah, both nomadic tribes of the Arabian Desert. They come from Sheba at the southern tip of Arabia. They bring gold and "incense" (or "frankincense," cf. 43:23). This is a representative list of the gifts given as the nations offer their worship. The people who come offer "praises" ($t^ehill\hat{a}$, see 42:8) to the Lord, v. 6.

Flocks come from Kedar, a nomadic tribe near Syria. Rams come from Nebaioth, a nomadic tribe located near Kedar in Arabia.[5] These "minister unto thee" in providing sacrifices for the people.[6] As in 56:7, the sacrifices are causes for remembrance. They recall the atoning sacrifice of the Lord.[7] He accepts these offerings and glorifies the temple, where the people make their sacrifices. For the first time in the chapter, the Lord reveals Himself as the one speaking through the prophet. He refers to "mine altar," the altar dedicated to His worship, v. 7.

Isaiah asks for the identity of these people.[8] He describes them as flying "as a cloud" moving across the sky.[9] They are like "doves" flying to

---

[5]Delitzsch, II, 413–14; Rawlinson, II, 401; and Wade, p. 381, identify Nebaioth with the Nabatæans. While the Nabatæans may have come from the stock of Nebaioth, they did not rise to power until the sixth century B.C. Nebaioth was the firstborn son of Ishmael, Gen. 25:13; I Chron. 1:29. The records of the Assyrian emperor Ashur-banipal (669–626 B.C.) mention both Kedar and Nebaioth as tribes in Arabia.

[6]Henry, p. 351, makes the "flocks" and "rams" represent "precious souls" because they have a ministry. The reference to being offered "on mine altar," however, suggests that these are sacrifices. Giving themselves as pictures of Christ's sacrifice at Calvary is certainly as much a ministry as that carried on by human beings.

[7]Young, III, 448, holds that the passage describes NT worship using OT figures. It is wrong "to interpret this verse as teaching a revival or reinstitution of animal sacrifices." This reflects his theological view rather than the teaching of the OT. Such passages as 56:6–7; Ezek. 20:40–41; 43:18–27, teach that the priests will offer blood sacrifices in the Millennium. These sacrifices are memorial, looking back to the death of Christ, rather than typical as in the OT, looking forward to His death.

[8]Watts, *Isaiah 34–66,* p. 295, makes Jerusalem the one who asks the question. This is unlikely. Nothing here indicates that the personified city speaks at this point.

[9]Whitehouse, II, 283, and Barnes, II, 363, understand the "cloud" as a word picture of the number of people coming into the land. Delitzsch, II, 415, and Motyer, *The Prophecy of Isaiah,* p. 495, understand it as a picture of speed. Slotki, p. 293; Wade, p. 382; and Leupold, II, 310, understand the cloud and dove as descriptions of the white sails of ships sailing across the Mediterranean. Vine, p. 174, relates the flight of the cloud and dove to that of airplanes today. He suggests that this is how the people will come to the land. There is no need to see anything more here than a word picture of motion. The clouds float across the sky; the doves fly to their nests. In the same way, the people of the world journey to Zion to worship the King.

10 *And the sons of strangers shall build up thy walls, and their kings shall minister unto thee: for in my wrath I smote thee, but in my favour have I had mercy on thee.*
11 *Therefore thy gates shall be open continually; they shall not be shut day nor night; that men may bring unto thee the forces of the Gentiles, and that their kings may be brought.*
12 *For the nation and kingdom that will not serve thee shall perish; yea, those nations shall be utterly wasted.*
13 *The glory of Lebanon shall come unto thee, the fir tree, the pine tree, and the box together, to beautify the place of my sanctuary; and I will make the place of my feet glorious.*
14 *The sons also of them that afflicted thee shall come bending unto thee; and all they that despised thee shall bow themselves down at the soles of thy feet; and they shall call thee, The city of the Lord, The Zion of the Holy One of Israel.*

their "windows" (*ᵃrubbâ*, or "openings," see 24:18). Strictly speaking, the word *ᵃrubbâ* refers to an opening, here the small opening through which the dove flies to its nesting place, v. 8. The Lord responds that the "isles" (*ʾîyim*, see 11:11), the area surrounding the Mediterranean, "wait," eagerly anticipate coming to the Lord.[10] The large "ships of Tarshish," cf. 2:16, will come first to bring "thy sons," the dispersed Israelites. They bring gold and silver as an offering to the Lord. They recognize what He has done to "thee," their homeland, by giving it glory, and they honor Him for it, v. 9.

b. Gifts to the Nation 60:10–22

10–14 The "sons of strangers," Gentiles, will help the Jews. They will assist in building the walls of Jerusalem. Gentile kings will "minister" to them, no doubt giving offerings to help in their building. In the past, God has smitten Israel in His wrath toward them for their sin. Now, however, He will extend mercy to them, v. 10. The gates of the city will remain open "continually" because of the peace that exists there. They will not shut the gates "day nor night." John likely rests his statement in Revelation 21:25 on this promise. The people will bring the "forces of the Gentiles" (or "wealth of the nations," cf. v. 5). Gentile kings will visit them,

---

[10]Watts, *Isaiah 34–66*, p. 296, understands the pronoun "thee" to refer to Artaxerxes, the Persian ruler, 465–425 B.C. This view, however, does not satisfy the context. The chapter is eschatological, looking forward to events in the reign of Christ over the earth.

15 *Whereas thou hast been forsaken and hated, so that no man went through thee, I will make thee an eternal excellency, a joy of many generations.*
16 *Thou shalt also suck the milk of the Gentiles, and shalt suck the breast of kings: and thou shalt know that I the Lord am thy Saviour and thy Redeemer, the mighty One of Jacob.*
17 *For brass I will bring gold, and for iron I will bring silver, and for wood brass, and for stones iron: I will also make thy officers peace, and thine exactors righteousness.*

no doubt coming to honor the Lord, v. 11.[11] Any nation or kingdom that will not serve Israel will perish and be "utterly wasted" (*harob yeḥᵉrabû*), completely devastated. The repetition of the root *harab* gives emphasis to the statement. The fact that this is the Millennium does not mean that the Lord will overlook rebellion. He will punish sin, cf. 65:20; Zechariah 14:16–19, v. 12. The "glory of Lebanon," its cedar trees, will be brought for use in the temple. The "fir" (probably the cypress tree), the "pine" (possibly the boxwood tree but uncertain), and the "box" (an unidentified tree) will lend beauty to His rebuilt sanctuary. "The place of my feet," the temple, will be "glorious" (*kabed*, see 3:5). Similar phrases refer to the temple elsewhere, cf. I Chronicles 28:2; Psalm 99:5; 132:7; Ezekiel 43:7, v. 13.[12] The "sons... of them that afflicted [*ᶜanâ*, see 31:4] thee," the Gentiles, will prostrate themselves before the Jews. They will humble themselves in recognizing that Jerusalem is indeed "the city of the Lord." It is the "Zion of the Holy One of Israel." The word "Zion" refers to the city of Jerusalem; cf. 1:26, 27; II Samuel 5:6–7. Here, it is the city that belongs to the "Holy One of Israel," the King who rules the world from it, v. 14.

15–17a In the past, Jerusalem has been oppressed. She has been "forsaken and hated" because of her low condition. Men would not walk through her ruins. The Lord will now make her "an eternal excellency,"

---

[11]Von Orelli, p. 321, and Näglesbach, p. 560, explain the coming of the kings as the coming of captive rulers. There is no reason, however, to understand the visit as anything other than voluntary. Verse 3 mentions the coming of the Gentiles to Zion. Verses 10, 16, refer to help coming from the Gentile kings. It is reasonable that these kings accompany their tribute as they come freely to worship the King of kings. Delitzsch, II, 417, explains the visit as that of kings who have been conquered by the church, i.e., "inwardly conquered." While this is possible, it forces us to read the church into the passage.

[12]Cowles, p. 493, makes the "place of his feet" the city of Jerusalem. Smith, p. 434, spiritualizes the phrase into the place in which there are poor or sick. The use of similar phrases and related words elsewhere argue that we should limit it to the rebuilt temple here.

18 Violence shall no more be heard in thy land, wasting nor destruction within thy borders; but thou shalt call thy walls Salvation, and thy gates Praise.

an object of national pride for generations to come, v. 15. She will feed upon the resources of the Gentiles. The ideas of sucking the "milk of the Gentiles [or 'nations']" and the "breast [*šod*][13] of kings" are idiomatic. They picture Israel's drawing upon the wealth of others.[14] Israel will then experientially "know" (*yadac*, cf. 1:3) that the Lord is their "Saviour" (*yašac*, see 17:10) and "Redeemer" (*goʾel*, see 35:9). This refers to the conversion of Israel. The Lord is the mighty God of "Jacob," a name that refers to the nation. The combination of names occurs again at 49:26 with the same sense, v. 16. Instead of "brass" (better "bronze") and iron, He will give them gold and silver. Instead of wood and stone, He will give them bronze and iron. The idea is that He will give them more valuable and stronger building materials in place of the common materials used in the past, v. 17*a*.

17*b*–18 "Peace" (*šalôm*, see 9:6) and "righteousness" (*sedakâ*, see 1:21) will rule the land. The word "exactors" (*nagaś*, see 3:5) is better "overseers," v. 17*b*. The violence of war, "wasting" (or "desolation"), and "destruction" will no longer come into the land. Instead, her walls of defense will be in the "salvation" given by the Lord. Her gates, again a defense of the city, will be in her attitude of "Praise" (*tehillâ*, see 42:8) to God, v. 18.

---

[13]The word *šod* normally means "violence, destruction," e.g., 51:19; 59:7; 60:18, while *šad* means "breast." There is also a variant reading *šed*, "devil," found here. The parallelism here with v. 16*a* forces us to understand *šod* as "breast." Stanley Schneider and Joseph H. Berke, "שׁד Breast, Robbery or the Devil?" in *JBQ* 23:86–90, explain this variance psychologically. The breast is desirable "both as a physical object unto itself and for its function." When access to the breast is hindered, causing frustration, "the breast will be feared and rejected." The authors apply this to v. 16. As Zion sucks the "breast" of the nations, it takes their riches. If this is given involuntarily, it is "robbery" (the meaning assigned by the authors rather than "violence" or "destruction"). This "devilish" behavior leads to the third sense of "devil" being given to *šod*. The authors fail to note that *šod*, "breast," also occurs at 66:11 and Job 24:9. For this reason, it is likely that *šod* is simply a variant spelling of *šad*.

[14]The awkwardness of nursing at the breast of kings has led some to understand nursing at "royal breasts." Pieper, p. 591; Leslie, p. 222; and Von Orelli, p. 322, along with the NIV adopt this view. Aside from the fact that *šod* is singular, "breast," the word *melek* occurs as "king" more than 2,500 times. Only twice, Gen. 49:20 and I Kings 10:13, do the translators give "royal" for this word. The translation "breast of kings" accurately reflects the idiom *šod melakîm*.

19 *The sun shall be no more thy light by day; neither for brightness shall the moon give light unto thee: but the Lord shall be unto thee an everlasting light, and thy God thy glory.*

20 *Thy sun shall no more go down; neither shall thy moon withdraw itself: for the Lord shall be thine everlasting light, and the days of thy mourning shall be ended.*

21 *Thy people also shall be all righteous: they shall inherit the land for ever, the branch of my planting, the work of my hands, that I may be glorified.*

22 *A little one shall become a thousand, and a small one a strong nation: I the Lord will hasten it in his time.*

19–22 Isaiah now moves beyond the Millennium. Verse 19 clearly sets the time and place of fulfillment in the New Jerusalem and the eternal ages. During the Millennium, there will be day and night. Here, the sun and moon will no longer shine. The Lord will be "an everlasting light"; cf. Revelation 21:23; 22:5. God will be glorious. The description marks this as belonging to the eternal ages, cf. 51:6, 16, v. 19. The people will not depend upon the changeable light of the sun and moon. The Lord will be their "everlasting light." There will be no more sorrow over the grief caused by their sin, v. 20. The people will be righteous. They will receive the land as their inheritance forever. Although nations war over Palestine today, the time will come when the Lord will give it perpetually to His chosen people. The Lord calls the people "the branch of my planting" and "the work of my hands."[15] The picture of God Himself planting the people occurs elsewhere; cf. 61:3; Matthew 15:13. Likewise, the people are "the work of [His] hands"; cf. 29:23; Psalm 138:8; Philippians 1:6. The nation receives these things "that I may be glorified" (*pa'ar*, better "that I may glorify myself," see 44:23), v. 21. God will bless them abundantly. The "little one" (*qaton*, or "insignificant") will become a "thousand" (*'elep*, or "clan").[16] The

---

[15]The MT reads *matta'aw*, "his planting." 1QIsa^a adds the name *y^{e}hwah*. This makes the *ketîb* reading possible, "the guardian of His plantation is the Lord." I. F. M. Brayley, "'Yahweh Is the Guardian of His Plantation' A Note on Is. 60,21," *Biblica* 41:275–86; Westermann, p. 355; Childs, p. 499; and Watts, *Isaiah 40–66*, p. 293, accept the MT. There is little support for the addition of *y^{e}hwah*. The AV follows the *q^{e}rê matta'ay*. This brings the phrase into agreement with the following phrase, "the work of My hands." The Targum and Vulgate support the *q^{e}rê*.

[16]The word *'elep* can mean either "thousand" or "clan." Skinner, *Isaiah XL–LXVI*, p. 203, and Watts, *Isaiah 34–66*, p. 293, translate as "clan." Whitehouse, p. 289, and Vine, p. 176, opt for "thousand." No matter which translation is used, the point is that there will be great numerical increase.

"small one" (*ṣaʿîr*, or "youngest") will become a "strong nation."[17] The implication is that Israel will have the strength to dominate the Gentile nations. The Lord Himself will "hasten" (*ḥûš*)[18] the fulfillment of this promise, v. 22.

Practical Application from Chapter 60

The Future Glory of Israel
1. The Nature of the Kingdom
   a. Blessings in Israel. The glory of the Lord shines in Israel, v. 1, as He rescues them from the darkness of the Tribulation, v. 2. Gentile kings now bring their tribute to Israel, v. 3. Jews from around the world return to the land, v. 4. This fills the Jews in the land with emotion at the sight, v. 5*a*. The wealth of the earth comes to Israel, v. 5*b*. The desert nations send their tribute on camels. Those who come offer praise to God, v. 6. The flocks of the nations come to provide memorial sacrifices in the temple, v. 7. Jews from around the Mediterranean bring their gifts to God because of His work on behalf of the nation, vv. 8–9.
   b. Work of the Gentiles. Gentile nations help build Jerusalem, v. 10. The city remains open day and night to receive the gifts of the Gentiles, v. 11. Any nation that will not submit to Israel will perish under God's judgment, v. 12. Different woods will be brought to beautify the temple, v. 13. The Gentiles humble themselves before the Jews, v. 14. Jerusalem has been oppressed in the past. The Lord now exalts her, v. 15. She draws upon the resources of the Gentiles. This gives her a new knowledge of God, v. 16. He gives Israel more valuable and stronger building material, v. 17*a*. This land enjoys peace and righteousness, v. 17*b*. The people recognize the salvation given by God and they praise Him, v. 18.

---

[17]There is not a clear distinction between *qaṭon* and *ṣaʿîr*. Both occur with similar senses of last born, weak, and insignificant.

[18]Watts, p. 293, understands the verb as *ḥûš*, "to enjoy." The Lord will enjoy His people. While this is possible, the verb *ḥûš* II occurs elsewhere only once, in the *qal* at Eccles. 2:25. The verb *ḥûš*, "to hasten," occurs more widely both in the *qal* and, as here, in the *hipʿîl*.

2. The Nature of the Eternal Ages

The sun and moon no longer shine. The Lord is the light of His people, vv. 19–20a. There is no more grief, v. 20b. The people will be righteous. They will possess the land forever, no more to be driven out by enemy nations, v. 21a. The Lord Himself plants the people in the land for His glory, v. 21b. He will make them a strong nation, v. 22.

1 *The Spirit of the Lord God is upon me; because the Lord hath
anointed me to preach good tidings unto the meek; he hath sent me
to bind up the brokenhearted, to proclaim liberty to the captives, and
the opening of the prison to them that are bound;*
2 *To proclaim the acceptable year of the Lord, and the day of
vengeance of our God; to comfort all that mourn;*

ISAIAH 61

The chapter continues to describe the end-time events introduced in
c. 60. The Lord surveys His ministry, giving seven different aspects of it,
vv. 1–2. He then focuses on His millennial rule over the nations of the
world. The grief of this age will be reversed and the wasted areas of
Palestine will be renewed, vv. 3–4. The Gentile nations will serve Israel,
v. 5, while the Jews serve the Lord, v. 6. They will receive payment for
the shame that they once endured, v. 7. The Lord will establish justice.
He will bless Israel with a new covenant, v. 8. All will know of His
blessing upon Israel, v. 9. The Lord will establish righteousness in the
earth and He will receive praise, vv. 10–11.

C. Blessing of the People 61:1–63:14
1. Return of the Messiah 61:1–11

1–2 Although the title "servant of the Lord" does not occur here,
many consider these words to be from the Servant of the Lord as in
42:1–9; 49:1–13; 50:4–11; and 52:13–53:12.[1] Whether we formally clas-
sify it as a Servant passage, there is no question but that the Lord speaks
here.[2] Isaiah nowhere speaks of himself as filled with the Spirit. Other
passages that mention the anointing of the Holy Spirit, e.g., 11:2; 42:1,
are messianic.[3] No person and certainly not Israel had such a purpose as

---

[1]Among others, Leupold, Näglesbach, Hailey, Rawlinson, and Delitzsch attribute the
passage to the Servant of the Lord.

[2]Watts, *Isaiah 34–66*, p. 299, tentatively suggests that Ezra is the author. Herbert,
Isaiah 40–66, p. 163, and Wright, p. 149, think that the speaker is Israel. Brueggemann,
Isaiah 40–66, p. 213, says that it is an unknown person with "immense theological authority." Among others, Kelley, p. 362; McKenzie, p. 181, cf. p. 150; and Westermann,
p. 365, cf. p. 296, hold that the speaker is Trito-Isaiah. See the discussion in the Introduction for the arguments against this idea.

[3]Slotki, p. 298, understands the anointing as a metaphorical expression for "appointed."
He argues that "only kings and high priests were actually anointed." Aside from the fact
that Elisha was "anointed" to be a prophet, I Kings 19:16, Slotki also ignores the messianic psalms that speak of Christ's anointing, Ps. 2:2; 45:7 (cf. Heb. 1:8–9); and 89:20.
Hab. 3:13 is also normally understood as messianic.

given in vv. 1–2. In addition, and conclusively, the Lord applies this passage to Himself in Matthew 11:5 (Luke 7:22) and in Luke 4:18–19, 21.[4] It is worth noting that Isaiah mentions here all three members of the Godhead ("Spirit . . . Lord God . . . me").[5]

There is a sevenfold purpose of the anointing. (1) He declares the good news of salvation to the "meek" (or "afflicted"). This repeats the message of 52:7, expanded by Paul in Romans 10:13–15 into the declaration of the gospel. (2) He binds up the "brokenhearted" (*nišbᵉrê-leb*), those whose hearts have been broken by repentance over sin.[6] The thought here is of consoling individuals who grieve over their sin. (3) He proclaims "liberty to the captives," cf. Leviticus 25:10, a part of the Year of Jubilee, a celebration that foreshadows the work of Christ by ending bondage, forgiving debts, and establishing rest. The emphasis here is on relieving the bondage to sin. (4) He proclaims the "opening of the prison" (*pᵉqaḥ-qôaḥ*) for those who have been imprisoned for righteous actions.[7] This promise repeats the thought introduced earlier in 42:7. From Luke 4:18, we should limit the thought here to freedom from the blindness of sin, v. 1. (5) He announces the "acceptable year" of God's grace, the church age.[8] (6) He proclaims the day of God's "vengeance," the judgments of the Tribulation

---

[4]It is significant that the Lord stopped in Luke 4:18–19 without mentioning the phrase "the day of vengeance of our God." The Lord's first coming was for a ministry of comfort. His Second Coming will include the judgment of this wicked world, II Thess. 1:8–9. Herbert, *Isaiah 40–66*, p. 163, objects to this: "There seems little justification for the suggestion that Jesus did not include this clause in order to avoid the idea of divine 'vengeance', since he includes precisely this in Luke 18:7–8." He thinks that the Lord simply "quoted enough to call the whole passage to mind." This misunderstands the purpose of the quote in Luke. This took place at the Lord's first sermon. It was an announcement of His immediate ministry, not a statement of His whole future work. Additional revelation to His followers expanded the scope of His ministry later, e.g., Matt. 25:41; John 5:27–29. The Lord's quotation comes from the LXX version of 61:1. This paraphrase interprets the Hebrew.

[5]See also 11:2; 42:1; 48:16; 59:19–21; 63:7–14 for other passages in Isaiah that mention the Trinity.

[6]The thought of repentance from sin may be seen where the phrase *nišbᵉrê-leb* occurs elsewhere, cf. Ps. 34:18; 51:17; and probably 147:3. In Ps. 69:20; Jer. 23:9; and Ezek. 6:9, the phrase refers to grief.

[7]The Isaiah Scroll reads *pᵉqahqôaḥ*, a reduplicated form from *paqah*, "to open the eyes." The sense is of gaining sight after being freed from the gloom of prison. If we retain the *maqqep*, we must explain *qôaḥ* as an irregular infinitive absolute from *laqah*. Since this form does not occur elsewhere, the explanation is doubtful. The LXX translates τυφλοῖς ἀνάβλεψιν, "recovery of sight to the blind." The NT gives authority to this interpretation.

[8]Wade, p. 387, claims that there is no distinction between the "acceptable year of the Lord" and the "day of vengeance of our God." He views both expressions as "merely

3 *To appoint unto them that mourn in Zion, to give unto them beauty for ashes, the oil of joy for mourning, the garment of praise for the spirit of heaviness; that they might be called trees of righteousness, the planting of the Lord, that he might be glorified.*
4 *And they shall build the old wastes, they shall raise up the former desolations, and they shall repair the waste cities, the desolations of many generations.*

period.[9] (7) He gives "comfort" (*naham*, see 1:24) to those who "mourn" (*°abal*, see 57:18) over the burdens of life. If we consider the sevenfold anointing as a sequence, this seventh promise refers to the Millennium. God's people will indeed receive comfort during this time, v. 2.

3–4 Verse 3 develops the point just made. The Lord will "appoint" (or "establish") those who "mourn" (*°abal*) in Zion. The idea is that the Lord replaces the sorrow of the people with desirable things. He moves on in the verse to describe these things. He will give them "beauty" (*$p^{e}°er$*, or "a beautiful headdress," see 3:20) for "ashes" (*°eper*). The interchange of *$p^{e}°er$* and *°eper* is a play on words, typical of Isaiah's style of writing. The Israelites put ashes on their head to show their grief, II Samuel 13:19; cf. Job 42:6. The *$p^{e}°er$*, on the other hand, was a headdress worn at occasions of joy; cf. v. 10. It serves here as an appropriate symbol of the joy given to the people to replace their grief; cf. Ezekiel 24:17, 23.

In addition, the Lord will give the people the "oil of joy" to replace their "mourning" (*°ebel*). The phrase "oil of joy" occurs again only in Psalm 45:7 ("oil of gladness"). An anointing with oil or ointment was normal, Ruth 3:3; II Samuel 12:20; Esther 2:12. Such anointing was a way of showing joy, Psalm 104:15; Proverbs 27:9; Ecclesiastes 9:7–8; Amos 6:6. The lack of an anointing showed grief, II Samuel 14:2; Daniel 10:3.[10]

---

rhetorical expressions." The significance, however, is clear in Luke 4:18–19. The Lord ends His quotation of vv. 1–2 after mentioning the "acceptable year of the Lord." He came to usher in the church age, not to proclaim the Tribulation judgments.

[9]Whitehouse, II, 291, thinks that the "day of vengeance" was a time of judgment upon those Jews who were products of the mixed marriages between the Jews and Samaritans. There is no evidence to support the view. Moreover, the use of the same phrase in 34:8 and 63:4 suggests rather that this is the end-time judgment rather than a limited judgment in Jewish history.

[10]Slotki, p. 299, states that oil "temper[ed] the effects of the heat" and was therefore a comfort. On the other hand, Merrill F. Unger, "Oil," *Unger's Bible Dictionary*, p. 805, states that the use of oil was cosmetic. It gave a "smooth and comely appearance" to the skin. Pieper, p. 605, refers to the "aromatic oils" used at joyous times. The people did not use oil in times of grief.

5 *And strangers shall stand and feed your flocks, and the sons of the alien shall be your plowmen and your vinedressers.*

6 *But ye shall be named the Priests of the Lord: men shall call you the Ministers of our God: ye shall eat the riches of the Gentiles, and in their glory shall ye boast yourselves.*

7 *For your shame ye shall have double; and for confusion they shall rejoice in their portion: therefore in their land they shall possess the double: everlasting joy shall be unto them.*

The Lord will also give His people the garments of "praise" ($t^ehillâ$, see 42:8) instead of a spirit of "heaviness" (or "dimness"), i.e., a weakened spirit as in discouragement or despair. They will be as "trees" (or "terebinths," see the description at 1:29) giving off the fruits of "righteousness" ($sedeq$, see 1:21). The Lord plants these for the purpose of bringing glory to Himself. They are the "planting of the Lord," cf. 60:21, growing up as healthy plants bringing forth fruit and beauty. Israel receives these gifts "that He might be glorified" ($pa^{\gamma}ar$, better "that He might glorify Himself," see 44:23), v. 3. Israel will build the wasted and desolate areas of the land. They will raise up the ruined cities, even those that have lain waste for many generations, v. 4.[11]

5–7 The "strangers" (zar, see 1:7), Gentile nations, will serve Israel throughout the Millennium. They will feed the flocks and care for the fields and vineyards. These are representative examples of service, not an exhaustive list, v. 5. The Jews themselves will be a kingdom of priests serving the Lord; cf. Exodus 19:6. Others will recognize them as "the Ministers of our God." They will live from the gifts of the Gentiles.[12] They will "boast" ($yamar$) in the "glory" (better "wealth") given them by the Gentiles, v. 6.[13] Israel will have "double" payment for the past

---

[11]Young, III, 462, spiritualizes the passage and makes it refer to the building up of the church from the ravages of sin. Henry, p. 359, also spiritualizes the thought. He makes this refer to the building up of the "unsanctified soul." There is no support for these views.

[12]Young, III, 463, again spiritualizes the passage to make Israel the church. He makes the Gentiles converts to Christianity and states that "the Church will thrive on the goods of those who are converted to her." Both Israel and the Gentiles are rather nations.

[13]The *hitpaᶜel* of *yamar* occurs only here. KB, II, 67, and BDB, p. 56, both relate *yamar* to *ᵓamar*. This gives rise to the sense "boast yourselves." Gerhard Lissowsky, *Konkordanz zum Hebräischen Alten Testament,* p. 613, relates it to *mar*, "to exchange" and thus "substitute," i.e., "you will succeed to their glory." The Targum gives "delight yourselves" and the Vulgate *superbietis*, "you shall pride yourselves," both interpretive. The LXX gives Θαυμασθήσεσθε, "you will be wondered at" or "you will be admired." The Isaiah Scroll gives the irregular spelling *ttyᵓmrû*, which supports the relationship to *ᵓamar*.

8 *For I the Lord love judgment, I hate robbery for burnt offering; and
I will direct their work in truth, and I will make an everlasting
covenant with them.*

9 *And their seed shall be known among the Gentiles, and their offspring among the people: all that see them shall acknowledge them,
that they are the seed which the Lord hath blessed.*

"shame" they have endured.[14] Although the Hebrew words differ, this has
the same sense as in 40:2. It represents full blessing of the land to replace the shame the nation has endured.[15] The 2mp pronoun here refers
to individual Israelites. The 3mp pronoun refers to the nation. They will
rejoice in the "portion" given them in place of the past "confusion"
(*kalam*, or "disgrace," see 30:3). They will enjoy "double" fruit from the
land and know "everlasting joy," v. 7.

8–9 The Lord loves "judgment" (*mišpaṭ*, better "justice," see 1:17) and
hates "robbery for [better 'in'] burnt offering."[16] The phrase refers to the
days when captive Israel was not able to make sacrifices. The Lord now
will "direct [better 'give'] their work [*peᶜullâ*, better 'recompense,' see
40:10] in truth," i.e., He will restore that which they had lost in the judgment. He will make an "everlasting covenant" with the nation, v. 8. Their

---

[14]The change in pronouns has caused confusion. Leupold, II, 323, and Westermann,
p. 368, change the pronouns to the second person. Wade, p. 389, and McKenzie, p. 180,
change them to the third person. Alexander, II, 403, explains the "ye" as referring to the
Jews and the "they" to the Gentiles of v. 6. Fausset, pp. 752–53, explains the change as
marking the transition from spiritual Israel to Israel in general. Dunlop Moore, editing
Näglesbach, p. 660, explains it as "an enallage of persons, the second giving place to the
third." Such pronominal changes, however, are not rare. G.K. 144 *p* notes that "abrupt
transition from one person to another" occurs often in poetic or prophetic language.

[15]Delitzsch, II, 431, explains "double" as double possession of the land. The Jews will
not only possess the land within the borders of the nation but will also possess land that
extends "far beyond the borders of their former possession." Näglesbach, p. 660, however, rejects the view that "double" refers to land. He feels that this refers to "double
honor." Cowles, p. 502, refers to "double strength and glory." Kelley, p. 363, suggests
that Israel is the "firstborn among the nations" and therefore receives "a double portion
of the Lord's inheritance." He does not explain what this is.

[16]Among others, Leupold, II, 324; Young, III, 463; and Skinner, *Isaiah XL–LXVI,* p. 208,
understand ᶜôlâ as wickedness. The Lord hates robbery that comes from unjust actions. The
view requires repointing ᶜôlâ to ᶜawᵉlâ. The LXX reads ἁρπάγματα ἐξ ἀδικίας, "rob-
beries of injustice." The Targum gives *šqrᵓ wᵓwnsᵓ*, "lying and oppression." The Vulgate
translates *rapinam in holocausto,* "robbery in burnt-offerings." The Isaiah Scroll supports
the MT. It is likely that misunderstanding the phrase "robbery in the burnt offering" led to
repointing the noun.

10 I will greatly rejoice in the Lord, my soul shall be joyful in my God; for he hath clothed me with the garments of salvation, he hath covered me with the robe of righteousness, as a bridegroom decketh himself with ornaments, and as a bride adorneth herself with her jewels.

11 For as the earth bringeth forth her bud, and as the garden causeth the things that are sown in it to spring forth; so the Lord God will cause righteousness and praise to spring forth before all the nations.

offspring will be known throughout the world as God's people. Others will recognize that the Jews receive special blessing from Him, v. 9.

10–11 Messiah speaks, expressing His joy in the Lord.[17] The "garments of salvation [*yašaᶜ*, see 17:10]" figuratively portray the salvation that He gives to mankind. Likewise, the "robe of righteousness" speaks of the righteousness that He imparts to those who follow Him. His clothing is elaborate. It is like the groom who clothes himself with "ornaments" (*pᵉᵓer*, "a beautiful headdress," cf. v. 3) and the bride who adorns herself with jewels, v. 10. Just as the earth brings forth buds and garden plants, so the Lord will cause righteousness and praise to spring up in the nations. The verse looks forward to the blessings of the kingdom, when mankind will worship the Lord. His "praise" (*tᵉhillâ*, see 42:8) will then abound throughout the earth, v. 11.

---

[17]Goldingay, p. 348; Barnes, II, 378; and Herbert, p. 164, see Isaiah as the speaker here. Knight, p. 59; Kelley, p. 363; and Kraeling, p. 215, make Israel the speaker here. Young, III, 465, and Pieper, p. 613, identify the speaker as the church, true Israel. McKenzie, p. 181, understands the speaker as Jerusalem. Watts, *Isaiah 34–66*, p. 304, continuing his view of dating this section late, makes the speaker Artaxerxes. Nothing in the context, however, makes the speaker here different from the one speaking in vv. 1–3.

Practical Applications from Chapter 61

1. The Ministry of the Messiah, vv. 1–2
   a. Declaration of salvation, cf. Romans 10:13–15
   b. Comfort for the repentant
   c. Proclamation of liberty, cf. Leviticus 25:10–11
   d. Proclamation of freedom, v. 1, cf. 42:7
   e. Proclamation of the church age, cf. Luke 4:18–19
   f. Proclamation of the Tribulation judgments
   g. Comfort for the mourners, v. 2
2. The Joy of the Lord, v. 3
   a. A symbol of joy to replace the symbol of sorrow
   b. An anointing of joy to replace the lack of anointing that comes from grief
   c. The garments of praise to replace the spirit of despair
3. The Kingdom of the Lord, vv. 5–12
   a. The service of the Gentiles, v. 5
   b. The priesthood of Israel, v. 6
   c. The blessing of Israel, vv. 7, 9
   d. The word of the Lord, vv. 8, 11
   e. The joy of the Lord, v. 10

1 *For Zion's sake will I not hold my peace, and for Jerusalem's sake I will not rest, until the righteousness thereof go forth as brightness, and the salvation thereof as a lamp that burneth.*

2 *And the Gentiles shall see thy righteousness, and all kings thy glory: and thou shalt be called by a new name, which the mouth of the Lord shall name.*

3 *Thou shalt also be a crown of glory in the hand of the Lord, and a royal diadem in the hand of thy God.*

4 *Thou shalt no more be termed Forsaken; neither shall thy land any more be termed Desolate: but thou shalt be called Hephzi-bah, and thy land Beulah: for the Lord delighteth in thee, and thy land shall be married.*

5 *For as a young man marrieth a virgin, so shall thy sons marry thee: and as the bridegroom rejoiceth over the bride, so shall thy God rejoice over thee.*

ISAIAH 62

The chapter continues the millennial theme of c. 60–61. The Jews become a righteous nation and the Gentile nations see this new character, vv. 1–2. The Lord gives His blessing to them and rejoices in the nation, vv. 3–5. The Lord commissions a group of men to pray night and day for His blessing upon Jerusalem, vv. 6–7. He promises to protect the nation from its enemies, vv. 8–9. He commands them to prepare a highway to assist those who wish to come to Jerusalem, v. 10. The nations of the world acknowledge the presence of Israel's Redeemer and His work of redemption for His people, vv. 11–12.

2. Restoration of the Enemies 62:1–12

1–5 The Lord speaks once more to the nations.[1] He determines that He will not "hold [His] peace" (better "be silent") or "rest" (*šaqaṭ*, better "be quiet," see 7:4) until He has delivered His people. The "righteousness" (*ṣedeq*, see 1:21) of Jerusalem will then shine forth brightly and her "salvation" will burn as a "lamp" (or "torch"), v. 1. The nations will then see her "righteousness" (*ṣedeq*, see 1:21). Gentile kings will see the

---

[1]As with the previous chapters, there is debate over the speaker. The most common position is that Isaiah (or "the prophet") speaks. Among others, Grogan, p. 337; Von Orelli, p. 328; and Smart, p. 264, adopt this position. Whitehouse, II, 296, argues for "some prophet" since vv. 2, 3, 4, 5, 6, 8, and 9 refer to the Lord "in the third [sic] person." This, however, is not unusual, e.g., 54:1, cf 54:5; 56:1, cf 56:3; 65:13, cf. 65:15. Ibn Ezra, p. 283, makes the speaker captive Israel. Watts, *Isaiah 34–66,* p. 309, views the speaker as "Judah's civil administrator." The spokesman here, however, continues the theme of c. 61. The personal pronoun "I" indicates that this is the Lord, the same speaker as in 61:8, 10.

glory of Israel. This stamps the time as during the Millennium, when the Gentile nations will recognize Israel's new relationship to the Lord.

The Lord in that time will give them a new name to reflect the new relationship to Him. Names in the Bible have theological significance. We see this in changes of names: Abram ("high father") to Abraham ("father of a multitude"), Genesis 17:5; Jacob ("one who overreaches," i.e., a "supplanter") to "Israel" ("he who wrestles with God"), Genesis 32:27. Verse 2 does not mention a new name. It is possible that the name "Hephzi-bah" in v. 4 expresses the new identification.[2] Revelation 2:17 and 3:12 also mention the "new name" of the believer, v. 2.

The nation will be a "crown of glory" (or "beautiful crown") held in the Lord's hand.[3] It will be a "royal [*melûkâ*, see 34:12] diadem [*ṣᵉnôp*]"[4] in God's hand. Since the hand often serves as an emblem for power, e.g., 11:11; 26:11; 41:13, it is likely that this is the figure here. The Lord holds

---

[2]Vine, p. 180, thinks that the new name is "Jehovah is our righteousness," found in Jer. 33:16. It is unlikely that the identification of the name comes from another prophet more than a century later. Alexander, II, 407, suggests that "the expression may be understood more generally as denoting change of condition for the better." But this is not what is said. New names elsewhere indicate some change in character or office. It is reasonable that the Lord gives His people a new name here to reflect their new relationship to Him.

[3]Vine, p. 180, notes that two different words occur here for the "hand." The first, *yad*, indicates "the open hand." The second, *kap*, is "that which is held out for display." Together, they "set forth the intense delight in the heart of the Lord in manifesting the effects of His grace and redeeming power." Slotki, p. 302, understands the *kap* as a closed hand. He concludes, "This denotes God's support and protection of Israel, as one who holds an article tightly in his hand, lest it fall." Both of these views overstate the case. The word *kap* indicates the "palm." There is no intent here to indicate "intense delight . . ." or to show "support and protection. . . ." The combination of *yad* and *kap* occurs regularly in poetic variation, e.g., Ps. 18:1; 71:4; Prov. 31:20; Jer. 15:21, and that is the case here.

[4]The *kᵉtîb ṣᵉnôp* occurs elsewhere only at 22:18, in which the construction is emphatic. The *qᵉrê ṣᵉnîp* occurs at 3:23; Job 29:14; and Zech. 3:5. We should read it here since the verb form is out of place. The idea of "turban" found in Herbert, *Isaiah 40–60*, p. 165, and Vine, p. 180, comes from the verb *ṣanap*, "to wind." We may as well translate "diadem," the circular emblem that often indicates royalty. The Lord holds this in His hand. Leupold, II, 330, suggests that He is inspecting it. Whitehouse, II, 297, gives the possibility that the crown is the city's wall, placed in the Lord's hand. Knight, p. 64, makes the Lord's hand the emblem of His power. He tentatively states the idea that He is about to place the diadem on Zion's head. Kraeling, p. 216, thinks the Lord holds the crown in His hand because it is pagan; cf. II Sam. 12:30. Motyer, *The Prophecy of Isaiah,* p. 506, sees the crown worn on the head as the "exercise of royal power." Held in the hand, it is "the possession of royal worth and dignity." Rawlinson, II, 430, suggests that the Lord holds the crown of Israel in His hand to exhibit it to an admiring world. Without further explanation, Ibn Ezra, p. 283, states that "in some countries, people wear crowns on their hands." We cannot be certain in explaining why the Lord holds the diadem in His hand. I have given my view above.

6 *I have set watchmen upon thy walls, O Jerusalem, which shall never hold their peace day nor night: ye that make mention of the Lord, keep not silence,*

7 *And give him no rest, till he establish, and till he make Jerusalem a praise in the earth.*

8 *The Lord hath sworn by his right hand, and by the arm of his strength, Surely I will no more give thy corn to be meat for thine enemies; and the sons of the stranger shall not drink thy wine, for the which thou hast laboured:*

9 *But they that have gathered it shall eat it, and praise the Lord; and they that have brought it together shall drink it in the courts of my holiness.*

the diadem representing Israel to help and protect it, v. 3. Others will no longer scoff at Israel as a nation "Forsaken" and "Desolate." They will call her "Hephzi-bah" ("My delight is in her"), an indication of the Lord's attitude toward the nation. They will call the land "Beulah" ("married"), recognizing the relationship between the people and the land. The name "Beulah" (*bᵉᶜûlâ*) is a passive participle of *baᶜal*, "to marry." The nation was forsaken; now the Lord delights in them. The land was desolate; now it is wed to its inhabitants, v. 4. Just as a young man "marrieth" (*baᶜal*) a virgin in the marriage relationship, so shall the "sons," i.e., the descendants, "marry" (*baᶜal*) "thee," the land of Palestine.[5] As the groom rejoices over his bride, so the Lord will rejoice in this new relationship, v. 5.

6–9 The Lord has set "watchmen" to pray for Jerusalem. The verse does not identify the watchmen. The parallelism to "ye that make mention of the Lord" suggests that these are humans, perhaps the prophets, given the special burden of prayer for Jerusalem.[6] They are commis-

---

[5]There is difficulty in understanding the marriage to a land. To avoid this, Knight, p. 66; Westermann, p. 372; and Goldingay, p. 352, among others, repoint *banayik*, "thy sons," to *bonayik*, "your builders." The plural noun *bonayik* refers to the Lord, who has rebuilt the land. The versions, however, do not support this. The LXX reads οὕτως κατοικήσουσιν οἱ υἱοί σου, "so your sons will dwell in thee." The Vulgate reads *et habitabunt in te filii tui*, "and your sons will dwell in you." The Targum reads, "Just as a young man cohabits with a virgin, so shall your sons cohabit in your midst." This consistent understanding by the early versions argues against repointing the word. Ibn Ezra, p. 284, understands the expression figuratively, "the kingdom will be restored to thee." The marriage relationship, however, is appropriate to show the joining of the people to the land. The Lord rejoices in this.

[6]Pieper, p. 620, and Henry, p. 364, spiritualize the passage. They make the watchmen ministers of the church. This interpretation ignores the context, which refers to Zion and Jerusalem, v. 1; Gentiles, v. 2; the "land," v. 4; and "Jerusalem," v. 6. Among others, Alexander, II, 409; Kraeling, p. 216; and Kissane, II, 282, suggest that the watchmen are angels; cf. Dan. 4:13, 17, 23. Nothing elsewhere, however, indicates that the angels pray for mankind. The context favors human watchmen.

sioned to pray continually, to "make mention of" (better "remind") the Lord, to "keep not silence" ($d^omî$, better "take no rest"), v. 6.[7] They should give the Lord no "rest" ($d^omî$) until He establishes Jerusalem, making it the "praise" ($t^ehillâ$, see 42:8) of the earth.[8] The thought is similar to that of Psalm 122:6, with Israel's peace coming only when Christ reigns over the world. While we cannot give the details of the fulfillment of this command, the context sets it in the future. Logically, it comes at the start of the Lord's rule over the earth, during the transition between the Tribulation and the Millennium, v. 7.[9] The Lord swears by His "right hand" and the "arm of his strength," emblems of His power. He will not let others overcome the nation again. Israel's enemies will not take their "corn" (better "grain") and "wine" (better "new wine") that they have labored to bring forth, v. 8.[10] Those who have worked to bring in the harvest will eat it. They will praise God for His goodness to them. They will drink wine in the "courts of my holiness" (better "courts of my sanctuary") as they keep the feasts once more, v. 9.

---

[7]Smith, p. 440, understands this as the restoration of prophecy. The description, however, sounds more like prayer than prophecy. It is, of course, possible that the prophets also pray as part of their ministry.

[8]Brueggemann, *Isaiah 40–66,* p. 222, wrongly states, "This nagging insistence suggests that Yahweh's loud resolve of verse 1 is not quite reliable and at least needs constant reinforcement." We do not pray, however, because God needs to be reminded. Real prayer begins with God Himself; cf. Rom. 8:26–27. As the Spirit intercedes with us to reveal God's will, we pray and thereby agree that we want God's will to be done.

[9]Delitzsch, II, 440; Von Orelli, p. 329; and Leupold, II, 334, make the command to captives in Babylon, preparing them for the first return. Whitehouse, II, 300, and Leupold, II, 334, refer it to later returns from Babylon. The captives should not remain behind but should also return to Palestine. Knight, p. 68; Wright, p. 150; and Herbert, *Isaiah 40–66,* p. 168, apply the command to Jews. They should leave the gates of Jerusalem to build a road by which others may come to the city. Vine, p. 182, spiritualizes the command, saying that obstacles to spiritual blessing should be removed. Alexander, II, 410, spiritualizes it differently pointing out that nothing should be allowed to stand in the way of nations entering the church. Price's view, p. 266, is similar, explaining that the gospel must be kept simple. He says, "The stumbling stones of human prejudices or private opinions" should not clutter the message to the lost. These views ignore the context. Verse 2 speaks of Israel's righteousness. Verse 7 refers to the praise of Jerusalem throughout the earth. Since vv. 11–12 are clearly eschatological, it is reasonable to make v. 10 eschatological as well.

[10]Whitehouse, II, 299, identifies the enemies as either the Samaritans or Edomites. His view rests upon the late dating of c. 56–66 and sees the passage as historical. From an eschatological view, the enemies are the nations of the world that gather against Israel at the close of the Tribulation.

10 *Go through, go through the gates; prepare ye the way of the people; cast up, cast up the highway; gather out the stones; lift up a standard for the people.*
11 *Behold, the Lord hath proclaimed unto the end of the world, Say ye to the daughter of Zion, Behold, thy salvation cometh; behold, his reward is with him, and his work before him.*
12 *And they shall call them, The holy people, The redeemed of the Lord: and thou shalt be called, Sought out, A city not forsaken.*

10–12 Isaiah urges the nation to "go through, go through" the gates of the city, most likely Jerusalem. The doubled command emphasizes the commission. They should "prepare" (or "make clear") a highway for dispersed Jews to use as they return; cf. 11:16; 19:23; 35:8–10; 40:3; 57:14.[11] They are to "cast up, cast up" (or "raise up, raise up") the road, building it above the surrounding land. The doubled command again emphasizes the nature of the work. They should free the road from stones that would hinder people from their travel. They are to raise a standard to mark the way for the people; cf. 5:26; 11:12; 49:22. The final word is plural, "peoples," referring to those coming from various parts of the world, v. 10. The Lord has proclaimed to the world that they are to tell Israel that her "salvation [*yaša*, see 17:10] cometh," i.e., her Savior comes. He brings His "reward" and His "work" (*p*ᵉ*ullâ*, better "recompense," see 40:10) for the faithful, v. 11. Other nations will call Israel "the holy people" (*ʿam⁻haqqodeš*)[12] and "the redeemed of the Lord." They will call Jerusalem "Sought out, A city not forsaken." This recognizes that the Lord has made it His own city, the capital of His kingdom, v. 12.

---

[11]Price, p. 266, spiritualizes the passage. He refers it to "spiritual highways" that lead sinners "to the heart of God." He is, however, inconsistent. At 11:16; 19:23; 35:8–10; and 40:3, he understands a literal highway. At 57:14 and here, he understands the removal of sin. The repeated emphasis in Isaiah on constructing a road argues that this is a literal road along which the redeemed travel as they journey to Jerusalem.

[12]Brueggemann, *Isaiah 40–66,* p. 224, understands *ʿam⁻haqqodeš* as "people belonging to the holy (one)." Pieper, p. 624, suggests the possibility "people of the sanctuary"; cf. v. 9. While these are possible translations, the parallelism with the phrase "redeemed of the Lord" argues for understanding "holy people."

Practical Application from Chapter 62

The New Position
1. A New Name. The Lord determines to deliver His people. His righteousness and salvation will then be seen by all, v. 1–2a. He will give them a new name, v. 2b.
2. A New State
    a. A new appearance. Israel will be a "crown of glory" and a "royal diadem," a beautiful object. He will hold the nation in His hand to protect her, v. 3.
        (1) The protection of prayer. The Lord appoints men to pray day and night for Jerusalem, v. 6. They will not stop until the Lord gives Jerusalem its position of praise in the earth, v. 7.
        (2) The protection of God's power. The Lord has sworn that their enemies will no more overcome the people, v. 8. They will eat their crops and praise the Lord for His goodness. They will drink the wine as they worship in the sanctuary, v. 9.
    b. A new delight. The nations call Israel "Hephzi-bah" to acknowledge the Lord's attitude toward His people, v. 4a.
    c. A new relationship. The nations will call the land "Beulah." They recognize that the people now are joined to the land, v. 4b. Just as a young man marries his bride, so the people now are married to the land, v. 5a.
        (1) The preparation of the way. A way is prepared, joining Egypt, Israel, and Assyria, so that people may journey to Jerusalem, v. 10.
        (2) The proclamation of the Savior. He comes bringing His reward to the faithful and His recompense to the unfaithful, v. 11.
        (3) The recognition of the nation. The nations understand that Israel has a special relationship with the Lord, v. 12.
    d. A new joy. Just as the groom rejoices in his bride, so the Lord rejoices over Israel, v. 5b.

1 Who is this that cometh from Edom, with dyed garments from
  Bozrah? this that is glorious in his apparel, travelling in the greatness of his strength? I that speak in righteousness, mighty to save.
2 Wherefore art thou red in thine apparel, and thy garments like him
  that treadeth in the winefat?
3 I have trodden the winepress alone; and of the people there was
  none with me: for I will tread them in mine anger, and trample them
  in my fury; and their blood shall be sprinkled upon my garments,
  and I will stain all my raiment.

ISAIAH 63

The opening paragraph continues the eschatological theme introduced in c. 60 and developed more fully in c. 61–62. The Lord foretells
the Tribulation judgments on the Gentile nations that oppose Him,
vv. 1–6. Isaiah, speaking for Israel, responds with prayer. After first
praising God for His work on their behalf, vv. 7–9, he confesses the sin
of the nation against Him, v. 10. The people recall His deliverances in
the past, vv. 11–14. Speaking for the people, Isaiah seeks God's favor
once more, vv. 15–16. The people ask why He has let them go in their
own ways, vv. 17–19.

3. Judgment of the Enemies 63:1–14
a. Promise of Judgment 63:1–6

1–3 Isaiah sees in a vision a figure coming from Edom.[1] He asks the
person to identify himself. The person in the vision wears "dyed"
(ḥamaṣ, better "red")[2] garments from Bozrah. This was an important
Edomite city about twenty-five miles southeast of the Dead Sea. It grew
up around an oasis. The clothing of the person in the vision is glorious in
appearance. His strength is great. The person identifies Himself to Isaiah.

---

[1]Barnes, II, 387, and Vine, p. 182, identify the spokesman as Israel. Motyer, *The
Prophecy of Isaiah,* p. 509, thinks this is a watchman of Israel, looking for the coming
king mentioned in 62:11. Westermann, p. 380, more generally makes the person a watchman challenging someone who approaches the gate. The narrative seems to come from a
vision. Necessarily, the spokesman must be an individual, likely Isaiah rather than an unknown watchman.

[2]Skinner, *Isaiah XL–LXVI,* p. 215, and Young, III, 476, translate ḥamaṣ as "bright."
They draw, however, on the root for ḥamaṣ III, "sharp, piercing" and conclude that it
means "bright" from this. The word here is from ḥamaṣ II. This root occurs elsewhere
only at Ps. 68:23, in which it must mean "red" ("your foot will be red with blood").
Verse 2 uses the synonym ʾadom, which can only be translated "red."

He is one who speaks in "righteousness" (*ṣ^edaqâ*, see 1:21) and is mighty to "save" (*yaša^c*, see 17:10). From the description, it is clear that this is the Lord, v. 1.[3]

Isaiah asks why the Lord's garments are red. Why are they like clothing spattered with the juice of grapes from walking in the "winefat" (*gat*)? The *gat* was the upper vat in the winepress, used for pressing the grapes. The juice drained to the lower vat, v. 2. The Lord answers that He has walked alone in the winepress of judgment upon people. He will judge them because of His anger over their sin. As occurs so often in the book, this is a prophetic perfect. The act is certain in the mind of God, so He states it as an accomplished fact. The "blood" (*neṣaḥ*) of His enemies is "sprinkled" (*nazah*, see 52:15) on His garments. It has "stain[ed]" (*^ɔeg^ɔaltî*) His clothing.[4] The word *neṣaḥ*, "juice," has a figurative sense here, "juice-colored," i.e., blood. This description of judgment recalls that given earlier in 34:5–17. The judgment of Edom represents the Tribulation judgments that will come on the earth; cf. Revelation 14:17–20; 19:13, 15.[5] This verse inspired Julia Ward Howe to write, "He is trampling out the vintage where the grapes of wrath are stored" in the "Battle Hymn of the Republic," v. 3.

---

[3]Watts, *Isaiah 34–66*, p. 321, keeping to his late dating of this part, sees the person as "a symbol of Persian imperial power fighting Jerusalem's and Yahweh's battles for them." He identifies the warrior as Megabyzus, the Persian general who governed Palestine in the mid-fifth century B.C. There is, however, no reason to abandon the Isaianic authorship of the passage.

[4]The *hip^cîl* verb *^ɔeg^ɔaltî* is irregular with a prefixed *^ɔalep* rather than a *he*. KB, I, 170, calls it a mixed form from the *hip^cîl* and *aphel*. BDB, p. 146, suggests reading it as a *pi^cel*. G.K. 53 *k* suggests a "scribal error," but 53 *p* says to read it as a *pi^cel* imperfect. Delitzsch, II, 447, calls the verb a *hip^cîl* with "an Aramæan inflexion." Näglesbach, p. 670, likewise calls it a "Hiphil form imitating the Aramaic." Ibn Ezra, p. 287, accepts it as a *hip^cîl* but makes it "a compound of the past and future," a rather strange conclusion. Cyrus H. Gordon and Edward J. Young, "אגאלתי (Isaiah 63:3)," *WTJ* 14:54, give several forms from the OT that combine "the prefix of the imperfect and the suffix of the perfect." They conclude that there is no reason to emend the verse.

[5]Ibn Ezra, p. 286, understands Edom as "the empire of Rome and Constantinople, who are called Edomites, because they adopted the Edomite religion—that is, the Christian religion—which was first established among the Edomites." This view rewrites history since Christianity was never prevalent in Edom. Kraeling, p. 218, thinks that the mention of Edom is important only as it indicates the direction from which the Lord comes. The use of the judgment of Edom elsewhere, however, argues that this represents the Tribulation judgments that will come on the earth.

4 *For the day of vengeance is in mine heart, and the year of my re-deemed is come.*

5 *And I looked, and there was none to help; and I wondered that there was none to uphold: therefore mine own arm brought salvation unto me; and my fury, it upheld me.*

6 *And I will tread down the people in mine anger, and make them drunk in my fury, and I will bring down their strength to the earth.*

7 *I will mention the lovingkindnesses of the Lord, and the praises of the Lord, according to all that the Lord hath bestowed on us, and the great goodness toward the house of Israel, which he hath bestowed on them according to his mercies, and according to the multitude of his lovingkindnesses.*

4–6 The Lord has His timetable for judging His enemies and for redeeming His people. The expressions "day of vengeance" and "year of my redeemed" recall the promise at 61:2. Putting the two passages together gives three divisions of history: (1) "the acceptable year of the Lord," the church age; (2) the "day of vengeance," the Tribulation, which follows the church age; and (3) the "year of my redeemed [or 'redemption']," the kingdom, that follows the Tribulation, v. 4.

The Lord has looked and found no one to help Him. He "wondered" (or "was astonished") that no one would uphold righteousness. For this reason, He Himself has acted. With His "arm," the emblem of His strength, He has brought "salvation" (*yašaᶜ*, see 17:10), deliverance, to His people and wrath to His enemies, v. 5. He will tread upon His enemies. They will stagger as though "drunk" (*šakar*)[6] from His wrath. He "will bring down their strength to the earth," causing their death as He brings judgment on them. This promise of judgment is eschatological, looking to the Tribulation judgments, v. 6.

b. Prayer for Deliverance 63:7–14

7–9 Isaiah begins his prayer with a note of praise.[7] He will "mention" (or "cause to be remembered") the "lovingkindnesses" (or "loyalties,"

---

[6]Whitehouse, II, 305; Westermann, p. 380; and McKenzie, p. 186, follow the Targum and several manuscripts in reading *šabar*, "to break, shatter," for *šakar*, "to be drunk." The LXX and Vulgate, along with other versions, support the MT. It is likely that the Targum is interpretive. Their change parallels the first phrase and explains the drunkenness as breaking or shattering the people. It is, however, unnecessary.

[7]Young, III, 480, spiritualizes the verse. Without any supporting arguments, he sees Israel as the church. He jumps back to Israel in the rest of the passage since it cannot refer to the church.

8 *For he said, Surely they are my people, children that will not lie: so he was their Saviour.*

9 *In all their affliction he was afflicted, and the angel of his presence saved them: in his love and in his pity he redeemed them; and he bare them, and carried them all the days of old.*

ḥesed, see 16:5) of the Lord. The word ḥesed occurs widely with a variety of meanings. In all of these, there is a strong component of loyalty. The Lord is loyal to His own. Isaiah praises Him for this. In addition, he recalls the "praises" (tᵉhillâ, or "praiseworthiness," see 42:8) of the Lord. Isaiah also recognizes the "great goodness" of the Lord. All of these have come to Israel from the "mercies" (or "compassions") and "lovingkindnesses" (ḥesed, again, "loyalties") of God, v. 7. The Lord had claimed Israel for His people. He had looked upon them as "children that will not lie," having the potential for faithfulness. In view of Israel's history, this commendation may seem strange. The Lord, however, has the future in His view. Israel will accept the Lord as their "Saviour" (yašaʿ, see 17:10), Zechariah 13:1, and will become faithful to Him. The Lord sees this potential and, therefore, becomes their Savior, v. 8. In their trials, the Lord also suffered.[8] He sent the "angel of his presence" to deliver and sustain them. The phrase "angel of his presence" is similar to "angel of the Lord," e.g., Genesis 16:7–11; 22:11–17, and "angel of God," e.g., Genesis 21:17; Judges 13:6, 9. It refers here to the second person of the Trinity. He "saved" (yašaʿ) Israel at such times as the crossing of the Red Sea, Exodus 14:19–20; the guidance through the wilderness, Exodus 33:14–15; and the entrance into Palestine, Joshua 5:14. All these were in "the days of old." He "redeemed them . . . bare them . . . carried them." The multiplied description of God's work shows the greatness of His love for the people, v. 9.

---

[8]The kᵉtîb is loʾ ṣar, "he did not afflict." The qerê reads lô ṣar, "He was afflicted." Watts, *Isaiah 34–66*, p. 326, accepts the kᵉtîb. He concludes that Israel's afflictions did not come from God. The position is difficult to defend. Alexander, II, 418, also accepts the kᵉtîb. He translates, "In all their enmity, He was not an enemy." This is better but still awkward. Overwhelmingly, the word ṣar is "affliction, trouble." In addition, the fact that He saves them suggests that they are going through trials. With the AV, I accept the qᵉrê here as best suiting the context.

10 But they rebelled, and vexed his holy Spirit: therefore he was turned to be their enemy, and he fought against them.

11 Then he remembered the days of old, Moses, and his people, saying, Where is he that brought them up out of the sea with the shepherd of his flock? where is he that put his holy Spirit within him?

12 That led them by the right hand of Moses with his glorious arm, dividing the water before them, to make himself an everlasting name?

13 That led them through the deep, as an horse in the wilderness, that they should not stumble?

14 As a beast goeth down into the valley, the Spirit of the Lord caused him to rest: so didst thou lead thy people, to make thyself a glorious name.

10–14 Isaiah recalls the history of the nation. Despite God's grace, Israel rebelled against Him. They "vexed his holy Spirit," rejecting His guidance.[9] Paul likely drew his challenge to the Ephesians from this verse: "grieve not the holy Spirit of God," Ephesians 4:30. Stephen's comment that the Jews "resist[ed] the Holy Ghost," Acts 7:51, may also have come from here. Israel's rebellion caused God to turn against them. He "fought against them" by bringing them into judgment, v. 10.

Finally, "he," Israel, remembered God's grace in former times. The people recalled the deliverance of the nation from Egypt by Moses.[10] They ask a series of questions. (1) Where is God, the one who brought His people through the Red Sea with their "shepherd" (lit. "shepherds"), the civil leaders of the nation? (2) Where is the one who gave His Holy Spirit to guide them, Numbers 11:25, v. 11? (3) Where is the one who

---

[9]Knight, p. 77, identifies the Spirit here with the Word of God. The fact, however, that the Spirit here is "grieved" indicates personality. Herbert, *Isaiah 40–66*, p. 176, says, "it would be a mistake to read into the phrase the fuller Christian meaning of the New Testament." He considers the phrase an "emphatic expression for 'him', as if to draw attention to God's presence and activity." Brueggemann, *Isaiah 40–66*, p. 229, likewise rejects "any developed theological sense that eventuated in a later Christian doctrine of the Trinity." The phrase "holy Spirit" occurs only here, vv. 10–11, and Ps. 51:11. This rare use suggests that this is more than another name for God the Father. The OT does not emphasize the work of the Holy Spirit, but it does not omit it entirely. If the phrase only renames God, v. 11 is tautologous, God putting God in the people. It is best to recognize this as the Holy Spirit. This completes the mention of the Trinity in vv. 9–11: "the angel of His presence" (the Son), v. 9; the "holy Spirit," vv. 10, 11; and "he" (the Father), v. 11.

[10]The AV translates according to the word order and the accents of the MT. Barnes, II, 394; Motyer, *The Prophecy of Isaiah*, p. 514; and Goldingay, p. 357, understand God as the subject. From the following question, it is clear that "His people" is the subject: "Then His people remembered the days of old, the days of Moses." This neglects the Hebrew accents but better fits the overall context.

15 Look down from heaven, and behold from the habitation of thy holi-
ness and of thy glory: where is thy zeal and thy strength, the sound-
ing of thy bowels and of thy mercies toward me? are they restrained?
16 Doubtless thou art our father, though Abraham be ignorant of us,
and Israel acknowledge us not: thou, O Lord, art our father, our re-
deemer; thy name is from everlasting.

led them through the Red Sea? (4) Where is the one whose "glorious arm" enabled Moses to part the Red Sea with his "right hand," Exodus 14:21?[11] This gained an "everlasting name," i.e., reputation, for the Lord, v. 12. (5) Where is the one who led Israel through the "deep," the divide in the Red Sea; cf. Psalm 106:9? God had removed the obstacles from them. They were as a horse walking through the wilderness without stumbling, v. 13. Like the "beast" (*b^ehemâ*, see 18:6) grazing in the valley, the Lord had given Israel rest. The noun *b^ehemâ* here refers to the domesticated animals: cattle, sheep, goats, and so forth. The Lord had led His people and gained a "glorious name," a reputation for Himself. If God had done these things for Israel before, why does He withhold His grace now, v. 14?

Note that vv. 7–14 mention all three members of the Godhead. Verses 7–9a, 10b, 11a, 12–14b refer to the work of the Father on Israel's behalf. Verse 9b refers to the "angel of his presence," the Son of God. Verses 10a, 11b, 14a refer to the work of the Holy Spirit.[12]

D. Prayer of the People 63:15–65:16
1. Confession of the People 63:15–19

15–16 Speaking on behalf of the nation, Isaiah pleads with the Lord. He asks Him to look from the "habitation of thy holiness and of thy glory," heaven, and to remember them once more. He asks where His zeal for them and His strength to deliver have gone. The last half of the verse is a statement rather than a question. "The sounding of thy bowels," idiomatic for the emotional response of God's heart, is restrained.

---

[11]The word "where" (*'ayyeh*) introduces the first two questions. Isaiah introduces the final questions with *hip^îl* participles. The sense that they are questions comes from continuing the thought of v. 11. It is common to divide the fourth question into two questions: "Who caused His glorious arm to go at the right hand of Moses?" and "Who divided the waters before them to make an everlasting name for Himself?" The verb "dividing" is a *qal* participle. Rather than making the final phrase of v. 12 a separate question, I have chosen to let it continue the action introduced in the question.

[12]See also 11:2; 42:1; 48:16; 59:19–21; 61:1 for other passages in Isaiah that mention the Trinity.

17 *O Lord, why hast thou made us to err from thy ways, and hardened our heart from thy fear? Return for thy servants' sake, the tribes of thine inheritance.*

18 *The people of thy holiness have possessed it but a little while: our adversaries have trodden down thy sanctuary.*

19 *We are thine: thou never barest rule over them; they were not called by thy name.*

His "mercies" (or "compassions") toward them are restrained. Isaiah, acting as the representative of Israel, uses the first person pronoun "me," v. 15. He acknowledges that God is the nation's Father. Although Abraham and "Israel," Jacob, have died and no longer know of the nation, the Lord is still Israel's father. The final part of the verse is separate from the rest. The phrase "our redeemer [*go²el*, see 35:9]; thy name is from everlasting" is better "our Redeemer from everlasting is your name." This acknowledges the redemptive work of God in the past on their behalf, v. 16.[13]

17–19 The people question why God has made them "err" from His ways. The Lord has made them "err" in that He has let them go in their own way. He has let them harden their hearts against Him. It is not that He has caused these things. Rather, He has permitted the people to go their own way. The people now ask Him to return to them for the sake of those who serve Him. They want Him again to consider them His inheritance, v. 17. They have possessed "it," the temple, where they could meet with Him, only a "little while" (*lammiṣ²ar*).[14] Their enemies have now broken it down, v. 18. Verse 19 reads better, "We are as those over whom you have never ruled, as those who were not called by your name." The statement confesses their rebelliousness in the past, v. 19.

---

[13]The Masoretic accents join *go²el* and *ᶜôlam*, "our Redeemer from old [or 'everlasting']." This is the name to which Isaiah refers. Paraphrasing for clarity, the phrase says, "Your name is 'our everlasting Redeemer.'"

[14]The verse is open to several interpretations. The phrase "but a little while" understands *lammiṣᶜar* to refer to time. Elsewhere, it refers to something small or insignificant. The phrase "people of thy holiness" may be either the subject or the object of the verb "possessed." It is not clear what the supplied word "it" refers to. These difficulties have led to three main interpretations. (1) For an insignificant reason, the heathen have possessed the holy people. This requires supplying "the heathen" as the subject. (2) Israel has possessed the "Holy Land" only a short time. This requires supplying "Holy Land" as the object of the verb. Alternately, the word "inheritance" in v. 17 may refer to Canaan. We may understand the supplied "it" to refer to this. (3) Israel has possessed the temple (or holy place) only a short time. This understands the supplied word "it" to refer to "sanctuary" in 18*b*. Both conservative and liberal authors hold all three views. I have adopted the last view because of the parallelism with "sanctuary" in the second half of the verse.

Practical Application from Chapter 63

1. Judgment of the Wicked

   a. Announcement of the judgment. Isaiah sees the Lord come from Edom in glorious array. The Lord identifies Himself as one who is "righteous" and "mighty to save," v. 1. Isaiah asks why the Lord's garments are red, v. 2. The Lord responds that He judges His enemies. The announcement looks forward to the Tribulation judgments, v. 3.

   b. Details of the judgment. The Lord looks forward to the "year of my redeemed," the church age, and the "day of vengeance," the Tribulation, v. 4. He alone will deliver His people and bring wrath to His enemies, v. 5. He will bring about their deaths, v. 6.

2. Prayer for Deliverance

   a. Recognition of God's protection. Isaiah praises the Lord for His loyalty, His praiseworthiness, and His goodnesses. These have come from the compassions and loyalty of the Lord, v. 7. He has claimed Israel as His own and has therefore delivered them, a promise for the future, v. 8. He has delivered them by His Son, v. 9.

   b. Prayer for God's protection. Israel has rebelled against the Lord. This has caused God to punish them, v. 10. Israel remembers the past deliverances by God. They ask where He has gone, vv. 12–14. The implied thought is "Why does God not work on our behalf now?"

3. Confession of Israel's Plight

   a. Isaiah pleads with God to remember His people again, v. 15. He acknowledges God as the Father of the nation. He is their everlasting Redeemer, v. 16.

   b. The people ask God why has He let them go from Him. They ask Him to return to them again, v. 17. They have possessed the sanctuary only a short time, v. 18. They are estranged from the Lord, v. 19.

1 *Oh that thou wouldest rend the heavens, that thou wouldest come
   down, that the mountains might flow down at thy presence,*
2 *As when the melting fire burneth, the fire causeth the waters to boil,
   to make thy name known to thine adversaries, that the nations may
   tremble at thy presence!*
3 *When thou didst terrible things which we looked not for, thou camest
   down, the mountains flowed down at thy presence.*

ISAIAH 64

Verse 1 is 63:19*b* in Hebrew, indicating that the rabbis thought that
the prayer of the verse concluded c. 63. Many present-day commentators
understand the verse this way.[1] It is true that the prayer continues into
c. 64. The thought of the Lord's appearance, however, leads nicely into
the similes of v. 2. In the prayer that follows, the plural pronouns, e.g.,
vv. 3, 5, 6, refer to Israel. It is, however, the prophet Isaiah who speaks
for the nation. The Lord will bless those who live righteously, vv. 4–5*a*.
He will, however, judge those who continue in sin, vv. 5*b*–7. God has
formed the nation, v. 8. Isaiah pleads with Him to hold back His anger,
v. 9. The nation has already undergone devastation, vv. 10–11. They need
His care, v. 12.

2. Request of Israel 64:1–12

1–3 Isaiah prays for an awesome revelation of God. He does not think
of a theophany but of a display of God's power such as would cause the
mountains to "flow down" (better "quake") before Him, v. 1.[2] Just as the
"melting [*hᵃmasîm*][3] fire burneth" (better "fire kindles brushwood") and

---

[1] Among others, McKenzie, p. 191; Alexander, II, 429; and Young, III, 490, understand
v. 1 (19*b*) as closing c. 63. There was early disagreement on this. The Vulgate made it
v. 1 in c. 64.

[2] Ibn Ezra, p. 291, makes the "mountains" symbols of kings. The context of "heavens,"
"water," and "fire," together with the historical reference to Sinai in v. 3, argue that the
verse refers to actual mountains.

[3] The word *hᵃmasîm* occurs only here. We must derive the meaning from the parallelism
to "fire boiling water," i.e., the word refers to something that fire operates on. The LXX
translates κηρὸς ἀπὸ πυρὸς τήκεται, "wax melts before a fire." The Vulgate is similar.
It gives *sicut exustio ignis tabescent,* "they would melt as at the burning of fire." The
Targum reads *rgzk bʾštʾ,* "your anger in the fire." The AV makes the noun *hᵃmasîm* modify "fire." This is unlikely since the phrase does not parallel 2*b*. The Isaiah Scroll reads
ʾeš ᶜamasîm, "burden of fire." This was undoubtedly an attempt to explain an unfamiliar
word. Guillaume, p. 42, relies on 1QIsaᵃ. He interprets ᶜ*msym* as "brushwood" although
BDB, p. 770, suggests "load, burden." Delitzsch, II, 464, bases the meaning "broken,

4 *For since the beginning of the world men have not heard, nor perceived by the ear, neither hath the eye seen, O God, beside thee, what he hath prepared for him that waiteth for him.*
5 *Thou meetest him that rejoiceth and worketh righteousness, those that remember thee in thy ways: behold, thou art wroth; for we have sinned: in those is continuance, and we shall be saved.*
6 *But we are all as an unclean thing, and all our righteousnesses are as filthy rags; and we all do fade as a leaf; and our iniquities, like the wind, have taken us away.*
7 *And there is none that calleth upon thy name, that stirreth up himself to take hold of thee: for thou hast hid thy face from us, and hast consumed us, because of our iniquities.*

boils the water, so the enemies of God will know His "name." God's "name" reveals His nature. This will cause the heathen to tremble in His presence, v. 2. In time past, God had worked in an awesome manner on Israel's behalf. He did things they had not "looked" (*qawâ*, see 5:2) for. He came down, meeting with Moses on Mt. Sinai, and the mountains "flowed down" (better "quaked") at His presence, Exodus 19:8, v. 3.

4–7 No one has ever heard or paid attention to or seen the extent to which God can work on behalf of His people. The Lord alludes to this in speaking with His disciples, Matthew 13:17. Paul loosely quotes the verse as he shows that Christians have a new revelation of God's Holy Spirit, I Corinthians 2:9, v. 4. God "meeteth" (*paga*ᶜ, see 47:3) with the one who "rejoiceth and worketh righteousness [*ṣedeq*, see 1:21]." The phrase is a hendiadys, "rejoices in doing righteousness." These workers of righteousness remember the works of God with mankind, v. 5*a*.

God, however, is "wroth" (*qaṣap*, see 8:21) over man's sin. Not only has man sinned but also "in those is continuance," i.e., they have continued in their sin. The statement "and we shall be saved" is better a rhetorical question, "and shall we be saved?" The answer is clearly no! God cannot look with favor on those who fail to repent, v. 5*b*. Isaiah confesses Israel's sins. The nation is vile and an "unclean thing" (*ṭame*ᵓ, see 6:5). Their righteousness is as "filthy rags" (ᶜ*iddîm*, or "menstrual cloth"), idiomatically showing their sin.[4] They "fade" (or "wither") like a

---

dry wood" on an Arabic cognate *hašim*, "dry twigs," i.e., "brushwood." Since this meaning parallels 2*b* nicely, most authors follow this today.

[4]The word ᶜ*iddîm* is a *hapax legomenon* from the unused root ᶜ*dd*. There is an Aramaic cognate ᶜ*iddan*, "time." The Akkadian root *adannu* means "fixed time." This connection with time suggests the menstrual period. Henry, p. 377, takes the word in a general sense, "filthy rags, fit to be cast to the dunghill." Ibn Ezra, p. 292, derives the word from

8 But now, O Lord, thou art our father; we are the clay, and thou our potter; and we all are the work of thy hand.
9 Be not wroth very sore, O Lord, neither remember iniquity for ever: behold, see, we beseech thee, we are all thy people.
10 Thy holy cities are a wilderness, Zion is a wilderness, Jerusalem a desolation.
11 Our holy and our beautiful house, where our fathers praised thee, is burned up with fire: and all our pleasant things are laid waste.
12 Wilt thou refrain thyself for these things, O Lord? wilt thou hold thy peace, and afflict us very sore?

leaf, not able to cling to health because of sin. Their "iniquities" (ʿawon, see 1:4), like the wind, have taken them away, v. 6. No one calls on God. They do not rouse themselves to cling to Him. God has hidden Himself from them. He has "consumed [mûg, or 'melted,' see 14:31] us, because of [better 'into the hand of'] our iniquities [ʿawon]." The verb mûg expresses the fact that God has weakened the people. The result is their deliverance into the "hand," i.e., the power, of their sin, v. 7.

8–12 The thought now changes. Isaiah pleads with God as the nation's "father," the one who brought them into being. He is the potter who shaped the nation, v. 8. Isaiah begs the Lord to "be not wroth" (qaṣap, see 8:21). He asks Him not to remember their "iniquity" (ʿawon, see 1:4) forever. He pleads with the Lord to look upon them as His people, v. 9. He reminds God that the "holy cities," holy because they lie in land dedicated to God, now lie waste. He mentions "Zion," i.e., "Jerusalem," as the most prominent of the cities in the land. Even Jerusalem, the nation's capital, is desolate, v. 10. The "holy and . . . beautiful house," the temple, where the fathers had offered praise to God, has been burned. The "pleasant things" of the nation, probably referring to the temple furniture and vessels, are ruined, v. 11.[5] Isaiah closes the prayer with a plea. Will the Lord refrain from working on Israel's behalf? Will He "hold [His] peace" (better "remain silent") and continue to "afflict" (ʿanâ, see 31:4) them greatly? The rhetorical questions imply that the Lord will not remain aloof from His people, v. 12.

ʿad, "prey," Gen. 49:27. He argues that the garment used to wrap the spoil is stained with blood. While the derivation differs, this also leads to a "menstrual cloth."
[5]Henry, p. 379, broadens the term. He includes not only the temple furniture but also the religious feasts and worship days throughout the year. The view is possible. Brueggemann, Isaiah 40–66, p. 236, refers the "pleasant places" to the "loveliness of the city." Fausset, p. 759, understands the phrase to describe "our homes, our city, and all its dear associations." The parallelism with v. 11a argues for something associated with the temple.

Practical Application from Chapter 64

Relying on God

1. Prayer for God's Work. Isaiah prays that God would reveal Himself in power: the quaking of the mountains, v. 1; the burning of wood; or the boiling of water, v. 2*a*. This will cause the heathen to tremble before Him, v. 2*b*. He recalls the awesome work of God at Sinai, when the mountain quaked at His presence, v. 3.

2. Contrast in God's Actions

   a. No one knows what God has prepared for those who look for Him, v. 4. The Lord meets those who rejoice in righteousness, v. 5*a*.

   b. God is angry, however, with those who continue in their sin, v. 5*b*. The nation is vile, blown about with their sin, v. 6. No one seeks God. He therefore hides from them and delivers them into the power of their sin, v. 7.

3. Plea for God's Help. Isaiah acknowledges God as the nation's "father," v. 8. He begs Him to limit His wrath and to look on them as His people again, v. 9. He reminds God of the devastation that has come on the nation, v. 10. Even the temple lies under judgment, v. 11. Will God continue to remain aloof? The questions imply Israel's need of God's help, v. 12.

1 *I am sought of them that asked not for me; I am found of them that*
   sought me not: I said, Behold me, behold me, unto a nation that was
   not called by my name.
2 *I have spread out my hands all the day unto a rebellious people,*
   which walketh in a way that was not good, after their own thoughts;
3 *A people that provoketh me to anger continually to my face; that*
   sacrificeth in gardens, and burneth incense upon altars of brick;
4 *Which remain among the graves, and lodge in the monuments, which*
   eat swine's flesh, and broth of abominable things is in their vessels;
5 *Which say, Stand by thyself, come not near to me; for I am holier than*
   thou. These are a smoke in my nose, a fire that burneth all the day.

ISAIAH 65

The first part of the chapter naturally follows the prayer of c. 64. The Lord now responds to Isaiah's plea. While the heathen have turned to Him, v. 1, Israel has not, v. 2. They have worshiped idols, v. 3, and followed wicked practices in their worship, v. 4. They were self-righteous and God will judge them, v. 5. He will not ignore their sins but will judge them, vv. 6–7. He will, however, spare a remnant to inhabit Palestine, vv. 8–9. He will bless the land, v. 10. The unfaithful, however, will receive judgment, vv. 11–12. He will bless those who serve Him but judge the wicked, vv. 13–15. The righteous will enjoy the blessing of God, v. 16.

Verse 17 begins the final part of the book. This looks at the end times, including both the Lord's rule on the earth and the eternal ages. The Lord will create "new heavens and a new earth," v. 17. His people will rejoice in the new creation, v. 18, and the Lord will rejoice in them, v. 19*a*. There will be no more grief, v. 19*b*. There will be no more premature death although sinners will die, v. 20. People will build houses and raise crops, v. 21. There will be peace in the earth, vv. 22–23. The Lord will hear the prayers of His people, v. 24. Even the animal kingdom will be at peace, v. 25.

3. Answer of the Lord 65:1–16

1–5 The Lord is "sought" (*nidraští*, better "allowed Myself to be sought") by those who were not seeking Him. Further, He has been "found" (*nimṣeʾtî*, better "allowed Myself to be found") by those not looking for Him.[1] He had announced Himself to the people "that was not

---

[1] In both clauses, the context argues that Isaiah uses the *nipʿal* verb with the tolerative sense rather than the passive. The Lord was not found accidentally by the Gentiles. He allowed Himself to be found. This creates an interesting paradox. The Lord revealed

540

called by my name" (better "to a nation that did not call on My name").
While the immediate context might suggest that this is Israel, the NT use
argues that the Gentiles are in view here. Paul quotes the passage in
Romans 10:20–21. He applies v. 1 to the Gentiles and v. 2 to the Jews.
Even at their worst, Israel continued to follow the temple ritual. They
continued to look upon themselves as chosen by God. For this reason,
they cannot be the nation that failed to call on the Lord. It is appropriate
to apply the verse to the heathen. The statement is a prophetic perfect,
certain in God's mind. It looks forward to the conversion of the Gentiles
in the church age, v. 1.[2]

The Lord has also reached out to Israel. He has held out His hands in
invitation to a rebellious people who walked in their own evil ways. This
gets at the heart of Israel's problem. While they carried out the temple
worship, they continued to practice wicked behavior. They walked "in a
way that was not good, after their own thoughts," v. 2. The Lord lists
some of Israel's sins. They continually vexed Him. They carried out their
sinful practices "to [His] face." They sacrificed to idols in the gardens.
They burned incense "upon altars of brick." This is lit. "upon the bricks
[*lebenîm*]," referring to altars made from bricks. The parallelism with
"sacrific[ing] in gardens" tells us that this was some form of worship.
Other than that, we do not know the exact meaning of the statement, v. 3.[3]

Himself to those who claimed to seek Him only to be rejected. He allowed Himself to be
found by those who did not seek Him and was accepted.

[2]Knight, p. 90, applies the verse to the Jews. He suggests that many of the Jews knew
nothing of the Lord. During the captivity, those who dwelled in the land came under heathen influence. It is to this group that Isaiah writes. The view assumes that the author is
Trito-Isaiah, who writes after the captivity. Skinner, *Isaiah XL–LXVI*, p. 232, takes basi-
cally the same position. He suggests that Paul's interpretation reflects a later view that had
become "traditional in the Apostle's time." Delitzsch, II, 475–76, also understands the
verse to have the "estranged" nation in view. As might be expected, the Jewish commentators also apply the verse to Israel. Slotki, p. 313, argues that Israel spurned "God's ready
accessibility." Ibn Ezra, p. 293, refers to the rejection of God by Israel although he mentions the view that v. 1 applies to all nations. In my judgment, the relative clause *ʾel gôy
loʾ-qoraʾ bišmî*, "unto a nation that [lit.] did not call on my name," argues that he writes of
heathen people. As a nation, Israel continued to go through their ritual of worship.

[3]Among others, Whitehouse, II, 319; Price, p. 282; and Rawlinson, II, 470, mention the
possibility that the "bricks" refer to the tiles on the roofs of the houses. Such verses as
II Kings 23:12; Jer. 19:13; 32:29; and Zeph. 1:5 show that the heathen carried out worship
on their housetops. Barnes, II, 409; Näglesbach, p. 689; and Von Orelli, p. 337, understand that the Jews had built altars from brick, violating Exod. 20:24–25. Verse 7 may
support this view, the father burning incense upon altars set up in the high places in the
mountains. Leupold, II, 360, suggests that this involved "the use of incense jars." On the

> 6 *Behold, it is written before me: I will not keep silence, but will rec-*
> *ompense, even recompense into their bosom,*
> 7 *Your iniquities, and the iniquities of your fathers together, saith the*
> *Lord, which have burned incense upon the mountains, and blas-*
> *phemed me upon the hills: therefore will I measure their former*
> *work into their bosom.*

The people "remain" (or "sit") among the graves, a place frequented by demons, Matthew 8:28. This may have been an effort to consult the dead, a practice forbidden elsewhere, e.g., Deuteronomy 18:11; cf. I Samuel 28:7–9 (I Chron. 10:13). They "lodge" (or "pass the night") among the "monuments" (*naṣar*, see 1:8). The participle form of *naṣar* refers to something that is watched. It has the sense here of a "guarded place," i.e., a place not open to casual visits. Perhaps this was a place of idol worship, limited to those devoted to the particular god involved. They seek the gods in that place through some ritual. They eat the flesh of swine, which were ritually impure, Leviticus 11:7–8; Deuteronomy 14:8. They eat the "broth of abominable things" (or "foul things") cooked in their pots.[4] While we do not know the nature of what they ate, it clearly violated the Mosaic Law. Leviticus 7:18 and 19:7, cf. Ezekiel 4:14, suggest that this may have been broth made from decayed meat, v. 4. Consumed with a self-righteous spirit, they would not let others near them lest their touch should defile them. This self-righteous attitude brings God's judgment. They are as "smoke" (*ʿašan*) in God's "nose" (*ʾap* or "wrath").[5] They are as a fire that burns all day as it consumes the fuel. The thought is that they cause the burning wrath of God to flare up in judgment, v. 5.

6–7 Their deeds have been written for the Lord to read, Revelation 20:12. He will not "keep silence," ignoring their sin. No, He will judge

---

basis of archaeological information, Dahood, *CBQ* 22:407–8, concludes that *lᵉbenîm* "might allude to some practice honoring Asherah." There is not enough information from archaeology to be certain of this. We cannot be sure of the nature and purpose of the "bricks" because the text does not give us enough information.

[4]The AV properly translates the *qᵉrê*, *mᵉraq*, "broth," rather than the *kᵉtîb*, *pᵉraq*, "fragments." The LXX, Vulgate, Targum, and 1QIsaᵃ all support the *qᵉrê*.

[5]The same word *ʾap* may mean "nose" or "anger." The connection lies in the fact that the nostrils of an angry person may dilate. This parallels the last phrase, "fire that burneth all the day." God's wrath will consume these enemies. The words *ʾap* and *ʿašan* occur together in II Sam. 22:9 (Ps. 18:8). Although the AV translates there "a smoke out of his nostrils," the grammatical construction is the same as here. God breathes out the smoke of His wrath as a picture of fiery judgment. Slotki, p. 314, understands the phrase to

8 *Thus saith the Lord, As the new wine is found in the cluster, and one saith, Destroy it not; for a blessing is in it: so will I do for my servants' sakes, that I may not destroy them all.*

9 *And I will bring forth a seed out of Jacob, and out of Judah an inheritor of my mountains: and mine elect shall inherit it, and my servants shall dwell there.*

10 *And Sharon shall be a fold of flocks, and the valley of Achor a place for the herds to lie down in, for my people that have sought me.*

them for their sin, repaying them for their actions. He will "recompense into [or 'upon'] their bosom [*ḥêq*, see 40:11]." The Lord uses the word picture of a lap filled with judgment, v. 6. He will judge the "iniquities" (*ʿawon*, see 1:4) of the children and the "iniquities" (*ʿawon*) of the fathers alike. They have "burned incense" to the gods in the high places on the mountains. They have "blasphemed [God]" on the hills of the land by their worship of the false gods. This combination of worshiping on the "mountains" and "hills" occurs elsewhere to describe Israel's idolatrous worship, Deuteronomy 12:2; Jeremiah 50:6; Ezekiel 6:3, 13; Hosea 4:13. Once more, the Lord will recompense them. He will measure out the judgment of their former "work" (*peʿullâ*, see 40:10) into their "bosom" (*ḥêq*, see v. 6), their lap, according as they have done, v. 7.

8–10 A cluster of grapes with bad grapes in it may be spared for the sake of the good grapes. In the same way, the Lord will not totally destroy Israel, v. 8. He will preserve a "seed" (or "offspring"), a remnant, from Jacob. He will bring forth an "inheritor" of the mountainous land from Judah. The names "Jacob" and "Judah" occur in poetic variation here. Both names refer to the faithful who will occupy the land. These are the "elect," chosen by the Lord to receive the land. They are His "servants," called to dwell in Palestine, v. 9. The Plain of Sharon extends south about fifty miles along the Mediterranean between Mt. Carmel and Joppa. This will be a sheepfold to hold the flocks of the nation. The Valley of Achor is best known as the place Achan received his punishment, Joshua 7:24, 26; 15:7. We cannot identify it specifically other than to place it near Jericho. The place of sin was a place of judgment. The place in which sin is judged now becomes a place of safety and peace in which the herds may lie down; cf. Hosea 2:15. Both Sharon and Achor

---

refer to actions that serve as "a source of provocation." The statement here is stronger than mere provocation. This is burning wrath that consumes the self-righteous.

11 *But ye are they that forsake the Lord, that forget my holy mountain, that prepare a table for that troop, and that furnish the drink offering unto that number.*

12 *Therefore will I number you to the sword, and ye shall all bow down to the slaughter: because when I called, ye did not answer; when I spake, ye did not hear; but did evil before mine eyes, and did choose that wherein I delighted not.*

13 *Therefore thus saith the Lord God, Behold, my servants shall eat, but ye shall be hungry: behold, my servants shall drink, but ye shall be thirsty: behold, my servants shall rejoice, but ye shall be ashamed:*

14 *Behold, my servants shall sing for joy of heart, but ye shall cry for sorrow of heart, and shall howl for vexation of spirit.*

15 *And ye shall leave your name for a curse unto my chosen: for the Lord God shall slay thee, and call his servants by another name:*

16 *That he who blesseth himself in the earth shall bless himself in the God of truth; and he that sweareth in the earth shall swear by the God of truth; because the former troubles are forgotten, and because they are hid from mine eyes.*

are only representative places. The idea is that God's people will occupy the whole land, v. 10.

11–16 In contrast with the faithful, the Lord rebukes the unfaithful. They have forsaken Him. They have turned away from His "holy mountain," the location of the temple among His people. They have offered sacrifice to the "troop" (better "Gad"), a Babylonian god of fortune, represented by the planet Jupiter. The name occurs elsewhere in the OT in compound names, e.g., Hor-hagidgad, Numbers 33:32, 33; Dibon-gad, Numbers 33:45–46; Baal-gad, Joshua 11:17; 12:7; 13:5; Migdal-gad, Joshua 15:37; Azgad, Ezra 2:12; 8:12; Nehemiah 7:17; 10:15. They pour out their drink offering to the "number" (better "$M^e n\hat{\imath}$"), a Babylonian god of destiny represented by the planet Venus. We know little about $M^e n\hat{\imath}$, v. 11.

The Lord will judge these idolaters. He will "number" (*manâ*, better "destine") them to face the sword of judgment. The verb *manâ* plays on the name $m^e n\hat{\imath}$, both coming from the same root. They had refused to bow before God; they will now bow before the "slaughter" of judgment. He develops this in vv. 13–16, in which he gives some specifics of their punishment. He has called them but they did not answer. He has spoken to them but they did not hear His words. They continued to do "evil" (*ra^c*, see 3:9) and to choose things not pleasing to God, v. 12.

To heighten the judgment of the wicked, the Lord contrasts it with the blessing that He will give to the faithful. There is a series of four comparisons, each introduced with "behold" to draw attention to the statement. The presentation of judgment is similar to that in Haggai 1:6. (1) Those who have served the Lord will eat; the wicked will starve. (2) The Lord's servants will drink; the wicked will thirst. (3) His servants will rejoice; the wicked will "be ashamed" (*bôš*, see 1:29), v. 13. (4) His servants will sing with joy; the wicked will cry with grief. They will howl "for vexation of spirit" (better "from a broken spirit"), v. 14. Isaiah does not single out the fifth comparison with the word "behold." The name of the wicked will become a curse for God's people. They will use it as an example of those judged by God. Jeremiah 29:22 illustrates this practice. The Lord will slay them. His servants, however, will receive a new name, probably describing their relationship to Him, cf. 62:2, 4, v. 15.[6] He who "blesseth himself" (*hammitbarek*),[7] i.e., invokes a blessing upon himself, does so "in" (or "by") the "God of truth." He who "sweareth," taking an oath, does so by the "God of truth." The name "God of truth" is appropriate here since the passage looks forward to the time that God has fulfilled all of His promises. The wicked have been judged and the righteous enjoy the presence and blessing of God on the redeemed earth. The "former troubles" of Israel have been "forgotten," completely blotted out. They are "hid" from God's eyes, nevermore to be brought up as evidence of His people's sin, v. 16.

---

[6]Cowles, p. 532, suggests that the "new name" is Christian. Formerly known as Israelites and Jews, the people of God are now known as Christians. While this is possible, those who follow God are also called "believers," Acts 5:14; I Tim. 4:12. In all likelihood, neither of these names is the new name in view here; cf. Rev. 2:17; 3:12. The Lord will reveal that name in His time.

[7]The NASB translates the *hitpaᶜel* verb *barak* as a passive both times in the first part of v. 16, "is blessed" and "be blessed." The *hitpaᶜel*, however, is normally reflexive. In each of the other occurrences of *barak* in the *hitpaᶜel*, Gen. 22:18; Deut. 29:19; Jer. 4:2; and Ps. 72:17, a reflexive sense is appropriate. The verb *barak* does occur elsewhere as a passive in the *nipᶜal*, the normal passive tense.

17 *For, behold, I create new heavens and a new earth: and the former shall not be remembered, nor come into mind.*

18 *But be ye glad and rejoice for ever in that which I create: for, behold, I create Jerusalem a rejoicing, and her people a joy.*

19 *And I will rejoice in Jerusalem, and joy in my people: and the voice of weeping shall be no more heard in her, nor the voice of crying.*

20 *There shall be no more thence an infant of days, nor an old man that hath not filled his days: for the child shall die an hundred years old; but the sinner being an hundred years old shall be accursed.*

E. Promises to the People 65:17–66:24
1. The New Creation 65:17–25

17–20 The Lord will create "new heavens and a new earth." This looks to the eternal ages to come, 66:22; II Peter 3:13; Revelation 21:1. The redeemed believers will not remember the sin-cursed earth that has passed away, v. 17.[8] He commands His people to "rejoice for ever" ($^c\!d\hat{e}^{-c}ad$) in the new creation.[9] He singles out renewed Jerusalem and the people living there as a new source of joy. The rejoicing of redeemed Israel is a constant theme in this part of the book, e.g., 42:10–12; 49:13; 51:11; 52:9, v. 18. The Lord Himself will rejoice in Jerusalem and her people, cf. 42:4–5; Jeremiah 32:41; Zephaniah 3:17, v. 19*a*.

---

[8]Ibn Ezra, p. 297, understands the "new heavens" as a new and healthier atmosphere. He rejects any reference to an eternal age since "in the future life there is neither eating nor drinking"; cf. v. 21. This is a rabbinical teaching, *Berachoth* 17*a*. The view forces him to interpret 66:22 in the same way. Cowles, pp. 534–35, understands the "new heavens and a new earth" as a *moral* change. The hearts of mankind come back to the Lord and receive full pardon and blessing. He identifies the period with the "gospel age," a better period than the Mosaic period. The NT, however, makes it clear that this is a *physical* change although, of course, redeemed believers enjoy it. The earth is renovated by fire, II Pet. 3:10–13; cf. Matt. 24:35; Heb. 1:10–12. There is a new city of Jerusalem, Rev. 3:12; 21:2. There is no longer a curse upon the earth, Isa. 11:6–9; 35:7–9; 65:25. Kraeling, p. 225, views the phrase as "more symbolical than real." There is no justification for this position. Both OT and NT testify to the eternal ages to come for those who sincerely follow the Lord. Slotki, pp. 317–18, varies this by calling it "metaphorical for a new world order." As mentioned above, the NT argues for an actual physical change in the earth. Price, p. 285, suggests that this refers to life "on a totally different planet." This does away with the need for renovating the earth by fire. In keeping with his view that the latter chapters of Isaiah fall during the Persian period of history, Watts, *Isaiah 34–66,* p. 353, places the fulfillment during the time "in which Persia holds sway over the entire area so that Jerusalem can be rebuilt." The view does not accept a single Isaiah as the author.

[9]Only Isaiah and Psalms use the expression $^c\!d\hat{e}^{-c}ad$, "for ever." See also Ps. 83:17; 92:7; 132:12, 14; and Isa. 26:4. This is one more place that the supposedly different authors of Isaiah use a relatively scarce expression.

21 *And they shall build houses, and inhabit them; and they shall plant vineyards, and eat the fruit of them.*

22 *They shall not build, and another inhabit; they shall not plant, and another eat: for as the days of a tree are the days of my people, and mine elect shall long enjoy the work of their hands.*

23 *They shall not labour in vain, nor bring forth for trouble; for they are the seed of the blessed of the Lord, and their offspring with them.*

24 *And it shall come to pass, that before they call, I will answer; and while they are yet speaking, I will hear.*

25 *The wolf and the lamb shall feed together, and the lion shall eat straw like the bullock: and dust shall be the serpent's meat. They shall not hurt nor destroy in all my holy mountain, saith the Lord.*

As evidence of God's blessing, the city will never again hear the sounds of grief, cf. 25:8; 51:11; Revelation 21:4, v. 19*b*. The prophecy now blends the millennial kingdom with the eternal state. Death is not a part of the eternal state, 25:8. Verse 20, therefore, must refer to the kingdom. Babies will not die nor will there be premature death. Those who die at the age of one hundred will be considered youths. A person who dies at this age is a sinner, cursed by God for His failure to receive Jesus Christ as His Savior, v. 20.

21–25 People will build houses to live in. They will plant crops and enjoy the fruits of them, v. 21. It is a time of peace. The people will not suffer the loss of their homes or crops to enemies. They will live as long as the trees; cf. Psalm 1:3; Jeremiah 17:8.[10] They will "long enjoy" (better "wear out") the results of their work. The idea is that no one will take from them the full use of their accomplishments. Idiomatically, we could translate "consume," v. 22. They will not labor in vain nor "bring forth" (or "give birth to") with "trouble" (*behalâ*, better "terror") resulting.[11] These are the children of those blessed by God. The parents will see their descendants blessed with them, v. 23. The Lord will answer their prayers. He will answer their prayer before they ask and hear them as they speak, v. 24. There will be peace on the earth as in the original creation. Ancient enemies such as the lion and the lamb will now lie

[10]The mention of "trees" is an illustration. It is *not* that man will live only as long as a tree. It is rather that the long life of a tree illustrates the long life of man. Trees include the longest lifespan of any living thing, e.g., giant sequoia, redwood, and bristlecone pines.

[11]The noun *bêhalâ* refers to the terror that comes from something unexpected or threatening. The children that come will have no defects or behavior problems that would bring disturbed feelings.

down together; cf. 11:6. The lion will eat the same diet as the "bullock" (or "ox"). The serpent's meat will be "dust," i.e., he will find his food on the ground and not strike at men.[12] There will be no "hurt" (raᶜaᶜ II, see 11:9) done to anyone in God's "holy mountain," Mt. Zion, v. 25.[13]

---

[12]Leupold, II, 368, understands "eat dust" metaphorically of tasting defeat. The serpent is no longer able to strike at man. This is possible, but the idea expressed above better parallels the first part of the verse. Cowles, p. 538, makes the serpent an emblem of Satan, "the great dragon . . . that old serpent," Rev. 12:9. In making the serpent eat the dust, Cowles sees Satan trodden under the foot of Messiah. While it is true that Satan will be defeated, there is no reason to spiritualize the passage here. In leaving the serpent to crawl in the dust, there is a continuing reminder to man of God's curse upon the Devil.

[13]Leupold, II, 369, refers the "holy mountain" to the whole land of Palestine. The phrase occurs six times in Isaiah: 11:9; 56:7; 57:13; 65:11, 25; and 66:20. At 56:7; 65:11; and 66:20 it can refer only to Mt. Zion, the temple location, since these speak of offering sacrifice. Since these verses clearly speak of Mt. Zion, it is better to understand the temple location here as well.

Practical Applications from Chapter 65

1. God's Plan for Israel, vv. 1–10

   a. The contrast with the Gentiles. The Lord has let the Gentiles find Him, v. 1. Israel, on the other hand, has ignored the Lord's invitation to come to Him, v. 2.

   b. The sins of the Jews. They practice idolatry and other wicked forms of worship, vv. 3, 7*b*. They consult the spirits of the dead or false gods, v. 4*a*. They violate the clear prohibitions of the Law, v. 4*b*. They have a self-righteous attitude that irritates God, v. 5.

   c. The judgment of God. He will not ignore the sin of the people. He will judge them, v. 6. Both the children and the fathers will suffer for their sins., v. 7*a*. He will measure judgment out to them according to what they have done, v. 7*c*.

   d. The preservation of a remnant. The Lord will not totally destroy His people, v. 8. He will preserve some to inherit the Promised Land, v. 9. He will then bless the land, v. 10.

2. The Faithful vs. the Unfaithful, vv. 13–15

   a. Provision for the faithful, starvation for the unfaithful

   b. Drink for the faithful, thirst for the unfaithful

   c. Joy for the faithful, shame for the unfaithful, v. 13

   d. Singing with joy for the faithful, crying with grief for the unfaithful, v. 14

   e. A new name from God for the faithful, a name that is cursed for the unfaithful, v. 15

3. The Glorious Future, vv. 17–25

   a. The eternal ages. The redeemed will not remember the sin-cursed earth, v. 17. They will rejoice in the new creation, v. 18. The Lord Himself will rejoice in His city and His people, v. 19*a*. There will be no more sorrow, v. 19*b*.

   b. The Millennium. Long life will be natural with only sinners dying, vv. 20, 22*b*. The people will live in peace, vv. 21–22*a*. They will enjoy the work of their hands, vv. 22*c*–23. The Lord will meet their needs, supplying them even before the people call to Him in prayer, v. 24. Even the animal kingdom will be at peace, v. 25.

1 Thus saith the Lord, The heaven is my throne, and the earth is my footstool: where is the house that ye build unto me? and where is the place of my rest?

2 For all those things hath mine hand made, and all those things have been, saith the Lord: but to this man will I look, even to him that is poor and of a contrite spirit, and trembleth at my word.

3 He that killeth an ox is as if he slew a man; he that sacrificeth a lamb, as if he cut off a dog's neck; he that offereth an oblation, as if he offered swine's blood; he that burneth incense, as if he blessed an idol. Yea, they have chosen their own ways, and their soul delighteth in their abominations.

4 I also will choose their delusions, and will bring their fears upon them; because when I called, none did answer; when I spake, they did not hear: but they did evil before mine eyes, and chose that in which I delighted not.

ISAIAH 66

Several authors find the final chapter of Isaiah hard to understand.[1] The problem they face comes from their refusal to admit the existence of prophecy. When an author tries to make this material historical, he makes insoluble problems for himself. When, however, we recognize that Isaiah looks into the future, these problems disappear. The chapter displays harmony as it presents some of the end-time events that involve God's people.

2. The New Worship 66:1–4

1–4 The Lord asks rhetorically how His worship can be limited to a single building. He picturesquely describes the "heaven," i.e., all of space, as His throne and the earth as His footstool. How can Israel build a house in which a God this mighty can dwell; cf. I Kings 8:27? Stephen used this as part of his sermon, Acts 7:48–50, v.1. The Lord has made "those things," the whole of the visible creation mentioned in v. 1. For this reason, He will not look to material things for His dwelling. He will look for those with a "poor" (ʿanî, see 3:14) and "contrite" (nakeh) spirit. The word nakeh refers to someone who has been beaten. Metaphorically, this refers to the crippled spirit of the man who fears God's Word; cf. 57:15. No longer arrogant, he submits to the direction of God.

---

[1]Among others, Wright, p. 156; Herbert, p. 190; and Brueggemann, p. 251, understand the chapter as made up of a series of "fragments."

5 *Hear the word of the Lord, ye that tremble at his word; Your
brethren that hated you, that cast you out for my name's sake, said,
Let the Lord be glorified: but he shall appear to your joy, and they
shall be ashamed.*
6 *A voice of noise from the city, a voice from the temple, a voice of the
Lord that rendereth recompence to his enemies.*

The passage does not condemn the building of a temple. There will in
fact be a temple in which men will worship in the millennial kingdom;
cf. 2:3; Ezekiel 37:26. The Lord here, however, shows that His more important dwelling is within the believer. He will dwell within those who
humble themselves before Him, v. 2.

Having stated the positive development of the new worship, the Lord
now describes it negatively. Sacrifice by a wicked man will be an abomination. He who offers an ox will be no better than a murderer. He who
offers a lamb will be no better than if he had sacrificed a dog; cf. Deuteronomy 23:18. He who makes an "oblation," a gift to God, will be as
though he had offered the blood of swine, 65:4. He who burns "incense"
(or "frankincense," cf. 43:23) will be as though he blessed an "idol" (or
"vanity," that which does not exist). These have chosen to worship in
their own way. They delight in abominable ways of worship, v. 3.[2]

The Lord will choose their "delusions" (or "abuses"), i.e., their pun-
ishments. He will bring their "fears" (*magôr*, see 31:9, "terrors") on
them. They have ignored Him to go after their evil desires. When He
called them through the prophets, they did not answer. When He spoke
to them through His Word and the prophets, they refused to hear. They
openly did "evil" (*raʿ*, see 3:9) in God's sight and chose things that He
hated, v. 4.

3. The New Nation 66:5–14

5–6 The Lord encourages the godly that "tremble at his word." Their
own countrymen have hated them. They have "cast you out" (*nadâ*) for
"my name's sake," i.e., they refuse to honor the Lord and so turn away

---

[2]The Hebrew sets four righteous actions opposite four ungodly actions. The verse literally reads: "He who kills an ox, he who slays a man; he who sacrifices a lamb, he who
breaks the neck of a dog; he who offers a grain offering, he who offers the blood of a pig
[the verb in the first clause governs the second clause also]; he who burns frankincense,
he who blesses an idol." The last part of the verse makes it clear that this refers to wicked
actions. For this reason, the AV supplies the comparison words "as if." Wade, p. 415,
supplies the word "also," one who kills an ox also slays a man, etc. Jack Murad Sasson,

7 Before she travailed, she brought forth; before her pain came, she was delivered of a man child.
8 Who hath heard such a thing? who hath seen such things? Shall the earth be made to bring forth in one day? or shall a nation be born at once? for as soon as Zion travailed, she brought forth her children.
9 Shall I bring to the birth, and not cause to bring forth? saith the Lord: shall I cause to bring forth, and shut the womb? saith thy God.

from those who honor His name. The word *nadâ* occurs only here and at II Kings 17:21 and Amos 6:3. In Amos, it refers to putting the time of judgment far away. In II Kings, it refers to keeping Israel from worshiping the Lord. That is its sense here. Having turned the worship of the Lord into an abominable ritual, they refuse to allow the true worship of God.[3] They have taunted them, saying, "Let the Lord be glorified [*kabed*, see 3:5]: but he shall appear to your joy" (better "Let the Lord be glorified that we may see your joy"). This is a scornful statement, something they thought would never happen. He shall, however, indeed appear. Those who had rejected Him will "be ashamed" (*bôš*, see 1:29), v. 5. The voice of the Lord announces judgment. There is a threefold reference to the "voice" of God. It comes first from within the "noise" (*ša'ôn*) of the city.[4] It next comes from the temple. Isaiah finally identifies it as being the "voice of the Lord." It announces the punishment of His enemies. The repeated mention of God's "voice" emphasizes the divine pronouncement of judgment, v. 6.

7–9 The subject of the verse, "she," is Israel. Before the nation travails, she brings forth a child. This refers to the birth of Christ; cf. Revelation 12:1–5. Her travail will come in the Tribulation, thus the birth of

---

"Isaiah LXVI 3–4a," *VT* 26:199–202, is similar. He supplies the connecting link "would now." The thought is that the wicked combine lawful and unlawful acts of worship. The view is possible. Alexander, II, 461, projects the verse into the time after Christ's death. Those who continue to offer sacrifice, rejecting the great sacrifice of Christ, are themselves rejected by God. Cowles, p. 542, agrees that "the Mosaic ritual is no longer obligatory, but is indeed repulsive to him, and therefore must be abolished at once and forever." The problem with this view is that the apostles continued to carry out the ritual after the death and resurrection of Christ, e.g., Acts 2:46; 3:1; 21:26. Although these actions were part of the Jewish ritual, the Christians worshiped the true God through them. In addition, there will be sacrifices in the millennial temple, 19:21; 56:6–7.

[3]Leupold, II, 373, understands this as putting them "out from the community." McKenzie, p. 207, and Slotki, p. 321, agree with this position. The last half of the verse, however, relates more to worship than to mere companionship in the community.

[4]Alexander, II, 463–64, and Cowles, p. 543, are wrong in making *ša'ôn* the noise of war. While *ša'ôn* may mean the noise of war, it as often refers simply to the noise of

10 *Rejoice ye with Jerusalem, and be glad with her, all ye that love her: rejoice for joy with her, all ye that mourn for her:*

11 *That ye may suck, and be satisfied with the breasts of her consolations; that ye may milk out, and be delighted with the abundance of her glory.*

12 *For thus saith the Lord, Behold, I will extend peace to her like a river, and the glory of the Gentiles like a flowing stream: then shall ye suck, ye shall be borne upon her sides, and be dandled upon her knees.*

13 *As one whom his mother comforteth, so will I comfort you; and ye shall be comforted in Jerusalem.*

14 *And when ye see this, your heart shall rejoice, and your bones shall flourish like an herb: and the hand of the Lord shall be known toward his servants, and his indignation toward his enemies.*

"the man child" precedes it, v. 7.[5] The birth and sacrificial death of Christ logically precedes v. 8. The Lord there declares something unheard of and unseen before. Can the earth bring forth a nation "in one day?" Can a nation come into existence "at once," i.e., at the same time? The word "day" refers to the time of the Tribulation, as in 61:2 and 63:4. The nation of Israel will turn to Christ in that "day," Zechariah 12:10. In her travail at that time, she will bring forth "her children," believing Israelites, v. 8. Will the Lord bring the nation to the point of giving birth and not accomplish it? Will the one who gives delivery shut the nation's womb? Clearly, the answer to these questions is no, v. 9.

10–14 God's people should rejoice with Jerusalem. Those who love Israel and who weep over her trials should rejoice at her conversion,

---

people, e.g., 5:14 ("pomp"); 17:12 ("rushing"); 24:8. Birks, p. 321, understands the "noise" as the "warcry" of the Lord as He displays His anger. It is rather an announcement, not a cry of war. The phrase here does not describe a cry from outside the city but a voice coming from within the noise of the city.

[5]Among others, Leupold, II, 374; Barnes, II, 431; and Hailey, p. 524, understand the child as the church, born at Pentecost. Rawlinson, II, 486; Skinner, *Isaiah XL–LXVI,* pp. 248–49, and Slotki, p. 322, refer it to the return from captivity to establish a new nation of Zion. There are enough differences between v. 7 and v. 8 that I hesitate to accept either of these interpretations. The first view requires Zion to give birth before her travail, v. 7, and after her travail, v. 8. The "man child" in v. 7 must be a collective singular representing the church. In v. 8, however, the plural "children" occurs. Verse 8 requires the nation to be born "in one day." But the church did not come into existence in a single day. Pentecost cannot satisfy this since the apostles were already the foundation of the church. The prophetic context virtually eliminates the second view. The passage looks at eschatological events, not at OT happenings. Price, p. 291, relates the birth to the Balfour Declaration, which made possible the modern nation of Israel in 1948. The emphasis here, however, is on "children" being born rather than Zion being born.

v. 10.[6] From her, other nations may "suck" (*yanaq*, or "nurse," see 53:2) and be satisfied. They will "milk out" (*maṣaṣ*, or "suck").[7] This will let them find nourishment from "the abundance [*zîz*, or 'bosom']"[8] of her glory" (or "her glorious [i.e., 'abundant'] bosom"), v. 11. Unending "peace" (*šalôm*, see 9:6), compared to a flowing river, will come to Jerusalem. The "glory" (*kᵉbôd*, see 3:5)[9] of the Gentiles, like a "flowing stream" (*naḥal šôṭep*, better "overflowing torrent") with abundant water, will likewise come to her. The *naḥal šôṭep* is a wadi, filled with a raging stream of water that spills over the bounds of the channel, see 7:19. The "glory of the Gentiles" includes all of the diverse resources of the nations.

The pronoun "ye" continues the thought of vv. 10–11. The Gentiles will "suck," drawing spiritual nourishment from Israel. She will carry them on her "sides" (lit. "side"), at the hip; cf. 60:4.[10] They will "be dandled" (or "fondled") on her knees, v. 12. Like a mother "comforteth" (*naḥam*, see 1:24) her child, so the Lord will "comfort" (*naḥam*) His own. In Jerusalem, His city, He will extend comfort (*naḥam*) to His people, v. 13. This comfort will bring blessing to His own. The "heart," the seat of the emotions, will rejoice. The bones, standing by synecdoche for the body, will flourish like an "herb" (or "new grass"). The "hand of the Lord," His power, will go forth on behalf of His people. His wrath, however, will fall upon His enemies, v. 14.

---

[6]The Jewish commentators refer the phrase "mourn for her" to Israel. Slotki, p. 322, understands it of the fasts that remembered "the destruction of Jerusalem, cf. Zech. 7:3." Ibn Ezra, p. 303, refers it to the sorrow over the nation's exile. The parallelism with "all ye that love her" suggests that the phrase refers to the Gentiles.

[7]The verb *maṣaṣ* occurs only here. It is apparently related to *maṣâ*, "to drain, drain out," a root that occurs often in the OT. From the parallelism, *maṣaṣ* must be similar in meaning to *yanaq*.

[8]The word *zîz* is a *hapax legomenon*. The parallelism virtually demands a meaning similar to "breasts." The LXX translates ἀπὸ εἰσόδου δόξης αὐτῆς, "from the entrance of his glory." The Targum reads *mḥmr yqrh*, "from the wine of her glory." The Vulgate translates from the context, *ab omnimoda gloria ejus,* "from the fulness of her glory." These are obvious interpretations of a rare word. Cohen, p. 46, relates *zîz* to an Akkadian cognate *zîzu,* "teat."

[9]Leupold, II, 375, translates *šalôm* as "prosperity" and *kᵉbôd* as "wealth." While "wealth" is possible for *kᵉbôd*, we should retain the traditional rendering of "peace" for *šalôm*. The emphasis is not solely on the material. The Lord here includes both the emotional blessing of peace and the material blessing of wealth.

[10]Slotki, p. 323, sees this as drawing upon the "nations that had hitherto oppressed them." Ibn Ezra, p. 303, likewise understands Israel relying on the nations during the return from exile. The earlier context supports the view given above.

15 *For, behold, the Lord will come with fire, and with his chariots like a whirlwind, to render his anger with fury, and his rebuke with flames of fire.*

16 *For by fire and by his sword will the Lord plead with all flesh: and the slain of the Lord shall be many.*

17 *They that sanctify themselves, and purify themselves in the gardens behind one tree in the midst, eating swine's flesh, and the abomination, and the mouse, shall be consumed together, saith the Lord.*

18 *For I know their works and their thoughts: it shall come, that I will gather all nations and tongues; and they shall come, and see my glory.*

4. The New Kingdom 66:15–24

15–18 The Lord will come with the fires of judgment; cf. II Thessalonians 1:7–9. His chariots move like a whirlwind. The OT associates chariots with the power of God; II Kings 6:17; Habakkuk 3:8. The heathen likewise linked their gods to chariots, II Kings 23:11. In II Kings 2:12 and 13:14, the word occurs figuratively to indicate that both Elijah and Elisha had demonstrated divine power to the nations. The chariots here represent the heavenly hosts that accompany the Lord at His coming in judgment; cf. Psalm 68:17.

His anger goes forth with "fury" and with "flames of fire." This pictures the wrath of the Lord that falls on the nations at the end of the Tribulation. The Lord will overthrow the dominion of the heathen and take up the rule Himself, cf. Zechariah 12:8–9, v. 15. He will unleash His "fire" and His "sword," both emblems of judgment. He will "plead" (*nip⁽al* of *šapaṭ*, see 59:4) with "all flesh." The phrase "all flesh" indicates that this is a worldwide judgment. Many will fall before Him, v. 16. Those who "sanctify" and "purify" themselves for the worship of false gods will fall. These have practiced their rituals in the "gardens"; cf. 65:3. The phrase "behind one [*²eḥad*] tree in the midst" is better "behind one in the middle," a reference to following the leader of their ritual.[11] These have eaten swine's flesh, cf. 65:4, unidentified abominable

---

[11] The *qᵉrê* substitutes *²aḥat* (feminine) for the *kᵉtîb*, *²eḥad* (masculine). If we read the *qᵉrê*, the reference must be to a priestess who leads the worship or to an idol of a goddess, Ashtoreth or some other being. There is, however, no reason to omit the name of the goddess. This leaves the possibility of a priestess. The Isaiah Scroll and several other manuscripts follow the *qᵉrê* but this may be interpretive. In any case, the sense does not differ greatly from the *kᵉtîb*. The NEB translates, "one after another in a magic ring." This is extremely interpretive and without support.

19 *And I will set a sign among them, and I will send those that escape of them unto the nations, to Tarshish, Pul, and Lud, that draw the bow, to Tubal, and Javan, to the isles afar off, that have not heard my fame, neither have seen my glory; and they shall declare my glory among the Gentiles.*

20 *And they shall bring all your brethren for an offering unto the Lord out of all nations upon horses, and in chariots, and in litters, and upon mules, and upon swift beasts, to my holy mountain Jerusalem, saith the Lord, as the children of Israel bring an offering in a clean vessel into the house of the Lord.*

21 *And I will also take of them for priests and for Levites, saith the Lord.*

22 *For as the new heavens and the new earth, which I will make, shall remain before me, saith the Lord, so shall your seed and your name remain.*

23 *And it shall come to pass, that from one new moon to another, and from one sabbath to another, shall all flesh come to worship before me, saith the Lord.*

24 *And they shall go forth, and look upon the carcases of the men that have transgressed against me: for their worm shall not die, neither shall their fire be quenched; and they shall be an abhorring unto all flesh.*

things, even mice; cf. Leviticus 11:29. These will "be consumed together" (better "come to an end"), v. 17. The Lord knows the works and the thoughts of the heathen. At the judgment, occurring at the end of the Tribulation, He will gather the nations together. He will reveal His "glory" to them in His judgment, v. 18.[12]

19–24 The Lord will set a "sign" (*ʾôt*, see 7:11) among the nations.[13] The word *ʾôt* almost always refers to a religious sign of some kind. It

---

[12]Gill, III, 395, understands the gathering here of the nations turning to Christ. They "see [His] glory" in the person of Christ and His gospel. The context leading up to this, however, does not support this view. This is a statement of judgment upon the heathen. Fausset, p. 766, correctly sees the gathering of the nations for judgment. He makes the gathering of "tongues" a turning of the nation's languages back to a common language. The view is inconsistent with the grammatical structure. The gathering of nations and gathering of tongues are parallel thoughts with no significant difference between them.

[13]Pieper, pp. 695, 697, argues that the combination of *śîm ʾôt* and the *bᵉ*-preposition should be translated "do a wonderful thing among them." This combination occurs again at Exod. 10:2; Ps. 78:43; 105:27; and Jer. 32:20, all referring to the miracles in Egypt. The *bᵉ*-preposition merely locates the work within a group. It has no effect on the translation of *ʾôt*. The word *ʾôt* occurs seventy-nine times. It is overwhelmingly translated "sign" or its equivalent. Only at Num. 14:22 and Deut. 11:3 is it translated "miracles." In both places, it refers to the miracles in Egypt that were meant as signs to Pharaoh. There is no context here to indicate that this is anything other than a sign. Cowles, p. 458, over-

apparently here indicates some call to God's people to come out from among the heathen nations. He will send them throughout the earth as His representatives. Tarshish, later called Tartessus, lay on the southwest coast of Spain at the mouth of the Bætis River. This was possibly the place that gave its name to the "ships of Tarshish," 2:16; 23:1, 14; 60:9. We cannot identify "Pul" unless we read *pûṭ*, an African nation south of Egypt. The nations of *pûṭ* and *lûd* occur together in Jeremiah 46:9 ("Libyans . . . Lydians"); Ezekiel 27:10 ("Lud and of Phut"); and Ezekiel 30:5 ("Libya, and Lydia"). There is limited support for *pûṭ*.[14] "Lud" is Lydia in Asia Minor. The Hebrew accents make both Pul and Lud warlike people who "draw the bow." "Tubal" lay south of the Black Sea in Asia Minor. Javan occupied the southeastern coast of Greece. The "isles [*ʾîyîm*, see 11:11] afar off" represent the coastal areas at the distant west end of the Mediterranean. These places have not heard of the Lord nor seen His glory. Now, however, His representatives will declare His glory to the heathen, v. 19.

The heathen will bring dispersed Jews with them as an offering to the Lord. They will come from all nations, using various means to travel to the Lord's "holy mountain," where Jerusalem stands. The means of transportation includes horses, chariots, "litters" (a wagon that is covered to protect its cargo), mules, and "swift beasts" (*kirkarâ*, or "dromedaries").[15] Isaiah compares this offering of redeemed Gentiles to an offering brought in a clean vessel to the temple, v. 20. The Lord will place some of the returning dispersed Jews as priests and Levites in the temple. These will carry out the worship ritual during the kingdom. This ritual has as its purpose the remembrance of Christ's sacrificial work, v. 21.[16] Just as the "new heavens and the new earth" continue through eternity, so the people of Israel will continue, v. 22. Month by month and week

---

states things when he says that *ʾôt* is "the usual word for miracles." The word "miracles" occurs only five times in the OT, but it translates three different Hebrew words. Among these, *ʾôt* occurs twice.

[14]The LXX reads φουδ, "Put." The Vulgate gives *Africam,* "Africa," the location of Put. We cannot tell if these readings were interpretive.

[15]The word *kirkarâ* occurs only here. The root is apparently *karar*, "to whirl, dance," possibly "to move about." The noun relates to the side-to-side swaying movement of the camel.

[16]Among others, Motyer, *The Prophecy of Isaiah,* p. 543; Young, III, 535; and Leupold, II, 378, understand that priests will come from both Gentiles and Jews. The view ignores the OT qualification for the priesthood of descent from Aaron, Exod. 28:1; cf. Ezra 2:61–62.

by week, the people will worship the Lord. This includes "all flesh," Jews and Gentiles alike joining in their worship of the Lord, v. 23. In sharp contrast with this worship of God, there will also be the unending torment of those who have rejected His salvation.[17] The fact that the worshipers can see the torments of the damned supports the location of this as being in the New Jerusalem, Revelation 21:2, 10. Those suffering the torments of an unquenchable fire are in the lake of fire, Revelation 20:14–15; 21:8. The Lord used the same description in Mark 9:44, 46, 48. The undying worm illustrates the unending torment of the damned.[18] The sight of the eternally damned is a continuing object lesson to the believers of the grace given them by God, v. 24.[19]

---

[17]While it is not a thing to rejoice in, the damnation of the lost is real and heartbreaking. The eternal punishment of the lost ought to challenge Christians to be faithful in telling others of their need to receive Jesus Christ as their Savior. His sacrificial death at Calvary makes possible the salvation of all that trust Him to take away their sin.

[18]Delitzsch, II, 517, aptly explains the figure: "He is speaking of the future state but in figures drawn from this present world."

[19]According to Jewish custom, the reading of the chapter should not end on the unhappy note of v. 24. Many Bibles repeat part of v. 23 after v. 24. For the same reason, the Jews follow a similar practice at the end of Ecclesiastes, Lamentations, and Malachi.

Practical Applications from Chapter 66

1. Acceptable or Unacceptable Worship, v. 3
   a. Righteous (sacrifice of an ox [or "bullock"], Lev. 4:10; 9:4), vs. wicked (murder, Exod. 20:13; Lev. 24:17)
   b. Honoring (sacrifice of a lamb, the symbol of our Lord, 53:7; John 1:29, 36) vs. insulting (a dog, an unclean animal, I Sam. 17:43; II Sam. 3:8; 9:8)
   c. Acceptable (oblation [or "offering"], Lev. 6:20–21; I Chron. 16:29) vs. unacceptable (65:4; Lev. 11:7; Deut. 14:8)
   d. Worthy (frankincense, Lev. 2:1–2, 15–16) vs. unworthy (idol [or "vanity"], 41:29; 44:9)
2. God's Plan for His People, vv. 5–14
   a. Encouragement of the godly. The Lord encourages the godly. Others have hated them because they refused to worship God, v. 5. The Lord will judge His enemies, v. 6.
   b. Salvation of the nation. The birth of Christ will take place, v. 7. During the Tribulation judgments, the nations will turn to Him, v. 8. The Lord will not fail to accomplish His plan for Israel, v. 9.
   c. Blessing of the Gentiles. Believers will rejoice over the salvation of the Jews, v. 10. They will be delighted in the abundance of glory found in her, v. 11. Jerusalem will experience unending peace. Gentile nations will make their resources available to Israel. They, in turn, will receive spiritual nourishment from Israel, v. 12. The Lord will comfort His own, v. 13. He will bless His people and judge His enemies, v. 14.
3. Revelation of the Future, vv. 15–24
   a. Judgment of the wicked, vv. 15–18
   b. Return of God's people, vv. 19–20
   c. Worship of the Jews, vv. 21–23
   d. Torments of the damned, v. 24

Selected Bibliography

COMMENTARIES AND OTHER BOOKS ON ISAIAH

Alexander, Joseph A. *Commentary on Isaiah*. 2 vols. 1867. Reprint, Grand Rapids, Mich.: Kregel Classics, 1992.

Barnes, Albert. *Notes on the Old Testament: Isaiah*. 2 vols. Ed. Robert Frew. Grand Rapids, Mich.: Baker Book House, 1950.

Birks, T. R. *Commentary on the Book of Isaiah*. London: Church of England Book Society, 1870.

Box, G. H. *The Book of Isaiah*. London: Sir Isaac Pitman and Sons, Ltd., 1908.

Brueggemann, Walter. *Isaiah 1-39* in *Westminster Bible Companion*. Ed. Patrick D. Miller and David L. Bartlett. Louisville, Ky.: Westminster John Knox Press, 1998.

_____. *Isaiah 40-66* in *Westminster Bible Companion*. Ed. Patrick D. Miller and David L. Bartlett. Louisville, Ky.: Westminster John Knox Press, 1998.

Childs, Brevard S. *Isaiah*. Louisville, Ky.: Westminster John Knox Press, 2001.

Chilton, Bruce D., trans. *The Isaiah Targum*. Vol. 11, *The Aramaic Bible*. Ed. Kevin Cathcart, Michael Maher, and Martin McNamara. Wilmington, Del.: Michael Glazier, Inc., 1987.

Chisholm Jr., Robert B. "Structure, Style, and the Prophetic Message: An Analysis of Isaiah 5:8-30," in *Vital Old Testament Issues*. Ed. Roy B. Zuck. Grand Rapids, Mich.: Kregel Resources, 1996.

Cowles, Henry. *Isaiah*. New York: D. Appleton and Company, 1869.

Cundall, Arthur E. *Proverbs—Isaiah 39*, in *Bible Study Books*. Grand Rapids, Mich.: William B. Eerdmans Publishing Company, 1968.

_____. *Isaiah 40—Jeremiah*, in *Bible Study Books*. Grand Rapids, Mich.: William B. Eerdmans Publishing Company, 1969.

Delitzsch, Franz. *Isaiah*, in *Commentary on the Old Testament*. 2 vols. Trans. James Martin. Reprint, Grand Rapids, Mich.: William B. Eerdmans Publishing Company, 1978.

Driver, G. R. "'Another Little Drink'—Isaiah 28:1-22," in *Words and Meanings*. Ed. Peter R. Ackroyd and Barnabas Lindars. New York: Cambridge University Press, 1968.

Eitan, Israel. "A Contribution to Isaiah Exegesis," in *Hebrew Union College Annual*, XII-XIII. New York: Ktav Publishing House, 1968.

Engnell, Ivan. *The Call of Isaiah*. Uppsala: A.-B. Lundequistska Bokhandeln, 1949.

Erlandsson, Seth. *The Burden of Babylon: A Study of Isaiah 13:2–14:23*. Trans. George J. Houser. Lund, Sweden: C. W. K. Gleerup, 1970.

Fausett, A. R. *Isaiah*, in *A Critical and Experimental Commentary on the Old and New Testaments*. 1866. Reprint, Grand Rapids, Mich.: Wm. B. Eerdmans Publishing Co., 1967.

Friedländer, M., ed. *The Commentary of Ibn Ezra on Isaiah*. 1873. Reprint, New York: Philipp Feldheim, Inc. n.d.

Gill, John. *An Exposition of the Books of the Prophets of the Old Testament*. 1810. Reprint, Streamwood, Ill.: Primitive Baptist Library, 1979.

Goldingay, John. *Isaiah*, in *New International Biblical Commentary*. Ed. Robert L. Hubbard Jr. and Robert K. Johnston. Peabody, Mass.: Hendrickson Publishers, Inc., 2001.

Gray, George Buchanan. *A Critical and Exegetical Commentary on the Book of Isaiah, I-XXXIX*, in *The International Critical Commentary*. Ed. Samuel Rolles Driver, Alfred Plummer, and Charles Augustus Briggs. 1911. Reprint, Edinburgh: T. and T. Clark, 1980.

Grogan, Geoffrey W. *Isaiah*, in *The Expositor's Bible Commentary*. Vol. VI. Ed. Frank E. Gaebelein. Grand Rapids, Mich.: Zondervan Publishing House, 1986.

Hailey, Homer. *A Commentary on Isaiah*. N.p.: Religious Supply, Inc., 1992.

Henry, Matthew. *Commentary on the Whole Bible*. Vol. IV. 1910. Reprint, New York: Fleming H. Revell Company, 1935.

Herbert, A. S. *The Book of the Prophet Isaiah, Chapters 1-39*, in *Cambridge Bible Commentary*. Ed. P. R. Ackroyd, A. R. C. Leaney, and J. W. Packer. Cambridge: Cambridge University Press, 1973.

_____. *The Book of the Prophet Isaiah, Chapters 40-66*, in *Cambridge Bible Commentary*. Ed. P. R. Ackroyd, A. R. C. Leaney, and J. W. Packer. Cambridge: Cambridge University Press, 1975.

Irwin, William Henry. *Isaiah 28-33: Translation with Philological Notes*. Rome: Biblical Institute Press, 1977.

Kaiser, Otto. *Isaiah 1-12*. Trans. R. A. Wilson, in *The Old Testament Library*. Ed. Peter Ackroyd, James Barr, John Bright, G. Ernest Wilson. Philadelphia: The Westminster Press, 1972.

_____. *Isaiah 13-39*. Trans. R. A. Wilson, in *The Old Testament Library*. Ed. Peter Ackroyd, James Barr, John Bright, G. Ernest Wilson. Philadelphia: The Westminster Press, 1974.

Kelley, Page H. *Isaiah*, in *The Broadman Bible Commentary*. Vol. V. Ed. Clifton J. Allen. Nashville: Broadman Press, 1971.

Kelly, William. *Exposition of the Book of Isaiah*. London: F. E. Race, 1916.

Kidner, Derek. *Isaiah*, in *The New Bible*. Ed. D. A. Carson, *et al.* Downers Grove, Ill.: InterVarsity Press, 1994.

Kissane, Edward J. *The Book of Isaiah*, 2 vols. Dublin, Ireland: The Richview Press, 1941.

Knight, George A. F. *The New Israel: A Commentary on the Book of Isaiah 56-66*, in the *International Theological Commentary*. Ed. George A. F. Knight and Fredrick Carlson Holmgren. Grand Rapids, Mich.: Wm. B. Eerdmans Publishing Company, 1985.

Kraeling, Emil G. *Commentary on the Prophets*. Vol. 1. Camden, N.J.: Thomas Nelson and Sons, 1966.

Leslie, Elmer A. *Isaiah*. New York: Abingdon Press, 1963.

Leupold, H. C. *Exposition of Isaiah*. 2 vols. Grand Rapids, Mich.: Baker Book House, 1968.

Lindsey, F. Duane. *The Servant Songs*. Chicago: Moody Press, 1985.

Lowth, Robert, *Isaiah: A New Translation*. London: T. T. and J. Tegg, 1833.

Mauchline, John. *Isaiah 1-39*. New York: The Macmillan Company, 1962.

McKenzie, John L. *Second Isaiah*, in *The Anchor Bible*. Ed. William Foxwell Albright and David Noel Freedman. Garden City, N.Y.: Doubleday and Company, 1968.

Mettinger, Tryggve N. D. "The Elimination of a Crux? A Syntactic and Semantic Study of Isaiah XL 18-20," in *Vetus Testamentum Supplements*. Vol. XXVI. Leiden: E. J. Brill, 1974.

Motyer, J. Alec. *The Prophecy of Isaiah*. Downers Grove, Ill.: Inter-Varsity Press, 1993.

_____. *Isaiah: An Introduction and Commentary*, in *Tyndale Old Testament Commentaries*. Ed. D. J. Wiseman. Downers Grove, Ill.: InterVarsity Press, 1999.

Näglesbach, Carl Wilhelm Eduard. *The Prophet Isaiah*. Trans. with additions by Samuel T. Lowrie and Dunlop Moore in *Commentary on the Holy Scriptures*. Ed. John Peter Lange. Reprint. Vol. XI. Grand Rapids, Mich.: Zondervan Publishing House, 1960.

North, Christopher R. *Isaiah 40-55*, in *Torch Bible Commentaries*. Ed. John Marsh and Alan Richardson. London: SCM Press Ltd., 1956.

Orlinsky, Harry M. "The So-called 'Servant of the Lord' and 'Suffering Servant' in Second Isaiah," *Vetus Testamentum Supplements*. Vol. XIV. Leiden: E. J. Brill, 1967.

Pieper, August. *Isaiah II: An Exposition of Isaiah 40-66*. Trans. Erwin E. Kowalke. Milwaukee, Wis.: Northwestern Publishing House, 1979.

Price, Ross E. *Isaiah*, in *Beacon Bible Commentary*. Ed. A. F. Harper and W. T. Purkiser. Kansas City, Mo.: Beacon Hill Press, 1966.

Rawlinson, George. *Isaiah*, in *The Pulpit Commentary*. 2 vols. Ed. H. D. M. Spence and Joseph S. Exell, New York: Funk and Wagnalls, n.d.

Scott, R. B. Y. *The Book of Isaiah*, in *The Interpreter's Bible*. Vol. V. Ed. George Arthur Buttrick. New York: Abingdon Press, 1956.

Skinner, J. *Isaiah Chapters I-XXXIX*, in *The Cambridge Bible*. Ed. A. F. Kirkpatrick. Cambridge: Cambridge University Press, 1905.

_____. *Isaiah Chapters XL-LXVI*, in *The Cambridge Bible*. Ed. A. F. Kirkpatrick. Cambridge: Cambridge University Press, 1963.

Slotki, Israel Wolf. *Isaiah*. Rev. A. J. Rosenberg, in *Soncino Books of the Bible*. Ed. A. Cohen. New York: The Soncino Press, 1983.

Smart, James D. *History and Theology in Second Isaiah*. Philadelphia: The Westminster Press, 1965.

Smith, George Adam. *The Book of Isaiah*. 2 vols. London: Hodder and Stoughton, 1896.

Snaith, Norman H. "A Study of the Teaching of the Second Isaiah and Its Consequences," in *Vetus Testamentum Supplements*. Vol. XIV. Leiden: E. J. Brill, 1967.

Stacey, David. *Isaiah 1-39*. London: Epworth Press, 1993.

Torrey, C. C. *The Second Isaiah*. Edinburgh: T. and T. Clark, 1928.

Vine, William Edwy. *Vine's Expository Commentary on Isaiah*. Reprint, Nashville, Tenn.: Thomas Nelson Publishers, 1997.

Von Orelli, C. *The Prophecies of Isaiah*. Trans. J. S. Banks. Edinburgh: T. and T. Clark, 1889.

Wade, George W. *The Book of the Prophet Isaiah*, in *Westminster Commentaries*. Ed. Walter Lock. London: Methuen and Co. Ltd., 1911.

Watts, John D. W. *Isaiah 1-33*, in *Word Biblical Commentary*. Ed. David A. Hubbard and Glenn W. Barker. Waco, Tex.: Word Books, 1987.

_____. *Isaiah 34-66*, in *Word Biblical Commentary*. Ed. David A. Hubbard and Glenn W. Barker. Waco, Tex.: Word Books, 1987.

Westermann, Claus. *Isaiah 40-66*. Trans. David M. G. Stalker, *The Old Testament Library*. Ed. Peter Ackroyd, James Barr, Bernhard W. Anderson, James L. Mays. Philadelphia: The Westminster Press, 1969.

Whitehouse, Owen C. *Isaiah* in *The Century Bible*. 2 vols. Ed. Walter F. Adeney. Edinburgh: T. C. and E. C. Jack, Ltd., n.d.

Wright, G. Ernest. *The Book of Isaiah*, in *The Layman's Bible Commentary*. Ed. Balmer H. Kelly. Atlanta: John Knox Press, 1982.

Young, Edward J. *The Book of Isaiah*. 3 vols. Reprint, Grand Rapids, Mich.: William B. Eerdmans Publishing Company, 1999.

LINGUISTIC AIDS

Brown, Francis, S. R. Driver, and Charles A. Briggs, eds. *A Hebrew and English Lexicon of the Old Testament*. Reprint, Oxford: Clarendon Press. 1974.

Cohen, Harold R. (Chaim). *Biblical Hapax Legomena in the Light of Akkadian and Ugaritic*. Missoula, Mont.: Scholars Press, 1978.

Harris, R. Laird, ed. *Theological Wordbook of the Old Testament*. 2 vols. Chicago: Moody Press, 1980.

Hulst, A. R. *Old Testament Translation Problems*. Leiden: E. J. Brill, 1960.

Kautzsch, E., ed. *Gesenius' Hebrew Grammar*. Trans. and rev. A. E. Cowley. Oxford: Clarendon Press, 1970.

Koehler, Ludwig, and Walter Baumgartner. *The Hebrew and Aramaic Lexicon of the Old Testament*. 5 vols. Rev. Walter Baumgartner and Johann Jakob Stamm. Ed. M. E. J. Richardson. New York: E. J. Brill, 1995.

Lissowsky, Gerhard. *Konkordanz Zum Hebräischen Alten Testament*. Stuttgart: Württembergische Bibelanstalt, 1958.

Nestle, Eberhard, Erwin Nestle, Kurt Aland, and Barbara Aland. *Novum Testamentum Graece*. Stuttgart: Deutsche Bibelstiftung, 1979.

Waltke, Bruce, and M. O'Connor. *An Introduction to Biblical Hebrew Syntax*. Winona Lake, Ind.: Eisenbrauns, 1990.

Williams, Ronald J. *Hebrew Syntax: An Outline*. Toronto: University of Toronto Press, 1974.

GENERAL WORKS

Chisholm Jr., Robert B. "Wordplay in the Eighth Century Prophets," in *Vital Old Testament Issues*. Ed. Roy B. Zuck. Grand Rapids, Mich.: Kregel Resources, 1996.

Driver, Samuel R. *An Introduction to the Literature of the Old Testament*. Edinburgh: T. and T. Clark, 1913.

Herodotus. *The Histories*. Trans. Robin Waterfield. New York: Oxford University Press, 1998.

Pentecost, J. Dwight. *Things to Come: A Study in Biblical Eschatology*. Grand Rapids, Mich.: Zondervan Publishing House, 1958.

Pritchard, James B., ed. *Ancient Near Eastern Texts.* Princeton, N.J.: Princeton University Press, 1969.

Whiston, William, trans. *The Works of Josephus: New Updated Edition.* Peabody, Mass.: Hendrickson Publishers, Inc., 2000.

PERIODICALS

Ahlström, G. W. "Isaiah VI. 13." *JSS* 19 (1974): 169–72.

_____. "Notes to Isaiah 53:8f." *BZ* 13 (1969): 95–98.

Albright, W. F. "The Son of Tabeel (Isaiah 7:6)." *BASOR* 140 (1955): 34–35.

Althann, Robert. "*Yôm*, 'Time' and Some Texts in Isaiah." *JNWSL* 11 (1983): 3–8.

Blythin, Islwyn. "A Note on Isaiah XLIX 16–17." *VT* 16 (1966): 229–30.

Brayley, I. F. M. "'Yahweh Is the Guardian of His Plantation' A Note on Is. 60,21." *Biblica* 41 (1960): 275–86.

Christensen, D. L. "The March of Conquest in Isaiah X 27c–34." *VT* 26 (1976): 385–99.

Cross Jr., Frank M. "The Council of Yahweh in Second Isaiah." *JNES* 12 (1953): 274–77.

Dahood, Mitchell. "'Weaker than Water': Comparative *beth* in Isaiah 1,22." *Biblica* 56 (1975): 91–92.

_____. "Accusative *ʿēṣāh*, 'Wood', in Isaiah 30,1b." *Biblica* 50 (1969): 57–58.

_____. "הֲדֵל 'Cessation' in Isaiah 38,11." *Biblica* 52 (1971): 215–16.

_____. "Textual Problems in Isaia." *CBQ* 22 (1960): 400–409.

Darr, Katheryn Pfisterer. "Like Warrior, like Woman: Destruction and Deliverance in Isaiah 42:10–17." *CBQ* 49 (1987): 560–71.

Davidson, R. "The Interpretation of Isaiah II 6ff." *VT* 16 (1966): 1–7.

Driver, G. R. "Isaiah I-XXXIX: Textual and Linguistic Problems." *JSS* 13 (1968): 36–57.

_____. "Two Misunderstood Passages of the Old Testament." *JTS* 6 (1955): 82–87.

Edwards, Janet. "Prophetic Paradox: Isaiah 6:9–10." *Studia Biblica et Theologica* 6 (1976): 48–61.

Evans, Craig A. "An Interpretation of Isa 8, 11–15 Unemended." *ZAW* 97 (1985): 112–13.

Flamming, James. "The New Testament Use of Isaiah." *Southwestern Journal of Theology* 11 (1968): 89–103.

Goldingay, John. "The Compound Name in Isaiah 9:5(6)." *CBQ* 61 (1999): 239–44.

Gordon, Cyrus H. and Edward J. Young. "אנאלתי" (Isaiah 63:3)." *WTJ* 14 (1951): 54.

Guillaume, Alfred. "Some Readings in the Dead Sea Scroll of Isaiah." . *JBL* 76 (1957): 40–43.

Hillers, Delbert R. "A Hebrew Cognate of *unuššu/ʾunt* in Is. 33:8." *Harvard Theological Review* 64 (1971): 257–59.

Hoffer, Vicki. "An Exegesis of Isaiah 38:21." *JSOT* 56 (1992): 69–84.

Holladay, W. L. "Isa. III 10-11: An Archaic Wisdom Passage." *VT* 18 (1968): 481–87.

Holter, Knut. "The Wordplay on אל ("God") in Isaiah 45, 20–21." *Scandinavian Journal of the Old Testament* 7 (1993): 88–98.

Irvine, Stuart A. "Isaiah's *She'ar-Yashub* and the Davidic House." *Biblische Zeitschrift* 37 ns (1995): 78–88.

Irwin, W. H. "'The, [*sic*] Smooth Stones of the Wady'? Isaiah 57, 6." *CBQ* 29 (1967): 31–40.

Janzen, J. Gerald. "An Echo of the Shema in Isaiah 51:1-3." *JSOT* 43 (1989): 69–82.

Jensen, Joseph. "The Age of Immanuel." *CBQ* 41 (1979): 220–39.

Jepson, A. "Die Nebiah in Jes 8 3." *ZAW* 72 (1960): 267–68.

Johnson, Hollis R. and Svend Holm-Nielsen. "Comments on Two Possible References to Comets in the Old Testament." *Scandinavian Journal of the Old Testament* 7 (1993): 99–107.

Joines, Karen Randolph. "Winged Serpents in Isaiah's Inaugural Vision." *JBL* 86 (1967): 410–15.

Jones, Douglas R. "Exposition of Isaiah Chapter One Verses One to Nine." *SJOT* 17 (1964): 469.

Kaiser Jr., Walter C. "The Unfailing Kindnesses Promised to David: Isaiah 55:3." *JSOT* 45 (2001): 91–98.

Key, Andrew F. "The Magical Background of Isaiah 6 9–13." *JBL* 86 (1977): 198–204.

Kleinig, John. "The Holy Way: An Exegetical Study of Isaiah 35:1–10." *Lutheran Theological Journal* 17 (1983): 115–20.

Knierim, Rolf. "The Vocation of Isaiah." *VT* 18 (1968): 47–68.

Knox, Sir T. M. "The Computer and the New Testament." *Svensk Exegetisk Årsbok* 28–29 (1963-64): 111–16.

Kselman, John S. "A Note on wᵓnḥhw in Isa 57:18." *CBQ* 43 (1981): 539–42.

Kuyper, L. J. "The Meaning of הסדו Isa. XL 6." *VT* 13 (1963): 489–92.

Lacheman, E. "The Seraphim of Isaiah 6." *JQR* 59 (1968): 71–72.

Lambdin, Thomas O. "Egyptian Loan Words in the Old Testament." *JAOS* 73 (1953): 145–55.

Leene, Henk. "Isaiah 46.8—Summons to Be Human?" *JSOT* 30 (1984): 111–21.

Litwak, Kenneth D. "The Use of Quotations from Isaiah 52:13–53:12 in the New Testament." *JETS* 26 (1983): 385–94.

Loewenstamm, Samuel E. "Isaiah I 31." *VT* 22 (1972): 246–48.

Lubetski, Meir. "Beatlemania of Bygone Times." *JSOT* 91 (2000): 3–26.

McRae, Allan A. "The Servant of the Lord in Isaiah." *Bibliotheca Sacra* 121 (1964): 125–32.

Maalstad, Kari. "Einige Erwägungen zu Jes. XLIII 4." *VT* 16 (1966): 512–14.

Moran, William L. "The Putative Root ᶜtm in Is. 9:18." *CBQ* 12 (1950): 153–54.

Morganstern, Julian. "'The Oppressor' of Isa 51 13—Who Was He?" *JBL* 81 (1962): 25–34.

Murtonen, A. "The Use and Meaning of the Words lᵉbårek and bᵉråkåʰ in the Old Testament." *VT* 9 (1959): 158–77.

Niessen, Richard. "The Virginity of the עַלְמָה in Isaiah 7:14." *Bibliotheca Sacra* 137 (1980): 133–50.

Oiley, J. W. "Notes on Isaiah XXXII 1, XLV 19, 23 and LXIII 1." *VT* 33 (1983): 446–53.

Orlinsky, Harry M. "*MADHEBAH* in Isaiah XIV 4." *VT* 7 (1957): 202–3.

Phillips, Anthony. "Double for All Her Sins." *ZAW* 94 (1982): 130–32.

Polaski, Donald C. "Reflections on a Mosaic Covenant: The Eternal Covenant (Isaiah 24:5) and Intertextuality." *JSOT* 77 (1998): 55–73.

Price, Charles P. "Immanuel: God with Us." *Christianity and Crisis* 23 (1963): 222–23.

Reymond, Robert L. "Who Is the עלמה of Isaiah 7:14?" *Presbyterion* 15 (1989): 1–15.

Rice, Gene. "The Interpretation of Isaiah 7:15–17." *JBL* 96 (1977): 363–69.

Roberts, J. J. M. "The Meaning of 'צמת הי' in Isaiah 4:2." *JBQ* 28 (2000): 20–27.

Rogers, Jeffrey S. "An Allusion to Coronation in Isaiah 2:6." *CBQ* 51 (1989): 232–36.

Sasson, Jack Murad. "Isaiah LXVI 3–4a." *VT* 26 (1976): 199–207.

Scheiber, Alexander. "Zwei Bemerkungen zu Jesaja." *VT* 11 (1961): 455–56.

Schneider, Stanley and Joseph H. Berke. "שׁד Breast, Robbery or the Devil?" *JBQ* 23 (1995): 86–90.

Schwantes, Siegfried J. "A Historical Approach to the ʾrʾlm of Is 33:7." *Andrews University Seminary Studies* 3 (1965): 158–66.

Southwood, Charles H. "The Problematic hᵃdurîm of Isaiah xlv 2." *VT* 25 (1975): 801–2.

Stampfer, Judah. "On Translating Biblical Poetry." *Judaism* 14 (1965): 501–10.

Talmage, Frank. "אנרשׁ תרט in Isaiah 8:1." *HTR* 60 (1967): 465–68.

Tate, Marvin E. "Satan in the Old Testament." *Review and Expositor* 89 (1992): 461–74.

Tsevat, M. "Isaiah I 31." *VT* 19 (1969): 261–63.

Van der Toorn, Karel. "Echoes of Judaean Necromancy in Isaiah 28, 7–22." *ZAW* 100 (1988): 199–217.

Van Selms, A. "Isaiah 28 9–13: An Attempt to Give a New Interpretation." *ZAW* 85 (1973): 332–39.

Vasholz, Robert I. "Isaiah and Ahaz: A Brief History of Crisis in Isaiah 7 and 8." *Presbyterion* 13 (1987): 79–84.

Watson, Wilfred G. E. "Tribute to Tyre (Is. XXIII 7)." *VT* 26 (1976): 372–74.

Watts, R. E. "The Meaning of *ʿālāw yiqpᵉṣû mᵉlākîm pîhem* in Isaiah LII 15." *VT* 40 (1990): 327–35.

Whitley, C. F. "The Language and Exegesis of Isaiah 8 16–23." *ZAW* 90 (1978): 28–43.

Williamson, H. G. M. "Isaiah 40,20—A Case of Not Seeing the Wood for the Trees." *Biblica* 67 (1986): 1–19.

Wolf, Herbert M. "A Solution to the Immanuel Prophecy in Isaiah 7:14–8:22." *JBL* 91 (1972): 449–56.

Wong, G. C. I. "Is 'God with Us' in Isaiah VIII 8?" *VT* 49 (1999): 426–32.

Zimmerman, Frank. "The Immanuel Prophecy." *JQR* 52 (1961): 154–59.

LIST OF HEBREW WORDS